Fo[...]

The Netherlands, Belgium, Luxembourg

"When it comes to information on regional history, what to see and do, and shopping, these guides are exhaustive."

—*USAir Magazine*

"Usable, sophisticated restaurant coverage, with an emphasis on good value."
—Andy Birsh, *Gourmet Magazine* columnist

"Valuable because of their comprehensiveness."
—*Minneapolis Star-Tribune*

"Fodor's always delivers high quality...thoughtfully presented...thorough."

—*Houston Post*

"An excellent choice for those who want everything under one cover."

—*Washington Post*

Fodor's Travel Publications, Inc.
New York • Toronto • London • Sydney • Auckland
http://www.fodors.com/

Fodor's The Netherlands, Belgium, Luxembourg

Editor: Carmen Anthony

Editorial Contributors: Robert Andrews, Robert Blake, Rodney Bolt, David Brown, Linda Burnham, Nancy Coons, Audra Epstein, Robert I. C. Fisher, Heidi Sarna, Helayne Schiff, Mary Ellen Schultz, M. T. Schwartzman (Gold Guide editor), Eric Sjogren, Dinah Spritzer, Nancy van Itallie

Creative Director: Fabrizio La Rocca

Associate Art Director: Guido Caroti

Photo Researcher: Jolie Novak

Cartographer: David Lindroth

Cover Photograph: Peter Guttman

Text Design: Between the Covers

Copyright

Third Edition

ISBN 0–679–03260–6

Special Sales

CONTENTS

Maps

ON THE ROAD WITH FODOR'S

WE'RE ALWAYS THRILLED to get letters from readers, especially one like this:

It took us an hour to decide what book to buy and we now know we picked the best one. Your book was wonderful, easy to follow, very accurate, and good on pointing out eating places, informal as well as formal. When we saw other people using your book, we would look at each other and smile.

Our editors and writers are deeply committed to making every Fodor's guide "the best one"—not only accurate but always charming, brimming with sound recommendations and solid ideas, right on the mark in describing restaurants and hotels, and full of fascinating facts that make you view what you've traveled to see in a rich new light.

About Our Writers

Our success in achieving our goals—and in helping to make your trip the best of all possible vacations—is a credit to the hard work of our extraordinary writers and editors.

Rodney Bolt was born in Africa, has an Irish passport, a British degree, and a Dutch driving license. After reading English at Cambridge University, he taught English on a Greek Island for two years, directed for the stage, and ran a theater in London for most of the 1980s. Then, after the Berlin Wall came down, he set off in a battered Volkswagen van to tour a newly united Germany—an experience that resulted in his Travel Writer of the Year award from the German National Tourist Office (along with a steep learning curve in mechanics). At the start of the '90s he realized a long-term ambition, finally coming to roost in Amsterdam. Since then he has written several books about Amsterdam and the Dutch, edited the city's England-language magazine, and made plentiful contributions to publications in the Netherlands, Great Britain, and the United States.

Linda Burnham began her love affair with Amsterdam—and travel—perched on a settee in the lobby of the Amstel Hotel at the beginning of a post-college Eurorail tour. Six years on staff with KLM later turned Holland into more than a destination: It became a second home. Her Dutch friends say she knows their country better than they do. She has co-authored several books about the Netherlands, the Caribbean, and the United States, and has written for *Travel & Leisure, Harper's Bazaar, Modern Bride,* and *Condé Nast Traveler.*

Nancy Coons has been following ancestral trails in Switzerland since moving to Europe in 1987. Having grown up in Michigan and worked as a writer and editor in New York, Chicago, and Little Rock, she contributes regularly to Fodor's publications and has written features on European topics for the *Wall Street Journal, Opera News,* and *National Geographic Traveler.*

After 25 years in Belgium, **Eric Sjogren** knows most of its nooks and crannies. He has lived in Stockholm, New York, London and Frankfurt, but Brussels to him is "the most liveable city I know." Wherever you live in Brussels, he claims, you can get to concert halls, theaters, and restaurants in less than half an hour—"not that you really need to leave your neighborhood to find a superior restaurant in this city of gourmands." Eric is a contributor to the *New York Times* Travel Section and writes on travel, food, business, and the arts for magazines in Scandinavia and the United States. A graduate of Iowa's Writers' Workshop, he admits to authorship of "a couple of early novels," short stories, and a travel book about his native country, *The Color of Sweden.*

New This Year

This year we've reformatted our guides to make them easier to use. Each chapter of *Fodor's The Netherlands, Belgium, Luxembourg* contains brand-new recommended itineraries to help you decide what to see in the time you have; a section called When to Tour points out the optimal time of day, day of the week, and season for your journey. You may also notice our fresh graphics, new in 1996. More readable and more helpful than ever? We think so—and we hope you do, too.

On the Web

Also check out Fodor's Web site (http://www.fodors.com/), where you'll find travel information on major destinations around the world and an ever-changing array of travel-savvy interactive features.

How to Use This Book

Organization

Up front is the Gold Guide. Its first section, **Important Contacts A to Z**, gives addresses and telephone numbers of organizations and companies that offer destination-related services and detailed information and publications. **Smart Travel Tips A to Z**, the Gold Guide's second section, gives specific information on how to accomplish what you need to in the Netherlands, Belgium, and Luxembourg, as well as tips on savvy traveling. Both sections are in alphabetical order by topic.

Chapters in *Fodor's The Netherlands, Belgium, Luxembourg* focus on the countries' main cities and the most interesting provinces within each country. The sections on the **major metropolises** of Amsterdam, Brussels, and Antwerp begin with exploring the sights, subdivided by neighborhood; after an introductory overview, each subsection recommends a walking tour then lists the top sights in alphabetical order. This allows you to find must-sees in a snap and helps chart a personalized itinerary. Following the exploring highlights of each main city are sections on dining, lodging, nightlife and the arts, outdoor activities and sports, and shopping. A single, comprehensive walking tour is suggested for **smaller urban centers**—such as Ghent, Brugge, and Luxembourg City. **Regional sections** are divided by geographical area and each kicks off with a suggested itinerary; within each area, towns are covered in logical geographical order, and attractive stretches of road and minor points of interest between them are indicated by the designation *En Route*. Throughout, Off the Beaten Path sights appear after the places from which they are most easily accessible. And within town sections, all restaurants and lodgings are grouped together.

To help you decide what to visit in the time you have, all chapters contain **recom-mended itineraries**—both countrywide and regional; you can mix and match these to create a complete vacation. The **A to Z section** that ends all city and regional sections covers essential information about the area: getting there, getting around, and helpful contacts and resources. And each chapter concludes with countrywide A to Z information on similar topics along with specifics such as language, currency, phones and mail, and tipping.

Icons and Symbols

★	Our special recommendations
✕	Restaurant
🏠	Lodging establishment
✕🏠	Lodging establishment whose restaurant warrants a detour
✪	Good for kids (rubber duckie)
☞	Sends you to another section of the guide for more information
✉	Address
☎	Telephone number
☉	Opening and closing times
💷	Admission prices (those we give apply only to adults; substantially reduced fees are almost always available for children, students, and senior citizens)

Numbers in white and black circles that appear on the maps, in the margins, and within the tours correspond to one another.

Dining and Lodging

The restaurants and lodgings we list are the cream of the crop in each price range. Price charts appear near the beginning of each chapter in our country-wide overviews, "The Pleasures of Dining and Lodging."

Hotel Facilities

We always list the facilities that are available—but we don't specify whether they cost extra: When pricing accommodations, always ask what's included. Assume that hotels operate on the European Plan (EP, with no meals) unless we note that they require full- or half-board arrangements.

Restaurant Reservations and Dress Codes

Reservations are always a good idea; we note only when they're essential or when they are not accepted. Book as far ahead as you can, and reconfirm when you get to town. Unless otherwise noted, the restaurants listed are open daily for lunch and dinner. We mention dress only when men are required to wear a jacket or a jacket and tie.

Credit Cards

The following abbreviations are used: **AE,** American Express; **DC,** Diners Club; **MC,** MasterCard; and **V,** Visa.

Please Write to Us

You can use this book in the confidence that all prices and opening times are based on information supplied to us at press time; Fodor's cannot accept responsibility for any errors. Time inevitably brings changes, so always confirm information when it matters—especially if you're making a detour to visit a specific place. In addition, when making reservations be sure to mention if you have a disability or are traveling with children, if you prefer a private bath or a certain type of bed, or if you have specific dietary needs or any other concerns.

Were the restaurants we recommended as described? Did our hotel picks exceed your expectations? Did you find a museum we recommended a waste of time? If you have complaints, we'll look into them and revise our entries when the facts warrant it. If you've discovered a special place that we haven't included, we'll pass the information along to our correspondents and have them check it out. So send your feedback, positive *and* negative, to the Netherlands/Belgium/Luxembourg editor at Fodor's, 201 East 50th Street, New York, New York 10022—and have a wonderful trip!

Karen Cure
Editorial Director

The Netherlands, Belgium, and Luxembourg

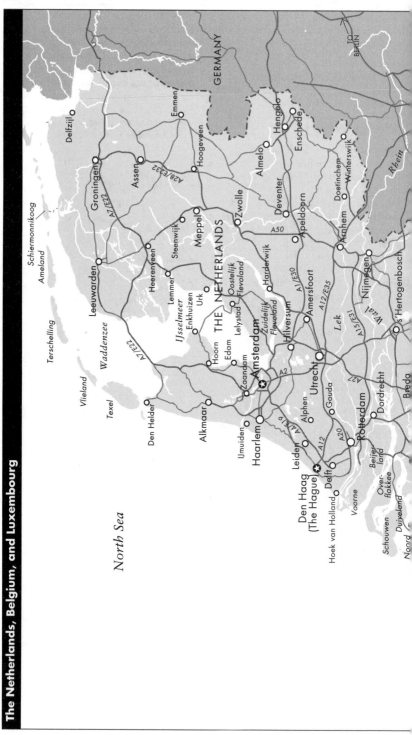

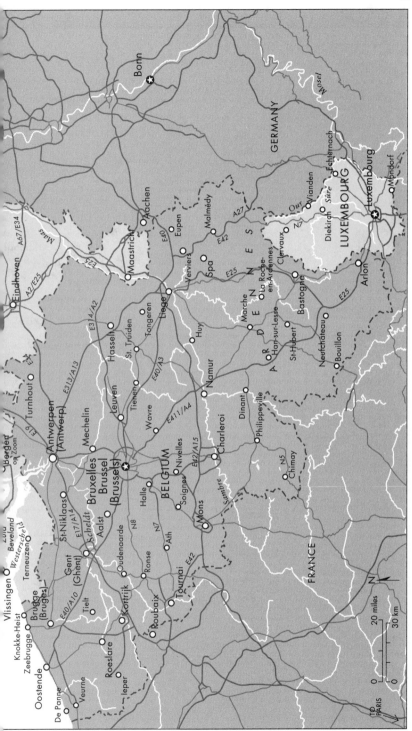

Europe

Reykjavík
ICELAND

NORWA
Bergen

NORTHERN
IRELAND
SCOTLAND
Edinburgh

*North
Sea*

Skage

IRELAND
Belfast
*Irish
Sea*
DENMAR

Dublin

UNITED
KINGDOM

WALES

ENGLAND
NETHERLANDS
Hambu

Cardiff
The Hague
Amsterdam

London
Rotterdam

G E R

*ATLANTIC
OCEAN*

English Channel
Brussels
Bonn

BELGIUM

Paris
Frankfurt

LUXEMBOURG

F R A N C E
Zürich
Mu

Bern
Bonn

SWITZERLAND

Lyon
LIECHTENS

Milan
V

Monte
Carlo

PORTUGAL
ANDORRA
Marseille
Nice
MONACO
Florence

Madrid
Corsica

Lisbon
Barcelona

S P A I N

Seville
Granada
Sardinia

*Balearic
Islands*
Tyrrh

Gibraltar
Mediterranean Sea

MOROCCO
ALGERIA

0   400 miles

0   600 km

TUNISIA

IMPORTANT CONTACTS A TO Z

An Alphabetical Listing of Publications, Organizations, and Companies That Will Help You Before, During, and After Your Trip

A

AIR TRAVEL

The major gateways to the Netherlands, Belgium, and Luxembourg are **Schiphol Airport** in Amsterdam, **Brussels National Airport** at Zaventem, and **Findel Airport** in Luxembourg-Ville. Flying time to the Netherlands and Belgium is about seven hours from New York and 10½ hours from Los Angeles (there are no nonstop flights to Luxembourg).

CARRIERS

Carriers serving the Netherlands, Belgium, and Luxembourg include **Air Canada** (☎ 800/776–3000), **American** (☎ 800/433–7300), **British Airways** (☎ 800/247–9297; to Netherlands only), **Delta** (☎ 800/221–1212), **Icelandair** (☎ 800/223–5500), **KLM Royal Dutch** (☎ 800/777–5553), **Martinair** (☎ 800/366–4655), **Sabena** (☎ 800/955–2000), **TWA** (☎ 800/892–4141), and **United** (☎ 800/241–6522).

COMPLAINTS

To register complaints about charter and scheduled airlines, contact the U.S. Department of Transportation's **Office of Consumer Affairs** (✉ 400 7th St. NW, Washington, DC 20590, ☎ 202/366–2220 or 800/322–7873).

CONSOLIDATORS

Established consolidators selling to the public include **BET World Travel** (✉ 841 Blossom Hill Rd., Suite 212-C, San Jose, CA 95123, ☎ 408/229–7880 or 800/747–1476), **Euram Tours** (✉ 1522 K St. NW, Suite 430, Washington, DC 20005, ☎ 800/848–6789), **TFI Tours International** (✉ 34 W. 32nd St., New York, NY 10001, ☎ 212/736–1140 or 800/745–8000), **Uni-Travel** (✉ Box 12485, St. Louis, MO 63132, ☎ 314/569–0900 or 800/325–2222), and **Travac Tours and Charter** (✉ 989 6th Ave., New York, NY 10018, ☎ 212/563–3303 or 800/872–8800; ✉ 2601 E. Jefferson, Orlando, FL 32803, ☎ 407/896–0014 or 800/872–8800). **FLY–ASAP** (✉ 3824 E. Indian School Rd., Phoenix, AZ 85018, ☎ 800/359–2727) isn't a discounter but gets good deals from among published fares and gets discount tickets from consolidators.

PUBLICATIONS

For general information about charter carriers, ask for the Office of Consumer Affairs' brochure **"Plane Talk: Public Charter Flights."** The Department of Transportation also publishes a 58-page booklet, **"Fly Rights"** ($1.75; ✉ Consumer Information Center, Dept. 133B, Pueblo, CO 81009).

For other tips and hints, consult the Consumers Union's monthly, **"Consumer Reports Travel Letter"** ($39 a year; ✉ Box 53629, Boulder, CO 80322, ☎ 800/234–1970) and the newsletter **"Travel Smart"** ($37 a year; ✉ 40 Beechdale Rd., Dobbs Ferry, NY 10522, ☎ 800/327–3633); *The Official Frequent Flyer Guidebook,* by Randy Petersen ($14.99 plus $3 shipping; ✉ 4715-C Town Center Dr., Colorado Springs, CO 80916, ☎ 719/597–8899 or 800/487–8893); *Airfare Secrets Exposed,* by Sharon Tyler and Matthew Wonder (✉ Sandcastle Publishing, Box 3070-A, South Pasadena, CA 91031, ☎ 213/255–3616 or 800/655–0053; $16.95 plus $3.75 shipping); and **202 Tips Even the Best Business Travelers May Not Know,** by Christopher McGinnis (✉ Irwin Professional Publishing, 1333 Burr Ridge Pkwy., Burr Ridge, IL 60521, ☎ 800/634–3966; $10 plus $3 shipping).

WITHIN THE NETHERLANDS, BELGIUM, & LUXEMBOURG

Both **KLM** and **Sabena** airlines (☞ Carriers, *above*) have flights between Amsterdam and Brussels, KLM has flights from Amsterdam to Luxembourg, and Sabena has flights from Brussels to Luxembourg. While the Netherlands has domestic air service, Belgium and Luxembourg do not.

B
BETTER BUSINESS BUREAU

For local contacts in the headquarters of a tour operator you may be considering, consult the **Council of Better Business Bureaus** (✉ 4200 Wilson Blvd., Arlington, VA 22203, ☎ 703/276–0100).

BUS TRAVEL

You can travel from London and between Brussels and Amsterdam (but not between cities in the same country) by **Eurolines** (✉ 52 Grosvenor Gardens, London SW1W 0AU, ☎ 0171/730–8235, FAX 0171/730–8721).

If you're planning to travel extensively in Europe, it may make sense to invest in a **Eurolines Pass** for unlimited travel between 16 major cities including Amsterdam and Brussels. The 1996 price for a 30-day pass was $339 ($299 for ages under 26 and over 60).

A newly established company, **Eurobus** (☎ 800/EUROBUS in the U.S., 0181/991–1021 in the U.K.), operates a "hop-on/hop-off" service on buses that travel along a one-way circuit—including Amsterdam, Brussels, and Luxembourg (in that order)—through Central Europe. The service is geared primar-

ily to younger people. A one-month pass costs $199 for those ages under 27; $260 for older passengers.

C
CAR RENTAL

Major car-rental companies represented in the Netherlands, Belgium, and Luxembourg include **Alamo** (☎ 800/327–9633, 0800/272–2000 in the U.K.), **Avis** (☎ 800/331–1084, 800/879–2847 in Canada), **Budget** (☎ 800/527–0700, 0800/181–181 in the U.K.), **Dollar** (known as Eurodollar outside North America, ☎ 800/800–4000, 0181/952–6565 in the U.K.), **Hertz** (☎ 800/654–3001, 800/263–0600 in Canada, 0181/679–1799 in the U.K.), and **National** (sometimes known as Europcar InterRent outside North America, ☎ 800/227–3876, 0181/950–5050 in the U.K.).

Rates in the Netherlands, Belgium, and Luxembourg vary from company to company; daily rates for budget companies start approximately at $55 (for an economy car including collision insurance, but with added charges for mileage, airport fee, and 17.5% VAT tax); weekly rates often include unlimited mileage.

RENTAL WHOLESALERS

Contact **Auto Europe** (✉ Box 7006, Portland, ME 04112, ☎ 207/828–2525 or 800/223–5555), **Europe by Car** (✉ 14 W. 49th St., New York, NY 10020, ☎ 212/581–3040, 212/245–1713, or 800/

223–1516; ✉ 9000 Sunset Blvd., 90069, Los Angeles, CA 90069, ☎ 800/252–9401 or 213/272–0424), **Foremost Euro-Car** (✉ 5658 Sepulveda Blvd., Suite 201, Van Nuys, CA 91411, ☎ 818/786–1960 or 800/272–3299), or the **Kemwel Group** (✉ 106 Calvert St., Harrison, NY 10528, ☎ 914/835–5555 or 800/678–0678).

THE CHANNEL TUNNEL

For information, contact **Le Shuttle** (☎ 01345/353535 in the U.K., 800/388–3876 in the U.S.), which transports cars, or **Eurostar** (☎ 0171/922–4486 in the U.K., 800/942–4866 in the U.S.), the high-speed train between London (Waterloo) and Paris (Gare du Nord). Eurostar tickets are available in the United Kingdom through **InterCity Europe,** the international wing of BritRail (✉ London Victoria Station, ☎ 0171/834–2345 or 0171/828–8092 for credit-card bookings), and in the United States through **Rail Europe** (☎ 800/942–4866) and **BritRail Travel** (✉ 1500 Broadway, New York, NY 10036, ☎ 800/677–8585).

☞ Driving *and* Rail Travel, *both below and in* Smart Travel Tips A to Z.

CHILDREN & TRAVEL

FLYING

Look into **"Flying With Baby"** ($5.95 plus $1 shipping; ✉ Third

Street Press, Box 261250, Littleton, CO 80126, ☎ 303/595–5959), co-written by a flight attendant. **"Kids and Teens in Flight,"** free from the U.S. Department of Transportation's Office of Consumer Affairs, offers tips for children flying alone. Every two years the February issue of **Family Travel Times** (☞ Know-How, *below*) details children's services on three dozen airlines.

KNOW-HOW

Family Travel Times, published four times a year by Travel With Your Children (✉ TWYCH, 45 W. 18th St., New York, NY 10011, ☎ 212/206–0688; annual subscription $40), covers destinations, types of vacations, and modes of travel.

The **Family Travel Guides** catalog ($1 postage; ✉ Box 6061, Albany, CA 94706, ☎ 510/527–5849) lists about 200 books and articles on family travel. Also check **Take Your Baby and Go! A Guide for Traveling with Babies, Toddlers and Young Children,** by Sheri Andrews, Judy Bordeaux, and Vivian Vasquez ($5.95 plus $1.50 shipping; ✉ Bear Creek Publications, 2507 Minor Ave., Seattle, WA 98102, ☎ 206/322–7604 or 800/326–6566). **Innocents Abroad: Traveling with Kids in Europe,** by Valerie Wolf Deutsch and Laura Sutherland ($15.95 hardcover, $5.95 paperback plus $2 shipping; ✉ Penguin USA, 120

Woodbine St., Bergenfield, NJ 07621, ☎ 201/387–0600 or 800/253–6476), covers child- and teen-friendly activities, food, and transportation.

LODGING

At the **Best Western** hotels (reservations ☎ 800/528–1234) in Brussels, Oostende, and Brugge in Belgium; Luxembourg-Ville; and more than 40 cities in the Netherlands, children under 12 may stay free when sharing a room with two paying adults. A maximum of five persons is allowed per room. The **Intercontinental** hotels (reservations ☎ 800/327–0200) in Amsterdam, The Hague, and Luxembourg allow one child of any age to stay free in his or her parents' room. **Hilton** hotels (reservations ☎ 800/445–8667) in Amsterdam, Rotterdam, Antwerp, and Brussels also allow one child of any age to stay free in his or her parents' room. Many hotels throughout the region have family rooms.

In Luxembourg, the National Tourist Office (☞ Visitor Information, *below*) publishes a free pamphlet listing available holiday apartments and houses and all their facilities. There's also a new brochure for "Rural Holidays" listing a number of farms that take in visitors.

TOUR OPERATORS

Grandtravel (✉ 6900 Wisconsin Ave., Suite 706, Chevy Chase, MD 20815, ☎ 301/986–0790 or 800/247–7651) has tours for people

traveling with grandchildren ages 7 to 17.

CUSTOMS

U.S. CITIZENS

The **U.S. Customs Service** (✉ Box 7407, Washington, DC 20044, ☎ 202/927–6724) can answer questions about duty-free limits and publishes a helpful brochure, **"Know Before You Go."** For information on registering foreign-made articles call 202/927–0540.

CANADIANS

Contact **Revenue Canada** (✉ 2265 St. Laurent Blvd. S, Ottawa, Ontario K1G 4K3, ☎ 613/993–0534) for a copy of the free brochure **"I Declare/Je Déclare"** and for details on duties that exceed the standard duty-free limit.

U.K. CITIZENS

HM Customs and Excise (✉ Dorset House, Stamford St., London SE1 9NG, ☎ 0171/202–4227) can answer questions about U.K. customs regulations and publishes **"A Guide for Travellers,"** detailing standard procedures and import rules.

D

DISABILITIES & ACCESSIBILITY

EUROPEAN ORGANIZATIONS AND ASSISTANCE

NETHERLANDS➤ The Netherlands leads the world in providing facilities for people with disabilities. Train and bus stations are equipped with special telephones, elevators, and toilets. Visitors can obtain special passes to ensure free escort service on Dutch trains (☎ 030/235–5555). For general assistance at railway stations, contact the **NS/Nederlandse Spoorwegen** (✉ Netherlands Railways, ☎ 030/235–5555 weekdays 8–4) before 2 PM at least one day in advance, or by 2 PM Friday for travel on Saturday, Sunday, Monday, or public holidays. Modern intercity train carriages have wheelchair-accessible compartments, and many have a free Red Cross wheelchair available. Train timetables are available in Braille, and some restaurants have menus in Braille. Some tourist sites also have special gardens for visitors with vision impairments. For information on accessibility in the Netherlands, and for general information relevant to travelers with disabilities, contact the national organization **De Gehandicaptenraad** (✉ Postbus 169, 3500 AD Utrecht, ☎ 030/230–6603 or 030/231–3454).

Each year the **Netherland Board of Tourism** (☞ Visitor Information, *below*) publishes a booklet listing hotels, restaurants, hostels and campsites, museums and tourist attractions, as well as gas/petrol stations with 24-hour services and boat firms with adapted facilities. For travelers with visual impairments, all Dutch paper currency is embossed with different symbols for each denomination. For information on tours and exchanges for travelers with disabilities, contact **Mobility International**

Nederland (✉ Postbus 9002, 5660 GC Groesbeek, ☎ 024/399–7138).

BELGIUM➤ For information on facilities, contact the **Fédération Francophone pour la Promotion des Handicapés** (✉ Rue St. Jean 32, 1000 Brussels, ☎ 02/515–0265) or **Vlaamse Federatie voor Gehandicapten** (VFG; ✉ same address, ☎ 02/511–5076).

Two holiday complexes have facilities built especially for people with disabilities: **De Ceder** (✉ Parijsestraat 34, 9800 Astene-Deinze, ☎ 09/386–3028) in Flanders and **Les Riezes et les Sarts** (✉ Rue Grande 84, 6404 Cul-des-Sarts, Couvin, ☎ 060/370311) in the Ardennes.

LUXEMBOURG➤ The Ministry of Health handles provisions for people with disabilities. Most trains and buses have special seats for riders with disabilities, and parking lots have spaces reserved for people with disabilities. Contact **Info–Handicap** (☎ 366466).

COMPLAINTS

To register complaints under the provisions of the Americans With Disabilities Act, contact the U.S. Department of Justice's **Public Access Section** (✉ Box 66738, Washington, DC 20035, ☎ 202/514–0301, TTY 202/514–0383, FAX 202/307–1198).

LODGING

The **Ramada Inns** (reservations ☎ 800/228–2828) in Liège and Amsterdam have rooms for guests with disabili-

ties. The **Intercontinental Hotel** (reservations ☎ 800/327–0200) in Luxembourg has two wheelchair-accessible rooms. Accessible rooms are also available at the **Hilton** hotels (reservations ☎ 800/531–5900) in Brussels, Amsterdam, and Rotterdam.

The following hotels in Brussels (listed from most expensive to least) have rooms for guests with disabilities: Conrad, Hilton, Jolly Hotel Grand Sablon, Meridien, Radisson SAS, Renaissance, Sodehotel La Woluwe, Bristol Stephanie, Sheraton Brussels, Sheraton Brussels Airport, Arctia, Cadetdt Mövenpick, Métropole, Holiday Inn Brussels Airport, Jolly Atlanta, Mercure, Novotel Brussels (off Grand'Place), Novotel Airport, Aris, Atlas, Palace, Albert Premier, Astrid, Capital, Green Park, Fimotel Airport, Fimotel Expo, Ibis (Brussels Centre, Sainte-Catherine and Airport), Balladins, Orion, Campanile, Comfort Inn, Gerfaut, France.

The same applies for a number of hotels outside Brussels, including the Ramada Hotel in Liège, the Switel and Hilton hotels in Antwerp, Hotel Pullman in Brugge, and Hotel des Ardennes in Spa-Balmoral.

ORGANIZATIONS

FOR TRAVELERS WITH HEARING IMPAIRMENTS➤ Contact the **American Academy of Otolaryngology** (✉ 1 Prince St., Alexandria, VA 22314, ☎ 703/836–4444, FAX 703/683–5100, TTY 703/519–1585).

THE GOLD GUIDE / IMPORTANT CONTACTS

FOR TRAVELERS WITH MOBILITY PROBLEMS➤ Contact the **Information Center for Individuals with Disabilities** (✉ Fort Point Pl., 27–43 Wormwood St., Boston, MA 02210, ☎ 617/727–5540, 800/462–5015 in MA, TTY 617/345–9743); **Mobility International USA** (✉ Box 10767, Eugene, OR 97440, ☎ 503/343–1284 and TTY, FAX 503/343–6812), the U.S. branch of an international organization based in Belgium (☞ Mobility International, *below*) that has affiliates in 30 countries; **MossRehab Hospital Travel Information Service** (✉ 1200 W. Tabor Rd., Philadelphia, PA 19141, ☎ 215/456–9603, TTY 215/456–9602); the **Society for the Advancement of Travel for the Handicapped** (✉ 347 5th Ave., Suite 610, New York, NY 10016, ☎ 212/447–7284, FAX 212/725–8253); the **Travel Industry and Disabled Exchange** (TIDE; ✉ 5435 Donna Ave., Tarzana, CA 91356, ☎ 818/344–3640, FAX 818/344–0078); and **Travelin' Talk** (✉ Box 3534, Clarksville, TN 37043, ☎ 615/552–6670, FAX 615/552–1182).

FOR TRAVELERS WITH VISION IMPAIRMENTS➤ Contact the **American Council of the Blind** (✉ 1155 15th St. NW, Suite 720, Washington, DC 20005, ☎ 202/467–5081, FAX 202/467–5085) or the **American Foundation for the Blind** (✉ 15 W. 16th St., New York, NY 10011, ☎ 212/620–2000, TTY 212/620–2158).

IN THE U.K.

Contact the **Royal Association for Disability and Rehabilitation** (RADAR; ✉ 12 City Forum, 250 City Rd., London EC1V 8AF, ☎ 0171/250–3222) or **Mobility International** (✉ Rue de Manchester 25, B1070 Brussels, Belgium, ☎ 00–322–410–6297), an international clearinghouse of travel information for people with disabilities.

PUBLICATIONS

Several free publications are available from the U.S. Information Center (✉ Box 100, Pueblo, CO 81009, ☎ 719/948–3334): **"New Horizons for the Air Traveler with a Disability"** (address to Dept. 355A), describing legally mandated changes; the pocket-size **"Fly Smart"** (Dept. 575B), good on flight safety; and the Airport Operators Council's worldwide **"Access Travel: Airports"** (Dept. 575A).

The 500-page *Travelin' Talk Directory* ($35; ✉ Box 3534, Clarksville, TN 37043, ☎ 615/552–6670) lists people and organizations who help travelers with disabilities. For specialist travel agents worldwide, consult the *Directory of Travel Agencies for the Disabled* ($19.95 plus $2 shipping; ✉ Twin Peaks Press, Box 129, Vancouver, WA 98666, ☎ 206/694–2462 or 800/637–2256).

TRAVEL AGENCIES, TOUR OPERATORS

The Americans With Disabilities Act requires that travel firms serve the needs of all travelers. However, some agencies and operators specialize in making group and individual arrangements for travelers with disabilities, among them **Access Adventures** (✉ 206 Chestnut Ridge Rd., Rochester, NY 14624, ☎ 716/889–9096), run by a former physical-rehab counselor. In addition, many general-interest operators and agencies (☞ Tour Operators, *below*) can also arrange vacations for travelers with disabilities.

FOR TRAVELERS WITH HEARING IMPAIRMENTS➤ One agency is **International Express** (✉ 7319-B Baltimore Ave., College Park, MD 20740, ☎ and TTY 301/699–8836, FAX 301/699–8836), which arranges group and independent trips.

FOR TRAVELERS WITH MOBILITY PROBLEMS➤ A number of operators specialize in working with travelers with mobility impairments: **Accessible Journeys** (✉ 35 W. Sellers Ave., Ridley Park, PA 19078, ☎ 610/521–0339 or 800/846–4537, FAX 610/521–6959), a registered nursing service that arranges vacations; **Flying Wheels Travel** (✉ 143 W. Bridge St., Box 382, Owatonna, MN 55060, ☎ 507/451–5005 or 800/535–6790), a travel agency that specializes in European cruises and tours; **Hinsdale Travel Service** (✉ 201 E. Ogden Ave., Suite 100, Hinsdale, IL 60521, ☎ 708/325–1335 or 800/303–5521), a travel agency that will give you access to the services of wheelchair traveler Janice Perkins; and **Wheelchair Journeys** (⊠ 16979 Redmond Way, Redmond, WA 98052, ☎ 206/885–2210), which can handle arrangements worldwide.

FOR TRAVELERS WITH DEVELOPMENTAL DISABILITIES➤ Contact the nonprofit **New Directions** (⊠ 5276 Hollister Ave., Suite 207, Santa Barbara, CA 93111, ☎ 805/967–2841), as well as the general-interest operators, *above.*

DISCOUNTS

CLUBS

Options include **Entertainment Travel Editions** (fee $28–$53, depending on destination; ⊠ Box 1068, Trumbull, CT 06611, ☎ 800/445–4137), **Great American Traveler** ($49.95 annually; ⊠ Box 27965, Salt Lake City, UT 84127, ☎ 800/548–2812), **Moment's Notice Discount Travel Club** ($25 annually, single or family; ⊠ 163 Amsterdam Ave., Suite 137, New York, NY 10023, ☎ 212/486–0500), **Privilege Card** ($74.95 annually; ⊠ 3391 Peachtree Rd. NE, Suite 110, Atlanta, GA 30326, ☎ 404/262–0222 or 800/236–9732), **Travelers Advantage** ($49 annually, single or family; ⊠ CUC Travel Service, 49 Music Sq. W, Nashville, TN 37203, ☎ 800/548–1116 or 800/648–4037), and **Worldwide Discount Travel Club** ($50 annually for family, $40 single; ⊠ 1674 Meridian Ave., Miami

Beach, FL 33139, ☎ 305/534–2082).

PASSES

☞ Bus Travel, *above,* and Rail Travel, *below.*

DRIVING

The Channel Tunnel has revolutionized road traffic between the United Kingdom and the Continent, making it independent of weather conditions and ferry restrictions. For information, contact **Le Shuttle** (☎ 0990/353535 in the U.K., 800/388–3876 in the U.S.), which transports cars on specially built railway carriages. Reservations are not needed, but tickets may be bought in advance from travel agencies. ☞ The Channel Tunnel, *above, and* Rail Travel, *below, plus* Driving *and* Rail Travel *in* Smart Travel Tips A to Z.

MAPS

Michelin maps are regularly updated and are the best countrywide maps; they offer the advantage of being consistent with Michelin maps of other countries you may visit. They are available at newsdealers and bookshops. Free city maps are generally available at tourist offices, and more complete city guides can be bought in bookshops. Gas stations near borders generally sell a variety of more detailed maps.

E

ELECTRICITY

Send a self-addressed, stamped envelope to the **Franzus Company** (⊠ Customer Service, Dept. B50, Murtha Industrial

Park, Box 142, Beacon Falls, CT 06403, ☎ 203/723–6664) for a copy of the free brochure, **"Foreign Electricity Is No Deep Dark Secret."**

EMERGENCIES

In **Belgium,** dial 101 for police; dial 100 for accidents and ambulance. In **Luxembourg,** dial 113 for police; dial 112 for ambulance, doctor and dentist. In **the Netherlands,** dial 06/11 for police, ambulance and fire.

F

FERRY TRAVEL

Holyman Sally (⊠ Argyle Centre, York St., Ramsgate CT11 9DS, ☎ 01843/595522), a new joint venture, has announced the startup of catamaran services between Ramsgate and Oostende from March 1, 1997, with up to eight daily round trips. The new service replaces previous ferry and jetfoil services. **P&O North Sea Ferries** (⊠ King George Dock, Hedon Rd., Hull HU9 5QA, ☎ 01482/377177) operates overnight ferry services from Hull to Zeebrugge and Rotterdam, and **Stena Line** (⊠ Charter House, Park St., Ashford, Kent TN24 BEX, ☎ 01233/647047) operates the car ferry service between Harwich in Essex and Hoek van Holland.

G

GAY & LESBIAN TRAVEL

ORGANIZATIONS

There are several gay and lesbian organizations in Brussels, including the **English–**

THE GOLD GUIDE / IMPORTANT CONTACTS

Speaking Gay Group (EGG; ✉ B.P. 198, 1060 Brussels), **Brussels Gay Professionals** (☎ 02/735–1759), **Brussels Gay Sports** (☎ 02/219–3779), and **Shalhomo** (✉ Avenue Besme 127, 1190 Brussels), for Jewish gays and lesbians.

Helpful gay and lesbian organizations in the Netherlands include the **SAD Schorerstichting** (✉ P.C. Hooftstraat 5, 1071 BL Amsterdam, ☎ 020/662–4206), for general information and HIV advice; **COC Nederland** (✉ Nieuwezijdzs Voorburgwal 68/70, 1012 SE Amsterdam, ☎ 020/623–4596), the national gay organization; and the **Gay & Lesbian Switchboard** (☎ 020/623–6565).

The **International Gay Travel Association** (✉ Box 4974, Key West, FL 33041, ☎ 800/448–8550), a consortium of 800 businesses, can supply names of travel agents and tour operators.

PUBLICATIONS

The premier international travel magazine for gays and lesbians is *Our World* ($35 for 10 issues; ✉ 1104 N. Nova Rd., Suite 251, Daytona Beach, FL 32117, ☎ 904/441–5367). The 16-page monthly, *"Out & About"* ($49 for 10 issues; ☎ 212/645–6922 or 800/929–2268), covers gay-friendly resorts, hotels, cruise lines, and airlines.

TOUR OPERATORS

Cruises and resort vacations are handled by **R.S.V.P. Travel Productions** (✉ 2800 University Ave. SE, Minneapolis, MN 55414, ☎ 800/328–7787) for gay men, **Olivia** (✉ 4400 Market St., Oakland, CA 94608, ☎ 800/631–6277) for lesbian travelers. For mixed gay and lesbian travel, contact **Hanns Ebensten Travel** (✉ 513 Fleming St., Key West, FL 33040, ☎ 305/294–8174), one of the nation's oldest operators in the gay market, and **Toto Tours** (✉ 1326 W. Albion, Suite 3W, Chicago, IL 60626, ☎ 312/274–8686 or 800/565–1241), which offers group tours worldwide.

TRAVEL AGENCIES

The largest agencies serving gay travelers are **Advance Travel** (✉ 10700 Northwest Freeway, Suite 160, Houston, TX 77092, ☎ 713/682–2002 or 800/695–0880), **Islanders/Kennedy Travel** (✉ 183 W. 10th St., New York, NY 10014, ☎ 212/242–3222 or 800/988–1181), **Now Voyager** (✉ 4406 18th St., San Francisco, CA 94114, ☎ 415/626–1169 or 800/255–6951), and **Yellowbrick Road** (✉ 1500 W. Balmoral Ave., Chicago, IL 60640, ☎ 312/561–1800 or 800/642–2488). **Skylink Women's Travel** (✉ 746 Ashland Ave., Santa Monica, CA 90405, ☎ 310/452–0506 or 800/225–5759) works with lesbians.

H

HEALTH ISSUES

FINDING A DOCTOR

For members, the **International Association for Medical Assistance to Travellers** (IAMAT; ✉ 417 Center St., Lewiston, NY 14092, ☎ 716/754–4883; in Canada, ✉ 40 Regal Rd., Guelph, Ontario N1K 1B5, ☎ 519/836–0102; ✉ 1287 St. Clair Ave., Toronto, Ontario M6E 1B8, ☎ 416/652–0137; in Switzerland, ✉ 57 Voirets, 1212 Grand-Lancy, Geneva, Switzerland; membership free) publishes a worldwide directory of English-speaking physicians meeting IAMAT standards.

MEDICAL-ASSISTANCE COMPANIES

Contact **International SOS Assistance** (✉ Box 11568, Philadelphia, PA 19116, ☎ 215/244–1500 or 800/523–8930; ✉ Box 466, Pl. Bonaventure, Montréal, Québec, H5A 1C1, ☎ 514/874–7674 or 800/363–0263), **Medex Assistance Corporation** (✉ Box 10623, Baltimore, MD 21285, ☎ 410/296–2530 or 800/573–2029), **Near Travel Services** (✉ Box 1339, Calumet City, IL 60409, ☎ 708/868–6700 or 800/654–6700), and **Travel Assistance International** (✉ 1133 15th St. NW, Suite 400, Washington, DC 20005, ☎ 202/331–1609 or 800/821–2828). Because these companies also sell death-and-dismemberment, trip-cancellation, and other insurance coverage, there may be some overlap with other travel-insurance policies (☞ Insurance, *below*).

I

INSURANCE

Travel insurance covering baggage, health, and trip cancellation or interruptions is available from **Access America** (⊠ Box 90315, Richmond, VA 23286, ☎ 804/285–3300 or 800/284–8300); **Carefree Travel Insurance** (⊠ Box 9366, 100 Garden City Plaza, Garden City, NY 11530, ☎ 516/294–0220 or 800/323–3149), **Near** (⊠ Box 1339, Calumet City, IL 60409, ☎ 708/868–6700 or 800/654–6700), **Tele-Trip** (⊠ Mutual of Omaha Plaza, Box 31716, Omaha, NE 68131, ☎ 800/228–9792), **Travel Insured International** (⊠ Box 280568, East Hartford, CT 06128-0568, ☎ 203/528–7663 or 800/243–3174), **Travel Guard International** (⊠ 1145 Clark St., Stevens Point, WI 54481, ☎ 715/345–0505 or 800/826–1300), and **Wallach & Company** (⊠ 107 W. Federal St., Box 480, Middleburg, VA 22117, ☎ 703/687–3166 or 800/237–6615).

IN THE U.K.

The **Association of British Insurers** (⊠ 51 Gresham St., London EC2V 7HQ, ☎ 0171/600–3333; ⊠ 30 Gordon St., Glasgow G1 3PU, ☎ 0141/226–3905; ⊠ Scottish Provident Bldg., Donegall Sq. W., Belfast BT1 6JE, ☎ 01232/249176; and other locations) gives advice by phone and publishes the free **"Holiday Insurance,"** which sets out typical policy provisions and costs.

L
LODGING

APARTMENT & VILLA RENTAL

If you're making your own travel arrangements, you can have hotel reservations in Belgium made for you free of charge by writing or faxing **Belgian Tourist Reservations** (BTR; ⊠ Boulevard Anspach 111, 1000 Brussels, ☎ 02/513–7484, FAX 02/513–9277). For self-catering accommodations and B&Bs in Wallonia, contact **Belsud Réservation** (⊠ Rue Marché-aux-Herbes 61, 1000 Brussels, ☎ 02/504–0280, FAX 02/514–5335). For hotel as well as B&B reservations in Antwerp, contact the **Tourist Board** (⊠ Grote Markt 15, 2000 Antwerp, ☎ 03/232–0103, FAX 03/231–1937).

For apartment and villa rentals in the Benelux countries, companies include **Europa-Let** (⊠ 92 N. Main St., Ashland, OR 97520, ☎ 503/482–5806 or 800/462–4486), **Hometours International** (⊠ Box 11503, Knoxville, TN 37939, ☎ 615/588–8722 or 800/367–4668), **Interhome** (⊠ 124 Little Falls Rd., Fairfield, NJ 07004, ☎ 201/882–6864), **Property Rentals International** (⊠ 1008 Mansfield Crossing Rd., Richmond, VA 23236, ☎ 804/378–6054 or 800/220–3332), **Rent-a-Home International** (⊠ 7200 34th Ave. NW, Seattle, WA 98117, ☎ 206/789–9377 or 800/488–7368), and **Vacation Home Rentals Worldwide** (⊠ 235 Kensington Ave., Norwood, NJ 07648, ☎ 201/767–9393 or 800/633–3284).

HOME EXCHANGE

Principal clearinghouses include **HomeLink**

International/Vacation Exchange Club ($60 annually; ⊠ Box 650, Key West, FL 33041, ☎ 305/294–1448 or 800/638–3841), which gives members four annual directories, with a listing in one, plus updates; **Intervac International** ($65 annually; ⊠ Box 590504, San Francisco, CA 94159, ☎ 415/435–3497), which has three annual directories; and **Loan-a-Home** ($35–$45 annually; ⊠ 2 Park La., Apt. 6E, Mount Vernon, NY 10552-3443, ☎ 914/664–7640), which specializes in long-term exchanges.

M
MONEY MATTERS

ATMS

Call for specific foreign **Cirrus** locations (☎ 800/424–7787); for foreign **Plus** locations, consult the Plus directory at your local bank.

CURRENCY EXCHANGE

If your bank doesn't exchange currency, contact **Thomas Cook Currency Services** (⊠ 41 E. 42nd St., New York, NY 10017, or 511 Madison Ave., New York, NY 10022, ☎ 212/757–6915 or 800/223–7373 for locations) or **Ruesch International** (☎ 800/424–2923 for locations).

WIRING FUNDS

Funds can be wired via **American Express MoneyGram℠** (☎ 800/926–9400 from the U.S. and Canada for locations and information) or **Western Union** (☎ 800/325–6000 for agent locations or to send using MasterCard

THE GOLD GUIDE / IMPORTANT CONTACTS

or Visa; 800/321–2923 in Canada).

P

PASSPORTS & VISAS

U.S. CITIZENS

For fees, documentation requirements, and other information, call the **Office of Passport Services** information line (☎ 202/647–0518).

CANADIANS

For fees, documentation requirements, and other information, call the Ministry of Foreign Affairs and International Trade's **Passport Office** (☎ 819/994–3500 or 800/567–6868).

U.K. CITIZENS

For fees, documentation requirements, and an emergency passport, call the **London passport office** (☎ 0171/271–3000).

PHONE MATTERS

The country code for **Belgium** is 32; for **the Netherlands,** 31; followed by the area code minus the initial "0" (which must be used for domestic long-distance calls). The country code for **Luxembourg** is 352; in this country there are no area codes.

For local access numbers abroad, *see* individual country chapters or contact **AT&T** USA Direct (☎ 800/874–4000), **MCI** Call USA (☎ 800/444–4444), or **Sprint** Express (☎ 800/793–1153).

PHOTO HELP

The **Kodak Information Center** (☎ 800/242–2424) answers consumer questions about film and photography.

R

RAIL TRAVEL

The big news in international is the **Eurostar** (☎ 01233/617575 in the U.K., 800/942–4866 in the U.S.), the high-speed train service that uses the Channel Tunnel to link London (Waterloo) with Brussels (Midi) in 3¼ hours. Eurostar tickets are available in the United Kingdom through **InterCity Europe,** the international wing of BritRail (London Victoria Station, ☎ 0171/834–2345 or 0171/828–8092 for credit-card bookings), and in the United States through **Rail Europe** (☎ 800/942–4866) and **BritRail Travel** (✉ 1500 Broadway, New York, NY 10036, ☎ 800/677–8585). The recently privatized Eurostar is operated by London & Continental Railways, a consortium that will also build the high-speed rail link between London and Dover; when completed, this will cut another 40 minutes from total travel time.

All 13 daily rail services between Paris and Brussels are now operated with **Thalys** high-speed trains (2 hours, 6 minutes). Four trains per day continue to Amsterdam and two to Liège; the Liège service is scheduled to be extended to Cologne in late 1997. Thalys is a joint venture between the Belgian, French, and Dutch railways (in Belgium ☎ 0800–95777).

DISCOUNT PASSES

For train passes in the Netherlands, *see* The Netherlands A to Z *in* Chapter 2.

The **EurailPass**—valid for unlimited first-class train travel through 20 countries, including the Netherlands, Belgium, and Luxembourg—is an excellent value if you plan to travel around the Continent. Standard passes are available for 15 days ($522), 21 days ($678), one month ($838), two months ($1,148), and three months ($1,468).

Eurail Saverpasses, valid for 15 days, cost $452 per person; for 21 days, $578; for one month, $712. You must do all your traveling with at least one companion (two companions from April through September). **Eurail Youthpasses,** which cover second-class travel, cost $598 for one month, $798 for two; you must be under 26 on the first day you travel. **Eurail Flexipasses** allow you to travel first class for 10 ($616) or 15 ($812) days within any two-month period. **Eurail Youth Flexipasses,** available to those under 26 on their first travel day, allow you to travel second class for 10 ($438) or 15 ($588) days within any two-month period. Apply through your travel agent or **Rail Europe** (✉ 226–230 Westchester Ave., White Plains, NY 10604, ☎ 914/682–5172 or 800/848–7245; or ✉ 2087 Dundas E, Suite 105, Mississauga, Ont. L4X 1M2, ☎ 416/602–4195), **DER Tours** (✉ Box 1606, Des Plaines, IL 60017, ☎ 800/782–2424, ✉ 800/282–7474), or **CIT Tours Corp.** (✉ 342 Madison Ave.,

Suite 207, New York, NY 10173, ☎ 212/697–2100 or 800/248–8687; in western U.S. ☎ 310/670–4269 or 800/248–7245).

Rail Europe also offers the **Benelux Tourrail Pass,** a special unlimited-mileage ticket for travel in the Netherlands, Belgium, and Luxembourg, good for any five days in a one-month period, for $217 first class, $155 second class. The **Benelux Junior Pass** costs $104/$143 second class for travelers under 26 years old and is free for children under 4.

S
SENIOR CITIZENS

ORGANIZATIONS

Contact the **American Association of Retired Persons** (AARP; ⊠ 601 E St. NW, Washington, DC 20049, ☎ 202/434–2277; $8 per person or couple annually). Its Purchase Privilege Program gets members discounts on lodging, car rentals, and sightseeing.

For other discounts on lodgings, car rentals, and other travel products, along with magazines and newsletters, contact the **National Council of Senior Citizens** (membership $12 annually; ⊠ 1331 F St. NW, Washington, DC 20004, ☎ 202/347–8800) and **Mature Outlook** (subscription $9.95 annually; ⊠ 6001 N. Clark St., Chicago, IL 60660, ☎ 312/465–6466 or 800/336–6330).

PUBLICATIONS

The 50+ Traveler's Guidebook: Where to Go, Where to Stay, What
to Do, by Anita Williams and Merrimac Dillon ($12.95; ⊠ St. Martin's Press, 175 5th Ave., New York, NY 10010, ☎ 212/674–5151 or 800/288–2131), offers many useful tips. **"The Mature Traveler"** ($29.95; ⊠ Box 50400, Reno, NV 89513, ☎ 702/786–7419), a monthly newsletter, covers travel deals.

SPORTS

Bicycling, boating, camping, and hiking rate high among the outdoor activities available in the Benelux countries (☞ Chapters 2, 3, and 4).

STUDENTS

GROUPS

Major tour operators include **Contiki Holidays** (⊠ 300 Plaza Alicante, Suite 900, Garden Grove, CA 92640, ☎ 714/740–0808 or 800/466–0610).

HOSTELING

Contact **Hostelling International-American Youth Hostels** (⊠ 733 15th St. NW, Suite 840, Washington, DC 20005, ☎ 202/783–6161) in the United States, **Hostelling International–Canada** (⊠ 205 Catherine St., Suite 400, Ottawa, Ontario K2P 1C3, ☎ 613/237–7884) in Canada, and the **Youth Hostel Association of England and Wales** (⊠ Trevelyan House, 8 St. Stephen's Hill, St. Albans, Hertfordshire AL1 2DY, ☎ 01727/855215 or 01727/845047) in the United Kingdom. Membership ($25 in the U.S., C$26.75 in Canada, £9 in the U.K.) gets you access to 5,000 hostels worldwide that
charge $7–$20 nightly per person.

I.D. CARDS

For discounts on transportation and admissions, get the **International Student Identity Card** (ISIC) if you're a bona fide student, or the **International Youth Card** (IYC) if you're under 26. In the United States, the ISIC and IYC cards cost $16 each and include basic travel accident and illness coverage, plus a toll-free travel hot line. Apply through the Council on International Educational Exchange (☞ Organizations, *below*). Cards are available for $15 each in Canada from **Travel Cuts** (☞ Organizations, *below*) and in the United Kingdom for £5 each at student unions and student travel companies.

ORGANIZATIONS

A major contact is the **Council on International Educational Exchange** (CIEE; ⊠ 205 E. 42nd St., 16th floor, New York, NY 10017, ☎ 212/661–1450) with locations in Boston (⊠ 729 Boylston St., Boston, MA 02116, ☎ 617/266–1926), Miami (⊠ 9100 S. Dadeland Blvd., Miami, FL 33156, ☎ 305/670–9261), Los Angeles (⊠ 1093 Broxton Ave., Los Angeles, CA 90024, ☎ 310/208–3551), 43 college towns nationwide, and the United Kingdom (⊠ 28A Poland St., London W1V 3DB, ☎ 0171/437–7767). Twice a year, it publishes *Student Travels* magazine. The CIEE's Council Travel Service is the exclusive U.S. agent for several student-discount cards (☞ I.D. Cards, *above*).

Campus Connections (✉ 325 Chestnut St., Suite 1101, Philadelphia, PA 19106, ☎ 215/625–8585 or 800/428–3235) specializes in discounted accommodations and airfares for students. The **Educational Travel Centre** (✉ 438 N. Frances St., Madison, WI 53703, ☎ 608/256–5551) offers rail passes and low-cost airline tickets, mostly for flights departing from Chicago. For air travel only, contact **TMI Student Travel** (✉ 100 W. 33rd St., Suite 813, New York, NY 10001, ☎ 800/245–3672).

In Canada, also contact **Travel Cuts** (✉ 187 College St., Toronto, Ontario M5T 1P7, ☎ 416/979–2406 or 800/667–2887).

PUBLICATIONS

Check out the **Berkeley Guide to Europe** ($18.95; Fodor's Travel Publications, ☎ 800/533–6478, or from bookstores).

T

TOUR OPERATORS

Among the companies selling tours and packages to the Netherlands, Belgium, and Luxembourg, the following have a proven reputation, are nationally known, and offer plenty of options.

GROUP TOURS

Super-Deluxe➤ **Travcoa** (✉ Box 2630, 2350 S.E. Bristol St., Newport Beach, CA 92660,

☎ 714/476–2800 or 800/992–2003, FAX 714/476–2538).

Deluxe➤ **Globus** (✉ 5301 S. Federal Circle, Littleton, CO 80123-2980, ☎ 303/797–2800 or 800/221–0090, FAX 303/795–0962) and **Tauck Tours** (✉ Box 5027, 276 Post Rd. W, Westport, CT 06881, ☎ 203/226–6911 or 800/468–2825, FAX 203/221–6828).

First-Class➤ **Brendan Tours** (✉ 15137 Califa St., Van Nuys, CA 91411, ☎ 818/785–9696 or 800/421–8446, FAX 818/902–9876), **Caravan Tours** (✉ 401 N. Michigan Ave., Chicago, IL 60611, ☎ 312/321–9800 or 800/227–2826), **Central Holidays Tours** (✉ 206 Central Ave., Jersey City, NJ 07307, ☎ 201/798–5777 or 800/935–5000), **Collette Tours** (✉ 162 Middle St., Pawtucket, RI 02860, ☎ 401/728–3805 or 800/832–4656, FAX 401/728–1380), **DER Tours** (✉ 11933 Wilshire Blvd., Los Angeles, CA 90025, ☎ 310/479–4140 or 800/937–1235), and **Gadabout Tours** (✉ 700 E. Tahquitz Canyon Way, Palm Springs, CA 92262, ☎ 619/325–5556 or 800/952–5068).

Budget➤ **Cosmos** (☞ Globus, *above*).

PACKAGES

Central Holidays Tours and **DER Tours** (☞ Group Tours, *above*) have the greatest variety of independent vacation packages. Among the U.S. airlines offering packages are **Delta Dream Vacations**

(☎ 800/872–7786) and **United Vacations** (☎ 800/328–6877). **Funjet Vacations,** based in Milwaukee, Wisconsin, and **Gogo Tours,** based in Ramsey, New Jersey, sell packages to the Netherlands, Belgium, and Luxembourg only through travel agents.

FROM THE U.K.

British Airways Holidays (✉ Astral Towers, Betts Way, London Rd., Crawley, West Sussex RH10 2XA, ☎ 01293/723–100) and **Travelscene** (✉ Travelscene House, 11–15 St. Ann's Rd., Harrow, Middlesex HA1 1AS, ☎ 0181/427–8800) offer city breaks in Amsterdam, Brussels, Brugge, and Luxembourg. **Cosmos** (✉ Tourama House, 17 Homesdale Rd., Bromley, Kent BR2 9LX, ☎ 0181/464–3477 or 0161/480–5799) offers tours by air and coach. **Stena Line** (✉ Charter House Park St. Ashford Kent TN24 8EX, ☎ 0990/747–747) books holidays by car, rail, sea, and air.

THEME TRIPS

Adventure➤ **Himalayan Travel** (✉ 112 Prospect St., Stamford, CT 06901, ☎ 203/359–3711 or 800/225–2380, FAX 203/359–3669) operates a range of active adventure tours.

Art and Architecture➤ **Endless Beginnings Tours** (✉ 9825 Dowdy Dr., #105, San Diego, CA 92126, ☎ 619/566–4166 or 800/822–7855, FAX 619/549–9655) explores the art of the Dutch Masters.

BARGE/RIVER CRUISES➤ Contact **Etoile De Champagne** (⊠ 88 Broad St., Boston, MA 02110, ☎ 800/280–1492, FAX 617/426–4689), **European Waterways** (⊠ 140 E. 56th St., #4C, New York, NY 10022, ☎ 212/688–9489 or 800/217–4447, FAX 212/688–3778 or 800/296–4554), **Kemwel's Premier Selections** (⊠ 106 Calvert St., Harrison, NY 10528, ☎ 914/835–5555 or 800/234–4000, FAX 914/835–5449), and **Le Boat** (⊠ Box E, Mawood, NJ 07507, ☎ 201/342–1838 or 800/922–0291).

BEER➤ **MIR Corporation** (⊠ 85 S. Washington St., #210, Seattle, WA 98104, ☎ 206/624–7289 or 800/424–7289, FAX 206/624–7360) leads you to the famous pubs and breweries of Holland and Belgium.

BICYCLING➤ For bike tours, contact **Backroads** (⊠ 1516 5th St., Berkeley, CA 94710-1740, ☎ 510/527–1555 or 800/462–2848, FAX 510/527–1444), **Butterfield & Robinson** (⊠ 70 Bond St., Toronto, Ontario, Canada M5B 1X3, ☎ 416/864–1354 or 800/678–1147, FAX 416/864–0541), **Classic Adventures** (⊠ Box 153, Hamlin, NY 14464-0153, ☎ 716/964–8488 or 800/777–8090, FAX 716/964–7297), and **Euro-Bike Tours** (⊠ Box 990, De Kalb, IL 60115, ☎ 800/321–6060, FAX 815/758–8851).

GARDENS➤ **Expo Garden Tours** (⊠ 101 Sunrise Hill Rd., Norwalk, CT 06851, ☎ 203/840–1441 or 800/448–2685, FAX 203/840–1224) visits Holland's multicolored tulip gardens.

VILLA RENTALS➤ Contact **Villas International** (⊠ 605 Market St., San Francisco, CA 94105, ☎ 415/281–0910 or 800/221–2260, FAX 415/281–0919) for properties in Belgium.

ORGANIZATIONS

The **National Tour Association** (⊠ 546 E. Main St., Lexington, KY 40508, ☎ 606/226–4444 or 800/755–8687) and **United States Tour Operators Association** (⊠ USTOA, 211 E. 51st St., Suite 12B, New York, NY 10022, ☎ 212/750–7371) can provide lists of member operators and information on booking tours.

PUBLICATIONS

Consult the brochure **On Tour,** and ask for a current list of member operators from the National Tour Association (☞ Organizations, *above*). Also get a copy of the **"Worldwide Tour & Vacation Package Finder"** from the USTOA (☞ Organizations, *above*) and the Better Business Bureau's **"Tips on Travel Packages"** (publication No. 24-195, $2; ⊠ 4200 Wilson Blvd., Arlington, VA 22203).

TRAVEL AGENCIES

For names of reputable agencies in your area, contact the **American Society of Travel Agents** (⊠ 1101 King St., Suite 200, Alexandria, VA 22314, ☎ 703/739–2782).

U

U.S. GOVERNMENT TRAVEL BRIEFINGS

The U.S. Department of State's Overseas Citizens Emergency Center (⊠ 2201 C St. NW, Room 4817, Washington, DC 20520; enclose SASE) issues **Consular Information Sheets,** which cover crime, security, political climate, and health risks, as well as embassy locations, entry requirements, currency regulations, and other routine matters. For the latest information, stop in at any U.S. passport office, consulate, or embassy; call the interactive hot line (☎ 202/647–5225 or FAX 202/647–3000); or, with your PC's modem, tap into the Bureau of Consular Affairs' computer bulletin board (☎ 202/647–9225).

V

VISITOR INFORMATION

The **Netherlands Board of Tourism** (in the U.S., ⊠ 355 Lexington Ave., New York, NY 10017, ☎ 212/370–7360; ⊠ 225 N. Michigan Ave., Suite 326, Chicago, IL 60601, ☎ 312/819–0300, FAX 312/819–1740; ⊠ 9841 Airport Blvd., 10th floor, Los Angeles, CA 90045, ☎ 310/348–9333, FAX 310/348–9344; in Canada, ⊠ 25 Adelaide St. E, Suite 710, Toronto, Ont. M5C 1Y2, ☎ 416/363–1577, FAX 416/363–

Important Contacts A to Z

THE GOLD GUIDE / IMPORTANT CONTACTS

1470; in the U.K., ⊠ 25–28 Buckingham Gate, London SW1E 6LD, ☏ 0171/828–7900).

Contact the **Belgian Tourist Office** (for the U.S. and Canada, ⊠ 780 3rd Ave., Suite 1501, New York, NY 10017, ☏ 212/758–8130, FAX 212/355–7675; in the U.K.,

⊠ 29 Princes St., London W1R 7RG, ☏ 0171/629–0230).

The **Luxembourg National Tourist Office** (for the U.S. and Canada, ⊠ 17 Beekman Pl., New York, NY 10022, ☏ 212/935–8888, FAX 212/935–5896; in the U.K., ⊠ 122 Regent St., London W1R 5FE, ☏ 0171/434–2800).

W
WEATHER

For current conditions and forecasts, plus the local time and helpful travel tips, call the **Weather Channel Connection** (☏ 900/932–8437; 95¢ per minute) from a touch-tone phone.

SMART TRAVEL TIPS A TO Z

Basic Information on Traveling in the Netherlands, Belgium, and Luxembourg and Savvy Tips to Make Your Trip a Breeze

A
AIR TRAVEL

If time is an issue, **always look for nonstop flights,** which require no change of plane and make no stops. If possible, **avoid connecting flights,** which stop at least once and can involve a change of plane, although the flight number remains the same; if the first leg is late, the second waits.

CUTTING COSTS

The Sunday travel section of most newspapers is a good source of deals (☞ Travel Passes, *below*).

MAJOR AIRLINES➤ The least-expensive airfares from the major airlines are priced for round-trip travel and are subject to restrictions. You must usually **book in advance and buy the ticket within 24 hours** to get cheaper fares, and you may have to **stay over a Saturday night.** The lowest fare is subject to availability, and only a small percentage of the plane's total seats are sold at that price. It's good to **call a number of airlines, and when you are quoted a good price, book it on the spot**—the same fare on the same flight may not be available the next day. Airlines generally allow you to change your return date for a $25 to $50 fee, but most low-fare tickets are non-refundable. However, if you don't use it, you can apply the cost toward the purchase price of a new ticket, again for a small charge.

CONSOLIDATORS➤ Consolidators, who buy tickets at reduced rates from scheduled airlines, sell them at prices below the lowest available from the airlines directly—usually without advance restrictions. Sometimes you can even get your money back if you need to return the ticket. Carefully read the fine print detailing penalties for changes and cancellations. If you doubt the reliability of a consolidator, **confirm your reservation with the airline.**

TRAVEL PASSES➤ You can save on air travel within Europe if you **plan on traveling to and from Brussels aboard Sabena.** As part of their Euro Flyer program, you can then buy between three and nine flight coupons, which are valid on those airlines' flights to more than 100 European cities. At $120 each, these coupons are a good deal, and the fine print still allows you plenty of freedom.

ALOFT

AIRLINE FOOD➤ If you hate airline food, **ask for special meals when booking;** these can be vegetarian, low-choles-terol, or kosher, for example. Commonly prepared to order in smaller quantities than standard catered fare, they can be tastier.

JET LAG➤ To avoid this syndrome, which occurs when travel disrupts your body's natural cycles, try to maintain a normal routine. At night, **get some sleep.** By day, move about the cabin to **stretch your legs, eat light meals, and drink water—not alcohol.** On arrival, go to bed when the clock, not your body, tells you to.

SMOKING➤ Smoking is not allowed on flights of six hours or less within the continental United States. Smoking is also prohibited on flights within Canada. For U.S. flights longer than six hours or international flights, **contact your carrier regarding its smoking policy.** Some carriers have prohibited smoking throughout their system; others allow smoking only on certain routes or even certain departures of that route. If smoking bothers you, **request a seat far from the smoking section.**

B
BUS TRAVEL

Bus service among the Benelux countries is minimal. *See* individual country chapters for specific availability.

C

CAMERAS, CAMCORDERS, & COMPUTERS

IN TRANSIT

Always **keep your film, tape, or disks out of the sun**; never put these on the dashboard of a car. Carry an extra supply of batteries, and **be prepared to turn on your camera, camcorder, or laptop computer for security personnel** to prove that it's real.

X RAYS

Always **ask for hand inspection at security.** Such requests are virtually always honored at U.S. airports and are usually accommodated abroad. Photographic film becomes clouded after successive exposure to airport X-ray machines. Videotape and computer disks are not harmed by X rays, but **keep your tapes and disks away from metal detectors.**

CUSTOMS

Before departing, **register your foreign-made camera or laptop with U.S. Customs.** If your equipment is U.S.-made, call the consulate of the country you'll be visiting to find out whether it should be registered with local customs upon arrival.

THE CHANNEL TUNNEL

The Channel Tunnel provides the fastest route across the Channel—35 minutes from Folkestone to Calais, 60 minutes from motorway to motorway, or 3 hours from Waterloo, London, to Paris, Gare du Nord. It consists of two large 50-kilometer- (31-mile-) long tunnels for trains, one in each direction, linked by a smaller service tunnel running between them.

Le Shuttle, a special car, bus, and truck train, operates a continuous loop, with trains departing every 15 minutes at peak times and at least once an hour through the night. No reservations are necessary, although tickets may be purchased in advance from travel agents. Most passengers travel in their own car, staying with the vehicle throughout the "crossing," with progress updates via radio and display screens. Motorcyclists park their bikes in a separate section with its own passenger compartment, while foot passengers must book passage by coach. At press time, prices for a one-day round-trip ticket began at £107–£154 for a car and its occupants. Prices for a five-day round-trip ticket began at £115.

Eurostar operates high-speed passenger-only trains, which whisk riders between new stations in Paris (Gare du Nord) and London (Waterloo) in three hours, and between London and Brussels (Midi) in 3¼ hours. At press time, fares were $154 for a one-way, first-class ticket and $123 for an economy fare.

The Tunnel is reached from Exit 11a of the M20/A20. You may **purchase tickets for either tunnel service in advance** (☞ The Channel Tunnel *in* Important Contacts A to Z).

CHILDREN & TRAVEL

BABY-SITTING

For recommended local sitters, **check with your hotel desk.**

DRIVING

If you are renting a car, **arrange for a car seat when you reserve.** Sometimes they're free.

FLYING

Always **ask about discounted children's fares.** On international flights, the fare for infants under age 2 not occupying a seat is generally either free or 10% of the accompanying adult's fare; children ages 2–11 usually pay half to two-thirds of the adult fare. On domestic flights, children under 2 not occupying a seat travel free, and older children currently travel on the lowest applicable adult fare.

BAGGAGE➤ In general, the adult baggage allowance applies for children paying half or more of the adult fare. Before departure, **ask about carry-on allowances,** if you are traveling with an infant. In general, those paying 10% of the adult fare are allowed one carry-on bag, not to exceed 70 pounds or 45 inches (length + width + height) and a collapsible stroller; you may be allowed less if the flight is full.

SAFETY SEATS➤ According to the Federal Aviation Administration (FAA), it's a good idea to **use safety seats aloft.** U.S. carriers allow FAA-approved models, but airlines usually require that you buy a ticket, even if your child would otherwise ride free, because the seats must be strapped into regular passenger seats. Foreign carriers may not allow infant seats, may charge the child's rather than the infant's fare for their use, or may require you to hold your baby during takeoff and landing, thus defeating the seat's purpose.

FACILITIES➤ When making your reservation, **ask for children's meals or freestanding bassinets** if you need them; the latter are available only to those with seats at the bulkhead, where there's enough legroom. If you don't need a bassinet, **think twice before requesting bulkhead seats**—the only storage for in-flight necessities is in the inconveniently distant overhead bins.

LODGING

Most hotels allow children under a certain age to stay in their parents' room at no extra charge, while others charge them as extra adults; be sure to **ask about the cut-off age** (☞ Lodging, *below*).

CUSTOMS & DUTIES

For specific regulations in the Netherlands, Belgium, and Luxembourg, *see* individual chapters.

IN THE U.S.

You may bring home $400 worth of foreign goods duty-free if you've been out of the country for at least 48 hours and haven't already used the $400 exemption, or any part of it, in the past 30 days.

Travelers 21 or older may bring back 1 liter of alcohol duty-free, provided the beverage laws of the state through which they re-enter the United States allow it. In addition, 100 non-Cuban cigars and 200 cigarettes are allowed, regardless of your age. Antiques and works of art more than 100 years old are duty-free.

Duty-free, travelers may mail packages valued at up to $200 to themselves and up to $100 to others, with a limit of one parcel per addressee per day (and no alcohol or tobacco products or perfume valued at more than $5); outside, identify the package as being for personal use or an unsolicited gift, specifying the contents and their retail value. Mailed items do not count as part of your exemption.

IN CANADA

Once per calendar year, when you've been out of Canada for at least seven days, you may bring in C$300 worth of goods duty-free. If you've been away less than seven days but more than 48 hours, the duty-free exemption drops to C$100 but can be claimed any number of times (as can a C$20 duty-free exemption for absences of 24 hours or more). You cannot combine the yearly and 48-hour exemptions, use the C$300 exemp-

tion only partially (to save the balance for a later trip), or pool exemptions with family members. Goods claimed under the C$300 exemption may follow you by mail; those claimed under the lesser exemptions must accompany you.

Alcohol and tobacco products may be included in the yearly and 48-hour exemptions but not in the 24-hour exemption. If you meet the age requirements of the province through which you re-enter Canada, you may bring in, duty-free, 1.14 liters (40 imperial ounces) of wine or liquor *or* 24 12-ounce cans or bottles of beer or ale. If you are 16 or older, you may bring in, duty-free, 200 cigarettes, 50 cigars or cigarillos, and 400 tobacco sticks or 400 grams of manufactured tobacco. Alcohol and tobacco must accompany you on your return.

An unlimited number of gifts valued up to C$60 each may be mailed to Canada duty-free. These do not count as part of your exemption. Label the package "Unsolicited Gift— Value under $60." Alcohol and tobacco are excluded.

IN THE U.K.

If your journey was wholly within EU countries, you no longer need to pass through customs when you return to the United Kingdom. If you plan to bring large quantities of alcohol or tobacco, check in advance on EU limits.

D

DISABILITIES & ACCESSIBILITY

The Netherlands provides excellent facilities for people with disabilities. Most train and bus stations are equipped with special lifts and toilets. Modern intercity train carriages have wheelchair-accessible compartments, and the majority of theaters and hotels have been designed with an understanding of special needs. Dutch paper currency is specially embossed so that notes can be identified by touch.

In Belgium and Luxembourg, hotels with facilities to receive guests with disabilities are identified in guides published by national and local tourist offices. Awareness of the sensitivities of people with disabilities is generally high but has not yet impacted on the language; the words *handicapé* (French) and *gehandicapt* (Dutch) are still commonly used. Visitors with disabilities should be aware that many Belgian streets are cobblestone.

In general, when discussing accessibility with an operator or the reservations desk, **ask hard questions.** Are there any stairs, inside *or* out? Are there grab bars next to the toilet *and* in the shower/tub? How wide is the doorway to the room? To the bathroom? For the most extensive facilities, meeting the latest legal specifications, **opt for newer facilities,** which more often have been designed with access in mind. Older properties or ships must usually be retrofitted and may offer more limited facilities as a result. Be sure to **discuss your needs before booking.**

DISCOUNT CLUBS

Travel clubs offer members unsold space on airplanes, cruise ships, and package tours by as much as 50% below regular prices. Membership may include a regular bulletin or access to a toll-free hot line giving details of available trips departing from three or four days to several months in the future. Most also offer 50% discounts off hotel rack rates. Before booking with a club, **make sure the hotel or other supplier isn't offering a better deal.**

DRIVING

A network of well-maintained superhighways and other roads covers the three countries, making car travel convenient. Traffic can be heavy around the major cities, especially on the roads to southern Europe in late June and late July, when many Belgians begin their vacations, and on those approaching the North Sea beaches on summer weekends.

From Calais, you can choose to drive along the coast in the direction of Oostende or via Lille and Tournai toward Ghent, Antwerp, and Amsterdam; or toward Mons and Brussels; or toward Namur and Luxembourg.

Be sure to **observe speed limits.** In the Netherlands, the speed limit is 120 kph (75 mph) on superhighways, 100 kph (60 mph) on urban-area highways, and 50 kph (30 mph) on surburban roads. On motorways in Belgium, the speed limit is 130 kph (80 mph), but the cruising speed is mostly about 140 kph (about 87 mph). In Luxembourg, the speed limit on motorways is 120 kph (75 mph), but most drivers seem to treat that as a minimum!

For safe driving, **go with the flow, stay in the slow lane unless you want to overtake, and make way for faster cars wanting to pass you.** In cities and towns, approach crossings with care; local drivers may exercise the principle of priority for traffic from the right with some abandon.

G

GAY & LESBIAN TRAVEL

The Netherlands is one of the most liberal countries in the world in its social and legal attitude toward gays and lesbians. The age of consent is 16, there are stringent anti-discrimination laws, and gay couples registered as living together have the same rights as heterosexual couples. At press time legislation was before parliament to fully legalize same-sex marriage.

Social attitudes in Belgium toward gays and lesbians are about the same as in the Netherlands, especially in bigger cities, but there's no equally far-reaching legislation. Luxembourg is the most conservative of the three countries, but in Luxembourg City similar attitudes apply as in the other two countries.

I
INSURANCE

Travel insurance can protect your investment, replace your luggage and its contents, or provide for medical coverage should you fall ill during your trip. Most tour operators, travel agents, and insurance agents sell specialized health-and-accident, flight, trip-cancellation, and luggage insurance as well as comprehensive policies with some or all of these features. Before you make any purchase, **review your existing health and home-owner policies** to find out whether they cover expenses incurred while traveling.

BAGGAGE

Airline liability for your baggage is limited to $1,250 per person on domestic flights. On international flights, the airlines' liability is $9.07 per pound or $20 per kilogram for checked baggage (roughly $640 per 70-pound bag) and $400 per passenger for unchecked baggage. Insurance for losses exceeding the terms of your airline ticket can be bought directly from the airline at check-in for about $10 per $1,000 of coverage; note that it excludes a rather extensive list of items, shown on your airline ticket.

FLIGHT

You should **think twice before buying flight insurance.** Often purchased as a last-minute impulse at the airport, it pays a lump sum when a plane crashes, either to a beneficiary if the insured dies or sometimes to a surviving passenger who loses eyesight or a limb. Supplementing the airlines' coverage described in the limits-of-liability paragraphs on your ticket, it's expensive and basically unnecessary. Charging an airline ticket to a major credit card often automatically entitles you to coverage and may also include travel by bus, train, and ship.

HEALTH

If your own health insurance policy does not cover you outside the U.S., **consider buying supplemental medical coverage.** It can provide from $1,000 to $150,000 worth of medical and/or dental expenses incurred as a result of an accident or illness during a trip. These policies also may include a personal-accident, or death-and-dismemberment provision, which pays a lump sum ranging from $15,000 to $500,000 to your beneficiaries if you die or to you if you lose one or more limbs or your eyesight, and a medical-assistance provision, which may either reimburse you for the cost of referrals, evacuation, or repatriation and other services, or may automatically enroll you as a member of a particular medical-assistance company (☞ Health Issues *in* Important Contacts A to Z, *above*).

FOR U.K. TRAVELERS

You can buy an annual travel-insurance policy valid for most vacations during the year in which it's purchased. If you go this route, make sure it covers you if you have a pre-existing medical condition or are pregnant.

TRIP

Without insurance, you will lose all or most of your money if you must cancel your trip due to illness or any other reason. Especially if your airline ticket, cruise, or package tour is non-refundable and cannot be changed, it's essential that you **buy trip-cancellation-and-interruption insurance.** When considering how much coverage you need, look for a policy that will cover the cost of your trip plus the non-discounted price of a one-way airline ticket should you need to return home early. Read the fine print carefully, especially sections defining "family member" and "pre-existing medical conditions." Also **consider default or bankruptcy insurance,** which protects you against a supplier's failure to deliver. However, such policies often do not cover default by a travel agency, tour operator, airline, or cruise line if you bought your tour and the coverage directly from the firm in question.

L

LANGUAGE

Belgium has three official languages: Flemish, French, and German (spoken by a small minority). In Luxembourg the official language is French, but German is a compulsory subject in schools, and everybody speaks Luxembourgish, the native tongue (a language descended from an ancient dialect of the Franks); most people also know a fair amount of English. In the Netherlands, Dutch is the official language, but almost everybody knows at least some English and many speak it very well.

LODGING

All three countries offer a range of choices, from the major international hotel chains and small, modern local hotels to family-run restored inns and historic houses, to elegant country châteaux and resorts. Prices in metropolitan areas are significantly higher than those in outlying towns and the countryside.

Most hotels that cater to business travelers will grant substantial weekend rebates. These discounted rates are often available during the week as well as in July and early August, when business travelers are thin on the ground. Moreover, you can often qualify for a "corporate rate" when hotel occupancy is low. The moral is, **always ask what's the best rate a hotel can offer before you book.** No hotelier was ever born who will give a lower rate unless you ask for it.

APARTMENT & VILLA RENTALS

If you want a home base that's roomy enough for a family and comes with cooking facilities, **consider a furnished rental.** It's generally cost-wise, too, although not always—some rentals are luxury properties (economical only when your party is large). Home-exchange directories do list rentals—often second homes owned by prospective house swappers—and some services search for a house or apartment for you (even a castle if that's your fancy) and handle the paperwork. Some send an illustrated catalogue and others send photographs of specific properties, sometimes at a charge; up-front registration fees may apply.

HOME EXCHANGE

If you would like to find a house, an apartment, or other vacation property to exchange for your own while on vacation, **become a member of a home-exchange organization,** which will send you its annual directories listing available exchanges and will include your own listing in at least one of them. Arrangements for the actual exchange are made by the two parties to it, not by the organization.

M

MAIL & POSTAL RATES

See individual country chapters.

MEDICAL ASSISTANCE

No one plans to get sick while traveling, but it happens, so **consider signing up with a medical assistance company.** These outfits provide referrals, emergency evacuation or repatriation, 24-hour telephone hot lines for medical consultation, dispatch of medical personnel, relay of medical records, cash for emergencies, and other personal and legal assistance.

MONEY & EXPENSES

The monetary unit in Belgium is the Belgian franc (BF); in Luxembourg, the Luxembourg franc (Flux); and in the Netherlands, the guilder (Fl). The currency exchange rates quoted in the following chapters fluctuate daily, so check them at the time of your departure.

ATMS

Cirrus, Plus, and many other networks connecting automated-teller machines operate internationally. Chances are that you can **use your bank card at ATMs** to withdraw money from an account and get cash advances on a credit-card account if your card has been programmed with a personal identification number, or PIN. Before leaving home, **check in on frequency limits** for withdrawals and cash advances. Also **ask whether your card's PIN must be reprogrammed** for use in the Netherlands, Belgium, or Luxembourg. Four digits are commonly used overseas. Note that Discover is accepted only in the United States.

On cash advances you are charged interest from the day you receive the money from ATMs as well as from tellers. Although transaction fees for ATM withdrawals abroad may be higher than fees for withdrawals at home, Cirrus and Plus exchange rates are excellent because they are based on wholesale rates only offered by major banks.

EXCHANGING CURRENCY

For the most favorable rates, **change money at banks.** You won't do as well at exchange booths in airports, rail, and bus stations, nor in hotels, restaurants, and stores, although you may find their hours more convenient. To avoid lines at airport exchange booths, **get a small amount of currency before you leave home.**

TAXES

AIRPORT➤ The Brussels National Airport tax is BF525, levied on all tickets and payable with your ticket purchase.

HOTEL➤ All hotels in the Netherlands charge a 6% Value Added Tax, which is usually included in the quoted room price. In addition, some local city authorities impose a "tourist tax." This is added to your bill, but usually amounts to just an extra dollar or two a day.

All hotels in Belgium charge a 6% Value Added Tax (TVA), included in the room

rate; in Brussels, there is also a 9% city tax.

Hotels in Luxembourg charge a visitor's tax of 5%, included in the room rate.

SALES/VAT TAX➤ In the Netherlands a sales tax (BTW/VAT) of 17.5% is added to most purchases, such as clothing, souvenirs, and car fuel. Certain items (books among them) fall into a 6% band, as do hotel tariffs and restaurant meals.

In Belgium, VAT ranges from 6% on food and clothing to 33% on luxury goods. Restaurants are in between; 21% VAT is included in quoted prices.

To **get a VAT refund** you need to be resident outside the European Union and to have spent Fl 300 or more in the same shop on the same day. Provided that you personally carry the goods out of the country within 30 days, you may claim a refund. Systems for doing this vary. Most leading stores will issue you a "VAT cheque" as proof of purchase (and charge a commission for the service). Then have these tax-refund forms stamped at customs as you leave the final European Union country on your itinerary; send the stamped form back to the store. Alternatively and for a simpler procedure, if you shop at a store that displays a Europe Tax Free Shopping sticker, ask for a refund check at the store, have it validated at customs at the airport, and claim a cash refund (minus

20% handling) at an ETS booth.

TRAVELER'S CHECKS

Whether to buy traveler's checks depends on where you are headed; **take cash to rural areas and small towns, traveler's checks to cities.** The most widely recognized are American Express, Citicorp, Thomas Cook, and Visa, which are sold by major commercial banks for 1% to 3% of the checks' face value—it pays to **shop around.** Both American Express and Thomas Cook issue checks that can be countersigned and used by you or your traveling companion, and they both provide checks, at no extra charge, denominated in Dutch guilders. You can cash them in banks without paying a fee (which can be as much as 20%) and use them as readily as cash in many hotels, restaurants, and shops. So you won't be left with excess foreign currency, **buy a few checks in small denominations** to cash toward the end of your trip. Record the numbers of the checks, cross them off as you spend them, and keep this information separate from your checks.

WIRING MONEY

You don't have to be a cardholder to send or receive funds through MoneyGram^SM from American Express. Just **go to a MoneyGram agent,** located in retail and convenience stores and in American Express Travel Offices. Pay up to $1,000 with cash or a credit card, anything over that, cash only. The money can be picked up within 10 minutes in the form of U.S. dollar traveler's checks or local currency at the nearest Money-Gram agent, or, abroad, the nearest American Express Travel Office. There's no limit, and the recipient need only present photo identification. The commission runs from 3% to 10%, depending on the amount sent, the destination, and how you pay.

You can also **send money using Western Union.** Money sent from the United States or Canada will be available for pickup at agent locations in 100 countries within 15 minutes. Once the money is in the system, it can be picked up at any one of 25,000 locations. Fees range from 4% to 10%, depending on the amount you send.

P

PACKAGES & TOURS

A package or tour to the Netherlands, Belgium, and Luxembourg can make your vacation less expensive and more convenient. Firms that sell tours and packages purchase airline seats, hotel rooms, and rental cars in bulk and pass some of the savings on to you. In addition, the best operators have local representatives to help you out at your destination.

A GOOD DEAL?

The more your package or tour includes, the better you can predict the ultimate cost of your vacation. Make sure you know exactly what is included, and **beware of hidden costs.** Are taxes, tips, and service charges included? Transfers and baggage handling? Entertainment and excursions? These can add up.

Most packages and tours are rated deluxe, first-class superior, first class, tourist, and budget. The key difference is usually accommodations. If the package or tour you are considering is priced lower than in your wildest dreams, **be skeptical.** Also, **make sure your travel agent knows the hotels** and other services. Ask about location, room size, beds, and whether it has a pool, room service, or programs for children, if you care about these things. Has your agent been there or sent others you can contact?

BUYER BEWARE

Each year consumers are stranded or lose their money when operators go out of business—even very large operators with excellent reputations. If you can't afford a loss, take the time to **check out the operator**—find out how long the company has been in business, and ask several agents about its reputation. Next, **don't book unless the firm has a consumer-protection program.** Members of the United States Tour Operators Association and the National Tour Association are required to set aside funds exclusively to cover your

payments and travel arrangements in case of default. Nonmember operators may, instead, carry insurance; look for the details in the operator's brochure—and the name of an underwriter with a solid reputation. Note: When it comes to tour operators, **don't trust escrow accounts.** Although there are laws governing those of charter-flight operators, no governmental body prevents tour operators from raiding the till.

Next, **contact your local Better Business Bureau and the attorney general's office** in both your own state and the operator's; have any complaints been filed? Last, **pay with a major credit card.** Then you can cancel payment, provided that you can document your complaint. Always **consider trip-cancellation insurance** (☞ Insurance, *above*).

BIG VS. SMALL➤ An operator that handles several hundred thousand travelers annually can use its purchasing power to give you a good price. Its high volume may also indicate financial stability. But some small companies provide more personalized service; because they tend to specialize, they may also be experts on an area.

USING AN AGENT

Travel agents are an excellent resource. In fact, large operators accept bookings only through travel agents. But it's good to **collect brochures from several agencies,** because some agents' suggestions may be skewed by promotional relationships with tour and package firms that reward them for volume sales. If you have a special interest, **find an agent with expertise in that area;** the American Society of Travel Agents can give you leads in the United States. (Don't rely solely on your agent, though; agents may be unaware of small niche operators, and some special-interest travel companies only sell direct.)

SINGLE TRAVELERS

Prices are usually quoted per person, based on two sharing a room. If traveling solo, you may be required to pay the full double-occupancy rate. Some operators eliminate this surcharge if you agree to be matched up with a roommate of the same sex, even if one is not found by departure time.

PACKING FOR THE NETHERLANDS, BELGIUM, & LUXEMBOURG

The best advice for a trip to the Netherlands in any season is to **pack light, be flexible, bring an umbrella** (and trench coat with a liner in winter), and **always have a sweater or jacket available.** For daytime wear and casual evenings, turtlenecks and flannel shirts are ideal for winter, alone or under a sweater, and cotton shirts with sleeves are perfect in summer. Blue jeans are popular and are even sometimes worn to the office;

sweat suits, however, are never seen outside of fitness centers. For women, high heels are nothing but trouble on the cobblestone streets of Amsterdam and other old cities, and sneakers or running shoes are a dead giveaway that you are an American tourist; a better choice is a pair of dark-colored walking shoes or low-heeled pumps.

In Belgium and Luxembourg, **bring a woolen sweater,** even in summer; if you hit a rainy spell, a raincoat and umbrella may prove indispensable. Practical **walking shoes are important,** whether for rough cobblestones or forest trails. Women here wear skirts more frequently than do women in the United States, especially those over 35. Men would be wise to include a jacket and tie, especially if you're planning to visit one of the upper-echelon restaurants.

Regardless of your destination, pack an extra pair of eyeglasses or contact lenses in your carry-on luggage, and if you have a health problem, **take enough medication** to last the trip, or have your doctor write a prescription using the drug's generic name, because brand names vary from country to country (otherwise you'll need a prescription from a local doctor). In case your bags go astray, **don't put prescription drugs or valuables in luggage to be checked.** To avoid problems with customs officials, carry medications in original

packaging. Also don't forget the addresses of offices that handle refunds of lost traveler's checks.

ELECTRICITY

To use your U.S.-purchased electric-powered equipment, **bring a converter and an adapter.** The electrical current in the Netherlands, Belgium, and Luxembourg is 220 volts, 50 cycles alternating current (AC); wall outlets take Continental-type plugs, with two round prongs.

If your appliances are dual voltage, you'll need only an adapter. Hotels sometimes have 110-volt outlets for low-wattage appliances marked "For Shavers Only" near the sink; don't use them for high-wattage appliances such as blow-dryers. If your laptop computer is older, carry a converter; new laptops operate equally well on 110 and 220 volts, so you need only an adapter.

LUGGAGE

Free airline baggage allowances depend on the airline, the route, and the class of your ticket; ask in advance. In general, on domestic flights and on international flights between the United States and foreign destinations, you are entitled to check two bags— neither exceeding 62 inches (158 centimeters), length + width + height, or weighing more than 70 pounds (32 kilograms). A third piece may be brought aboard; its total dimensions are generally limited to less than 45 inches (114 centimeters), so it will fit easily under the seat in front of you or in the overhead compartment. In the United States, the FAA gives airlines broad latitude to limit carry-on allowances and tailor them to different aircraft and operational conditions. Charges for excess, oversize, or overweight pieces vary.

If you are flying between two foreign destinations, note that baggage allowances may be determined not by piece but by weight—66 pounds (30 kilograms) in business class, and 44 pounds (20 kilograms) in economy. If your flight between two cities abroad *connects* with your transatlantic or transpacific flight, the piece method still applies.

SAFEGUARDING YOUR LUGGAGE➤ Before leaving home, **itemize your bags' contents** and their worth, and label them with your name, address, and phone number. (If you use your home address, cover it so that potential thieves can't see it.) Inside your bag, **pack a copy of your itinerary.** At check-in, **make sure that your bag is correctly tagged** with the airport's three-letter destination code. If your bags arrive damaged or not at all, file a written report with the airline before leaving the airport.

PASSPORTS & VISAS

If you don't already have one, **get a passport.** While traveling,

keep one photocopy of the data page separate from your wallet and leave another copy with someone at home. If you lose your passport, promptly call the nearest embassy or consulate, and the local police; having the data page can speed replacement.

U.S. and Canadian residents do not require visas to visit the Benelux countries for pleasure or business trips not exceeding three months. British citizens do not require visas regardless of the length or purpose of their visit, but will be required to register with local authorities if they take up residence.

U.S. CITIZENS

All U.S. citizens, even infants, need a valid passport to enter the Netherlands, Belgium, or Luxembourg for stays of up to 90 days. New and renewal application forms are available at any of the 13 U.S. Passport Agency offices and at some post offices and courthouses. Passports are usually mailed within four weeks; allow five weeks or more in spring and summer.

CANADIANS

You need a valid passport to enter the Netherlands, Belgium, or Luxembourg for stays of up to 90 days. Application forms are available at 28 regional passport offices as well as post offices and travel agencies. Whether for a first or a subsequent passport, you must apply in person. Children under 16 may be included on a

parent's passport but must have their own to travel alone. Passports are valid for five years and are usually mailed within two to three weeks of application.

U.K. CITIZENS

Citizens of the United Kingdom need a valid passport to enter the Netherlands, Belgium, or Luxembourg for stays of up to 90 days. Applications for new and renewal passports are available from main post offices as well as at the passport offices, located in Belfast, Glasgow, Liverpool, London, Newport, and Peterborough. You may apply in person at all passport offices, or by mail to all except the London office. Children under 16 may travel on an accompanying parent's passport. All passports are valid for 10 years. Allow a month for processing.

R
RAIL TRAVEL

Rail travel in Europe, even first-class including supplements, is consistently 60%–75% cheaper than the lowest available one-way airline fare.

To save money, **look into rail passes** (☞ Rail Travel *in* Important Contacts A to Z). But if you don't plan to cover many miles, you may come out ahead by buying individual tickets.

Many travelers assume that rail passes guarantee them seats on the trains they wish to ride—not so. You need to **book seats ahead even if you are using a** rail pass; seat reservations are required on some European trains, particularly high-speed trains, and are a good idea on trains that may be crowded—particularly in summer on popular routes. You will also need a reservation if you purchase overnight sleeping accommodations.

Eurostar operates high-speed passenger-only trains, which whisk riders between new stations in London and Brussels (Midi) in 3¼ hours. At press time, fares were $180 for a one-way, first-class ticket and $123 for an economy fare. A number of promotional return fares are available.

On the new Thalys high-speed trains, a one-way ticket from Brussels to Paris costs $90 in first class and $60 in economy.

RENTING A CAR

The major car rental firms have booths at the airports. This is convenient, but the airports charge rental companies a fee that is passed on to customers, so you may want to **wait until you arrive at the downtown locations of rental firms.** Consider also whether you want to get off a transatlantic flight and into an unfamiliar car in an unfamiliar city.

Renting a car becomes competitive with other forms of transportation if at least two people traveling together cover a distance of 1,000 miles a week. There are of course many other reasons for having wheels, but if your stay is limited to major cities, you don't need them. **Look for special weekend deals and weekly rates** (and make sure you keep the car at least five days so you're not socked with a daily rate).

CUTTING COSTS

To get the best deal, **book through a travel agent and shop around.** When pricing cars, **ask where the rental lot is located.** Some off-airport locations offer lower rates—even though their lots are only minutes away from the terminal via complimentary shuttle. You may also want to **price local car-rental companies,** whose rates may be lower still, although service and maintenance standards may not be up to those of a national firm. Also **ask your travel agent about a company's customer-service record.** How has it responded to late plane arrivals and vehicle mishaps? Are there often lines at the rental counter, and, if you're traveling during a holiday period, does a confirmed reservation guarantee you a car?

Always **find out what equipment is standard** at your destination before specifying what you want; **do without automatic transmission or air-conditioning** if they're optional. In Europe, manual transmissions are standard and air-conditioning is rare and often unnecessary.

Also in Europe, **look into wholesalers—** companies that do not own their own fleets but rent in bulk from those that do and often offer better rates than traditional car-rental operations. Prices are best during low travel periods, and rentals booked through wholesalers must be paid for before you leave the United States. If you use a wholesaler, **know whether the prices are guaranteed** in U.S. dollars or foreign currency, and if unlimited mileage is available; find out about required deposits, cancellation penalties, and drop-off charges; and confirm the cost of any required insurance coverage.

INSURANCE

When you drive a rented car, you are generally responsible for any damage or personal injury that you cause as well as damage to the vehicle. Before you rent, **see what coverage you already have** by means of your personal auto-insurance policy and credit cards. For about $14 a day, rental companies sell insurance, known as a collision damage waiver (CDW), that eliminates your liability for damage to the car; it's always optional and should never be automatically added to your bill.

REQUIREMENTS

In the Netherlands, Belgium, and Luxembourg your own driver's license is acceptable. An International Driver's Permit, available from the American or Canadian Automobile Association, is a good idea.

SURCHARGES

Before picking up the car in one city and

leaving it in another, **ask about drop-off charges or one-way service fees,** which can be substantial. Note, too, that some rental agencies charge extra if you return the car before the time specified on your contract. To avoid a hefty refueling fee, **fill the tank just before you turn in the car.**

S
SENIOR CITIZENS

DISCOUNTS

To qualify for age-related discounts, **mention your senior-citizen status up front** when booking hotel reservations, not when checking out, and before you're seated in restaurants, not when paying your bill, also when buying tickets for museums and other attractions. Note that discounts may be limited to certain menus, days, or hours. When renting a car, **ask about promotional car-rental discounts**—they can net lower costs than your senior-citizen discount.

LODGING

Radisson SAS hotels in Brussels and Amsterdam offer reductions for senior citizens and traveling companions based on age. If you're 65 years old, you qualify for a 65% reduction, those age 75 are eligible for a 75% reduction, and so on. Travelers age 100 stay for free. These rates are available both weekends and during the week, but book early, as availability is limited. For other hotels, **check on the availability of senior rates when you book.**

STUDENTS ON THE ROAD

To save money, **look into deals available through student-oriented travel agencies.** To qualify, you'll need to have a bona fide student I.D. card. Members of international student groups also are eligible (☞ Students *in* Important Contacts A to Z).

T
TAXIS

Generally, you can't flag a taxi in the street in the Benelux countries. If you're not close to a cab stand, call for one. Generally, passengers give a 10% tip.

AT THE AIRPORT

Plenty of taxis are available outside arrival halls. You may be tired when you arrive, but **do not accept the offers of "help" you may get from unlicensed taxi drivers** who may accost you in the arrival hall.

TELEPHONES

LONG-DISTANCE

The long-distance services of AT&T, MCI, and Sprint make calling home relatively convenient and let you avoid hotel surcharges; typically, you dial a local number. Before you go, **find out the local access codes** for your destinations.

TIPPING

For specific tipping practices, *see* individual country chapters.

W
WHEN TO GO

The best times to visit these three countries are late spring—when the

northern European days are long and the summer crowds have not yet filled the beaches, the highways, or the museums—and in fall.

THE NETHERLANDS

The Netherlands' high season begins in late March to late April, when the tulips come up, and runs through October, when the Dutch celebrate their Autumn Holiday. June, July, and August are the most popular months with both international visitors and the Dutch themselves—it can be difficult to obtain reservations, particularly in beach towns on the North Sea coast and at campgrounds, during mid-summer. The cultural season lasts from September to June, but there are special cultural festivals and events scheduled in summer months.

The Netherlands has a mild maritime climate, with bright, clear summers and damp, overcast winters. The driest months are from February through May; the sunniest, May through August. In the eastern and southeastern provinces, winters are colder and summers warmer than along the North Sea coast.

BELGIUM

Because Belgians take vacations in July and August, these months are not ideal for visiting the coast or the Ardennes, but summer is a very good time to be in Brussels, Antwerp, or Liège. In summer you will also be able to get a break on hotel prices; on the other hand, this is also vacation time for many restaurants. For touring the country and visiting much-frequented tourist attractions such as Brugge, the best times are April–June and September–October.

LUXEMBOURG

Luxembourg is a northern country—parallel in latitude to Newfoundland, Canada—with the same seasonal extremes in the amount of day-light. In late spring, summer, and early fall, you have daylight until 10 PM; in winter, however, be prepared for dusk closing in before 4 PM. There's rarely a long spell of heavy snow, but winters tend to be dank and rainy. Many attractions, especially outside the city, maintain shortened visiting hours (or close altogether) from late fall to Pentecost (late spring), except for a brief time around Easter. Summer is the principal tourist season, when Luxembourg polishes up its sightseeing train and restaurants set out terrace tables under the sycamores; gardens are in full bloom and weather can be comfortably hot. Spring and early fall are attractive as well.

Climate in the Netherlands, Belgium, and Luxembourg

What follows are average daily maximum and minimum temperatures:

AMSTERDAM

Jan.	40F	4C	May	61F	16C	Sept.	65F	18C
	34	1		50	10		56	13
Feb.	41F	5C	June	65F	18C	Oct.	56	13C
	34	1		56	13		49	9
Mar.	47F	8C	July	70F	21C	Nov.	47F	8C
	38	3		59	15		41	5
Apr.	52F	11C	Aug.	68F	20C	Dec.	41F	5C
	43	6		59	15		36	2

BRUSSELS

Jan.	40F	4C	May	65F	18C	Sept.	70F	21C
	31	−1		47	8		52	11
Feb.	45F	7C	June	72F	22C	Oct.	59	15C
	32	0		52	11		45	7
Mar.	50F	10C	July	74F	23C	Nov.	49F	9C
	36	2		54	12		38	3
Apr.	58F	14C	Aug.	72F	22C	Dec.	43F	6C
	41	5		54	12		34	1

LUXEMBOURG

Jan.	38F	3C	May	65F	18C	Sept.	67F	19C
	31	− 1		47	8		50	10
Feb.	40F	4C	June	70F	21C	Oct.	56	13C
	31	− 1		52	11		43	6
Mar.	50F	10C	July	74F	23C	Nov.	45F	7C
	34	1		56	13		38	3
Apr.	58F	14C	Aug.	72F	22C	Dec.	40F	4C
	40	4		54	13		32	0

THE GOLD GUIDE / SMART TRAVEL TIPS

1 Destination: The Netherlands, Belgium, and Luxembourg

REFLECTIONS IN A PEWTER BOWL

SLATE-COLORED SKIES CURVE like a pewter bowl over an undulating landscape, the long, low horizon punctuated by blunt steeples and a scattering of deep-roofed farmhouses that seem to enfold the land like a mother goose spreading wings over her brood. Inky crows wheel over spindle-fingered pollards, jackdaws pepper the ocher grainfields, and a magpie, flashing black and white, drags a long, iridescent tail through the damp air. These are the 16th-century landscapes of Pieter Bruegel the Elder—stained-glass planes in sepia tones, leaded by black branches, crooked spires, dark-frozen streams.

And these, too, are the 20th-century landscapes of Belgium, the Netherlands, and Luxembourg—a wedge of northern Europe squeezed between the massive and ancient kingdoms of France and Germany, bounded by the harsh North Sea to the northwest, defined by the rough, high forests of the Ardennes to the southeast. No wonder so much of their appeal, past and present, is interior—bountiful, sensual still lifes, the glowing chambers of Vermeer, the inner radiance in the portraits of Rembrandt: Their weather-beaten cultures have turned inward over the centuries, toward the hearth. Indoors, Bruegel's otherwise sepia scenes warm subtly with color—earthy browns, berry reds, loden greens, muted indigos, coral cheeks. So it is today: The Netherlanders gather in gold-lit, smoke-burnished "brown cafés," old bentwood chairs scraping across weathered stone floors; the Flemish nurse goblets of mahogany beer by candlelight in dark-beamed halls, a scarlet splash of paisley runner thrown over the pine tabletop; red-vested Walloons—French-speaking Belgians—read the newspaper in high-backed oak banquettes polished blue-black by generations of rough tweed. In Luxembourg, the glass of light beer and *drüp* of eau-de-vie go down behind the candy-colored leaded glass of spare, bright-lit *stuff* or pubs, where village life finds its social focus, day in, day out. In each of these small northern lands, so often lashed by rain, soaked by drizzle, wrapped in fog, with winter dark closing in at 4 PM and winter daylight dawdling until 9 AM, the people live out the rich-hued interior scenes of the Old Masters.

Yet the skies do clear, come spring, and at last the light lingers until well after 10 at night. Then the real pleasure begins—an intense appreciation that residents of moderate climates would be hard-put to understand. As if the people's gratitude took physical form, it manifests itself in flowers, a frenzy of color spilling from every windowsill, spreading like ocean waves across tulip fields, over rose trellises, through wisteria-woven archways. Fruit trees explode like fireworks, and whole orchards shimmer pink. Chestnut branches sag under the weight of their leaves and the heavy, grapelike clusters of blossom that thrust upward, defying gravity. In the midst of this orgy of scent and color, Dutch university students bicycle along canals in loose batik-print cotton; Flemish farmers in blue overalls open their half-doors and bask; the international bankers of Luxembourg swing their Versace suit coats over their shoulders and head for the benches in the green Petrusse Valley.

Then café society, and home life with it, moves lock, stock, and barrel outdoors, to bask, lizardlike in the rare warmth. Terrace cafés on the Grote Markts and Grand'Places rival any piazza in Italy. And when there's no café around, the family simply sets out a cluster of folding chairs, perhaps a checkered-cloth-covered card table, whether smack on the sidewalk or behind the barn door, to make the most of fine weather. A suntan remains (as it does in sun-starved North Germany) the most sought-after of status symbols—doubly prestigious if flaunted in midwinter, as northerners, once pale and prune-skinned, return from the ski slopes of the Alps or the beaches of the Canary Islands.

The extremes of their climate, from inexorable gray to luxurious sun, may form a common bond, but the three countries of the Netherlands, Belgium, and Luxembourg sustain sharply different cultures, languages, and terrain. The Netherlands itself is a tangle of inner conflicts—Catholic versus Protestant (they lean 60–40 toward the latter, that 60 percent still functioning as one of Europe's Reformation strongholds); puritanical versus prurient (though you can't buy liquor on Sunday in some areas, in others prostitutes sit, whalebone-stayed, in display windows like so much grade-A beef). In fact, in narrow, low row houses up and down town streets, whole blocks-full of ordinary people live without curtains, their evening lives and possessions open to viewing by passersby. Each summer the Netherlanders turn their backs on the beach, load up their trailers, and migrate south; though they're leaving behind the most heavily populated land on the Continent, they flock together in crowded trailer parks wherever they go, rank on cozy rank decked with lace curtains and black-and-yellow Dutch license plates.

THE BELGIAN SITUATION goes beyond mere contradiction: It is a country torn in two, split by two tongues and two distinct cultures. The division between Wallonie and Flanders traces back to Merovingian times, and the Walloon patois and Belgian French represent the last northward wave of the Roman empire and its lingual residue. Twice in this century Flemish citizens (and possibly a king) were known to collaborate with German invaders, allying themselves against what they saw as French-speaking domination. And today the bickering over bilingual rights leaves Brussels a no-man's-land, with extra-wide enamel signs naming every street and alley in two tongues. The cultures are as different as their languages: The Flemish are proud and tidy, their homes filled with the exterior light that pours in through tall, multipaned windows; a spare, avant-garde current in fashion, film, and literature shows their Dutch leanings. The Walloons, on the other hand, remain more laissez-faire, their homes often dark, cozy, and cluttered with knickknacks and lace. A women's clothing shop in Ghent is likely to include progressive, trendy, severe clothing, while the equivalent in Liège will show cardigans, A-line skirts, and fussy floral prints. These two separate worlds share a Catholic culture that, beyond the spiritual realm, finds expression in a shared appreciation of the good things in life, such as the pleasures of the table.

If Belgium and the Netherlands show inner conflict, the natives of little Luxembourg present a solid front to the outside, interacting in French, German, or English, but maintaining their private world in their own native *Lëtzebuergesch* (Luxembourgish). Thus, having survived centuries of conquest and occupation, they can open their country to European Union "Eurocrats" and more than a hundred international banks, and still keep to themselves. Luxembourg sustains two parallel cultures, with some cafés catering to trendy, international, or tourist crowds and others reserved for the loden-coated locals, who may greet an aberrant visitor with stunned silence as thick as the cigarette smoke that fills the air.

The Netherlands, Belgium, and Luxembourg—as diverse within themselves as they are to one another. And yet all this diversity has been thrown together by the dominant cultures pressing in at the borders—France and Germany. Having been conquered and economically dwarfed for generations, the three little countries felt compelled, in 1958, to form an alliance, an economic union that served as a foundation for the European Union. Since then, "Benelux" has become a convenient abbreviation for a small, independent wedge of northern Europe where even fruit juice is labeled in French and in Dutch.

But, of course, Benelux is considerably more than an arbitrary economic unit. It is a rich and varied region, laced with canals, sprinkled with orchards, its cities burnished with age, where museum visitors can browse through the landscapes of Bruegel and Van Ruisdael and the interiors of Van Eyck, Vermeer, and Rembrandt—then experience their inspiration firsthand, in the magnificent, brooding countryside and time-polished interiors that remain much unchanged since they first inspired the Old Masters.

—Nancy Coons

Since moving to Europe in 1987, Nancy Coons has contributed regularly to Fodor's publications and has written features on European topics for *National Geographic Traveler*, the *Wall Street Journal*, and *Opera News*.

WHAT'S WHERE

Here is a quick overview to help you travel civilized roads, both back in time and forward.

The Netherlands

"God made the world," say the citizens of Holland, "but the Dutch made the Netherlands." Nearly half of this democratic monarchy's 15,450 square miles has been reclaimed from the sea, and the doughty inhabitants have been working for generations to keep it from slipping back. Hence the special look of the Dutch landscape, the subject of some of the most beautiful Old Master paintings ever created. In scenery and structure, the country's north and south regions differ little, for both have the same North Sea beachline on side, the same sand dunes and bulb-fields in the center, and the same type of rivers on its land borders. Yet each of the country's four main regions—Amsterdam, the Randstad, the Green Heart, and the Border Provinces—possesses its own distinct flavor. There is the capital, Amsterdam, one of the most amazing cities in Europe and the Netherlands' Shop Window. South of the capital is the Randstad (Ridge City), comprised of four adjacent urban centers—Leiden, The Hague, Rotterdam, and Utrecht; together they make up the true cultural and economic heart of the nation. To the east of the Randstad is the "Green Heart," with vast national parks studded with lovely museums and palaces. Near the Belgian and German borders are the Border Provinces and Maastrict—where billiard-table flatness gives way to gentle hills, and a more cosmopolitan and convivial way of life. Everywhere, of course, you'll find the Dutch people—at one and the same time *deftig* (dignified, respectable, and decorous) and *gezellig* (cozy, comfortable, and enjoying themselves).

In most areas, the biggest slopes are those leading up to the canal bridges; the tallest objects are the windmills with their white cloth sails stretched to pick up the slightest breeze. Everywhere, you will find cozy villages—the kind painted by Hobbema—and shining, immaculate cities (the whole country looks as though it had been scrubbed with Dutch cleaner). In the end, although it is one of Europe's smallest countries, the Netherlands manages to pack within its borders as many pleasures and treasures as countries five times its size.

Amsterdam

One of the great historic cities of the world, Amsterdam has also embraced modernity with a passion. Although called the City of Canals—it has more than a thousand of them—Amsterdam is no Venice, content to live on gondolas, moonlight serenades, and its former glory. It is one of the most forward-looking, cosmopolitan, and bustling cities around; on every street the delicious dichotomies of old and new stand side by side. Built on a lattice work of concentric canals arching from the IJ river like a great aquatic rainbow, Amsterdam is held together by the linchpins of its great public squares—the Dam, the Rembrandtplein, the Munt, and the Leidseplein. Most travelers begin at the **Dam,** abutting the Royal Dam Palace—to visitors, a godsend as a landmark, for even the worst student of foreign languages can easily obtain help if lost by asking for the "Dom" (as it is pronounced). Once you get settled, your first excursion should be a sightseeing tour in a glass-roofed canal boat: This is a city you have to get to know on water in order to be properly introduced.

After navigating the neighborhoods—literally—explore the main monuments on foot: the **Royal Dam Palace**; the **Tower of Tears,** from which Hendrik Hudson set sail in the *Half Moon* in 1609 to discover New York; **Rembrandt's House**; the fascinating attic **church of the Amstelkring**; the **Begijnhof**—the most peaceful corner of the city; the **Gouden Bocht** (Golden Bend), replete with stately burgher mansion of stepped gables and Daniel Marot doorways; and, of course, the famous **Rijksmuseum** and the **Vincent van Gogh museum.** With 22 Rembrandts, including the great *Night Watch,* and more than 200 van Goghs, Amsterdam is a prime destination for art lovers. Diamonds galore are found in the shops and factories of the historic **Jewish Quarter** east of the Zwanenburgwal. No one should miss the **Anne Frank house**—guaranteed to have you moved. Along the way, take time to sip *koffie* in one of the thousands of *bruine kroegjes* (Brown Cafés). Then at night, take in the Netherlands' hottest nightlife, impressive concerts, and fine restaurants—

with every sunset, Amsterdam reinvents itself. For a quick country escape, head west and slow down to smell the flowers on **"Die Bloemen Route"** (The Flower Road) from Aalsmeer—the greatest floral village in Europe—to the gorgeous Keukenhof Gardens and the town of Lisse. This is the Holland of tulips, hyacinths, and narcissi, ablaze with the colors of Easter in the spring and generally a rainbow of color year-round.

Metropolitan Holland and the Hague

Like filings around the end of a magnet, six major urban centers cluster in an arc just to the south of Amsterdam. While the capital remains a world-class city, these six cities offer a truer look at Dutch culture and society. It is a short step from the ocean of annual color of "Die Bloemen Route" to a haven of perennial color—the city of **Haarlem,** which is the earliest center of Dutch art and which gave rise to one of the most important schools of landscape painting in the 17th century. Today, you can still pursue the ghost of Frans Hals through its city streets while taking in the noted Frans Hals and Teyers museums and St. Bavo's Cathedral. **Leiden,** the birthplace of Rembrandt and site of a great university, remains a charming town where windmills rise over the cityscape. New Englanders are fond of making a pilgrimage here to the Pieterskerk, church of the Pilgrim Fathers who worshiped here for ten years before setting sail for America in 1620. **The Hague,** called 's-Gravenhage or Den Haag by the Dutch (and "the Largest Village in Europe" by residents), is a royal and regal city—filled with patrician mansions and gracious parks, and home to Queen Beatrix and the International Court of Justice. Here, you'll find the Mauritshuis (much more intimate that the Rijksmuseum) with canvases on display so uniformly excellent—Vermeer's *View of Delft* and *Girl with the Pearl* are just two—that you can see more beauty in a single hour here than probably anywhere else in the Netherlands.

After taking in the windswept beach resort of **Scheveningen**—and some of its herring (the best in the world)—head for **Delft,** a lovely old town whose tree-lined canals, humpbacked bridges, and step-gabled houses preserve the atmosphere of the 16th and 17th centuries better than

any other city in the country, captured unforgettably in the canvases of Vermeer and Pieter de Hoogh. Delft, of course, colored the world with its unique blue, best found in its famous blue-and-white Delftware china. Next up is **Rotterdam,** a true phoenix of a city that rose from the ashes of World War II to become one of the busiest ports in Europe. Rounding your way back to Amsterdam, stop a while in **Utrecht**'s history-soaked town center, climb the 338-foot tower of "the Cathedral that is Missing," and study its Oude Gracht (Old Canal). This city is the centerpiece of a region that is considered by many Dutch to be the most beautiful in the country: the landscape fairly bursts with lovely old trees (a rarity in the polders, or reclaimed countryside from the sea) and storybook castle-châteaux.

The Border Provinces and Maastricht

In most Dutch provinces the sea presses in to the land, constantly striving to win a foothold; Zeeland to the contrary pushes out into the water, invading the invader's territory and looking for trouble. On strips of land, like thumbs of a right hand, pointing westward toward the North Sea, Zeeland remains an ancient and romantic place. From the yachting port of **Zierikzee** you can explore **Veere,** a relentlessly picturesque town, then move on to the historic towns of **Middelburg, Breda,** and **'s-Hertogenbosch.** Heading south through Limbourg province, you'll enter **Maastricht,** the oldest city in the Netherlands. Wedged somewhat hesitatingly between Belgium and Germany, the town remains an intoxicating mixture of three languages, times, currencies, and customs. There are imposing Romanesque and Gothic churches, hundreds of historic gable-stone houses, and fabulous French food (where else can you enjoy breakfast with champagne in the Netherlands?). Each March, the European Fine Art Fair—some say this is the best art fair in Europe—draws in such high-rollers as Baron Thyssen-Bornemisza, Prince Bernhard, and J. Paul Getty, Jr.

The Green Heart: From Apeldoorn to Arnhem

Although as steeped in history as any other Dutch region, Gelderland seems to put the emphasis on the beauties of outdoor life, for it is a province studded with national parks and Edenic forests. Glorying in the title "The Largest Garden City in the Netherlands," **Apeldoorn** is so lavishly endowed with trees, natives challenge visitors to find the place! Thousands do every year, mostly to visit the **Palace Het Loo**—a legendary Dutch-Baroque castle and hunting lodge that was home to William and Mary (who went on to become king and queen of England). Set within **De Hoge Veluwe,** the nation's largest natural preserve, is the world-famous **Kröller-Müller Museum,** which has extraordinary paintings of the post-Impressionists as well as a multitude of works by van Gogh, including his *Sunflowers* and *Potato Eaters.* This region is, above all, a walking and bicycling paradise, and hikes through lush woods and moors can often delightfully end at grand country mansions, such as Het Wezenveld, Bruggenbosch, and Hunderen, outside Apeldoorn. The major towns of the region—**Zwolle, Deventer, Zutphen**—all have historic churches or town squares. The capital of the region is **Arnhem**—best known for "the bridge too far" of World War II. Its chief attractions are the battlefields, memorials, and war cemeteries that have become sacred places of pilgrimages, set in a region rich in scenic beauty.

The North

In this off-the-beaten-track region, you can be certain to see things that countless other visitors to the Netherlands miss. **Leeuwarden** is the capital of Friesland and birthplace of Saskia, Rembrandt's wife, and also of the mysterious Mata Hari. Crafts are a highlight here: You'll find the fine Netherlands Ceramic Museum, while nearby in **Makkum,** you can explore Tichelaar's Royal Makkum Pottery and Tile Factory. Farther north is **Groningen,** a famous university town, filled with architectural delights, pretty canals, and the magnificent gardens of the Prinsenhoftuin, where 250 years of topiary, lawn-making, and hedge-growing have produced a masterpiece on nature's canvas. Here and there, you'll find those distinctive storks' nests mounted atop wheels high upon poles—a fitting icon for this lovely, almost Adamic region of the Netherlands.

Belgium

Visitors continue to flock to Belgium, for this stamp-size country has tourist attractions out of all proportions to its size. Old World charm, a great cuisine, golden beaches, and the scenic forest of the Ardennes: these are but a few. The rest is art, to which Belgium, at the cultural crossroads of Europe, has been one of the supreme contributors. Jan van Eyck, said to have invented oil painting, heads a distinguished list of Flemish artists that includes Roger Van der Weyden, Dirck Bouts, Hugo Van der Goes, Hans Memling, Quentin Matsys, Pieter Bruegel, Peter Paul Rubens, and Anthony Van Dyck. Their work still shines with the mystic aura of the 15th century, the rich humanism of the Renaissance, the decorative exuberance of the Baroque. You can still find the people and the landscapes of Flanders almost unchanged since Pieter Bruegel brought his extraordinary powers of observation to focus on scenes of Flemish peasant life.

The top two cities are Brussels, a lively capital, a great shopping center, and the site of several fine museums, and Antwerp, a bustling port that is also a notable museum city. Probably the two most visited attractions aside from these are the so-called "picture-book towns," Ghent and Brugge (or Bruges), gems of medieval reminiscence. If you are interested in military history, you have your choice: from Kortrijk (Courtrai), where Flemish foot soldiers defeated French horsemen in 1302, to Waterloo, where Wellington confronted Napoleon, to Ieper, or Ypres (World War I), and Bastogne (World War II). There are any number of other cities of historic and artistic interest that are worth visiting— Liège, Leuven (Louvain), Namur, Mechelen (Malines), and Tournai. The ancestor of all health resorts is Spa. On the seacoast, Ostende and Knokke-Heist are the two main lures. To get away from the teeming life of Belgium's cities, journey into the rolling hills, dark woods, and green fields of the Ardennes, where you will find Belgium's greatest natural curiosity, the grottos of Han-sur-Less and of neighboring Rochfort.

Brussels

In Belgium, all roads lead to Brussels— and this goes for the railroads and airlines, too. Brussels is now the capital of the European Union, the boomtown home of international businessmen, Eurocrats and lobbyists with their legendary expense accounts. However, side by side with the

European institutions lies the old traditional capital, the ancient heart of the Brabant. In many respects, it is a thoroughly modern city, with shining steel-and-glass office blocks jostling Gothic spires and Art Nouveau town houses.

Everyone begins a city tour at the **Grand'-Place,** which Victor Hugo once called "the most beautiful square in the world." Flanked by flamboyantly decorated 17th-century guild houses, it's dominated by the Hôtel de Ville (town hall), which is in regal Brabant Gothic–style. After you've had a beer in one of the many superb cafés on the *place* (in summertime, return to see the square spectacularly floodlit at night), walk three blocks behind the town hall to pay respects to Belgium's "oldest inhabitant," the charming *Manneken Pis*—many amusing legends surround this statue of a peeing boy. The city's superlatives then await: Magnificent Rubenses and Bruegels at the **Musée d'Art Ancien,** the grand **Cathédrale de St. Michel et Ste. Gudule,** the delightful museum devoted to the art of comic strips, the fashionable square of the **Grand Sablon** (great antiques, pastry shops and restaurants), the opulent **Théâtre de la Monnaie** for the best concerts and ballet, and the haunting Magritte and Delvaux paintings on view at the **Musée d'Art Moderne.** No one will want to miss the **Victor Horta house,** the finest Art Nouveau building on the continent, now a museum, and other treasures of both Art Nouveau and Art Deco in the residential areas to the south and southeast of the city center. Along the way, of course, you'll be seasoning your sightseeing with some of Europe's finest cuisine: from *biftec et frites* (steak and fries) in a bistro to *waterzooi* (an elegant chicken stew) in a brasserie to *gaufres* (waffles) or death-by-chocolate pralines on the sidewalk.

Outside the Capital: From Waterloo to Hainaut

The countryside around Brussels offers a delightful atmosphere of historic interest and rural calm. Take in **Waterloo** by packing along an account of the historic battle in your picnic hamper; then stop at Wellington's Headquarters before surveying the battlefield, most of which remains as it was that fateful day in 1815. Head on to explore **Mechelen** (Malines in French), once famed as Margaret of Austria's court city, and discover Saint Rombout's Cathedral's great carillon, which reawakened modern worldwide interest in this art. Call on the town of **Leuven** (Louvain), home to the great university where Erasmus taught, and then head toward **Gaasbeek** to see one of Belgium's most beautiful châteaux, set within a landscape that inspired the great Bruegel.

Ghent, Brugge, and the Coast

"The Art Cities of Flanders" is a phrase that conjures up images of proud Ghent, now becalmed but in the past often torn by civil strife, and medieval Brugge (Bruges), contemplating its weathered beauty in the dark mirror of its calm canals. In the 15th century, these were among the richest cities in Europe, and the aura of that golden age still seems to emanate from their cloth halls, opulent merchants' homes, and cathedrals. **Ghent** is a city—one of Belgium's largest—not an inanimate museum, as is often said of Brugge. While much is medieval in this city, every stone is, in fact, part of 20th-century life. On a summer evening, viewed from Sint-Michielsbrug (St. Michael's Bridge), Ghent's noble medieval buildings assume a fairy-tale quality under the floodlights. One of the three great medieval spires is that of **St. Bavo's Cathedral,** where you'll find that world-wonder, the 15th-century *Adoration of the Mystic Lamb* altarpiece, which Jan van Eyck must have painted with a magnifying glass, so miraculous is its detail. Then take in the Gravensteen, the grand castle of the counts of Flanders; the imposing Town Hall; the proud Belfort (Belfry); and many other centuries-old buildings.

If it were not for people in modern clothes (and the fact that certain portions of the city are modern business districts), it would be difficult to realize you are living in the 20th century in **Brugge.** Scarcely a facade on any street or canal fails to conjure up visions of the past. Like a northern Venice, it is laced with tranquil canals and quaint bridges (Brugge, indeed, means bridges). This town is most famed as the birthplace of Flemish painting, and in the **Groeninge Museum** on the Dijver you'll find some of the finest masterpieces of Jan van Eyck (his magnificent *Madonna with Canon Van der Paele*), Van der Goes, Memling, Gerard David, and Hieronymus Bosch. Nearby, you can walk to such sights as the **Memling Museum** (with just six paintings—but they are six of the greatest Memlings in the world) within the walls of the 12th-century St. John's Hospice. Nothing remains of the castle that gave the **Burg** its name, but even so this is an extraordinary square, with its Gothic town hall and Romanesque chapel. The highways south from Brugge and Ghent point to Flanders Fields—there are countless military cemeteries in the area surrounding **Ieper** (Ypres), risen from the ashes of World War I. The **North Sea Coast** has more than 20 resorts, where holidaymakers can laze in deck chairs, take in the James Ensor Museum in **Oostende,** and enjoy some of the best seafood in the country.

Antwerp

For the visitor to Belgium with a taste for atmosphere and history, it may be that Antwerp will fill the bill even better than Brussels. For all that the city has grown and modernized at a rapid pace—today it is a mighty port and diamond mecca (60% of the world's diamond dealing is done here)—it still preserves a great deal of yesterday's glories. Most visitors come to the city to enjoy the afterglow of Antwerp's greatest period, the late 17th century, when three painters—Peter Paul Rubens, Jacob Jordaens, and Anthony van Dyck—made it into a standard bearer of style second only to Rome. Begin your explorations at the **Cathedral,** where three great Rubens altarpieces dazzle the eye and will probably fill you with enthusiasm to see the house occupied by the artist from 1610 for the last quarter century of his life. Off the Meir, the **Rubenshuis** is a truly patrician palace, marked by a large Flamboyant Baroque portico and lovely garden. Nearby is the **Mayer van den Bergh Museum,** a connoisseur's delight, with several masterpieces on view, including Bruegel's unforgettable *Dulle Griet* (Mag Meg). Two other august houses are a few blocks away: the **Rockoxhuis,** home of Rubens's patron, and the **Plantin-Moretus Museum,** once the home and print shop of Europe's most noted 17th-century publisher. After these famous homes, explore Antwerp's famed **Diamond District,** then discover the city's opulent churches, Renaissance guild halls, and the **Koninklijk Museum voor Schone Kunsten,** with its noted Rubens masterworks and four centuries of Dutch and Flemish art on view. From Antwerp you can make an excursion through the province of **Limbourg** with

its prosperous farms and orchards, dotted with ancient towns.

The Ardennes and the Black Country

Perhaps more than any other part of historic Belgium, the **Meuse Valley** is marked by centuries of man's long effort to survive and protect himself. Here, side by side, are the graves of stone age hunters and the tombs of soldiers killed in every war since the days of Charlemagne. Next to each town are hilltop forts that sought to hold up invaders, French as well as German. Signs of the great Belgian craft of metalwork are everywhere, especially in **Dinant,** squeezed between the river and the cliffside, in 17th-century **Namur,** at the confluence of the Meuse and the Sambre, and in **Huy,** "the epitome of romantic towns." The symbol of Walloon independence and pride is **Liège,** hard hit by the international steel crisis but still an important industrial center (Val-St-Lambert crystal is made here). Its old city is riddled with secret courtyards, narrow medieval lanes, steeply stepped streets, and *café chantants,* where everyone bursts into song.

The Ardennes is a rolling forest region, full of fast-flowing streams and wooded glens, one of Belgium's most favored vacationlands. It is the enchanted Forest of Arden of Shakespeare's *As You Like It,* and it offers the double charm of quaint villages and a beautiful landscape, still only half discovered by overseas visitors. The Ardennes forms an arc through the Belgian provinces of Namur, Liège, and Luxembourg, and on to the neighboring Grand Duchy. It remains one of the finest places to fill your lungs with fresh mountain air in Europe.

To the west, ancient **Tournai** beckons, with its great museum of tapestries, fabulous five-tower cathedral, and the **château of Beloeil,** Belgium's greatest garden. Nearby, too, is **the Borinage,** the area south of Mons, where Vincent van Gogh went as a preacher to the poor in 1878, and **Chimay,** where the lure is Madame Tallien's legendary Chateau de Chimay.

Luxembourg

When you try to locate Luxembourg on a map, look for "Lux." at the heart of Western Europe. Even abbreviated, the name runs over—west into Belgium, east into Germany, south into France—as the country's influence has done for centuries. The Grand Duchy of Luxembourg is a thriving, Rhode Island–size land that offers variety and contrasts out of all proportion to its size. On the northern borders of the country and down along the Our and Súre rivers is a rugged, wildly beautiful highland country studded with castles, rich in history. Castles abound as you travel south through rich farmlands lying in the broad, central river valleys, giving way to lush vineyards as you follow the southeastern frontier down the Wine Route through the Moselle Valley. If you turn back north from the French border, a 20-minute drive will bring the capital into view, its ancient fortress towering above the south central plain. Seen through early morning mists, it revives the magic of Camelot. It is the nerve center of a thousand-year-old seat of government, a functional working element of the European Union, a spot where the past still speaks, the present interprets, and the future listens.

There is an old saying that describes the life of the Luxembourgers—or *Luxembourgeois*, if you prefer the more elegant French appelation: "One Luxembourger, a rose garden; two Luxembourgers, a kaffeeklatsch; three Luxembourgers, a band." This is a country of parades and processions, good cheer, and a hearty capacity for beer and Moselle wine. Everybody here speaks French and German, and English is widely understood, which is fortunate because the official language, Letzeburgesch, is like nothing else you ever heard before.

Luxembourg City

The capital of the country will not disappoint you. It looks just like a setting for Franz Lehar's operetta, *The Count of Luxembourg,* and you would never suspect from its medieval aura that this city is a major European Union center. All periods exist together in a kind of helter-skelter harmony, and yet the place seems ageless: Centuries-old bridges, watchtowers, and ramparts reassert themselves to the exclusion of all incongruities. The city itself is small, a perfect place to explore on foot. With a little imagination, a walk outside the ramparts will recreate the past when this was one of the impregnable citadels of Europe.

You'll soon know why Luxembourg has been called the "Gibraltar of the North" as you approach the thousand-year-old fortress known as the **Bock.** Nearby is the 17th-century **Citadelle du St-Esprit** (Citadel of the Holy Spirit). Some may wish to explore the historic military **Casemates** (tunnels); all will wish to head for the **Place d'Armes,** the most welcoming corner of town. Then discover the **Grand Ducal Palace,** the **Musée National,** and the **Grand'rue,** the city's leading shopping street, which overflows with luxury boutiques. Cap off a day with a walk along the beautiful scenic ramparts of **the Corniche,** with its magnificent views over the deep valley below.

The Luxembourg Ardennes

The northern part of the country, called the Luxembourg Ardennes, is similar in many ways to its Belgian namesake. Romantic winding valleys of fast rivers, ideal for angling, cut into the plateau of high hills. Here and there are magnificent medieval castles—such as those at **Vianden, Bourscheid, Wiltz,** and **Clervaux.** The last was virtually reduced to rubble (but now amazingly restored) by an event that shook the world just over 50 years ago—the devasting Battle of the Ardennes, or Bulge. In **Diekirch** and **Wiltz** are museums devoted to this heroic battle.

The Petite Suisse and the Moselle

In the region that is regarded as their own Switzerland, Luxembourgers head for **Müllerthal,** not exactly the Alps but still a hiker's paradise, with its leafy hills, flowering fields, and rustling streams. At **Echternach,** a major center of pilgrimage and the arts, explore the town's exquisite abbey, once famed for its fine medieval school of illumination. Heading south you can enter the **Moselle Valley,** where vines cover every exposed slope in sight. The method of making sparkling Moselle wine is illustrated by local vintners in the most refreshing way—by offering you several glasses of the bubbly stuff!

NEW AND NOTEWORTHY

The Netherlands

The Netherlands' newest **museums** are drawing in the crowds and making use of their expanded facilities to host exceptional exhibitions. In the northern provinces the Groninger Museum is getting a reputation for excellent modern art shows, while the Fries Museum in Leeuwarden promises a new, permanent multimedia exhibition on Mata Hari, the dancer and spy who was born in the city. **Amsterdam's skyline** gets a remarkable new addition early in 1997 with the ship-shape Impuls Science & Technology Center, designed by Renzo Piano, architect of the equally eye-catching Pompidou Centre in Paris. On the other side of town an old favorite has had a bit of a face-lift—after years of careful restoration, the south wing of the **Rijksmuseum** finally reopened during 1996. At long last, the museum's excellent Asian collection is back on view, alongside gems of 18th- and 19th-century Dutch art.

The **magnificent old buildings** that comprise a good deal of the Netherlands' charm need constant care and renovation; often restorers hit upon unexpected problems, such as crumbling stonework or roofs. Worse, the coffers occasionally run dry during the process of rebuilding, meaning even further delay. But triumphantly emerging from shrouds and scaffolding during 1996 were the delightfully wonky Oude Kerk at Delft and the soaring Gothic tower of the Grote Kerk at Breda. Still languishing under wraps is the Walburgskerk at Zutphen, with its famous library—though (bar mishaps) this is finally due to open in 1997. Amsterdam's medieval Waag (weighhouse) has just gotten a new lease on life as a restaurant and café, after having been shut up for decades.

Russo-Dutch relations get a boost in 1997 with a series of **exhibitions and events** held nationwide in celebration of the tercentenary of the visit of Czar Peter the Great, who came to Amsterdam to brush up on his knowledge of things maritime. Early in 1997, you'll still be able to catch the blockbuster exhibition on Jan Steen, the first major retrospective of this Golden Age painter of rowdy tavern scenes to be held since the 1950s. In the summer, the Amsterdam Arts Adventure attracts a glittering array of opera, ballet, and music stars to town, and the capital is already girding its loins in preparation for the 1998 international Gay Games.

Belgium

To honor the centenary of the painter's birth, 1997 will be the **Paul Delvaux Year,** highlighted by a retrospective at Brussels' Musée d'Art Moderne. Delvaux is one of the leading lights in Belgian modern art—his paintings, filled with odd assemblages of skeletons, railroad stations, and vacantly staring nudes, are among the more unforgettable images of 20th-century art. Along with Magritte, Delvaux offered a uniquely Belgian take on surrealism. The retrospective and accompanying gallery shows, seminars, and concerts will be among the most important celebrations in the European art world in 1997.

The **Europalia festival**—which focuses on a different country every year—has become an important cultural showcase. This year it will spotlight Turkey, with major exhibitions, concerts, and theatrical performances from September to December 1997, both in Brussels and other major cities.

Luxembourg

The tremendous efforts put into creating the infrastructure for Luxembourg's year as European City of Culture back in 1995 are yielding lasting benefits, as visitors discover that the Grand Duchy is more than a tax haven with a pretty face. One example is the old **Neumünster Abbey.** Located below the cliffs of Luxembourg's old castle, in the region known as the Grund, the abbey was sacked by the French and later used for many years as a men's and women's prison. Today, it is becoming a very different kind of center. The women's prison is now the Museum of Natural History, and its *Tutesall* (workshop) was turned into an attractive exhibition space. Work is under way to convert the men's prison into the city's new Cultural Center.

FODOR'S CHOICE

No two people will agree on what makes a perfect vacation, but it's fun and helpful to know what others think. We hope you'll have a chance to experience some of Fodor's Choices yourself while visiting the Benelux countries. For detailed information about each entry, refer to the appropriate chapters within this guidebook.

The Netherlands

Quintessential Holland

★**Begijnhof, Amsterdam.** Feel the gentle breeze of history in the solitude of a quiet courtyard that seems hardly to have changed since the Pilgrim Fathers worshiped here all those centuries ago. This place is the very soul of serenity.

★**Amsterdam canals at night.** Walking along the canals of Amsterdam after dark is one of the simplest, cheapest, and most memorable experiences that Holland has to offer. Pedestrians (and cyclists) rule over traffic, the most beautiful gables are subtly lit up, and the pretty hump-backed bridges are festooned with lights. Alternatively, get up early and stroll out before the city is awake, as the mist is gently rising off the water.

★**Anne Frank House, Amsterdam.** The swinging bookcase that hid the door is still there, also the magazine pictures that young Anne pasted on the walls for decoration. It is impossible not to be moved as you wander through the secret apartment where the Frank family hid from the Nazis.

★**Portuguese Synagogue, Amsterdam.** A gracious survivor of the ravages wrought by World War II on the city's Jewish Quarter, this 17th-century synagogue is suffused with light on sunny days. After a contemplative moment or two, exit to enjoy the bustling flea market nearby.

★**Prinsenhof, Delft.** Sit quietly in the courtyard garden, then explore the atmospheric 15th-century convent before strolling off along what is probably the oldest—and certainly one of the most attractive—canal in the Netherlands. At times it seems that you are stepping right into Vermeer's *View of Delft*.

★**St. John's Cathedral, Hertogenbosch.** Pilgrims set off from here to San Tiago de Compostela in Spain, but you can stay behind to see the richly carved pulpit and ornate 17th-century organ.

★**Caves of Mount St. Peter, Maastricht.** Wander along some of the 20,000 passages and into the dim, echoing halls of a vast subterranean complex of caves that provided a refuge for the people of Limburg from 50 AD up to the Second World War.

★**Dom Tower, Utrecht.** Climb through a puzzling complexity of twisting stairways to find yourself atop the tallest church tower in the Netherlands, with panoramic views across city and countryside.

Where Art Comes First

★**Rijksmuseum, Amsterdam.** As if the best collection of Dutch Golden Age art in the world were not enough, "the Rijks" also offers a cornucopia of other aesthetic delights, from medieval Buddhas to embroidered four-poster beds. Most visitors first head, however, to Rembrandt's *Night Watch*—a hot contender for the title of "the world's most famous painting." The enormous canvas has a room all to itself (and a strategically placed bench for those who wish to linger).

★**Vincent van Gogh Museum, Amsterdam.** It is difficult to pick a favorite from the more than 200 paintings by this great artist on view here, but *Sunflowers* will probably top most visitors' lists. None of the versions you may have seen in reproduction can match the lustre of the original, where brilliant blues appear unexpectedly between the bright yellows and greens.

★**Paleis Het Loo, Apeldoorn.** Pace through the elegant formal gardens, admire the sumptuous Dutch Baroque palace that was home to the Dutch royal family until the 1960s, then pop inside to feast your eyes on the rich furnishings.

★**Nieuwe Kerk, Delft.** Here, typically Dutch building materials of brick and wood give even soaring Gothic buildings a down-to-earth feel. Inside, however, you'll find the magnificent marble mausoleum of the royal House of Orange.

★**Sint Servaas Basilik, Maastricht.** Restorers have done a wonderful job in bringing back to life the bright colors and delicate floral designs inside this 7th-century basilica, and the treasury brims with jewel-encrusted reliquaries and other precious objects.

★**Kröller-Müller Museum, Otterloo.** Art collections based on the quirks of one person's taste are often the choicest ones, as is here proved by Hélène Müller's stash of van Goghs and modern art. Not only is the art world-class, the museum is in the heart of the Netherlands' most beautiful nature reserve.

★**Rietveld-Schroeder House, Utrecht.** A pinnacle of Dutch modernism awaits you in a suburb of Utrecht. With its white walls, plate-glass windows, and clean straight lines, this villa—designed by Gerrit Rietveld—set the mark for much 20th-century European design.

Great Hotels

★**The Grand Hotel, Amsterdam.** The Grand's last incarnation was as Amsterdam's City Hall, and it is resplendent with decor by some of the top artists of the 1920s and 1930s. Ask to see the Wedding Room and keep an eye open for the mural by Karel Appel. $$$$

★**Amstel Inter-Continental, Amsterdam.** The Grand Duchess of Amsterdam hotels is quite at home with royal guests and stands, quietly proud of her most recent face-lift, at a prime spot on the river Amstel. Take the hotel luxury launch for a classy trip on the canals. $$$$

★**Hotel Derlon, Maastricht.** After you have unpacked your suitcase and admired the original artworks on the walls, go downstairs for a look at the hotel's private museum of antiquities, then saunter outside for a coffee on the most beautiful square in Maastricht. $$$$

★**Auberge Corps de Garde, Groningen.** Small is beautiful in this 17th-century barracks house. The hotel rooms have a homey atmosphere, while the restaurant downstairs ranks with the most elegant in town—a veritable honeypot to the gourmets of the northern provinces. $$

★**Canal House, Amsterdam.** Experience the gracious life in a genuine Amsterdam canal house, overflowing with antiques. Linger over breakfast beneath a crystal chandelier, and then enjoy the calm of the quiet garden courtyard. $$

★**Kasteel Elsloo, Elsloo.** Wine, dine, and spend the night in the castle where an erstwhile Prince of Monaco lived with his bride. The next morning take a promenade in the castle park—lovingly landscaped in the picturesque English style. $$

Memorable Restaurants

★**Excelsior, Amsterdam.** Enjoy a view across the Amstel to the delicate spire of the old Munttoren, as waiters in stiff formal attire glide up to serve you with the very best haute cuisine and *grand vin*. $$$$

★**Prinses Juliana, Valkenburg aan de Geul.** Various heads of state have feasted here before you, including members of the Dutch royal family. So sit back, enjoy the plush surrounds, and order up the vintage champagne. $$$$

★**Nolet's Restaurant, Het Reymerswale.** Climb upstairs for a table that has a view over the dike to the very waters that have provided your meal. Oysters and mussels are the specialty here; and the lobster bisque is so popular that Danny Nolet has taken to bottling it for guests to take home. $$–$$$$

★**Café Américain, Amsterdam.** The painted-glass Art Deco lamps here once cast their light on the cream of Amsterdam's intelligentsia. Today, even though most tables are occupied by tourists, the café-society atmosphere lingers. $$$

★**De Silveren Spiegel, Amsterdam.** Two tiny rooms in a crooked, 17th-century house offer space for just a handful of diners. The owner lives upstairs and serves at table, his shaggy dog sits obediently in one corner, and the chef works wonders. $$$

★**Kastel Doorwerth, Arnhem.** Step across the drawbridge of a diminutive stone castle for a fine meal in the onetime stables; then explore the ramparts or go for a walk in the surrounding woods. $$$

★**Polman's Huis, Utrecht.** Tall windows and an impossibly distant stucco ceiling dwarf the coffee drinkers in this grandest of Grand Cafés. $$

★**Haesje Claes, Amsterdam.** The epitome of *gezelligheid* is chock-full of solid wooden furniture, adorned with brass trinkets, and renowned for its slap-up meals. This is the place, on a cold day, for pea soup so thick that your spoon stands upright. $

Special Memories

⭐ **Bikes on dikes (most anywhere).** Trundling along the top of a dike on a sit-up-and-beg Dutch bicycle, with the sea to one side of you, wetlands (alive with birdlife) on the other, and the wind in your hair, is transporting in more ways than one. Enhance the delight by stopping over at one of myriad waterside cafés or charming villages along the way.

⭐ **Carnival, Maastricht.** Medieval Christian pageantry combines with pagan revelry in the last days before Lent. Join the merriment of parades and parties as the ebullient southern Dutch go all out for a jolly good time.

⭐ **Oosterschelde, Zeeland.** For an awesome insight into how this low-lying country keeps constant battle with water, visit the Delta Storm Barrier, and then stroll in the bracing breeze along the shores of the Oosterschelde before stopping off at a harbor restaurant for oysters fresh from the water's edge.

Belgium

Quintessential Belgium

⭐ **The canals of Brugge.** If you wake up at dawn to view these canals without people, they will look like three-dimensional Hans Memling paintings. Passing under hump-backed bridges and along quay-side merchant's homes, visitors can glimpse an intimate view of the city—complementing the grand façades that are its public face.

⭐ **Grand'Place, Brussels.** This jewel box of a square ranks among Europe's great treasures. The soaring lines of the Gothic Town Hall dominate one side, in contrast with the elaborately decorated Baroque guild halls that surround it. Several of the guild halls have sidewalk cafés where locals and visitors soak up the atmosphere along with potent Trappist beer. All tours start here—this is Brussels ground zero.

⭐ **Sint-Michielsbrug, Ghent.** From this vantage point, the spiritual, mercantile, and military glory that was Ghent is spread out before you. To the east are the three great medieval spires of the gray St. Nicholas Church, the honey-colored St. Bavo's

Cathedral, and the gilt-encrusted Belfry. To the north, on either side of the River Leie, note the grand old quays of Korenlei and Graslei, with, in the background, the ancient fortress of s'-Gravensteen. At night, under floodlights, the view assumes a fairy-tale quality.

⭐ **La Roche-en-Ardenne, Ourthe River Valley.** This is the vacation land Belgians dream about. Deep down between wooded hills, the lively river winds a meandering course, carrying kayaks that seem to move now toward you, now away. Families camp on the riverside while kids splash in the chilly water. A small village clings to the hillside, its farms and church built of stone and slate. From above, look out over an undulating vista of green hills.

⭐ **Malmedy, Les Hautes Fagnes.** These "High Fens" are mossy, waterlogged moors—a windswept, desolate landscape punctuated by bushes and copses of beech and oak trees, rich in bird life and mountain vegetation. The frequent mist adds to the mystery for those addicted to this type of solitude, and trekkers are urged not to stray from the well-marked paths.

⭐ **The North Sea Coast.** One long, wide beach, the North Sea Coast often looks like a scene from an Impressionist painting: couples strolling arm-in-arm, riders galloping along the water's edge, kites flying high above, tiny tots digging sand castles to be swallowed by the tide. Out at sea—pleasure craft and fishing vessels. Behind the dike—vacation apartment houses, sand dunes, and cafés serving pancakes and waffles.

Where Art Comes First

⭐ **Museum Mayer Van den Bergh, Antwerp.** If you think of Pieter Bruegel as a painter of jolly village scenes, you're in for a surprise. His *Dulle Griet* (badly translated to "Mad Meg," as if she were some 16th-century bag lady) strides angrily across a landscape of surrealist horrors, a sword in one hand and a cooking pot in the other. Many interpretations have been advanced, but it certainly can be read as a prophetic antiwar statement, as pertinent to the war in Bosnia as to the Thirty Years' War, which in Bruegel's day was just around the corner.

⭐ **St. Bavo's Cathedral, Ghent.** Van Eyck's *Adoration of the Mystic Lamb,* completed in 1432, inspires all the awe that its creator could have hoped for. This mother of all oil paintings was executed with brilliant, miniaturist realism. Though the brushstrokes are microscopic, they are brilliantly held together by a unifying view of the redemption of mankind.

⭐**St. Bartholomew's Church, Liège.** Under the prince-bishops of Liège in the 11th and 12th centuries there flourished *L'Art Mosan*—one of the most distinctive of all medieval styles. The leader of the school was Renier de Huy, and here you will find his masterpiece, a huge baptismal bronze font decorated with sculpted reliefs. Note, in particular, the high-relief scenes of St. John the Baptist and of the baptisms of Christ—sculptures of extraordinary plasticity and emotion.

⭐**St. John's Hospital, Brugge.** The small Memling Museum is installed in this vast hospital, which served Brugge's sick and poor for 800 years. This is the most important collection of the few works by Memling to have survived. The realism of the so-called Flemish Primitives is present in all meticulously rendered details, but just as some of his women's faces are covered by a delicately painted veil, so there is in his work a gossamer veil of mysticism that points up the spirituality of the subject.

Lodging and Dining Gems

⭐**Amigo, Brussels.** Even diplomats feel at home here thanks to personalized service (and even bankers appreciate that a junior suite costs no more than a double in the top price category). Although a mere 50 years old, the Amigo blends perfectly into its Old Town surroundings. $$$

⭐**Die Swaene, Brugge.** Chandeliers, Louis XV furniture, four-poster beds, Burgundy wallpaper, ancient tapestries, candlelit dinners, open fireplaces, marble nymphs, canalside setting: if romance is what you crave, you'll find it here. The cuisine keeps getting better and now ranks as one of the best in the gourmet heaven that is Brugge. $$$ (hotel), $$$$ (restaurant)

⭐**Firean, Antwerp.** There's a small hotel in Antwerp where every detail is authentic Art Déco, and this is it. It is family-owned with family service and wonderful attention to details, including its own-brand toiletries. Just inside the Ring Road, it is well located for drivers who would rather not negotiate Antwerp's one-way maze,

but you have to hop a tram to get to the Old Town from here. $$$

⭐**Welcome/Truite d'Argent, Brussels.** The smallest hotel in Brussels is one of its most charming. It owes its double name to the fact that taxi drivers are more familiar with the name of its 100-year-old restaurant, the Truite d'Argent ($$$). The good news: Michel and Sophie Smeesters are working on expanding from 6 to 10 rooms. Wearing his chef's hat, Michel prepares great seafood specialties, with Sophie in charge of the dining room. $

Taste Treats

⭐**Neuze Meuze, Antwerp.** The ever-present, mustachioed Domien Sels has transformed several small 16th-century houses in the shadow of the cathedral into one stylish restaurant that seems to consist exclusively of nooks and crannies. His is a cuisine of surprises: goose liver meunière with caramelized pineapple, sole with a purée of shrimps. And he pulls it off! $$$

⭐**Ogenblik, Brussels.** Slap in the historic center, in the Galeries Saint-Hubert, this rough-and-ready bistro has been packing them in for more than 20 years. Marble-topped tables, green-shaded lamps, and superior grub all add up to a delightfully friendly ambience. $$$

⭐**Léon de Bruxelles, Brussels.** Léon has celebrated its first century by changing its name from plain old Chez Léon; prices have started to edge upward but little else has changed. Most diners opt for the specialty, a heaping bowl of blue-shelled mussels accompanied by lots of super fries, but Léon does a mean *filet américain* (tartar steak to you) as well. $

Special Memories

⭐**The Grottes de Han, Han-sur-Lesse.** As you wander through the dark, cool caves, where Neolithic man found shelter and later generations found a hiding place from marauding armies, you come upon a vast hall under a dome-like rock roof 400 feet high. Suddenly, on the guided tour, a single torch-carrier appears, running a slalom-like course down the steeply slanting wall: You feel transported thousands—not hundreds—of years back in time.

⭐**The Last Post, Ieper.** Every night at 8, buglers sound the Last Post at the Menin Gate in memory of the 300,000 British soldiers who passed through here to their death in the trenches of "Flanders Fields." For one poignant moment, traffic is stopped, as Ieper remembers.

⭐**The Ommegang, Brussels.** Once a year, in July, the noble ladies and gentlemen of Belgium revert to the pomp and circumstance of yore, as they reenact the stately procession, with standards flying, that greeted the Holy Roman Emperor Charles V on the self-same Grand'Place in 1549. Horsemen, acrobats, fire-eaters, and stilt-walkers participate with gusto.

⭐**Vlaeykensgang, Antwerp.** Linger in the alley that progress forgot—where small whitewashed houses stand shoulder to shoulder along a narrow cobblestone alleyway—and listen to the Monday evening carillon concert from the great cathedral. As you emerge into Pelgrimstraat, you're rewarded by the best possible view of the white cathedral spire, whose Gothic lines sweep upward to an incomparable, open-work summit.

Luxembourg

Quintessential Luxembourg

⭐**Luxembourg City.** The 1,000-year-old fortress city, classified as a World Heritage Monument by the United Nations, was once thought so formidable a stronghold that its mere presence was considered a threat to international peace. The European powers of the day once tried to dismantle the fortress but it turned out to be a greater task than they thought, and a vast panorama of medieval stonework and fortified towers remain. Today they guard Luxembourg's considerable wealth as one of the world's leading financial centers and its political clout within the European Union as home to the European Court of Justice.

⭐**The Château of Vianden.** It's difficult to imagine a more dramatic sight than your first view of this grandiose castle, which suddenly looms from the top of a hill as you approach Vianden. It has a special significance to Luxembourgers: It was the ancestral home of the ruling Orange-Nassau dynasty and was the last part of Luxembourg to be liberated by U.S. troops.

Dining and Lodging Gems

⭐**Clairefontaine, Luxembourg City.** Tony and Margot Tintinger have served one

pope, several presidents, and lots of prime ministers in their swank restaurant, decorated with restrained opulence. It is located on the handsomest square in town, a stone's throw from the ministries that supply much of their clientele, and on fine days tables spill out over the square. The menu begins with five different preparations of *foie gras d'oie,* which suggests that this is far from your garden-variety bar-and-grill. $$$$

⭐**La Bergerie, Geyershof, Luxembourg.** A soufflé of brill, flavored with basil, may not be what you expect in the middle of the Luxembourg forest, but that's what Claude Phal has in mind for you in his pastoral hideaway. They don't come any more idyllic than this, and if you wish, they'll whisk you off for an overnight at the villa/hotel of the same name in nearby Echternach. $$ (hotel), $$$$ (restaurant)

⭐**La Cascade, Luxembourg City.** A splendid, turreted villa from the turn of the century has been converted into this delightful hotel on the banks of the Alzette. An Italian-inspired lunch on the comfortable, sunny riverside terrace is a special treat. $$

Special Memories

⭐**The Bock, Luxembourg City.** This is Sigefroid's 1,000-year-old castle, the rock on which the "Gibraltar of the North" was built, protected in its heyday by three rings of defense and 53 forts. As you wander through the casemates—underground corridors tunneled through the rock—stop at an aperture to look out over the valley below, and imagine the thousands of banner-topped tents and campfires of an army laying siege to the impenetrable fortress.

⭐**Müllerthal, Luxembourg.** Spread your picnic of dark bread, pink Ardennes ham, and smoky sausage alongside a twisting brook in Luxembourg's "Little Switzerland." Butterflies flutter over the meadow, swallows dart about in the sky, and the only sounds are the drone of the bees and the rustle of the stream rushing between high bluffs. If you feel drowsy, it's not just because of the Moselle you drank with your meal.

GREAT ITINERARIES

Haute Cuisine and Country Air

The peripatetic gourmet first chooses overnight stops to ensure that each evening meal is a feast. It is a bonus that many of the finest small hotels with outstanding restaurants are in out-of-the-way places that you might not otherwise visit. This kind of travel obviously does not come cheap.

Duration

14 days

Getting Around

BY CAR➤ In the Netherlands, the drive from Amsterdam to Kerkrade, by way of Oisterwijk, is 380 kilometers (228 miles). In Belgium, highways link Antwerp and Noirefontaine, by way of the coast, for an arc of some 600 kilometers (360 miles). To travel from meal to meal in Luxembourg, a car is indispensable.

BY TRAIN➤ In the Netherlands there are good train and taxi connections from Amsterdam, by way of Middelburg and Den Bos. Trains in Belgium connect, through Brussels, with the main towns on the route; a car is necessary in the Ardennes. In Luxembourg, only Luxembourg City is easily reached by direct rail lines.

The Main Route

3 NIGHTS: THE NETHERLANDS➤ From Amsterdam, travel south toward Middelburg; take the Yerseke-Kruiningen exit on the highway toward Kruiningen. **Restaurant Inter Scaldes** sits alone in the countryside, offering fine French cuisine and luxury accommodations. The following day can be a leisurely drive to **Oisterwijk** between Tilburg and 's-Hertogenbosch, for an overnight stay at **Hotel-Restaurant De Swaen** in the town square. The following day, travel south through Limbourg province to **Kerkrade** for dinner in the castle at **Hotel Kasteel Erenstein** and overnight in its luxury accommodations across the road, a half-timbered, former Limbourg farmstead. A word of advice: Book your overnight stays well in advance.

9 NIGHTS: BELGIUM➤ Start the Belgian portion of your trip in **Antwerp**, where **'t Fornuis** is the top restaurant. The 10 exquisite rooms of De Rosier are only minutes away. Make your next stop **Brugge**, to eat at the revered **De Karmeliet** or the young, imaginative **Den Gouden**, both within easy walking distance of the aristocratic rooms of De Tulierieen. From Brugge, head for the coast and **Oostende**, where you can stay and dine at the sumptuous **Oostendse Compagnie**, overlooking the sea. At the west end of the coast, dine and stay in **De Panne** at the exquisite **Le Fox.**

As you head inland, stop first at **Eddy Vandekerckhove's Gastronomic Village** just outside **Kortrijk**, where the rooms have views of a tropical garden or the Flemish countryside, and the cuisine will delight you. **Brussels** would be an obvious stop, with its **Comme Chez Soi** and other renowned restaurants. For something more unusual, stop instead at **Genval**, near Brussels, where the Château du Lac's restaurant, **Le Trèfle à Quatre,** offers lake views and superb food. Farther east, just west of **Hasselt,** the world-class **Scholteshof** restaurant provides extraordinary dining and superb accommodations. The **Clos Saint-Denis** in nearby **Tongeren** runs a close second, but offers no lodging. Head south to **Noirefontaine** in Belgian Luxembourg, and treat yourself to an overnight stay at the luxurious **Moulin Hideux,** where you can savor fine, leisurely meals and work off the calories by taking enchanting walks in the woods.

3 NIGHTS: LUXEMBOURG➤ In **Luxembourg City,** settle for the night in either the traditional Hotel Cravat or the modern luxury of Le Royal. You'll dine in the splendid **Clairefontaine**, on the charming square of the same name. The next day, head south toward the French border for **Frisange,** where Lea Linster will serve a world-class lunch, and dine at super chef Franky Steichen's **L'Agath,** just south of the city. Next day, explore the castle country of the Ardennes, lunching at **Le Châtelain** in Vianden. Book for the night at the pleasant little Bergerie in **Echternach.** They provide shuttle service to the idyllic restaurant, also called **Bergerie,** in the middle of the woods, where Claude Phal's cooking reaches new heights.

Ancient Crafts of the Low Countries

The extraordinary flourishing of decorative crafts in the Low Countries during the Middle Ages was the result of the rulers' insatiable appetite for ornamentation, an appetite shared by local gentry and wealthy burghers. The clothing and jewelry lovingly depicted in 15th-century Flemish paintings indicate the very high standards of the artisans of the era, whose traditions continue to the present.

Duration

10 days

Getting Around

BY CAR➤ Luxembourg City is easy to reach by car. The Villeroy & Boch complex lies just outside the center, on the northwest edge, toward Wiltz. The Belgian section of the itinerary (Luxembourg City to Rotterdam) is about 780 kilometers (468 miles), some 10 hours' driving time. The Dutch section (Antwerp to Delft to Amsterdam to Hindeloopen) is about 290 kilometers (174 miles).

BY TRAIN➤ If you're visiting Luxembourg by train, city buses pass the Villeroy & Boch outlet. All Belgian cities on this itinerary are accessible by train, but you'll have to double back from Brugge to Brussels to get to Antwerp. Train travel in the Netherlands is efficient.

The Main Route

1 NIGHT: LUXEMBOURG➤ A weekday stop in Luxembourg will give you a chance to visit the on-site factory outlet store of Villeroy & Boch, whose popular vitroporcelain sells here at discount prices. Watch for specials on patterns being phased out, and be sure to dig through the bargain bin. The factory does not ship, so be prepared to schlep. If you can round up a group of 20, you can take a guided tour of the factory.

1 NIGHT: LIÈGE➤ Arriving from Luxembourg, start your Belgian crafts tour in Liège. The Val Saint-Lambert glassworks in Seraing, on the outskirts of the city, is one of the finest in the world; you can visit the showroom and watch glassblowers in action. As usual, the factory outlet offers great value for the money.

3 NIGHTS: BRUSSELS➤ **Mechelen,** halfway between Brussels and Antwerp, has the only workshops in Belgium where traditional tapestry weaving is still practiced; Gaspard De Wit's Royal Tapestry Manufacture (open for visits Saturday mornings only) is at the Refuge van Tongerlo. In **Brussels,** some of the finest examples of Belgian tapestry, from the 14th to 16th centuries, are on view in the Musées Royaux d'Art et d'Histoire (Royal Museums of Art and History), and lace and needlework are on view in the Musée du Costume et de la Dentelle (Costume and Lace Museum). **Tournai** (southwest of Brussels) is one of the old centers of tapestry; at the new Museum of Tapestry (and Textile Arts) you can see how it is done.

1 NIGHT: BRUGGE➤ Brugge is intimately associated with lace-making, and there are a large number of shops selling everything from lace souvenirs to works of art. The best place to get a real understanding of the craft is the Kantcentrum (Lace Center), incorporating a museum and a lace-making school.

1 NIGHT: ANTWERP➤ Diamonds are big business in Antwerp, where the origins and history of diamond cutting are shown at the Provincial Diamond Museum, while Diamondland, where you can also see diamond-cutting demonstrations, is probably the most spectacular diamond showroom in the world.

3 NIGHTS: THE NETHERLANDS➤ Begin in **Delft** with a visit to the factory De Porcelyn Fles to watch artists paint the famous blue-and-white ceramic ware known as Delft. Continue to **Amsterdam** for a visit to a diamond factory. Then go north to the village of **Makkum** in Friesland, where the prized Dutch multicolor ceramic ware is produced at the factory of Tichelaars Koninklijk Makkumer Aardewerk en Tegelfabriek (Tichelaars Royal Makkum Pottery and Tile Factory). In nearby **Hindeloopen** you can see the traditional painted furniture of Friesland in the Museum Hidde Nieland Stichting.

Information

☞ Chapters 2, 3, and 4.

The Ardennes

To experience the Ardennes fully, you owe it to yourself to take your time. Explore the hamlets and river valleys off the highway. Stop in the small towns along the way for a meal of hearty Ardennaise fare—smoked ham, cheese and farm bread, crayfish and trout from the rushing streams—enjoy the inns, visit the churches and castles. You will be amply rewarded!

Duration

8 days

Getting Around

BY CAR➤ The Belgian portions of the trip add up to about 430 kilometers (258 miles). Much of this is on secondary routes, so expect driving time of about eight hours. To see the best of the Luxembourg Ardennes, you'll need a car for the *routes nationales* and secondary roads that snake through the forests.

BY TRAIN➤ The cities on the itinerary are accessible by train, but they are not necessarily interconnected in the same sequence. Rail connections in Luxembourg are minimal, though a train does run from Luxembourg City to Clervaux, in the north.

The Main Route

2 NIGHTS: BELGIUM➤ From **Liège,** go by way of Eupen toward Malmedy, stopping to explore the high moorland known as the **Hautes Fagnes.**

1 NIGHT: LA-ROCHE-EN-ARDENNE➤ Passing Stavelot, continue to La-Roche-en-Ardenne in the heart of the Belgian mountain range. Here, in the valley of the River Ourthe, you will see the finest scenery the Ardennes has to offer.

2 NIGHTS: LUXEMBOURG➤ Enter the Grand Duchy of Luxembourg from the north, stopping to visit **Clervaux**'s castle museum before winding through rolling countryside toward **Vianden,** where the spectacular castle dominates the hill village. Head south to **Diekirch** to visit the Romanesque church, with its Merovingian sarcophagi, and the evocative Battle of the Bulge museum. Then, though it falls just below the Ardennes plateau, drive on into **Luxembourg City,** for the medieval fortifications, cathedral, and Old Town streets.

3 NIGHTS: BELGIUM➤ Driving west from Luxembourg City, follow the Semois River, with a stop to see the romantic ruins of

Orval Abbey, and then to **Bouillon** with its mountaintop fort. Through dense woods you reach **Saint-Hubert,** going on to **Han-sur-Lesse,** with its remarkable caves and nature reserve. Follow the Lesse to **Dinant**—part of the way by kayak, if you wish—spectacularly situated on the River Meuse. As you drive along the Meuse, sheer cliffs line the riverbank on the opposite side. Continuing along the river, with stops in **Huy** and **Modave,** you arrive back in **Liège.**

FURTHER READING

Netherlands

A visit to the Netherlands is greatly enhanced by a knowledge of the nation's history and a familiarity with its rich art heritage. Books of particular value and interest include *Amsterdam: The Life of a City,* by Geoffrey Cotterell (Little, Brown; 1972), a comprehensive history of the city; *Diary of Anne Frank,* by Anne Frank, the diary of a young Jewish girl that details the experience of living in hiding in Amsterdam during World War II; and *Images of a Golden Past,* by Christopher Brown (Abbeville, 1984), a guide to Dutch genre painting of the 17th century.

Some worthwhile histories include *The Dutch Revolt,* by Geoffrey Parker (Peregrine/Penguin, 1977), a history of the development of the Dutch nation; *The Dutch Seaborne Empire 1600–1800,* by C.R. Boxer (Penguin, 1965), which traces the development of the great Dutch trading companies in the 17th and 18th centuries; and *The Embarrassment of Riches,* by Simon Schama (Alfred A. Knopf, 1987/University of California Press, 1988), which interprets the Dutch culture in its Golden Age. *Evolution of the Dutch Nation,* by Bernard H.M. Vlekke (Roy, 1945), is a comprehensive history of the Netherlands.

In addition, Janwillem Van de Wetering's mystery novels (Ballantine), set in Amsterdam, can make for good light reading on the plane.

Luxembourg

The Grand Duchy of Luxembourg: The Evolution of a Nationhood by James

Newcomer (University Press of America, Lanham, MD, 1984) is an extensive, fairly readable history of the Grand Duchy's early woes. *A Time for Trumpets* by Charles B. MacDonald (William Morrow and Company, New York, 1985) gives a blow-by-blow account of the Ardennes offensive, as does *The Battle of the Bulge* by Roland Gaul (two volumes, Schiffer Military Books).

Belgium

Barbara Tuchman's *A Distant Mirror*, describing 14th-century European affairs, gives valuable insights, illuminated by memorable vignettes, into the conflicts between Flemish towns and the Crown of France. *The Guns of August* applies Tuchman's narrative technique to the events, largely in Belgium, of the first month of World War I. John Keegan's *The Face of Battle* includes a brilliant analysis of the Battle of Waterloo. Leon Wolff's *In Flanders Fields* is a classic account of the catastrophic campaign of 1917, while John Toland's *No Man's Land* covers the events on the Western Front in 1918.

Toland has also written *Battle: The Story of the Bulge*. William Wharton's *A Midnight Clear* is a fictional account of the Ardennes battle as seen by American GIs. *Outrageous Fortune* by Roger Keyes is a sympathetic account of the role played by Leopold III up to 1940. Hugo Claus's *The Sorrow of Belgium,* an outstanding novel of life during the occupation, has been translated into many languages from the original Dutch.

Two 19th-century novels well worth dipping into are Georges Rodenbach's *Bruges-la-Morte,* which was contemporaneous with the rediscovery of Brugge, and Charles de Coster's picaresque *La legende d'Ulenspiegel,* which captures the spirit of Belgian defiance of outside authority. Both have been translated into English.

Maurice Maeterlinck, Marguerite Yourcenar, and Georges Simenon were all Belgian writers working in French. So was Jacques Brel, many of whose songs also contain outstanding poetry. Hergé set many of the *Tintin* cartoon adventures in foreign lands, but Tintin himself remained always the quintessential *bon petit Belge.*

FESTIVALS AND SEASONAL EVENTS

Benelux's top seasonal events are listed below, and any one of them could provide the stuff of lasting memories. Contact each country's tourist agency for complete information.

THE NETHERLANDS

Winter

JAN.–FEB.➤ The international **Filmfestival Rotterdam** celebrates avant-garde cinema.

FEB. (WEEK BEFORE LENT)➤ **Carnival** dances through the cities of Brabant and Limbourg provinces.

MAR.➤ **European Fine Arts Fair** gathers artists and works in Maastricht, and international crews compete in Amsterdam's **Head of the River Race.**

Spring

APR.➤ **Rotterdam Marathon** draws runners from around the globe, and the **Flower Parade** passes through Lisse to open the **National Floral Exhibition** at Keukenhof gardens.

MAY➤ **National Bicycle Day** races through the Netherlands; an international modern dance festival, **Spring Dance,** bounces into Utrecht; and the **International Traditional Jazz Festival** makes Breda jump.

MAY/JUNE➤ The **Eleven Cities by Bicycle Race** and the five-day **Eleven Cities Walking Tour** circle Friesland.

Summer

JUNE➤ **Holland Festival of the Performing Arts** cap-

tures Amsterdam, spilling over to The Hague, Rotterdam, and Utrecht; **Parkpop,** a pop music festival, livens up The Hague; and **Pinkpop** bursts into Landgraf.

JULY➤ The Hague hosts the **North Sea Jazz Festival;** the **International Organ Competition** brings musicians to Haarlem in even-numbered years; and the **International Four Days Walking Event** strides through Nijmegen.

JULY/AUG.➤ **Skutsjesilen Sailing Regattas** skim the lakes in Friesland.

AUG.➤ Utrecht enjoys the **Festival of Ancient Music.**

Autumn

SEPT.➤ The **Floral Parade** makes a day-long procession of floats from Aalsmeer to Amsterdam; **Gaudeamus Muziekweek** honors music in Amsterdam; and the **Opening of Parliament** takes place in The Hague on the third Tuesday—the queen arrives in her golden coach.

OCT.➤ **Delft Art and Antiques Fair** fills the Prinsenhof with treasures.

NOV.➤ With the **St. Nicolas Parade** in Amsterdam and in cities throughout the country, the arrival of Sinterklaas launches the Christmas season.

BELGIUM

Winter

END JAN.➤ Brussels' **International Film Festival,** which gains in prestige each year, takes place at the Palais des Congrès (☎ 02/513–4130).

EARLY FEB.➤ **Carnival** is celebrated with great gusto, especially at Binche with its extravagantly costumed Gilles, and at Malmedy, Oostende, and Eupen.

MAR. 9➤ In Stavelot, the hilarious Blancs Moussis, with their long red noses, swoop through town during the **mid-Lent carnival.**

Spring

END APR.➤ One of the world's leading flower shows, the **Floralies** (☎ 09/222–7336), is held every five years in the Flanders Expo Hall in Ghent: next in 2000.

LATE APR.–EARLY MAY➤ The **Royal Greenhouses** (☎ 02/513–0770), at Laeken Palace near Brussels, with superb flower and plant arrangements, are open to the public for a limited period.

EARLY MAY➤ On **Ascension Day,** the Procession of the Holy Blood (☎ 050/448664) in Brugge is one of the oldest and most elaborate religious and historical processions in Europe. Early seat reservations are recommended.

MAY➤ The **Queen Elisabeth International Music Competition** (☎ 02/513–0099) is one of the most demanding events of its kind. In 1997, the focus is on young violinists. No competition in 1998; piano 1999, singing 2000.

MAY➤ The **Kunsten-FESTIVALdesArts** (☎ 02/512–7450) in Brussels is a month-long international celebration of contemporary drama, dance, and music.

LATE MAY➤ The **Brussels Jazz Marathon** (☎ 0900/00606) encompasses gigs and informal sessions in more than 50 clubs and pubs, plus outdoor concerts in the Grand'Place and Grand Sablon featuring leading jazz musicians. One ticket for all events, plus free shuttle between venues and public transport.

LATE MAY➤ **Trinity Sunday** in Mons features a procession of the Golden Carriage and St. George's battle with Lumeçon the dragon.

Summer

LAST WEEKEND IN JUNE➤ The **Folklore and Shrimp Festival** (☎ 058/511189) in Oostduinkerke features shrimp fishermen on horseback, brass bands, floats, and folklore ensembles.

1ST TUES. AND THURS. IN JULY➤ The **Ommegang** (☎ 02/512–1961) takes over Brussels' Grand'Place. It's a sumptuous and stately pageant reenacting a procession that honored Emperor Charles V in 1549. Book early.

MID-JULY➤ The **Ghent Festivities** (☎ 091/241555) start, a 10-day sequence of music-making, entertainment, and assorted happenings in the streets of the city.

JULY 21➤ **Belgium's National Day** is celebrated in Brussels with a military march, followed by a popular feast in the Parc de Bruxelles and brilliant fireworks.

AUG.➤ The **Francorchamps Formula I Grand Prix** is one of the key events in the annual cycle of international motor racing.

MID-AUG.➤ A **Flower Carpet,** painstakingly laid out, covers and transforms the entire Grand'-Place of Brussels for two days. Even years only; next in 1998.

AUG. 15➤ The **Outremeuse Festival** in Liège combines religious and folkloric elements in a joyous tide that sweeps through this section of town.

END AUG.➤ In the **Canal Festival** (☎ 050/448686) in Brugge, events from the city's past are re-created alongside the romantic canals. It is celebrated every third year; next in 1998.

Autumn

SEPT.–MID-OCT.➤ The **Festival of Flanders** (✉ Eugeen Flageyplein 18, 1050 Brussels, ☎ 02/640–1525) brings hundreds of concerts to all the old Flemish cities.

SEPT.–DEC.➤ Every other year, the **Europalia Festival** honors a different country with exhibitions, concerts, and other events amounting to a thorough inventory of its cultural heritage. In 1997, the country thus honored in Brussels and in other cities will be Turkey (☎ 02/507–8550).

2ND WEEKEND IN SEPT.➤ On **National Heritage Day** (☎ 02/511–1840) buildings of architectural or historical interest throughout Belgium that are not normally accessible to the public open their doors to all who come.

NOV.➤ The **European Union Championship** (☎ 03/326–1010) in Antwerp is a major event on the international tennis circuit.

2ND WEEKEND IN DEC.➤ The **European Christmas Market** in the Grand'Place in Brussels features the traditions and products of many different European countries.

LUXEMBOURG

Winter

FEB. 9–11➤ **Carnival** Processions and masked balls are especially festive in Vianden, Echternach, and Wormeldange.

EARLY MAR.➤ On Laetare Sunday, **Bretzelsonndeg** is dedicated to lovers and features folk art displays along the Moselle.

EASTER MON.➤ At the **E'maischen** fair in old Luxembourg, lovers give each other "whistling" clay birds (*Peckvillchen*) to usher in spring.

Spring

OCTAVE➤ For two weeks, beginning the third Sunday after Easter, grateful villagers have, since the 17th century when the Holy Mother spared the devout from a raging plague, walked from their local church to the cathedral in Luxembourg City, accompanied by chants, incense, and often the community band. During Octave, a fair holds forth in the Place Guillaume, featuring arcade games, crafts, and food stands selling the traditional batter-fried *merlan* (whiting). On the final Sunday, the royal family participates in a solemn procession.

MAY–JUNE➤ The **Echternach Music Festival** features classical music concerts by renowned soloists and groups in the city's churches.

WHIT TUESDAY (LATE MAY)➤ During Echternach's **Spring Procession** (Dance-Procession), the most famous spring pageant, pilgrims and townspeople dance through the streets, leaping from one foot to the other and chanting prayers to St. Willibrord, each group accompanied by musicians who all play the same haunting melody.

Summer

JUNE 23➤ **Luxembourg's National Day** honors its beloved Grand-Duke with parades, ceremonies, and gun salutes; the night before, there's a torchlight military exercise and spectacular fireworks.

JULY➤ International **Festival of Open-Air Theater and Music** in Wiltz always attracts thousands.

END AUG.➤ The **Schueberfouer** (a former shepherds' market begun in 1340) has become the capital's giant funfair, interspersed with a procession of sheep with colorful ribbons being herded through the city streets.

Autumn

2ND WEEKEND IN SEPT.➤ Three-day **Wine and Grape Festival** in Grevenmacher is a popular September event.

2ND SUN. IN OCT.➤ **Walnut Market** is held in Vianden: outdoor sale of fresh walnuts, walnut cake, walnut candy, and walnut liqueur to the music of popular bands.

2 The Netherlands

The tulip fields and windmills are here and so are the canals, but there's more to the Netherlands than just these delights. Small enough to drive through in a day, but interesting enough to take weeks to explore, the Netherlands is a colorful array of lush countryside, historic towns, and beach resorts that have inspired artists from Vermeer to van Gogh. Amsterdam, with its narrow, canalside houses; The Hague, center of international justice; and Rotterdam, with the world's largest port, are filled with historic neighborhoods, art museums, and restaurants and cafés serving everything from Indonesian "rijsttafel" to seafood plucked from local waters.

By Linda
Burnham

Updated by
Rodney Bolt

IF YOU COME TO THE NETHERLANDS expecting to find its residents shod in wooden shoes, you're years too late; if you're looking for windmills at every turn, you're looking in the wrong place. The bucolic images that brought tourism here in the decades after World War II have little to do with the Netherlands of the '90s. Sure, tulips grow in abundance in the bulb district of Noord and Zuid Holland provinces, but today's Netherlands is no backwater operation: This tiny nation has an economic strength and cultural wealth that far surpass its size and population. Sophisticated, modern Netherlands has more art treasures per square mile than any other country on earth, as well as a large number of ingenious, energetic people with a remarkable commitment to quality, style, and innovation.

The Netherlands, with 41,526 square kilometers (15,972 square miles), is almost half the size of the state of Maine, and its population of 15 million is slightly less than that of Texas. Size is no measure of international clout, however. Only Great Britain and Japan invest more than the Netherlands in the American economy. The Netherlands encourages internal accomplishments as well, particularly of a cultural nature. Within a 120-kilometer (75-mile) radius are 10 major museums of art and several smaller ones that together contain the world's richest and most comprehensive collection of art masterpieces from the 15th to the 20th centuries, including the works of Rembrandt and Vincent van Gogh. In the same small area are a half dozen performance halls offering music, dance, and internationally known performing arts festivals.

The marriage of economic power and cultural wealth is nothing new to the Dutch; in the 17th century, for example, money raised through their colonial outposts overseas was used to buy or commission portraits and paintings by young artists such as Rembrandt, Hals, Vermeer, and van Ruisdael. But it was not only the arts that were encouraged: The Netherlands was home to the philosophers Descartes, Spinoza, and Comenius; the jurist Grotius; the naturalist van Leeuwenhoek, inventor of the microscope; and others like them who flourished in the country's enlightened tolerance. The Netherlands continues to subsidize its artists and performers, and it supports an educational system in which creativity in every field is respected, revered, and given room to express itself.

The Netherlands is the delta of Europe, where the great Rhine and Maas rivers and their tributaries empty into the North Sea. Near the coast, it is a land of flat fields and interconnecting canals; the center of the country is surprisingly wooded, and the far south has rolling hills. The country is too small for there to be vast natural areas, and it's too precariously close to sea level, even at its highest points, for there to be dramatic landscapes. Instead, the Netherlands is what the Dutch jokingly call a big green city. Amsterdam is the focal point of the nation; it also is the beginning and end point of a 50-kilometer (31-mile) circle of cities that includes The Hague (the Dutch seat of government and the world center of international justice), Rotterdam (the industrial center of the Netherlands and the world's largest port), and the historic cities of Haarlem, Leiden, Delft, and Utrecht. The northern and eastern provinces are rural and quiet; the southern provinces that hug the Belgian border are lightly industrialized and sophisticated. The great rivers that cut through the heart of the country provide both geographical and sociological borders. The area "above the great rivers," as the Dutch phrase it, is peopled by tough-minded and practical Calvinists; to the south are more ebullient Catholics. A tradition of tolerance pervades this densely populated land; aware that they cannot survive alone, the

Dutch are bound by common traits of ingenuity, personal honesty, and a bold sense of humor.

The Pleasures of Dining and Lodging

Dining

The Dutch have a dining advantage over other Europeans in the quantity and quality of the fresh ingredients available to them. Their national green thumb produces the Continent's best and greatest variety of vegetables and fruits, and their dairy farms supply a rich store of creams, cheeses, and butter for sauces. The forests yield a wide range of game meats, and the sea dikes are covered with rare herbs and other vegetation that offer a rich diet to their lambs and calves, resulting in exceptionally tasty, tender meats year-round. The waters of the Netherlands, both salt and fresh, are well known for the extraordinary quality and variety of the fish and shellfish they yield. Remarkably, for centuries Dutch cuisine failed to take advantage of this national bounty. Today, even in rural areas, imaginative dishes are prepared with the high-quality fresh ingredients so readily available. Many Dutch chefs also have spent time in the kitchens of France and Belgium to learn the techniques of both traditional and nouvelle cuisine. The rest of the population travels as well, and that fact has influenced dining in the Netherlands. You find Chinese, Italian, Mexican, and Indian restaurants even in small cities, and Indonesian restaurants are found everywhere because the Dutch, having colonized the country, developed a taste for the multi-dish Indonesian meal rijsttafel (rice served with several small, spicy meat, poultry, and vegetable dishes). Potatoes, cabbage, sausage, and other ingredients of traditional cooking can still be found in Old Dutch restaurants; soup continues to be the appropriate, and delicious, beginning of a meal on a daily basis. Also unchanging in the Netherlands is fresh flowers on the tables.

In Amsterdam and major cities, dinner is served until 10 PM in most restaurants, though most diners eat between 7 and 9 PM; elsewhere, dining hours vary by local custom. In the northern and eastern provinces, people dine from as early as 6, while in the southern provinces, dinner is later: from 8 to 9. However, even in Amsterdam and other large cities, it is difficult to find anywhere that will serve you after 10:30.

Fixed-price and pre-theater menus are found at restaurants throughout the country; vegetarian menus also are available, particularly in university cities.

CATEGORY	AMSTERDAM, THE HAGUE, & ROTTERDAM	METRO CITIES & MAASTRICHT	OTHER CITIES
$$$$	over Fl 85	over Fl 75	over Fl 65
$$$	Fl 60–Fl 85	Fl 55–Fl 75	Fl 45–Fl 65
$$	Fl 35–Fl 60	Fl 35–Fl 55	Fl 30–Fl 45
$	under Fl 35	under Fl 35	under Fl 30

per person for a three- or four-course meal, including service and taxes but excluding drinks

Lodging

Accommodations in the Netherlands range from Old Dutch "cozy," through modern European cosmopolitan to the splendid and luxurious. There are attractive family-run hotels in canal houses and historic buildings, smart international chain hotels, and historic castles and manor houses that have been converted into sumptuous resorts, many with their own golf courses and gourmet restaurants. Standards are high. Behind a 17th-century facade, the rooms come equipped with all modern conveniences. Even small hotels and family-owned inns may be decorated in trendy colors and have televisions in the guest rooms.

CATEGORY	AMSTERDAM, THE HAGUE, & ROTTERDAM	METRO CITIES & MAASTRICHT	OTHER CITIES
$$$$	over Fl 450	over Fl 400	over Fl 300
$$$	Fl 400–Fl 450	Fl 300–Fl 400	Fl 200–Fl 300
$$	Fl 300–Fl 400	Fl 200–Fl 300	Fl 150–Fl 200
$	under Fl 300	under Fl 200	under Fl 150

for a double room, including tax and service

Exploring the Netherlands

Amsterdam, the capital of the Netherlands, combines its extraordinarily rich cultural heritage with an adventurous, cosmopolitan verve. It's known as the youth capital (and the gay capital) of Europe, yet it also has the largest historical town center on the Continent and some of the most august art collections in the world. South of Amsterdam, the borders of a number of cities—Leiden, The Hague, Rotterdam, and Utrecht—run so close to each other that the Dutch have given the area a single name, the Randstad (Ridge City). This metropolitan conglomerate forms the cultural, economic, political, and social heart of the nation; it is also home to the world's largest port (Rotterdam) and the International Court of Justice (in The Hague).

To the east of the Randstad is the country's green heart, yet even amidst the forests and duneland of vast national parks there are palaces and museums that can take your breath away. Life up north is even more sedate, with old trading ports and fishing villages dotted in between prosperous farms. At its northernmost point, the Netherlands finally admits defeat in its battle against the sea and tapers off in a series of sandy islands.

The region along the Belgian and German borders, south of the Randstad, is, as the Dutch will often remind you, "another country." Northern Calvinists find their southern Catholic cousins (with their softly accented speech and ebullient ways) quite another breed. Even the countryside is different, as billiard-table flatness gives way to gentle hills—many of them adorned with castles and grand manor houses. The paved squares and busy sidewalk cafés of Maastricht are more reminiscent of France than of towns to the north.

Great Itineraries

The Netherlands is small and has a superb road and rail network. A couple of hours' traveling will take you halfway across the country. But a lot is packed into this compact land. You could happily spend a week just getting to know Amsterdam. Two to three weeks would be ideal for exploring the rest of the country.

Numbers in the text correspond to numbers in the margin and on the maps.

IF YOU HAVE 3 DAYS

After arriving in ⚌ **Amsterdam** ①–㉙ and viewing the famous gables from the comfort of a canal boat (tours take from one to two hours), feast your eyes on Rembrandts and van Goghs in the city's museums. Your first night is spent in Amsterdam, so there's plenty of time to explore the back streets of the Jordaan (Amsterdam's Greenwich Village) and to find a cozy restaurant. Next morning, check out some of Amsterdam's quirkier shops—or visit a diamond-cutting factory if that's more your style. Then set off along the A4 for ⚌ **The Hague** ㊶ to visit a palace or two and the Madurodam miniature village. End the day with a *rijsttafel* in one of The Hague's excellent Indonesian restaurants. In the morning, take a tram to nearby **Delft** ㉝ (20 minutes), and visit its renowned porcelain factory, then set off back along the A4 to 🏛 **Leiden** ㊵. If it's springtime, take the N206 out of town and through the bulb fields to the spectacular Keukenhof Gardens. Otherwise, spend the afternoon exploring this attractive old university town, for many years home to the Pilgrim Fathers. Leiden is just half an hour from Schiphol Airport, along the A4.

IF YOU HAVE 5 DAYS

Your first night is in 🏛 **Amsterdam** ①–㉙. This gives you a day on either side for exploring canals, museums, bustling markets, and the Jordaan district. In the afternoon of your second day, head off along the A4 to 🏛 **Leiden** ㊵. If it's springtime, follow instead the A9 and the N208 through the bulb fields, allowing an hour for visiting the Keukenhof Gardens on the way. After a morning spent seeing Leiden's 15th-century church and beautifully restored windmill, continue along the A4 to 🏛 **The Hague** ㊶, seat of the government and home to some excellent art collections. Next day, take a tram to **Delft** ㉝, one of the most beautifully preserved historic towns in the country, conveniently situated on the outskirts of The Hague. Then take the A12 to 🏛 **Utrecht** ㊺, where you can climb the Gothic Domtoren, the highest church tower in the Netherlands, for a panoramic view of the countryside. Back on ground level, you can visit a delightful museum of music boxes, player pianos, and barrel organs. On the fifth day take the A28, then the A1, out to the Hoge Veluwe National Park, near **Apeldoorn** ㉞, where you can spend time walking in the forest or visiting the Kröller-Müller Museum with its world-class collection of van Goghs and modern art. From Apeldoorn, you can continue your journey into Germany or take the A1 back to Amsterdam.

IF YOU HAVE 9 DAYS

Two days and two nights in 🏛 **Amsterdam** ①–㉙ give you time for a leisurely exploration of the city. On the third day, follow the A4 to **Leiden** ㊵ (or take the N208 bulb route if it's springtime), and then travel on to 🏛 **The Hague** ㊶. Visit the historic center and porcelain factory of **Delft** ㉝ on the morning of the fourth day, then head across to 🏛 **Utrecht** ㊺ on the A12. On the way, stop off for a moment in Gouda, famed not only for its cheeses but also for its medieval city hall and the magnificent stained glass in the St. Janskerk. From Utrecht take the A2 south, stopping for the night in an ancient Limburg manor house or castle, such as the medieval Kasteel Wittem near 🏛 **Heerlen** ㉟. Spend day six in 🏛 **Maastricht** ㉓–㉟ (just a short drive from Wittem on the N278), which has an abundance of sidewalk cafés and a carefree French air. Maastricht also boasts the Bonnefantenmuseum, which is well stocked with superb religious carvings and intriguing contemporary art. Then travel along the German border to the Hoge Veluwe National Park near **Apeldoorn** ㉞ (take the A2 out of Maastricht, then turn off onto the N271 and follow it up to Nijmegen, from where the A325 and the A50 take you into the park). The pretty little town of 🏛 **Zutphen** ㊿, which has a library of rare and beautiful early manuscripts, makes a good overnight stop (follow the N345 out of Apeldoorn). On day eight travel north to 🏛 **Leeuwarden** ㉟ (follow the A50 to Zwolle, then the A28 to Meppel, and turn finally onto the A32). After visiting the National Ceramics Museum and viewing some of Leeuwarden's elegant 18th-century facades, you can take the A31 to the coast. Take the dike road (N31), exploring coastal towns such as **Harlingen** and the pottery town of **Makum** ㊏ along the way. Then head back to Amsterdam along the A7, which takes you over the Afsluit-dijk, the long dike that closes off the IJsselmeer from the North Sea.

When to Tour the Netherlands

All those popular songs about tulips and springtime have a point. The Netherlands is at its most beautiful in the spring. The bulb fields south-west of Amsterdam burst out in vast blocks of bright color, parks and gardens all over the country display brilliant spreads of blossoms, and there's a flower parade through the town of Lisse in early April to mark the opening of the flower exhibition season at Keukenhof Gardens. Keukenhof, and other popular parks, is best seen in the dewy early morn-ing, before the crowds set in.

Summertime in the Netherlands is festival time. The Holland Festival in Amsterdam in June attracts a glittering array of international stars in the fields of music, opera, theater, and dance. The North Sea Jazz Festival in The Hague in July is one of the premier jazz events in the world. Rotterdam has a massive street festival in August, Utrecht hosts a Festival of Ancient Music, and pop festivals sprout up in country areas throughout the season. The long summer evenings are ideally spent sit-ting outside on café terraces or strolling along the canals (in Amster-dam the facades of the more elegant canal houses are softly lit at night).

In early September there is a massive Flower Parade from Aalsmeer to Amsterdam, and even winter has something to offer. Maastricht holds a lively pre-Lent carnival (February–March), and Rotterdam hosts an internationally renowned Film Festival (January–February). Devotees of Dutch architecture will find that they get a much better view of the rows of decorative gables once the trees lining the canals have lost their leaves.

AMSTERDAM

Amsterdam is a city with a split personality: It's a gracious, formal cul-tural center built on canals, and it's the most offbeat metropolis in the world. There is an incomparable romance about the canals at night, and a depth of cultural heritage in its great art museums; but there is also a houseboat crawling with stray cats permanently parked in front of an elegant gabled canal house, and prostitutes display their wares in the windows facing the city's oldest church. Only in Amsterdam can you marvel at the acoustics of the Concertgebouw one evening and be greeted by a hurdy-gurdy barrel organ pumping out happy tunes on the shopping street the next morning. When you know what to expect, Am-sterdam is a delight to visit; when you don't, it can be disconcerting.

The city is laid out in concentric rings of canals around the old center, crosscut by a network of access roads and alleylike connecting streets; visitors easily can see the city on foot, though there are also trams and water taxis for the weary. Most of the art museums are clustered con-veniently at the edge of the canal district. This cobweblike layout of the city means that you can dart back and forth with ease, rather than having to confine your sightseeing to one specific area of town.

To help you along with your choices, the sights that follow are arranged in three thematic groups. The first deals with cultural high points and Amsterdam's major museums. The second traces two important strands of Amsterdam's past—the crucial contribution that the Jewish popu-lation made to the life of the city, and the history of Amsterdam as a prosperous port, once the headquarters of the powerful Dutch East India Company. The final group focuses on notable architectural attrac-tions and on Amsterdam's romantic canals.

Pleasures and Pastimes

Amsterdam has delights for all—cozy cafés, elegant canals, and some of the greatest art produced in Western civilization. The city also has an exciting cosmopolitan edge and an abundance of cuisines to suit the gourmand and gourmet alike.

BROWN CAFÉS

Coffee and conversation are the two main ingredients of "a good time" for an Amsterdammer, and perhaps a beer or two as the evening wears on. The best place for these pleasures is a traditional Brown Café. Wood paneling, wooden floors, comfortably worn furniture, and walls and ceilings stained with eons' worth of tobacco smoke give the cafés their name—though today a little carefully applied paint achieves the same effect. Traditionally, there is no background music, just the hum of chitchat. You can meet up with friends or sit alone and undisturbed for hours, enjoying a cup of coffee and a thorough read of the newspapers and magazines from the pile in the corner.

CITY OF PAINTERS

Amsterdam is a city of artists and for artists. Its museums are filled with some of the best art in the western world. Not only are there the home-grown Old Masters and van Gogh, but there's also a wealth of contemporary art. Long an inspiration for generations of artists, the attractive canals and gabled houses are a popular subject for today's Sunday painters. In the galleries and art museums, keep an eye open for works by Georg Breitner, who roamed Amsterdam with his friend Vincent van Gogh and produced atmospheric-night and winter-city scenes.

One of Amsterdam's most lasting gifts is the quiet delight you experience as the life of an artist, such as Rembrandt, begins to unfold for you as you visit his house and walk along canals that have changed little since his day. After that, a visit to the Rijksmuseum becomes quite a different experience from the usual visit to an art museum. You will recognize his wife, Saskia, who modeled for him, and perhaps even fancy that one of the guardsmen in *The Nightwatch* is an ancestor of the man who had lunch opposite you in a canalside café.

The art scene continues to thrive, attracting young painters from all over the world who want to live and work in Amsterdam. To fully appreciate the abundance and high quality of local art, stroll through the commercial art galleries. Occasionally, artists working in one area of town will open their studios to the public. Then you can wander from one to the other, watching work in progress and perhaps even making a purchase before the paint is hardly dry.

DINING AND LODGING

Amsterdam has more than 700 restaurants, spanning a wide variety of ethnic cuisines. Along the canals and tucked away in side streets, you'll find elegant dining rooms and cozy, chef-owned restaurants. The city also has plenty of fast-food chains.

There are some 270 hotels from which to choose in Amsterdam, though most are small mom-and-pop operations, best described as pensions, found along and among the canals or in residential neighborhoods beyond the center. These smaller canalside hotels, often in historical buildings with antique furniture, capture the charm and flavor of Amsterdam. The larger hotels, including the expensive international chains, are clustered in the area around Centraal Station, at Dam Square, and near Leidseplein. Amsterdam is a busy city; reservations are advised at any time of the year and are absolutely necessary in tulip season (late March–June).

NIGHTLIFE

Amsterdam nightlife centers mainly on two city squares: Leidseplein, where the cafés and discos tend to attract young visitors to the city, and Rembrandtplein, which fills up with a more local crowd. Trendier nightspots and many of Amsterdam's gay venues are on the streets in between the two squares; Reguliersdwarsstraat is a particularly happy hunting ground, while Warmoestraat and other streets in the red-light district are the scene of heavier gay bars and throbbing rock clubs.

SHOPPING

The variety of goods available here and the convenience of a shopping district that snakes through the city in a continuous parade of boutiques and department stores are the major joys of shopping in Amsterdam. Be sure to visit the year-round outdoor flea market at Waterlooplein, a holdover from the pushcart days in the Jewish Quarter. Shopping hours in the Netherlands are regulated by law: One night a week is reserved for late shopping. In Amsterdam, department stores and many other shops are closed Monday morning but open Thursday evening. Increasingly, following an easing of legislation governing shopping hours, you'll find main branches of major stores in the center of the city open on Sunday afternoon.

Exploring Amsterdam

Great Itineraries

Amsterdam is compact, its canals laid out somewhat like the bottom half of a spider's web. A walk from the center of the web (Central Station) directly down to the bottom edge takes you through the heart of town to the museum district. To the right (somewhat east of the center of town) lie the Old Town and the former Jewish Quarter, and to the left, you'll find the charming area of the Jordaan. At the bottom are the grandest canals, forming a semicircle around the entire area.

Amsterdam deserves time. You can skim the surface of the museums and get a glimpse of the canals in two to three days, but to really savor the city's charm, you need a week or more.

IF YOU HAVE 3 DAYS

Start with a boat trip around the canals to get an overview of the city; then head for the museum district. Visit the **Rijksmuseum** first and save the others for later, unless time is really short. Dinner is on a canalside terrace, or in one of the cozy "eetcafes." Next day, head for the **Vincent van Gogh Museum**; then spend some time wandering around the **Jordaan.** If you enjoy modern art, visit the **Stedelijk Museum** on your third day, or pop into one of the diamond-cutting factories before visiting the **Anne Frank House** and the **Waterlooplein Fleamarket.** Don't forget to try a Rijsttafel on one of your dinners out, and round off the evening with a visit to a Brown Café.

IF YOU HAVE 5 DAYS

Begin, as in the three-day itinerary, with a canal trip. Apart from viewing the Old Masters at the **Rijksmuseum,** you'll have time to take in some of the other delights, such as the 17th-century doll's houses—even if this means returning to the museum on day two. On the second day, you can also wander around the **Vincent van Gogh Museum** before relaxing in **Vondel Park** and heading off to the **Fleamarket.** Spend the third day exploring the **Jordaan** and wandering along the historic canals, with a visit to one of the canal house museums, and also to the **Stedelijk** for a taste of modern art. On day four, start with a visit to the **Rembrandt House** and explore the **Jewish Quarter** before heading across town to the **Anne Frank House.** On your last day, visit some of Amsterdam's older churches, have a peek at the red-light district (which surrounds the Oudekerk), and pop into the curious **Amstelkring Museum.**

IF YOU HAVE 7 DAYS

Follow the five-day itinerary described above, and on day six enjoy a taste of the nation's maritime history by visiting the **Scheepvaartmuseum,** having a look at the historic boats moored nearby and then heading off to the old **Kromhout Shipyard** and the surrounding harbor islands. Spend your final day wandering some of the quieter canals, such as the **Brouwersgracht,** and checking out the city's early-20th-century architectural delights, such as the **Beurs van Berlage** and the **American Hotel.**

When to Tour Amsterdam

Although Amsterdam is a good place to be at any time of the year, it's best in the spring when the parks and window boxes are filled with flowers and you can get a clear view of the gables between the branches of trees not yet in full leaf. Winters can be icy, with biting winds, but one of the compensations—if the canals freeze over—is ice skating on them. Amsterdam's best festival is Queen's Day, a street party to celebrate the queen's birthday on April 30. June sees the star-studded Holland Festival of the Arts, which is part of a longer Amsterdam Arts Adventure, lasting well into the summer.

City of the Arts: From the Dam to the Golden Bend

From inauspicious beginnings as a small fishing settlement built beside a dam in a muddy estuary, Amsterdam had developed, by the 17th century, into one of the richest and most powerful cities in the world. This Golden Age left behind it a tide-mark of magnificent buildings and some of the greatest paintings in western art. Amsterdam's wealth of art— from Golden Age painters through van Gogh up to the present day— is concentrated on the area around the grassy Museumplein, which also serves as the transition point between the central canal area and the modern residential sections of the city. On the way from the site of the original dam to the museum quarter, you encounter some of the grand mansions built over the ages by Amsterdam's prosperous merchants.

Numbers in the text correspond to numbers in the margin and on the Amsterdam map.

A Good Walk

Begin where Amsterdam began, at the seething hub of the **Dam** ① (Dam Square). On the south side, where Kalverstraat and Rokin meet the square, is **Madame Tussaud's** ②, a branch of the famous wax museum. People interested in ancient cultures might enjoy a brief diversion to the **Allard Pierson Museum** ③ farther down Rokin, on the left. Otherwise, follow the busy pedestrian shopping street, Kalverstraat, south to the entrance to the **Amsterdam Historisch Museum** ④ (or get there through the Enge Kapelsteeg alley if you have visited the Allard Pierson Museum). Here you can get an enjoyable, easily accessible lesson on the city's past. Passing through the painting gallery of the Historisch Museum brings you to the entrance of the **Begijnhof** ⑤, a blissfully peaceful residential square, where the Pilgrim Fathers once worshiped. Behind the Begijnhof you come to an open square, the Spui, lined with popular sidewalk cafés, and to the Singel, the first of Amsterdam's concentric canals. Cut through the canals by way of the romantic alley Heisteeg and its continuation, the Wijde Heisteeg, to the corner of Herengracht and Leidsegracht, part of the prestigious **Gouden Bocht** ⑥, the grandest stretch of canal in town. Follow Herengracht left to Vijzelstraat and turn right. Cross the Keizersgracht and turn left to find the **Museum van Loon** ⑦, an atmospheric canal house that is still occupied by the family that has owned it for centuries but is open to the public. Turn left and follow Keizersgracht to Nieuwe Spiegelstraatou; take another right and walk toward Museumplein. Rising up in front of you is the glittering **Rijksmuseum** ⑧, housing the world's greatest collection of Dutch art. When you leave the Rijksmuseum, walk through the covered gallery that divides the building. Directly ahead is Museumplein itself; to your right is Paulus Potterstraat (look for the diamond factory on the far corner), where you'll find the **Vincent van Gogh Museum** ⑨, which contains nearly all of that tortured artist's work. Continuing along Paulus Potterstraat, at the corner of Van Baerlestraat, you reach the **Stedelijk Museum** ⑩, where you can see modern art from Picasso to the present day. Just around the corner, facing the back of the Rijksmuseum across Museumplein is the magnificent 19th-century concert hall, the **Concertgebouw** ⑪. A short walk back up along Van Baerlestraat will bring you to Amsterdam's "green lung," the **Vondelpark** ⑫—acre after acre of parkland that buzzes in the summer months with all manner of live entertainment.

TIMING

To see only the buildings, allow about an hour. Expand your allotment depending on your interest in the museums en route. At minimum, each deserves 30–45 minutes. At the Rijksmuseum allow at least that just to see the main Dutch paintings. You could easily pass most of the day there if you want to investigate the entire collection.

The best time to visit the Vondelpark is in late afternoon or evening, especially in summer, as this is when the entertainment starts. In the busy season (July–September), queues at the Vincent van Gogh Museum are long, so it's best to go early or allow for an extra 15 minutes' waiting time.

Sights to See

❸ Allard Pierson Museum. The fascinating archaeological collection of the University of Amsterdam is housed here, tracing the early development of Western civilization, from the Egyptians to the Romans, and of the Near Eastern cultures (Anatolia, Persia, Palestine) in a series of well-documented, interestingly presented displays. ⊠ *Oude Turkmarkt 127,* ☎ *020/525–2556.* ⌑ *Fl 6.* ☉ *Tues.–Fri. 10–5, weekends and holidays 1–5.*

★ **❹ Amsterdam Historisch Museum** (Amsterdam Historical Museum). Housed in a former orphanage, this museum will help you learn all you need to know about the history of Amsterdam, from its beginnings in the 13th century as a marketplace for farmers and fishermen through the glorious period in the 17th century when Amsterdam was the richest, most powerful trading city in the world. A tall, skylighted gallery is filled with the guild paintings that document that period of power. In one of the building's tower rooms you can have a go on an old church carillon. ⊠ *Kalverstraat 92,* ☎ *020/523–1822.* ⌑ *Fl 7.50.* ☉ *Weekdays 10–5, weekends 11–5.*

❺ Begijnhof (Beguine Court). The absolute soul of serenity—and called the most peaceful corner in this bustling metropolis by many—the Begijnhof is the courtyard of a residential hideaway, built in the 14th century as a conventlike residence for unmarried lay women. It's typical of many found throughout the Netherlands. The court is on a square where you'll also find No. 34, the oldest house in Amsterdam and one of only two remaining wooden houses in the city center. After a series of disastrous fires, laws were passed in the 15th century putting a stop to buildings made entirely from timber. The small **Engelse Kerk** (English Church) in one corner of the square dates back to 1400 and was

34

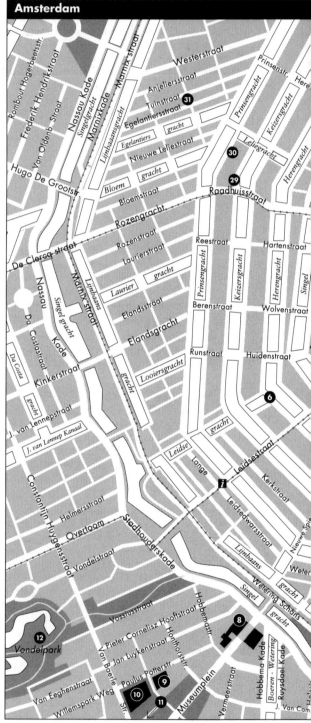

Amsterdam

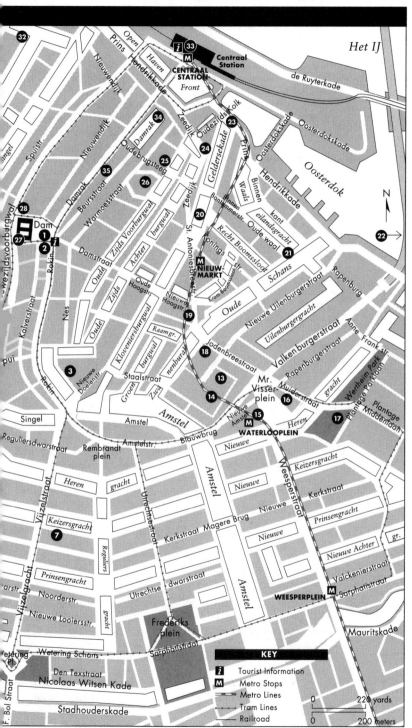

Het IJ

CENTRAAL
STATION
Front

Centraal
Station

de Ruyterkade

Oosterdokskade

Oosterdok

Oosterdoksstraat

Prins Hendrikkade

Binnen kant
Binnen
Bantammerstr. Oude waal
Recht Boomssloot
Krom Boomssloot
Oude Schans

Waals eilandsgracht

N

Nieuwe Uilenburgerstraat
Uilenburgergracht
Valkenburgerstraat

Rapenburg

Anne Frank str.
Rapenburgerstraat

Wertheim Park
Plantage Parklaan

Plantage
Middenlaan

Jodenbreestraat

Mr.
Visser-
plein

Muiderstraat

Heren

WATERLOOPLEIN

Nieuwe Amstel

Oude

NIEUW-
MARKT

St. Antoniesbreestraat
Koningstr.
Nieuwe Hoogstr.

Zeedijk

Oudezijds Kolk

Geldersekade

Kloveniersburgwal

Raamgr.

nieuwburg

Staalstraat

Groen
Zwa.

Amstel

Blauwbrug

Amstel

Nieuwe Doelenstr.

Nes

Oude
Zijds
Hoogstr.
Oude
Zijds

Achter
burgwal

Zijds Voorburgwal

Damstraat

Oude

Dam

Rokin

Kalverstraat

Singel

Reguliersdwarsstraat

Rembrandt
plein

Amstelstr.

Heren gracht

Keizersgracht

Vijzelstraat

Reguliers gracht

Prinsengracht
Noorderstr.
Nieuwe Looiersstr.

Wetering

Wetering Schans

Den Texstraat
Nicolaas Witsen Kade

Stadhouderskade

Amstel

Utrechtsestraat

Kerkstraat Magere Brug

Utrechtse dwarstraat

Frederiks
plein

Sarphatistraat

Weesperstraat

Kerkstraat

Prinsengracht

Nieuwe

Nieuwe

Nieuwe

Nieuwe Achter gr.

Nieuwe Keizersgracht

Valckenierstraat

WEESPERPLEIN

Sarphatistraat

Mauritskade

F. Bol Straat

Singel

Rokin

Spui

Nieuwendijk

Damrak

Beursstraat

Warmoesstraat

Oudebrugsteeg

Open Haven
Prins Hendrikkade

Nieuwezijds Voorburgwal

Nieuwendijk

Spuistr.

Open

KEY

i   Tourist Information
M   Metro Stops
Metro Lines
Tram Lines
Railroad

0   220 yards
0   200 meters

used by the Pilgrim Fathers during their brief stay in Amsterdam in the early 17th century. ✉ *Begijnhof 29,* ☎ *020/623–3565.* ▣ *Free.* ☼ *Weekdays 11–4.*

NEED A
BREAK? The Spui is an open square that is the focal point of the University of Amsterdam. Several of the pubs and eateries here are good places to take a break, including **Caffe Esprit** (✉ Spui 10, ☎ 020/622–1967), attached to the store of the same name. Try **Broodje van Kootje** (✉ Spui 28, ☎ 020/623–7451) for a classic Amsterdam *broodje* (sandwich). The Spui is at the end of the alley that passes out of the Beguine Court.

⑪ **Concertgebouw** (Concert Building). The Netherlands' premier concert hall, the world famous Concertgebouw, has been filled since the turn of the century with the music of the Royal Concertgebouw Orchestra, as well as visiting international artists. There are two concert halls in the building, Grote (large) and Kleine (small). The larger hall is well known to music lovers and musicians around the world as one of the most acoustically perfect anywhere. You will recognize the building at once (it is topped with a lyre); enter through the glass extension along the side. There are no tours of the building, so you will need to buy a ticket to a concert to see beyond the broad lobby, or, if you visit on a Wednesday before 12:30 September–June, you can attend a free lunchtime concert. ✉ *Concertgebouwplein 2–6,* ☎ *020/675–4411 (24-hr concert schedule and hot line) or 020/671–8345 (box office). AE, DC, MC, V.*

NEED A
BREAK? **Small Talk** (✉ Van Baerlestraat 52, ☎ 020/671–4864), because of its situation midway between the Concertgebouw and the Sweelinck Music Conservatory, is popular with music students, musicians, and visitors alike, who all pack in for coffee and apple pie or a light meal and a chat.

❶ **Dam** (Dam Square). The Dam, the official center of town, traces its roots to the 12th century, when wanderers from central Europe came floating in their canoes down the Amstel River and stopped to build a dam. Soon this muddy mound became the focal point of the small settlement of Aemstelledam and the location of the local weigh house. The Dam is still the official center of town. Once, ships could sail right up to the weigh house, along the Damrak. But in the 19th century the Damrak was filled in to form the street leading to Centraal Station, and King Louis Napoleon had the weigh house demolished in 1808 because it spoiled the view from his bedroom window in the palace across the way. The monument in the center of the square was erected in 1956 to commemorate the liberation of the Netherlands at the end of World War II. ✉ *Go down the Damrak from Central Station. Raadhuisstraat leads from the Dam to intersect the main canals.*

❻ **Gouden Bocht** (Golden Bend). Named for a bend on the Herengracht, this is the grandest stretch of one of the city's three main canals and is Amsterdam at its most beautiful. Construction of these canals, the Prinsengracht (Princes' Canal), the Keizersgracht (Emperors' Canal), and the Herengracht (Gentlemen's Canal), began during the Golden Age. In true Dutch egalitarian style, the most prestigious of the three was the Herengracht. The section of this canal, stretching from Nieuwe Spiegelstraat to Leidsestraat, is known as the Golden Bend. The houses are wide, with elaborate gables and cornices, richly decorated facades, and heavy, centrally placed doors—an imposing architecture that suits the bank headquarters of today as well as it did the grandees of yore.

❷ **Madame Tussaud's.** A branch of the world-famous wax museum, this Madame Tussaud's—at Dam Square above the P&C department store—includes a life-size, 3-D rendering of a painting by Vermeer—

a remarkable vision or a kitschy delight, depending on your sensibility. ⊠ *P&C Bldg., Dam 20,* ☎ *020/622–9949.* ⊡ *Fl 17.50.* ☉ *Sept.–June, daily 10–5:30; July–Aug., daily 9:30–7:30.*

★ ❼ **Museum van Loon.** The city's best look at life in those magnificent canal houses, the Museum van Loon is still a private residence for a descendant of one of Amsterdam's powerful families. Today, the house is filled with portraits, many of them traditional, paired marriage portraits and paintings of children. ⊠ *Keizersgracht 672,* ☎ *020/624–5255.* ⊡ *Fl 7.50.* ☉ *Mon., Tues. 11–5, Sun. 1–5.*

★ ❽ **Rijksmuseum** (State Museum). Home to Rembrandt's *Night Watch* and many of the most beloved Vermeer, Hals, and Hobbema paintings extant, this is the Netherlands' greatest museum. When architect P.J. Cuypers came up with the museum's extravagant design in the late 1880s, it shocked Calvinist Holland. Cuypers was persuaded to tone down some of the more ostentatious elements of his neo-Renaissance decoration and to curb the excesses of his soaring neo-Gothic lines—but, while the building was being constructed, he managed to visit the site and reinstate some of his ideas. The result is a magnificent, turreted building that glitters with gold leaf—a fitting palace for the national art collection.

The Rijksmuseum has more than 150 rooms displaying paintings, sculpture, and objects from both the West and Asia, dating from the 9th through the 19th centuries. The primary collection is of 15th- to 17th-century paintings, mostly Dutch (the Rijksmuseum has the largest concentration of these masters in the world); there are also extensive holdings of drawings and prints from the 15th to the 20th centuries.

If your time is limited, then head directly for the Gallery of Honor on the upper floor. Here you'll find the main attraction of the museum, Rembrandt's *The Night Watch,* as well as a selection of other well-known Rembrandt paintings, and works by Vermeer, Frans Hals, and other great Golden Age artists. A clockwise progression through the rooms of the adjoining East Wing will take you past works by some of the greatest Dutch painters of the 15th to the 17th centuries—meticulous still lifes, jolly tavern scenes, and rich portraits full of character.

The South Wing, renovated and restored to its former glory in 1996, contains 18th- and 19th-century paintings, costumes, and textiles, and the museum's impressive collection of Asiatic art, which includes some 500 statues of Buddha from all over the East.

The Rijksmuseum's collection of drawings and prints is far too vast to be on display, and only a small selection is shown in the Print Room at any one time. Here you might catch a glimpse of Italian Renaissance sketches, Rembrandt engravings, or early-19th-century photographs.

Elsewhere in the museum you can wander through room after room of antique furniture, silverware, and exquisite porcelain, including Delftware. The 17th-century Doll's Houses—made not as toys but as showpieces for wealthy merchant families—are especially worth seeing. ⊠ *Stadhouderskade 42,* ☎ *020/673–2121.* ⊡ *Fl 12.50.* ☉ *Daily 10–5.*

★ ❾ **Rijksmuseum Vincent van Gogh** (Vincent van Gogh Museum). This museum honors van Gogh as the Rijksmuseum honors Rembrandt. The light-filled building, based on a design by Gerrit Rietveld and opened in 1973, venerates the short but prolific career of the 19th-century Dutch painter with a collection that includes nearly all of his paintings, drawings, and letters. The galleries present, step by step, van Gogh's development as an artist, from the early dark and rough-hewn drawings of potato farmers he did in the Dutch province of Drenthe to his brooding final painting of crows circling above a wheat field. ⊠ *Paulus Potterstraat 7,* ☎ *020/570–5200.* ⊡ *Fl 12.50.* ⊙ *Daily 10–5.*

⑩ Stedelijk Museum (Municipal Museum). Hot and happening modern art has one of its most respected homes here at the Stedelijk. Works by such trendy contemporary artists as Jeff Koons are displayed alongside a collection of paintings and sculptures by granddaddies of modernism, including Chagall, Cézanne, Picasso, Monet, and others, dating from 1850 to the present. Major movements that are well documented here are COBRA (Appel, Corneille), American pop art (Johns, Oldenburg, Liechtenstein), American action painting (de Kooning, Pollock), and neorealism (de Saint-Phalle, Tinguely). ⊠ *Paulus Potterstraat 13,* ☎ *020/573–2911.* ⊡ *Fl 11.* ⊙ *Daily 11–5.*

⑫ Vondelpark. Known as the Green Lung of Amsterdam, the Vondelpark was first laid out in 1865 as a 25-acre "Walking and Riding Park." It soon expanded to cover some 120 acres. In the process, it was renamed after Joost van den Vondel, the "Dutch Shakespeare." Landscaped in the informal English style, the park is an irregular patchwork of copses, ponds, and fields linked by winding pathways. In good weather the park buzzes with activity. People come to rollerskate and play tennis. Dutch families string up flags between the branches and party under the trees. Lovers stroll through the fragrant formal Rose Garden. Children sit transfixed by colorful acrobatics in the outdoor theater. Later, the clowns give way to jazz bands and cabaret artists who play well into the night, and the Vondelpark takes on the atmosphere of a giant outdoor café.

Over the years a range of sculptural and architectural delights have made their appearance in the park. There's an elegant 19th-century bandstand, and the famous **Round Blue Teahouse,** a rare beauty of functionalist architecture built beside the lake in 1937. **Picasso** himself donated a sculpture (which stands in the middle of a field) to commemorate the park's centenary in 1965. An elegant 19th-century entertainment pavilion has been converted into the **Nederlands Filmmuseum** (Netherlands Film Museum). Although there is no permanent exhibition, the museum has shows every day in its two cinemas, drawing on material from all over the world as well as from its substantial archive (which includes such gems as hand-tinted silent movies). On summer Saturdays there are free outdoor screenings on the terrace. ⊠ *Filmmuseum, Vondelpark 3,* ☎ *020/589–1400.*

Historic Amsterdam: From the Jewish Quarter to Rembrandt's House

From the time in the 15th century when the diamond cutters of Antwerp first arrived to find refuge from the Spanish Inquisition, the area east of the Zwanenburgwal has traditionally been Amsterdam's Jewish Quarter. In the 16th and 17th centuries, Jewish refugees from Spain, Portugal, and Eastern Europe also found a haven in Amsterdam. By 1938, 10% of Amsterdam's population was Jewish, but this community of 130,000 people was reduced to just 30,000 by the devastation of the Nazi occupation.

The area to the north and northeast of the Jewish Quarter is the oldest part of Amsterdam. This is the site of Amsterdam's original harbor and the core of the Old Town, an area steeped in the history and romance of exotic trade and exploration, much of it conducted under the auspices of the immensely wealthy Dutch East India Company (VOC).

A Good Walk

Start your walk at what was once the heart of Amsterdam's Jewish Quarter, **Waterlooplein** ⑬. Today the square is dominated by the imposing modern **Muziektheater** ⑭, which is surrounded by a large and lively flea market. East of Waterlooplein, on Jonas Daniel Meyerplein, is the **Joods Historisch Museum** ⑮, skillfully converted out of a number of old synagogues. Just to the east of that, on the corner of Mr. Visserplein and Jonas Daniel Meyerplein, is the stately **Portugees Israelitische Synagogue** ⑯. Its interior is simple but awe-inspiring because of its vast size and floods of natural light. From here, you might like to make a short diversion, especially if you have children in tow. Tram 9 or 14 will take you along Plantage Middenlaan to the **Hortus Botanicus** ⑰ (Botanical Gardens), to the **Artis Zoo** (which was attractively laid out in park-like surroundings in the 19th century and has a well-stocked aquarium), and on to the **Tropenmuseum,** which has riveting displays on tropical cultures and a special children's section. Alternatively, you can walk from the synagogue up Jodenbreestraat, where—in the second house from the corner by the Zwanenburgwal—you'll find the **Museum het Rembrandthuis** ⑱, the mansion that Rembrandt lived in at the height of his prosperity, which now houses a large collection of his etchings. Cross the bridge to St. Antoniesbreestraat and follow it to the **Zuiderkerk** ⑲, whose rather Asian spire is the neighborhood's chief landmark. Cut through on Zandstraat to Kloveniersburgwal and follow it north to **Nieuwmarkt** ⑳. Take Koningsstraat to the Kroomboomsloot and turn left, then right at Rechtboomsloot (both pretty, leafy canals) and follow it through its homey neighborhood to Montelbaans Straat; turn left and cut through to Oudewaal canal. Follow it right to the **Montelbaanstoren** ㉑, a tower that dates back many centuries. Up Kalk Markt from the tower is Prins Hendrikkade, which runs along the eastern docks. Following Prins Hendikkade east will bring you into the 20th century with a bang, at the **Impuls Science & Technology Center** ㉒. A little farther on is the **Rijksmuseum Nederlands Scheepvaart,** where there is a fascinating replica of an old Dutch East India ship. Across the bridge on Hoogte Kadijk is the **Museumwerf 't Kromhout,** where wooden sailing boats are still restored and repaired. If, on the other hand, you go west along Prins Hendrikkade to Gelderskade, you can see the **Schreierstoren** ㉓, where legend has it that women used to stand weeping and waiting for their men to return from sea. Follow Oudezijds Kolk, beside the Schreierstoren, south to the small alley of **Zeedijk** ㉔, once the seedy haunt of drug dealers but now lined with cafés and galleries. From Zeedijk, take Oudezijds Voorburgwal south to **Museum Amstelkring** ㉕, a tiny but atmospheric canal house that has a church hidden in its attic. Continue south on Oudezijds Voorburgwal through part of the red-light district to the **Oude Kerk** ㉖, Amsterdam's oldest church, which grew up haphazardly over three centuries. From here you can continue south on Oudezijds Voorburgwal through more of the red-light district to Damstraat and the Dam.

TIMING

To see only the buildings along the main route, block out an hour and a half. Detours to Artis and the Tropenmuseum will need an extra 30 minutes' traveling time; and to the Scheepvaartsmusem and Museumwerf 't Kromhout, another 45 minutes. Museums along this route need at least a 30-minute visit, though the Museum Amstelkring and the Tropenmuseum deserve a little longer.

Note that the flea market does not operate on Sunday and that the children's section of the Tropenmuseum has very specific visiting times. Although the Zeedijk has been considerably cleaned up of late, it is still advisable to take care when visiting this area and the red-light district. Don't carry too many valuables, and avoid the district late at night.

Sights to See

🕐 **Artis** (The Amsterdam Zoo). Keep young travelers entertained with a visit to Amsterdam's zoo. Built in the mid-19th century, Artis is a 37-acre park that is home to a natural history museum, a zoo with an aviary, an aquarium, and a planetarium. A special Artis Express canal boat from the central railway station provides a fun means of getting there. ⊠ *Plantage Kerklaan 40,* ☏ *020/523–3400.* ☜ *Fl 21.* ☉ *Zoo daily 9–5; planetarium Mon. 12:30–5, Tues.–Sun. 9–5.*

⑰ Hortus Botanicus. An attractive botanical garden, the Hortus Botanicus was laid out as an herb garden for doctors and pharmacists in 1638. It has since been expanded to incorporate a covered swamp and an ornamental garden, where 6,000 species are represented. ⊠ *Plantage Middenlaan 2,* ☏ *020/625–8411.* ☜ *Fl 7.50.* ☉ *Apr.–Sept., weekdays 9–5, weekends and holidays 11–5; Oct.–Mar., weekdays 9–4, weekends and holidays 11–4.*

🕐 **㉒ Impuls Science & Technology Center.** Opened in early 1997, this is already a new landmark. Designed by Renzo Piano, the architect of the Pompidou Centre in Paris, this new science and technology museum is shaped like the prow of a gigantic ship, poking up into the skyline from above the entrance to the IJ Tunnel in the city's Eastern Docks. Inside is a high-tech, hands-on world of historic, present-day, and exciting futuristic technology. Addicted button-pushers and screen-gogglers will be in raptures. ⊠ *Oosterdok, Prins Hendrikkade,* ☏ *020/ 570811 for prices and entry times.*

⑮ Joods Historisch Museum (Jewish Historical Museum). Composed of four synagogues, dating from the 17th and 18th centuries, the Joods skillfully combines them into one museum for documents, paintings, and objects related to the history of the Jewish people in Amsterdam and the Netherlands. Across from the entrance to the museum is a statue erected after World War II to honor a solidarity strike by Amsterdam's dock workers in protest of the deportation of Amsterdam's Jews during the war. ⊠ *Jonas Daniel Meyerplein 2–4,* ☏ *020/626–9945.* ☜ *Fl 7.* ☉ *Daily 11–5.*

㉑ Montelbaanstoren (Montelbaans Tower). A tilting tower dating from 1512, the Montelbaanstoren now houses the City Water Office. Since 1878, this department has maintained the water levels in the canals and engineered the nightly flushing of the entire city waterway system, closing and opening the sluices to change the direction of the flow and cleanse the waters. (The canals remain murky green despite the process, due to algae.) The elegant clock tower was added early in the 17th century. ⊠ *Oude Schans 2.*

㉕ Museum Amstelkring ("Our Lord in the Attic" Museum). This appears to be just another canal house, and on the lower floors it is, but the attic of this building contains something unique—a small chapel that dates from the Reformation in Amsterdam, when open worship by Catholics was outlawed. ⊠ *Oudezijds Voorburgwal 40,* ☏ *020/624– 6604.* ☜ *Fl 5.* ☉ *Mon.–Sat. 10–5, Sun. 1–5.*

★ **⑱ Museum het Rembrandthuis** (Rembrandt's House). One of Amsterdam's most remarkable sights, this was the house that Rembrandt, flush with success, bought for his family. He chose a house on what was once the main street of the Jewish Quarter because he felt that he could then experience daily and at first hand the faces he would use in his religious paintings. Later Rembrandt lost the house to bankruptcy when he fell from popularity following his wife's death. He came under attack by the Amsterdam burghers, who refused to accept his liaison with his housekeeper. The house today is a museum of Rembrandt prints and etchings and includes one of his presses. ⊠ *Jodenbreestraat 4–6,* ☎ *020/624–9486.* ☞ *Fl 7.50.* ☼ *Mon.–Sat. 10–5, Sun. and holidays 1–5.*

☾ **Museumwerf 't Kromhout** (Museum Wharf The Kromhout). Head to one of Amsterdam's oldest shipyards, the Museumwerf 't Kromhout, and you'll immediately notice the smell of tar, wood shavings, and varnish still lingering in the air. Although the shipyard is run as a museum, old boats are still restored here, and the yard is sure to hold the attention of nautically minded youngsters. There's a whiff of diesel in the air, too. During the first part of the 20th century, 't Kromhout produced the diesel engine used by most Dutch canal boats. Models of old engines are on display. ⊠ *Hoogte Kadijk 147,* ☎ *020/627–6777.* ☞ *Fl 3.50.* ☼ *Weekdays 10–4.*

⑭ **Muziektheater/Stadhuis** (Music Theater/Town Hall). A brick and marble complex known locally as the Stopera (from Stadhuis and opera), this is the cornerstone of the revival of the Jewish Quarter, which was derelict and devastated after World War II. Built as a home for everything from opera performances to welfare applications, it is a multifunctional complex that includes theaters, offices, shops, and even the city's wedding chamber (Dutch marriages all must be performed in the Town Hall, with church weddings optional). Feel free to wander through the lobbies; there is interesting sculpture as well as a display that dramatically illustrates Amsterdam's position below sea level. Tours of the backstage areas are run twice weekly. ⊠ *Waterlooplein 22,* ☎ *020/551–8054.* ☞ *Fl 8.50.* ☼ *Tours Wed. and Sat. at 3.*

⑳ **Nieuwmarkt** (New Market). Dating to the 17th century—when farmers from the province of Noord-Holland began setting up stalls here—the Nieuwmarkt soon became a busy daily market. The **Waag** (Weigh House) in the center of the square was built between 1488 and 1614 as a town gate, and it was part of the city walls in 1500. After 1617 this was the weighing house; one of its towers became a teaching hospital for the academy of surgeons of the Surgeons' Guild. It was here that Rembrandt came to watch Professor Tulp in action prior to painting *The Anatomy Lesson.* ⊠ *East of the Dam, down Damstraat, along Oude Doelenstraat and Oude Hoogstraat, then up Kloveniersburgwal.*

㉖ **Oude Kerk** (Old Church). Amsterdam's oldest church, the Oude Kerk was built between 1366 and 1566 and restored from 1955 to 1979. It is a pleasing hodge-podge of styles and haphazard side buildings. Rembrandt's wife, Saskia, is buried here. Seminude women display their wares in the windows around the church square and along the surrounding canals—the neighborhood has doubled as a red-light district for nearly six centuries. ⊠ *Oudekerksplein 23,* ☎ *020/625–8284.* ☞ *Fl 5.* ☼ *Apr.–Oct., Mon.–Sat. 11–5, Sun. 1–5; Nov.–Mar., Fri.–Sun. 1–5.*

⑯ **Portugees Israelitische Synagogue** (Portuguese Israeli Synagogue). A square brick building behind brick courtyard walls, this noted synagogue was built between 1671 and 1675 by the Sephardic Jewish community that emigrated from Portugal during the preceding two centuries. Its spare, elegantly proportioned wood interior has remained virtually unchanged since it was built and still is lighted by candles in two immense candelabra during services. ⊠ *Mr. Visserplein 3,* ☎ *020/624–5351.* ☞ *Fl 5.* ☼ *Apr.–Oct., Sun.–Fri. 10–4; Nov.–Mar., Mon.–Thurs. 10–4, Fri. 10–3, Sun. 10–noon. Closed for lunch 12:30–1.*

☾ **Rijksmuseum Nederlands Scheepvaart** (State Museum of Netherlands Shipping). This is the place to go if you want to learn about the Dutch role in the development of world trade. Once the warehouse from which trading vessels were outfitted for their journeys, with everything from cannons to hardtack, the building now incorporates room after room of displays related to the development and power of the Dutch East and West Indies companies, as well as the Dutch fishing industry. Moored alongside the building at the east end of Amsterdam Harbor is a replica of the VOC (Dutch East India Company) ship **Amsterdam.** ⊠ *Kattenburgerplein 1,* ☎ *020/523–2311.* 🎟 *Fl 12.50.* ۞ *Tues.–Sat. 10–5, Sun. and holidays 1–5, June–Sept. also Mon. 10–5.*

㉓ **Schreierstoren** (Weeper's Tower). Although today this is a shop for nautical instruments, maps, and books, in the 16th century it was a lookout tower for the women whose men were fishing at sea. This gave rise to the mistaken belief that the name meant "weeper's" or "wailer's" tower. But the word "Schreier" actually comes from an old Dutch word describing the position of the tower astride two canals. A plaque on the side of the building tells you that it was from this location that Henry Hudson set sail on behalf of the Dutch East India Company to find a shorter route to the East Indies, discovering instead Hudson's Bay in Canada and, later, New York harbor and the Hudson River. The Schreierstoren overlooks the old **Oosterdok** (Eastern Dock) of Amsterdam Harbor. ⊠ *Prins Hendrikkade 94-95.*

Tropen Museum (Tropical Museum). This museum honors the Netherlands' link to Indonesia and the West Indies. It is a magnificent tiered, galleried, and skylighted museum decorated in gilt and marble. Displays and dioramas portray everyday life in the world's tropical environments. Upstairs in the **Kindermuseum** (Children's Museum) children can participate directly in the life of another culture through special programs involving art, dance, song, and sometimes even cookery. Adults may visit the children's section, but only under the supervision of a child age 6–12. ⊠ *Linnaeusstraat 2,* ☎ *020/568–8295.* 🎟 *Fl 10.* ۞ *Mon. and Wed.–Thurs., 10–5, Tues. 10–9:30, weekends and holidays noon–5; Kindermuseum activities Wed. at 2 and 3:30, weekends at 12:30, 2, and 3:30.*

⑬ **Waterlooplein flea market.** The wooden pushcarts that were used when the market began (before World War II) are gone, but the Waterlooplein remains a bustling shopping arena, wrapped around two sides of the Music Theater/Town Hall complex. A stroll past the stalls provides a colorful glimpse of Amsterdam entrepreneurship in action, day in and day out, in every sort of weather. ⊠ *Waterlooplein.* 🎟 *Free.* ۞ *Weekdays 9–5, Sat. 8:30–5:30.*

NEED A   Grab a bite in the **Waterlooplein** flea market or in the café of the
BREAK?   **Muziektheater.**

㉔ **Zeedijk.** Once known throughout the country as the black hole of Amsterdam for its concentration of drug traffickers and users, the Zeedijk began a new lease on life one night in the late 1980s when the city fathers cleared the area with an onslaught of horse patrols and fire hoses. These attackers were immediately followed by a brigade of carpenters, who reclaimed the area's dilapidated buildings; many of these buildings now house shops, restaurants, and galleries. No. 1 Zeedijk, now a café, is one of only two timbered houses left in the city. ⊠ *Zeedijk runs from Oudezijds Kolk (near Central Station) to Nieuwmarkt.*

⑲ **Zuiderkerk** (South Church). Built between 1603 and 1611 by Hendrick de Keyser, the Zuiderkerk is one of the most prolific architects of the Golden Age. This church is said to have inspired the great British architect Christopher Wren. The Zuiderkerk was one of the earliest

churches built in Amsterdam in the Renaissance style and was the first
in the city to be built for the Dutch Reformed Church. The city planning office maintains a display here that offers a look at the future of
Amsterdam. ⊠ *Zandstraat.* ⌧ *Free.* ☉ *Tower June–Oct., Wed. 2–5,
Thurs.–Fri. 11–2, Sat. 11–4.*

The Canals: City of 1,001 Bridges

One of Amsterdam's greatest pleasures is also one of its simplest—a
stroll along the canals. The grand, crescent-shaped waterways of the
grachtengordel (belt of canals) are lined with splendid buildings and
pretty, gabled houses. But you can also wander off the main thoroughfares, along the smaller canals that crisscross them, sampling the
charms of such historic city quarters as the Jordaan.

A Good Walk

Begin at the busy **Dam** ① square, where the imposing **Koninklijk
Paleis** ㉗ (Royal Palace) fills the western side of the square. The richly
decorated marble interiors are open to the public when the queen is
not in residence. To the right of the palace looms the Gothic **Niewe
Kerk** ㉘. Circle around behind the palace, follow the tram tracks into
the wide and busy Raadhuisstraat, and continue along it to the Westermarkt. The **Westerkerk** ㉙, on the right, facing the next canal, is another Amsterdam landmark, and Rembrandt's burial place. Make a
right past the church and follow the Prinsengracht canal to the **Anne
Frankhuis** ㉚, where you can visit the attic hideaway where Anne Frank
wrote her famous diary. Continue north along the Prinsengracht canal.
The neighborhood to your left, across the canal, is the **Jordaan** ㉛, full
of curious alleys and pretty canals, intriguing shops and cafés. At the
intersection of the Prinsengracht and Brouwersgracht canals, turn right
onto the **Brouwersgracht** ㉜, which many believe is the most beautiful
canal in Amsterdam. Cross the canal and follow it back to the Singel
canal. On the other side, follow the tram tracks to the left toward the
harbor. Ahead of you is the palatial **Centraal Station** ㉝. From Centraal
Station the Damrak leads past the **Beurs van Berlage** ㉟—the building
that is seen as Amsterdam's first significant venture into modern architecture—and back to the Dam.

TIMING

The timing for this walk is difficult to pin down, for the walk takes
you through areas that invite aimless wandering and exploration of
side streets. If you were brisk and determined, you could manage the
route in about an hour. But you could also easily while away an afternoon in the Jordaan, or take a leisurely stroll along the Prinsengracht.
Allow a minimum of half an hour each for the Royal Palace and the
Anne Frank House. Waiting in line to get into the Anne Frank House
can add another 10 to 20 minutes to your time (get there early to beat
the mid-day crowds).

The best time for canal walks is in late afternoon and early evening—
or early in the morning, when the mists still hang over the water. If
you're planning to go shopping in the Jordaan, remember that shops
in the Netherlands are closed Monday mornings. With its many restaurants and cafés, the Jordaan is also a fun place to visit at night.

Sights to See

★ ㉚ **Anne Frankhuis** (Anne Frank House). This unimposing canal house where
two Jewish families hid from the Nazis for more than two years during World War II is one of the most frequently visited places in the world.
The families were eventually discovered and sent to concentration
camps, but young Anne's diary survived as a detailed record of their

life in hiding. If you have time to see nothing else in Amsterdam, don't miss a visit to this house. The swinging bookcase that hid the door to the secret attic apartment is still there, you can walk through the rooms where Anne and her family lived, and there is also an exhibition on racism and oppression. ✉ *Prinsengracht 263,* ☎ *020/556–7100.* 🎫 *Fl 8.* ☉ *June–Aug., Mon.–Sat. 9–7, Sun. 10–7; Sept.–May, Mon.–Sat. 9–5, Sun. 10–5.*

NEED A BREAK? Sugared or fruit-filled crepes are a Dutch specialty, and the **Pancake Bakery** (✉ Prinsengracht 191, ☎ 020/625–1333) is one of the best places in Amsterdam to try them; the menu offers a choice of more than 30 combinations.

㉟ Beurs van Berlage (Berlage's Stock Exchange). Completed in 1903, the Stock Exchange is considered Amsterdam's first modern building. In 1874, when the Amsterdam Stock Exchange building on the Dam showed signs of collapse, the city authorities held a competition for the design of a new one. The architect who won was discovered to have copied the facade of a French town hall, so he was disqualified and the commission was awarded to a local architect, H.P. Berlage. The building that Berlage came up with proved to be an architectural turning point. Gone are all the fripperies and ornamentations of the 19th-century "neo" styles. The new Beurs, with its simple lines, earned Berlage the reputation of being the "Father of Modern Dutch Architecture." Today it serves as a concert and exhibition hall. ✉ *Damrak 213,* ☎ *020/626–5257.*

㉜ Brouwersgracht (Brewers Canal). A tree-lined canal considered one of the prettiest in Amsterdam, the Brouwersgracht is lined with homes and former warehouses of the brewers who traded here in earlier centuries. It is blessed with long views down the main canals and plenty of sunlight, all of which makes the Brouwersgracht one of the most photographed spots in town. The canal runs westward from the end of the Singel (a short walk along Prins Hendrikkade from Central Station).

㉝ Centraal Station (Central Station). Designed by P.J. Cuyper, the architect of Amsterdam's Rijksmuseum, this imposing building is a landmark of Dutch neo-Renaissance style (and bears a distinct resemblance to the museum on the other side of town). It opened in 1885 and has been the hub of transportation for the Netherlands ever since. From time to time the sumptuous **Koninklijle Wachtkamer** (Royal Waiting Room) on Platform 2 is opened to the public—and is certainly worth a visit. ✉ *Stationsplein,* ☎ *31/6–9292 or 06–9292 locally (public transport information).*

㉞ Damrak (Dam Port). This busy street leading up to Centraal Station is now lined with a curious assortment of shops, attractions, hotels, and eating places. It was once a harbor bustling with activity, its piers loaded with fish and other cargo on their way to the weigh house at the Dam. During the 19th century it was filled in, and the only water that remains is a patch in front of the station that provides mooring for canal tour boats.

★ **㉗ Het Koninklijk Paleis te Amsterdam** (Royal Palace at Amsterdam). Built in the mid-17th century as the city's town hall, the Koninklijk Paleis stands solidly on 13,659 pilings sunk deep into the marshy soil of the former riverbed. Designed by Jacob van Campen, one of the most prominent architects of the time, the Stadhuis (City Hall) is a high point of the Dutch Classicist style. Inside and out, the building is adorned with rich carvings. The prosperous burghers of the Golden Age wanted a city hall that could boast of their status to all visitors—and indeed, the Amsterdam Stadhuis became known as "the Eighth Wonder of the World." When you walk into what was originally the public entrance hall, the earth is quite literally at your feet. Two maps inlaid in the marble floor show Amsterdam not just at the center of the world, but of the universe as well.

During the French occupation of the Netherlands, Louis Napoleon, who had been installed as king in 1808, decided that this was the building most suitable for a royal palace. It has been the official residence of the House of Orange ever since. Louis filled his new palace with fashionable French Empire furniture, much of which remains.

Queen Beatrix, like her mother and grandmother before her, prefers to live in the quieter environment of a palace in a park outside The Hague and uses her Amsterdam residence only on the highest of state occasions. So, once again, the former Stadhuis is open to the public. If you are in Amsterdam while it is open, be sure to visit; this is the Dutch equivalent of touring the White House. ⊠ *Dam,* ☎ *020/624–8698.* 🎫 *Fl 5.* ☉ *Tues.–Thurs. 1–4; June –Sept., daily 12:30–5.*

★ ❸ **Jordaan.** The renovation generation has helped make the Jordaan—Amsterdam's "Greenwich Village"—the winner in the revival-of-the-fittest sweepstakes. Located in the western part of town, it is one of the most charming neighborhoods in a city that defines charm, basking in centuries-old patina and yet address to chic eateries and boutiques. It was originally called *jardin,* French for "garden." During the French occupation of Amsterdam, the vegetable gardens to the west of the city center were developed as a residential area. The new city quarter was referred to as the jardin, and the streets and canals (which follow the lines of the original irrigation ditches) were named for flowers and trees. In the mouths of the local Dutch, *jardin* became Jordaan, the name by which the quarter is known today.

The Jordaan was a working-class area and the scene of odorous industries, such as tanning and brewing. Its inhabitants developed a reputation for rebelliousness, but their strong community spirit also gave them a special identity, rather like London's cockneys. Until a generation ago, native Jordaaners would call their elders "uncle" or "aunt"—and they still have a reputation for enjoying a rousing sing-a-long.

Since the 1980s, the Jordaan has gone steadily upmarket, and now it is one of the trendiest parts of town. The narrow alleys and leafy canals are lined with quirky specialty shops, good restaurants, and designer boutiques. Students, artists, and the fashionable set fill the cafés. But many of the old Jordaaners are still here—as the sound of jolly singing emanating from some local pubs will testify. The Jordaan is bounded by the Prinsengracht, Looiersgracht, Lijnbaansgracht, and Brouwersgracht canals. After a visit to the Anne Frank House, you could cross the bridge to Egelantiersgracht, the canal that runs through the heart of the Jordaan. Then zigzag through pretty side streets, such as 3e (Derde) Egelantiersdwarsstraat, Tuinstraat, and 1e (Eerste) Tuinwarsstraat, for coffee on the Noordermarkt (Northern Market). Weave back south along alleys you haven't explored yet to the antiques markets on Looiersgracht.

❷❽ **Nieuwe Kerk** (New Church). Begun in the 14th century, the Nieuwe Kerk is a soaring Gothic church that was never given its spire because the authorities ran out of money. Inside are the graves of the poet Vondel (known as the "Dutch Shakespeare") and Admiral Ruyter, who sailed his invading fleet up the river Medway in England in the 17th century, becoming a naval hero in the process. Dutch monarchs are not crowned but are "inaugurated." This church is where the ceremony has taken place for every monarch since 1815. In between times it serves as a venue for special exhibitions. ⊠ *Dam,* ☎ *020/626–8168.* ⊠ *Free (except special exhibitions).* ⊙ *Daily 11–5.*

㉙ Westerkerk (Western Church). Built between 1602 and 1631, the Westerkerk has a tower topped by a copy of the crown of the Hapsburg emperor Maximilian I. Maximilian gave Amsterdam the right to use his royal insignia in gratitude for help from the city in his struggle for control of the Low Countries. The tower, with its gaudy yellow crown, is an Amsterdam landmark. Its carillon is the comforting "clock" of the canal area of Amsterdam, its chiming mentioned often in the diary of Anne Frank, who lived around the corner. Rembrandt and his son Titus are buried here; the philosopher René Descartes lived on the square facing the church. ⊠ *Prinsengracht (corner of Westermarkt),* ☎ *020/624–7766.* ⊙ *Tower June–Sept., Tues.–Wed. and Fri.–Sat. 2–5.*

Dining

Amsterdammers enjoy good food, particularly when shared with good company. In couples or small groups, they seek out the quieter, cozy places or go in search of the new culinary stars of the city; to celebrate or entertain, they return to the institutions that never disappoint them with the quality of their cuisine or service; and in large groups, you invariably find the Dutch trooping into their favorite Indonesian restaurant to share a rijsttafel. The city's more than 700 restaurants span a wide variety of ethnic cuisines; you'll find everything from international fast-food joints to chandeliered waterfront dining rooms frequented by the royal family. In between are small, chef-owned establishments on the canals and their side streets, restaurants that have stood the test of time on the basis of service, ambience, and consistency. For a dining chart that explains the range of price categories, *see* The Pleasures of Dining and Lodging at the beginning of this chapter.

$$$$ ✕ **Beddington's.** The decor is eye-catching, and the location is good. Near the Concertgebouw and the art museums, Beddington's sits at the junction between the business district and the city's most prestigious modern residential neighborhoods. The chef, an Englishwoman, takes a multicultural approach in the kitchen, mixing Japanese and other East Asian flavors and concepts with those from England, Spain, and the West Indies. The sort of imaginative meal you might put together for yourself here would be *zeeduivel* (monkfish) tandoori followed by— why not?—trifle. ⊠ *Roelof Hartstraat 6–8,* ☎ *020/676–5201. Jacket required. AE, DC, MC, V. Closed Sun.*

$$$$ ✕ **De Kersentuin.** The name of this cheerful, high-ceiling restaurant, which means "cherry orchard," signals the color scheme that extends from the dinnerware to the decor. It is a good place for a leisurely meal. Although there are large windows overlooking a residential street, the focal point is the kitchen, open behind glass panels. As you dine, you can watch chef Rudolf Bos and his staff prepare French dishes with a Far Eastern twist, such as perch flavored with coconut and spicy Thai sauce, or calves' sweetbreads marinated in soy sauce and ginger. ⊠ *Dijsselhofplantsoen 7,* ☎ *020/664–2121. Reservations essential. Jacket and tie. AE, DC, MC, V. Closed Sun. No lunch.*

$$$$ ✕ **De Trechter.** This very small restaurant beside a canal in the residential part of the city has a very big reputation and a devoted following. Chef Jan de Wit offers such specialties as carpaccio of Angus beef and Scotch salmon, fillet of lamb in potato crust with ratatouille and rosemary sauce, and smoked oxtails with cubes of goose liver, garlic mayonnaise, and croutons. ⊠ *Hobbemakade 62–63,* ☎ *020/671–1263.*

Reservations essential. Jacket and tie. AE, DC, MC, V. Closed Sun.–Mon. No lunch.

$$$$ ✕ **Excelsior.** The Excelsior's view over the Amstel River, to the Munt-
★ plein on one side and the Music Theater on the other, is the best there is in Amsterdam. The dining room is a gracious, chandeliered hall with plenty of room for diners, waiters, dessert trolleys, preparation carts, towering palms, tall candelabra, and a grand piano. The approach is traditional French with a twist: You might choose a lobster bisque or an adventurous dish such as duck liver gratin with pumpkin, or cod with olive tapenade. For dessert, try the delicious lemon tart or poached figs. There are five fixed-price menus. ⊠ *Hotel de L'Europe, Nieuwe Doelenstraat 2–8,* ☎ *020/623–4836. Jacket and tie. AE, DC, MC, V. No lunch Sat.*

$$$$ ✕ **'t Swarte Schaep.** This cozy upstairs restaurant overlooking the noisy
★ Leidseplein is named after a legendary black sheep that roamed the area in the 17th century. It's a study in traditional Dutch decor, with cop-per pots hanging from the wooden beams and heavily framed paint-ings on the walls. Together with this Old Holland atmosphere, the excellent French cuisine—which includes chateaubriand with béar-naise sauce and lobster mousse with asparagus salad—sometimes at-tracts members of the Dutch royal family during their incognito visits to the capital. Dinner orders are accepted until 11—late even for Am-sterdam. ⊠ *Korte Leidsdwarsstraat 24,* ☎ *020/622–3021. Reserva-tions essential. AE, DC, MC, V.*

$$$–$$$$ ✕ **Le Garage.** On April 1, 1990, a backstreet garage near the Con-certgebouw began a new lease on life. Oil stains and engine parts had given way to mirrored walls, plush seating, and clinking cutlery. Chef Joop Braakhekke, who is famed in the Netherlands as the zany pre-senter of a TV cooking show, comes up with superb New Dutch cui-sine, including a few old family recipes, such as eel stewed with raisins, barley, and herbs. Media stars, politicians, and such leading lights in the Dutch art world as the novelist Harry Mulisch eat here, making this a hot spot for celebrity spotters. ⊠ *Ruysdaelstraat 54,* ☎ *020/679–7176. Reservations essential. Jacket and tie. AE, DC, MC, V.*

$$$ ✕ **Café Americain.** Though thousands of buildings in Amsterdam are
★ designated as historic monuments, the one that houses this restaurant is the only structure whose interior, an Art Deco treasure, is also pro-tected. Opened in 1882 and said to have been the site of Mata Hari's wedding reception, the Americain is a hybrid restaurant-café serving everything from light snacks to full dinners. To one side are formal ta-bles draped with white linens, where traditional entrées such as medal-lions of beef with béarnaise sauce are served; to the other side are tiny bare-topped tables, perfect for a quick coffee and pastry. There is a well-stocked buffet complete with hot dishes, salads, and desserts. ⊠ *Amer-ican Hotel, Leidsekade 97,* ☎ *020/624–5322. Reservations not accepted. AE, DC, MC, V.*

$$$ ✕ **Christophe.** After Algerian-born Christophe Royer opened his *eet tempel* (eating temple) on a small cross canal between the Keizersgracht and Prinsengracht, not far from the Anne Frank House, he and his French kitchen staff quickly became recognized for their fine French cuisine. When Christophe arrived in Amsterdam in the early 1980s he was ad-vised to adapt his cuisine to Dutch taste, but instead he has been in-fluential in changing the style of local restaurant fare. Specialties include Indian corn soup with oysters, *crevettes à l'orange* (shrimp with orange sauce), and *pigeon à la marocaine* (pigeon cooked with coriander and other tangy spices); there is also a selection of vegetarian dishes, including a delicious aubergine prepared with cumin. Not only is the menu special, but so are Christophe's welcoming atmosphere and per-sonalized service. ⊠ *Leliegracht 46,* ☎ *020/625–0807. Reservations*

48

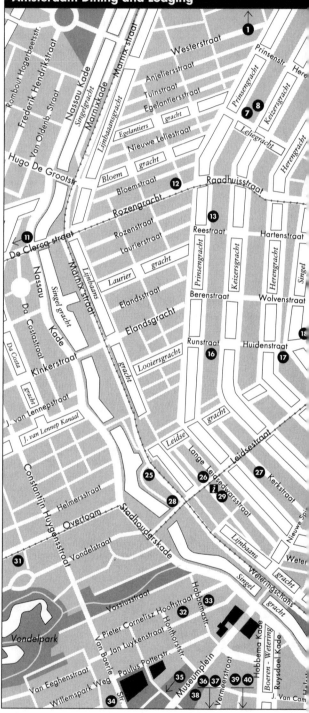

Amsterdam Dining and Lodging

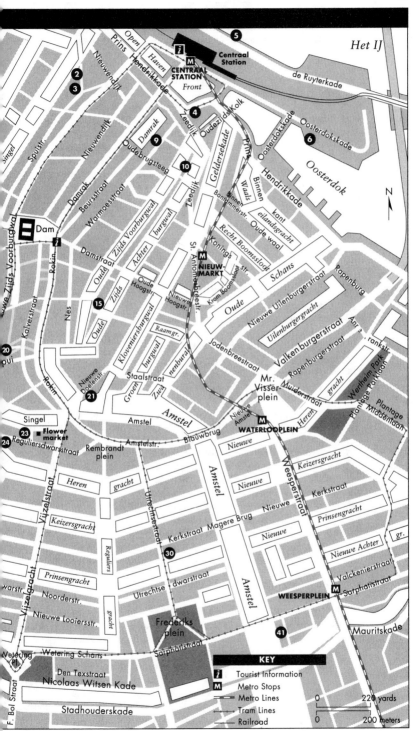

Het IJ

de Ruyterkade

Centraal
Station

CENTRAAL
STATION
Front

Oosterdokskade

Oosterdok

Oudezijds Kolk

Prins Hendrikkade

Waals
Binnen kant
eilandsgracht
Binnen
Bontemmersm.
Oude waal

Recht Boomssloot

Konings str.

Schans

Oude

Nieuwe Uilenburgerstraat

Rapenburg

Uilenburgergracht

Valkenburgerstraat

Krom Boomssloot

Jodenbreestraat

Rapenburgerstraat

Anne . ranksir.

Wertheim Park

Plantage Parklaan

Plantage Middenlaan

Mr.
Visser-
plein

Muiderstraat

gracht

Heren

Amstel

Nieuwe
Amstel

WATERLOOPLEIN

Keizersgracht

Weesperstraat

Kerkstraat

Prinsengracht

Nieuwe

Nieuwe Achter

gr.

Nieuwe

Valckenierstraat

WEESPERPLEIN

Sarphatistraat

Mauritskade

Sarphatistraat

KEY

ℹ️ Tourist Information

Ⓜ Metro Stops

- - - Metro Lines

↔ Tram Lines

— Railroad

0   220 yards

0   200 meters

Nieuwe Zijds Voorburgwal

Nieuwendijk

Prins Hendrikkade

Open
Haven

Singel

Spuistr.

Damrak

Beursstraat

Warmoesstraat

Oudebrugsteeg

Zeedijk

Zijds Voorburgwal

Achter burgwal

Geldersekade

St. Antoniesbreestr.

NIEUW-
MARKT

Nieuwe
Hoogstr.

Oude
Hoogstr.

Zijds Hoogstr.

Oude

Kloveniersburgwal

Raamgr.

burgwal

Zuid nenburgwal

Nieuwe
Doelenstr.

Staalstraat

Groen

Zuid

Amstel

Amstel

Blauwbrug

Amstelstr.

Rembrandt
plein

Singel

Flower
market

Reguliersdwarsstraat

Vizelstraat

Heren

gracht

Keizersgracht

Reguliers

Amstel

Utrechtsestraat

Kerkstraat   Magere Brug

Nieuwe

Amstel

Prinsengracht

gracht

Utrechtse dwarsstraat

Noorderstr.

Nieuwe Looiersstr.

Vizelgracht

Wetering
Pl.

Wetering Schans

Den Texstraat

Nicolaas Witsen Kade

Stadhouderskade

F. Bol Straat

Frederiks
plein

Dam

Rokin

Kalverstraat

Nes

Rokin

Singel

Damstraat

Oude

Pui

2

3

5

4

6

9

10

15

20

21

23

24

30

41

N

essential. Jacket and tie. AE, DC, MC, V. Closed Sun., Mon., 1st wk in Jan., and 2 wks in July–Aug.

$$$ ✕ **De Silveren Spieghel.** Owner Ben van den Nieuwboer gives you his
★   personal attention, including offering wines from his own French vineyard, as you sit at one of the scattered tables of this restaurant in a delightfully crooked 17th-century house. The cuisine is French-influenced but uses the best of local ingredients, including lamb from the island of Texel and the honey of Amsterdam's Vondelpark. The seasonal game dishes are always worth trying, especially those that come with rose-petal sauce, and the fixed-price menus represent excellent value for the money. ⊠ *Kattengat 4–6, ☎ 020/624–6589. Reservations essential. AE, MC, V. Closed weekends. Lunch by appointment (phone a day ahead).*

$$$ ✕ **D'Vijff Vlieghen.** Dining in a traditional canal-house environment is part of the Amsterdam experience, though you are more likely to find yourself seated among closely packed tables of Swedes and Japanese than among Dutch diners. But don't let that stop you; the "Five Flies" is a charming spot that in the 1950s and 1960s was frequented by the likes of Walt Disney and Orson Welles. Set in five adjoining houses that date from 1627, the restaurant incorporates a series of small, timbered dining rooms, each well adorned with mementoes and bric-a-brac, ranging from music boxes, liqueur kegs, and violin cases to two etchings by Rembrandt. The kitchen, long a bastion of traditional Dutch meat-and-potatoes cooking, is now drawing on fresh local ingredients in such dishes as suckling pig cutlets coated in pastry, and grilled halibut with a mussel ragout. Judge for yourself whether it's overpriced, as some diners attest. ⊠ *Spuistraat 294–302, ☎ 020/624–8369. Jacket and tie. AE, DC, MC, V.*

$$$ ✕ **Dynasty.** At this trendy, interesting spot, the decor is a fanciful mating of Asian and Art Deco. A mural in red, white, and black encircles the room, and dozens of amber and dove-gray Chinese paper umbrellas hang upended from the ceiling. Chef K.Y. Lee's menu is as fascinating as the decor: The medley of Asian cuisines includes authentically prepared, classic Chinese dishes, such as Three Meats in Harmony, and selections from the cuisines of Thailand, Malaysia, and Vietnam. There are two fixed-price menus. ⊠ *Reguliersdwarsstraat 30, ☎ 020/626–8400. Jacket required. AE, DC, MC, V. Closed Tues.*

$$$ ✕ **Tout Court.** Chef John Fagel, who hails from a well-known Dutch
★   family of chefs, has stuck by his intention to serve "good food without a fuss." This comfortable, casual restaurant is tucked away on a side street between the canals: You'll know it by the napkins that hang in the window, as if strung on a laundry line. The menu is direct and uncomplicated, with selections such as saddle of lamb filled with spinach, guinea fowl stuffed with mushrooms, roast brill with leeks, and a heavenly bouillabaisse. At dinner there are three menus, including a seven-course feast. ⊠ *Runstraat 13, ☎ 020/625–8637. AE, DC, MC, V. Closed Sun.–Mon.*

$$$ ✕ **Yamazoto.** The chef at this Japanese restaurant, lauded by Japanese residents as the best in town, tempers his fidelity to the traditions in which he has been trained with a few concessions to local taste—there are more beef dishes than usual on a traditional Japanese menu. A full seasonal set menu costs Fl 120, but there are scores of less pricey options. There is a separate sushi bar and a teppanyaki restaurant, which specializes in table-side grilling. ⊠ *Hotel Okura, Ferdinand Bolstraat 333, ☎ 020/678—7111. Reservations essential. AE, DC, MC, V.*

$$–$$$ ✕ **Lonny's.** Lonny Gerungan offers Indonesian cuisine at its best. His
★   family have been cooks on Bali for generations, and the recipes used for the feasts in his restaurant are those that his forefathers used to prepare for royal banquets on the island. Treat yourself to a Selamatan Puri Gede, more than 15 succulently spicy dishes served with rice. The

waiters wear sarongs, and the restaurant is decorated with silky fabrics and colorful parasols. ⊠ *Rozengracht 46-48,* ☏ *020/623–8950. Reservations essential. AE, DC, MC, V. No lunch.*

$$–$$$ ✕ **Lucius.** The plain setting and the simple service belie the fact that this is one of the best fish restaurants in town. On the marine menu, your choices range from fishburgers with gorgonzola cheese to grilled lobster. The wine list includes a good selection from California and even a Dutch wine from Apostlehoeve in Limburg province, the country's only vineyard. ⊠ *Spuistraat 247,* ☏ *020/624–1831. Reservations essential. AE, DC, MC, V. Closed Sun.*

$$–$$$ ✕ **Pier 10.** This intimate restaurant, perched on the end of a pier behind
★ Centraal Station, was built in the 1930s as a shipping office. Ask for a table in the tiny glass-enclosed room at the far end of the restaurant, where you can see the water lap gently beneath the windows and the harbor lights twinkle in the distance. Owner-chef Steve Muzerie sometimes comes up with odd combinations, such as licorice mousse with a sauce made from *advocaat* (a liqueur made with beaten egg yolks, sugar, and spirit), but his culinary inventions are usually delicious. Try the goose with wild mushrooms, or a monstrous Caesar salad. ⊠ *De Ruyterkade Steiger 10,* ☏ *020/624–8276. Reservations essential. AE, MC, V.*

$$ ✕ **Bistro Izmir.** Tops among the many Turkish restaurants in Amsterdam, the Izmir offers delicious, authentic Turkish cuisine. Inside, traditional stained-glass Turkish lanterns dapple spots of bright color over walls lined with pink fabric. Try the *meze*—a feast of small dishes—or succulent grills. ⊠ *Kerkstraat 66,* ☏ *020/627–8239. AE, DC, MC, V.*

$$ ✕ **Bodega Keyzer.** After 85 years spent serving musicians, concert
★ goers, and residents of the neighborhoods surrounding the art museums and Concertgebouw, this half restaurant, half café-bodega has evolved into something as familiar and comfortable as an old shoe. You can come in almost any attire, at almost any hour, for a simple drink or a full meal. The interior is paneled with dark wood, the lights are dim, and Oriental carpets cover the tables. The menu is equally traditional—among the meat and fish selections are tournedos, schnitzel, and sole meunière—though you may also come across a more adventurous *ris de veau* (veal sweetbreads) with orange and green pepper sauce or fricassee of veal with nut-basil sauce. ⊠ *Van Baerlestraat 96,* ☏ *020/671–1441. AE, DC, MC, V. Closed Sun.*

$$ ✕ **Brasserie van Baerle.** Begun as a neighborhood lunch and Sunday brunch restaurant, this bright, appealing spot with an uncomplicated European modern decor now even draws late diners who come in following performances at the nearby Concertgebouw. The chef's creativity is the main attraction. Imaginative dishes include spicy Asian salads and heavier fare, such as duck in truffle sauce. There is outdoor dining in good weather. ⊠ *Van Baerlestraat 158,* ☏ *020/679–1532. AE, DC, MC, V. Closed Sat. and Dec. 25–Jan. 2.*

$$ ✕ **De Compagnon.** Down a dimly lit alley in the red-light district and through an unmarked door, you'll find a gem of a restaurant crammed into an old, narrow house overlooking Damrak harbor. Odd chairs and tables that don't quite earn the designation "antique" make up the furnishings, and flea-market knickknacks adorn the walls. There's just one three-course set menu—though you may be offered a fish or vegetarian option if the main course is meat. The cuisine is French-country. Though the quality of the standard fare is variable, the atmosphere more than makes up for any shortfall. ⊠ *Guldehandsteeg 17,* ☏ *020/620–4225. AE, DC, MC, V.*

$$ ✕ **De Kooning van Siam.** This Thai restaurant, which is favored by the city's Thai residents, sits smack in the middle of the red-light district, but don't let that keep you away. Although the beams and wall panels are still visible in this old canal house, there is nothing Old Dutch about the furniture or the wall decorations. Choices are somewhat limited: Selections might include very hot stir-fried beef with onion and chili peppers, or a milder chicken and Chinese vegetables with coconut, curry, and basil. ⊠ *Oude Zijds Voorburgwal 42,* ☎ *020/623–7293. AE, DC, MC, V. Closed Feb.*

$$ ✕ **De Oesterbar.** "The Oyster Bar," like its namesake in New York, is a local institution. It's the first place to think of when you hanker for a half-dozen oysters fresh from the Oosterschelde or the simply prepared catch of the day. The choices are straightforward: grilled, baked, or fried fish served with tartar sauce, potatoes, and salad. Live lobster is also available in season. The no-nonsense room on the main floor has a small bar at the back, with white tile walls incorporating nautical murals and a long row of eerily lighted fish tanks along one side. In the upstairs dining room, the mood is oddly bordellolike, with elaborately patterned wallpaper and an assortment of innocuous paintings on the walls. ⊠ *Leidseplein 10,* ☎ *020/623–2988. Reservations essential. AE, DC, MC, V.*

$$ ✕ **Haesje Claes.** This is as Old Dutch cozy as you can get. The beams are dark and heavy, the walls are chockablock with copper pots and farmstead curios, and the lamp shades that hang low over the tabletops are draped with kerchiefs in the traditional way to shadow the light. The food, too, is Old Dutch. Come here for calves' liver with bacon and onions, or tournedos with pepper sauce, or a *stamppot* (meat and vegetables mashed with mounds of potato). A nightly tourist menu is served; there also is a children's menu. The prices are as basic as the food. ⊠ *Spuistraat 273–275,* ☎ *020/624–9998. AE, DC, MC, V. Closed Sun.*

$$ ✕ **Pakistan Restaurant.** When Khalid Seikh and Bobby Khawaja opened their restaurant in the early 1980s, it was the first of its kind in Amsterdam. From meals once set before Moguls to dishes you would find in the humblest Islamabad market, their food soon became the talk of the town. You can get searingly hot curries as well as deliciously marinated meats, cooked in subtle spices. The presentation can be spectacular (sometimes involving edible silver leaf), and the service is always charming. Although it is situated a little to the west of Amsterdam's historic center, this restaurant is well worth the detour. ⊠ *De Clercqstraat 65,* ☎ *020/618–1120. AE, DC, MC, V. No lunch.*

$$ ✕ **Rose's Cantina.** A perennial favorite of the sparkling set, this restaurant serves up spicy Tex-Mex food and lethal cocktails. The noise level can be lethal, too. Pop in for a full meal or sundowner. ⊠ *Reguliersdwarsstraat 38,* ☎ *020/625–9797. AE, DC, MC, V.*

$$ ✕ **Sluizer.** Sluizer is really two side-by-side restaurants—one serves only meat, the other only fish. Both are simply decorated and unpretentious; both are known for good food that is prepared without a lot of fanfare or creativity; both are reasonably priced; and, not surprisingly, both are crowded every night. ⊠ *Utrechtsestraat 43–45,* ☎ *020/622–6376 (meat) or 020/626–3557 (fish). AE, DC, MC, V.*

$$ ✕ **Toscanini.** This cavernous, noisy Italian restaurant is very popular with
★   local trendies. The food is superb. You'll find pasta with game sauce, subtle fresh fish dishes, such as trout with fresh basil, and other delights, as well as such familiar favorites as antipasto, which is scrumptious here. And there's not a pizza in sight. ⊠ *Lindengracht 75,* ☎ *020/623–2813. Reservations essential. No credit cards. Closed Tues. No lunch.*

$ ✕ **Caffe Esprit.** Clean-cut and popular, it has tall windows that over-
★   look the busy Spui square; the decor is simple black, white, and gray. There is just a handful of small tables, with a small counter to take care of overflow. The menu is contemporary American in character, with choices such as Surf Burger garnished with avocado and bacon, or a Yankee Doodle sandwich (crisp roll with pastrami, mustard, mayonnaise, and grilled paprika). Salads include Popeye's Favorite Salad—

wild Italian spinach, bacon, croutons, mushrooms, and egg, smothered in a warm tarragon vinaigrette. There also are pastas, pizzas, and standard sandwiches; at breakfast (served until noon) there's fresh-squeezed orange juice, as well as yogurt with muesli, and scones with butter and jam. There is a children's menu. ⊠ *Spui 10,* ☎ *020/622–1967. Reservations not accepted. No credit cards. Closed Sun.*

$ ✕ **De Keuken van 1870.** A soup kitchen throughout the Great Depression and two world wars, this "Kitchen of 1870" now serves up hearty Dutch food at unbeatably low prices. Tourists, punksters, and pensioners sit at plain wooden tables spread about a traditional black-and-white tile floor. The steamy kitchen maintains a constant outpouring of enormous white plates piled high with substantial meat stews, potatoes, and vegetables. Late-nighters take note: The kitchen closes at 8. ⊠ *Spuistraat 4,* ☎ *020/624–8965. Reservations not accepted. No credit cards.*

$ ✕ **Pizzeria Calzone.** Not all the restaurants on the Reguliersdwarsstraat are expensive. Calzone is a bright, cheerful place decorated in Italian red, white, and green, with small white tables and stiff black chairs that don't encourage anyone to linger. Pizzas, pastas, and simple grilled meats are on the menu. ⊠ *Reguliersdwarsstraat 55,* ☎ *020/627–3833. AE, DC, MC, V.*

$ ✕ **Sama Sebo.** Come to this small, busy, and relaxed neighborhood Indonesian restaurant near the State Museum for rijsttafel, a simple *bami goreng* (spicy fried rice with vegetables), or a lunch of *nasi goreng* (spicy fried noodles with vegetables). The colors are muted tans and browns with rush mats covering the walls. When things are busy, the restaurant can be cramped. ⊠ *P.C. Hoofstraat 27,* ☎ *020/662–8146. AE, DC, MC, V. Closed Sun.*

Lodging

Amsterdam is a pedestrian's paradise but a driver's nightmare. Few hotels have parking lots, and cars are best abandoned in one of the city's multistory lots for the duration of your stay. Most visitors prefer to stay inside the concentric ring of canals that surround the downtown area. Within this, the quiet museum quarter is a convenient choice, close to both the Rijksmuseum and Vondelpark. Most atmospheric is the historic canalside neighborhood with its gabled merchants' houses. Wherever you choose, one thing is certain: Most hotels offer up rooms that are spotlessly clean. For price categories, *see* The Pleasures of Dining and Lodging at the beginning of this chapter.

$$$$ ⊞ **Amstel Inter-Continental Hotel.** This grand 125-year-old hotel reopened
★ in 1992 with a completely new interior designed by Pierre Yves Rochon of Paris, who has created a Dutch atmosphere with a European touch. Rooms are still the most spacious in the city; the new decor resembles that of a gracious home, with Oriental rugs, brocade upholstery, Delft lamps, and a color scheme that borrows from the warm tones of Makkum pottery. Everything about this hotel has been redesigned, including the format of its well-known restaurant, La Rive, where there's now a special table from which you can watch your meal being prepared. ⊠ *Professor Tulpplein 1,* ☎ *020/622–6060,* ℻ *020/622–5808. 79 rooms. 2 restaurants, pool, sauna, exercise room. AE, DC, MC, V.*

$$$$ ⊞ **Golden Tulip Barbizon Palace.** One of the newest hotels in Amsterdam also has one of the most convenient locations, directly across from Centraal Station. The exterior was designed to blend with the neighboring row of old houses, which overlook the inner harbor. Inside, the historic mood disappears in the face of the towering, skylighted, Roman-atrium–style lobby, which stretches across the length of the hotel, with cafés, shops, restaurants, and club rooms opening to the sides. Guest rooms are small, but they are decorated nicely and support the

Old Dutch theme with dark beams across the ceilings. ✉ *Prins Hendrikkade 59–72,* ☎ *020/556–4564,* 🖷 *020/624–3353. 268 rooms. 2 restaurants, exercise room. AE, DC, MC, V.*

$$$$ ⊡ **The Grand Amsterdam.** This hotel is on a historically important site: It was built into a group of buildings dating from the 14th century that served for more than 185 years as the Town Hall of Amsterdam. Maria de Medici once stayed here, as did William of Orange, and it was the site of Queen Beatrix's wedding. Today's hotel is deluxe, with Gobelin tapestries, Jugendstil stained-glass windows, and, in the café, a mural by Karel Appel created early in his career to repay a debt to the city. The rooms, which vary in size, are attractively done in deep tones of burgundy damask and bold floral prints; the best of them overlook the garden courtyard. ✉ *Oude Zijds Voorburgwal 197,* ☎ *020/555–3111,* 🖷 *020/555–3222. 182 rooms. 2 restaurants, pool, sauna. AE, DC, MC, V.*

$$$$ ⊡ **Hotel de l'Europe.** Quiet, gracious, and understated in both decor
★   and service, this hotel overlooks the Amstel River, the Muntplein, and the flower market. It is near the Music Theater, in one of Amsterdam's most convenient locations. The city-side rooms, recently redecorated, are full of warm, rich colors; the riverside rooms are done in pastel shades and brilliant whites and have French windows to let in floods of light. The marble baths are large and luxurious. A junior suite might be a worthwhile choice here. ✉ *Nieuwe Doelenstraat 2–8,* ☎ *020/623–4836,* 🖷 *020/624–2962. 100 rooms. Restaurant, pool, sauna, exercise room. AE, DC, MC, V.*

$$$ ⊡ **American.** The American, one of the oldest hotels in Amsterdam,
★   is housed in one of the city's most fancifully designed buildings. Its location, directly on the Leidseplein, is ideal for anyone who likes to be in the middle of everything—nightlife, dining, sightseeing, and shopping are all at hand. Rooms are comfortable and furnished in an art deco style. ✉ *Leidseplein 28,* ☎ *020/624–5322,* 🖷 *020/625–3236. 188 rooms. Restaurant, exercise room. AE, DC, MC, V.*

$$$ ⊡ **Jan Luyken.** This small, out-of-the-way place is barely noticeable
★   among the homes and offices of a residential Amsterdam neighborhood. The personal approach is a relaxing alternative to the large hotels, yet it also is well equipped to handle the needs of the many business travelers who stay here regularly, with office services and small meeting rooms available. ✉ *Jan Luykenstraat 58,* ☎ *020/573–0730,* 🖷 *020/676–3841. 63 rooms. AE, DC, MC, V.*

$$$ ⊡ **Pulitzer.** Twenty-four 17th-century houses were combined to create this hotel, which faces both the Prinsengracht and the Keizersgracht canals and is just a short walk from Dam square; the place retains a historic ambience. Most guest rooms have beamed ceilings; there are gardens in the middle of the block. Refurbishment begun in 1996 will gradually replace modern furnishings with more appropriate antique styles. From here you may hear the hourly chiming of the nearby Westerkerk clock. Recent renovations have added comfort and convenience. ✉ *Prinsengracht 315–331,* ☎ *020/523–5235,* 🖷 *020/627–6753. 213 rooms, 7 suites, 1 apartment. Restaurant, bar. AE, DC, MC, V.*

$$ ⊡ **Ambassade.** Nine 17th- and 18th-century canal-side houses have
★   been joined to create this hotel, which is elegantly decorated with Oriental rugs, chandeliers, and antiques. The canal-side rooms are spacious, with large windows and solid, functional furniture. The rooms at the rear are quieter, but smaller and darker. Service is attentive and friendly. ✉ *Herengracht 341,* ☎ *020/626–2333,* 🖷 *020/624–5321. 44 rooms, 5 suites, 1 apartment. Lobby bar. AE, DC, MC, V.*

$$ ⊡ **Canal House.** This is what you imagine a canal-house hotel to be like:
★   a beautiful old home with high, plaster ceilings, antique furniture, old paintings, and a backyard garden bursting with plants and flowers. Every

room is unique in both size and decor. The elegant chandeliered breakfast room overlooks the garden, and there is a small bar in the front parlor. The American owners have put a lot of love and style into the Canal House—the result is an intimate hotel that seems more like the private home of a well-to-do family. ⊠ *Keizersgracht 148,* ☎ *020/622–5182,* 𝔽𝔸𝕏 *020/624–1317. 26 rooms with bath. AE, DC, MC, V.*

$$ 🏨 **Hotel de Filosoof.** This hotel, on a quiet street near the Vondel Park, attracts artists, thinkers, and people looking for something a little different; bona fide Amsterdam philosophers are regularly to be found in the salon's comfy armchairs. Each room is decorated with a different cultural motif—there's an Aristotle room furnished in Greek style, with passages from the works of Greek philosophers hung on the walls, and a Goethe room adorned with Faustian texts. ⊠ *Anna van den Vondelstraat 6,* ☎ *020/683–3013,* 𝔽𝔸𝕏 *020/685–3750. 29 rooms, 25 with bath. Lobby bar. AE, MC, V.*

$ 🏨 **Amstel Botel.** This floating hotel, moored near Centraal Station, is an appropriate lodging in watery Amsterdam. The rooms are cabin-like, but the portholes have been replaced by windows that provide fine views of the city across the water. Make sure you don't get a room on the land side of the vessel, or you'll end up staring at an ugly postal sorting office. ⊠ *Oosterdokskade 2,* ☎ *020/626–4247,* 𝔽𝔸𝕏 *020/639–1952. 176 rooms. AE, DC, MC, V.*

$ 🏨 **Quentin Hotel.** This small, family-run hotel is just a stone's throw from the hectic Leidseplein and attracts a young, alternative clientele. It is simply decorated in white and pastel shades and with modern prints. Large windows let in a flood of light. The best rooms are the spacious corner ones that overlook a canal. ⊠ *Leidsekade 89,* ☎ *020/626–2187,* 𝔽𝔸𝕏 *020/622–0121. 24 rooms, 19 with shower. AE, DC, MC, V.*

Nightlife and the Arts

Amsterdam's theater and music season begins in September and runs through June, when the Holland Festival of Performing Arts is held. *What's On in Amsterdam* is a comprehensive, English-language publication distributed by the tourist office that lists art and performing-arts events around the city. Reserve tickets to performances at the major theaters before your arrival through the **National Reservation Center** (⊠ Postbus 404, 2260 AK Leidschendam, ☎ 3170/320–2500, 𝔽𝔸𝕏 070/320–2611). Tickets can also be purchased in person at the tourist information offices through the **VVV Theater Booking Office** (⊠ Stationsplein 10) Monday through Saturday, 10–4; the **AUB Ticketshop** (⊠ Leidseplein/corner Marnixstraat, ☎ 020/621–1211) Monday through Saturday, 9–9; or at theater box offices.

Brown Cafés

Once the tasting house of an old family distillery, **De Admiraal** (⊠ Herengracht 319, ☎ 020/625–4334) still serves potent liqueurs—many with obscene names. A busy, jolly Brown Café, **In de Wildeman** (⊠ Kolksteeg 3, ☎ 020/638–2348), attracts a wide range of types and ages. **Nol** (⊠ Westerstraat 109, ☎ 020/624–5380) resonates with lusty-lunged, native Jordaaners having the time of their lives. **Rooie Nelis** (⊠ Laurierstraat 101, ☎ 020/624–4167) is one of the cafés that have kept their traditional Jordaan atmosphere despite the area's tendency toward trendiness. The high-ceilinged **'t Smalle** (⊠ Egelantiersgracht 12, ☎ 020/623–9617) has a waterside terrace and is a favorite after-work watering hole. **De Reiger** (⊠ Nieuwe Leliestraat 34, ☎ 020/624–7426) has a distinctive Jugendstil bar and serves food. If you want to hear the locals sing folk music on Sunday afternoon, stop by **De Twee Zwaantjes** (⊠ Prinsengracht 114, ☎ 020/625–2729).

Cocktail Bars

Le Bar (⊠ Hotel de l'Europe, Nieuwe Doelenstraat 2–8, ☎ 020/623–4836), cozy and stylish, is a favorite meeting place for businesspeople. Comfy leather chairs and soft lighting give the **Golden Palm Bar** (⊠ Grand Hotel Krasnapolsky, Dam 9, ☎ 020/554–9111) something of the atmosphere of a British gentlemen's club. **Ciel Bleu Bar** (⊠ Hotel Okura, Ferdinand Bolstraat 333, ☎ 020/678–7111) has a glass-walled lounge 23 stories high, where you can enjoy the sunsets over Amsterdam and watch the night lights twinkle to life.

Discos and Rock Clubs

Boston Club (⊠ Kattengat 1, ☎ 020/624–5561) is a mainstream hotel disco that plays mainly chart music. Unabashedly commercial, **Cash** (⊠ Leidseplein 12, ☎ 020/422–0808) attracts Dutch youth from the provinces and reveling tourists. The huge, popular **Escape** (⊠ Rembrandtplein 11–15, ☎ 020/622–1111) can handle 2,500 people dancing to a DJ or live bands. There are also laser light shows and videos here, and shops selling clubwear. Converted out of an old cinema, **Roxy** (⊠ Singel 465, ☎ 020/620–0354) is considered the trendiest discotheque in the Netherlands at the moment. Unless you are pretty fast-talking or spectacularly dressed, you might not get past the door. Wednesday is gay night. **36 Op de Schaal Van** (⊠ Reguliersdwarsstraat 36, ☎ 020/626–1573) is an intimate club with two small dance floors and soul and soul-derivative sounds. **It** (⊠ Amstelstraat 24, ☎ 020/625–0111) has four bars, special acts and bands, and celebrities in the crowd. This place tends toward a gay crowd on Friday and Saturday nights, straight on Thursday and Sunday nights. A group of artists runs **Seymour Likely Too** (⊠ Nieuwezijds Voorburgwal 161, ☎ 020/420–5663), giving vent to their creativity in the decor—such as the Beuys Bar, decorated in the style of Joseph Beuys, a father of the avant-garde. Sound is in the capable hands of some of Amsterdam's most popular DJs. If you feel like dancing in a gracious old canal house, head for **Odeon** (⊠ Singel 460, ☎ 020/624–9711), where jazz and rock play in various rooms, many of which retain their spectacular painted and stucco ceilings.

Film

Mainstream cinemas are concentrated near the Leidseplein; the largest is the seven-screen **City 1–7** (⊠ Kleine Garmanplantsoen 13–25, ☎ 020/623–4579). The four-screen **Alfa 1–4** (⊠ Kleine Gartmanplantsoen 4A, ☎ 020/627–8806) shows art films and movies not on the big-time commercial circuit. Worth visiting, if only for the pleasure of sitting in its magnificent Art Deco auditorium, is the **Tuschinski** (⊠ Reguliersbreestraat 26, ☎ 020/626–2633).

Gay Bars

Tankards and brass pots hang from the ceiling in the **Amstel Taveerne** (⊠ Amstel 54, ☎ 020/623–4254), and the friendly crowd of Amsterdammers around the bar burst into song whenever the sound system plays an old favorite. **Le Montmarte** (⊠ Halvemannsteeg 17, ☎ 020/620–7622) attracts a hip crowd of younger gay men, who crowd in for a drink before heading out clubbing. **Downtown** (⊠ Reguliersdwarsstraat 31, ☎ 020/622–9958) is a pleasant daytime coffee bar with a sunny terrace. Amsterdam's best women-only bar, **Saarein** (⊠ Elandsstraat 119, ☎ 020/623–4901) has a cozy Brown-Café atmosphere. **April's Exit** (⊠ Reguliersdwarsstraat 42, ☎ 020/625–8788) attracts a smart young crowd of gay men.

Jazz Clubs

At **Bimhuis** (⊠ Oude Schans 73–77, ☎ 020/623–3373), the best-known jazz place in town, you'll find top musicians, including avant-gardists, performing on Friday and Saturday nights, and weeknight jam sessions.

In the smoky, jam-packed atmosphere of **Alto** (⊠ Korte Leidsedwarsstraat 115, ☎ 020/626–3249), you can hear the pick of local bands. **Bamboo Bar** (⊠ Lange Leidsedwarsstraat 64, ☎ 020/624–3993) has a long bar and cool Latin sounds. **Bourbon Street Jazz & Blues Club** (⊠ Leidsekruisstraat 6–8, ☎ 020/623–3440) presents mainstream blues and jazz to a largely tourist clientele. **Joseph Lam** (⊠ Van Diemenstraat 242, ☎ 020/622–8086) specializes in Dixieland and is open only on Saturday.

Multicultural Performances

Akhnaton (⊠ Nieuwezijdskolk 25, ☎ 020/624–3396) is a multicultural stage and dance club renowned for its world music. African nights are especially good, but there's lots of salsa and jazz, too, and even hip-hop. **Paradiso** (⊠ Weteringschans 6, ☎ 020/623–7348), a former church, reverberates nightly to unusual sounds—anything from the latest rock band to a serious contemporary composer. Flexible staging arrangements make this a favorite venue for performance artists and multimedia events. **De Melkweg** (The Milky Way; ⊠ Lijnbaansgracht 234A, ☎ 020/624–1777 or 020/624–8492) is internationally known as a multicultural center for music, theater, film, and dance, with live music performances at least four nights a week and an innovative programming policy that tends increasingly toward multimedia events.

Music

There are two concert halls, large and small, under one roof at the **Concertgebouw** (⊠ Concertgebouwplein 2–6, ☎ 020/671–8345). In the larger one, Amsterdam's critically acclaimed **Koninklijk Concertgebouworkest** (Royal Concert Orchestra) is often joined by internationally known performers. The smaller hall is a venue for chamber music and up-and-coming musicians. There are free lunchtime concerts in the Concertgebouw on Wednesday. You need to start queuing at about 12:30. The **IJsbreker** (⊠ Weesperzijde 23, ☎ 020/668–1805) is at the cutting edge of contemporary music and often hosts festivals of international repute.

Nightclub and Casino

One of the best additions to the nightlife scene of Amsterdam in recent years is the **Lido Dinner Show** (⊠ Leidsestraat 105, ☎ 020/626–2106), which offers cabaret and light entertainment while you dine. The **Holland Casino Amsterdam** (⊠ Max Euweplein 62, ☎ 020/620–1006), which is part of the Lido complex near Leidseplein, is one of the largest in Europe (more than 90,000 square feet) and offers everything from your choice of French or American roulette to computerized bingo, as well as the obligatory slot machines to eat up your supply of loose guilders.

Opera and Ballet

The grand and elegant music theater, **Muziektheater** (⊠ Waterlooplein 22, ☎ 020/551 8911), is Amsterdam's equivalent of New York's Lincoln Center. It seats 1,600 people and hosts international opera, ballet, and orchestra performances throughout the year. The Muziektheater is home to **De Nederlandse Opera** (The Netherlands National Opera) and **Het Nationale Ballet** (The Netherlands National Ballet). Both offer largely classical repertoires, but the dance company has, in recent years, gained a large measure of fame throughout Europe for its performances of 20th-century ballets, and the opera company is known for its imaginative stagings.

Puppets and Marionettes

The young and the young at heart will enjoy puppet and marionette shows at **Amsterdam Marionettetheater** (⊠ Nieuwe Jonkerstraat 8, ☎ 020/620–8027).

Theater and Cabaret

Amsterdam's municipal theater, the **Stadsschouwburg** (⊠ Leidseplein 26, ☎ 020/624–2311), mainly stages theater in Dutch but sometimes hosts smaller visiting opera companies and is beginning to turn its eye to the profitable possibilities of multicultural programming. For lavish, large-scale productions, the place to go is **Koninklijk Theater Carre** (⊠ Amstel 115–125, ☎ 020/622–5225), built in the 19th century as permanent home to a circus. **Kleine Komedie** (⊠ Amstel 56–58, ☎ 020/624–0534) has for many years been the most vibrant venue for cabaret and comedy (mainly in Dutch). Amsterdam's Off-Broadway–type theaters are centered in an alley leading off the Dam and include **Frascati** (⊠ Nes 63, ☎ 020/623–5723 or 020/623–5724) and **Brakke Grond** (⊠ Nes 45, central box office ☎ 020/626–6866). **Boom Chicago** (⊠ Korte Leidsedwarsstraat 12, ☎ 020/422–1776) belongs to a bunch of zany ex-pat Americans who opened their own restaurant-theater to present improvised comedy inspired by life in Amsterdam. Dinner and seating begin at 7, showtime at 8:15.

Outdoor Activities and Sports

Beaches

After their long, dreary winter, Amsterdammers count the days until they can hit the beaches at **Zandvoort,** a beach community directly west of the city, beyond Haarlem, where clean beachfront stretches for miles and many of the dunes are open for walking. The train station is close by, and there are lifeguards on duty. Separate areas of the beach are reserved for nudists, though topless bathing is common practice everywhere in the Netherlands.

Biking

The most convenient places to rent a bicycle are **Centraal Station** (⊠ Stationsplein 12, 1012 AB, ☎ 020/624–8391) and **McBike** (⊠ Marnixstraat 220, 1016 TL, ☎ 020/626–6964). Expect to pay from Fl 10 per day, plus a deposit of Fl 50 to Fl 200 per bicycle. You'll need a passport or other identification.

Golf

The new and luxurious **BurgGolf** is outside Amsterdam in Noord Holland province. It is a 27-hole course, comprising a 9-hole course and a more difficult 18-hole course. ⊠ *Golden Tulip Hotel Purmerend, Westerweg 60, 1445 AD Purmerend,* ☎ *0299/481666. Greens fees: Fl 75 weekdays, Fl 95 weekends.*

Health Clubs

Several hotels in Amsterdam have fitness facilities for guests, usually including exercise machines, weights, sauna, and whirlpool. The **Holiday Inn Crowne Plaza** (⊠ N.Z. Voorburgwal 5, 1012 RC, ☎ 020/620–0500) has a large indoor swimming pool. Two of the more comprehensive hotel-based fitness facilities are **Splash Renaissance** (⊠ Kattengat 1, ☎ 020/621–2223) and **Barbizon Fit Palace** (⊠ Prins Hendrikkade 59–72, ☎ 020/556–4899), both of which offer personal training, aerobics, weight training, massage, solarium, Turkish bath, sauna, and whirlpool. **Sporting Club Leidseplein** (⊠ 18 Korte Leidsedwarsstraat, ☎ 020/620–6631) offers fitness facilities, sauna, and super-fast tanners. Day rates at all of the above are Fl 25, with extra charges for special services.

Jogging

Sunday morning is about the only time when Amsterdam's city center gets enough of a break from foot, bike, and car traffic to allow for a comfortable jog. **Vondelpark** (Vondel Park), near the art museums, and

Oosterpark (Eastern Park), behind the Tropenmuseum, are the only parks within the city proper. Beyond the city near the suburb of Amstelveen, **Amsterdamse Bos** (Amsterdam Woods) is a large, spacious place to run.

Squash

The **Sporting Club Leidseplein** (⊠ 18 Korte Leidsedwarsstraat, ☎ 020/ 620–6631) is a squash, fitness, and aerobics club. There are five courts; the use of a sauna is included, and you can rent equipment and take lessons. Day cards for all facilities are Fl 25 weekdays until 4 PM; services are priced separately on evenings and weekends.

Shopping

Shopping Districts and Streets

The **Dam** square is home to two of Amsterdam's main department stores. Several popular shopping streets radiate from the square, offering something for nearly all tastes. **Nieuwendijk** is a busy pedestrian mall, good for bargain hunters. **Rokin** is the place to go for high-price fashion and jewelry, Old Masters, and expensive antiques. **Kalverstraat** is the city's main pedestrians-only shopping street and where Amsterdam does its day-to-day shopping. **Leidsestraat** offers a range and variety of shopping similar to Kalverstraat's, but with more of an eye to the tourist trade. **Max Euweplein** is a small plaza-style shopping mall surrounding a summer café and adjacent to the Amsterdam Casino. The posh and prestigious **P.C. Hooftstraat,** generally known as the P.C. (pronounced "pay-say"), is home to chic designer boutiques; this is where diplomats and politicians buy their glad rags. **Van Baerlestraat,** leading to the Concertgebouw, is lined with smart clothing shops—but those that are not quite smart enough to have made it to the adjoining P.C. Hooftstraat. **Utrechtsestraat** offers a variety of opportunities for the trendier shopper.

Department Stores

De Bijenkorf (⊠ Dam 1, ☎ 020/621–8080) is the city's best-known department store and the stomping ground of its monied middle classes. **Peek & Cloppenburg** (⊠ Dam 20, ☎ 020/622–8837) specializes in durable, middle-of-the-road clothing. The gracious and conservative **Maison de Bonneterie en Pander** (⊠ Rokin 140–142, ☎ 020/626– 2162), all crystal chandeliers and silently gliding shop assistants, stocks an elegant range of clothing and household items. The Amsterdam branch of England's **Marks & Spencer** (⊠ Kalverstraat 66-72, ☎ 020/620– 0006) is a good bet for inexpensive clothing and expensive food. **C&A** (⊠ Damrak 79, ☎ 020/626–3132) offers discount clothing. **Vroom & Dreesmann** (⊠ Kalverstraat 203, ☎ 020/622–0171) is Amsterdam's third smartest department store after De Bijenkorf and Maison de Bonneterie and sells good quality clothing. **Metz & Company** (⊠ Keizersgracht 455, ☎ 020/624–8810) stocks up on textiles and household goods from **Liberty of London** and adds a range of breathtakingly expensive designer articles from all over the world.

Street Markets

Few markets compare with Amsterdam's **Waterlooplein** flea market. It is a descendant of the haphazard pushcart trade that gave this part of the city its distinct and lively character in the early part of the century. You're unlikely to find anything of value here, but it's a good spot to look for the secondhand clothing young Amsterdammers favor, and it is a gadget lover's paradise. The flea market is open Monday through Saturday 9:30 to 5. The **Bloemenmarkt** (along the Singel canal, between Koningsplein and Muntplein) is another of Amsterdam's must-see markets, where flowers and plants are sold from permanently moored barges. The market is open Monday through Saturday 9:30 to 5 (some flower stalls stay open until 6, and some are open Sunday). **Sunday**

art markets are held in good weather from April to October on Thorbeckeplein, and from April through November at Spui. The **Postzegelmarkt** stamp market is held twice a week (Wednesday and Saturday 1–4) on Nieuwezijds Voorburgwal.

Specialty Stores

ANTIQUES

Antiques always have been a staple item of shopping in Amsterdam, and the array of goods available at any time is broad. There are more than 150 antiques shops scattered throughout the central canal area. The greatest concentration of those offering fine antiques and specialty items is in the **Spiegel Quarter. Nieuwe Spiegelstraat** and its continuation, **Spiegelgracht,** constitute the main thoroughfare of the quarter, with shops on both sides of the street and canal for five blocks, from the Golden Bend of the Herengracht nearly to the Rijksmuseum, including several dealers under one roof in the **Amsterdams Antiques Gallery** (⊠ Nieuwe Spiegelstraat 34, ☎ 020/625–3371). **Rokin,** between Dam and Muntplein, is the location of the Amsterdam branch of **Sotheby's** (⊠ Rokin 102, ☎ 020/550–2200) and of a number of the sorts of art and antiques stores where museum curators do their shopping, including **Waterman** (⊠ Rokin 116, ☎ 020/623–2958). Shops on **Rozengracht** and **Prinsengracht,** near the Westerkerk, offer country Dutch furniture and household items; you'll also find antiques and curio shops along the side streets in that part of the city. For a broad range of vintage and antique furniture, curios, jewelry, clothing, and household items, try **Antique Market de Looier** (⊠ Elandsgracht 109, ☎ 020/624–9038), open Saturday through Wednesday 11–5 and Thursday 11–5, which houses more than 50 dealers. The indoor flea market, **De Rommelmarkt** (⊠ Looiersgracht 38, ☎ 020/627–4762), is a warren of stalls selling everything from Art Deco lamps to defunct electrical equipment; it's open Saturday through Thursday 11–5.

There are old maps and prints (including botanicals) in antiques shops all over Amsterdam, but for a broad selection of high quality, visit **A. van der Meer** (⊠ P.C. Hooftstraat 112, ☎ 020/662–1936), a gallery that has specialized in 17th-, 18th-, and 19th-century works for more than 30 years. Daumier etchings, hunt prints, and cityscape engravings can be found here.

Tangram (⊠ Herenstraat 9, ☎ 020/624–4286) is a good source for the Art Deco and Jugendstil items that are so popular in the Netherlands. **De Haas** (⊠ Kerkstraat 155, ☎ 020/626–5952) specializes in smaller pieces from the beginning of the 20th century. **Galerie Frans Leidelmeyer** (⊠ Nieuwe Spiegelstraat 58, ☎ 020/625–4627) is a good source of top-quality Art Deco and Jugendstil artifacts.

ART

Many of the galleries that deal in modern and contemporary art are centered on the **Keizersgracht** and **Spiegel Quarter.** *What's On in Amsterdam,* published by the tourist office, is a good source of information on current exhibitions; another is the Dutch-language publication *Alert,* which has the most comprehensive listings available. Among the dealers specializing in 20th-century art in Keizersgracht are **D'Art 1970** (⊠ Keizersgracht 516, ☎ 020/622–1511), **Kunsthandel M.L. De Boer** (⊠ Keizersgracht 542, ☎ 020/623–4060), and **Galerie Espace** (⊠ Keizersgracht 548, ☎ 020/624–0802). In the Spiegel Quarter, **E. Den Bieman de Haas** (⊠ Nieuwe Spiegelstraat 44, ☎ 020/626–1012), **Marie-Louise Woltering** (⊠ Nieuwe Spiegelstraat 53, ☎ 020/622–2240), **C.M. Kooring Verwindt** (⊠ Spiegelgracht 14–16, ☎ 020/623–6538), **Galerie Asselijn** (⊠ Lange Leidsedwarsstraat 200, ☎ 020/624–9030), **Wetering Galerie,** (⊠ Lijnbaansgracht 288, ☎

020/623–6189), and **Galerie Guido de Spa** (⊠ 2e Weteringdwarsstraat 34, ☎ 020/622–1528).

Eurasia Antiques (⊠ Nieuwe Spiegelstraat 40, ☎ 020/626–1594) is a treasure trove of old paintings, engravings, and Asian art. **Couzijn Simon** (⊠ Prinsengracht 578, ☎ 020/624–7691) specializes in molting teddies and other vintage toys. **Galerie Animation Art** (⊠ Berenstraat 39, ☎ 020/627–7600) offers original Disney and other cartoon sketches.

BOOKS

Allert de Lange (⊠ Damrak 60–62, ☎ 020/624–6744) has a good selection of books on travel, history, and fiction. **W.H. Smith** (⊠ Kalverstraat 152, ☎ 020/638–3821) has four floors of English-language books, from children's stories to computer manuals. **Premsela** (⊠ Van Baerlestraat 78, ☎ 020/662–4266) specializes in art books and stocks many luscious, tempting tomes. True to its name, the **American Book Center** (⊠ Kalverstraat 185, ☎ 020/625–5537) is strongly oriented to American tastes and expectations. **The English Bookshop** (⊠ Lauriersgracht 71, ☎ 020/626–4230) is a cozy canal-side bookshop with a good range of new and secondhand English travel books and novels.

CERAMICS AND CRYSTAL

Focke & Meltzer (⊠ P.C. Hooftstraat 65–67, ☎ 020/664–2311; ⊠ Hotel Okura Shopping Arcade, ☎ 020/678–7111) is the primary source in Amsterdam of authenticated Delft and Makkumware, as well as fine crystal.

CIGARS AND SMOKING

One of the best places in the world to buy cigars and other smoking materials is **Hajenius** (⊠ Rokin 92, ☎ 020/623–7494), in business since 1826. **Davidoff** (⊠ Van Baerlestraat 84, ☎ 020/671–1042), while not as exclusive as the famous Hajenius, nevertheless stocks fine cigars and other smokers' requisites.

COFFEE, TEA, AND SPICES

Jacob Hooy & Co. (⊠ Kloveniersburgwal 12, ☎ 020/624–3041) has been selling herbs, spices, and medicinal potions from the same shop beside the Nieuwmarkt since 1743. Gold-lettered wooden drawers, barrels, and bins contain not just spices and herbs but also a daunting array of *dropjes* (hard candies and medicinal drops) and teas. **S. Levelt's Koffie- en Theehandel N.V.** (⊠ Prinsengracht 180, ☎ 020/624–0823) offers nearly 100 different kinds of tea and more than two dozen coffees.

DIAMONDS AND JEWELRY

The **Amsterdam Diamond Center** (⊠ Rokin 1–5, ☎ 020/624–5787), houses several diamond sellers. **Coster Diamonds** (⊠ Paulus Potterstraat 2–4, ☎ 020/676–2222) not only sells jewelry and loose diamonds but gives free demonstrations of diamond cutting. You can see a replica of the most famous diamond cut in the factory—the Koh-I-Noor, one of the prize gems of the British crown jewels. **Van Moppes Diamonds** (⊠ Albert Cuypstraat 2–6, ☎ 020/676–1242) has an extensive diamond showroom and offers a glimpse of the process of diamond cutting and polishing. **Bonebakker** (⊠ Rokin 88/90, ☎ 020/623–2294) is one of the city's oldest and finest jewelers and carries an exceptionally fine range of watches and silverware. The century-old **Schaap and Citroen** (⊠ Kalverstraat 1, ☎ 020/626–6691) has an affordable range of jewelry and watches. **Premsela & Hamburger** (⊠ Rokin 120, ☎ 020/624–9688; closed weekends) has sold fine antique silver and jewelry since 1823.

DUTY-FREE

If you don't have time to shop in Amsterdam, save your guilders for the airport, as **Amsterdam Airport Shopping Centre** (⊠ Amsterdam

Schiphol Airport, Holland, ☎ 020/601–2497) is bigger, better, and cheaper than almost any other airport duty-free shopping area in the world. The airport's departure hall looks more like a shopping mall than a transportation facility, and auxiliary shops for the most popular items (liquor, perfume, chocolates) are found in every wing of the terminal.

MEN'S CLOTHING

Meddens (⊠ Heiligeweg 11–17, ☎ 020/624–0461) stocks a good range of fairly conservative men's casual and formal wear. **The English Hatter** (⊠ Heiligeweg 40, ☎ 020/623–4781) has tweed jackets, deerstalkers, and many other trappings of the English country gentleman. **McGregor and Clan Shop** (⊠ P.C. Hooftstraat 113, ☎ 020/662–7425) has a distinctly Scottish air, with chunky knitwear and the odd flash of tartan. **Mulberry Company** (⊠ P.C. Hooftstraat 46, ☎ 020/673–8086) sells stylish fashions from England. **Society Shop** (⊠ Van Baerlestraat 20, ☎ 020/664–9281) stocks good basics for businessmen. For highly styled apparel and designer togs, head to **Dik** (⊠ P.C. Hooftstraat 35, ☎ 020/662–4328). **Oger** (⊠ P.C. Hooftstraat 81, ☎ 020/676–8695) puts suits on the backs of leading Dutch politicians and TV personalities. **Gaudi** (⊠ P.C. Hooftstraat 116, ☎ 020/679–9319) is a mecca for the trendy and label conscious.

SHOES AND HATS

Smit Bally (⊠ Leidsestraat 41, ☎ 020/624–8862) sells classically smart shoes for men. **Bally Shoes** (⊠ Leidsestraat 8–10, ☎ 020/622–2888) is a byword for good taste in women's shoes. **Dr. Adams** (⊠ P.C. Hooftstraat 90, ☎ 020/662–3835) sells chunkier, more adventurous styles of shoes for men and women. **Shoebaloo** (⊠ Koningsplein 7, ☎ 020/626–7993) is the place for 8-inch heels, mock leopardskin boots, and other outrageous footwear. The well-stocked **Hoeden M/V** (⊠ 422 Herengracht, ☎ 020/626–3038), in a canal house, carries Borsalino hats for men and women as well as Dutch and international designer hats.

WOMEN'S CLOTHING

In the **Jordaan** neighborhood, generation after generation of experimental designers have set up shop to show their imaginative creations. Antique- and used-clothing shops are also in this part of town. Designer shops stand shoulder to shoulder in the **P.C. Hooftstraat** and include **Benetton** (⊠ P.C. Hooftstraat 72, ☎ 020/679–5706), **Max Mara** (⊠ P.C. Hooftstraat 110, ☎ 020/671–7742), **Leeser** (⊠ P.C. Hooftstraat 117, ☎ 020/679–5020), and **Edgar Vos** (⊠ P.C. Hooftstraat 134, ☎ 020/662–6336). **Claudia Sträter** (⊠ Beethovenstraat 9, ☎ 020/673–6605; ⊠ Kalverstraat 179–181, ☎ 020/622–0559) is part of a Dutch minichain that sells simply styled, well-made clothes for all occasions. **Boetiek Pauw** (⊠ van Baerlestrasse 66 and 72, ☎ 020/662–6253), which also operates men's and children's shops, is part of a chain that stands out for the quality of both design and craftsmanship of its clothing. The international fashion house **Esprit** (⊠ Spui 1c, ☎ 020/626–3624) has a large branch in central Amsterdam.

Spectator Sports

Rowing

Amsterdamse Bos (Amsterdam Woods), a large park south of the city, has monthly rowing events organized by Stedelijk Beheer Sport en Recreatie (☎ 020/643–1414) and canoeing events four times a year. The **Dutch Marine Academy** stages a rowing event (☎ 020/624–7699) on the city's canals in September.

Soccer

Soccer is a near obsession with the Dutch, and if you want to impress an Amsterdam host, you would best be advised to know the current standing of the local team, Ajax (pronounced *eye*-axe), relative to that of its archrivals, Rotterdam's Feyenoord (pronounced *fie*-nord) and PSV (Philips Sports Vereninging). The Dutch soccer season runs from August to June, with a short break in midwinter; matches are played at the **Amsterdam Arena** (⊠ Haaksbergweg 59, ☎ 020/691–2906).

Side Trips from Amsterdam

Numbers in the margin correspond to points of interest on the Excursions from Amsterdam map.

The Bulb Fields and Flower Auction

Though the bulb fields are in full bloom in April and May, flowers are a year-round business in the Netherlands: Visitors in the dead of winter can still gain a sense of the magnitude and magnificence of Dutch tulips and countless other varieties of flowers.

In the spring, the bulb fields to the southwest of Amsterdam blaze with color. Millions of tulips and other bulbs add technicolor streaks to the flat Dutch countryside. Great squares and oblongs of red, yellow, and white look like giant Mondrian paintings laid out on the ground. It is a spectacular sight, whether you travel through the fields by bike or bus, or pass by in the train on your way to Leiden.

The **Bollenstreek Route** (Bulb District Route) is a special itinerary through the heart of the flower-growing region that was designed by the Dutch auto club, ANWB. The route is marked with small blue and white signs that read "Bollenstreek." It begins in Oegstgeest, near Leiden, and circles through Rijnsburg (site of one of Holland's three major flower auction houses), where there is a colorful Flower Parade on the first Saturday in August. On the way you pass through **Lisse**, which has a Flower Parade on the last Saturday in April. Lisse is also the site of the famous Keukenhof Gardens.

35 **Keukenhof** is a 70-acre park and greenhouse complex where nearly 7 million flowers bloom every spring. In the last weeks of April you can catch tulips, daffodils, hyacinths, and narcissi all flowering simultaneously. In addition there are bright floral mosaics and some 50,000 square feet of more exotic blooms under glass. Dutch botanists use Keukenhof as a showcase for their latest hybrids, so black tulips and gaudy frilled varieties also make an appearance. ⊠ *West of the village of Lisse; follow main road out of town;* ☎ *0252/465–535.* 🎟 *Fl 16.* ⊙ *Late Mar.–late May, daily 8–8.*

After braving the crowds at Keukenhof, you can get lost in the dunes outside **Noordwijk.** The Lisse Flower Parade ends up here on the boulevard on Saturday evening and continues from here on Sunday. North of the village is a vast, sandy nature reserve, almost as big as the bulb district itself. Small canals and pools of water are dotted about in between the dunes, providing a haven for birdlife. In addition to Noordwijk, the Bulb Route passes through the beach community of **Katwijk** and through **Sassenheim**, where there is an imposing 13th-century ruined castle.

36 At any time during the year, it is an easy trip from Amsterdam to the small village of **Aalsmeer.** This is the site of the **Bloemenveiling Aalsmeer** (Aalsmeer Flower Auction) that is held five days a week from the predawn hours until midmorning. It is the largest flower auction in the world, with three auction halls operating continuously in a building

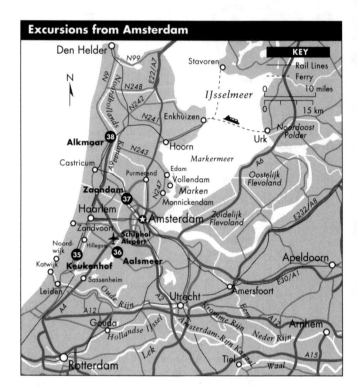

Excursions from Amsterdam

the size of several football fields. You walk on a catwalk above the rolling four-tier carts that wait to move on tracks past the auctioneers. The buying system is what is called a Dutch auction—the price goes down, not up, on a large "clock" on the wall. The buyers sit lecture-style with buzzers on their desks; the first to register a bid gets the bunch. ⊠ *Legmeerdijk 313,* ☎ *0297/393–939.* 🎫 *Fl 4.* ⊙ *Weekdays 7:30–11.*

Folkloric Holland

③⑦ Over the Noordzee Kanaal from Amsterdam and just beyond the city of **Zaandam** is the restored village of **Zaanse Schans,** gateway to the windmill-studded countryside of Noord Holland province. Many of the buildings here have been restored as private homes, but a small cluster along the river edge includes a clock museum, the shops of a clog maker and a cheese maker, a bakery museum, and a restaurant. ⊠ *Kraaienest 2,* ☎ *075/616–8218.* 🎫 *Free.* ⊙ *Daily 8:30–6.*

③⑧ An open-air cheese market is held in **Alkmaar** (☎ *072/114–284;* Apr.–Sept., Fri. mornings). To see how cheese is made, visit one of more than a dozen *kaasboerderij* (cheese farms) near Katwonde, including **Kaasboerderij De Irenehoeve** (⊠ Hogedijk 1, ☎ 0299/652–291), **Kaasboerderij De Wilg** (⊠ Hogedijk 8, ☎ 0299/655–151), and **Kaasboerderij Simonehoeve** (⊠ Wagenweg 2, ☎ 0299/365–828).

Amsterdam A to Z

Arriving and Departing

BY CAR

Major European highways leading into the city from the borders are E19 from western Belgium; E25 from eastern Belgium; and E22, E30, and E35 from Germany. Follow the signs for *Centrum* to reach center city. Traffic is heavy but not stationary at rush hour.

Amsterdam Schiphol Airport (☎ 06/350–34050) is 25 kilometers (15 miles) southeast of the city and directly linked to it by rail.

KLM Road Transport (☎ 020/649–5651 or 020/649–1393) operates a shuttle bus service between Amsterdam Schiphol Airport and major city hotels. The trip takes about half an hour and costs Fl 17.50 one-way.

The **Schiphol Rail Line** (☎ 06/9292) operates between the airport and the city 24 hours a day, with service to the central railway station or to stations in the south part of the city. The trip takes about 15 minutes and costs Fl 5.75.

There is a **taxi** stand directly in front of the arrival hall at Amsterdam Schiphol Airport. All taxis are metered, and the fare is approximately Fl 55 to various points within central Amsterdam. Service is included, but small additional tips are not unwelcome.

The city has several substations, but all major Dutch national, as well as European international, trains arrive at and depart from **Centraal Station** (☎ 06/9292 for national service information, ☎ 020/620–2266 for international). The station also houses the travel information office of **NS/Nederlandse Spoorwagen** (Netherlands Railways).

Getting Around

Amsterdam is a small city, and most major sites are within its central district. The canal-laced core is surrounded by concentric rings of 15th- to 17th-century canals, built following the pattern of earlier city walls and drainage ditches. Six roads link the city center with the more modern outer neighborhoods. Once you understand the fanlike pattern of Amsterdam's geography, you will have an easier time getting around. All trams and most buses begin and end their journeys at Centraal Station, sightseeing and shopping are focused at Dam square, and the arts and nightlife are centered in the areas of Leidseplein, Rembrandtsplein, and Waterlooplein.

Bicycling is the most convenient way to see Amsterdam. There are bike lanes on all major streets, bike racks in key locations, and special bike parking indentations in the pavement. For a list of rental shops, *see* Outdoor Activities and Sports, *above.*

Taxi stands are at the major squares and in front of the large hotels. Or you can call **Taxicentrale** (☎ 020/677–7777), the central taxi dispatching office. Fares are Fl 5.60, plus Fl 2.80 per kilometer. A 5-kilometer (3-mile) ride will cost about Fl 20.

The transit map published by **GVB** (main information office: ✉ Prins Hendrikkade 108–114, ☎ 020/551–4911) is very useful. It's available at the GVB ticket office across from the central railway station, or at the VVV tourist information offices next door. It is also reprinted as the center spread in *What's On in Amsterdam,* the weekly guide to activities and shopping published by the tourist office. The map shows the locations of all major museums, monuments, theaters, and markets, and it tells which trams to take to reach each of them.

Single-ride tickets valid for one hour can be purchased from the tram and bus drivers for Fl 3, but it is far more practical to buy a *strippenkaart* (strip ticket) that includes from 2 to 45 "strips," or ticket units. The best buy for most visitors is the 15-strip ticket for Fl 11. By tradition,

Dutch trams and buses work on the honor system: Upon boarding, punch your ticket at one of the machines situated in the rear or center section of the tram or bus. The city is divided into zones, which are indicated on the transit map, and it is important to punch the correct number of zones on your ticket (one for the basic tariff and one for each additional zone traveled). Occasional ticket inspections can be expected: A fine of Fl 60 is the price for "forgetting" to stamp your ticket.

BY WATER TAXI

A **Water Taxi** (☎ 020/622–2181) provides a novel, if pricey, means of getting about. Water taxis can be hailed anytime you see one cruising the canals of the city, or called by telephone. The boats are miniature versions of the large sightseeing canal boats, and each carries up to eight passengers. The cost is Fl 60 for the first 30 minutes, plus a Fl 30 pick-up charge. There is a flat rate of Fl 150 (including pick-up) for one hour, then Fl 30 per extra 15-minute period. The rate is per ride, regardless of the number of passengers.

Contacts and Resources

B&B RESERVATION AGENCIES

Should you arrive without a room, head for one of two **VVV Logiesservice** (VVV Accommodation Service) offices: Stationsplein 10, open daily 9–5, or Leidsestraat 106, open daily 9–7. This is a same-day hotel booking service that, for a modest charge of Fl 5, can help you find a room.

CAR RENTALS

Avis (✉ Nassaukade 380, ☎ 020/683–6061). **Hertz** (✉ Overtoom 333, ☎ 020/612–2441). **Budget** (✉ Overtoom 121, ☎ 020/612–6066).

CHANGING MONEY

GWK/Gdrenswisselkantoren (✉ Centraal Station, ☎ 020/627–2731) is a nationwide financial organization specializing in foreign currencies, where travelers can exchange cash and traveler's checks, receive cash against major credit cards, and receive Western Union money transfers. Many of the same services are available at banks, and cash can be exchanged at any post office.

CONSULATES

U.S. Consulate (✉ Museumplein 19, Amsterdam, ☎ 020/664–5661). **British Consulate** (✉ Koningslaan 44, Amsterdam, ☎ 020/676–4343).

DOCTORS AND DENTISTS

Referrals (☎ 06/350–32042), 24-hour service for all medical assistance. **Dentist Surgery AOC** (✉ W.G. Plein 167, ☎ 020/616–1234).

EMERGENCIES

National Emergency Alarm Number (☎ 06/112). **Police, ambulance, and fire** (☎ 555–5555). **Police only** (☎ 622–2222). **City police stations** (✉ Elandsgracht 117; Lijnbaansgracht 219; Warmoesstraat 44–46; and entrance to IJtunnel).

GAYS AND LESBIANS

Major newsstands carry specialized publications that include ads and listings for entertainment possibilities oriented to the interests of gays and lesbians. The gay scene in Amsterdam is concentrated mostly on Warmoesstraat, Reguliersdwarsstraat, Amstelstraat and along the Amstel, and Kerkstraat near Leidseplein. The **Gay & Lesbian Switchboard** (☎ 020/623–6565) can provide information from 10 AM to 10 PM, as can the **COC** action group (✉ Rozenstraat 14, ☎ 020/626–3087), which also operates as a coffee shop, youth café, and dance club.

Afternoon **bus tours** of the city operate daily. Itineraries vary, and prices range from Fl 25 to Fl 35. A three-hour city tour that includes a drive through the suburbs is offered by **Key Tours** (⊠ Dam 19, ☎ 020/624–5051). A 3½-hour tour, focusing on the central city and including a canal-boat cruise, is offered by **Lindbergh Excursions** (⊠ Damrak 26, ☎ 020/622–2766). However, it must be said that this city of narrow alleys and canals is not best appreciated from the window of a coach. Also, a number of visitors feel unhappy that part of some tours involves a visit to a diamond factory, where they feel pressured into listening to a sales pitch.

The quickest, easiest way to get your bearings in Amsterdam is to take a **canal-boat cruise.** Trips last from one to 1½ hours and cover the harbor as well as the main canal district; a taped commentary is available in four languages. Excursion boats leave from piers in various locations in the city every 15 minutes from March to October, and every 30 minutes in winter. Most launches are moored in the inner harbor in front of Centraal Station. Fares are about Fl 12–Fl 15. Operators of canal cruises include **Rederij D'Amstel** (⊠ Nicolaas Witsenkade, opposite Heineken Brewery, ☎ 020/626–5636), **Holland International** (⊠ Prins Hendrikkade, opposite Centraal Station, ☎ 020/622–7788), **Rederij P. Kooy B.V.** (⊠ Rokin, near Spui, ☎ 020/623–3810 or 020/623–4186), **Rederij Lovers B.V.** (⊠ Prins Hendrikkade 26, opposite Centraal Station, ☎ 020/622–2181), **Meyers Rondvaarten** (⊠ Damrak, quays 4–5, ☎ 020/623–4208), **Rederij Noord/Zuid** (⊠ Stadhouderskade 25, opposite Parkhotel, ☎ 020/679–1370), and **Rederij Plas C.V.** (⊠ Damrak, quays 1–3, ☎ 020/624–5406 or 020/622–6096).

The **VVV Amsterdam Tourist Office** (⊠ Stationsplein 10, ☎ 06/340–34066, FAX 020/625–2869) maintains lists of **personal guides** and can advise you on making arrangements. The costs are Fl 208 for a half day and Fl 333 for a full day. The tourist office also sells brochures outlining easy-to-follow **self-guided theme tours** through the central part of the city. Among them are "A Journey of Discovery Through Maritime Amsterdam," "A Walk Through the Jordaan," "Jewish Amsterdam," and "Rembrandt and Amsterdam."

Several **boat trips** to museums are available: **Canalbus** (⊠ Nieuwe Weteringschans 24, ☎ 020/623–9886), which makes six stops along two different routes between Centraal Station and the Rijksmuseum, costs Fl 12.50. Following a longer route is **Museumboot Rederij Lovers** (⊠ Stationsplein 8, ☎ 020/622–2181), which makes seven stops near 20 different museums. The cost is Fl 22 for a day ticket that entitles you to a 50% discount on admission to the museums.

From April through October, guided three-hour **bike trips** through the central area of the city are available through **Yellow Bike** (⊠ Nieuwezijds Kolk 29, ☎ 020/620–6940).

Walking tours focusing on art and architecture are organized by **Artifex** (⊠ Herengracht 342, 1016 CG, ☎ 020/620–8112), **Stichting Arttra** (⊠ Staalstraat 28, 1011 JM, ☎ 020/625–9303), and **Archivisie** (⊠ Postbus 14603, 1001 LC, ☎ 020/625–8908). For walking tours of the Jewish Quarter, contact **Joods Historisch Museum** (⊠ Jonas Daniel Meyerplein 2–4, Postbus 16737, 1001 RE, ☎ 020/626–9945, FAX 020/624–1721), and for a guided walk through the red-light district, contact **Stichting FIS** (⊠ Postbus 1566, 1001 ND, ☎ 020/624–5720).

Academisch Medisch Centrum (⊠ Meibergdreef 9, ☎ 020/566–9111). **Boven 't IJ Ziekenhuis** (⊠ Statenjachtstraat 1, ☎ 020/634–6346). **VU**

Ziekenhuis (⊠ de Boelelaan 1117, ☎ 020/548–9111). **Onze Lieve Vrouwe Gasthuis** (⊠ le Oosterparkstraat 197, ☎ 020/599–9111). **Slotervaartziekenhuis** (⊠ Louwesweg 6, ☎ 020/512–9333).

American Express International (⊠ Damrak 66, ☎ 020/520–7777). **Thomas Cook** (⊠ Damrak 1, ☎ 020/620–3236). **Holland International Travel Group** (⊠ Dam 6, ☎ 020/622–2550). **Key Tours** (⊠ Dam 19, ☎ 020/623–5051). **Lindbergh Excursions** (⊠ Damrak 26, ☎ 020/622–2766). For student travel, **NBBS** (⊠ Rokin 38, ☎ 020/624–0989).

The **VVV Amsterdam Tourist Office,** in front of Amsterdam's neo-Renaissance Centraal Station (⊠ Stationsplein 10, ☎ 06/340–34066, FAX 020/625–2869), is open daily 9–5. A second information office at Leidsestraat 106 operates daily 9–7 in summer.

METROPOLITAN HOLLAND AND THE HAGUE

Like filings around the end of a magnet, the population of the Netherlands clusters in the arc of Amsterdam's attraction. More than 25% of the country's 15 million residents live in and around 10 small- to medium-size cities that are within 80 kilometers (50 miles) of the capital. And that doesn't count the tulip growers, vegetable farmers, dairy farmers, and villagers who fill in what little open land remains in this area. The Dutch refer to the circle formed by the four cities of Amsterdam, Den Haag (The Hague in English), Rotterdam, and Utrecht as the Randstad (Ridge City) because the cities lie along the same ridge. The megalopolis also is called "The West" by young Randstad wanna-bes waiting for their opportunity to hit the big time in the same way young Americans and Britons dream of making it in New York, Los Angeles, or London. In addition to harboring the capital of international justice (The Hague) and the world's largest port (Rotterdam), Metropolitan Holland is the political and historic heart of the Dutch nation. Fodor's takes you around the circle, starting and ending at Amsterdam.

Pleasures and Pastimes

Metropolitan Holland has much to offer, from art treasures in the museums to the modern-day treasures at the porcelain factories of Delft. You'll also find architectural wonders aplenty, and many restaurants with exotic cuisines.

DELFT BLUE AND WHITE

Centuries ago, when traders brought the first porcelain back from China, Europeans eyed it with envy and amazement—and immediately set about trying to imitate it. The good burghers of Delft were among the first to crack the secret. True to the original inspiration, Delftware appeared first in blue and white, though the designs were westernized. Today, Delft porcelain is acknowledged as among the finest in the world. No visit to Delft is complete without stopping off at the Royal Porcelain Factory to see plates and tulip vases being painted by hand and perhaps picking up a souvenir or two. Whether you opt for ornate urns or tiny pairs of porcelain clogs, always make sure that you are getting the real thing—genuine Delftware has a distinctive mark underneath.

DINING

Like Amsterdam, the cities of the Randstad offer a tantalizing range of establishments and cuisines, from pancakes at canalside cafés in Delft to hearty meals beside the old harbor in Rotterdam to the haute cuisine of the restaurant in The Hague, where Mata Hari, the infamous World War I spy, once dined. Nicknamed "the Widow of Indonesia" for all the former colonials who live here, The Hague is a good place to try a *rijstaffel,* a spicy Indonesian feast that includes rice and up to 30 different small dishes. The coast, from nearby Scheveningen to IJmuiden, is a center of activity when the herring season opens on the last Saturday in May. Out comes the bunting, and fishermen race to see who can bring home the first catch. If you have the stomach for it, you can enjoy the national summer dish: *haring* (herring), eaten raw with onions. Simply hold the fillet by its tail and slip it whole down your throat, followed by a quick glass of *jenever* (Dutch gin).

One of Holland's national dishes, *hutspot,* comes from Leiden. Tradition has it that this stew-and-mash dish was left simmering on the fire by a fleeing Spanish army when William of Orange relieved the siege of Leiden in 1574, and (together with the *haring* that William brought with him) was much welcomed by the starving citizens.

LODGING

If your taste is for cozy, canal-house accommodations, head for Delft and Leiden. At the other end of the scale, The Hague offers some of the grandest, old-style hotels in the country, dripping with crystal chandeliers and redolent with a history of famous guests. Rotterdam is very much a commercial harbor city, with hotels aimed primarily at the business trade, though the Hotel New York, a converted shipping office from the first part of this century, is an atmospheric exception.

MODERN ANGLES ON ROTTERDAM

Of all Dutch cities, Rotterdam, with its important port, suffered particularly heavy bombing during World War II. The citizens responded by rebuilding their city with such verve and daring that it has become a display case of exciting modern architecture, much of which can be appreciated during a short walk around the city center. Look out especially for the Blaakse Bos, a group of curiously angled, cube-shaped apartments on stalks. Rotterdam is also home to the national Institute of Architecture, which houses intriguing exhibitions. The local tourist office can send you off on a specially planned "modern architecture walk."

PAINTERS' PROSPECTS

Even in the largest cities there are corners where time seems to be holding its breath. Visit some of the larger museums, or browse through a book of Dutch art before you come, and have a look at paintings of church interiors by Saenredam and De Witte, and views of Delft (especially the famous ones by Vermeer), of Utrecht, or of Haarlem's St. Bavokerk. Store them away in your mind's eye and, sure enough, as you look across a market square from a certain angle, turn a corner of a canal, or wander through a church, the real world will appear to dissolve and, just for a moment, you will have the sensation of stepping into a 17th-century painting.

Exploring Metropolitan Holland

An arc south of Amsterdam, running near the coast, takes you through the heart of Metropolitan Holland, starting with Haarlem and ending at Rotterdam. Utrecht, the remaining city in the Randstad conurbation, sits inland from this arc. The land stretches flat for as far as the eye can see, though the coast west of Haarlem and Leiden undulates with long expanses of dunes, many of which are nature reserves. In spring, the farmland between these two towns is bright with tulips and other blooms.

Great Itineraries

Each of the cities in the region could detain you for at least a day. If you don't have a week at your disposal, you will have to be disciplined and selective and begin drawing up plans for a return trip.

Numbers in the text correspond to numbers in the margin and on the Metropolitan Holland map.

IF YOU HAVE 3 DAYS
Head straight for ⌖ **The Hague** ㊶ and take day trips from there. Your first day is spent exploring the main museums and viewing the palaces in the center of town. On day two, visit the seaside resort of **Scheveningen** ㊼ and the historic town of **Delft** ㊷, both within easy reach (in fact, there's a tram connecting the two). Save most of your time for exploring Delft's romantic canals and visiting the porcelain factory before heading back to The Hague. Next day, travel to **Rotterdam** ㊸, where the magnificent art collection at the Boymans-van Beuningen Museum is a must and the old harbor area around Delfshaven is a nice spot for a quiet lunch.

IF YOU HAVE 5 DAYS
On your way out of Amsterdam stop off at Haarlem, if only for a look at the St. Bavo's Church and the intriguing Teylers museum, then make tracks for ⌖ **Leiden** ㊵, where old windmills, grand houses, and a cheery university-town atmosphere await you. Over the next two days enjoy a leisurely exploration of ⌖ **The Hague** ㊶ and **Scheveningen** ㊼; then on the evening of the third day pop next door to ⌖ **Delft** ㊷. Spend day four lingering in this historic city, before heading off to the more cosmopolitan attractions of ⌖ **Rotterdam** ㊸.

IF YOU HAVE 7 DAYS
Follow the five-day itinerary outlined above, but spend two days exploring **Haarlem** ㊴ and ⌖ **Leiden** ㊵, taking time to visit the Frans Hals Museum in Haarlem and to wander through Leiden's charming Hortus Botanicus. After your night in ⌖ **Rotterdam** ㊸, set off for ⌖ **Utrecht** ㊺ and such contrasting delights as a magnificent Gothic cathedral and a museum of musical boxes.

When to Tour Metropolitan Holland

Bright fields of flowers make the springtime ideal for a trip around Haarlem and Leiden. If you're into the arts, you might prefer to schedule your trip to catch one of the area's two world-renowned festivals: the Rotterdam Film Festival, in late January and early February, and the North Sea Jazz Festival in The Hague, which blasts away for three days in July.

Haarlem

㊴ *20 km (13 mi) west of Amsterdam, 41 km (26 mi) north of The Hague.*

Often eclipsed by Amsterdam, Haarlem is an important small city in its own right. It is home to one of the finest church organs in the world, and its museums contain art that fills in gaps or expands upon the collections of Amsterdam's major museums. The heart of Haarlem lies, as it does with many a Dutch town, in its market square. Surrounding Haarlem's Grote Markt are the medieval town hall and the old fish- and meat-market halls dating from the 17th century and frequently used by the Frans Hals Museum for special exhibitions. In its center is the imposing Grote Kerk, often painted by the masters of the Golden Age.

The late Gothic St. Bavo's Church, more commonly called the **Grote Kerk** (Great Church), was built on the square in the 15th century and is the burial place of Frans Hals. The church is the home of the world-famous Müller Organ, on which both Handel and Mozart played (Mozart at age 10). Installed in 1738, and long considered to be the finest in the world, this gilded and gleaming instrument has been meticulously maintained and restored through the years to protect the

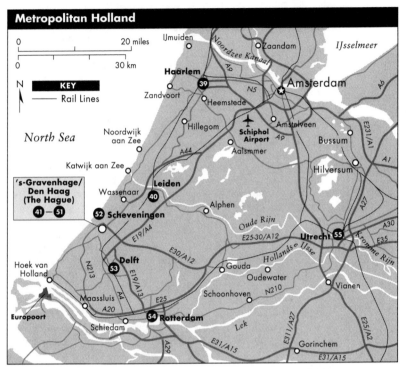

Metropolitan Holland

```
0          20 miles
0          30 km
```

KEY
— Rail Lines

North Sea

IJmuiden
Zaandam
IJsselmeer
Noordzee Kanaal
Haarlem
39
Amsterdam
Zandvoort
Heemstede
N5
Noordwijk aan Zee
Hillegom
Amstelveen
Schiphol Airport
Bussum
A44
Aalsmeer
Katwijk aan Zee
Hilversum
's-Gravenhage/ Den Haag (The Hague)
41 - 51
Leiden
40
Wassenaar
Alphen
52 Scheveningen
Oude Rijn
E25-30/A12
Utrecht 55
E19/A4
E30/A12
Hollandse IJsse
Hoek van Holland
Delft
53
Gouda
Oudewater
Vianen
Maassluis
A20
Schoonhoven
N210
Europoort
Schiedam
54 Rotterdam
Lek
Gorinchem
E31/A15

---

sound planned by its creators, the master organ builder Christian Müller and the sculptor Jan van Logteren. Between May and October the official town organists of Haarlem give free weekly or twice-weekly concerts. ⌧ *Grote Markt.* ☎ *023/533–0877.* ⌫ *Fl 2.50.* ☉ *Apr.–Aug., Mon.–Sat. 10–4; Sept.–Mar., Mon.–Sat. 10–3:30.*

NEED A BREAK?

The spacious **Grand Café Brinkmann** (⌧ Grote Markt 9–13, ☎ 023/532–3111), adorned with cherubic ceiling paintings, offers baguettes, tacos, and other light snacks. You look out windows edged with Art Deco stained glass onto the Grote Markt and across the square to St. Bavo's Church.

Just off the Grote Markt, tucked into a small gabled town building above a shop is the **Corrie ten Boom House,** which honors a family of World War II resistance fighters who successfully hid a number of Jewish families before being captured themselves by the Germans in 1944. Most of the ten Boom family members lost their lives in the concentration camps, but Corrie survived and returned to Haarlem to tell the story in her book, *The Hiding Place.* The family clock shop is preserved on the street floor, and their living quarters now contain displays, documents, photographs, and memorabilia. Visitors can also see the hiding closet, which the Gestapo never found, although they lived six days in the house hoping to starve out anyone who might be hiding there. ⌧ *Barteljorisstraat 19,* ☎ *023/310–823.* ⌫ *Free.* ☉ *Apr.–Nov., Tues.–Sat. 10–4; Nov.–Mar., Tues.–Sat. 11–3.*

The **Frans Hals Museum** spreads itself through a series of small houses that, in the 17th century, was an Old Men's Home. The cottages, arranged around an attractive garden courtyard, now form a sequence of galleries for paintings, period furniture, silver, and ceramics. The 17th-century collection of paintings that is the focal point of this museum includes the works of Frans Hals and other masters of the Haarlem School, including Hendrick Goltzius, Judith Leyster, Johannes Verspronck, Pieter Claesz, Willem Heda, Adriaen van Ostade, and Jacob van Ruisdael. The museum has a modern art collection as well, with the works of Dutch impressionists and expressionists, including sculpture, textiles, and ceramics, as well as paintings and graphics; there are also an 18th-century dollhouse and a re-created 18th-century pharmacy. From the Grote Markt, the museum can be found by taking Warmoesstraat and its continuations, Schagchelstraat and Groot Herlig Land. ⊠ *Groot Heilig Land 62,* ☎ *023/531–9180.* ☑ *Fl 7.50.* ☉ *Mon.–Sat. 11–5, Sun. and public holidays 1–5.*

⟳ Having first opened its doors in 1784, the **Teylers Museum** is one of the most curious in the world. The museum itself is a grand old building with mosaic floors and wooden cabinets; its major artistic attraction is the superb collection of master drawings and prints by Michelangelo, Rembrandt, and others, based on a collection that once belonged to Queen Christina of Sweden. Among the scientific curiosities are collections of fossils and crystals and examples of early machines and scientific tools. There is also a collection of coins and medals and even a rare 31-tone Fokker organ. In the beautiful oval library you can use brass parabolic mirrors (dating from 1800) to reflect the soft ticking of a watch right across the room; the Luminescence Cabinet is stocked with fluorescent and phosphorescent rocks and minerals that glow with extraordinary colors in the dark. To find the Teylers from the Hals Museum, follow the canals past the Turfmarkt to Spaarne. ⊠ *Spaarne 16,* ☎ *023/531– 9010.* ☑ *Fl 7.50.* ☉ *Tues.–Sat. 10–5, Sun. and public holidays noon–5.*

Dining and Lodging

$$$ ✕ **Peter Cuyper.** This small but gracious restaurant has a traditional beamed dining room that is brightened with flowers, crisp linens, and light from an enclosed garden (open in summer) filtering through the windows. Try a fillet of corn-fed hen stuffed with wild mushrooms, or one of the delicious soups. The restaurant is convenient to both the Frans Hals and the Teyler museums. ⊠ *Kleine Houtstraat 70,* ☎ *023/532– 0885. Reservations essential. AE, DC, MC, V. Closed Sun.–Mon.*

$$$ ▦ **Carlton Square Hotel.** This modern high-rise, in a residential district beyond the center, has rooms that are bright and spacious with white, Art Deco–inspired furniture. ⊠ *Baan 7, 2012 DB,* ☎ *023/319091,* ℻ *023/329853. 106 rooms. Restaurant, bar. AE, DC, MC, V.*

$$–$$$ ▦ **Golden Tulip Lion d'Or.** This traditional hotel near the railway station has been here since the early 18th century. Thoroughly modernized, it has spacious guest rooms and meeting rooms. A jogging path runs behind the hotel. ⊠ *Kruisweg 34–36, 2011 LC,* ☎ *023/532–1750,* ℻ *023/532–9543. 36 rooms with bath. Restaurant, business services, parking (fee). AE, DC, MC, V.*

$ ▦ **Hotel Faber.** Within walking distance of the beaches of Zandvoort, this is a small, family-style hotel with bright, tidy rooms and a summer terrace. ⊠ *Kostverlorenstraat 15, 2042 PA Zandvoort,* ☎ *023/571– 2825,* ℻ *023/571–6886. 30 rooms with shower or bath. Lobby bar, terrace. AE, MC, V.*

Nightlife and the Arts

Haarlem hosts the **International Organ Competition** in even-numbered years during the first week of July, giving people ample opportunity to hear the renowned Müller organ at full throttle.

Outdoor Activities and Sports

AUTO RACING

One of Europe's best-known auto racing tracks is near Haarlem at **Circuit Park Zandvoort** (⊠ Burgemeester van Alphenstraat, ☎ 023/571–6004 or 023/571–8284); the racing season runs from March to October.

BEACHES

Near Haarlem, **Zandvoort** is also the principal beach for Amsterdam. It is busy, but very large, and if you wander south for 10 minutes or so you can find isolated spots among the dunes; after about 20 minutes, you come to the nude sunbathing beach.

BIKING

You can rent bicycles in Haarlem from **Van Bentum** (⊠ Stationsplein, ☎ 023/531–7066) and **De Volkenfietser** (⊠ Koningstraat 36, ☎ 023/532–5577)

Leiden

40 *35 km (22 mi) south of Haarlem, 45 km (28 mi) south of Amsterdam, and 16 km (10 mi) northeast of The Hague.*

Birthplace of Rembrandt and site of the nation's oldest and most prestigious university, Leiden is also noted for its significant historic role. In 1574, Leiden was the object of a major siege at the hands of the Spanish; the story of that siege, and the city's deliverance by the uniquely Dutch tactic of breaching the dikes to flood out an invader, is an important part of national lore. Leiden is also the town that was home to the Pilgrim Fathers for some 12 years, before they set off for the New World. A place where windmills still rise over the cityscape, Leiden derives its charm today from its relaxed and spirited university-town atmosphere.

Following the wide Rapenburg canal from the center of town, you'll discover Leiden University's **Hortus Botanicus** (botanical garden), the oldest in Europe, which includes extensive beds of flowers, rare plants, and towering trees; there is an orangery, a Japanese garden, and several greenhouses. ⊠ *Rapenburg 73,* ☎ *071/527–5188.* ☜ *Fl 5.* ☉ *Apr.–Sept., Mon.–Sat. 9–5, Sun. 10–5; Oct.–Mar., weekdays 9–4:30, Sun. 10:30–3.*

Founded in 1575, **Leiden University** soon became a mecca for the great thinkers and scientists of the 16th and 17th centuries, including the philosopher René Descartes. Today it is still one of the most respected academic establishments in the country, and the students preserve many time-honored traditions. The old university buildings are not open to the public, but in the "Academic Quarter," between the Rapenburg and Singel canals, students give Leiden a lively atmosphere.

Within a stone's throw of the university is **Pieterskerk** (St. Peter's Church), often surrounded by students sunning themselves in the church square. It is the oldest church in the city, dating from 1428. Inside the church you'll find the graves of the painter Jan Steen and of Rembrandt's parents. There is also a mysterious dried-up mummy that was discovered in a secret room under the pulpit, exciting tales of murder and illicit lovers. Genealogists might be intrigued by a family tree showing how former U.S. president George Bush was descended from the Pilgrim Fathers. Also on the church square is the Gravensteen, which once was the home of the Counts of Holland. ⊠ *Pieterskerkhof,* ☎ *071/512–4319.* ☜ *Free.* ☉ *Daily 1:30–4.*

A few of the houses occupied by the Pilgrim Fathers still stand in the quarter around the Pieterskerk. Among them is the former home of

William Brewster, spiritual leader of the Pilgrims. At the entrance is a small plaque placed by the Society of Mayflower Descendants. The house is just behind the church on Pieterskerkchoorsteeg.

The **Rijksmuseum van Oudheden** (National Museum of Antiquities) has a particularly fine Egyptian and classical collection, as well as Dutch archaeological artifacts. Pass through a soaring gallery in which the Egyptian temple of Taffah has been reconstructed, and continue through two floors of Greek and Roman sculpture, Egyptian tombs, funerary urns, and collections of everyday items from the pre-Christian eras, including glassware, ceramics, jewelry, and weapons. ⊠ *Rapenburg 28,* ☎ *071/516–3163.* 🎟 *Fl 5.* ☉ *Tues.–Sat. 10–5, Sun. noon–5.*

<table>
<tr><td>NEED A
BREAK?</td><td>**De Waterlijn** (⊠ Prinsessekade, ☎ 071/512–1279) occupies one of the most attractive spots in town. Just past the end of the Rapenburg canal (which is itself lined with gracious buildings), this strikingly modern, glass-walled café on a moored boat offers views of old boats, gabled houses, and a windmill. The Dutch apple tart is good here.</td></tr>
</table>

De Lakenhal museum contains an impressive collection of paintings, furniture, and silver and pewter pieces, set in the sumptuous surrounds of a 17th-century Cloth Hall. Leiden was once a center of the wool trade, and this is the building where the cloth was inspected and traded, and where the Guild Governors met. The galleries are hung with paintings by Rembrandt, Gerrit Dou, Jan Steen, and Salomon van Ruysdael, as well as a grand collection of the works of Lucas van Leyden, including his triptych, *Last Judgment.* Also of interest here are the reconstructed guild rooms. ⊠ *Oude Singel 28–32,* ☎ *071/516–5361.* 🎟 *Fl 5.* ☉ *Tues.–Sat. 10–5, Sun. and public holidays noon–5.*

★ ☾ Leiden's **Molenmuseum de Valk** (Windmill Museum de Valk) began grinding grain in 1743. You can wander around the perfectly preserved living quarters on the ground floor, then clamber past the massive millstones and climb seven stories to the top of the mill. On the way up you can pop out onto the "reefing-stage"—the platform than runs around the outside of the mill halfway up its length. This is a wonderful place to get an insider's view of the windmill heritage of the Netherlands. ⊠ *2e Binnenvestgracht 1,* ☎ *071/516–5353.* 🎟 *Fl 5.* ☉ *Tues.–Sat. 10–5, Sun. and holidays 1–5.*

☾ Europe's first permanent space exhibition, **Noordwijk Space Expo,** includes real satellites, engines, and space stations, as well as models and pieces of moon rock. ⊠ *Keplerlaan 3, Noordwijk, 13 km (8 mi) from Leiden,* ☎ *071/364–6460.* 🎟 *Fl 12.50.* ☉ *Tues.–Sun. 10–6.*

Dining and Lodging

$$$ ✕ **Bistro La Cloche.** This chic, attractive French-Dutch restaurant, just off the Rapenburg canal on the small street leading to St. Peter's Church, is done up in soft pastels, with flowers everywhere. It has a pleasant but small streetside café area and quieter dining upstairs. ⊠ *Kloksteeg 3,* ☎ *071/512–3053. Reservations essential. AE, DC, MC, V.*

$$$ ✕ **Oudt Leyden.** This formal Dutch-style restaurant has a traditional menu of simple grilled and sautéed meats and fishes. It shares a kitchen with its neighbor, Pannekoekenhuysje (☞ *below*). ⊠ *Steenstraat 51–53,* ☎ *071/513–3144. AE, DC, MC, V. Closed Sun.*

$$ ✕ **Mangerie de Koekop.** Just a few minutes from the old De Valk Windmill, near the center of old Leiden, this restaurant is popular with students and locals. The turn-of-the-century building was gutted and has been refurbished with tasteful but no-frills decor, including cream ceramic-tile floors, apple-green tablecloths, and wicker chairs. The good-value, excellent food draws the crowds: Less than Fl 45 buys a

three-course meal that includes such mouthwatering dishes as mushrooms with goat's cheese and mustard sauce, baked in a fluffy filo pastry case. ⊠ *Lange Mare 60,* ☎ *071/514–1937. AE, DC, MC, V.*

$$ ✗ **M'n Broer.** Run by a pair of twins, "My Brother" is a cozy brasserie with a Brown Café atmosphere. The kitchen serves up such hearty meals as seafood pie, and roast duck with port sauce; the portions are generous, and the food is good. ⊠ *Kloksteeg 7,* ☎ *071/512–5024. Reservations not accepted. No credit cards.*

$–$$ ✗ **Annie's Verjaardag.** This restaurant consists of a low-ceilinged, arched cellar, often full of chatty students, and a water-level canal-side terrace. During the day, there is a modest selection of salads and sandwiches on baguettes, and at least one more substantial offering. After 6 you can choose from a fuller menu that includes cheese fondue, grilled trout, and spareribs. ⊠ *Hoogstraat 1a,* ☎ *071/512–5737. Reservations not accepted. No credit cards.*

$ ✗ **Pannekoekenhuysje.** This restaurant, a traditional Dutch pancake house, shares a kitchen with its neighbor, Oudt Leyden (☞ *above*), but it has a totally different menu and environment. It has red-checked tablecloths, a relaxed mood, and easy-on-the-budget prices. ⊠ *Steenstraat 51–53,* ☎ *071/513–3144. AE, DC, MC, V. Closed Sun.*

$$$ 🏨 **Holiday Inn Leiden.** Just off the secondary highway between Leiden and The Hague and not far from the beaches at Katwijk, this is more a resort than a hotel. There is a vast interior garden lobby, and the decor of the guest rooms carries out the garden theme with bold colors and floral curtains. ⊠ *Haagse Schouwweg 10, 2332 KG,* ☎ *071/535–5555,* 𝔽𝔸𝕏 *071/535–5553. 200 rooms. Restaurant, bar, pool, sauna, 7 tennis courts, bowling, squash. AE, DC, MC, V.*

$ 🏨 **De Ceder.** This is a small, friendly, and very tidy family-style hotel in a converted home out near the teaching hospital of Leiden University. The garden rooms are particularly desirable, and the breakfast room overlooks the garden. ⊠ *Rijnsburgerweg 80, 2333 AD,* ☎ *071/517–5903,* 𝔽𝔸𝕏 *071/515–7098. 16 rooms, 10 with bath/shower. Bar. AE, DC, MC, V.*

Outdoor Activities and Sports

BEACHES
Leiden's coastal resorts are at **Katwijk** and **Noordwijk,** in the dunes beside the North Sea.

BIKING
The place to rent a bicycle in Leiden is the **Rijwiel Shop** (☎ 071/513–1304), next to the railroad station.

CANOEING
A canoe may be the very best way to get a close view of the bulb fields that fill the countryside between Haarlem and Leiden. The **VVV Leiden Tourist Office** (☎ 071/514–6846) has mapped out four different routes of varying lengths through the Dune and Bulb Area. Ask, too, about the Singel sightseeing route through Leiden's canals and moats. For information on canoe rentals contact **Jac. Veringa** (☎ 071/514–9790).

TENNIS AND SQUASH
You can play tennis and squash at the **Holiday Inn Racket Center** (⊠ Haagse Schouwweg 10, ☎ 071/535–5100).

Shopping
Thursday is the night the shops stay open late here. Leiden's street market is held in the city center on the Nieuwe Rijn on Wednesday and Saturday, 9–6, and at Vijf Mei plein on Tuesday, 9–2.

The Hague and Its Environs

16 km (10 mi) southwest of Leiden, 57 km (36 mi) southwest of Amsterdam.

41 As becomes an aristocrat, Den Haag has several names. The French call it La Haye, whereas the official Dutch name is 's-Gravenhage or, literally, the Count's Hedge, while Den Haag is favored by the Dutch in conversation. In English it is known as **The Hague.** The business about the hedge recalls the early 13th century when the Counts of Holland had a hunting lodge in a small woodland village called Die Haghe. Then, around 1248, Count Willem II built a larger house; the noted Knights' Hall, or Ridderzaal, was added in 1280; and gradually Den Haag became the focus of more and more government functions. Today, while Amsterdam remains the official capital of the Netherlands, 's-Gravenhage/Den Haag is the seat of government and home of the reigning monarch, Queen Beatrix. An elegant city dotted with parks and open squares, it exudes a graciousness that Amsterdam lacks and has a formal and traditional lifestyle that befits its role as a diplomatic capital and world center of international peace and justice. Almost seamlessly connected to The Hague is the popular beach and fishing resort of Scheveningen, nicknamed "our national bathing place," and aglitter with all the bright lights and entertainments of a seaside holiday town.

Numbers in the margin correspond to points of interest on The Hague map and the Metropolitan Holland map.

42 The governmental heart of the Netherlands, in the very center of The Hague, is the **Binnenhof** (Inner Court). For many centuries the court of the Counts of Holland, the Binnenhof is now a complex of buildings from a spectrum of different eras. It incorporates the halls used by the First and Second Chambers of the Staten Generaal (States General, equivalent to the U.S. Senate and House of Representatives). Beside the Bin-
43 nenhof is the **Hofvijver** (Court Lake), a long, rectangular reflecting pool, complete with tall fountains. The oldest building in the complex
44 is the late-13th-century **Ridderzaal** (Knight's Hall), which is where the queen comes each fall to address her government at the annual Opening of Parliament (third Tuesday in September). There are guided tours into the legislative chambers (when they are not in session) and the Knight's Hall, with its provincial flags and stained-glass windows displaying the coats of arms of the major Dutch cities. You can also see a special exhibition on the origin and methods of the Dutch governmental system. ☏ *070/364–6144. Reservations essential.* ✉ *Tour Fl 6; Parliament exhibition free.* ⊙ *Mon.–Sat. 10–4; last guided tour at 3:45.*

NEED A
BREAK?   **'t Goude Hooft** (✉ De Groenmarkt 13, ☏ 070/346–9713) is the oldest restaurant in The Hague, with both a traditional Dutch dining room and a street café looking out on the old Town Hall.

---

45 The **Mauritshuis,** a small 17th-century palace tucked into a corner behind the Parliament Complex and overlooking the Court Lake, contains one of the nation's choicest collections of art. Known as the Royal Gallery of Paintings, this is an outstanding collection of Dutch masterpieces, including three Rembrandt self portraits and his breakthrough painting, *The Anatomy Lesson.* Also here are three highly prized paintings by Vermeer (*Girl with the Pearl, View of Delft, Diana with the Nymphs*); more than a dozen works by Jan Steen, who portrayed daily life and ordinary people in the Netherlands in the 17th century; and paintings by other Dutch and Flemish masters, including Hals, Ruysdael, Potter, Rubens, and Van Dyck. ✉ *Korte Vijverberg 8,* ☏ *070/346–9244.* ✉ *Fl 10.* ⊙ *Tues.–Sat. 10–5, Sun. 11–5.*

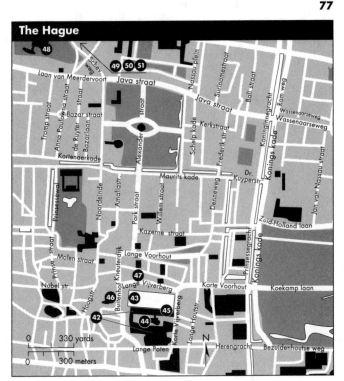

The Hague

In 1773, Willem V built a new gallery in his palace and allowed the general public in for a look three days a week, thus earning the **Painting Gallery of Prince Willem V** the reputation of being the Netherlands' first public museum. The small gallery has fine Louis XVI stucco ceilings but keeps an intimate, homey atmosphere. It is rather as if a friend, who happened to have a good collection of 17th-century masters, had invited you over to see them. ⊠ *Buitenhof 35,* ☎ *070/318–2487.* 🎟 *Fl 2.50.* ☉ *Tues.–Sun. 11–4.*

The **Museum Bredius** illustrates the point that private collections are often the most delightful. Housed in an 18th-century mansion, the collection of traveler and art connoisseur Abraham Bredius includes works by the likes of Rembrandt and Jan Steen, as well as lesser-known works of the period, all held together by the thread of a personal vision. The house itself, an 18th-century patrician mansion overlooking the Hofvijver (Court Lake), makes a magnificent context for the paintings. ⊠ *Lange Vijverberg 14,* ☎ *070/362–0729.* 🎟 *Fl 6.* ☉ *Tues.–Sun. noon–5.*

Facing the world across a broad lawn, the **Vredespaleis** (Peace Palace) houses the International Court of Justice. The court was initiated in 1899 by Czar Nicolas II of Russia, who invited 26 nations to meet in The Hague to set up a permanent world court of arbitration. The present building was constructed in 1903 with a $1.5 million gift from the Dutch-American industrialist Andrew Carnegie. Gifts from each of the participating nations embellish the architecture with examples of their national craftsmanship in the form of statuary, stained-glass windows, gates, doors, clocks, and such. ⊠ *Carnegieplein 2,* ☎ *070/320–4137.* 🎟 *Fl 5.* ☉ *May–Oct., weekdays 10–4; Nov.–Apr., weekdays 10–3; guided tours at 10, 11, 2, and 3 (May–Oct. additional tour at 4).*

49 The **Haags Gemeentemuseum** (Hague Municipal Museum) is best known for housing the world's largest collection of works by Piet Mondrian, as well as 50 drawings by Karel Appel. In addition, there are paintings by The Hague School and an arts-and-crafts section that displays magnificent local silverware, old glass, earthenware, ceramics, and Dutch and Chinese porcelain. ⊠ *Stadhouderslaan 41,* ☎ *070/ 351–2873.* ▣ *Fl 8.* ☉ *Tues.–Sun. 11–5.*

50 The **Museon** incorporates science exhibits on the origins of the universe and evolution with three themes: Earth, Our Home; Between Man and the Stars; and Ecos, an environmental show. Special exhibitions are frequent here and are always excitingly presented, with lots of hands-on and interactive displays. Archaeological and intercultural subjects are common themes. The Museon adjoins the Haags Gemeentemuseum (☞ *above*). ⊠ *Stadhouderslaan 41,* ☎ *070/338–1338 and 070/338–1305.* ▣ *Fl 5.* ☉ *Tues.–Fri. 10–5, weekends and public holidays noon–5.*

51 The IMAX theater **Omniversum** shows a rotating program of spectacular presentations, including several with natural and futuristic themes, on a film screen that is six stories high. ⊠ *Pres. Kennedylaan 5,* ☎ *070/ 354–5454.* ▣ *Fl 17. Tues.–Thurs. hourly 11–4, Fri.–Sun. and holidays hourly 11–4 and 6–9.*

52 At the seaside resort of **Scheveningen,** you can enjoy a variety of relaxing pleasures, including a walk on the beach promenade or a swim in a wave pool. The famous and grand old hotel, the **Kurhaus** (☞ Dining and Lodging, *below*), houses a casino as well as several restaurants. There is also shopping seven days a week. Scheveningen is the departure point for deep-sea fishing trips.

In the **Scheveningen Sea Life Centre** you will encounter hundreds of exotic sea creatures from starfish to stingrays. The imaginative design features of this aquarium include a transparent tunnel, 30 feet long, where sharks swim above your head. ⊠ *Strandweg 13,* ☎ *070/354– 2100.* ▣ *Fl 14.* ☉ *Sept.–June, daily 10–6; July–Aug., daily 10–9.*

The miniature village of **Madurodam** comes complete with a collection of small reproductions of typically Dutch buildings set in a sprawling "village" with pathways, tram tracks, and railway stations. All of the most important buildings of the Netherlands have been reproduced; if you are here at sunset you will see the lights come on in the houses. In July and August, there is also an after-dark sound-and-light presentation, free to park visitors. ⊠ *Haringkade 175,* ☎ *070/355–3900.* ▣ *Fl 19.50.* ☉ *Apr.–Sept., daily 9 AM–10 PM; Oct.–Mar., daily 9–5.*

June is the time to visit **Westbroek Park** in The Hague, when its 20,000 rosebushes are in magnificent bloom. ⊠ *Kapelweg.* ▣ *Free.* ☉ *Daily 9–hr before sunset.*

Dining and Lodging

$$–$$$ ✕ **Le Haricot Vert.** In a 1638 former staff house for the nearby palace, this intimate, candlelit restaurant combines Dutch simplicity and French flair. Succulent meats covered with sauces are served on large white plates with tangles of colorful vegetables. The menu changes seasonally. ⊠ *Molenstraat 9a–11,* ☎ *070/365–2278. AE, MC, V.*

$$ ✕ **Greve.** You sit at long trestle tables, and the waiters arrive with steaming loaves of pumpernickel served on a board. Then come such mouthwatering delights as grilled swordfish with guacamole, or hearty chicken soup, thick with fresh vegetables. Service is quick and friendly, and the atmosphere chatty and informal. Greve has both a restaurant and a café section. ⊠ *Torenstraat 138,* ☎ *070/360–3919. Reservations essential. AE, DC, MC, V (restaurant only).*

$$$$ ×⌸ **Kurhaus Hotel.** Holding the prime position at the center of the beach at Scheveningen, this grand hotel of the old school is fully modernized and bustling. Now engulfed by shops and apartments on the street side, it still has its famous turn-of-the-century profile from the amusement pier, and you still can dine in the magnificent Kurzaal with its fancifully painted, coffered ceiling high overhead. Rooms here are grand and grandly decorated in a variety of modern and traditional styles. ✉ *Gevers Deynootplein 30, 2586 CK, Scheveningen,* ☎ *070/416–2636,* ⨳ *070/416–2646. 231 rooms, 8 suites, 2 bridal suites. 2 restaurants, sauna, casino. AE, DC, MC, V.*

$$$ ×⌸ **Hotel Des Indes Inter-Continental.** Once a private mansion built principally for grand balls and entertainment, the Des Indes has a grace and graciousness that make it one of the world's very special hotels. It sits on one of The Hague's most prestigious squares. The former inner courtyard is now a towering reception area leading to the restaurant. The spacious, stylish rooms were renovated in 1993–94. One suite, which enjoys a magnificent view over the city toward the beach, is fought over by rock stars who come to perform in nearby Rotterdam. The superlative restaurant is enjoyed by all. ✉ *Lange Voorhout 54–56, 2514 EG,* ☎ *070/363–2932,* ⨳ *070/345–1721. 76 rooms. Restaurant, bar. AE, DC, MC, V.*

$$$ ⌸ **Corona Hotel.** Elegant lodging seems appropriate to an elegant city of diplomacy, and this hotel fits in perfectly. It is conveniently located across from the Parliament Complex, near the Mauritshuis and Museum Bredius at the edge of the shopping district. The rooms are restfully decorated in a muted scheme of white, cream, and dove gray. ✉ *Buitenhof 39–42, 2513 AH,* ☎ *070/363–7930,* ⨳ *070/361–5785. 26 rooms with bath. Restaurant, bar, brasserie. AE, DC, MC, V.*

$$ ⌸ **Novotel Hotel.** Well located for both the sights and the shopping of The Hague, Novotel is a new and well-appointed full-service hotel with modestly sized rooms; the decor is a bland but tranquilizing beige and white. ✉ *Hofweg 5–7, 2511 AA,* ☎ *070/364–8846,* ⨳ *070/356–2889. 106 rooms. Restaurant, bar. AE, DC, MC, V.*

$–$$ ⌸ **Hotel Petit.** On a residential boulevard between the Peace Palace and The Hague Municipal Museum, this quiet, family-style brick hotel is operated by a young couple. Bright and graciously furnished, it has a pleasant guests-only bar-lounge for relaxing after a day of sightseeing. ✉ *Groot Hertoginnelaan 42, 2517 EH,* ☎ *070/346–5500,* ⨳ *070/346–3257. 20 rooms with bath. Bar. AE, DC, MC, V.*

$–$$ ⌸ **Hotel Sebel.** The friendly owners of this hotel have expanded into two buildings between the city center and the Peace Palace. Tidy and comfortable, the rooms are large and have high ceilings and tall windows for lots of light and air. ✉ *Zoutmanstraat 38, 2518 GR,* ☎ *070/360–8010,* ⨳ *070/345–5855. 14 rooms with bath. Bar. AE, DC, MC, V.*

$ ⌸ **City Hotel.** Just off the beach in Scheveningen, this spanking clean, brightly decorated, and very friendly small family hotel spreads through several houses on a main street leading to the waterfront. ✉ *Renbaanstraat 1–3 and 17–23, 2586 EW, Scheveningen,* ☎ *070/355–7966,* ⨳ *070/354–0503. 20 rooms with bath. Restaurant, bar. AE, DC, MC, V.*

Nightlife and the Arts

For information on cultural events, call the **Uit** (*Going Out*) **information** numbers in The Hague (✉ Uitpost Den Haag, ☎ 070/363–3833). In addition, you can pick up the monthly *Info: Den Haag, Scheveningen en Kijkduin (Day to Day Tourist Information),* which lists (in Dutch) what's going on in major theaters in that area, with English copy describing major events.

CAFÉS

In the beach community of Scheveningen, **Plaza Bar** (✉ Gevers Deynoot-plein 118, ☎ 070/351–5426) is a chic and exclusive place that offers all sorts of music, live and recorded.

CLASSICAL MUSIC

The Hague's **Residentie Orkest** is an excellent orchestra with a world-wide reputation. It performs at **Dr. Anton Philipszaal** (✉ Houtmarkt 17, ☎ 070/360–9810) and **Nederlands Congresgebouw** (✉ Churchillplein 10, ☎ 070/354–8000).

DANCE

The **Nederlands Danstheater** is the national modern dance company of the Netherlands and makes its home at the **AT&T Danstheater** (✉ Schedeldoekshaven 60, ☎ 070/360–4930).

DISCOS

The huge **Marathon** (✉ Wijndaelerweg 3, ☎ 070/368–0324) offers a wide variety of music and attracts a young, energetic crowd. The latest local and international bands can be heard at **Het Paard** (✉ Prin-sengracht 12, ☎ 070/360–1618), where you can also dance and watch multimedia shows. **Club Exposure** (✉ Westduinweg 232, ☎ 070/356–1289) in Scheveningen has a trendy clientele and organizes special party and theme nights. **Thahiti** (✉ Strandweg 43, ☎ 070/350–2068) in Scheveningen offers live performances as well as hot recorded sounds.

JAZZ

One of the festivals for which the Netherlands is well known is the annual **North Sea Jazz Festival** (☎ 015/214–8900), which is the largest of its kind in the world. It is held in The Hague and Scheveningen for four days in July and regularly attracts the greats of jazz as well as thousands of jazz lovers from around the world.

THEATER AND OPERA

Mainstream Dutch theater is presented by the national theater company **Het Nationale Toneel,** which performs at the **Royal Schouwburg** (✉ Korte Voorhout 3, ☎ 070/346–9450). **De Appel** company has a lively, experimental approach to theater and performs at its own **Ap-peltheater** (✉ Duinstraat 6–8, ☎ 070/350–2200). **Musicals,** including occasional world tours from Broadway, can be seen at **Nederlands Congresgebouw** (✉ Churchillplein 10, ☎ 070/354–8000) or in the adjoining beach resort community of Scheveningen at **Circustheater** (✉ Circusstraat 4, ☎ 070/351–1212).

Outdoor Activities and Sports

BEACHES

The beach at **Scheveningen** is one of the most popular in the country and has a boardwalk and amusement pier as well as numerous cafés and sunbathing terraces.

BIKING

You can rent bicycles in The Hague at the **Rijwiel Shop** (✉ Hollands Spoor, ☎ 070/389–0830; ✉ Centraal Station ☎ 070/385–3235) and **Garage du Nord** (✉ Keizerstraat 27, Scheveningen, ☎ 070/355–4060).

HORSE RACING

Near The Hague, **Duindigt Racecourse** (✉ Waalsdorperlaan 29, Wasse-naar, ☎ 070/324–4427) is one of two racetracks in the Netherlands (the other is in Hilversum, between Utrecht and Amsterdam). The racing season runs from mid-March to mid-November and includes both flat and trotting races with betting. Race days are Wednesday and Sunday.

SEA FISHING

Sea fishing is one of the main reasons many people visit Scheveningen. For information and reservations, contact **Sportviscentrum Trip** (✉ Dr. Lelykade 3, Scheveningen, ☎ 070/354–1122 or 070/354–0887).

Shopping

Late shopping in **The Hague** is on Thursday; in **Scheveningen** on Friday and, during the summer at the Palace Promenade, Monday through Saturday. In **The Hague** there's a Farmers' Market on Wednesday 10 to 6, and there is an antiques market on Lange Voorhout on summer Thursdays and Sundays.

Delft

★ ⑤ *14 km (9 mi) from The Hague and 71 km (45 mi) from Amsterdam.*

Perhaps more than any other city in the Netherlands, Delft preserves a historic look that is best appreciated by simply wandering along its small canals with their graceful, humpbacked bridges. In some places, so little has changed that you can recognize the views made famous by the Golden Age painter Johannes Vermeer. Delft rivals Leiden in its importance to the history of the Netherlands; it was here that William of Orange (known as William the Silent), founder of the nation, was assassinated in 1584. The Dutch monarchs that followed him are all buried here in the Nieuwe Kerk (New Church), in the shadow of which Vermeer was born and lived. And, of course, Delft also is the crafts center known around the world for its blue-and-white porcelain.

Delft's **Stadhuis** (Town Hall) stands grandly at one end of the large market square. Behind the lavishly embellished building designed by Hendrick de Keyser, one of the most prolific architects of the Golden Age, rises a simpler, more stolid 14th-century tower. Behind the Town Hall is a row of buildings that formerly served as the butter market, the town weigh house, and the guild halls of gold- and silversmiths and pharmacists. ✉ *Markt 87.*

All but a few of the Dutch monarchs of the House of Orange lie buried in the **Nieuwe Kerk** (New Church), located on the market square. The mausoleum of William the Silent, a massive and ornate structure of black marble and alabaster, dominates the chancel. Nearby in the floor is the stone that covers the entry to the royal crypt, and throughout the church are paintings, stained-glass windows, and memorabilia associated with the Dutch royal family. In summer it is possible to climb the church tower for a view that stretches as far as The Hague and Scheveningen. ✉ *Markt,* ☎ *015/212–3025.* ✉ *Combination card (Old and New Churches) Fl 4; tower Fl 2.50.* ☉ *Mar.–Oct., Mon.–Sat. 9–6; Nov.–Apr., Mon.–Sat. 11–4.*

Pretty, tree-lined, and with an abundance of historic gabled houses along its banks, the **Oude Delft** takes the honors for being the first canal dug in the city and probably the first city canal to be dug anywhere in the Netherlands. It is located one canal over from the Stadhuis.

NEED A
BREAK?

Kleyweg's Stads-Koffyhuis (✉ Oude Delft 133, ☎ 015/212–4625) looks out over the oldest and one of the most beautiful canals in Delft. Inside, you'll find a "stamtafel," a large table laid out with newspapers and magazines, where anyone may sit and chat. There are also smaller individual tables where you can enjoy good coffee and delicious pancakes.

The tower of the **Oude Kerk** (Old Church) manages to lean in four directions at once. But then, this is the oldest church in Delft, having been founded in 1200. It is the final resting place of several important Dutch military and naval heroes, and of Antonie van Leeuwenhoek, the Delft resident who invented the microscope. The tower, which now leans too precariously to be ascended, holds the largest carillon bell in the Netherlands; weighing nearly 20,000 pounds, it now is used only on state occasions. ⊠ *Heilige Geestkerkhof,* ☎ *015/212–3015.* ⌨ *Combination card (Old and New Churches) Fl 4.* ☉ *Apr.–Nov., Mon.–Sat. 10–5.*

Delft's most famous sight, **Het Prinsenhof** (Prince's Court), was built as a convent in the early 15th century and is located directly across the Oude Delft from the Oude Kerk. The complex of buildings was taken over by the government of the new Dutch Republic in 1572 and given to William of Orange for his use as a residence. It was here that William was assassinated. The complex now houses a museum devoted to the history of the Dutch Republic; there is also a museum of ethnology and a church. ⊠ *St. Agathaplein 1,* ☎ *015/260–2358.* ⌨ *Fl 5.* ☉ *Tues.–Sat. 10–5, Sun. 1–5.*

Dining and Lodging

$$$ ✕ **De Prinsenkelder.** In the old storerooms of a former convent that now is the Prinsenhof Museum, this restaurant has a sedate, elegant atmosphere. Classic French dishes, such as duck with apple and raisins and a creamy Calvados sauce, are wonderfully prepared and beautifully presented. Entry is by way of a small alley opening onto the Oude Delft canal. ⊠ *Schoolstraat 11,* ☎ *015/212–1860. Reservations essential. AE, DC, MC, V. Closed Sun.*

$$$ ✕ **L'Orage.** The owner-chef of this bright and gracious small French restaurant facing the Old Canal is Jannie Munk, who won the Netherlands' Lady Chef of the Year award in 1994. She creates delicious fish dishes, many based on recipes from her native Denmark. Try the red bass, grilled in its skin and served with risotto and sun-dried tomatoes. ⊠ *Oude Delft 111b,* ☎ *015/212–3629. Reservations required. Jacket and tie. AE, DC, MC, V. Closed Sun.–Mon.*

$–$$ ✕⊡ **Les Compagnons.** This is a one-family hospitality package in the heart of Delft. The younger generation operates a small and comfortable hotel on the market square that offers a variety of brightly decorated rooms with a range of amenities that you wouldn't expect in so small a hotel. Dad hosts a restaurant on the next canal, and Mom operates a deli and tearoom in the adjoining store. In the early 1990s the family took over a pension farther along the market square and a four-star hotel on the other side of town. ⊠ *Markt 61, 2611 GS,* ☎ *015/214–0102,* ℻ *015/212–0168. 10 rooms with bath. AE, DC, MC, V.*

$$ ⊡ **Delft Museumhotel & Residence.** This small, elegant hotel has been created within a complex of 11 historic buildings in the prime neighborhood of Delft. Among the choices are small apartments in the adjacent Residence building that opens onto the side alley. ⊠ *Oude Delft 189, 2611 HD,* ☎ *015/214–0930,* ℻ *015/214–0935. 50 rooms. Bar, lobby lounge, meeting room. AE, DC, MC, V.*

$–$$ ⊡ **Hotel Leeuwenbrug.** Facing one of Delft's canals, this traditional hotel has an Old Dutch–style canal-side lounge. The rooms are large, airy, and contemporary in decor; those in the annex are particularly appealing. ⊠ *Koornmarkt 16, 2611 EE,* ☎ *015/214–7741,* ℻ *015/215–9759. 37 rooms with bath/shower. Bar. AE, MC, V.*

Outdoor Activities and Sports

BIKING

Bike rentals are available at the **railway station** (☎ 015/214–3033).

SQUASH

Squash courts are available at **Squash Delft** (⊠ Sportring 3, ☎ 015/214–6983).

Shopping

In Delft, market day is Thursday, from 9 to 5, and there is a flea market on the canals in the town center on summer Saturdays.

DELFTWARE

De Porceleyne Fles (⊠ The Royal Delftware Factory, Rotterdamseweg 196, ☎ 015/256–0234) is home to the popular blue-and-white Delft pottery. The galleries here exhibit famous pieces from throughout Delft's history, and regular demonstrations of molding and painting pottery are given by the artisans. The pottery factories of **De Delftse Pauw** (⊠ Delftweg 133, ☎ 015/212–4920 or 015/212–4743), while not as famous as De Porceleyne Fles, produce work of equally high quality. **Atelier de Candelaer** (⊠ Kerkstraat 13, ☎ 015/131848) makes a convenient stop-off for those who want to compare Delftware with other pottery before making a purchase.

Rotterdam

54 *12 km (8 mi) southeast of Delft, 77 km (48 mi) south of Amsterdam.*

Were it not for the devastation of World War II, when the city and its port were leveled in the cross fire between Hitler's forces and the Allies, Rotterdam might never have become the dynamic and influential world port it is today. A busy harbor since the 17th century, it built bigger facilities in the 19th and early 20th centuries, playing a key role in European trade. Today, its **Europoort** is the world's largest port, a massive complex of piers, warehouses, and refineries stretching for 48 kilometers (30 miles), an awe-inspiring sight from a boat at night. An imaginative program of postwar building has given Rotterdam an extraordinary concentration of adventurous modern architecture.

As you walk along the Leuvehaven inner harbor past several old ships moored along the quay, you'll come to Rotterdam's noted nautical museum located at the head of the harbor. The history of Rotterdam harbor and its historic role in world trade come to life in the **Prins Hendrik Maritime Museum.** The museum building contains both changing exhibitions and a permanent collection of models and memorabilia; the warship *De Buffel,* moored alongside the museum, is part of the collection, and there are several other intriguing old ships moored along the quay. ⊠ *Leuvehaven 1,* ☎ *010/413–2680.* 🎫 *Fl 6.* ☉ *Tues.–Sat. 10–5, Sun. and holidays 11–5.*

Perhaps the oddest building in this city of bold architecture is the **Kijk-Kubus,** one of a series of cube-shaped apartments that have each been turned to balance on one corner on the top of tall stems. The precarious-looking Kijk-Kubus is just east of the center of town and is open to the public. ⊠ *Overblaak 70,* ☎ *010/414–2285.* 🎫 *Fl 2.50.* ☉ *Tues.–Fri. 10–5, weekends 11–5.*

The **Boymans-van Beuningen Museum** stands shoulder to shoulder with the Rijksmuseum in Amsterdam in the line-up of the Netherlands' exceptional fine-arts museums. Its collection spans the 15th to 20th centuries and includes a number of extraordinary early primitives by painters such as Hieronymus Bosch, Sint Jans, and the van Eycks, as well as Bruegel the Elder and van Scorel. Later painters, including Rubens and Van Dyck, are also represented. Rembrandt's portrait of his son Titus is part of the collection, as are prints and drawings by Dürer, da Vinci, and later artists such as Cézanne and Picasso. Add to this a remarkable collection of Impressionist, surrealist, and contemporary art, and as the final fillip, a fine collection of objects that includes glassware, silverware, and earthenware. ⊠ *Museumpark 18–20,* ☎ *010/441–9400.* ☒ *Fl 7.50.* ☉ *Tues.–Sat. 10–5, Sun. and holidays 11–5.*

Fittingly, for a city of exciting modern architecture, Rotterdam is the site of the **Nederlands Architectuurinstituut** (Netherlands Architectural Institute). The eyebrow-raising glass and metal building hosts changing exhibits on architecture and interior design. ⊠ *Museumpark 25,* ☎ *010/440–1200.* ☒ *Fl 7.50.* ☉ *Tues.–Sat. 10–5, Sun. 11–5.*

The **Kunsthal** hosts all manner of major temporary exhibitions—from an Andy Warhol retrospective to rows of compact cars—in a massive, multistoried exhibition center, built in 1992. ⊠ *Westzeedijk 341,* ☎ *010/440–0300.* ☒ *Fl 10.* ☉ *Tues.–Sat. 10–5, Sun. 11–5.*

Delfshaven, the last remaining nook of old Rotterdam, has rows of gabled houses lining the waterfront, and even a windmill. Today Delfshaven is an up-and-coming area of trendy galleries, cafés, and restaurants.

☾ The **Euromast** tower, more than 600 feet high, not only affords panoramic views of Rotterdam Harbor but also packs in a number of other attractions. The most exciting is the Space Cabin at the tip of the tower, in which you can experience the sensation of a rocket launch. ⊠ *Parkhaven 20,* ☎ *010/436–4811.* ☒ *Fl 14.50.* ☉ *Apr.–June and Sept., daily 10–7; Oct.–Mar., daily 10–5; July–Aug., Tues.–Sat. 10 AM–10:30 PM, Sun.–Mon. 10–7.*

The charming old city of **Dordrecht,** at the busiest river junction in Europe, has medieval town gates, a 15th-century church with a leaning tower, and an 18th-century period house museum. It is the oldest town in Holland, given its charter in 1220. ⊠ *23 km (15 mi) southeast of Rotterdam.*

Dining and Lodging

$$$$ ✕ **Raden Mas of Rotterdam.** At this elegant and exotically decorated Indonesian restaurant, rijsttafel is served both traditional style (from a number of small dishes) and Asian style (all on your plate from the kitchen). Among the traditional elements of a rijsttafel, you will find *sate* (a kebob of chicken or pork in peanut sauce), *gado-gado* (Asian vegetables), and *sambal* (a red-pepper condiment that is very, very hot). ⊠ *Kruiskade 72,* ☎ *010/411–7244. AE, DC, MC, V.*

$$$ ✕ **La Gondola.** In this Italian restaurant there is a picture wall that reads like a history of modern pop music. Directly across from the Rotterdam Hilton, where pop stars tend to stay, it is a relaxing, friendly place with a good selection of traditional Italian specialties. ⊠ *Kruiskade 6,* ☎ *010/411–4284. Reservations essential. Jacket required. AE, DC, MC, V.*

$$–$$$ ✕ **Het Heerenhuys De Heuvel.** Resplendent beside a lake in the city's Maas Park, this airy 19th-century mansion has one of the most attractive locations—and the sunniest terrace—in town. In one wing is a restaurant serving such curiosities as lamb with anchovy butter; in the other is a café offering simpler fare. ⊠ *Baden-Powellaan 12,* ☎ *010/436–4249. AE, DC, MC, V.*

$$–$$$ ✕ **Millers.** This restaurant in attractive Delfshaven is in a converted warehouse dating from 1620. There's a spacious bistro downstairs for drinks and light meals, and intimate nooks under the rafters upstairs for dining by candlelight. There is also a small canal-side terrace. The menu includes such delights as snapper cooked in saffron, and marinated swordfish. ⊠ *Voorhaven 3,* ☎ *010/477–5181. AE, DC, MC, V.*

$$$$ ✕⊡ **Rotterdam Hilton.** Don't be surprised if you run into Mick Jagger or Diana Ross if you stay here. This is the hotel of choice for many of the pop and rock performers who bring their tours to Holland; it provides top facilities, a number of suites, a fine restaurant, and luxury appointments and amenities. It also has one of the best downtown locations in Rotterdam. ⊠ *Weena 10,* ☎ *010/414–4044,* FAX *010/411–8884. 247 rooms, 7 suites. Restaurant, bar, café, barbershop, beauty salon, dance club, parking (fee). AE, DC, MC, V.*

$$$–$$$$ ✕⊡ **Park Hotel.** An old town house and a glittering metallic skyscraper are yoked together to form an elegant hotel. The rooms are tastefully furnished in a modern style and most offer panoramic views of the city. It is a few minutes' walk to the Boymans-van Beuningen Museum, and the staff offer the sort of apparently effortless, unobtrusive attention to your every need that makes a stay here a delight. The restaurant nicely balances nouvelle with traditional selections. ⊠ *Westersingel 70,* ☎ *010/436–3611,* FAX *010/436–4212, 189 rooms. Restaurant, bar, lobby lounge, sauna, exercise room, free parking. AE, DC, MC, V.*

$–$$ ✕⊡ **Hotel New York.** The twin towers rising over the water of the Nieuwe Maas, across from the city center, for decades were known to Rotterdammers as the headquarters of the Holland-America Line. In 1993, the old building was renovated and opened as a hotel. Rooms are individually decorated and modern. The enormous restaurant (it seats 400) somehow maintains an intimate, café atmosphere, and the fine, eclectic cuisine attracts Rotterdam's fashionable set. ⊠ *Koninginnenhoofd 1,* ☎ *010/486–2066,* FAX *010/484–2701. 73 rooms. Restaurant, exercise room, meeting rooms. AE, DC, MC, V.*

$ ✕⊡ **Hotel van Walsum.** On a residential boulevard within walking distance of the Boymans-van Beuningen Museum, Hotel van Walsum is not far from the Euromast. The gregarious owner proudly restores and re-equips his rooms, floor by floor, on a continuously rotating basis, with the always-modern decor of each floor determined by that year's best buys in furniture, carpeting, and bathroom tiles. There is a bar-lounge and a small restaurant that has a summer garden extension. ⊠ *Mathenesserlaan 199–201,* ☎ *010/436–3275,* FAX *010/436–4410. 25 rooms. Restaurant, café. AE, DC, MC, V.*

$$$ ⊡ **Hotel Inntel Rotterdam.** All the rooms in this modern high-rise, built at the opening to the Leuvehaven inner harbor in 1990, have water views, as do the restaurant and the rooftop health club. ⊠ *Leuvehaven 80,* ☎ *010/413–4139,* FAX *010/413–3222. 150 rooms. Restaurant, café, indoor pool, sauna. AE, DC, MC, V.*

Nightlife and the Arts

You can book tickets and find out what's on around town through Uit Promotie Rotterdam (☎ 010/413–6540) or VVV Rotterdam (☎ 06/3403–4065). The free publication *Inside Out,* available in many cafés, also has listings of what's on.

CAFÉS

Café De Heuvel (⊠ Baden-Powellaan 12, ☎ 010/436–4249), in the middle of Het Park beside the Maas River, has a busy terrace, casual café, and smart restaurant. **Carrera** (⊠ Karel Doormanstraat 10–12, ☎ 010/213–0534) attracts a fashionable young crowd and has an all-night French terrace serving snacks. **De Consul** (⊠ Westersingel 28B, ☎ 010/436–3323) offers movies, New Age and pop music. **Hallo** (⊠ Stadhuisplein 43, ☎ 010/414–6400) has a well-stocked bar and an intimate dance floor and plays a wide range of music. A big dance floor and great live music make **Nighttown** (⊠ West Kruiskade 28, ☎ 010/436–4534) *the* place to be in Rotterdam. There are frequent special party nights.

CLASSICAL MUSIC

In Rotterdam, the concert orchestra is the fine **Rotterdam Philharmonic Orchestra,** which performs at the large concert hall **Concert-en Congresgebouw de Doelen** (✉ Kruisstraat 2/Schouwburgplein 50, ☎ 010/217–1700).

DANCE

Rotterdam's resident modern dance company, **Scapino Ballet** has the reputation of being one of the most formidably talented troupes in the country. They perform at **Rotterdamse Schouwburg** (✉ Schouwburgplein 25, ☎ 010/411–8110), which was designed by Dutch architect Wim Quist.

FILM

In addition to the annual avant-garde **Film Festival Rotterdam** (☎ 010/413–6540), Rotterdam offers mixed media and film performances at **Lantaren/Venster** (✉ Gouvernestraat 129–133, ☎ 010/436–1311) and has a special publication for film listings titled *Cargo,* available in bars, cafés, and some shops.

GAY BARS

Very much part of the late-night scene, **Gay Palace** (✉ Schiedamnsesingel 139, ☎ 010/414–1486) attracts crowds of young gay Rotterdammers to its large dance floor. New on Rotterdam's gay scene is **d'Groove** (✉ Westblaak 81, ☎ 010/414–8796). It plays the latest club music and is already attracting gay Rotterdam celebrities.

JAZZ

In August the **Heineken Jazz Festival** (☎ 010/413–3972) fills Rotterdam's streets and cafés with music and bopping youth. **De Twijfelaar** (✉ Mauritsstraat 173, ☎ 010/413–2671) is a cozy, friendly place with jazz sessions on Wednesday. **Dizzy** (✉ 's Gravendijkswal 127A, ☎ 010/477–3014) is a jazz café with a big terrace out back that has performances by Dutch and international musicians every Tuesday and Sunday.

POP AND ROCK

When the big stars come to Rotterdam, they perform either at the **Sportpaleis Ahoy** (✉ Zuiderparkweg 20–30, ☎ 010/410–4204) or at the major soccer stadium, **Feyenoord Stadion** (✉ Van Zandvlietplein 1, ☎ 010/492–9499 or 010/492–9444).

THEATER

The leading theater company of Rotterdam is **RO-theatergroup,** which performs (mainly in Dutch) at the new **Rotterdamse Schouwburg** (✉ Schouwburgplein 25, ☎ 010/411–8110). **Cabaret and musicals** in Rotterdam are performed at **Luxor Theater** (✉ Kruiskade 10, ☎ 010/413–8326).

Outdoor Activities and Sports

BIKING

You can rent bicycles in Rotterdam from the **Rijwiel Shop** (✉ Stationsplein 1, ☎ 010/412–6220).

MARATHON

Run in late April each year (in close time proximity to both the Boston and London marathons), the **City of Rotterdam Marathon** is the major European running event of the year, where world records are routinely broken.

SOCCER

Rotterdam's Feyenoord (pronounced *fie*-nord) team is one of the best in the country and plays at **Feyenoord Stadion** (✉ Van Zandvlietplein 1, ☎ 010/492–9499 or 010/492–9444).

Shopping

Late shopping in Rotterdam is on Friday. An antiques, curiosities, and general market is held on Mariniersweg on Tuesday and Saturday, 9–5, and the stamp, coin, and book market on Grotekerkplein is on Tuesday and Saturday, 9:30–4; there is also a Sunday market at Schiedamsedijk April through September, 11–5.

Utrecht

⑤⑤ *Utrecht is 58 km (36 mi) northeast of Rotterdam, and 40 km (25 mi) southeast of Amsterdam.*

Birthplace of the 16th-century pope Adrian VI, the only Dutch pope, Utrecht has been a powerful bishopric since the 7th century and is still a major religious center. It was here that the Dutch Republic established in 1579 with the signing of the Union of Utrecht. Although the surrounding city is among the busiest and most modern in the Netherlands, the central core of Utrecht retains a historic character, particularly along its two main canals. If you arrive by train, you might be forgiven for thinking that Utrecht is one enormous covered shopping mall: The railway station is surrounded by the biggest mall in the country.

There are pleasant views up and down the **Oude Gracht** (Old Canal), which winds through the central shopping district. The unique feature of this lively esplanade is that there are upper and lower levels, with shops opening onto the street level, restaurants and cafés opening onto the walkway that is just above water level. The best place to begin a tour of the historic city center is from the bridge that connects Lange Viestraat to Potterstraat just beyond Vredenburg Square.

NEED A BREAK?	For a tasty lunch, visit **De Soepterrine** (✉ Zakkendragerssteeg 40, ☎ 030/231-7005), a snug restaurant that serves bowls of steaming homemade soups and hefty salads. Some 10 varieties of soup are made daily, including the traditional Dutch *erwtensoep* (thick pea soup). Soups come with crusty bread and herb butter.

An old church houses one of the most delightful museums in the Netherlands, the **Rijksmuseum van Speelklok tot Pierement** (National Museum from Musical Clock to Street Organ). It is a happy place filled with ticking clocks, music boxes, player pianos, and traditional Dutch barrel organs. To find the museum, follow the Oude Gracht to Steenweg and follow the signs. ✉ *Buurkerkhof 10,* ☎ *030/231–2789.* ⊡ *Fl 7.50.* ☉ *Tues.–Sat. 10–5, Sun. and public holidays 1–5; guided tours every hr.*

Take a deep breath and prepare to tackle the 465 steps of the **Domtoren** (Dom Tower), located at the Oude Gracht and the Zadelstraat bridge. Climbing the highest church tower in the Netherlands (367 feet tall) is well worth the effort for the panoramic view of the city and surrounding countryside of Utrecht province. Built in the late 14th century, the stone tower was originally the bell tower of a cathedral that was destroyed in a hurricane late in the 17th century (the outline of its nave can still be seen in the paving squares of the Domplein). Soaring lancet windows add to the impression of majestic height. ✉ *Domplein,* ☎ *030/231–0403.* ⊡ *Fl 4.* ☉ *Apr.–Nov., weekdays 10–5, weekends and public holidays noon–5; Dec.–Mar., weekends and public holidays noon–5. View by tour only; last tour at 4.*

Holding its own against the imposing Domtoren across the square, the grand Gothic **Domkerk** (Dom Church) was built in the 13th and 14th centuries and designed after the pattern of the Tournai Cathedral in Belgium. It has five chapels radiating around the ambulatory of the chancel, as well as a number of funerary monuments, including that of a 14th-century bishop. The 15th-century cloister garden adjacent to the Dom Church, the **Pandhof** (House Garden), is planted with herbs and offers a peaceful respite. ⊠ *Domplein,* ☎ *030/231–0403.* 🎫 *Free; guided tours Fl 4.* ☉ *May–Sept., weekdays 10–5, Sat. 10–3:30, Sun. 2–4; Oct.–Apr., weekdays 11–4, weekends 2–4.*

Het Catharijneconvent, a vast and comprehensive museum of religious history and sacred art, occupies a former convent near the Nieuwe Gracht (New Canal). There are magnificent altarpieces, ecclesiastical garments, manuscripts, sculptures, paintings, and the country's primary collection of medieval art. ⊠ *Nieuwegracht 63,* ☎ *030/231–7296.* 🎫 *Fl 7.* ☉ *Tues.–Fri. 10–5, weekends and public holidays 11–5.*

Primarily dedicated to painting and the decorative arts, the **Centraal Museum** contains collections of costumes, coins, and medals, as well as an archaeological section. The paintings here include excellent works from the 16th-century Utrecht School, reflecting the strong Italian influence on painters such as van Scorel, van Heemskerk, and Terbrugghen. There are also examples of the 20th-century Dutch de Stijl movement, perhaps best known to the rest of the world through the straight black lines and blocks of primary colors seen in the paintings of Mondrian. ⊠ *Agnietenstraat 1,* ☎ *030/231–7296.* 🎫 *Fl 6.* ☉ *Tues.–Sat. 11–5, Sun. and public holidays noon–5.*

The **Rietveld–Schroder House** exemplifies several key principles of the de Stijl movement that affected not only art, but modern architecture, furniture design, and even typography in the early part of the 20th century. The house was designed for the Schroder family by Gerrit Rietveld (one of the leading architects of De Stijl), who is best known outside the Netherlands for his design of a brightly painted, angular chair. The open plan, the direct communion with nature from every room, and the use of neutral white or gray on large surfaces, with primary colors to identify linear details, are typical de Stijl characteristics. The house is just a few blocks away from the Centraal Museum. ⊠ *Prins Hendriklaan 50A,* ☎ *030/332–6310. Reservations essential.* 🎫 *Fl 9 (includes guided tour).* ☉ *Wed.–Sat. 11–5.*

Dining and Lodging

$$$–$$$$ ✕ **Het Grachtenhuys.** There is the feeling of being in a gracious home at this restaurant in a canal house that overlooks the fashionable New Canal. The young owners offer a choice of four- or five-course menus of French-influenced Dutch cuisine. Tempting selections might include rabbit fillet with a puree of various nuts, or truffle and potato soup with smoked eel. ⊠ *Nieuwegracht 33,* ☎ *030/231–7494. Reservations essential. AE, DC, MC, V. Closed Mon. No lunch.*

$$ ✕ **De Zakkendrager.** Students, concert goers from the nearby Vredenburg Music Centre, and come fashionable young locals come here for generous grills smothered in scrumptious sauces. The restaurant is cozy, friendly, and informal. Outside, in the tiny walled garden, a 175-year-old beech tree towers over all. ⊠ *Zakkendragerstraat 22-26,* ☎ *030/231–7578. AE, DC, MC, V. Closed Mon.*

$$ ✕ **Polman's Huis.** This grand café of the old school is a Utrecht institution. Its Jugendstil/Art Deco interior is authentic. Other reasons to find your way to Polman's are its relaxing atmosphere and range of meal choices, from a simple quiche to a steamed fish dinner. ⊠ *Keistraat 2,* ☎ *030/231–3368. Reservations not accepted. MC, V. Closed Dec. 25.*

$$$ 🏨 **Holiday Inn.** Primarily a business hotel (it looks like an office building), it serves visitors to the convention and exhibition hall next door and makes a convenient choice for other travelers as well. It has the

only hotel swimming pool in town. ⊠ *Jaarbeursplein 24,* ☎ *030/291–0555,* FAX *030/294–3999. 280 rooms. Restaurant, bar, exercise room. AE, DC, MC, V.*

\$\$ 🔄 **Hotel Smits.** On the main square between the station and the old city center, this medium-size hotel has all the comforts of the larger, business-oriented establishments. The rooms are bright, comfortable, and decorated in soothing plum and burgundy. ⊠ *Vredenburg 14,* ☎ *030/233–1232,* FAX *030/232–8451. 85 rooms. Restaurant, bar, no-smoking rooms. AE, DC, MC, V.*

\$–\$\$ 🔄 **Malie Hotel.** On a quiet residential street in a 19th-century row house, ★ this is a modern and attractive family hotel. Rooms are brightly decorated, though simply furnished. The bar-lounge doubles as a small art gallery. ⊠ *Maliestraat 2–4,* ☎ *030/231–6424,* FAX *030/234–0661. 29 rooms with bath. Bar. AE, DC, MC, V.*

\$ 🔄 **Hotel Ouwi.** A convivial family hotel, it is just off one of the main transit routes to the city center. The rooms are tight and simple in furnishings and decor, but they're very clean and tidy. ⊠ *F.C. Dondersstraat 12,* ☎ *030/271–6303,* FAX *030/271–4619. 24 rooms, 18 with bath/shower. No credit cards.*

Nightlife and the Arts

Contact the VVV tourist information office in Utrecht (⊠ Vredenburg 90, ☎ 06/3403–4085) for both schedules and ticket information. *Uit in Utrecht* is a free publication, available at various venues and cafés, that will let you know what is happening in Utrecht.

CAFÉS

Het Oude Pothuis (⊠ Oude Gracht 279, ☎ 030/318970) has both music and meals six nights a week, plus a stage with instruments available for jam sessions. **Polman's Huis** (⊠ Keistraat 2, ☎ 030/231–3368) attracts a lively crowd of students and thirty-somethings.

DANCE

In Utrecht you will find dance on the programs of **Stadsschouwburg** (⊠ Lucas Bolwerk 24, ☎ 030/232–4125), which has a major performance hall as well as the Blauwe Zaal (Blue Room) for small productions.

DISCO AND DANCING

Fellini (⊠ Stadshuisbrug 3, ☎ 030/231–7271) is a popular rock and dancing club in the cellars of the old town hall. **Trianon Union Salsa** (⊠ Oudegracht 252, ☎ 030/233–1154) is a hot 'n' jumping salsa club that organizes great weekend parties. On some nights there are salsa classes earlier in the evening before the party starts.

GAY AND LESBIAN

De Roze Wolk (⊠ Oude Gracht 45, ☎ 030/232–2066) is a cozy canalside gay and lesbian bar with a friendly atmosphere and a dance space in the cellar.

JAZZ AND BLUES

Zeezicht (⊠ Nobelstraat 2, ☎ 030/319957) is a crowded bar that resonates with jazz and blues on Tuesday.

MUSIC

Utrecht is the site of an exceptionally good **Festival of Early Music** (☎ 030/236–2236) late in summer each year. It also offers a full program of concerts in its fine churches, including the Dom Church (☎ 030/231–0403), St. Peter's Church (☎ 030/231–1485), and St. Catharine's Church (☎ 030/231–4030 or 030/231–8526); and there are programs including both concerts and master classes in the Conservatory of the **K&W-gebouw/Arts and Sciences Building** (⊠ Mariaplaats 27, ☎ 030/231–4044).

Visiting opera companies and talented local musicians keep up a high standard at the **Stadsschouwburg** (⊠ Lucas Bolwerk 24, ☎ 030/232–4125).

Outdoor Activities and Sports

You can rent a bike from **Rijwiel Shop** (⊠ Centraal Station Utrecht, ☎ 030/311159) and **Verleun and Co.** (⊠ Van Bijnkershoeklaan 413, ☎ 030/936368).

The sports center **De Vechtsebanen** (⊠ Mississippidreef 151, ☎ 030/627878) offers bowling, badminton, volleyball, squash, curling, and a number of other sports; there is a small running track, as well as both indoor and outdoor tennis courts and ice-skating rinks.

Both tennis and squash are available at the **De Vechtsebanen** (☞ Sports Complex, *above*).

Shopping

Late shopping night in Utrecht is Thursday. A general market is held at Vredenburg on Wednesday 9–5 and Saturday 8–5; the antiques market at the Ossekop (⊠ Voorstraat 19) is Saturday 9–5; flowers and plants are sold at Janskerkhof on Saturday 7–4, and by the Old Canal on Saturday 8–5; there is a health-food market at Vredenburg on Friday noon–6; and a flea market at Waterstraat on Saturday 8–2.

Metropolitan Holland and The Hague A to Z

Arriving and Departing

N5/A5 goes to Haarlem from Amsterdam (from there N208 leads through the bulb district to Leiden); to reach Leiden, The Hague, Delft, and Rotterdam directly from Amsterdam, take E19 via Amsterdam Schiphol Airport; to continue to Utrecht from Rotterdam, take A15 and then the A27, or to reach Utrecht directly from Amsterdam, take E25. Take E30/A12 from The Hague to Utrecht to bypass the congestion of Rotterdam.

Getting about by rail is the ideal means of intercity transport in the Metropolitan area. Trains are fast, frequent, clean, and reliable, and stations in all towns are centrally located, usually within walking distance of major sights.

Intercity express trains (☎ 06/9292) run twice an hour between Amsterdam and Leiden, The Hague, and Rotterdam; and four times an hour between Amsterdam and Haarlem and Utrecht. To get to Delft from Amsterdam, change trains in The Hague. Four trains an hour also run between The Hague and Rotterdam, and three per hour between The Hague and Utrecht, and Rotterdam and Utrecht.

There are two **railway stations** in The Hague: one in the central business district and the other in the residential area. For reasons that have more to do with politics than practicality, trains from Amsterdam do *not* stop at the central station, which means you must either change trains in Leiden to disembark directly at the central station or take a bus from the high station into the center.

Getting Around

BY BICYCLE

Bicycles can be rented at railway stations or by contacting local rental facilities. In this flat land, a bicycle is an ideal means of getting around, and cities have safe cycle lanes on busy roads.

BY BUS OR TRAM

In combination with trains, the efficient system of buses and trams in the Metropolitan area will easily take care of most of your transportation needs. Bus service is available in all cities in this region, and trams run in The Hague, between Delft and The Hague, in Rotterdam, and in Utrecht; Rotterdam also has an excellent underground metro system with two major lines (east–west and north–south) that extend into the suburbs and cross in the city center for easy transfers from one to the other. For information on public transportation (trains, buses, trams, and ferries) in all major Dutch cities, call 06/9292 from anywhere in the country.

BY TAXI

Taxis are available at railway stations, at major hotels, and, in larger cities, at taxi stands in key locations. Call to order a taxi in Delft (☎ 015/262–0621), Haarlem (☎ 023/515–1515), The Hague (☎ 070/390–7722), Leiden (☎ 071/521–2144), Rotterdam (☎ 010/462–6060 or 010/425–7000), or Utrecht (☎ 030/251–5151 or 030/233–1122).

Contacts and Resources

EMERGENCIES

National Emergency Alarm Number for police, fire, and ambulance: ☎ 06/112.

GUIDED TOURS

In Leiden, **Jaap Slingerland** (☎ 071/541–3183) runs 3½-hour boat trips, including a windmill cruise, every summer afternoon except Saturday from the *haven* (harbor) across the Braassemer Lake and the Kager Lakes; the fare is Fl 17.50. In July and August there are day trips across Braassemer Lake to visit the bird and recreation center, **Avifauna** (☎ 0172/487–575), in Alphen aan den Rijn; the cost is Fl 7.50, plus admission to the park, Fl 9.50. In The Hague, a **Royal Tour** (☎ 06/340–35051) that takes in the palaces and administrative buildings associated with Queen Beatrix operates April through September; the cost is Fl 27.50. The **Rotterdam Tourist Hopper** (✉ Coolsingel, ☎ 06/3403–4065) is available twice daily from May through September: Fl 14.50. The best way to see Rotterdam's waterfront is by boat. **Spido Harbor Tours** (✉ Willemsplein, ☎ 010/413–5400) offers excursions lasting from just over an hour to a full day. In Utrecht, carriages drawn by Gelderland horses tour the city on weekends, April through October. Another option in Utrecht is the **Walkman Tour,** available from the tourist office (✉ Vredenburg 90, ☎ 06/340–34805) for Fl 5.

HOSPITAL EMERGENCY ROOMS

Delft (✉ R. De Graafweg 3–11, ☎ 015/260–3060). **Haarlem** (✉ Velserstraat 19, ☎ 023/522–4466). **The Hague** (✉ Bronovolaan 5, ☎ 070/312–4141). **Leiden** (✉ Rijnsburgerweg 10, ☎ 071/526–9111). **Rotterdam** (✉ Dr. Molewaterplein 40, ☎ 010/463–9222). **Utrecht** (✉ Heidelberglaan 100, ☎ 030/250–9111).

LATE-NIGHT PHARMACIES

Delft (☎ 015/212–1568). **Haarlem** (☎ 023/531–9148). **The Hague** (☎ 070/345–1000). **Rotterdam** (☎ 010/411–0370). **Utrecht** (☎ 030/244–1228). Pharmacies stay open late on a rotating basis. Call for addresses on a given night.

VISITOR INFORMATION

VVV Delft (⊠ Markt 85, ☎ 015/212–6100) is open April–September, weekdays 9–6, Saturday 9–5, Sunday 10–3; October–March, weekdays 9–5:30, Saturday 9–5. **VVV Haarlem** (⊠ Stationsplein 1, 2011 LR, ☎ 06/320–24043, FAX 023/534–0537) is open April–September, Monday–Saturday 9–5:30; October–March, weekdays 9–5:30, Saturday 9–4. **The Hague Information Office** (⊠ Koningin Julianaplein 30, Babylon shopping center, ☎ 06/340–35051) is open Monday–Saturday 9–5:30 and Sunday, July–August, 10–5. **Scheveningen Information Office** (⊠ Gevers Deynootweg 1134, Palace shopping center Promenade, ☎ 070/354–6200) is open January–mid-April and October–December, Monday–Saturday 9–5:30; mid-April–June and September, Monday–Saturday 10–6:30, Sunday 10–5; July–August, Monday–Saturday 10–8, Sunday 10–5. **VVV Leiden** (⊠ Stationsplein 210, ☎ 071/514–6846) is open weekdays 9–5:30 and Saturday 9–4. **VVV Rotterdam** (⊠ Coolsingel 67, ☎ 06/340–34065, FAX 010/413–0124) is open Monday–Thursday 9–7, Friday 9–9, Saturday 9–7, and Sunday 10–5. **VVV Utrecht** (⊠ Vredenburg 90, ☎ 06/340–34085, FAX 030/233–1544) is open weekdays 9–6, Saturday 9–4.

THE BORDER PROVINCES AND MAASTRICHT

The long border between the Netherlands and Belgium runs like a drunkard's test path from the North Sea coast to the German frontier. The shared heritage of religion, architecture, food, and lifestyle makes Brussels as alluring as Amsterdam to the residents of the southern provinces of the Netherlands: These southern Dutch are more gregarious and outspoken than those of the north; they also pursue the good life of food, drink, and conviviality with more gusto, and less guilt, than their Calvinist-influenced countrymen who live "above the Great Rivers." When Amsterdammers want to spend a weekend eating well and being pampered in elegant hotels, they think first of the southern provinces of their own country. The freshness of Zeeland shellfish and the Burgundian lifestyle and French kitchens of the border provinces make for restaurants of exceptional quality, and Limburg's castles are often the site of luxurious hotels.

Three provinces hug the Belgian border: Zeeland (Sea Land) is a collection of flat, open, and windswept islands and peninsulas, known for its agriculture and shellfish; Noord Brabant, also known simply as Brabant, is a wooded and water-laced industrial area bordered on both east and north by the river Maas; Limburg is a region of hills and half-timbered farmhouses that extends along the river Maas deep into the south. The capital city of the region, Maastricht nestles in a peninsula surrounded on one side by Belgium and the other by Germany. This sophisticated small city is a mecca for goods from all over Europe, drawing merchants and shoppers from as far as Amsterdam, Brussels, and Cologne.

Pleasures and Pastimes

The Border Provinces, and especially the tongue of land around Maastricht, offer an atmosphere quite different from the rest of the Netherlands. You'll find hills and castles here, and a cosmopolitan population whose cuisine and way of life reflect influences from across the borders of Belgium and Germany.

CARNIVAL CAPERS

In February, in a last fling of indulgence before Lent, the Catholics of the south throw a Carnival. The villages elect a Prince in November who leads the revels for the four days prior to Ash Wednesday. Most towns have parades (the most spectacular are in Maastricht and Den Bosch) and people in cafés party all night. On the streets, revelers guzzle pancakes and *nonnevotten* (deep-fried doughballs) to ward off the cold. Visitors are made especially welcome, whirled up into the merrymaking in no time at all.

DINING

Most Netherlanders agree that the best food to be had in their country is found "south of the rivers"—from the fat, succulent oysters and mussels of Zeeland to the French- and German-influenced cuisine of Limburg (around Maastricht). *Limburg vla,* a delicious custard flan, appears on dessert menus all over the country but is tastiest on home turf. The mushrooms and asparagus that grow in Limburg are superb and serve as both ingredient and inspiration for those master chefs in their hillside château restaurants.

LODGING

The castles of the south are more akin to French châteaux or British stately homes than to the rock-solid, fortified edifices of Germany. Many an elegant *kasteel* has been converted into a hotel, and not all of them are pricey. Most, though, do belong in the upper price brackets, but these usually come with top-class restaurants and are incomparably romantic. If you are on a limited budget, save this part of the Netherlands for your extravagant blow-out.

WATERY WAYS

That much of the Netherlands is land reclaimed from the water is nowhere so evident as in the Zeeland, a patchwork of rivers, estuaries, and islands. You can brace yourself against the breezes on the North Sea with windsurfing and sailing, or opt for the quieter pleasures of bird-watching, canoeing around the backwaters of the Oosterdchelde or Westerschelde, or exploring small riverside towns. Alternatively, you can park yourself on a peaceful river bank for a day's fishing. If you prefer a little drama, head for Delta Expo, where the the Dutch struggle against the rising waters is revealed in a waterworks exhibition.

Exploring the Border Provinces and Maastricht

Zeeland, in the southwestern part of the Netherlands, is almost entirely taken up by sprawling estuaries. Travel in this area is often circuitous, along many bridges and dikes. As you head eastward, the land begins to undulate until, in Limburg (around Maastricht), the terrain becomes—for the Netherlands at least—quite hilly. Since Maastricht is situated on a slip of land that juts far down into Belgium and Germany, you can reach it faster by going from Zeeland directly across Belgium. Not only is this quicker, but you can stop off for a look at Antwerp along the way.

Great Itineraries

The border provinces are spread out, so allow yourself at least a week to really get a feel for the area. Otherwise, concentrate on the eastern and western extremes of the region—Zeeland and Maastricht.

Numbers in the text correspond to numbers in the margin and on the Border Provinces and Maastricht maps.

IF YOU HAVE 3 DAYS

Start your visit wandering through the old cobblestone streets of the pretty port of **Zierikzee** ㊋, and then head off across the water to the marvels of the waterworks exhibition at **Delta Expo** ㊌. There's just enough of the day left to visit the historic abbey at 🎖 **Middelburg** ㊎ before retiring for the night. Next day make a brief detour through

Veere ⑤⑧, one of the most beautiful villages in the country, then lunch on fresh mussels from the farms at Yerseke. Cut through Belgium to spend the night at ☷ **Maastricht** ⑥③, so that you can spend all of day three visiting its excellent museums and handsome churches.

IF YOU HAVE 5 DAYS

After a visit to **Zierikzee** ⑤⑥ and the **Delta Expo** ⑤⑦, take time off to putter about the waterways or try your hand at windsurfing. Then head for bed in ☷ **Middelburg** ⑤⑨. Next day, explore Middelburg's ancient abbey and check out the traditional costumes in the local museum, and make a round-trip to **Veere** ⑤⑧ and Yerseke. On day three, travel up to ☷ **'s-Hertogenbosch** ⑥① to triple your cholesterol count with a scrumptious *Bossche bol* cream-puff pastry in the shadow of the Gothic St. Janskathedraal. If you like modern art, stop off on the fourth day to view the magnificent collection at the Van Abbemuseum in **Eindhoven** ⑥②, before heading off to ☷ **Maastricht** ⑥③, where visiting museums, whiling away time in historic squares, and viewing churches can easily take up the rest of your time.

IF YOU HAVE 7 DAYS

Check in at ☷ **Veere** ⑤⑧, and use this as a base for two days of exploration and watersports around **Zierikzee** ⑤⑥ and the Oosterschelde, visiting the **Delta Expo** ⑤⑦. Transfer to ☷ **Middelburg** ⑤⑨ for your second night, and spend the third day exploring the town before traveling to ☷ **Breda** ⑥⓪, perhaps stopping along the way for a feast of mussels at Yerseke. After a quick look around Breda's attractive Old Town, head up to ☷ **'s-Hertogenbosch** ⑥①. Next day, stop off in **Eindhoven** ⑥② to view the modern art in the Abbemuseum. Then head south to the hills, and for your last three days, book into one of the castle hotels near ☷ **Maastricht** ⑥③. Spend your time exploring the city, visiting other castles in the area, or rent a bike for country jaunts (it's not *that* hilly).

When to Tour Maastricht and the Border Provinces

The region is at its liveliest at Carnival time, the few days leading up to Ash Wednesday (usually in mid-February). Gourmets come in the summer for the asparagus season (early May to June 24). The mussels season (mid-August to April) usually starts off with parties in village squares around Zeeland, where you'll find steaming cauldrons boiling up as many mussels as you can eat.

Zeeland: The Land of the Sea

On the fingerlike peninsulas and islands of the province of Zeeland you are never more than a few miles from a major body of water. You also are never more than a few inches above sea level, if you are above it at all: Floods have put this province almost completely under water on several occasions, most recently in 1953. Today, major dikes, dams, and bridges connect the four chief islands and peninsulas of Zeeland, guarding against the possibility of the sea's reclaiming the land already reclaimed by the Dutch.

Zierikzee

⑤⑥ *67 km (40 mi) southwest of Rotterdam.*

Traveling south from Rotterdam across the islands and frail peninsulas, following A29 to N59, you come to the small old city of Zierikzee, a yachting port with an attractive Old Town, cobblestone streets, three historic gateways, and a canal connecting it to the open waters of the Oosterschelde. Zierikzee, founded in 849, is reputed to be the best-preserved town in the Netherlands. The chief center of Schouwen-Duiveland, Zierikzee's most spectacular attraction is the great tower of the cathedral, **Sint Lievens Monstertoren,** begun in 1454 but never completed (when it reached 199 feet, the townspeople ran out of money). After Zierikzee, the road crosses the Oosterscheldekering dam, reached by continuing on N59 to Serooskerke, where you can turn onto N57 and over the dam. This dramatic ride may be restricted in times of high winds; the North Sea to one side, the Oosterschelde bay to the other, and the looming storm-surge barriers beside the road remind you that it requires massive constructions of steel and concrete to resist the forces of the sea.

☜ ⑤⑦ **Delta Expo** documents the 2,000-year history of Dutch hydraulic engineering. There are films and slide shows, working scale models, and displays of materials used to construct dikes, dams, and underwater supports. The visit includes a boat trip in good weather, and there is an opportunity to walk inside a sample of one of the multistory pilings that make up the support system of the storm-surge barriers. Delta Expo is on Neeltje Jans Island, which was used as a work island during the 20 years it took to build this massive dam and flood barrier. ⊠ *Eiland Neeltje Jans, Burgh-Haamstede,* ☎ *0111/652–702.* ✍ *Fl 16.50 Apr.–Oct.; Fl 12.50 Nov.–Mar.* ☉ *Apr.–Oct., daily 10–5:30; Nov.–Mar., Wed.–Sun. 10–5:30.*

Veere

★ ⑤⑧ *106 km (67 mi) southwest of Rotterdam, 7 km (4 mi) north of Middelburg.*

One of the prettiest small towns in the Netherlands, Veere is well worth a few hours' stopover to explore its quiet streets and admire its elegant architecture. Now the principal sailing port of the Veerse Meer (Veerse Lake), the town was an important seaport in the 16th century, with a busy trade in items such as wool, linen, and salt. Reach Veere by crossing both the Oosterscheldekering and the Veersegatdam dams and then following the dike road.

Veere's fairy-tale Gothic **Stadhuis** (Town Hall), begun in 1474, sports a facade that harks back to the town's glory days and seems surprisingly grand for the sleepy town of today. The building has a minaret-style tower, added in 1599.

The **Museum De Schotse Huizen** (The Scots' Houses) stands beside 16th-century buildings, facing the town's small inner harbor, that once were the offices and warehouses of Scots wool merchants. Highly ornate, the buildings are named Het Lammetje (The Little Lamb) and De Struys (The Ostrich); you'll know which is which by the facade stones. Inside is a collection of local costumes, porcelain, household items, and paintings. Unfortunately, at press time, the museum was closed due to lack of funding. Although it is expected to reopen in 1997, it is likely to do so with restricted hours. ⊠ *Kaai 25–27, Veere,* ☎ *0118/501–744.*

Outdoor Activities and Sports

SAILING

The lakes and dams of Zeeland are great sailing territory, and there's much fun to be had yachting between the area's attractive small harbors. To arrange a day on the water in Zeeland, contact **Jachtwerf Oostwatering** (⊠ Polredijk 13 B, Veere, ☎ 0118/501–665), **WSVW en RYCB** (⊠ Wolphaartsdijk, ☎ 0113/581–565), **Marina Veere B.V.** (⊠ Kanaalweg wz 5, Veere, ☎ 0118/501–223), or **Jachtwerf Wolphaartsdijk** (⊠ Zandkreekweg 5, Wolphaartsdijk, ☎ 0113/581–562).

The Border Provinces

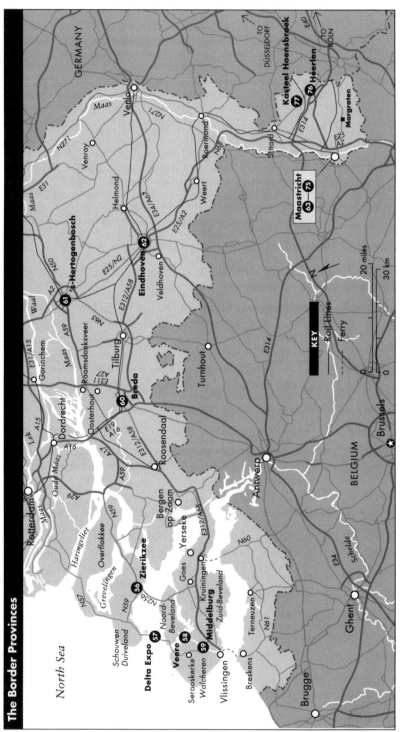

Middelburg

59 *98 km (62 mi) southwest of Rotterdam, 89 km (56 mi) northwest of Antwerp.*

The capital of the province of Zeeland, Middelburg was an important trading post of the Dutch East and West India companies in the 17th century. Today it is a bustling, friendly town that—despite severe bombing during the World War II—preserves many impressive monuments.

A testimony to Middelburg's past grandeur, the elaborately decorated **Stadhuis** (Town Hall) stands resplendent on the market square. Begun in the mid-15th century, it is a showpiece of southern-Dutch Gothic architecture and is adorned with statues of past counts and countesses of Zeeland. ⊠ *Markt,* ☎ *0118/675–450,* 🎫 *Fl 4.* ☉ *Tours Mar.–Oct., Mon.–Sat. 10–5, Sun. noon–5.*

The heart of Middelburg is the 12th-century **Abdij** (Abbey Complex), which incorporates three churches, countless provincial government offices, a major research library, the provincial cultural and historical museum, and a tall tower that overlooks the city and surrounding countryside. Although it was badly damaged in World War II, the entire complex has been faithfully reconstructed. *Onze Lieve Vrouwe Abdij* (Our Beloved Lady Abbey) was founded in 1150 as a Premonstratensian abbey and served as a monastery until 1574. The **Historama,** a multimedia presentation about the design and history of Middelburg and the abbey, includes a 20-minute video in English. ⊠ *Abdij 9,* ☎ *0118/616–851.* 🎫 *Fl 6.* ☉ *Apr.–Nov., Mon.–Sat. 10–6, Sun. noon–6.*

The **Zeeuws Museum** (Zeeland Museum) is best known for its series of tapestries illustrating the major Dutch sea battles with Spain during the 16th century. The varied collection also includes an Egyptian mummy, votive stelae dating from the Roman period, a collection of rare seashells of the Royal Zeeland Science Association, and a costume hall that is one of the best in the Netherlands. The museum is part of the Abdij complex. ⊠ *Abdij,* ☎ *0118/626–655.* 🎫 *Fl 6.* ☉ *Mon.–Sat. 10–5, Sun. noon–5.*

NEED A BREAK? | **Restaurant De Abdij** (⊠ Abdijplein 5, ☎ 0118/635–022 or 0118/636–196) is a convenient place to stop for lunch. Within the Abbey Complex, next to the Zeeuws Museum, it offers sandwiches, salads, and light meals.

Of particular interest to American visitors to Zeeland is the **Roosevelt Studiecentrum** (Roosevelt Study Center), a library, research center, and exhibition hall. Theodore Roosevelt and Franklin Delano Roosevelt were descendants of a Zeeland family; the purpose of this center is to make known the historical links between the United States and the Netherlands and particularly to publicize the role of the United States in Europe during the 20th century. The study center is part of the Abdij complex. ⊠ *Abdij 9,* ☎ *0118/631–590.* 🎫 *Free.* ☉ *Weekdays 10–12:30 and 1:30–4:30.*

You can climb the 207 steps to the top of the octagonal **"Lange Jan" Abdijtoren** ("Long John" Abbey Tower), which is attached to the Choral Church of the Abbey Complex. The stone tower, 280 feet high, was constructed in the 14th century and is topped with an onion-shaped dome from the 18th century. ⊠ *Abdij,* ☎ *0118/682–255.* 🎫 *Fl 3.* ☉ *Apr.–Oct., Mon.–Sat. 10–5, Sun. noon–5.*

Typical buildings and landmarks of the area have been duplicated in 1/20th of actual size in **Miniatuur Walcheren** (Miniature Walcheren), a miniature city in a garden. The skillfully made models include houses, churches, and windmills, and a reconstruction of Veerse Lake with motorized boats. Even the trees and plants are in miniature. This toy town is just a short walk from the Abdij complex. ⊠ *Molenwater, Middelburg, Zeeland,* ☎ *0118/612–525.* ☞ *Fl 11.* ☉ *Daily 10–5 (July–Aug. until 6).*

🔄 The **Remschip de Schorpioen** (Ramship *Scorpion*) is one of only three iron ramming ships of its kind in the world and the oldest surviving Dutch naval vessel. ⊠ *Loskade, Middelburg, Zeeland,* ☎ *0118/639–649.* ☞ *Fl 5.* ☉ *Apr.–Oct., daily 10–5.*

Dining and Lodging

$$$$ ✕ **Het Groot Paradys.** Facing the market square in a house that dates from the mid-16th century, this intimate restaurant retains a traditional town-house decor. Dishes feature ingredients from the region, including delicious oysters. Fresh-baked breads are the pride of the kitchen. ⊠ *Damplein 13,* ☎ *0118/626–764. Reservations essential. Jacket required. AE, DC, MC, V. No lunch Sat.*

$$–$$$$ ✕ **Nolet's Restaurant Het Reymerswale.** After a stroll along the harbor, stop in at the Nolet family's restaurant for a bite. The traditional, beamed, second-floor dining room overlooking the water is spacious and graciously decorated. It has a comfortable lounge area with a fireplace and a summer porch in back. The menu's focus is on seafood, traditionally and simply prepared to finest French standards. In a separate building, with shared kitchen, is an informal bistro. ⊠ *Jachthaven 6,* ☎ *0113/571–642. Reservations essential. AE, DC, MC, V. Closed Feb. and Tues.–Wed.*

$$$$ ✕🏨 **Restaurant Inter Scaldes.** In the past 25 years the owner-chef of this small, gracious country restaurant has regularly earned "best restaurant" awards from the European culinary world for her imaginative use of the products of her region. To accommodate the diners who were traveling from all over the Netherlands and Belgium to sample her French cooking, a luxuriously appointed 12-room *manoir* was added on the far side of the small formal garden beyond the windows of the restaurant. ⊠ *Zandweg 2, 4416 NA in Kruiningen, 35 km (22 mi) from Middelburg,* ☎ *0113/381–753,* 🖷 *0113/381–763. Reservations essential. Jacket and tie. AE, DC, MC, V. Closed Mon.–Tues.*

$–$$ 🏨 **Le Beau Rivage.** This attractive hotel occupies a gabled, brick, turn-of-the-century canal-side building near the city center. The rooms are comfortable and decorated in pale colors with modern prints on the walls; the management is efficient and friendly. ⊠ *Loskade 19, 4331 HW,* ☎ *0118/638–060,* 🖷 *0118/629–673. 9 rooms with shower. Restaurant. AE, MC, V.*

Outdoor Activities and Sports

BEACHES

In the vicinity of Middelburg, you will find the best beaches at **Domburg, Kouderkerke, Oostkapelle, Vrouwenpolder/Serooskerke, Westkapelle,** and **Zoutelande;** all have beach houses to rent, and all but Vrouwenpolder/Serooskerke have beach pavilions.

BIKING

You can rent a bicycle from **Stationsrijwielstalling** (⊠ Kanaalweg 22, ☎ 0118/612–178) or **L. Petiet** (⊠ Kinderdijk 92, ☎ 0118/624–394).

Shopping

Middelburg's market day is Thursday, and the fruit market is held on Saturday. The summer antiques and curiosities market is at the Vismarkt from mid-June through August, Thursday 9–4. Late shopping is on Thursday.

En Route   On your way east to Breda, take time for a quick detour to **Yerseke,** a small fishing port that is the oyster nursery of Europe. Along the waterfront, you'll see lobster boats docked at the piers; below the seawalls, in pits, are the beds in which are nurtured some of the finest, sweetest, and most flavorful oysters and mussels in the world. Peek into the small buildings on the docks and you will see shellfish being sorted and packed for shipment.

Breda

㉒   *96 km (60 mi) east of Middelburg, 147 km (93 mi) northwest of Maastricht.*

In the 15th and 16th centuries Breda was the seat of the powerful Counts of Nassau, ancestors of the present Dutch royal family. Today, dotted with parks, this small city maintains a quiet medieval charm that is unexpected in a city that is also a major manufacturing center.

The **Stadspark Valkenburg** (Valkenburg Park) dates from 1350 and was originally the castle garden of the counts of Breda. The former castle, **Kasteel van Breda** (Breda Castle), sits majestically beyond the moat; it now houses the KMA (Royal Military Academy) and can be visited only on the city walks organized by the VVV during the summer. It's not far from the railroad station.

The imposing 15th- and 16th-century **Grote Kerk** (Great Church), built in the French-influenced Brabant Gothic style in brick and sandstone, was the family church of the House of Orange-Nassau. William of Orange's first wife and child are buried here, as are several of his ancestors. The church was looted of its brass ornamentation when Napoléon's soldiers used it as a barracks. The splendor of the architecture remains, as does the magnificence of the blue-and-gold-painted 18th-century organ. ⊠ *Kerkplein,* ☎ *076/521–8267.* 🎫 *Fl 2.* ☉ *May–Oct., Mon.–Sat. 10–5, Sun. 1–5; Nov.–Apr., weekdays 10–5.*

Breda's **Stadhuis** (Town Hall), which has pride of place on the market square, counts among its treasures a copy of the celebrated Velázquez painting of the surrender of Breda in 1625.

NEED A
BREAK?
   You'll find a good selection of restaurants and cafés surrounding the Grote Markt. **Brasserie-Café Beecker & Wetselaar** (⊠ Grote Markt 45–49, ☎ 076/522-1100), next to the Great Church, is a traditional high-ceilinged café with a brasserie upstairs.

The entrance to the **Begijnhof** (Beguine Court) is several blocks from the Grote Markt, along Catharinastraat, marked by the austere **Waalse Kerk** (Walloon Church). A home for unmarried or widowed lay women who dedicate their lives to prayer and charitable works, this peaceful and attractive courtyard is one of only two remaining cloisters of this type in the Netherlands (the other is in Amsterdam). A fragrant formal herb garden occupies the center of the court, and in one corner is a sculpture of two Beguines. ⊠ *Catharinastraat 83a; Walloon Church information* ☎ *076/541–1303.*

OFF THE
BEATEN PATH
   DE EFTELING – This fairy-tale park offers a wealth of rides and amusements enhanced by the fanciful and witty depiction of classic fairy tales by Dutch artist Anton Pieck. Sleeping Beauty's chest heaves as she breathes, and there are elves and goblins galore. ⊠ *Kaatsheuvel, Brabant,* ☎ *0416/288-111,* 𝖥𝖠𝖷 *0416/288-318.* 🎫 *Fl 32.50.* ☉ *Mid-Apr.–late Oct., daily 10–6; July–Aug., 10–10.*

OFF THE
BEATEN PATH

SAFARIPARK BEEKSE BERGEN – This park is home to hundreds of animals living in an open, naturalistic environment. There is a safari bus to take you through the park, or you can rent your own safari Jeep. There is also a children's farm. ⊠ *Beekse Bergen 1, Hilvarenbeek, Brabant,* ☎ *013/536–0035.* ☞ *Fl 21; Jeep Fl 50 for 1½ hrs.*

Dining and Lodging

$$–$$$ ✕ **Auberge De Arent.** The ceiling murals in this elegant, white, step-gabled 15th-century house, thought to be among the oldest in western Brabant, are of pheasants, rabbits, and snails, all of which are found on the menu in wild season (the fall and winter months). The Arent has a French kitchen, but the adventurous chefs also experiment with piquant sauces and Asian flavors. There is a separate bistro and also a wine cellar with a tasting room. ⊠ *Schoolstraat 2,* ☎ *076/514–4601. Jacket and tie. AE, DC, MC, V. No lunch Sat. Closed Sun.*

$$–$$$ 🏨 **Hotel Mercure.** Next to the railway station in a building that formerly housed the offices of the telephone company, this member of the French hotel chain is a straightforward business hotel with a no-nonsense approach to decorating. Still, rooms are spacious, and the staff exhibits a certain degree of Gallic charm. ⊠ *Stationsplein 14,* ☎ *076/ 522–0200,* ℻ *076/521–4967. 40 rooms. Restaurant, bar. AE, DC, MC, V.*

$$ 🏨 **De Klok.** This small hotel is a busy and friendly part of the lively market square of Breda. There is a café on the street in summer, and a bar and restaurant take up the lobby. Double rooms are generously sized, and beds have *dekbedden* (comforters) to keep you warm. Baths may have shower or tub; some quads are available. ⊠ *Grote Markt 26–28,* ☎ *076/521–4082,* ℻ *076/514–3463. 28 rooms with bath/shower. Bar, café. AE, DC, MC, V.*

Nightlife
The **Holland Casino Breda** (⊠ Bijster 30, ☎ 076/227600) is stylish and offers blackjack, roulette, and other favorites.

Outdoor Activities and Sports
BIKING
To rent a bicycle, contact **Rijwielstalling NS** (⊠ Stationsplein 16–20, ☎ 076/521–0501).

CANOEING AND KAYAKING
The **Biesbosch** area near Breda combines small creeks with stretches of open water (busy with powerboats in the summer season), and the tiny **Dommel River** meanders through the countryside between 's Hertogenbosch and Eindhoven and beyond. To rent a canoe in the Biesbosch area, contact **Nion Watersport** (⊠ Oosterhoutseweg 20, Raamsdonksveer, ☎ 0162/512–997); along the Dommel, contact **Adventure Trips** (⊠ Sint Oedenrode, ☎ 0413/477–267), **De Kanovriend** (⊠ Geenhovensedreef 10, Valkenswaard, ☎ 040/201–4632), or **Kanobouw/kanoverhuur Rofra** (⊠ Luikerweg 74, Valkenswaard, ☎ 043/363–8339).

Shopping
Breda has a general market at Grote Markt Tuesday through Friday, and a secondhand market on Wednesday. Late shopping is on Thursday.

Oisterwijk

28 km (18 mi) east of Breda, 39 km (25 mi) northwest of Eindhoven.

Oisterwijk is a wooded community and resort town that's perfect for a weekend getaway or a quiet day in the country. There's a charming central square planted with lime trees, and a bird sanctuary with a number of exotic species.

Dining and Lodging

$$$ ✕⌷ **Hotel Restaurant De Swaen.** This French-Victorian town hotel, on a tree-shaded square, is more the sort of place you expect to see in the American Southwest, not in the middle of the Netherlands. The shallow front porch has rocking chairs and is used as a café terrace in the summer; there is also a patio terrace. The crystal-chandeliered restaurant, overlooking the elegant formal garden in back of the hotel, serves excellent French cuisine. There is also a small *auberge* (inn) restaurant, De Jonge Swaen (The Young Swan), that serves simpler, less expensive, traditional Dutch choices. The Swan's hotel rooms are gracious and homey; baths are marble. ⌧ *De Lind 47,* ☏ *013/521–9006,* FAX *013/528–5860. 18 rooms with bath. Restaurant, bar, lobby lounge. AE, DC, MC, V.*

's-Hertogenbosch

⊕ *45 km (28 mi) east of Breda, and 123 km (77 mi) northwest of Maastricht.*

The name 's-Hertogenbosch means "The Duke's Woods" in Dutch, and while that is the official name of this medieval city, the name you will hear more commonly is Den Bosch (pronounced "den boss"), "The Woods." Not much remains of the woods for which it was named, however: The forests have been replaced by marshes and residential and industrial development.

With spidery Gothic windows and a noble Romanesque tower, the magnificent **St. Janskathedraal** (St. John's Cathedral) stands out as Den Bosch's principle attraction and is the only cathedral in the Netherlands. Built between 1380 and 1520 in the Brabant Gothic style, it is a cruciform, five-aisle basilica with numerous side chapels around the apse. Abundantly decorated with statuary, sculptural details, and grotesques, its nave is supported by double flying buttresses that are unique in the Netherlands. ⌧ *Parade,* ☏ *073/613–9740.* ⌹ *Free.* ☉ *Mon.–Sat. 10–5, Sun. 1–5.*

NEED A BREAK? There is a very special sweet treat in store for you in 's-Hertogenbosch: A *Bossche bol* is a ball-shaped *choux* (cream puff) pastry, filled with whipped cream, dipped in dark chocolate, and served cool. **Patisserie Jan de Groot** (⌧ Stationsweg 24, ☏ 073/133830), on the road leading to the railway station, makes the best in town.

Noordbrabants Museum (North Brabant Museum) is the foremost provincial museum in the country. Housed in the imposing former residence of the provincial governor, the museum contains historical, archaeological, and cultural exhibits related to the history of Brabant, as well as an outstanding art collection that includes many 17th- and 18th-century Dutch floral paintings and works by Brabant artists of various periods. Reach the museum from the Parade by following Lange Putstraat to Verwersstraat and turning left. ⌧ *Verwersstraat 41,* ☏ *073/686-6877.* ⌹ *Fl 7.50.* ☉ *Tues.–Fri. 10–5, weekends noon–5.*

Dining and Lodging

$$ ✕ **Pilkington's.** In the shadow of the St. Janskerk tower, this informal restaurant has a British touch, with such old-fashioned favorites as shepherd's pie. But there's also duck breast, fresh grilled fish, and all manner of other delights. In good weather the walled garden, covered with climbing roses, is a must. You can also stop off here just for coffee and cake. ⌧ *Torenstraat 5,* ☏ *073/612-2923. AE, DC, MC, V.*

$$$ ✕🏨 **Golden Tulip Hotel Central.** This is more than just your typical full-service business hotel: The Hotel Central has a family-run atmosphere, especially reflected in the warmth of the service. The rooms have a modern, tailored look. The restaurant, De Leeuwenborgh, with a separate entrance on the square, is graciously appointed and intimate. Its mirrors are etched with views of the city's important buildings, and the menu is traditional and French. ⊠ *Burg. Loeffplein 98,* ☎ *073/612–5151,* 🗟 *073/614–5699. 124 rooms. Restaurant, bar. AE, DC, MC, V.*

Nightlife and the Arts

Once a week, 's-Hertogenbosch offers back-to-back **carillon recitals** from two sets of bells. The town-hall bells play every Wednesday morning from 10 to 11, followed by another carillon concert from the cathedral from 11:30 to 12:30.

CAFÉS

Sporty types and young businesspeople frequent **Silva Ducis** (⊠ Parade 6–7, ☎ 073/613–0405), an elegant grand café that looks out onto the most attractive square in town. There is a wide range of beer to choose from and jazz or classical music in the background. **King's Cross** (⊠ Vughterstraat 99a, ☎ 073/613–4479) is open late, plays loud music, and attracts a boisterous but good-natured crowd.

Outdoor Activities and Sports

BIKING

You can rent bicycles at **Stationsfietsstalling** (⊠ Stationsplein 22, 5211 AP, ☎ 073/613–4737 or 073/613–4033) or **Cyclepoint** (⊠ Hoek Zuid-Willemsvaart-Hinthamereinde, ☎ 073/613–9020).

Shopping

There is a large general market every Wednesday and Saturday on the market square. Late shopping is on Thursday.

ART BOOKS

The shop of the **North Brabant Museum** (⊠ Verwersstraat 41, ☎ 073/687–7800) offers an exceptional collection of art books covering many periods and styles of Dutch and international art.

Eindhoven

    ❻❷   *38 km (24 mi) south of 's-Hertogenbosch, 125 km (79 mi) north of Maastricht.*

A bustling, modern city, Einhoven has no traditional, historic center to explore, thanks to heavy bombing in World War II, but there are remarkable examples of contemporary architecture throughout the city (even the bus shelters are designed by well-known architects), and there is an exceptional museum of modern art.

The **Stedelijk Van Abbemuseum** (Municipal van Abbe Museum) began in 1936 as the simple wish of a local cigar maker, Henri van Abbe, to visit a museum in his own town. Today it has one of Europe's richest collections of contemporary art and owns more works than can be displayed at one time. The galleries and exhibitions are rotated and rearranged continually. The collection includes major works by artists such as Picasso and Christo. There are examples here of every major trend of the last 100 years, including cubism, constructivism, de Stijl, German expressionism, minimalism, and American pop. At press time, the museum occupied temporary premises. The building that houses the old museum is undergoing extensive and lengthy renovations, so it can do the collection more justice. In the meantime, only a small portion of the collection is on view. ⊠ *Vonderweg1,* ☎ *040/275–5275.* 🖼 *Fl 5.* ☉ *Tues.–Sun. 11–5.*

NEED A
BREAK? **Grand Cafe Berlage** (✉ Kleine Berg 16, ☎ 040/245–7481) is a spacious Art Deco brasserie with a streetside terrace that serves standard Dutch café fare, such as spareribs, salads, and *uitsmijters* (fried eggs on toast with a variety of accompaniments, including tomatoes, ham, bacon, and cheese).

Dining and Lodging

$$ ✕ **Ravensdonck.** The Ravensdonck is in a large and elegant house with tall windows. The dining room, on the second floor, with windows all around, serves a variety of simple but tasty grilled dishes. A café with a friendly atmosphere occupies the first floor. There is an amusing touch here, in that you can buy boxes of chocolates in the shape of light bulbs. Why not? It was a light-bulb factory that transformed Eindhoven from a sleepy village at the turn of the century into an international business mecca. ✉ *Ten Hagestraat 2,* ☎ *040/244–3142. Reservations essential. AE, DC, MC, V. No lunch weekends.*

$$$ ✕🏨 **The Mandarin Hotel.** Prepare yourself for a pleasant surprise: The Mandarin is unique in that it was designed to meet East Asian standards of service. Its Asian decor includes small bridges spanning water gardens, used as footpaths through the lobby. The restaurants are all Asian in theme and cuisine: One serves fine Chinese specialties, another offers a range of Indonesian and Asian dishes, and the third is a Japanese steak house; there also is a Parisian coffee shop. ✉ *Geldropseweg 17,* ☎ *040/212–5055,* 𝖥𝖠𝖷 *040/212–1555. 105 rooms and suites. 3 restaurants, café, indoor pool, saunas, no-smoking rooms, free parking. AE, DC, MC, V.*

Outdoor Activities and Sports

SOCCER

Eindhoven's soccer team, **PSV** (Philips Sport Vereniging), is one of the top three in the country and plays from September through May at **PSV-stadion Eindhoven** (✉ Frederiklaan 101A, ☎ 040/250–5505).

En Route As you travel south toward Maastricht, the small town of **Thorn** is well worth a detour. It is known as the "white village" because of its abundance of 18th-century houses and buildings painted white. Visit the 10th-century abbey church, which has an outstanding Baroque altar and three choirs (for canons, princesses, and noblewomen); there also is a small museum.

Maastricht: Capital of Limburg

★ ⑥₃ *207 km (130 mi) southeast of Amsterdam, 25 km (16 mi) west of Aachen (Germany).*

The oldest city in the Netherlands, established by the Romans more than 2,500 years ago, Maastricht has enjoyed a long history as a crossroads between Germanic and Latin cultures. As such, it was an appropriate venue for the signing of the latest major treaty regulating the affairs of the European Union. Wedged somewhat hesitatingly between Belgium and Germany, this town is an intriguing mixture of three languages, times, currencies, and customs. It is a miracle that it has remained Dutch—probably because the dignity of its capitalship (of Limburg Province) has weighed heavily upon its hoary head. Small, but quintessentially European, Maastricht offers a lighthearted lifestyle, meticulous attention to service, and exceptionally fine, French-influenced cuisine. Every March, jet-setters and millionaires arrive to buy Jordans drawings and Gothic tapestries at its sumptuous European Fine Art Fair, one of Europe's very best. It straddles the river Maas: The old city is on the river's western bank, and its newer neighborhoods and the railway station are on the eastern side.

64 The **St. Servaasbrug** (St. Servatius Bridge) spans the Maas between the old and new parts of town and offers the best views of the old city. Built solidly of gray Namur stone in the late 13th century to replace an even earlier wooden bridge, it is one of the oldest bridges in the Netherlands.

65 Maastricht's **Stadhuis** (Town Hall) stands imposingly at one end of the large market square. Built in 1662 as a proud statement of burgher prosperity, it is filled with fine tapestries, stucco, and paintings. The sumptuous entrance hall is open to the public. ⊠ *Markt 78,* ☎ *043/ 350–4000.* ✑ *Free.* ☉ *Weekdays 8:30–12:30 and 2–5:30.*

Wednesday and Friday are market days in Maastricht, and the **Grote Markt** is chockablock with stalls and stands offering fruits, vegetables, meats, and household items. Business here is conducted in three currencies (Dutch, Belgian, and German) and four languages (Dutch, French, German, and English). The jolly statue of a roly-poly woman carrying a basket of vegetables, which stands on one side of the market square, is known **66** affectionately in local dialect as the **Moosewief** (Greengrocer's Wife).

67 Each February, the enormous **Vrijthof** square explodes with the festivities of Carnival. Ringed with restaurants, grand cafés, discotheques, and traditional pubs, it is the major public gathering place of Maastricht, year-round.

NEED A BREAK?
A cheerful place to stop any time of day is the plant-filled **Cafe Britannique** (⊠ Vrijthof 6, ☎ 043/321–8691). It serves breakfast (with champagne if you like) as well as simple, light meals throughout the day and drinks, including a house beer, until midnight.

68 Beneath the magnificent and historic 7th-century **St. Servaasbasiliek** (St. Servatius Basilica) lie the bones of its namesake, the 4th-century saint whose choice of Maastricht for his see stimulated the development of the city following the departure of the Romans in 402. The basilica's 1993 restoration included a fresh paint job using the bright colors of the original interior design. The focal points of the church are the richly carved 13th-century **Berg Portal**, and the **Schatkamer van Sint Servaas** (Treasure Chamber of St. Servatius) in the 12th-century chapel. This extraordinary collection of treasures dates from 827 and contains religious relics (some of them donated by Charlemagne) and exquisitely wrought liturgical objects. The most important item in the collection is the 12th-century Noodkist, an elaborately decorated, gold-plated oak chest, adorned with gold and silver figures and containing the bones and relics of St. Servatius and other local bishops. ⊠ *Vrijthof,* ☎ *043/325–2121.* ✑ *Fl 3.50.* ☉ *Dec.–Mar., daily 10–4; Apr.–June and Sept.–Nov., daily 10–5; July–Aug., daily 10–6.*

69 The 14th-century Gothic **St. Janskerk** (St. John's Church) has a stark white interior and a tall, red tower that offers panoramic views of the city. ⊠ *Vrijthof (enter Henric van Veldekeplein),* ☎ *043/347–8880.* ✑ *Free, though donation appreciated from tower-climbers.* ☉ *Easter– Oct., Mon.–Sat. 11–4.*

70 Recent excavations around the **Onze Lieve Vrouwebasiliek** (Our Beloved Lady Basilica) indicate that the basilica may have replaced a Roman temple. The Westwork, a massive flat facade in Romanesque style that is topped with two round turrets, is the oldest part of the structure, dating from the 11th and 12th centuries. Inside is a two-story apse with a double row of columns and a half-domed roof. The church opens **71** out onto the tree-shaded, intimate **Onze Lieve Vrouweplein** (Our

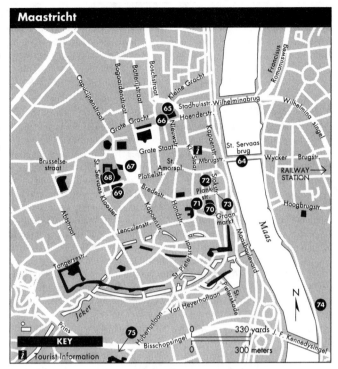

Beloved Lady Square). ⊠ *Onze Lieve Vrouweplein,* ☎ *043/325–1851.* 🎫 *Church free; treasure chamber Fl 3.50.* 🕙 *Easter–Oct., Mon.–Sat. 11–5, Sun. 1–5.*

72 **Op de Thermen** hints at the Roman heritage that lies deep beneath the surface of Maastricht. This small residential square, discovered in 1840, was the site of a Roman villa and baths. Recently laid paving stones indicate the outline of the ancient buildings—red for a 1st-century house with underfloor heating, gray for a 2nd-century bathhouse, **73** and white for a 4th-century bathhouse. **Stokstraat,** now a fashionable street lined with galleries and boutiques, was the heart of the original Roman settlement of Maastricht.

★ **74** Diversity is the keyword at the excellent **Bonnefantenmuseum** (Bonnefanten Museum), the provincial museum of Limburg. Not only do you find displays on the archaeological history of the province, but there is an art collection with gems from 13th- to 15th-century Romanesque and Gothic Mosan sculpture of the Meuse region; 14th- to 16th-century Italian painting; and 16th- to 18th-century paintings of the South Netherlands, including works by Jan Brueghel and Pieter Brueghel the Younger. The collection of medieval religious carving is unequaled in the Netherlands. And there's more: An intriguing and intelligently selected exhibition of contemporary art includes work by many important Dutch painters of the late 20th century, several of them from Limburg. ⊠ *Ave. Ceramique 250,* ☎ *043/329–0190.* 🎫 *Fl 10.* 🕙 *Tues.–Sun. 11–5.*

75 **Grotten St. Pieter** (Caves of St. Peter) are man-made corridors carved deep into the limestone hills since Roman times to produce building stone. There are approximately 200 kilometers (124 miles) of chambers and passageways here. In some areas the mining was so extensive that the ceiling height now is nearly 40 feet; this means that graffiti left by the Romans are now far above your head, while the signatures of such visitors as Napoléon can still be seen. The caves are complex and can be visited only with a guide; they are also chilly and damp, so bring a sweater. ⊠ *Grotten Noord (Northern System), Luikerweg 71; Zonneberg Caves, Slavante 1 (near Enci Cement Works);* ☎ *043/321–7878 for tour times and for English-speaking guide.* ☜ *Fl 5.25.* ☉ *Hrs vary; call ahead.*

Dining and Lodging

$$$$ ✕ **Chateau Neercanne.** Built in 1698, this gracious château was once visited by Czar Peter the Great. Today it is one of the top restaurants in the area, with a wine cellar that occupies old Roman caves that were carved into the hillside. Enjoying meals in the elegant and quietly decorated dining rooms is like attending a dinner party in a private home. The cuisine, regularly honored in European culinary circles, is French, with an emphasis on seasonal and country specialties. In a former chapel there is a second, less formal lunch restaurant, L'Auberge. A wide summer terrace looks out over the garden. ⊠ *Cannerweg 800,* ☎ *043/325–1359,* ℻ *043/321–3406. Reservations essential. Jacket and tie. AE, DC, MC, V. Closed Mon.*

$$$ ✕ **Old Hickory.** Named after the American regiment that liberated Maastricht in 1944, this spacious restaurant is focused around a large central fireplace. The emphasis is on traditional French gastronomy, and the quality is supreme. Fish and shellfish are the basis for many dishes, and game is served in season—sometimes the product of chef John Kuzelj's own hunting expeditions. John sometimes invites guests to visit his extensive, climate-controlled wine cellar. ⊠ *Meerssenerweg 372,* ☎ *043/362–0548. AE, DC, MC, V. Closed Sun.*

$$–$$$ ✕ **'t Hegske.** This romantic spot is near St. Amorsplein off Vrijthof. Window boxes full of flowering plants decorate the street side, and there is a bubbling fountain in the interior courtyard. The warmth of half-timbered walls, hanging baskets, and antique collectibles here and there add to the intimacy. The kitchen is open, the cuisine classic French. ⊠ *Heggenstraat 3a,* ☎ *043/325–1762. Reservations essential. AE, DC, MC, V. No lunch.*

$$ ✕ **De Blindgender.** Not far from Onze Lieve Vrouweplein, De Blindgender is a particularly warm and cheerful eating pub with large windows looking onto the street. The tables are plain and unadorned, the service is relaxed, and the menu has a good selection of fish dishes, including salmon cooked with sesame seeds. ⊠ *Koestraat. 3,* ☎ *043/325–0619. Reservations not accepted. AE, DC, MC, V.*

$$ ✕ **La Ville.** During the day you can take your pick of delicious salads and light meals. In the evening the friendly and enthusiastic staff serve up hearty, French-influenced cuisine, such as filet mignon with shallots and red wine sauce. The restaurant is on Maastricht's prettiest square and has tables under the trees in good weather. ⊠ *Onze Lieve Vrouweplein 28,* ☎ *043/321–9889. AE, DC, MC. Closed Tues. in winter.*

$$$$ ✕▥ **Hotel Derlon.** The relaxed and quiet elegance of Onze Lieve Vrouweplein is perfectly reflected in this small luxury hotel. Guest rooms are graciously sized and decorated in relaxing, sand-and-seashell tones, and each has its own work of art, most often a contemporary painting; they face either the medieval side street or, if you are particularly fortunate, the tree-filled square. A unique feature of this hotel is a private museum in the cellar, with exhibits ranging from the 1st century BC to the 15th century AD. There is a personal quality to the service, especially in the elegant restaurant. ⊠ *Onze Lieve Vrouweplein 6, 6211 HD,* ☎ *043/321–6770,* ℻ *043/325–1933. 44 rooms. Restaurant, shops. AE, DC, MC, V.*

$$$ ✕🏠 **Kasteel Elsloo.** This 16th-century manor house, with its own park and botanical garden, was once the property of one of Limburg's leading families and the scene of many glittering occasions, including the wedding of a daughter of the family to the Prince of Monaco in the 19th century. Rooms are spacious and restfully decorated. The restaurant, too, has a manor-house ambience; the kitchen is traditional French, serving such dishes as beef with onion confit and port sauce. ✉ *Maasberg 1, 10 km (6 mi) northeast of Maastricht,* ☎ *046/437–7666,* 🅵🅰🆇 *046/437–7570. 27 rooms with bath. Restaurant, bar. AE, DC, MC, V.*

$–$$ ✕🏠 **Hotel Bergere.** The family-owned Bergere occupies an elegant 19th-century building not far from the railway station. There's an elevator, a grand café with a separate entrance, and comfortable, well-appointed rooms. The color scheme is light and fresh in pinks, grays, and beiges. ✉ *Stationsstraat 40,* ☎ *043/325–1651,* 🅵🅰🆇 *043/325–5498. 40 rooms with bath/shower. Restaurant, parking. AE, MC, V.*

$ ✕🏠 **De Poshoorn.** Conveniently situated between the railway station and the Old Town, the Poshoorn has smallish rooms, but they are spotlessly clean and brightly decorated. The hotel is above a café with a friendly clientele, and service is attentive and efficient. ✉ *Stationsstraat 47,* ☎ *043/321–7334,* 🅵🅰🆇 *043/321–0747. 11 rooms with bath/shower. Café. AE, DC, MC, V.*

$$ 🏠 **Hotel Du Casque.** Smack-dab in the center of old Maastricht, this hotel has a tradition that dates back to a 15th-century inn, although today's building is a modern postwar structure. Some rooms overlook the Vrijthof square, and there's direct access to a steak house with a terrace on the square. ✉ *Helmstrat 14,* ☎ *043/321–4343,* 🅵🅰🆇 *043/325–5155. 38 rooms with bath/shower. Parking (fee). AE, DC, MC, V.*

Nightlife and the Arts

For information on what is going on during your visit, check *Maandagenda,* a monthly calendar you will find around town, or *Uit in Maastricht,* published biweekly by the VVV tourist office.

CAFÉS

In the heart of the city, with a terrace that hums with life on summer evenings, **De Lanteern** (✉ O.L. Vrouweplein 26, ☎ 043/321–4326) attracts everyone from tourists to the corner shopkeeper. Named for a type of pot-bellied gin bottle, **Sjinkerij De Bóbbel** (✉ Wolfstraat 32, ☎ 043/321–7413) is a traditional Maastricht pub, where there's a buzz of conversation rather than background music. It has sand on the floor, simple wooden chairs, and marble-topped tables—and a good choice of beers. A special pub to visit is the very old **In den Ouden Vogelstruys** (✉ Vrijthof 15, ☎ 043/321–4888), first mentioned in town records in the 13th century. It has remained virtually unchanged since 1730 (except, of course, for the modern conveniences of electricity and beer on tap).

CARILLON CONCERTS

In the summer the air rings with a series of evening concerts played by carillonneurs on various church bells of the city; and throughout the year there are midday concerts every Friday from 11:30 to 12:30 from the cheerful 43-bell carillon on the town hall in the market square.

CARNIVAL

The Catholic heritage of the southern provinces of the Netherlands is most dramatically felt during the days preceding Ash Wednesday. The public celebration of Carnival survives in its full bloom of conviviality and relative recklessness in Maastricht, with parades, parties, and fancy dress.

CASINOS

The **Holland Casino Valkenburg** (✉ Odapark, ☎ 076/525–1100), not far from Maastricht, offers blackjack, roulette, and Punto Banco in chic surrounds.

CLASSICAL MUSIC

In Maastricht, the **Limburgse Symfonie Orkest** (Limburg Symphony Orchestra), the leading regional orchestra, performs at the Theater aan Het Vrijthof (✉ Vrijthof 47, ☎ 043/321–0380); the box office is open Monday through Saturday 11–4. Maastricht has a thriving and talented **student and amateur** music scene. Performances are at both the Conservatoire Concert Hall (✉ Bonnefanten 15, ☎ 043/346–6680) and the Kumulus Auditorium (✉ St. Maartenspoort 2, ☎ 043/329–3141).

DISCOS

Momus (✉ Vrijthof 8, ☎ 043/321–1937) is a big, Top 40 discotheque with neoclassical decor of marble and statues. Fraternized by students and young arty types, **Satyricon** (✉ St. Bernardusstraat 16, ☎ 043/321–0321) is a mellow, jazz-oriented "dance-café" that sometimes lets rip with funkier sounds and live concerts.

GAY BARS

Near the railway station, and decorated with Dutch Rail flotsam and jetsam, **La Gare** (✉ Spoorweglaan 6, ☎ 043/325–9090) has a long bar, a tiny dance floor, and chatty customers. **La Ferme** (✉ Rechtestraat 29, ☎ 043/321–8928) has a lights show, offers the latest music, and is a vortex of south-Netherlands gay life.

THEATER

The main theater of Maastricht, the **Theater aan Het Vrijthof** (✉ Theater at Vrijthof, Vrijthof 47, ☎ 043/321–0380) has a reputation for exciting programming that extends beyond the city limits. Top quality national and international companies all play here. In addition, there is a small theater hall, **Podium** (✉ Het Generaalshuis, Vrijthof 47, ☎ 043/321–0380), and next door, **Het Vervolg Theater** (✉ Vrijthof 47a, ☎ 043/325–5333), which stage more experimental and esoteric work

Outdoor Activities and Sports

BIKING

Rent bicycles at the **Railway Station** (✉ Stationsplein, Maastricht, ☎ 043/321–1100).

CANOEING AND KAYAKING

Kayaking is especially pleasant on the river Maas, through the gently hilly countryside. Contact **Kayak Tours Limburg** (✉ Grote Dries 8, 6223 AE Borgharen, ☎ 043/363–8339) for rentals.

TENNIS AND SQUASH

To play tennis or squash in Maastricht, visit **Squash Centre Erik van der Pluijm** (✉ Brusselsestraat 74a, ☎ 043/321–6387) or **Sportpark Mulder** (✉ Mockstraat 36–38, ☎ 043/363–7295). Rates are about Fl 20 per hour of court time during the day, Fl 40 after 5 PM.

Shopping

Shopping in Maastricht is concentrated in the pedestrian cross streets that connect and surround the three main squares of the city. Maastrichter Brugstraat takes you into the network of shopping streets from the St. Servaasbrug. Maastrichter Smedenstraat and Plankstraat are lined with exclusive shops, with Wolfstraat and the exceptionally fashionable Stokstraat intersecting both of them. In the other direction, Kleine Staat and Grote Staat lead to Vrijthof, with a mixed bag of shopping opportunities. Off Grote Staat is a trio of small shopping streets—Spilstraat, Nieuwestraat, and Muntstraat—that end at the

Markt. Off Helmstraat is a shopping square, W.C. Entre Deux. Late-night shopping is on Thursday.

Maastricht has a tri-country general market in front of the Town Hall on Wednesday and Friday mornings, and a flea market opposite the railway station on Saturday.

ART AND ANTIQUES FAIR

Each year Maastricht's MECC Congress and Exhibition Hall is the site of the **European Fine Art Fair** (⊠ European Fine Art Foundation, Box 1035, 5200BA, 's-Hertogenbosch, ☎ 073/614–5165), for a week beginning in mid-March. Major dealers in antiques and fine art from all over Europe participate, showing paintings, drawings, and prints (traditional and contemporary), furniture and objects, textiles, tapestries, and rugs; there also are music programs and lectures.

En Route   On the way out of Maastricht toward the German border, near the town of Margraten, you will find the entrance to the 65-acre **Netherlands American Cemetery and Memorial.** This is the only American military cemetery in the Netherlands and is the final resting place of more than 8,000 Americans killed in World War II. ⊠ *Rijksweg 2, 10 km (6 mi) east of Maastricht,* ☎ *043/458–1208.* ☞ *Free.* ☉ *Summer, daily 9– 6; winter, daily 9–5.*

Heerlen

⑦ *23 km (14 mi) east of Maastricht.*

Heerlen is the second of the Roman cities in this part of the Netherlands. The discovery in 1940 of the foundations of a large and elaborate Roman bathhouse was proof of the importance of Heerlen as a meeting place for the Roman troops stationed in this northern outpost.

Now enclosed in a large, glass-encircled building, the **Thermenmuseum** (Thermae Museum) has catwalks over a perfectly preserved Roman bath complex. The *thermae* (baths) incorporated open-air sports fields, a large swimming pool, shops, restaurants, and the enclosed bathhouse complex, which included a large dressing room, the hot-air sweating room, and a series of baths (warm, lukewarm, cold, and immersion). ⊠ *Coriovallumstraat 9,* ☎ *045/560–4581.* ☞ *Museum Fl 3.* ☉ *Tues.–Fri. 10–5, weekends and holidays 2–5.*

⑦ From the 14th up to the 20th century, **Kasteel Hoensbroek** (Hoensbroek Castle) belonged to the same family, who added on bits here and there as the years went by. Nowadays, it is open to the public as the largest and best preserved of the castles in South Limburg. You can see sections dating from the 14th century and products of various architectural styles, including Baroque and Maasland-Renaissance. There are several sparsely but appropriately furnished rooms, and various small galleries that show temporary exhibitions. ⊠ *Klinkertstraat 118, 5 km (3 mi) northeast of Heerlen city center,* ☎ *045/522–7272.* ☞ *Fl 6.* ☉ *Daily 10–5:30.*

Dining and Lodging

$$$$ ✕☒ **Prinses Juliana.** Food is everything here; the classic French haute cuisine served here was recognized internationally more than 10 years ago and continues to be honored by even the harshest French food critics. Members of the Dutch royal family, and foreign dignitaries, such as the German chancellor Helmut Kohl and the late French president François Mitterrand, have all stopped off for a meal. The decor is elegant in an unadorned way so you can pay attention to the food. The suite-style rooms are bright and spacious. ⊠ *Broekhem 11, Postbus 812, 6300 AV Valkenburg a/d Geul, 11 km (7 mi) east of Maastricht,*

12 km (8 mi) west of Heerlen, ☎ *043/601–2244,* ⒻⒶⓍ *043/601–4405. 25 rooms with bath. Restaurant, lobby lounge. AE, DC, MC, V.*

$$$ ✕ 🏨 **Hotel Kasteel Erenstein.** A 14th-century moated château houses the restaurant; across the road, a traditional whitewashed Limburg farmstead houses the luxury hotel. Many of the rooms have beamed ceilings, and some are bilevel and skylighted; others have rooftop balconies. The menu and the wine cellar are French. ⊠ *Oud Erensteinerweg 6, 8 km (5 mi) east of Heerlen,* ☎ *045/546–1333,* ⒻⒶⓍ *045/546–0748. 44 rooms. Restaurant, bar, massage, sauna, exercise room. AE, DC, MC, V.*

$$$ ✕ 🏨 **Kasteel Wittem.** This fairy-tale castle hotel, with its duck-filled moat, spindle-roofed tower, and series of peekaboo dormers dotting the roof, is human in scale. The family that has owned it for more than 25 years welcomes you to a comfortable environment of vintage Dutch furnishings. The intimate dining room, where the cuisine is French, has towering windows open to views of gardens and fields. There is a summer terrace beside the moat. ⊠ *Wittemer Allee 3, 15 km (9 mi) east of Maastricht, 14 km (9 mi) south of Heerlen,* ☎ *043/450–1208,* ⒻⒶⓍ *043/450– 1260. 12 rooms with bath. Restaurant, lobby lounge. AE, DC, MC, V.*

$$$ 🏨 **Kasteel Geulzicht.** Built in the 19th century, this Disneylike hotel is set in gentle hills. Despite its grand appearance and sumptuous period entrance hall, the hotel has a cozy, family-run atmosphere. The rooms are stylishly furnished, often with antiques; some rooms occupy the castle turrets. The flagstone garden terrace is open only to hotel guests. ⊠ *Vogelzangweg 2, Berg en Terblijt, 6 km (4 mi) east of Maastricht, 3 km (2 mi) from the Thermae 2000 Spa,* ☎ *043/604–0432,* ⒻⒶⓍ *043/ 604–2011. 16 rooms with bath/shower. Restaurant, bar, lobby lounge. AE, DC, MC, V.*

Spa

One of the special treats of South Limburg is **Thermae 2000,** a luxurious hill spa that offers a complete range of services, including indoor and outdoor spring-fed pools, sauna, steam bath, yoga/meditation, hydrogymnastics, aerobics, sports massage, herbal and mud baths, and more. ⊠ *Cauberg 27, Valkenburg aan de Geul, Valkenburg,* ☎ *043/601– 9419.* ⊙ *Daily 9 AM–11 PM.*

The Border Provinces and Maastricht A to Z

Arriving and Departing

BY CAR

To reach **Zeeland** take E19 from Amsterdam to Rotterdam and pick up A29 south; connect with N59 west to Zierikzee and N256 across the Zeelandbrug bridge to Goes, where you can pick up E312/A58 west to Middelburg, capital of Zeeland province.

To reach the provinces of **Brabant** and **Limburg,** take E25/A2 from Amsterdam south through Utrecht. Pick up A27 south to Breda, or stay on E25 through Den Bosch to reach Eindhoven and other points south. To travel from Zeeland across to Maastricht, it is far quicker to travel via Antwerp (in Belgium), taking the A4 and then the E313.

BY PLANE

There are airports in Eindhoven and Maastricht. In addition to regular flights to both cities from Amsterdam, **KLM City Hopper** (☎ 020/474– 7747) operates service direct from London Gatwick to Maastricht and from London Heathrow to Eindhoven. Additional services to Eindhoven from the United Kingdom are scheduled by **Base Business Airlines** (☎ 061/489–2988) from Birmingham and Manchester.

BY TRAIN

There are **Intercity express trains** (☎ 06/9292) twice each hour from Amsterdam direct to 's-Hertogenbosch and Eindhoven, and once each hour direct to Middelburg or Maastricht. To reach Breda by train, it is necessary to connect either in Roosendaal or 's-Hertogenbosch.

Getting Around

BY BUS

Local and regional buses leave from and return to the Dutch railway stations, but bus travel can be slow. The **national bus information** number is 06/9292. Operators can also give you information about local bus routes.

BY TRAIN

As always in the Netherlands, traveling by train between cities is fast and efficient. There is an **Intercity** train line (☎ 06/9292) that crosses the country, west to east within the Border Provinces, twice each hour. From Breda there also is twice-hourly service direct to Eindhoven, for connections to Maastricht.

BY TAXI

If you are not traveling under your own steam, you will need to hire a taxi to get to some of the more far-lying castles. To summon a taxi, call Breda (☎ 076/522–2111), Eindhoven (☎ 040/252–5252), 's-Hertogenbosch (☎ 073/631–2900), Maastricht (☎ 043/347–7777), and Middelburg (☎ 0118/412–600).

Contacts and Resources

EMERGENCIES

National Emergency Alarm Number for police, fire, or ambulance: ☎ 06/112.

GUIDED TOURS

The **Maastricht Tourist Office** (✉ Kleine Staat 1, ☎ 043/325–2121) offers a guided tour of the city for Fl 5.25. Tours last 1–1½ hours. For cruises on the river Maas, contact **Stiphout Cruises** (✉ Maaspromenade 27, 6211 HS Maastricht, ☎ 043/325–4151). Fares start at Fl 8.75.

The **Middelburg Tourist Office** (✉ Markt 65a, ☎ 0118/616–851) occasionally offers guided walking tours (1¼ hrs, daily Apr.–Oct.) for Fl 6.50 per person. Tours of the province also are available through **Holland International Reisbureau Van Fraassen** (✉ Londensekaai 19, ☎ 0118/627–758), **Carlier Tours** (✉ Elektraweg 9, ☎ 0118/615–015), and **Holland International Reisbureau** (✉ Langeviele 7, ☎ 0118/627–855).

HOSPITALS

Breda (☎ 076/525–8000). **Eindhoven** (☎ 040/233–5933). **'s-Hertogenbosch** (☎ 073/686–9111). **Maastricht** (☎ 043/387–6543). **Middelburg** (☎ 0118/425–000).

VISITOR INFORMATION

VVV Breda (✉ Willemstraat 17–19, 4811 AJ, ☎ 076/522–2444). **VVV Eindhoven** (✉ Stationsplein 17, 5611 AC, ☎ 040/244–9231). **VVV 's-Hertogenbosch** (✉ Markt 77, Box 1039, 5200 BA, ☎ 073/612–3071). **VVV Maastricht** (✉ Het Dinghuis, Kleine Staat 1, 6211 ED, ☎ 043/325–2121, FAX 043/321–3746). **VVV Middelburg** (✉ Markt 65a, Postbus 730, 4330 AS, ☎ 0118/416–851).

THE GREEN HEART

Like a mystery package that opens in a series of ever smaller, ever more intriguing boxes, the wooded heart of the Netherlands is an unfolding treasure. The national park is the wrappings; its ultimate and most precious gift is a museum of art that is buried deep in the forest; another of its surprises is a small palace. The Royal Game Reserve in the north and the fruit- and vegetable-growing region to the east provide the restaurants of the Green Heart with abundant, high-quality ingredients. The area is well supplied with hotels of all sizes and types, small resorts, and country inns in the woods.

Seven hundred years before the European Common Market or the European Union, there was an association of northern European trading cities called the Hanseatic League. It began as a pact among itinerant merchants to travel together for mutual safety, but in time it became an alliance of more than 80 cities scattered over the Continent, including major ports, such as London, Lübeck, Bremen, Hamburg, Cologne, Danzig, Stockholm, Novgorod, and Bergen, as well as 17 cities on the rivers and coastline of what is now the Netherlands. Their purpose was to consult with one another on matters of trading routes, tolls, and uniformity of regulations governing trade.

Three of the Dutch cities that were important members of that league are in the Green Heart, along the river IJssel, which connects the Rhine with the body of water known today as IJsselmeer, an open sea (the Zuider Zee) in the 13th century. After the national park and its captivating art museum, these Hansa towns make an interesting stopover.

Pleasures and Pastimes
The Green Heart offers forests for long summer walks, cozy restaurants for hearty fall and winter meals, a scattering of old-fashioned villages, and one or two first-class museums.

DINING
The forests of the Green Heart teem with game, much of which ends up in local cooking pots. The main game season is in the fall, though clever restaurateurs manage to find something for almost every month; some even go hunting themselves. Braised hare is a specialty, and local boar and venison are delicious, as is the pheasant. Whether cooked as a family-style stew in a simple restaurant or as the creation of one of the area's top chefs, sampling local game is a must.

LODGING
The Green Heart is great for getting away from it all. Rather than staying in a town, head for one of the village hotels—some are simple, others have a country-house atmosphere, but all have a special charm and relaxing sense of isolation.

MARRIAGE OF TRUE MINDS
When heiress Hélène Müller married industrialist Anton Kröller at the turn of the century, their combined wealth and complementary tastes were destined to give pleasure for generations to come. Today you can wander through the vast forests of the Hoge Veluwe National Park, land bought up by Anton, and see the descendants of the wild boar and deer with which he stocked the estate. Or you can visit the museum in the middle of the park, established by Hélène and containing one of the best collections of van Goghs in the world, as well as an excellent selection of late-19th-century and modern art. Children can caper about the extensive sculpture garden, and the whole family can pick up one of the free bikes that are available in the park and trundle off down wooded lanes.

VILLAGE HOPPING
You'll find some of the Netherlands' most charming villages nestled among the trees in the Green Heart. Pop into one of these, Hoog Soeren, in the middle of the forest, and you'll feel as though you've

landed in a woodcutters' village in a Grimm fairy tale; or take the punt over the river IJssel to Bronkhorst to see the smallest hamlet in the country. Driving from village to village, stopping off for lunch or afternoon tea and a stroll, then driving on through the forest to the next spot, is a delightfully lazy way to spend the day.

Exploring the Green Heart

The Hoge Veluwe National Park and the Royal Forest lie at the heart of the Netherlands. Farther east, arranged in an arc that stretches from north to south are the historic Hanseatic towns and Arnhem.

Great Itineraries

A visit to the Hoge Veluwe National Park and Kröller-Müller Museum can easily fill an entire day. Allow another day to explore the outskirts of the park and at least another two days to get the most out of the Hanseatic towns.

Numbers in the text correspond to numbers in the margin and on the Green Heart map.

IF YOU HAVE 3 DAYS

Start your tour with a visit to the sculpture park and van Gogh collection at the Kröller-Müller Museum, and spend the rest of the day in the beautiful natural surrounds of **De Hoge Veluwe** ⑦, stopping overnight in the forest village of 🏠 **Hoog Soeren,** near **Apeldoorn** ⑦. On the second day visit the historic town of **Deventer** ⑧, then head across to 🏠 **Zutphen** ⑧ for coffee in a 19th-century coffee house and a look at medieval manuscripts in the Librije. The tour ends on a sober note with a visit to the war memorial and museum in **Arnhem** ⑧.

IF YOU HAVE 5 DAYS

Spend the first day taking in the delights of the Kröller-Müller Museum and **De Hoge Veluwe** ⑦, spending two nights in 🏠 **Hooge Soeren,** near **Apeldoorn** ⑦. Walk among the primates at Apenheul on the edge of the park, and visit the magnificent Paleis Het Loo nearby. Then travel up to 🏠 **Zwolle** ⑧ to nibble spicy local candy and to see the 11th-century St. Michaelskerk. Spend the rest of the day canoeing or fishing in the surrounding waters. Your fourth night is in the romantic old town of 🏠 **Zutphen** ⑧. Stop off to view the medieval center of Deventer on the way there. On the last day, after exploring Zutphen, finish the tour at the war memorial and museum in **Arnhem** ⑧.

IF YOU HAVE 7 DAYS

Book two nights at 🏠 **Hoog Soeren,** and spend your first two days exploring **De Hoge Veluwe** ⑦, visiting the Kröller-Müller Museum, Paleis Het Loo, and the monkeys at Apenheul. Then head up to 🏠 **Zwolle** ⑧ for some canoeing and fishing. Allow some time to visit the attractive old port of Kampen with its 14th-century town hall, before making your way to 🏠 **Zutphen** ⑧ via Deventer. Next morning, after a look around Zutphen's historic center, transfer to 🏠 **Bronkhorst,** the smallest village in the Netherlands, filled with quaint old buildings and a tempting restaurant. Then head down to 🏠 **Arnhem** ⑧ for a visit to the war memorial and museum. Round off your tour with a meal at the moated Kasteel Doorwerth, just outside town.

When to Tour the Green Heart

Fall is the ideal time to visit this region. Not only do the restaurants offer all sorts of delicious game dishes, but De Hoge Veluwe is spectacular at this time of year. Hélène Kröller-Müller adored autumnal colors, and stretches of the park were especially planted with trees that make a mosaic of reds, oranges, and browns in the fall.

Apeldoorn

78 ✉ *89 km (56 mi) east of Amsterdam.*

Though not much of an attraction in itself, the small city of Apeldoorn is the gateway to the Royal Forest and other delights of the Green Heart.

Built in 1685 on the site of a 14th- and 15th-century castle and hunting lodge, and serving as a country residence for William III and his wife Mary Stuart (daughter of James II of England), **Palace Het Loo** expanded into a full-blown royal palace when the couple became king and queen of England. Mary's quarters were in the east wing and William's to the west. Constructed of brick and outfitted with what are said to be the world's first sash windows, the palace is Dutch Baroque and has formal French gardens. An avenue of tall beeches leads to the central courtyard, where you enter through a high, grilled fence. Exhibits fill some of the rooms, and there is a video that documents the building's history and restoration prior to its opening to the public in 1984. Many other rooms are furnished as they had been for William and Mary, but rooms are also maintained in the manner in which they were used by later Dutch monarchs, including Queen Wilhelmina, who was the grandmother of the current queen. Wilhelmina was the last regent to make this her home and died here in 1962. Queen Mary's kitchen, where she made jam, is particularly appealing for the sense of homeyness it gives to the palace. The four gardens, meticulously and formally planted, are decorated with statues and fountains, and lined with tall trees. There are separate King's and Queen's Gardens; the King's is dominated by plantings in blue and orange, the colors of the Dutch royal family. Don't miss the stable; it is full of old royal carriages, including the toy car used by the current crown prince of the Netherlands when he was a child. ✉ *Koninklijk Park 1,* ☎ *055/577–2400.* ✆ *Fl 12.50.* ☉ *Tues.–Sun. 10–5.*

79 The **De Hoge Veluwe** public nature reserve covers more than 13,000 acres of forest and rolling grassland. The traditional hunting grounds of the Dutch royal family, it is populated with deer, boar, and many birds; it is also filled with towering pines and hardwood trees (oak, beech, and birch), dotted with small villages (**Hoge Soeren,** near Apeldoorn, is particularly charming), and riddled with paths for cars, bicycles, and walkers. There is a landlocked, always shifting sand dune to marvel at; the world's first museum of all things that live (or have lived) underground; plus an old hunting lodge, beside a dam, that provides a nice stopping place. You'll find racks of bikes here and there in the park, available free of charge; just be sure to return the bike to any bike rack when you are finished using it. If you need an idea for a destination, there is a visitors center that contains exhibits on the park and an observation point for animal-watching. ✉ *Entrances at Hoenderloo, Otterloo, and Schaarsbergen,* ☎ *0318/591–627.* ✆ *Fl 8; cars Fl 8.* ☉ *Oct.–Mar., daily 9–6; Apr.–May, daily 8–8; June–Aug., daily 8–10; Sept., daily 9–8.*

The **Kröller-Müller Museum** ranks as the third most important museum of art in the Netherlands, after the Rijksmuseum and the Vincent van Gogh Museum in Amsterdam. Opened in 1938, it is the repository of a remarkable private collection of late-19th-century and early-20th-century paintings, including 278 works by van Gogh that, when combined with the collection in the Amsterdam museum, constitutes nearly his entire oeuvre. Hélène Kröller, née Müller, the wife of a prosperous industrialist, had a remarkable eye for talent and a sixth sense about which painters and paintings would be important. Her first purchase was van Gogh's *Sunflowers.* Among his other well-known paintings in her col-

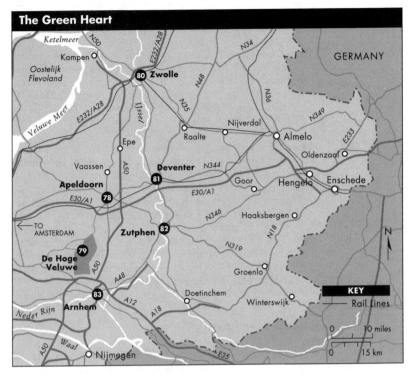

lection are *Potato Eaters, The Bridge at Arles,* and *L'Arlesienne,* copied from a drawing by Gauguin. But Hélène Kröller-Müller was not myopic in her appreciation and perception. She added to her collection of van Goghs with works by Seurat, Picasso, Redon, Braque, and Mondrian. The collection also contains 16th- and 17th-century Dutch paintings, ceramics, Chinese and Japanese porcelain, and contemporary sculpture. The museum building itself, which was designed by Henry van de Velde, artfully brings nature into the galleries through its broad windows, glass walkways, and patios. The gardens and woods around the museum form another gallery in the open air, with a collection of 20th-century sculptures by Aristide Maillol, Jean Dubuffet, Richard Serra, and Claes Oldenburg; works by Barbara Hepworth and Alberto Giacometti are under a special pavilion added in 1953. The museum is in the heart of the Hoge Veluwe National Park. ✉ *National Park De Hoge Veluwe,* ☎ *0318/591–041.* 🎫 *Park and museum Fl 8.* 🕑 *Park and museum Tues.–Sun. 10–5; sculpture garden Tues.–Sun. 10–4:30.*

More than 350 monkeys, apes, chimpanzees, and gorillas wander free in the woods at **Apenheul** park. Some saunter right up to the visitors, and there are also bright flocks of tropical birds. But don't come for a visit if the weather is cold, because the animals disappear into snug nooks in the forest. Watch your bags, too—some of the apes are adept pickpockets. ✉ *Park Berg en Bos,* ☎ *055/357–5757.* 🎫 *Fl 16.* 🕑 *Apr.–June, daily 9:30–5; July–Aug., daily 9:30–6, Sept.–Oct., daily 10–5.*

Dining and Lodging

$$$ ✕ **Echoput.** Not far from Palace Het Loo, Echoput is a much-honored and gracious country restaurant. The large fireplace in the lounge is welcoming in winter, the terrace in summer. With the royal hunting grounds nearby, the restaurant is able to offer fine game dishes nearly year-round. ⊠ *Amersfoortseweg 86,* ☎ *055/519–1248. Reservations essential. AE, DC, MC, V. Closed Mon.*

$ ✕⊡ **Hotel Oranjeoord.** In a small woodland village that seems to be right out of a Grimms fairy tale, the Oranjeoord is a relaxed country hotel with garden rooms, terraces, and a sunny dining room. It is a pleasant choice for a country weekend. ⊠ *Hoog Soeren 134, 7346AH, 5 km (3 mi) west of Apeldoorn,* ☎ *055/519–1227,* 𝔽𝔸𝕏 *055/519–1451. 27 rooms with bath. Restaurant. No credit cards.*

$$$ ⊡ **De Keizerskroon.** A nice cross between a business hotel and a country inn, it is within easy walking distance of Palace Het Loo. Renovations over the past 25 years have obliterated all traces of traditional architecture; in its place is a stylish hotel, with rooms decorated in pastels and furniture that, like the hotel, is a blend of business practical and weekend comfortable. ⊠ *Koningstraat 7,* ☎ *055/521–7744,* 𝔽𝔸𝕏 *055/521–4737. 101 rooms. Pool, sauna. AE, DC, MC, V.*

$ ⊡ **Astra.** On a quiet residential side street, Astra is a small pension-style family hotel that is comfortably furnished in the manner of a Dutch home. Rooms are large for this type of accommodation. There is a pleasant garden terrace behind the house. ⊠ *Bas Backerlaan 12–14,* ☎ *055/522–3022,* 𝔽𝔸𝕏 *055/522–3021. 27 rooms with bath. Exercise room. AE, DC, MC, V.*

Nightlife and the Arts

MUSIC

Incomparable for atmosphere are the concerts on the last Friday of every month at the beautiful **Paleis Het Loo** (⊠ Koninklijk Park 1, ☎ 055/521–2244).

Outdoor Activities and Sports

BIKING

Driving seems a shame in De Hoge Veluwe National Park. There are *free* bicycles (a total of 400 vehicles) for use on the 42 kilometers (26 miles) of bicycle paths and special cycles for people with disabilities.

TENNIS AND SQUASH

Facilities in the region include **De Maten Sports** (⊠ Ambachtsveld 2, ☎ 055/542–5044).

Shopping

Market days in Apeldoorn are Monday and Wednesday mornings, and Saturday at Marktplein in the city center. The late shopping nights are Thursday in the city center, Friday in the suburbs.

Zwolle

⑳ *41 km (26 mi) north of Apeldoorn, 103 km (65 mi) east of Amsterdam.*

Zwolle was an important depot for trade between the Netherlands and Germany during the time of the Hanseatic League, located as it is between the IJssel and another important Dutch river, the Vecht. Founded in 800, it officially became a town in the 12th century. An important Latin school was in Zwolle, and the religious philosopher Thomas à Kempis lived here in the early 1400s, when he wrote his influential work *Imitation of Christ.* Today Zwolle is an important center of cattle trading, grain processing, coffee roasting, and linen manufacturing.

The brick- and stone-embellished **Sassenpoort,** the only one of the original town gates of 1406 left standing, was for centuries a prison. Nowadays only exhibits and photographs on the theme of Zwolle's history are confined within its towers. ⊠ *Sassenstraat, no phone.* ☜ *Free.* ☉ *Weekdays 10–5, weekends noon–5.*

The **Grote Kerkplein** is the main square of Zwolle and the site of the Gothic **Stadhuis** (Town Hall). There is also a charming shop, **Zwolse Balletjes Huis** (⊠ Grote Kerkplein 13, ☎ 038/421–8815), that sells the local sweet specialty, *Zwollse balletjes* (fruit-and-spice-flavored hard candies).

The Gothic **St. Michaelskerk** dates from 1446 and contains a magnificent 18th-century organ made by the famous Schnitger brothers from Hamburg. The church is the final resting place of the 17th-century genre painter Gerard Terborch, who was born in Zwolle. ⊠ *Grote Kerkplein.* ☎ *06/911–22375.* ☉ *Limited visiting hrs.*

The **Stedelijk Museum Zwolle** (Zwolle Municipal Museum) is housed in a building that dates from the mid-16th century. Its principal display is the wainscoted living-dining Blokzil Room, which came from a house in the north part of the province and exemplifies the lifestyle of a prosperous 17th-century family. ⊠ *Broerenkerkplein 15,* ☎ *038/421–4650.* ☜ *Fl 2.50.* ☉ *Tues.–Sat. 10–5, Sun. 2–5.*

OFF THE
BEATEN PATH

KAMPEN – This attractive former herring port lies near the point where the IJssel River empties into IJsselmeer. The **Schepenzaal** (Magistrates' Hall) in the 14th-century Oude Raadhuis (Old Town Hall) is an excellent example of a medieval courtroom. To see the oft-painted skyline at its best, approach the city from across the river by way of the old bridge rather than on the highway: Take N50 and follow signs for IJsselmuiden.

Dining and Lodging

$$$ ✕ **De Librije.** Housed in the former library of a 15th-century monastery, this atmospheric restaurant is known far afield for the excellence of its cuisine. Try the delicious *polderduif,* wild pigeon from the surrounding waterlands, served with a sauce of local berries. ⊠ *Broerenkerkplein 13,* ☎ *038/423–2329. Reservations essential. Jacket required. AE, DC, MC, V. No lunch Sat. Closed Sun.*

$$$ 🏨 **Grand Hotel Wientjes.** Convenient to both the railway station and the city center, this hotel occupies a stately old building. Most rooms are in the modern wings and are both spacious and brightly decorated. It also has theme rooms, including one styled in Old Dutch and a Chinese-style bridal suite with a lacquered four-poster bed and a two-person bubble bath. ⊠ *Stationsweg 7, 8000 AM,* ☎ *038/425–4254,* 📠 *038/425–4260. 57 rooms. Restaurant. AE, DC, MC, V.*

Nightlife

Every Friday is Mellow Night at **Café 'T Zonnetje** (⊠ Luttekestraat 6, ☎ 038/423–5293), but other nights explode with live music as people knock back cut-price cocktails. **JC Hedon** (⊠ Papenstraat 5, ☎ 038/423–1423) is the hottest, hippest dance club in town, though at press time it was keeping an eye open for new premises.

Outdoor Activities and Sports

CANOEING

In summer it's possible, and highly pleasurable, to canoe on the waterways in and around Zwolle. **Vadesto Kanocentrum** (⊠ Veenrand 5, 8051 DW Hattem, ☎ 038/444–5428) at the Potgietersingel rents canoes. The **VVV** (⊠ Zwolle tourist information office; ☞ Visitor Information *in* The Green Heart A to Z, *below*) sells canoeing maps.

Fishing in the streams of Overijssel province near Zwolle is easy and pleasurable. The VVV Zwolle tourist information office (☞ Visitor Information *in* The Green Heart A to Z, *below*) sells one-day fishing licenses for Fl 5. The license includes a list of fishing sites. The tourist office also has a helpful map of the area.

JOGGING

There is a training circuit in Zwolle at the **Haersterveerweg.** Near the center of town are two places suitable for jogging, **Park De Weezenlanden** and **Park 't Engelse Werk.**

TENNIS AND SQUASH

There are good tennis and squash facilities at **Squash Zwolle** (⊠ Near Winkelcentrum Aalanden, ☎ 038/454–8485), **Sportpark Wilhelmina** (⊠ Wilhelminastraat, ☎ 038/421–4826), **Sportpark de Marslanden** (⊠ Marsweg, ☎ 038/421–7189), and **Tenniscentrum Zwolle** (⊠ Palestrinalaan, ☎ 038/454–5100).

Shopping

Market days in Zwolle are Friday morning and Saturday. On Friday, especially, the farmers come to town, and stalls spread through Melkmarkt, Sassenstraat, Grote Markt, Nieuwe Markt, and Grote Kerkplein. On Thursday morning there's an organically grown produce market on Grote Kerkplein. Late shopping is on Thursday.

En Route Leaving Zwolle, follow signs for Wijhe-Olst for a scenic drive along the IJssel River, passing rich marshes filled with wildlife and lush plants. This region, between the river and the German border, is known as the **Salland** and is in the Provence of the Netherlands. A quiet farming area, with its own dialect, it produces asparagus and offers food specialties such as *kruitmoes* (hot porridge with raisins).

Deventer

⑧ *35 km (22 mi) south of Zwolle, 18 km (11 mi) east of Apeldoorn, 107 km (67 mi) east of Amsterdam.*

Founded late in the 8th century by an English cleric named Lubuinus, whose mission in life was to convert the Saxons to Christianity, Deventer was a prosperous port and a powerful bishopric by the 9th century; the town center still reflects this medieval heritage. A center of learning as well, it had a printing industry to disseminate the thoughts of its scholars. It was home at various times to Thomas à Kempis, Pope Adrian VI, Erasmus, and, in the 17th century, French philosopher René Descartes. Deventer has won prizes for the meticulous renovation of its historic houses and public buildings.

Deventer's late Gothic **Waag** (Weigh House), begun in 1528, is a stately testament to the city's Hanseatic past. Inside, an exhibition on town history, from prehistoric times to the present day, includes the Netherlands' oldest bicycle, the spindly *Vélociède*, built in 1870. ⊠ Brink 56, ☎ 0570/693–780, ☉ Tues.–Sat. 10–5, Sun. 2–5.

Ⓒ Two huge medieval houses barely contain the **Speelgoed-en Blikmuseum** (Toys and Tin Museum), an enchanting collection of toys dating from the Middle Ages to the 20th century. There are dolls, puppets, and tin soldiers galore and an exceptional collection of mechanical toys and electric trains. In the museum's darkroom you can see a 17th-century magic lantern and a host of other optical playthings. ⊠ Brink 47, ☎ 0570/693–786. 🎟 Fl 5. ☉ Tues.–Sat. 10–5, Sun. 2–5.

The 13th-century Romanesque-Gothic **Bergkerk** (Church of the Berg Quarter) sits high on a square with pleasing views down medieval side streets (Bergstraat and Roggestraat are particularly appealing). ✉ *Free.* ☉ *Tues.–Fri. 11–5, weekends 1–5.*

NEED A BREAK? **Chez Antoinette** (✉ Roggestraat 10–12, ☎ 0570/016–630) is a restaurant-pub whose menu honors the owners' fascination with everything Portuguese. The building dates from 1303, and the pub (open for lunch and snacks) is the oldest in the city (from 1881).

The **Lubuinuskerk** (St. Lubuinus' Church), a huge stone cross basilica that was built in the 10th century on the site of Lubuinus's small wooden church, has some fine 16th-century murals and a 700-year-old paved floor. Hanging in the 15th-century tower is the oldest extant carillon made by the Hemony brothers, who in the 17th century were the most celebrated bellmakers in the world. The tower can be climbed in the summer months for a wide view of the town; the carillon is played at least twice a week. ✉ *Grote Kerkhof.* ✉ *Free.* ☉ *Weekdays 10–5, Sat. 1:30–5.*

Nightlife

De Waagschaal (✉ Brink 77, ☎ 0570/617–190) is one of the most popular of the concentration of Brown Cafés on Deventer's main square. A bicycle and other eccentric decor hang on the wall at **Lightenhill's Pub** (✉ Brink 50–51, ☎ 0570/619–889), which has a range of British beers, such curiously named snacks as Ma Baker's Bitterballs, and occasional live bands.

Outdoor Activities and Sports

TENNIS AND SQUASH

Energetic locals in Deventer head for the **Tennis en Squashcentrum** (✉ Bremenweg 29, ☎ 0570/622–107).

Shopping

Friday and Saturday are market days in Deventer, when the Brink is crowded with fresh-produce stalls and a few antiques dealers. On the first Sunday in August the largest Book Market in the Netherlands stretches for 3 kilometers (2 miles) along the IJsel.

Zutphen

82 *15 km (9 mi) south of Deventer, 22 km (14 mi) southeast of Apeldoorn, 107 km (67 mi) east of Amsterdam.*

Known as the Tower City for the many spires that rise above its city center, Zutphen is on a small hill at the juncture of the rivers IJssel and Berkel. It was one of the region's wealthiest towns in the 14th and 15th centuries. Today, the charming, once-walled town is a patchwork of medieval houses and courtyards, churches and towers, and the remnants of old city gates.

The small **Henriette Polak Museum** offers changing exhibitions from its substantial collection of 20th-century Dutch figurative art. Climb the stairs to the attic to see the tiny room used in the 17th century as a *schuilkerk*, a secret Roman Catholic church. ✉ *Zaadmarkt 88,* ☎ *0575/516–878.* ✉ *Fl 5.* ☉ *Tues.–Fri. 11–5, weekends 1:30–5.*

NEED A BREAK? **De Pelikaan** (✉ Pelikaanstraat 6, ☎ 0575/512–024), a coffee and tea emporium dating from the late 1880s, is filled with heady aromas. In the adjacent tearoom you can take your pick from a long list of tea and coffee blends.

St. Walburgskerk (St. Walburgis Church) was begun in the 12th century in Romanesque style and enlarged in the 16th century in Gothic style. It is busy with roofs and a wide variety of building materials. Within, the side walls and vaults are ornamented with 14th- and 15th-century frescoes; the richly decorated organ loft contains a Baeder organ. The **Librije** (library), in a side chapel, is where you'll find the true treasures of Zutphen: This library dates from 1561, and under its white, vaulted ceilings are rare and beautiful early manuscripts and incunabula, chained to rows of reading stands. At press time both church and Librije were undergoing extensive renovation, which is expected to be completed by May 1997. ⊠ *Kerkhof.* 🏛 *Fl 3.50.; combined with walking tour Fl 5.* ☉ *May–Sept., tours Mon. at 2 and 3, Tues.–Sat. at 11, 2, and 3.*

Dining and Lodging

$ ✕🏨 **Berkhotel.** With a stream running by outside, and rooms decorated in English country style (with pastels and floral prints), it's hard to believe that this hotel is almost in the heart of town. The restaurant has a grand ambience, with chandeliers, live piano music, palms, and candlelight; the cuisine is strictly vegetarian, prepared with an Asian touch. ⊠ *Marspoortstraat 19, 7201 JA,* ☎ *0575/511–135,* 🅵🅰🆇 *0575/541–950. 19 rooms, 10 with bath/shower. Restaurant, bar, lounge. AE, MC, V.*

Nightlife

Café 't Winkeltje (⊠ Groenmarkt 34, ☎ 0575/511–804) is a welcoming Brown Café with a mixed crowd, rock and golden oldies over the sound system, and a good assortment of specialty beers.

Shopping

On Thursday morning there's a busy market in the center of town. Late shopping is on Friday.

Bronkhorst

9 km (5 mi) south of Zutphen.

Bronkhorst, the tiniest town in the Netherlands, has a population of just 160. The entire town is protected by the national historic preservation program. There are curious little museums and shops here, as well as an exceptionally good restaurant. The 14th-century chapel is particularly attractive and peaceful.

Dining and Lodging

$$$ ✕🏨 **Herberg de Gouden Leeuw.** This is a peaceful country inn that happens to boast an excellent restaurant, with formal and informal dining areas and a fireplace in the lounge. On Saturday nights, diners are entertained with piano music. The cuisine is traditional Continental, with such choices as beef bourguignonne and veal cordon bleu. Game, asparagus, and lobster are served in season. Special three- to six-course menus cost between Fl 55 and Fl 130. The guest rooms are simple and are inexpensively priced. ⊠ *Bovenstraat 2,* ☎ *0575/451–231,* 🅵🅰🆇 *0575/452–566. 8 rooms, 2 with shower. Restaurant. AE, DC, MC, V.*

Arnhem

❽③ *25 km (16 mi) south of Apeldoorn, 92 km (58 mi) southeast of Amsterdam.*

Arnhem is best known as the "bridge too far." Near the end of World War II the Allies followed up the invasion of Normandy by seeking to cut off the German army entrenched in the eastern Netherlands. The battle involved the largest airborne operation of the war, and 3,000 British, American, and Canadian lives were lost in three weeks of fighting that left the Allies short of their goal, which was finally achieved seven months later.

The **Airborne Museum** includes a large scale model of the Arnhem region and incorporates memorabilia, weapons, and equipment to depict the crucial battle that took place here during World War II. Tanks and guns sit on the lawn, and an audiovisual presentation describes the progress of the battle. ⊠ *Utrechtseweg 232, Oosterbeek,* ☎ *026/333–7710.* ▣ *Fl 5.* ◷ *Mon.–Sat. 11–5, Sun. and holidays noon–5.*

Much of Arnhem was destroyed during World War II, but around the **Korenmarkt** old warehouses have become pubs, cafés, restaurants, and discotheques, preserving a sense of the old town in a cozy entertainment area. A weekly market is held in the shadows of Arnhem's **Grote Kerk** (Great Church), a three-aisled cross-basilica that dates back to the 15th century. The church is also the site of traveling exhibitions. Among Arnhem's chief attractions are its trolley buses (unique in the Netherlands) and its extensive surrounding parkland, including the 185-acre **Sonsbeek Park.**

The **Nederlands Openlucht Museum** (Open Air Museum), in a 44-acre park, re-creates Dutch country life through farm buildings typical of their regions, transported to the site from every province of the Netherlands. Here you can see furnished farmhouses, outbuildings, windmills, and crafts shops in a setting that reflects the varied nature of the Dutch landscape. The museum is on the northern outskirts of town. ⊠ *Schelmseweg 89,* ☎ *026/357–6111.* ▣ *Fl 16.* ◷ *Apr.–Oct., daily 10–5.*

☾ More than 3,000 animals inhabit **Burgers' Zoo** in Arnhem. Established in 1913 on the principle that there should be as few barriers as possible between human beings and animals, this zoo includes a large safari park with roaming lions, zebras, giraffes, and rhinos, plus a tropical rain forest and a subtropical desert. ⊠ *Schelmseweg 85,* ☎ *026/442–4534 or 026/445–0373.* ▣ *Fl 21.* ◷ *Summer 9–7, last safari at 5; winter 9–sunset, last safari at 4.*

Dining and Lodging

$$$ ✕ **Kasteel Doorwerth.** This restaurant offers a rare experience: dining in a moated castle near the Rhine, 8 kilometers (5 miles) from Arnhem. The timbered dining room, once the castle's coach house, is furnished with antiques, and the cuisine is in the new, French-inspired Dutch mode; vegetables and herbs come from the castle gardens. ⊠ *Fonteinallee 4, Doorwerth,* ☎ *026/333–3420. Reservations essential. AE, DC, MC, V. Closed Tues.*

$$–$$$ ✕ **Belvedere.** This noted eaterie is actually in the neighboring town of Nijmegen. Housed in a tall tower high on a hill in the middle of Belvedere Park, overlooking a wide bend in the river Waal, it has possibly the best river view in the Netherlands. In the beamed dining room are only a handful of tables; the menu is new Dutch cooking, including choices such as duck breast in an envelope of goose liver. ⊠ *Kelfkensbos 60,* ☎ *024/322–6861. Reservations essential. AE, DC, MC, V. No lunch Sat., Mon. Closed Sun.*

$ ✕▥ **Hotel Blanc.** This small hotel is not far from the railway station in central Arnhem. In a turn-of-the-century town house, the Blanc offers bright and comfortable rooms and a friendly café for guests. ⊠ *Coehoornstraat 4, 6811 LA,* ☎ *026/442–8072,* ℻ *026/443–4749. 22 rooms, 4 with bath, 18 with shower. Café, bar, lounge. AE, DC, MC, V.*

$$$ 🏨 **Hotel de Bilderberg.** In a wooded setting in the suburb of Oosterbeek, de Bilderberg caters to business travelers as well as weekenders. The rooms are spacious and bright, with comfortable modern furnishings. ⊠ *Utrechtseweg 261, 6862AK, Oosterbeek,* ☎ *026/334–0843,* 🅵🅰🆇 *026/333–4651. 144 rooms. Indoor pool, sauna, tennis court, exercise room. AE, DC, MC, V.*

$ 🏨 **Hotel Molendal.** In an Art Deco–era house in a residential neighborhood near Sonsbeek Park, the hotel has spacious and high-ceilinged rooms. Decorative elements in public spaces carry out the Art Deco heritage of the building, while the bedrooms have a more modern design. ⊠ *Cronjestraat 15,* ☎ *026/442–4858,* 🅵🅰🆇 *026/443–6614. 16 rooms with shower. Bar, lounge. AE, DC, MC, V.*

Shopping

Market days in Arnhem are Friday morning and Saturday at Kerkplein. Late shopping is on Thursday.

OFF THE BEATEN PATH   The pre-Roman city of **Nijmegen** is situated strategically near the junction of the Maas–Waalkanal and the river Waal. The river is the main branch of the Rhine and the second of the great rivers of the Netherlands that lead to the North Sea. Nijmegen is a lively university town and shopping center for the region, as well as gateway to the southern provinces. The city's **Belvedere Park** offers a splendid view of the river below and a restaurant in a tower. Nearby is the **Waalkade riverfront esplanade,** lined with restaurants, shops, and a casino, a pleasant place to stroll.

The Green Heart A to Z

Arriving and Departing

BY CAR

From Amsterdam, take A1 to Apeldoorn and Deventer or Zutphen; A2 and A12 to Arnhem; or A1 and A28 to Zwolle. Nijmegen is easily reached from Arnhem by A325.

BY TRAIN

There are **express Intercity trains** (☎ 06/9292) twice each hour from Amsterdam to Apeldoorn, Deventer, Zwolle, and Arnhem; there is hourly service to Nijmegen, with an additional train each hour connecting in Arnhem. To reach Zutphen by train, change in either Arnhem or Zwolle.

Getting Around

BY BICYCLE

Free bicycles are provided for visitors in the national park De Hoge Veluwe. In the cities of this region, you can also rent a bicycle at railway stations or from Blakborn (⊠ Soerenseweg 3, ☎ 055/521–5679), Harleman (⊠ Arnhemseweg 28, ☎ 055/533–4346), and M. Janssen (⊠ Koninginnelaan 54, ☎ 055/521–2582) in Apeldoorn; Mantel (⊠ 95 Lawick van Pabststraat, ☎ 026/442–0624), H. Matser (⊠ 784 Kemperbergweg, ☎ 026/442–3172), or R.W. Roelofs (⊠ 1 G.A. van Nispenstraat, ☎ 026/442–6014) in Arnhem; and Scholten (⊠ Luttekestraat 7, ☎ 038/421–7378) in Zwolle.

BY BUS

There is a comprehensive network of local and regional bus services in the Green Heart. They provide a useful supplement to the train service (for information, ☎ 06/9292).

BY TAXI

Taxis wait at city railway stations; additional stands may be available in central shopping and hotel districts. To call a taxi: Apeldoorn (☎

055/541–3413), Arnhem (☎ 026/445–0000), Deventer (☎ 0570/626–200 or 0570/622–537), Nijmegen (☎ 024/322–6000 or 024/323–3000), Zutphen (☎ 0575/525–345 or 05755/512–935), Zwolle (☎ 038/455–1133).

Contacts and Resources

EMERGENCIES

National Emergency Alarm Number for police, fire, and ambulance: ☎ 06/112.

GUIDED TOURS

The tourist offices (☞ Visitor Information, *below*) in most cities in the region organize walking tours in the summer months. Inquire for times, minimum group size, and whether or not English translation is offered or can be arranged.

In summer (late June–late Aug.) the **VVV Apeldoorn** (☎ 06/916–81636) offers a variety of tours through the surrounding nature parks, including a three-hour combined bus tour and evening walk through parts of the Royal Forest not usually open to the public (Fl 12.50).

HOSPITALS

Apeldoorn (☎ 055/581–8181). **Arnhem** (☎ 026/321–0000). **Deventer** (☎ 0570/646–666). **Zutphen** (☎ 0575/592–592). **Zwolle** (☎ 038/429–9911 or 038/426–2222).

VISITOR INFORMATION

VVV Apeldoorn (⊠ Stationstraat 72, ☎ 06/916–81636). **VVV Arnhem Region** (⊠ Stationsplein 45, ☎ 026/442–0330). **VVV Deventer** (⊠ Pikeursbaan 6, ☎ 0570/613–100). **VVV Zutphen** (⊠ Groenmarkt 40, ☎ 0575/519–355). **VVV Zwolle** (⊠ Grote-Kerkplein 14, ☎ 038/421–3900).

THE NORTH

In the northern provinces of the Netherlands, life is more peaceful; there are quiet streams and a chain of sparkling lakes 64 kilometers (40 miles) long to tempt you to sample the outdoor life. For the most part, museums are small and quiet but have surprisingly rich displays, and there are luxury resorts hidden in small wooded villages that rival the attractions of the more cosmopolitan parts of the country. The people of Friesland are proud of their ancient culture. Their language, *Fries,* is very different from Dutch and spoken even among young people. Street signs are often in both languages. Friesland has an unusual array of sporting activities, including sailing regattas, bike races, long-distance walks, a local version of pole-vaulting, and—*if* the canals freeze in the winter—one of the world's most famous ice-skating races, which flashes through 11 cities.

Whether the canals are frozen over or not, you can get a good taste of the area by beginning in Leeuwarden, the capital of Friesland, then looping through the Frisian countryside and heading eastward to the thriving city of Groningen.

Pleasures and Pastimes

This part of the country offers lots of water and open space, its own tradition of porcelain making, and the opportunity to take part in some unique sports.

DINING

The local pea soup, *Erwetensoep,* is the ideal culinary weapon against icy Frisian winters. It has the consistency of thick porridge and often has lumps of bacon or sausage floating in it. Fill up those extra corners with a slice of *karnemelkbrood* (buttermilk bread), and wash it down with warm milk, flavored with aniseed, or a mug of Frisian tea—served extra sweet. If your palate is accustomed to more delicate tastes, try lamb from the island of Texel, its flesh fragrant with the herbs that compose its main diet.

LODGING

Most of the main cities of the north are disappointing when it comes to finding interesting accommodations. If you're looking for something other than a standard, business-type hotel, turn your attention to smaller villages or to hotels converted from gracious old country houses, such as De Klinze at Oudkerk, or Lauswolt at Beetsterzwaag.

MADE IN MAKKUM

The people of Delft are not the only Netherlanders to make porcelain. At around the same time as the Delftians began making their famous blue-and-white Delftware, the people of Makkum put the soft clay that surrounded their village to similar use. Ten generations later, they're still at it. Makkumware is just as fine quality as Delftware but is multicolored. Watch patterns being painted by hand at the Tichelaar family factory in Makkum—a fascinating experience. From a shop attached to the factory, you can take home a souvenir that is a little different from everyone else's Delft.

MUD AND ICE

Northerners make the most of their climate. In the summer you can indulge in *wadlopen,* or "horizontal mountain climbing," as the locals jokingly call it—wading thigh-deep across the mudflats to the Wadden Islands. It is exhausting work, but done with tremendous good cheer. After much laughing, shrieking, and sweating, the group finally arrives at its destination, and everyone dives into a good Frisian feast. Each winter, as the weather worsens, a frisson of tension ripples through the country. Will this be a year for the *Elfstedentocht,* the "Eleven-Cities Tour"? This famous skating race—between 11 Frisian towns—is only possible during severe freezes. The last one was in 1996, but prior to that, no *Elfstedentocht* was held for 10 years. The origin of the race goes back hundreds of years, though it was only in 1909 that the present 200-kilometer (120-mile) course was agreed upon. As well as the official race, which attracts participants from all over the world, there is an unofficial *Elfstentocht* enjoyed by thousands. Spectators line the route, and wayside stalls sell copious amounts of warm food and drink. Whether you're up to such a gruelling ordeal or not, the race can be great fun, and no one says you have to finish it.

Exploring the North

Although a whole new province (Flevoland) has recently been reclaimed from the water, the northern Netherlands remains essentially split in two by an inland sea, the IJsselmeer. Today, a dike closes off the top of the IJsselmeer. A road runs over the dike, making transport between the two "halves" of the north much more direct than before. On the banks of the IJsselmeer, you'll find attractive towns with harbors and crafts shops; to the east are Leeuwarden and Groningen, the region's two main cities, and a scattering of lakes. Dotted along off the country's northern coastline are the Wadden Islands.

Great Itineraries

Groningen and Leeuwarden could each take up a full day, although it is possible to appreciate both in one day. At least another day or two can happily be spent exploring the old towns along the IJsselmeer.

Numbers in the text correspond to numbers in the margin and on The North map.

IF YOU HAVE 3 DAYS
Start at **Groningen** ⑧⑨, with a visit to its startlingly modern museum and a look-in at the market in the town center. Then cross over to **Leeuwarden** ⑧④ to see the national ceramics collection at Museum Het Princessehof. Spend the night out of town at De Klinze, in the village of 🏠 **Aldtsjerk/Oudkerk.** Next day, visit **Franeker** ⑧⑤ and the eccentric Eise Eisinga Planetarium, before going on to **Makkum** ⑧⑥ to see Makkumware in the making. The night is spent in nearby 🏠 **Beetsterzwaag.** On your last day, visit the museum at **Workum** ⑧⑦, dedicated to the work of another Dutch eccentric, Jopie Huisman; then finish up at **Hindeloopen** ⑧⑧, a port that seems lost in time.

IF YOU HAVE 5 DAYS
Spend your first day in 🏠 **Groningen** ⑧⑨, exploring its museums and market and getting a taste of the atmosphere of the university quarter. On day two travel to **Leeuwarden** ⑧④ to see ceramics and elegant 18th-century architecture, spending the night out of town in the village of 🏠 **Aldtsjerk/Oudkerk.** Then travel through **Franeker** ⑧⑤ to visit the porcelain factory at **Makkum** ⑧⑥. Base yourself at 🏠 **Beetsterzwaag** for the rest of your stay, exploring the towns of Workum and Hindelopen on the first day, and spending your remaining time enjoying watersports on the Frisian lakes.

IF YOU HAVE 7 DAYS
Take life slowly. After a day in 🏠 **Groningen** ⑧⑨, book into De Klinze at 🏠 **Aldtsjerk/Oudkerk** for two nights. Pay a day's visit to **Leeuwarden** ⑧④, and then go wading over the mudflats (or take a ferry) to visit one of the Wadden Islands. On the fourth day, meander through **Franeker** ⑧⑤, visit the pretty port of Harlingen, and then head down to the porcelain factory at **Makkum** ⑧⑥. Check into a country hotel, such as the Lauswolt at 🏠 **Beetsterzwaag** for your remaining three nights. Spend a day visiting the old fortified town of Sloten, together with **Hindelopen** ⑧⑧ and **Workum** ⑧⑦. While away your remaining time canoeing, sailing, or windsurfing on the Frisian lakes.

When to Tour the North

Summer is the time to come if you like watersports and dislike cold weather. Mudwalking to the islands is only possible from May to September. But to get a true feel of the north, why not brave the winter, take your chances in the *Elfstedentocht,* and experience the delicious warmth of *Erwetensoep* (pea soup) working its way throughout your body?

Leeuwarden

⑧④ *132 km (83 mi) north of Amsterdam.*

An odd mixture of distinctions identifies the small provincial capital of Leeuwarden. On one hand, it was the official residence of the first hereditary *stadhouder* (king) of the Netherlands; on the other, it is believed to have been the birthplace of the notorious dancer-spy, Mata Hari. The *stadhouders* left a legacy of elegant architecture; the town's most infamous citizen is honored by a small statuette beside the canal.

Leeuwarden is well known as the focal point of the Dutch dairy industry and site of one of the largest cattle markets in Europe. It also is home to one of the world's finest collections of Asian ceramics. The world-famous 200-kilometer (124-mile) *Elfenstedentocht* (Eleven Cities Tour) ice-skating race departs from Leeuwarden when—or if—there

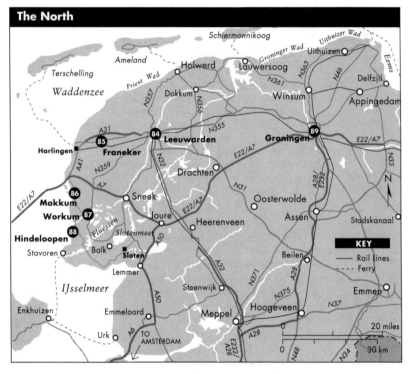

The North

is ice on the canals connecting the capital with 10 other cities of the province (including Harlingen, Franeker, Workum, Hindeloopen, Stavoren, and Sloten).

Pride of place in Leeuwarden goes to the **Museum het Princessehof,** the former residence of Marie-Louise of Hesse-Kassell, who was the widow of the first prince of Orange. Her gracious dining room has been preserved, but nowadays the house is given over to the Nederlands Keramiekmuseum (Netherlands Ceramic Museum), which documents the history of fine ceramics, Asian as well as European, and modern as well as ancient. The remarkable collection of Chinese stoneware and porcelain dates from the third millennium BC through the 20th century. Look closely at the plates and tiles commissioned in China by the Dutch East India Company; you'll notice decidedly Asian features on Dutch-costumed merchants and their women. To reach the museum from the railway station, follow the wide street across the Nieuwestade canal, and then jog left to the next bridge before continuing along Kleine Kerkstraat. ⊠ *Grote Kerkstraat 9–15,* ☎ *058/212–7438.* ⊠ *Fl 6.50.* ☉ *Mon.–Sat. 10–5, Sun. 2–5.*

Situated in a blissfully peaceful square, the 13th-century **Grotekerk** (Great Church), a Jacobin church, has been reconstructed and restored over the centuries, most recently in 1978; it is the traditional burial place of the Nassau line, ancestors of the royal family. ⊠ *Jacobinerkerkhof,* ☎ *058/215–1203.* ⊠ *Free.* ☉ *June–Aug., Tues.–Fri. 2–4.*

The ornate Renaissance building known as the **Kanselarij** (Chancellery), which was the residence of George of Saxony when he governed the region in the 16th century, today forms the heart of a small museum complex. From the Grotekerk, follow Bij de Put and its continuation, Sacramentsstraat, across the Voorstreek canal; follow Tuinen calan and turn right at Turfmarkt. In the attic of the Kanselarij is the **Verzetsmuseum Friesland** (Resistance Museum), an intriguing collection of memorabilia and exhibits honoring the strong Frisian resistance movement under the German occupation during World War II. The provincial **Fries Museum** (Frisian Museum) occupies the rest of the Kanselarij and buildings across the road (a tunnel links the two wings). Here you will find a varied collection documenting the history and culture of Friesland. Among its treasures is a portrait by Rembrandt of his wife, Saskia; she was the daughter of the mayor of Leeuwarden. The couple married in 1634 in the nearby village of St. Annaparochie. Mata Hari, that other famed daughter of Leeuwarden, is soon to have an exhibition to herself. A permanent multimedia display on her life is scheduled to open in 1997. ⊠ *Turfmarkt 11,* ☎ *058/212–3001.* 🖻 *Fl 6.50.* ⊙ *Mon.–Sat. 11–6, Sun. 3–5.*

Facing one another across the leafy **Hofplein** are Leeuwarden's **Stadhuis** (Town Hall) and the **Hof,** which was the former residence of the Frisian stadhouders. In the center of the square is a statue of Willem Louis, the first stadhouder, locally known as *Us Heit* (Our Father).

For many centuries, the commercial hub of Leeuwarden has been the Waagplein, which is dominated by the redbrick **Waag** (Weigh House), decorated with heraldic lions. Built at the end of the 16th century, it was used as a weigh house for butter and cheese until the late 19th century; it now houses a bank and a restaurant.

NEED A BREAK?

In an old wooden Dutch sailing boat, you can enjoy a variety of traditional Dutch pancakes, both sweet and savory. The **Pannekoekschip** (⊠ Pancake Ship, Willemskade 69, ☎ 058/212-0903) is moored midway between the railway station and the center of town.

If you happen to be in Leeuwarden on Friday morning, find your way to the Frieslandhal on the perimeter of town for the **weekly cow market.** It is one of the largest in Europe and offers a look into what this part of the Netherlands is really all about. ⊠ *FEC, Helikonweg,* ☎ *058/294–1500.*

Dining and Lodging

$ ✕ **Spinoza.** Three rooms and the shady garden courtyard of an 18th-century city mansion make up this popular restaurant. It is one of those cavernous spaces that, through the patina of age and subtle lighting, manages also to be intimate. The cuisine is an odd, though delicious, mixture of Frisian and Indonesian, so you can follow vegetable-and-cheese soup with chicken in a spicy peanut sauce. ⊠ *Eewal 50–52,* ☎ *058/212–9393. Reservations essential. V.*

$$$$ ✕🏨 **Landgoed De Klinze.** In a wooded town not far from Leeuwarden, De Klinze is a semiresort created from a 17th-century country estate. The roomy suites in the manor house are decorated with vintage furniture and antiques; the bright and spacious guest rooms, decorated in a cheerful lemon-yellow and white, are in a separate, modern wing that also includes the spa. Dinner is in the former parlors, with views of the woods. The cuisine is French. ⊠ *Van Sminiaweg 32–36, Oudkerk/Aldtsjerk, 10 km (8 mi) northeast of Leeuwarden,* ☎ *058/256–1050,* 🗷 *058/256–1060. 22 rooms with bath, 5 suites. Restaurant, indoor pool, beauty salon, sauna. AE, DC, MC, V.*

$$$ ✕🏨 **Oranjehotel.** Primarily a business hotel, Oranjehotel is directly across from the railway station. The rooms are comfortable; the hotel is a local gathering place with a busy pub and a fine restaurant serving traditional Continental cuisine. ⊠ *Stationsweg 4,* ☎ *058/212–6241,* 🗷

058/212–1441. 78 rooms. Restaurant, bar. AE, DC, MC, V. Closed Dec. 25–26.

Nightlife

The generally tame nightlife scene in Leeuwarden is enlivened by **De Brouwershoeck** (⊠ Poststraat 21, ☎ 058/215–2916), a music café that offers live jazz, blues, and funk. **Café Mukkes** (⊠ Grote Hoogstraat 26, ☎ 058/215–9800) brings a rousing selection of local bands to a crowd of enthusiastic young fans.

Outdoor Activities and Sports

If Leeuwarden remains the most cosmopolitan center of the North region, it also is a great base from which to set out to enjoy the area's rich outlets for water sports.

CANOEING

Friesland offers a wealth of canoeing opportunities, along quiet countryside waterways and following canals through attractive towns. Canoeing routes have been laid out and special maps have been printed. Check with the respective tourist offices. Three of the largest canoe renting facilities in Friesland are **Watersportbedrijf De Drijfveer** (⊠ U. Twijnstrawei 31, 8491 CJ Akkrum, ☎ 0566/652–789), **Makkumerstrand** (⊠ Suderseewei 19, 5784 GK Makkum, ☎ 0515/232–285), and **De Ulepanne/Balk** (⊠ Tsjamkedijkje 1, 8561 HA Balk, ☎ 0514/602–982).

KAATSEN

During the summer months, you will find local matches of the Frisian ball game *kaatsen* (similar to baseball) played in the villages throughout Friesland; major tournaments are held in August.

POLSSTOKSPRINGEN

Another uniquely Frisian sport is *polsstokspringen,* which involves pole-vaulting over canals. The main competition is held in Winsum in August.

SAILING AND BOATING

Friesland is bordered by the large and windswept IJsselmeer (Lake IJssel). The province is also cut with a swath of lakes, canals, and small rivers that offer sailing or boating opportunities. Throughout the summer you will find weekend racing on the Frisian lakes. The summer's main event, however, is the two-week series of **Skûtjesilen Races** (late July) using the uniquely Dutch vessels, *skûtjes,* which are wide-bottom sailing barges.

There are more than 150 companies throughout Friesland renting boats and sailboats, including **Watersportbedrijf Anja** (⊠ Meersweg 9a, 9001 BG Grou, ☎ 0566/621–373), **Botenverhuurbedrijf Grou** (⊠ Wilhelminastraat 9001 KE Grou, ☎ 0566/623–810), **A.E. Wester en Zn., 'De Blieken'** (⊠ Garde Jagersweg 4–5, Postbus 51, 9001 ZB Grou, ☎ 0566/621–335, ℻ 0566/623–840), **Watersportcamping Heeg** (⊠ De Burd 25a, 8621 JX Heeg, ☎ 0515/442–328), **Jachtwerf Frisia** (⊠ Oude Oppenhuizerw 79, 8606 JC Sneek, ☎ 0515/412–814, ℻ 0515/418–182), and **Top En Twel Zeilcentrum** (⊠ It Ges 6, 8606 JK Sneek, ☎ 0515/419–192).

WINDSURFING

Where there's water and a breeze there are Windsurfers. In Friesland the following firms rent both equipment and wet suits: **De Ulepanne/Balk** (⊠ Tsjamkedykje 1, 8571 MS Balk, ☎ 0514/602–982), **Jeugdherberg Oer 'T Hout** (⊠ Raadhuisstraat 18, 9001 AG Grou, ☎

0566/621–528), and **Top En Twel Zeilcentrum** (⊠ It Ges 6, 8606 JT Sneek, ☎ 0515/419–192).

Shopping

Market days are Friday (until 3:30) at Leeuwarden, Monday afternoon at Wilhelminaplein, and Wednesday morning at Akkerstraat. Late shopping is on Thursday.

Franeker

85 *17 km (11 mi) west of Leeuwarden.*

In the Middle Ages Franeker was a leading academic town. Although there is no university here today, there are Renaissance gables aplenty, pretty canals, and one or two curious museums.

The **Eise Eisinga Planetarium** is one man's attempt to demonstrate why the planets do not collide. In the late 18th century a local clergyman convinced the inhabitants that the end of the world was imminent, due to a collision of the planets. When his dire prediction failed to materialize, a local scoffer set out to help his neighbors understand why. One wonders what his wife must have thought, for Eise spent years turning his living-room ceiling into a continuously moving display of interplanetary action, and his home's closets and attic into storage for the workings needed to carry out his unusual experiment in education and home decoration. ⊠ *Eise Eisingastraat 3,* ☎ *0517/393–070.* 🖃 *Fl 4.* ☉ *Oct.–Apr. 14, Tues.–Sat. 10–12:30 and 1:30–5; Apr. 15–Sept., Mon.–Sat. 10–12:30 and 1:30–5, Sun. 1–5.*

En Route   Just a short drive through the flat Frisian waterlands brings you to the small port city of **Harlingen.** A walk along its main canal will remind you of Amsterdam in that several homes are copies of canal houses in the capital. After Harlingen, avoid the N31 main road, and take the smaller (unnumbered but signposted) road along the dike toward Zurich and Makkum. On one side sprawls farmland and waterlands rich in bird life. On the other, if you stop and climb the dike, you can look out across the Waddensee.

NEED A BREAK?   Facing the main canal in Harlingen is the pleasant, small hotel-restaurant **Anna Caspari** (⊠ Noorderhaven 69, ☎ 0517/412–065), where you can have lunch or dinner, or just a coffee while overlooking the canal.

Makkum

86 *20 km (13 mi) south of Franeker, 37 km (23 mi) southwest of Leeuwarden.*

If you are a lover of fine pottery, you will know that multicolored Makkumware is as important and treasured in Dutch homes as the better-known blue-and-white Delftware. This tiny Frisian town, where it is produced, has some fine old buildings and a sleepy, country atmosphere.

The small, family-owned factory, **Tichelaars Koninklijke Makkumer Aardewerk en Tegelfabriek** (Tichelaar's Royal Makkum Pottery and Tile Factory), which has made Makkumware under license from the royal family for 10 generations, invites you to watch the craftspeople at work; they also operate a shop where you can buy the products of the sole supplier of Makkumware to the world. ⊠ *Turfmarkt 63,* ☎ *0515/231–341.* 🖃 *Fl 4.* ☉ *Tours Mon.–Thurs. 10–11:30 and 1–4; Fri. 10–11:30 and 1–3; factory showrooms weekdays 9–5:30, Sat. 10–5.*

A late-17th-century weigh house now accommodates the **Fries Aardewerkmuseum DeWaag** (Frisian Pottery Museum), a small collection of ceramic tiles and other pottery that includes many contributions by the Tichelaar family. ✉ *Waaggebouw, Pruikmakershoek 2,* ☎ *0515/231–422.* ⊡ *Fl 3.* ⊙ *Apr.–mid-Sept., Mon.–Sat. 10–5, Sun. 1:30–5; Nov.–Mar., weekdays 10–noon and 1–4.*

Workum

87 *10 km (6 mi) south of Makkum, 38 km (24 mi) southwest of Leeuwarden.*

The small seaside town of Workum was once an important trading town and harbor. Today, all that hints at its past prosperity are a few streets of elegant 16th- and 17th-century architecture. But Workum is also home to one of the most-visited museums in Friesland.

One man's art fills the **Jopie Huisman Museum** and attracts 100,000 visitors a year to Workum. Jopie Huisman was born in Workum and lives here still in a house by an eel stream where he fishes every night. What is unusual about the man, and his art, is that he was a junk man all his life; sketching and painting every chance he had. Without benefit of formal instruction, he produced an abundance of fine canvases and drawings, many reminiscent of the careful duplication of fabric and texture in the work of the early Dutch masters. Jopie Huisman, however, has made haunting compositions of the rags, worn shoes, and discarded dolls he collected in his travels. ✉ *Noard 6,* ☎ *0515/543–131.* ⊡ *Fl 5.* ⊙ *Mar. and Nov., daily 1–5; Apr.–Oct., Mon.–Sat. 10–5, Sun. 1–5.*

Hindeloopen

88 *6 km (4 mi) south of Workum, 44 km (28 mi) southwest of Leeuwarden.*

On a slip of land projecting into the IJsselmeer, Hindeloopen is surrounded on three sides by water, crisscrossed by canals, and virtually stitched together by wooden bridges. Centuries ago, Hindeloopen was a spot favored by sea captains as a home base, and many old houses remain here. The town is also known for its colorful local costume and for its traditional painted furniture.

Housed in a building that served as Town Hall from 1683 to 1919, the **Museum Hidde Nijland Stichting** brims with the brightly painted wooden furniture that is Hindeloopen's specialty. Finely decorated period rooms give you an idea of how more prosperous mariners lived in past centuries, and the walls are covered in decorative 18th-century Frisian tiles. ✉ *Dijkweg,* ☎ *0514/521–420.* ⊡ *Fl 3.50.* ⊙ *Mar.–Oct., Mon.–Sat. 10–5, Sun. 1:30–5.*

En Route　From Hindeloopen you are within easy driving distance of the **Frisian Lakes,** which lure Dutch and international sailors and boating enthusiasts every summer. The N359, just outside Hindeloopen or Workum, takes you across the countryside and across the connecting land between one of the largest lakes and its outlet. The small fortified towns of **Sloten** and **Balk** are focal points in this area of southwestern Friesland, known as **Gaasterland.**

☾　From April through October you can follow the **Aldfaers Erf** (Our Forefathers' Heritage) route, which weaves through the Frisian countryside in a small area bounded by the towns of Makkum, Bolsward, and Workum, stopping at 12 restored buildings and workshops. In Exmorra you can visit the agricultural museum, a village grocery, and a schoolroom; in Allingawier, a farm, church, painter's workshop, forge, bakery, and two residences; in Piaam, an ornithological museum; and in Ferwoude, a carpenter's workshop. ⊠ *Postbus 176, Bolsward,* ☎ *0515/575–681.* ⊘ *Apr.–Oct., daily 10–5.*

<table>
<tr><td>OFF THE
BEATEN PATH</td><td>**WADDEN ISLANDS –** Of all the unexpected places in the Netherlands, these islands, which shelter the northern coastline from the North Sea, are perhaps the most intriguing. They offer varying degrees of seclusion or socialization and plenty of opportunity for water sports, beach walking, and birding. The need for dikes to hold back the sea makes broad beaches impossible along the long northern coastline of the Netherlands, but there are plenty of wide sandy beaches on these islands. *Ferries: from Harlingen to Terschelling (*☎ *0562/442–141); from Holwerd to Ameland (*☎ *0519/542–001); and from Lauwersoog to Schiermonnikoog (*☎ *0519/339–050). For accommodations on the islands contact VVV Friesland (*⊠ *Stationsplein 1, 8911 AC Leeuwarden,* ☎ *06/ 32024060,* ☒ *058/213-6555).*</td></tr>
</table>

Groningen

89 *141 km (89 mi) east of Leeuwarden, 184 km (116 mi) northeast of Amsterdam.*

Groningen is a university town as well as a major commercial center of the northern provinces of the Netherlands. A member of the Hanseatic League in medieval times, it enjoyed six centuries of prosperity as a grain market. The province still leads Western Europe in the production of sugar beets; another of its riches is a large supply of natural gas. Street life is busy in the city, and the region offers pleasant drives in the countryside.

Groningen's **Grote Markt,** the market square in front of the modern **Stadhuis** (Town Hall), is the scene of one of the biggest daily markets in the Netherlands, selling everything from vegetables to vintage clothing. Dominating the Grote Markt is the **Martinikerk,** which dates from 1230 and was begun as a Romanesque-Gothic cruciform basilica. Finished in the 15th century, it has an organ that was installed in 1470, as well as splendid murals from that period; the stained-glass windows date from the late 18th century. ⊠ *Martinikerkhof,* ☎ *050/ 318–3636.* ☑ *Fl 1.* ⊘ *June–Sept., Tues.–Sat. noon–5.*

The peaceful **Prinsenhoftuin** herb and rose garden sports an 18th-century sundial in its gate and hedges cut in the shapes of the letters *A* and *W,* after the first names of former governors of Friesland and Groningen provinces. The garden is tucked away behind the Martinikerk. ⊠ *Turfsingel.* ☑ *Free.* ⊘ *Apr.–mid-Oct.*

The **university quarter** invites exploration and carefree wandering. Founded in 1614, the university was chosen by Descartes in 1645 to arbitrate his conflicts with Dutch theologians. Today it is one of the largest in the Netherlands. The main university building is neo-Renaissance in style, built in 1909. Allegorical figures of Science, History, Prudence, and Mathematics adorn the gable. In the surrounding streets you will pass a number of fashionable homes built by prominent 18th-century citizens and, on the corner of the Broerstraat, a medieval stone house that is one of the oldest in town. The university quarter is centered on Oude Boteringestraat.

<table>
<tr><td>NEED A
BREAK?</td><td>The high ceilings, wall paintings, and stained glass of a stylish 18th-century mansion give **De Librije** (⊠ Oude Boteringestraat 9, ☎ 050/</td></tr>
</table>

318–3535) a *grand café* atmosphere. Here you can take tea and English scones as you page through magazines and eavesdrop on student gossip.

Ten sculptures on major city access roads are part of the **City Identification Project,** conceived by the Municipal Physical Planning Department to restore to the city the identity once derived from its medieval city gates. Two architects, three artists, a historian, a philosopher, a choreographer, a playwright, and an economist were each commissioned to design an "identification feature." Each was given an identifying letter spelling out *Cruoningae,* an ancient name for the city. The resulting sculptures and structures circle the city clockwise from the south and carry such mystifying titles as *Earth, Water and Gas Flames; A Steel Book on Posts;* and *The Missing Factor X.*

Groningen's newest landmark is the zanily designed, brightly colored **Groninger Museum.** A complex of three pavilions connected by walkways, it was conceived by Italian designer and architect Alessandro Mendini. The adventurous design, which includes flashy mosaics and rooms with trapezoid doors, was made even more irreverent by additions by several "guest architects." You'll find exhibits on Groningen history, art and crafts (including a good collection of Asian porcelain), and visual art from the 16th century to the present. ⊠ *Museumeiland 1,* ☎ *050/366–6555.* ▣ *Fl 9.* ☉ *Tues.–Sun. 10–5.*

☺ Children will enjoy a stop at **Abraham's Mosterdmakerij,** a museum-restaurant in the village of Eenrum/Pieterburen. The convivial manager invites diners and visitors into the mustard factory to see how mustard (a local specialty) and vinegar are made. ⊠ *Molenweg 5, Eenrum/Pieterburen, 20 km (12 mi) north of Groningen,* ☎ *0595/491–600.* ▣ *Museum Fl 2.50.* ☉ *Restaurant daily 10–9; museum daily noon–9.*

Dining and Lodging

$$$ ✕ **De Pauw.** This chic, highly styled restaurant, done in cream and soft yellows, with crisp white linen on the tables, has a sophisticated and imaginative menu influenced by the cuisines of Provence and other sunny climes. Dishes include fresh paprika soup, and cod poached in champagne. Art decorates the walls, and the vases are filled with peacock feathers. ⊠ *Gelkingestraat 52,* ☎ *050/318–1332. Reservations essential. Jacket required. AE, DC, MC, V.*

$$ ✕ **De Opera.** With its lush greenery and glass roof, this is an ideal spot in spring or early summer, when there's still a cold edge to the air in these northern climes. Waiters descend from the kitchen along a spiral staircase to bring you Asian crepes, creamy Swiss cheese fondue, or delicious vegetable casseroles. ⊠ *Poelestraat 17,* ☎ *050/313–1181. AE, DC, MC, V.*

$ ✕ **De Kleine Kasteleine.** Tiny, wood-paneled, and split over two levels, this traditional *eetcafé* has a friendly ambience. It offers simple but delicious meals, such as grilled beef with mushrooms and Groningen mustard sauce. Round off your meal with warm, homemade apple pie, and then call for the Scrabble or backgammon boards to while away the rest of the evening. ⊠ *Carolieweg 31,* ☎ *050/313–9561. No credit cards.*

$$$$ ✕▥ **Landgoed Lauswolt.** This golf and spa resort, with a sprawling manor-house hotel, sits behind a sweeping lawn in a quiet wooded village. The fine restaurant is a member of the Alliance Gourmandise Néerlandaise. The rooms are large, and suites have separate living rooms. Special golf, spa, and gastronomic packages are available. ⊠ *Van Harinxmaweg 10, Beetsterzwaag, 40 km (25 mi) southwest of Groningen,* ☎ *0512/381–*

245, FAX *0512/381–496. 58 rooms. Restaurant, pool, beauty salon, sauna, 9-hole golf course, 2 tennis courts. AE, DC, MC, V.*

$$$ ✕⊡ **'t Familiehotel Paterswolde.** In a comfortable suburb of Groningen, on the edge of the area's largest lake, this small family hotel has grown over the years into a semiresort. There is a spaciousness and an elegantly modern but homey feeling about the rooms and suites. The lakeside café is particularly busy and entertaining in summer; boats can be rented nearby. ✉ *Groningerweg 19, Paterswolde,* ☎ *050/309–5400,* FAX *050/309–1157. 72 rooms. 3 restaurants, indoor pool, sauna, 2 tennis courts, dock, bicycles. AE, DC, MC, V.*

$$ ✕⊡ **Auberge Corps de Garde.** This small family-owned hotel is in a gracious 17th-century barracks house facing the city center's encircling canal. Partially furnished with antiques, it is a congenial place with pleasant, spacious rooms that are brightly decorated in tones of green and rose. The restaurant (reservations essential, jacket required) serves excellent new Dutch cuisine, such as quail stuffed with sweetbreads. ✉ *Oude Boteringestraat 74,* ☎ *050/314–5437,* FAX *050/313–6320. 11 rooms, 6 with bath. Restaurant, lobby lounge. AE, DC, MC, V.*

$$ ✕⊡ **Schimmelpenninck Huys.** This grand old patrician mansion, the scene of revolutionary plotting in the 18th century, was requisitioned as an officers' barracks during the Eighty Years' War. It was also home to Groningen's first dentist. More recently, owner Paula Karistos-Smit rescued the building from occupation by squatters and lovingly restored it to its former glory. The decor reflects its checkered history. There's a Baroque Room, an Empire Dining Room, and a Jugendstil Grand Café—though the bedrooms are mostly decorated in a tasteful modern style. ✉ *Oosterstraat 53,* ☎ *050/318–9502,* FAX *050/318–3164. 12 rooms, 6 suites. Restaurant, café, garden terrace. AE, DC, MC, V.*

Nightlife

CASINO

Holland Casino (✉ Gedempte Kattendiep 150, ☎ 050/312–3400), the only casino in the northern half of the Netherlands, is in Groningen.

DANCING AND LIVE MUSIC

The most vibrant nightspots in Groningen are on or around **Peperstraat,** near the Grote Markt. The influence of 20,000 university students in town ensures that there is plenty of dancing to the latest music. **Jazz Café De Spieghel** (✉ Peperstraat 11, ☎ 050/312–6300) swings nightly to mainstream jazz, with live bands over the weekends. Up-to-the-minute DJs and a long happy hour attract hordes of students and other young Groningers to **De Blauwe Engel** (✉ Grote Markt 39, ☎ 050/313–7679). If your taste is for salsa and other Latin rhythms, then head for the lively **Troubadour** (✉ Peperstraat 19, ☎ 050/313–2690). **Warhol** (✉ Peperstraat 7, ☎ 050/312–1350) is dark and cavernous and throbs with heavy rock.

GAY BARS

Leto (✉ A Kerkstraat 20, ☎ 050/313–5960) has a terrace and art exhibitions and attracts a crowd of trendy younger gay men. Groningen's largest and most popular gay disco, **The Mac** (✉ Hoge der A–3, ☎ 050/312–7188) has a big dance floor, video screens, and live shows.

Outdoor Activities and Sports

SAILING AND CANOEING

Although less blessed with open water than neighboring Friesland, the province of Groningen offers opportunities for sailing and boating as well, particularly on the Schildmeer from the boating center at Steendam; contact **Hinrichs Watersport** (✉ Damsterweg 32, 9629 PD Schildmeer, ☎ 0596/629–137) for information on boat rentals.

Canoeing through the waterways of the province of Groningen can be great fun. Special canoeing routes have been laid out and maps have been printed. To rent canoes: **Horizon** (⊠ Witherenweg 26, 9977 SB Kleine Huisjes, ☎ 0595/481–980), **De Zijlsterhoeve** (⊠ Zijlsterweg 7, 9892 TE Aduarderzijl, ☎ 0594/621–423), and **Hinrichs Watersport** (⊠ Damsterweg 32, 9629 PD Schildmeer, ☎ 0596/629–137).

Shopping

In Groningen the market is held on the Grote Markt, Tuesday through Saturday; there also is a Sunday flea market between June and mid-October in Groningen on the Grote Markt. Late shopping night is Thursday.

ANTIQUES AND ANTIQUE BOOKS

A number of general antiques shops are clustered on the broad shopping street, **Gedempte Zuiderdiep.** Antique book dealers are especially thick in this university city. **De Groninger Boekverkoper** (⊠ Oude Kijk-in-'t-Jatstraat 60, ☎ 050/313–5858) has a good selection of old Dutch prints, as well as books on Groningen. **Isis Antiquarian Bookshop** (⊠ Folkingestraat 20, ☎ 050/318–4233) specializes in Asian studies, as well as translated and Dutch literature.

The North A to Z

Arriving and Departing

BY CAR

To reach the northern provinces from Amsterdam, you can take A6 across the province of Flevoland to Joure, and from there E22 to Groningen. Turn north on A32 for Leeuwarden. You can also follow E22 through Noord Holland province and across the 35-kilometer (22-mile) Afsluitdijk (Enclosing Dike) that divides the IJsselmeer from the North Sea; from the end of the Enclosing Dike, take A31 to Leeuwarden or continue on E22 to Groningen. A third option is to drive to Enkhuizen and take the car ferry to Urk (☞ By Ferry, *below*). From Urk, take N351 to A6 and continue as above.

BY FERRY

Two ferry lines cross the IJsselmeer from May to September to connect the town of Enkhuizen with the northern provinces of Friesland and Flevoland. Both lines are operated by **Rederij Naco B.V.** (⊠ de Ruyteskade, Steiger 7, Amsterdam, ☎ 020/626–2466), and both accept bicycles but not cars. One takes travelers to **Stavoren,** where there is a direct train connection to Leeuwarden; the ferry operates three times a day from May to September, and twice daily (except Monday) from October through April. There is no need for a reservation. Adult fare is Fl 10.50 one-way, Fl 16 round-trip; children, Fl 5.75 one-way, Fl 8.75 round-trip. The other goes to **Urk** in Flevoland province June through September, Monday through Saturday, twice daily. Adult fare one-way is Fl 12 one way, Fl 18 round-trip; children Fl 9 one-way, Fl 12 round-trip, bicycles Fl 6.50 each.

BY TRAIN

Intercity express trains (☎ 06/9292) operate once an hour direct from Amsterdam to both Leeuwarden and Groningen; there is an additional hourly Intercity service to both cities that requires a connection in Amersfoort. Whatever train you take, however, be sure you are in the right car; trains split en route, so there are separate cars for each destination in both classes of service.

Getting Around

BY CAR
Roads are excellent throughout the northern provinces of Friesland and Groningen. In Friesland signs are in two languages, however, with the town names shown in Frisian as well as in Dutch. For example, the provincial capital Leeuwarden also is seen on signs by its Frisian name, Ljouwert.

BY TAXI
Taxis wait at the railway stations in both Leeuwarden and Groningen. For a taxi in Leeuwarden, call 058/212–2222 or 058/212–3333; in Groningen, call 050/312–8044.

BY TRAIN
In addition to the national rail lines connecting Leeuwarden with the south, local trains link the Enkhuizen–Stavoren ferry service to Leeuwarden; another connects Leeuwarden with Harlingen (departure point for ferry and hydrofoil services to the Wadden Islands); and another links Leeuwarden with Groningen and continues to the German border. A small local train in Groningen province connects Groningen with Winsum (a canoeing center), Uithuizen (departure for guided walks to the Wadden Islands at low tide), and the port of Eemshaven. For **train information** in Leeuwarden or Groningen, call 06/9292.

Contacts and Resources

CAMPING
With more than 100 campgrounds in the province of Friesland alone, the North offers plenty of opportunity for camping. Unfortunately, there is no national central reservation service for campsites, so you have to contact sites individually. For camping in Leeuwarden, **De Kleine Wielen** (⌂ De Groene Ster 14, 8926 XE, ☎ 0511/431–660), open April–October, has sites for 350 tents and touring caravans and places for hikers. **Camping Stadspark** (⌂ Campinglaan 6, 9727 KH, ☎ 050/525–1624), open March–October, in Groningen has 200 sites; it also has accommodation for hikers.

EMERGENCIES
National Emergency Alarm Number for police, fire, and ambulance (☎ 06/112). **Groningen Police** (☎ 050/599–5995). **Groningen Breakdown and Towing Service** (☎ 06/0888). **Leeuwarden Police** (☎ 058/213–2423).

GUIDED TOURS
Canal cruise trips are available in summer; in Leeuwarden, contact **Party Cruise Prinsenhof** (⌂ Spanjaardstraat 29, ☎ 058/215–3737); in Groningen, **Rederij Kool** (⌂ Stationsweg 1012, ☎ 050/312–2713 or 050/312–8379).

Another guided option, as much sport as sightseeing, is to join a **wadlopen excursion,** walks across the sand at low tide, from the mainland to the Wadden Islands. Permissible *only* with a guide who knows well the timing of the tidal waters on the Wadden Sea, these walks are available from May through September. Don't even think about attempting this on your own; the tides are very, very tricky. The tourist offices can give you information and recommend qualified guides, or you can contact **De Stichting Wadlooppcentruem Pieterburen** (⌂ Postbus 1, Pieterburen, ☎ 0595/528–300, ℻ 0595/528–318).

HOSPITAL EMERGENCY ROOMS
Groningen (☎ 050/361–9111 or 050/524–5245). **Leeuwarden** (☎ 058/293–3333).

Groningen VVV (✉ Gedempte Kattendiep 6, 9711 PN, ☎ 06/32023050, FAX 050/313–6358), open weekdays 9–5:30, Saturday 9–4. **Leeuwarden VVV** (✉ Stationsplein 1, 8911 AC, ☎ 06/32024060, FAX 058/213–6555), open weekdays 9–5:30, Saturday 9–4.

THE NETHERLANDS A TO Z

This section details essential country-wide information: For further advice, also consult the A to Z sections throughout this chapter that follow each specific Netherlands region.

Arriving and Departing

From North America by Plane

AIRPORTS AND AIRLINES

Amsterdam Schiphol Airport (☎ 06/35034050) is 25 kilometers (15 miles) southeast of Amsterdam and linked by rail to every part of the country.

KLM Royal Dutch Airlines (☎ 800/374–7747) is the national carrier of the Netherlands. Other airlines serving the country include **Delta** (☎ 800/241–4141), **Northwest** (☎ 800/225–2525), **TWA** (☎ 800/221–2000), and **United** (☎ 800/241–6522).

DISCOUNT FLIGHTS

Martinair (☎ 800/366–4655) offers reduced-fare flights to Amsterdam from Detroit, Fort Lauderdale, Los Angeles, Miami, New York, Oakland, San Francisco, Seattle, Tampa, and Toronto.

FLYING TIME

Flying time to Amsterdam from New York is just over seven hours; from Chicago, closer to eight hours; and from Los Angeles, 10½ hours.

From the United Kingdom

BY PLANE

Airlines that serve the Netherlands from the United Kingdom include **KLM City Hopper** (☎ 0181/750–9000), **British Airways** (☎ 0181/897–4000), and **Aer Lingus** (☎ 0181/899–4747). Flying time to Amsterdam from London is one hour; from Belfast, 1½ hours.

BY CAR

The **Channel Tunnel** opened officially in May 1994, providing the fastest route across the Channel—35 minutes from Folkestone to Calais, or 60 minutes from motorway to motorway. It consists of two large 50-kilometer-long (31-mile-long) tunnels for trains, one in each direction, linked by a smaller service tunnel running between them. **Le Shuttle** (☎ 0345/353535 in the U.K., 800/388–3876 in the U.S.), a special car, bus, and truck train, which was scheduled to begin service in June 1994, operates a continuous loop, with trains departing every 15 minutes at peak times and at least once an hour through the night. No reservations are necessary, although tickets may be purchased in advance from travel agents. Most passengers stay in their own car throughout the "crossing"; progress updates are provided on display screens and radio. Motorcyclists park their bikes in a separate section with its own passenger compartment, while foot passengers must book passage by coach (☞ By Train, *below*).

The Tunnel is reached from exit 11a of the M20/A20. Drivers purchase tickets from toll booths, then pass through frontier control before loading onto the next available service. Unloading at Calais takes eight minutes. Five-day round-trip for a small car starts at Fl 130 (low season, night travel); high-season day travel is Fl 190.

BY TRAIN

British Rail International (☎ 0171/834–2345 or 0171/828–0892) runs three trains a day from London to Amsterdam.

Eurostar (☎ 0171/922–4486 in the U.K., 800/942–4866 in the U.S.) high-speed train service whisks riders through the "Chunnel" between new stations in Paris (Gare du Nord) and London (Waterloo) in three hours, and between London and Brussels (Midi) in 3¼ hours. There are eight connecting services a day from Amsterdam Centraal station to the Eurostar. Tickets for these services are available from international ticket counters at Dutch railway stations. Eurostar tickets are available in the United Kingdom through **British Rail International** (London/Victoria Station, ☎ 0171/834–2345 or 0171/828–0892 for credit-card bookings) and in the United States through **Rail Europe** (☎ 800/942–4866) and **BritRail Travel** (✉ 1500 Broadway, New York, NY 10036, ☎ 800/677–8585).

BY BUS

Bus/ferry combination service between the United Kingdom and the Netherlands is operated from London to Amsterdam by **Euro-City Tours** (☎ 0171/828–8361).

BY FERRY

Ferries are run between Harwich and Hook of Holland twice daily by **Sealink/Stena** (☎ 01233/646801), and overnight between Hull and Rotterdam by **North Sea Ferries** (☎ 01482/795141). The trip can last 6–14 hours, depending on the route taken.

Car Rentals

Major international car rental companies, including **Alamo, Avis, Hertz, Europcar/National,** and **Eurodollar/Dollar,** operate desks at Amsterdam Schiphol Airport and have rental offices in Amsterdam and other key cities throughout the Netherlands. In addition, the Dutch firm **Van Wijk Amsterdam** (Amsterdam Schiphol Airport, ☎ 020/601–5277) operates at the airport and other locations.

Customs and Duties

On Arrival

Customs barriers within the EU began to be removed in 1993. Today there are no limits on goods (such as perfume, cigarettes, or alcohol) brought into the Netherlands from another EU country, provided that they are bought duty-paid (i.e., not in a duty-free shop) and are for personal use. If you enter from a non-EU country, or have purchased goods duty-free, you may bring in 200 cigarettes or 50 cigars or 100 small cigars or 250 grams of tobacco; 1 liter of alcohol (more than 22%) or 2 liters (less than 22%) of other liquid refreshments, 50 grams of perfume and .25 liter cologne, 500 grams of coffee, 100 grams of tea, and other goods with a total value of up to Fl 125.

There are no restrictions regarding the import or export of currency.

On Departure

To export Dutch flower bulbs, a health certificate issued by the Nederlandse Planteziektenkundige Dienst (Dutch Phytopathological Service) is required; these are provided with packages you buy from specialized flower bulb companies.

Guided Tours

General-Interest Tours

Abercrombie & Kent (✉ 1520 Kensington Rd., Oak Brook, IL 60521, ☎ 708/954–2944 or 800/323–7308) runs six-night barge cruises through the waterways of Holland in the early spring. **Holland Approach, Inc.** (✉ 550 Mountain Ave., Gillette, NJ 07933, ☎ 908/580–9200 or 800/225–1699 outside NJ) offers nine-day tours. **Maupintour** (✉ Box 807, Lawrence, KS 66044, ☎ 913/843–1211 or 800/255–4266) offers eight-day tulip-time excursions through Holland while the flowers are blooming. **Olson Travelworld** (✉ Box 10066, Manhattan Beach, CA 90226, ☎ 310/546–8400 or 800/421–2255) tailors tours for individuals and groups.

Special-Interest Tours

The **Netherlands Board of Tourism** (NBT) offices in North America maintain a data bank for special-interest travel that includes specialized tours for senior citizens, gays, and travelers with disabilities; information is continually updated, and printouts are available.

ARCHITECTURE

Art Express (✉ 4500 Campus Dr., Suite 410, Newport Beach, CA 92660, ☎ 800/325–7103, FAX 714/852–1234). **Art Horizon International** (✉ 14 E. 63rd St., New York, NY 10021, ☎ 212/888–2299, FAX 212/888–2148). **Horizon Holidays** (✉ 160 John St., Toronto, Ontario M5V 2X8, ☎ 416/585–9911 or 800/387–2977, FAX 416/585–9614) all offer tours.

ARTS, CULTURE, AND MUSIC

Unitours (✉ 8 S. Michigan Ave., Chicago IL 60603, ☎ 312/782–1590 or 800/621–0557, FAX 312/726–0339). **International Education** (✉ 301 Alhambra Pl., Madison, WI 53713, ☎ 608/274–8574 or 800/558–0215, FAX 608/274–8421). **Travel Time** (✉ 203 N. Wabash Ave., Chicago, IL 60601, ☎ 312/726–7197 or 800/621–4725, FAX 312/726–0718). **Witte Travel** (✉ 3250 28th St. SE, Grand Rapids, MI 49512–1640, ☎ 616/957–8113 or 800/253–0210, FAX 616/957–9716). **Ciao! Travel** (✉ 810 Emerald St., Suite 107, San Diego, CA 92109, ☎ 619/272–5116 or 800/942–2426, FAX 619/272–1543).

BARGE CRUISING

The Barge Lady (✉ 230 E. Ohio St., Suite 210, Chicago IL 60611, ☎ 312/944–2779). **European Waterways** (✉ 230 S. Beverly Dr., Suite 203, Beverly Hills, CA 90212, ☎ 310/247–8612 or 800/438–4748, FAX 310/247–9460). **Waterways & Byways** (✉ 1027 S. Palm Canyon Dr., Palm Springs, CA 92264, ☎ 619/320–5754 or 800/925–0444). **SeaAir Holidays Ltd.** (✉ 733 Summer St., Stamford, CT 06901, ☎ 203/356–9033 or 800/732–6247). **Inclusive Tours** (✉ 2 Carleton St., Suite 910, Toronto, Ont. M5B 1J3, ☎ 416/977–5074, FAX 416/977–7759) offer cruising on Holland's waterways.

BIKING

Country Cycling Tours (✉ 140 W. 83rd St., New York, NY 10024, ☎ 212/874–5151 or 800/284–8954, FAX 212/874–5286). **International Bicycle Tours** (✉ Box 754, 7 Champling Sq., Essex, CT 06426, ☎ 203/767–7005, FAX 203/767–3090). **Four Seasons Cycling** (✉ Box 203, Williamsburg, VA 23187, ☎ 804/253–2985). **Revatours** (✉ 1256 Philips Sq., Suite 906, Montréal, Québec H3B 3G1, ☎ 514/392–9016 or 800/363–6339, FAX 514/392–9015) arrange cycling vacations.

HORTICULTURE

Quinn's International Holidays (✉ 333 Vaughn St., Suite 2, Winnipeg, Manitoba R3B 3J9, ☎ 204/942–5380 or 800/665–2626, FAX 204/957–

0322. **Silverline Tours** (✉ 112 Athol St., Suite 204, Whitby, Ontario H3B 3G1, ☎ 416/666–1404 or 416/436–2253, ℻ 416/430–2911).

PACKAGE DEALS FOR INDEPENDENT TRAVELERS

Jet Vacations (✉ 1775 Broadway, New York, NY 10019, ☎ 212/474–8700 or 800/538–0999) offers a Flexiplan Europe package, which includes a choice of hotels, car rentals, airport transfers, and sightseeing options for a number of cities in Holland. **Northwest WorldVacations** (call your travel agent or 800/692–8687) provides visitors to Amsterdam with hotel, car rental, and tour options for a minimum of two nights. **Travel Bound** (✉ 599 Broadway, Penthouse, New York, NY 10012, ☎ 212/334–1350 or 800/456–8656) offers packages for a minimum of three to six nights. **United Vacations** (✉ 106 Calvert St., Harrison, NY 10528, ☎ 800/678–0949) will plan customized itineraries.

Language

Dutch is the official language of the Netherlands, although local dialects are used in Friesland and Limburg provinces. Although many city residents speak good English, in rural areas you may need a phrase book, at least until the residents overcome their shyness about using the English they know.

Lodging

Netherlands Reservation Center (NRC, Postbus 404, 2260 AK Leidschendam, ☎ 070/320–2500, ℻ 070/320–2611) handles bookings for most lodgings in the Netherlands.

Camping

Prices at the country's numerous camping locations range from Fl 25 to Fl 75 per site per night. There is no central reservation bureau for campsites, but you can get general information from the **ANWB** (Royal Dutch Touring Club) in Amsterdam (✉ Museumplein 5, ☎ 020/673–0844).

Mail

Postal Rates

Airmail letters up to 20 grams (⅔ ounce) cost Fl 1.60 to the United States or Canada, Fl 1 to the United Kingdom; postcards to the United States or Canada cost Fl 1, to the United Kingdom 80¢. Aerograms cost Fl 1.30.

Money and Expenses

Currency

The official monetary unit of the Netherlands is the guilder, which may be abbreviated as Dfl, Fl, F, Hfl, and occasionally as NLG. There are 100 cents in a guilder; coins are minted in denominations of 5, 10, and 25 cents, and 1, 2½, and 5 guilders. Bank notes are printed in amounts of 10, 25, 50, 100, 250, and 1,000 guilders, with the denominations embossed in raised symbols on each bill. Bank notes in denominations of more than Fl 100 are seldom seen, and some shops refuse to accept Fl 1000 notes. In October 1996 the exchange rate was 1.70 guilders to the dollar, 1.28 to the Canadian dollar, and 2.65 to the pound sterling.

What It Will Cost

Prices in the Netherlands include a 17.5% BTW/VAT (value added tax). Residents of countries outside the European Union (EU) are entitled to a refund of the BTW on purchases over Fl 300 that are personally carried out of the country within 30 days of purchase. Shops have different systems for granting refunds: Some shops will credit your credit card account, but most require you to present some form of proof of purchase at the customs desk at Schiphol Airport on your way home. Some stores will give you a special "cheque" that may be cashed at the airport; otherwise, you'll receive your refund in the mail. The amount of the refund varies (some organizations deduct a commission), but a refund of 10% to 15% is standard.

SAMPLE COSTS

Cup of coffee, Fl 2.75; glass of beer, Fl 3.50; glass of wine, Fl 4; soda or juice, Fl 2.50–Fl 4; a sandwich, Fl 4–Fl 10; a pastry or dessert, Fl 4–Fl 8.

Opening and Closing Times

Banks are open weekdays from 8 or 9 to 4 or 5; post offices are open weekdays from 8:30 to 5 and often on Saturday from 8:30 to noon. Shopping hours, regulated by the government, are Monday from 1 to 6, Tuesday through Friday from 9 to 6, and Saturday from 9 to 5; each city may designate one night a week as a late shopping night, when stores are open until 9. Certain shops now have permission to open from noon to 5 on Sunday. This is administered at a local level and varies from city to city; it also depends on whether the individual shop manager thinks that opening is worthwhile. In the center of Amsterdam and other large cities, you can be fairly sure of finding major department stores, main branches of chain stores, and shops in larger malls open; but most stores still close on Sunday. Some branches of supermarkets now stay open until 7 or 8 on weekdays. Drugstores are open weekdays from 8 or 9 to 5:30, with a rotating schedule in each city to cover nights and weekends. Most national museums are closed on Monday.

Outdoor Activities and Sports

Boating and Sailing
ANWB (Royal Dutch Touring Club) stores in Amsterdam (✉ Museumplein 5, ☎ 020/673–0844) sell very good nautical maps.

Canoeing
For detailed information on canoeing in the Netherlands, contact the **Dutch Canoe Union** (✉ Postbus 1160, 3800 BD Amersfoort, ☎ 033/462–2341).

Golf
De Nederlandse Golf Federatie (✉ Postbus 221, 3454 ZL De Meern, ☎ 030/662–1888) can provide information on golfing around the country.

Rail Passes

If you plan to travel a lot by train throughout the Netherlands, consider buying one of the following passes. The **Benelux Tourrail** gives you unlimited travel throughout Holland, Belgium, and Luxembourg on any five days within one month (U.S. $217/C$299 first class, U.S. $155/C$213 second class). A **Holland Rail Pass** allows unlimited travel throughout Holland for 3, 5, or 10 days within any 30-day period (first class: 3-day U.S. $88/C$122; 5-day U.S. $140/C$194; 10-day U.S. $260/C$358; second class: 3-day U.S. $68/C$92; 5-day U.S. $104/C$144; 10-day U.S. $184/C$256). For an additional fee, the **Holland Rail Pass Transport Link** offers free travel on public transportation as well (3 days U.S. $14/C$19; 5 days U.S. $23/C$31; 10 days U.S. $36/C$49). A **Dagkaart** (day ticket) is available only in the Netherlands and entitles you to unlimited travel within Holland for one day (first class Fl 99, second class Fl 66). In addition, between June and the end of August, a **Zomertoer** (summer tour) ticket entitles you to three days of unlimited travel within any 10-day period (second class, Fl 85 for one person, Fl 115 for two; first class, Fl 105 for one, Fl 155 for two). The NBT offices have information on train services, as do overseas offices of Netherlands railways. You may need your passport to purchase these passes.

Student and Youth Travel

In addition to the YHA hostels, young visitors to Holland may want to consider staying at a **youth hotel,** or "sleep-in," which provides basic, inexpensive accommodations for young people. A list of these is available from the NBT (☎ 212/370–7367 in New York). In summer (and in some cases year-round), the Institute for Nature Protection Education (⊠ IVN, Postbus 20123, 1000 HC Amsterdam, ☎ 020/622–8115) organizes **work camps** in scenic locations, popular among English-speaking visitors age 15 to 30. Another organization to consider for **volunteer work** in Holland is S/W, International Volunteer Projects (⊠ Willemstraat 7, 3511 RJ Utrecht, ☎ 030/231–7721).

Telephones

The country code for the Netherlands is 31. Numbers with an 06 code are generally information numbers.

The area code for Amsterdam is 020 (or 20 if you are calling from outside the Netherlands), and it is used only when you call from other parts of the Netherlands to Amsterdam. Within the immediate environs of any municipality you do not need to use an area code.

Local Calls

Coin-operated telephones are becoming a rarity in the Netherlands; most public phones take PTT (Dutch telephone company) credit cards. The public telephones take Fl .25 and Fl 1 coins, and most modern ones also accept Fl 2.5 and Fl 5 coins. Short local calls may only require one *kwartje* (25-cent coin), but for longer calls or calls to other parts of the country insert several coins before dialing, and they will drop automatically as needed during your conversation. Calls will be cut off abruptly when all the coins are used, so keep an eye on how many are left and add more accordingly.

International Calls

To call outside the Netherlands, dial 00 followed by the country code (1 for the United States and Canada, 44 for the United Kingdom), area code, and number. In Amsterdam, **Telecenter** (⊠ Raadhuisstraat 28–50, ☎ 06/0402) is open daily 8 AM–2 AM; it also has a fax service. Dial 06/022–9111 to reach an **AT&T USA Direct** operator in the United States; 06/022–9122 to reach an **MCI Call USA** operator; 06/022–9119 for **Sprint**; or 06/0410 for an international operator.

Operators and Information

Dial 06/8008 for **directory assistance** within the Netherlands, 06/0418 for numbers elsewhere. Operators speak English.

Tipping

Service is included in the prices you pay in the Netherlands, though it is customary to round up to the nearest guilder or two on small bills, and up to the nearest 5, 10, or even 25 guilders for good service on large bills.

Transportation: Getting Around

By Plane
KLM City Hopper (☎ 020/474–7747) provides regular service between Amsterdam Schiphol Airport and Rotterdam, Eindhoven, and Maastricht, though air travel in a country this small is really unnecessary.

By Train
NS/Nederlandse Spoorwegen (Netherlands Railways) (☎ 06/9292 in the Netherlands, 020/620–2266 outside the Netherlands) operates a minimum of one train per hour throughout its system, and major cities are connected by three or more trains each hour. Nearly every corner of the country is covered, supplemented by local and regional bus services. The modern, clean trains have first- and second-class coaches and no-smoking and smoking cars. Rail fares are based upon distance; there are one-way fares, day-return fares for same-day round-trip travel, and multiday fares; bicycles may be carried aboard for a nominal fee. Children under 3 travel free and children under 11 are charged Fl 1 if they are accompanied by an adult.

When you purchase your rail ticket at a station ticket office, you can buy a "train-taxi" ticket for Fl 6 per person. Special "train-taxis" will take you from a special stand outside the station to anywhere within a certain area (usually defined by the town boundaries). Taxis are shared, but waiting time is guaranteed to be no longer than 10 minutes. The scheme also operates for journeys back to the station. Although not available in the large cities, "train-taxis" are ideal for getting to sights on the outskirts of smaller towns, such as Paleis Het Loo outside Apeldoorn.

By Ferry
An extensive ferry system serves the Netherlands. Ferries in **Zeeland** province operate from Breskens (☎ 0117/381–663), Vlissingen (☎ 0118/465–905), and Perkpolder (☎ 0114/681–234). In **Friesland** province they run from Lauwersoog (☎ 0519/349–050 or 0519/349–079), Harlingen (☎ 0562/442–969 or 0562/442–770), and Holwerd (☎ 0519/542–001) to the Frisian Islands, and from Den Helder (☎ 0222/369–600) in **Noord Holland** province. Ferries crossing the IJsselmeer run from Enkhuizen to Stavoren (☎ 020/626–2466; no cars) or Urk (☎ 0527/683–407).

By Car
The Dutch superhighway system is extensive and very well maintained; there are European, national, provincial, and local roads designated as E, A, N, and S, respectively. The **ANWB (Royal Dutch Touring Club)** operates telephone road information services (☎ 06/9622) and has a 24-hour fleet of bright yellow cars and trucks equipped to handle routine repairs free of charge for members of AAA, CAA, or any affiliate of Alliance International du Tourisme (☎ 06/0888). The speed limit in the Netherlands is 120 kilometers (75 miles) per hour, and driving is on the right. A valid driver's license from your home country is all that is required to operate a vehicle in the Netherlands.

Visitor Information

In the United States
Netherlands Board of Tourism (✉ 355 Lexington Ave., 21st floor, New York, NY 10017, ☎ 212/370–7367, FAX 212/370–9507; ✉ 90 New Montgomery St., Suite 305, San Francisco, CA 94105, ☎ 415/543–6772, FAX 415/495–4925; ✉ 225 N. Michigan Ave., Suite 326, Chicago, IL 60601, ☎ 312/819–0300, FAX 312/819–1740; ✉ 9841 Airport Blvd., 10th floor, Los Angeles, CA 90045, ☎ 310/348–9333).

In Canada
Netherlands Board of Tourism (✉ 25 Adelaide St., Suite 710, Toronto, Ontario. M5C 1Y2, ☏ 416/363–1577, FAX 416/363–1470).

In the United Kingdom
Netherlands Board of Tourism (✉ 25–28 Buckingham Gate, London SW 1E 6LD, ☏ 0171/828–7900).

3 Belgium

This stamp-size country packs a scenic and cultural wallop with its historic towns, sophisticated cuisine, and museums filled with works of the world's great Flemish artists. Brussels, its capital, and Antwerp, an important port city, are both art and shopping centers, while Ghent and Brugge are gems of well-preserved medieval architecture. For military history buffs, there are the battlefields of Waterloo and Bastogne; for nature lovers, the hills and green fields of the Ardennes; and for pleasure seekers, the beach resorts of Ostende and Knokke-Le Zoute, and the sulphur waters of Spa, the mother of modern health resorts.

BELGIUM IS A COUNTRY FOR CONNOISSEURS: This is the land of Van Eyck, Bruegel, and Rubens, and this is where their greatest work can be seen. The

By Eric Sjogren   spirit of the Middle Ages lives on in cities of great renown, such as Brugge and Ghent, and in others that are waiting to be discovered, such as Mechelen and Lier. The art of living well has been cultivated in Belgium since the days of the great Burgundian wedding feasts that celebrated dynastic marriages. Today, the country boasts an astonishing number of gourmet restaurants, including some of the world's finest.

Belgium packs just over 5 million Dutch-speaking Flemings and almost as many French-speaking Walloons into a country only slightly larger than the state of Vermont. The presence of two language cultures inevitably creates tension, but it also enriches. A diverse geography also enhances the country's attractions. The Belgian landscape ranges from the beaches and dunes of the coast and the tree-lined, placid canals of the "platte land" (flat land), to the sheer cliffs of Ardennes River valleys and the dense forests of the south.

A staunch, unapologetic middle-class culture thrives in Belgium. Dukes, counts, and lesser lords have built many a feudal castle on Belgian land, and abbots and cardinals have constructed towering religious edifices, but it was the merchants who built the cities and commissioned the works of art we admire today. The endless variations of Art Nouveau in the town houses of the Belle Epoque are another manifestation of middle-class individualism, as are the comfortable proportions of today's private homes and public spaces.

Until recently, the Belgians had no common history. Rather, their fate was determined by marriages whereby princely families sought to extend their influence and perpetuate their power. It was through marriage that the possessions of the dukes of Flanders passed into the hands of the dukes of Burgundy in the 14th century, and then to the Hapsburg family in 1477. A scion of that family, born in Ghent, became Emperor Charles V in 1519 when he inherited the Holy Roman Empire from his father and Spain from his mother. This was the beginning of 200 years of Spanish rule. When the Austrian branch of the Hapsburg family eventually gained the upper hand, the only real difference for Belgium was that it came to be ruled from Vienna instead of Madrid.

After the fall of Napoléon in 1815, the victorious powers tried to settle matters by awarding the Belgian provinces to the Netherlands. But a cultural divide had opened up between the Low Countries to the north and those to the south, and it was a foregone conclusion that the staunchly Roman Catholic southerners would not get along with the adamantly Protestant northerners. In military terms, Belgium's 1830 war of independence did not amount to more than a few skirmishes, but the purpose was served and a new nation was formed. It included the former principality of Liège, which under elected prince-bishops had maintained its independence for 800 years.

Colonialism, too, was thrust upon the Belgians. The Congo was the personal fiefdom of King Leopold II (son of Leopold I, first king of independent Belgium), who bequeathed it to the nation in 1908 shortly before his death. The Belgians may have reaped the rewards, but they also had to pay the consequences when colonialism came to a painful end and the independent Congo (now known as Zaire) was born 52 years later.

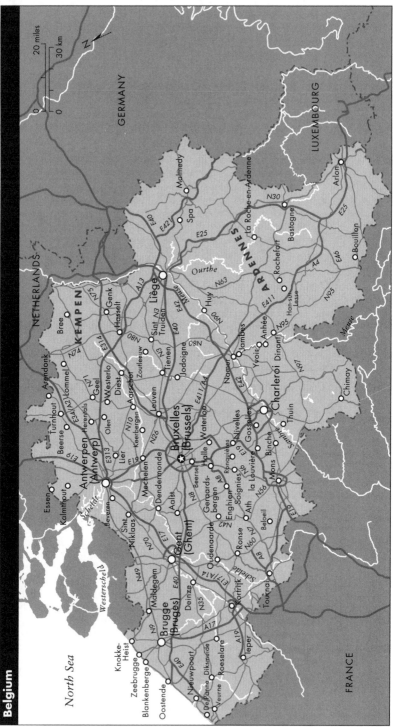

Belgium

20 miles
30 km

NETHERLANDS

GERMANY

LUXEMBOURG

FRANCE

North Sea

Westerschelde

Scheldt

KEMPEN

ARDENNES

Ourthe

Maas

Meuse

Lesse

Hoëgne

Semois

Knokke-Heist
Zeebrugge
Blankenberge
Oostende
De Panne
Nieuwpoort
Veurne
Diksmuide
Roeselare
Ieper
Brugge (Bruges)
Deinze
Kortrijk
Tournai
Gent (Ghent)
Maldegem
Oudenaarde
Ronse
Geraards-bergen
Enghien
Ath
Belœil
Mons
Binche
Soignies
Nivelles
Gosselies
Charleroi
Thuin
Chimay
Beauraing
Dinant
Yvoir
Anhée
Namur
Jodoigne
Tienen
Zoutleeuw
Waterloo
Halle
Bruxelles (Brussels)
Beersel
Ronquières
La Louvière
Aalst
Dendermonde
Mechelen
Lier
Sint-Niklaas
Beveren
Antwerpen (Antwerp)
Essen
Kalmthout
Turnhout
Beerse
Arendonk
Herentals
Geel
Olen
Westerlo
Diest
Aarschot
Leuven
Keerbergen
Lommel
Bree
Genk
Hasselt
Sint-Truiden
Liège
Huy
Tienen
Jambes
Rochefort
La Roche-en-Ardenne
Bastogne
Bouillon
Arlon
Spa
Malmedy

N9
N49
N70
E17
N35
A17
A19
N8
N60
N42
A8
N7
N56
E19
N5
E420
A54
N90
E411/A4
E42
A13
E313
E34/A21
N71
N10
N26
N2
N3
E40
N80
N74
N75
N63
N97
N95
A4
N30
E25
E421
E46
E40

FRANCE

When Belgian forces put up unexpected resistance against the Germans in 1914, the country became known, a little patronizingly, as "brave little Belgium." In 1940, during another war that Belgium basically had nothing to do with, the country was ravaged.

This is perhaps why Belgium is one of the strongest supporters of the European Union (EU). Brussels is the home of the European Commission, where most decisions affecting the EU are initiated. Writers and politicians tend to refer to "Brussels" as a synonym for the Commission, and this can be a mixed blessing. While being the capital of Europe is a heady sensation, it is of secondary importance to forging a commonality of interests. The EU will survive only if it is successful in fashioning unity out of diversity. Exactly the same thing applies to the Kingdom of Belgium.

The Pleasures of Dining and Lodging

Dining

The Belgians, by and large, take dining seriously and are discerning about fresh produce and innovative recipes. Because they put a high value on the pleasures of the table, they are prepared to pay a steep price for fine meals. Wherever you go, even in the most expensive restaurants, you will almost always find families or groups of friends sharing a celebratory meal.

In Belgium, as in France, the introduction of nouvelle cuisine meant a liberation of creative spirits. Now the trend is back to regional and traditional dishes, but with a modern twist. These may include such hearty dishes as *waterzooi* (a rich chicken or fish hot pot), *faisan à la brabançonne* (pheasant with braised chicory), *lapin à la bière* (rabbit cooked in beer), or *carbonnade* (chunky beef stew with beer).

The quintessential Belgian vegetable is not brussels sprout but endive, also known as chicory (*witloof* or *chicon* in French). We owe endive to an act of serendipity. During one of the many wars in Belgium, a farmer near Mechelen had to abandon the chicory roots (used to produce a coffee substitute) that he had just harvested. When he returned, he found they had sprouted leaves; he tried them, liked them, and thus, endive was born. You'll find it in many guises—braised, au gratin, or in salads, always with a slightly bitter edge. Many other good foods come from Belgium: superb asparagus, smoked ham and sausages, crayfish, and trout. But the mussels the Belgians eat with such gusto and proclaim as their own, actually come from Holland.

Belgians also swear by the humble *frites*—chips or fries. They are served in every restaurant and home; you can also get them on street corners and at roadside stands. Also known as *fritures* or *frituur*, they are served with mayonnaise, catsup, or, catering to more advanced tastes, béarnaise or curry sauce. You're not likely to encounter a cheaper or more typical Belgian dish.

Most hotels serve breakfast until 10. Belgians usually eat lunch between 1 and 3, but restaurants open at noon. The two-hour lunch is generally expense-account related. The main meal of the day is dinner, generally eaten between 8 and 10. Peak dining time used to be about 8 but seems to be getting later, and reservations are readily accepted for 9 or 9:30.

Belgians are becoming less formal, and conservative dress is now de rigueur only in the most expensive restaurants. The younger generation, in particular, favors stylish but casual dress when dining out.

Price categories for Belgium are as follows:

CATEGORY	BRUSSELS*	BELGIUM EXCEPT BRUSSELS*
$$$$	over BF3,500	over BF5,000
$$$	BF2,500–BF3,500	BF2,500–BF3,500
$$	BF1,500–BF2,500	BF1,500–BF2,500
$	under BF1,500	under BF1,500

per person for a three-course meal, including service, taxes, but not beverages

Lodging

You can trust Belgian hotels, almost without exception, to be clean and of a high standard. Modern hotels catering to business travelers, especially in Brussels, can be very expensive, but there is also a wide range of perfectly acceptable and reasonably priced hotels, where the only difference is the size of the room and number of amenities. Hotel prices in the rest of the country are considerably lower than in the capital. Taxes and service charges are always included in the quoted price. Hotel lists are available from local tourist offices.

Pensions offer a double room with bath or shower and full board from BF2,500 to BF3,500 in Brussels, about BF500 less elsewhere. There's often a minimum-stay requirement of two to three days. B&B accommodations are available for BF700 and up. For information, check the local tourist office. Youth hostels are also popular for the MTV generation, and, of course, Belgium is well supplied with camping and trailer sites.

CATEGORY	BRUSSELS*	BELGIUM EXCEPT BRUSSELS*
$$$$	over BF9,000–BF12,000	BF7,500–BF10,000
$$$	BF6,500–BF9,000	BF5,500–BF7,500
$$	BF3,500–BF6,500	BF2,500–BF5,500
$	under BF3,500	under BF2,500

for two persons sharing a double room, including service and tax

Exploring Belgium

Numbers in the text correspond to numbers in the margin and on the maps.

Great Itineraries

IF YOU HAVE 7 DAYS

Make **Brussels** ①–⑮ your headquarters, spending two days exploring the magnificent Grand'Place and its historic surroundings, then the area of the neoclassical Palace Royale with its museums, whose collections range from Bruegel and Rubens to Delvaux and Magritte. Then, make several one-day excursions: to medieval **Brugge** ㊳ with its romantic canals, the city where oil painting was invented and where some of the greatest masterpieces of 15th-century art have been preserved; to **Ghent** ㉘ to see Van Eyck's masterpiece, the *Adoration of the Mystic Lamb,* and the splendid towers and enchanting riverfronts; to **Antwerp** ㊺–㊲, the great port city, whose luminous cathedral contains Rubens' finest works; to Waterloo's brooding battlefield, where the history of Europe was forever changed; to **Han-sur-Lasse** ㊟ in the Ardennes, whose vast caves seem to echo prehistoric memories.

IF YOU HAVE 10 DAYS

Plan on five days in **Brussels** ①–⑮, adding a third day in the capital to see the Horta Museum, arguably the world's finest example of Art Nouveau, and the Comic Strip Museum, housed in another Horta building, honoring another Belgian art form whose best-known exponents are Tintin and Lucky Luke. From Brussels, take day trips to Waterloo and **Antwerp** ⑥–⑦. Then move on to 🔲 **Brugge** ㊳ for three days, with excursions to **Ghent** ㉘, the World War I battlefields around **Ieper** ㊱, and the North Sea Coast. Wind up your visit to Belgium with two days in the Ardennes, where, based in 🔲 **Namur** ㊥, you can visit the caves in Han-sur-Lesse and see the dramatic Meuse River valley; take a day-long drive over forest-clad hills and green plateaus to visit Roche-en-Ardenne and the meandering river Ourthe; to Bastogne of Battle of the Bulge fame; and north past Stavelot and Malmédy to the Hautes Fagnes (High Fens) nature reserve and Liège.

BRUSSELS

Brussels (Bruxelles in French, Brussel in Flemish) is a provincial city at heart, even though it has assumed a new identity as capital of the European Union (EU). Within Belgium, Brussels has equal status with Flanders and Wallonia as an autonomous region. It is a bilingual enclave just north of the "language border" that divides the country into Flemish- and French-speaking parts.

At the end of the 19th century, Brussels was one of the liveliest cities in Europe, known for its splendid cafés and graceful Art Nouveau architecture. That gaiety was stamped out by German occupation during the two world wars. The comeback of Brussels on the international scene was heralded by the World's Fair and the Universal Exposition of 1958.

International business has invaded the city in a big way since the 1960s, resulting in blocks full of steel-and-glass office buildings, but they are only a few steps from the cobbled streets and forgotten spots where the city's eventful past is plainly visible.

Over the centuries, Brussels has been shaped by the different cultures of the foreign powers that have ruled it. It has learned the art of accommodating them and, in the process, prepared itself for the role of political capital of Europe.

Pleasures and Pastimes

ARCHITECTURE

Art Nouveau flourished in Brussels as nowhere else. You'll find many a splendid town house in this fanciful style, with bay windows, turrets, and curlicues of all kinds, by Victor Horta and his pupils, especially in the boroughs of Saint-Gilles and Ixelles, to the south and southeast of the city center. Even more important, this style unleashed the imagination of lesser-known architects and, as a result, no two houses look alike on many residential streets. The locals often take pleasure in walking down streets, away from their habitual haunts, to admire or be amused by the inventiveness of house builders and owners.

CAFÉ SOCIETY

Café tables and chairs move out on Brussels sidewalks the first sunny day in March and often stay there until November. Most people drink beer rather than coffee, and the choice of beers is enormous, with some cafés stocking 200 or more different brands, many of them served only in their own specific type of glass. Although some of the most popular cafés are around the Grand'Place and the Grand Sablon, you'll find them all over the place, on virtually every street corner. Interiors range from bleak to cozy. Some are Art Nouveau showpieces with decor that hasn't changed for the past 100 years.

CHOCOLATES AND PASTRY

The *praline,* filled with differently flavored creams, nougat, nuts, or liqueur, was invented in Brussels about 150 years ago. The city's leading pastry shops still produce some of the world's finest, handmade

chocolates. They make wonderful gifts to take home. The pastry, however, is for local consumption and not to be missed: delicious crois-
sants, rich chocolate cakes, or light red-currant-flavored mousse.

DINING

The star-studded Brussels restaurant scene is a boon to visitors and
natives alike. It has been suggested that the reason the European
Commission chose Brussels for its headquarters is the excellence of
its restaurants. While this is not the entire truth, the top Brussels restaurants do, in fact, rival the best Parisian restaurants; so, alas, do the
prices. Most Belgians, however, value gourmet cooking as a work of
art and are prepared to part with a substantial sum for a special
occasion.

A number of neighborhood restaurants have risen to the challenge of
making dining out affordable. The choice of dishes may be more limited, and the ingredients less costly, but an animated ambience more
than makes up for it. And the tab is likely to be a quarter of what a
dinner would cost you in one of the grand restaurants.

You can reduce the check almost by half by choosing a set menu. Fixed-
price luncheon menus are often an especially good bargain. Menus and
prices are always posted outside restaurants. You should never feel that
you're under an obligation to eat a three-course meal; many people order
just a salad and a main course.

Tourist Information Brussels (TIB) publishes a booklet, "Gourmet
Restaurants," which contains food journalists' evaluations of some
250 restaurants. It's available for BF80 at the tourist office in Grand'-
Place. Listings include the cost of set menus and of *plats du jour*
(daily specials).

LODGING

As the capital of Europe, Brussels attracts a large number of high-pow-
ered visitors, and a disproportionate number of very attractive luxury
hotels have been built to accommodate them. Their prices are higher
than what most tourists would like to pay, but on weekends and during July and August, when there aren't many business travelers, prices
come down to below BF5,000 for a double room.

Happily, new hotels catering to cost-conscious travelers, priced at less
than BF3,000 for a double, have also been constructed over the last
few years. They may be less ostentatious, but they're squeaky clean,
with just as much attention to your comfort as the palatial five-star
hotels.

Brussels has seen a boom in hotel-building over the past few years in
response to the increase in business and diplomatic travel; two out of
four visitors come here on business. Most business travel takes place
in winter, so a number of hotels offer impressive discounts on weekends and in July and August.

Exploring Brussels

The historic center of Brussels is 1,000 years old. It is in the center of
a group of ring roads that form concentric circles around it. Crossing
them is like traveling back and forth across the centuries. The absence

of a river to "organize" the city in left and right banks can make orientation a bit difficult. The center sits in a bowl and is sometimes known as the Pentagon, from the shape of the oldest ring road, which roughly follows the ancient ramparts; all that's left of them is one of the gates, the Porte de Hal. On either side of the road you can see the cupolas of the Palais de Justice and the Basilique, and in the center, the slender belfry of the Hôtel de Ville rises like a beacon.

Brussels is a small city, and you can get a superficial impression of it from a car window in a single day. For more substantial appreciation, you need one day for the historic city heart, another for the uptown squares and museums, and additional days for off-the-beaten-path sights and excursions to the periphery. There are many attractive nooks and crannies to explore.

Great Itineraries

IF YOU HAVE 2 DAYS

Concentrate on the historic heart of Brussels, starting with a visit to "Brussels's oldest citizen," **Manneken Pis,** and the baroque grandeur of the **Grand'Place.** Discover the popular restaurant district of the **Ilôt Sacré** and the **Galeries St. Hubert,** with its old-fashioned but elegant shops. Visit the city's principal church, the 13th-century **Cathédrale de Saint-Michel et Sainte-Gudule,** and continue to the unique museum devoted to the art of the **Centre Belge de la Bande Dessinée** (Belgian Comic Strip Museum). Nearby is the attractive Baroque church of **Saint-Jean Baptiste,** the animated **Fish Market area,** the patrician, 18th-century Maison de la Bellone and the neo-Renaissance **Bourse.** The Grand'Place is just a block away.

Start the second day at the fashionable square, the **Grand Sablon,** and its prolongation, the sculpture-adorned Petit Sablon. Then stop (unless it's Monday, when museums are closed) at the twin **Musée d'Art Ancien** and **Musée d'Art Modern.** You're now at the white, 18th-century **Place Royale,** adjoined by the neoclassical Ancien Cour, the Palais Royal, and the formal Parc des Bruxelles. From here, proceed to the fashionable uptown **shopping area,** ending at the **Palais de Justice.**

IF YOU HAVE 4 DAYS

In addition to seeing the sights of the inner city, on the third day take a half-day trip to **Waterloo** to see the battlefields, monuments, and museums. In the afternoon, visit the beautifully restored 17th-century **Maison d'Erasme,** where the great humanist Erasmus sojourned in 1521. On the fourth day, tour some of the areas graced with fine Art Nouveau town houses in the boroughs of **Ixelles** and **Saint-Gilles.** In the afternoon, visit the home of **Victor Horta,** father of the Art Nouveau movement, or (if this is a Monday) the Art Deco home of **David and Alice Van Buuren.**

IF YOU HAVE 6 DAYS

Do all of the above and on the fifth day visit the old university town of **Lenven** (Louvain) and/or the ecclesiastical center, **Mechelen** (Malines), both with splendid Gothic churches and town halls and both, incidentally, with excellent restaurants. On the sixth day, rent a car for an all-day drive through the pleasing, hilly landscape of the province of **Brabant,** which surrounds the city, passing through the beech woods of the Forêt de Soignes, along smaller roads to Nivelles, with its collegiate church dating from the 7th century, and pausing at small towns and villages en route. The part of the province west of Brussels, known as **Pajottenland,** is where Bruegel painted many of his pictures; at its center is the magnificent château of Gaasbeek.

152

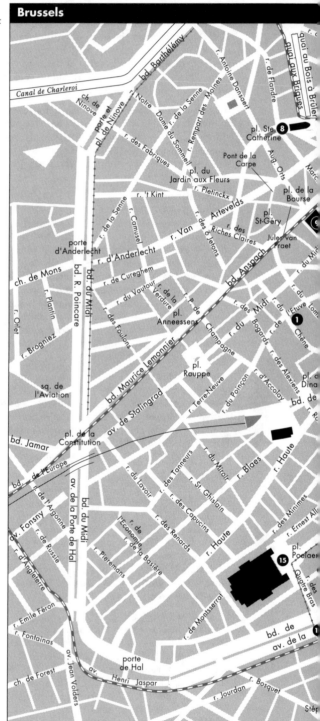

Brussels

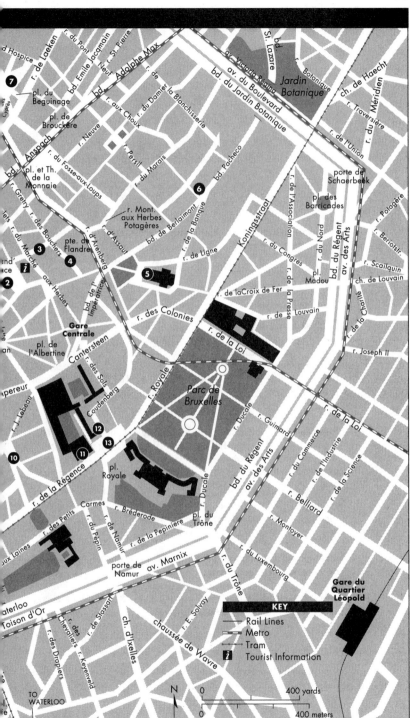

KEY

— Rail Lines
═ Metro
⋯ Tram
i Tourist Information

Lower Town: The Heart of Brussels

During the latter half of the 10th century, a village began to emerge on the site of present-day Brussels. A population of craftsmen and traders settled gradually around the castle of the counts of Leuven, who were later succeeded by the dukes of Brabant.

Philip the Good, Duke of Burgundy, took possession of Brussels, then known as Brabant, in 1430. Under him, Brussels became a center for the production of tapestry, lace, and other luxury goods. By 1555, when Charles V abdicated in favor of his son, Philip II of Spain, the Protestant Reformation was spreading through the Low Countries. Philip, a devout Catholic, dealt ruthlessly with advocates of the Reformation. His governor, the Duke of Alva, had the leaders of the revolt, the Counts of Egmont and Hoorn, executed in the Grand'Place. A monument to them stands in the square of the Petit Sablon.

In 1695, the French Marshal Villeroy bombarded the city with red-hot cannonballs. The ensuing fires destroyed 4,000 houses, 16 churches, and all of the Grand'Place, with the exception of the Town Hall. The buildings around the square were immediately rebuilt, in the splendor that we see today.

Numbers in the text correspond to numbers in the margin and on the Brussels map.

A Good Walk

Start at **Manneken Pis** ① (corner of Rue de l'Etuve and Rue du Chêne), for the bronze statue of a small boy urinating, which symbolizes the insouciant spirit of the *Bruxellois*. Thousands of copies are on sale in the souvenir shops along the three blocks of Rue de l'Etuve leading to the **Grand'Place** ②, the magnificent square surrounded by the Hôtel de Ville (Town Hall) and ornate guild houses. The alley next to the Maison du Roi (opposite the Town Hall) leads into the restaurant-lined Petite Rue des Bouchers with the highly original puppet theater, Théâtre Toone, in the **Quartier de l'Ilôt Sacré** ③. Turn right at the top of the street to reach the **Galeries St. Hubert** ④, an impressively engineered and decorated shopping gallery from 1847.

At the exit from the gallery, turn right on Rue d'Arenberg and cross the Boulevard de Berlaymont, heading for the twin Gothic towers of the **Cathédrale Saint-Michel et Sainte-Gudule** ⑤, a 13th-century edifice with outstanding stained-glass windows. Walk back down the hill and turn right on the uninspiring Boulevard de Berlaymont. Take the second flight of stairs on the left, down to the Rue des Sables and the **Centre Belge de la Bande Dessinée** ⑥, or Belgian Comic Strip Museum, as engrossing to adults as it is enchanting to kids. A left and a right takes you into Rue du Persil and the Place des Martyrs, currently under reconstruction. The pedestrian shopping street, Rue Neuve, is half a block away. It is filled with bargain-seeking shoppers in the daytime, but deserted at night. It leads to the Place de la Monnaie and the Théâtre de la Monnaie, one of Europe's leading opera stages.

As you cross the busy Boulevard Anspach onto the Rue des Augustins, the remnants of the Tour Noire are on the left; it was part of the 12th-century fortifications. To the right, the short Rue des Cyprès leads to the Flemish Baroque church of **Saint-Jean-du-Béguinage** ⑦. Walk down the block-long Rue du Peuplier, and you're in the old Fish Market area, although the canal has been replaced by ponds, and every house is now a seafood restaurant. Turn left toward the blackened church of Sainte-Catherine and you'll find a busy market in front of it on the **Place Sainte-Catherine** ⑧. Take the first right, Rue de Flandre. Halfway up the block is the gateway to the Maison de la Bellone with its fine Baroque facade, now a theater museum. Returning to the Place Sainte-Catherine, cross the square, and take the second street right. This is Rue Antoine Dansaert, with "in" fashion boutiques and art galleries. You are now facing the grandiose **Bourse** ⑨. Next to it is Bruxella 1238, an in-situ archaeological museum, and the small church of Saint-Nicolas, hemmed in by tiny houses. You are now on Rue au Beurre, half a block from the **Grand'Place** ②.

TIMING

Walking the route will take you about two hours (and those cobblestone streets call out for good walking shoes). You will probably want to linger in the Grand'Place for half an hour (more if you do your lingering in one of its cafés). Stops in churches and museums may add another hour and a half. With a break for lunch, this is a comfortable, one-day program any day of the week, especially Monday, when museums are closed (most of the city's must-see museums are located in the Upper Town).

Sights to See

Anderlecht Béguinage. The Beguines, lay sisters and mostly widows of Crusaders, lived here in a collection of small houses (one from the 13th century), grouped around a garden. ⊠ *Next door to the Maison d'Erasme, Rue du Chapître 31.*

Autoworld. Here, under a high glass roof of the south hall in the Parc de Cinquantenaire, you'll find one of the best collections of vintage cars—more than 450 of them—in the world. ⊠ *Parc du Cinquantenaire 11,* ☎ *02/736–4165.* 🎟 *BF150.* ☉ *Daily 10–5 (Apr.–Sept. until 6). Subway: Mérode.*

⑨ **Bourse** (Stock Exchange). The decorative frieze of allegorical statues in various stages of nudity, some of them by Rodin, forms a sort of idealization of the common man. Step inside if you feel like placing a bet on Belgian stocks. Right next to the Bourse, what looks like major roadwork is, in fact, an in-situ archaeological museum, **Bruxella 1238**, where you can inspect the excavation of a 13th-century church. ⊠ *Rue de la Bourse,* ☎ *02/279–4355.* 🎟 *BF80.* ☉ *Guided visits from the Town Hall Wed. at 10, 10:45, and 11:30; Fri. at 1:45, 2:30, and 3:15.*

⑤ **Cathédrale Saint-Michel et Sainte-Gudule.** Next to nothing is known about St. Gudule, the daughter of a 7th-century Carolingian nobleman, but this is where her relics have been preserved for the past thousand years. Construction of the cathedral began in 1226. Its twin Gothic towers are gleaming white again after the recent removal of centuries of grime, and restoration of the interior is under way. Because of the restoration, the choir is not accessible, but the remains of an earlier, 11th-century Romanesque church that was on the site can be glimpsed through glass apertures set into the floor. Among the windows in the cathedral, designed by various artists, those by Bernard van Orley, a 16th-century court painter, are outstanding. The window of *The Last Judgment,* at the bottom of the nave, is illuminated from within in the evening. ⊠ *Parvis Ste-Gudule,* ☎ *02/217–8345.* ☉ *Nov.–Mar., daily 7–6; Apr.–Oct., Mon.–Sat. 7–7, Sun. 8–7.*

★ ☺ ⑥ **Centre Belge de la Bande Dessinée** (Belgian Comic Strip Museum). It fell to the land of Tintin, a cherished cartoon character, to create the world's first museum dedicated to the art of the comic strip. It is an art that, despite its primary appeal to children, has been taken seriously in Belgium for many years, and in this museum it is wedded to another art form in which Belgium still excels, Art Nouveau. The building was designed, down to the smallest detail, by Victor Horta in 1903 for a textile wholesaler, and the lighting and stairs, always important to Horta, are impressive. They serve the purposes of the new owner equally well. Tintin, the creation of the late, great Hergé, became a worldwide favorite cartoon character, and his albums have sold an estimated 80 million copies. But many other artists have followed in Hergé's footsteps, some of them even more daringly original. The collection includes more than 400 original plates by Hergé and his successors and 25,000 cartoon works; those not exhibited can be viewed in the archive. There's also a large comic strip shop, library, and cafeteria. ⊠ *Rue des Sables 20,* ☎ *02/219–1980.* ☑ *BF120.* ☉ *Tues.–Sun. 10–6. Metro: Rogier/Botanique; Trams 90, 92, and 93; Bus 38.*

Eglise de Saint-Nicolas. This small church, surrounded by tiny houses that seem to huddle under it, is almost 1,000 years old. Little remains of its origins, but a cannonball fired by the French in 1695 is still lodged in one of the pillars. ⊠ *Rue au Beurre 1,* ☎ *02/513–8022.* ☉ *Daily 7:30–6:30; Mass in English, Sun. at 10 AM.*

NEED A BREAK? **Cirio** (⊠ Rue de la Bourse 18–20, ☎ 02/512–1395) is a peaceful café with an outstanding Art Nouveau decor that hasn't changed for generations; nor, apparently, has some of the clientele.

❼ Eglise Saint-Jean-du-Béguinage. Here is a quiet and peaceful spot to restore your serenity. Originally, this elegant, Flemish Baroque church served as the center for the *béguines* (lay sisters) who lived in houses clustered around it. The interior has preserved its Gothic style, with soaring vaults. The surprisingly different architectural styles combine to make this one of the most attractive churches in Brussels. A number of streets converge on the small, circular square, which is surrounded by buildings that help create a harmonious architectural whole. ⊠ *Place du Béguinage.* ☉ *Tues.–Fri. 10–5.*

NEED A BREAK? **A la Mort Subite** (⊠ Rue Montagne-aux-Herbes-Potagères 7, ☎ 02/513–13180) is a Brussels institution named for a card game called "Sudden Death." This café, untouched for 75 years, still serves Mort Subite draft beer, brewed on the premises.

European Institutions. The European Commission and related institutions have had an impact on Brussels, most easily seen in the form of entire neighborhoods being razed to make room for steel-and-glass buildings purpose-built to produce regulations. To be fair, what remains of the old blocks has also seen an influx of ethnic restaurants catering to the tastes of lower-level Eurocrats; the grandees eat in splendid isolation in their own dining rooms. The area is centered on **Rond Point Schuman.** The landmark, star-shaped Berlaymont building is closed for renovation, looking at the moment as if it had been wrapped by Christo. Meanwhile, the **European Commission** has temporary headquarters at Rue de Trèves 120, while the **European Council of Ministers** is at Rue de la Loi 170. The new and controversial **European Parliament** building—France still insists on regular Parliament meetings in Strasbourg—is at Rue Wiertz 43. Its central element, a rounded glass summit, looms behind the Gare de Luxembourg. *Subway: from Sainte-Cathérine via De Brouckère to Schuman.*

❹ Galeries Saint-Hubert. A visit to this arcade is like going shopping with your great-grandparents. There are three parts to it: *de la Reine, du Roi,* and *du Prince* (of the queen, the king, and the prince). They were built in 1847 as the world's first covered shopping galleries, using the new engineering techniques that allowed architects to use iron girders to design soaring constructions of glass. Neoclassical gods and heroes look down from their sculpted niches on the crowded scene below; flags of many nations billow ever so slightly; and the buskers play classical music, while diffused daylight penetrates the gallery from the glassed arches. The shops are interspersed with cafés, restaurants, and theaters.

★ ❷ **Grand'Place.** This jewel box of a square is arguably Europe's most ornate and most theatrical. You catch your breath the first time you see it, and the second and third time as well. It is close to the hearts of all the people of the city, and all ages come here from time to time. Especially at night, you experience the full theatrical effect of the burnished facades of the guild houses and their gilded statuary. From April to September, the square is floodlit after sundown with waves of changing colors, accompanied by music. Try to be here for the *Ommegang,* a magnificent historical pageant re-creating Emperor Charles V's reception in the city in 1549 (the first Tuesday and Thursday in July). There is a daily flower market in the Grand'Place, a bird market on Sunday morning, frequent jazz and rock concerts, and in December, under the majestic Christmas tree, a life-size crèche with sheep grazing around it.

Guild Houses of the Grand'Place. Built in ornate Baroque style soon after the 1695 bombardment, the guild houses have an architectural coherence that makes for a dramatic impact on the Grand'Place (☞ *above*). Among the buildings on the north side of the square, No. 1–2, **Le Roi d'Espagne,** belonged to the bakers' guild. It is surmounted by a cupola on which the figure of Fame is perched. **Le Sac,** No. 4, commissioned by the guild of joiners and coopers, and No. 6, **Le Cornet,** built for the boatmen, were both designed by Antoon Pastorana, a gifted furniture maker. **Le Renard,** No. 7, was designed for the guild of haberdashers and peddlers. A sculpture of St. Christopher, their patron, stands on top of the gable. **Le Cygne,** No. 9, was formerly a butcher's guild. Today, it is an elegant restaurant (☞ Maison du Cygne *in* Dining and Lodging, *below*), but before that it was a popular tavern often frequented by Karl Marx.

Hôtel de Ville (Town Hall). This Gothic building, which dates to the early 15th century, dominates the Grand'Place (☞ *above*). It is nearly 300 years older than the guild houses, which were rebuilt after the French bombardment of 1695. The left wing was begun in 1402 but was soon found to be too small. Charles the Bold laid the first stone for the extension in 1444, and it was completed four years later. The extension left the slender belfry off center (today, it's partially hidden by scaffolding). The belfry is topped by a bronze statue of St. Michael crushing the devil beneath his feet. During the current restoration, the weather-worn St. Michael was airlifted off the top of the tower and another archangel flown in to replace him. Over the gateway are statues of the prophets, female figures representing lofty virtues, and effigies of long-gone dukes and duchesses. Inside the Town Hall are some excellent Brussels and Mechelen tapestries, some of them in the Gothic Hall, where there are frequent recitals and chamber-music concerts. ✉ *Grand'Place,* ☎ *02/279–4365.* 🎫 *BF80.* ⊙ *English-speaking tours Tues. at 11:30 and 3:15, Wed. at 3:15, Sun. at 12:15.*

NEED A BREAK?
There are plenty of cafés to choose from on Grand'Place. On the ground floor of No. 1, there's the vast and popular **Au Roy d'Espagne,** with an open fire and solid wooden furniture.

L'Arbre d'Or. On the same side of the Grand'Place (☞ *above*) as the Town Hall, this was once the brewers' guild. Today it houses a modest Brewery Museum, appropriately enough in a country that still

brews 400 different beers. ⊠ *Grand'Place 10,* ☎ *02/511–4987.* ☜
BF100. ☺ *Daily 10–5.*

Maison de la Bellonne. This patrician 18th-century building was named
for the Roman goddess of war, whose effigy graces the Baroque facade.
It houses a Theater Museum and is often home to exhibitions and concerts. ⊠ *Rue de Flandre 46,* ☎ *02/513–333.* ☺ *Tues.–Fri. 10–6.*

Maison d'Erasme (Erasmus House). In the middle of a commonplace
neighborhood stands this remarkable redbrick building, which allows
us to enter the home of a 16th-century scholar and see how he lived
and worked. The house has been restored to its mint condition of 1521,
the year the great humanist came to Brussels for its fresh air. Erasmus
was out of tune with the ecclesiastical authorities of his day, and some
of the pages on view show where the censors stepped in to protect the
faithful. First editions of *In Praise of Folly,* and other books by Erasmus, can be inspected, and there are some extraordinary works of arts:
prints by Albrecht Dürer and oils by Holbein and Hieronymus Bosch.
⊠ *Rue du Chapître 31,* ☎ *02/521–1383.* ☜ *BF20.* ☺ *Wed.–Thurs.
and Sat.–Mon. 10–noon and 2–5. Subway: Sainte-Catherine to Saint-
Guidon station in borough of Anderlecht.*

Maison du Roi (House of the King). Although no king ever lived in this
house—a showplace on the Grand'Place (☞ *above*)—it was named for
its grandeur. Today, it houses the **Musée Communal,** which has some
fine tapestries, altarpieces, and paintings, notably the *Marriage Procession,* by Pieter Bruegel the Elder. On the top floor you can see the
extravagant wardrobe of costumes donated to clothe the little statue
of *Manneken Pis* on festive occasions. ⊠ *Grand'Place,* ☎ *02/279–4355.*
☜ *BF80.* ☺ *Mon.–Thurs. 10–12:30 and 1:30–4 (Apr.–Sept. until 5),
weekends 10–1.*

❶ Manneken Pis. For centuries, the small bronze statue of a chubby boy
urinating into a fountain has drawn visitors from near and far. (A rarely
remarked-upon fact is that he is left-handed.) The first mention of him
dates from 1377. Sometimes called "Brussels's Oldest Citizen," he has
also been said to symbolize what Belgians think of the authorities, especially those of occupying forces. The present version was commissioned from sculptor Jerome Duquesnoy in 1619. It is a copy; the original
was seized by French soldiers in 1747. In restitution, King Louis XV
of France was the first to present *Manneken Pis* with a gold-embroi-
dered suit. The statue now has 517 other costumes for ceremonial occasions. Tons of copies, in various materials and sizes, are sold as
souvenirs every year. One version serves as a kitchen utensil, with his
penis as a corkscrew.

Musée Royal d'Afrique Centrale (Royal Museum of Central Africa).
Here you'll find the final vestiges of Belgium's colonial adventure, an
incredible collection of 250,000 objects. Only 800 are displayed, including masks, sculpture, and memorabilia of the journeys of the ex-
plorers of Africa. The museum is in the middle of a beautifully
landscaped park. ⊠ *Leuvensesteenweg 13,* ☎ *02/767–5401.* ☜ *BF50.*
☺ *Mid-Mar.–mid-Oct., Tues.–Sun. 9–5:30; mid-Oct.–mid-Mar.,
Tues.–Sun. 10–4:30. Subway: to Montgomery Sq., then Tram 44 to
Tervuren.*

Musée Royal de l'Armée et de l'Histoire Militaire (Royal Museum of
Arms and Military History). The highlight of this vast museum is the
hall filled with 130 aircraft from World War I to the Gulf War. ⊠ *Parc
du Cinquantenaire 3,* ☎ *02/733–4493.* ☜ *Free.* ☺ *Tues.–Sun. 9–noon
and 1–4:45.*

Musées Royaux d'Art et de l'Histoire (Royal Museums of Art and History). This is one of many vast museums that flank Brussels's version of the Arc de Triomph, known as *Cinquantenaire.* Brussels needed an Arc de Triomphe like it needed a hole in the head. But Leopold II thought otherwise and planned one for the 50th anniversary of Belgian independence in 1880. Hence its name, *Cinquantenaire,* although it was not completed until 25 years later. For decades museums on this arch collected mostly dust. All this is changing. The museum has 140 rooms, many filled with important antiquities and ethnographic collections, but the most interesting sections are those devoted to Belgian archaeology and to the immense tapestries for which Brussels once was famous. ⊠ *Parc du Cinquantenaire 10,* ☎ *02/741–7211.* 🖃 *Free.* ☉ *Tues.–Fri. 9:30–5, weekends 10–5.*

Place des Martyrs. This square is dedicated to 445 patriots who died in the brief 1830 war of independence against the Dutch. The shrine to the patriots is underneath the square. The square itself is a neoclassical architectural ensemble built in 1795 in the cool style favored by the Austrian Hapsburgs. This noble square has also been a martyr to local political and real estate interests. After long neglect, it is now being restored according to the dubious principle of *façadisme,* a frequent choice in this city of compromise. It means that only the front of the building is preserved, while the rest is torn down and rebuilt. ⊠ *Rue du Persil, near the Belgian Comic Strip Museum.*

❽ Place Sainte-Catherine. If you find the Grand'Place overrun by tourists, come to this market square, which is devoid of tourists. This is a working market every weekday from 7 to 5, where people come to shop for necessities and banter with fishmongers. There's a stall where you can down a few oysters, accompanied by a glass of ice cold muscadet. In the evening the action moves to the old **Vismet** (Fish Market), which branches off from the (forgettable) Eglise de Sainte-Catherine. All that remains of the old canal is a couple of elongated ponds, but both sides are lined with good-to-excellent seafood restaurants. In good weather there's outdoor waterside dining.

★ ❸ Quartier de l'Îlot Sacré. Pickpockets, flimflam artists, and jewelry vendors mingle happily with the crowds in the narrow Rue des Buchers and even narrower Petite Rue des Buchers. Still, except for the pickpockets, it's all good-natured fun in the liveliest area in Brussels, where restaurants and cafés stand cheek by jowl, their tables spilling out onto the sidewalks. One local street person makes a specialty of picking up a heaped plate and emptying it into his bag. The waiters laugh and bring another plate. The restaurants make strenuous efforts to pull you in with huge displays of seafood and game. The quality, alas, is a different matter (for some outstanding exceptions, *see* Dining, *below*).

Rue Antoine Dansaert. In itself fairly nondescript, this street has a number of boutiques that sell Belgian-designed men's and women's postgrunge fashions, as well as avant-garde galleries and stylish furniture.

Théâtre Toone. A famous old puppet theater, now run by a seventh-generation member of the Toone family, this theater has a repertoire of 33 plays, including some by Shakespeare. The plays are performed in the local dialect (Bruxellois). You won't understand a word, but it's fun anyway. There's a puppet museum and a bar with great, old-fashioned ambience. ⊠ *Impasse Schuddeveld,* ☎ *02/511–7137.* 🖃 *Performance BF400, museum BF100.* ☉ *Performance, most evenings at 8:30.*

Upper Town: Royal Brussels

Uptown Brussels bears the hallmark of two rulers, Charles of Lorraine, from Austria, and Leopold II, Belgium's empire builder. The Peace of Utrecht of 1713, which distributed bits of Europe like pieces in a jigsaw puzzle at the end of one of Europe's interminable wars, handed the Low Countries to Austria. Fortunately for the Belgians, the man Austria sent here as governor was a tolerant and far-sighted man, who oversaw the construction of a new palace, the neoclassical Place Royale, and other buildings that transformed the Upper Town.

The next large-scale rebuilding of Brussels was initiated by Leopold II, the second king of independent Belgium, in the latter part of the 19th century. Cousin of both Queen Victoria and the Kaiser, he annexed the enormous Congo for Belgium and applied some of the profits to grand urban projects. Present-day Brussels is indebted to him for the wide avenues and thoroughfares.

Brussels needed no help from the outside to pull down much that was charming but not very productive, including some of the masterpieces of Art Nouveau, to make way for anonymous and monotonous glassed-in office buildings. Many of them stand half empty today, as recession inevitably followed the boom years. But Brussels has survived many invasions and fully intends to outlive the one by big business and Eurocrats.

A Good Walk

Start at the **Place du Grand Sablon** ⑩, but take care that you don't dawdle too long among its antiques shops and galleries. Cross the Rue de la Régence into its sister square, the peaceful **Place du Petit Sablon,** whose formal garden is filled with, and surrounded by, statuary. Turn right on the Rue de la Régence to the **Musée d'Art Ancien** ⑪, recently refurbished to show its Old Masters to better effect, and the spectacular **Musée d'Art Moderne** ⑫, which burrows underground for space to show its modern and contemporary art.

You're now on the gleaming-white **Place Royale** ⑬, a pearl of 18th-century neoclassicism, with the Eglise de Saint-Jacques. Walk down the Rue de la Montagne du Cour; on the left is the elegant courtyard of the Palace of Charles de Lorraine. Continue along the Rue Ravenstein around Victor Horta's **Palais des Beaux-Arts,** the city's premier concert and exhibition venue, and up the handsome steps to the formal **Parc du Bruxelles.** At its end, on the right, stands the vast hulk of Leopold II's **Palais Royal.**

Returning to Place Royale, pass through the gateway on the corner next to the church, and up the Rue de Namur to the Porte de Namur. You have now reached the city's most prestigious shopping area, and as you walk right on the **Boulevard de Waterloo,** you will pass the same high-fashion names that you find in Paris, London, and New York. The focus of the shopping district is the **Place Louise** ⑭, with the Avenue and Galerie of the same name.

For a fitting finale, walk down the short Rue des Quatre Bras toward the not-to-be-missed **Palais de Justice** ⑮. From the balustrade facing the old town, you have a panoramic view of the city, from the cupola of the Basilique on the left to the Atomium, the replica of a vastly enlarged molecule, on the right.

TIMING
Walking time, without stopping, is about an hour and a half. For stops in the art museums (closed Monday) add another couple of hours, plus

one hour for window shopping in the Grand Sablon and Place Louise areas.

Sights to See

☺ **Atomium.** A model of an iron molecule enlarged 165 billion times, built for the 1958 World's Fair, this is one of the Brussels landmarks. You're entitled to ask yourself why. There's an express elevator to the highest point, 400 feet up, where you have a panoramic view of Brussels. ⊠ *Boulevard du Centenaire,* ☎ *02/477–0977.* ☜ *BF160.* ☉ *Apr.–Aug., daily 9:30–8, Sept.–Mar. until 6. Metro: Heysel.*

☺ **Boulevard du Midi.** From mid-July until the end of August, all of Belgium's carnival barkers and showmen and their carousals, ghost trains, Ferris wheels, shooting galleries, rides, swings, and merry-go-rounds congregate along the Boulevard du Midi for this giant and hugely popular funfair. It extends for blocks and blocks. ⊠ *Both sides of Boulevard Gare du Midi.* ☜ *Each attraction separately priced.* ☉ *Morning–late night.*

Brussels Gueuze Museum. Connoisseurs of beer and the noble art of brewing flock to this living museum where Lambic is produced. This quintessential Brussels beer, created through spontaneous fermentation, is brewed nowhere else and is the basic ingredient in other popular Belgian beers, such as Gueuze, cherry-flavored Kriek, and raspberry-flavored Framboise: *santé,* cheers, and *gezondheit!* ⊠ *Rue Gheude 56,* ☎ *02/521–4928.* ☜ *BF70.* ☉ *Weekdays 8:30–4:30, Sat. 10–1 (until 6 mid-Oct.–May). Metro: Gare du Midi.*

David and Alice Van Buuren Museum. A perfect Art Deco interior from the 1930s is preserved in this museum. The made-to-order carpets and furnishings are supplemented by paintings by the Van Buurens, as well as Old Masters, including a Bruegel, *Fall of Icarus,* one of the three versions he painted. ⊠ *Avenue Leo Errera 41,* ☎ *02/343–4851.* ☜ *BF200.* ☉ *Mon. 2–4 and by appointment (groups only). Trams 23 and 90.*

★ ❿ **Grand Sablon.** Here's where the good people of Brussels come to see and be seen. Once, as the name implies, it was nothing more than a sandy hill. Today, it is an elegant square, surrounded by numerous restaurants, cafés, and exclusive antiques shops, some in intriguing alleys and arcades. Downhill from the square stands the **Eglise de la Chapelle,** dating from 1134. Inside, there's a memorial to Pieter Bruegel the Elder, who was married in this church and buried here just a few years later. Every Saturday and Sunday morning there's a lively antiques market of more than 100 stands at the upper end of the square. It's not for bargain hunters, however. At the eastern end stands the **Eglise Notre-Dame du Sablon,** a Flamboyant-Gothic church founded in 1304 by the guild of crossbowmen (the original purpose of the square was crossbow practice) and rebuilt in the 15th century. It's one of Brussels's most beautiful churches, and at night the stained-glass windows are illuminated from within.

NEED A BREAK? **Wittamer,** the finest of Brussels's many excellent pastry shops (⊠ Grand Sablon 12, ☎ 02/512-37420), has recently added an attractive upstairs tearoom, which also serves breakfast and light lunches, accompanied by Wittamer's unbeatable pastries.

Les Marolles. If the Grand'Place stands for old money, the neighborhood known as the Marolles stands for old poverty. Walk down the steps in front of the Palais de Justice, and you have arrived. This was where the workers lived who produced the luxury goods for which Brussels was famous. There may not be many left who still speak the old Brussels dialect, mixing French and Flemish with a bit of Spanish thrown in, but the area still has a somewhat raffish charm. The Marolles has welcomed many waves of immigrants, the most recent from Spain, North Africa, and Turkey. Many come to the daily **Flea Market** at the Place du Jeu de Balle, where old clothes are sold along with every kind of bric-a-brac, plain junk and the occasional gem.

Mini-Europe. This consists of a collection of 1:25 scale models of more than 300 famous European buildings and high-tech achievements, located in a 5-acre park next to the Atomium. ⊠ *Boulevard du Centenaire 20,* ☎ *02/478–0550.* ☜ *BF380.* ☉ *Daily 9:30–6 (July–Aug. until 8).*

★ ⓫ **Musée d'Art Ancien** (Museum of Ancient Art). Those who have trouble naming famous Belgians should turn to their art history books. In the first of the interconnected art museums, special attention is paid to the great, so-called Flemish Primitives of the 15th century, who invented the art of painting with oil. The Spanish and the Austrians pilfered some of the finest works, but there's plenty left by the likes of Memling, Petrus Christus, and Roger Van det Weyden. The collection of works by Pieter Bruegel the Elder is outstanding; it includes *The Fall of Icarus,* in which the figure of the mythological hero disappearing in the sea is but one detail of a scene in which people continue to go about their business. A century later Rubens, Van Dyck, and Jordaens dominated the art scene; their works are on the floor above. The 19th-century collection on the ground floor includes the *Assassination of Marat* by Jacques-Louis David, who, like many other French artists and writers, spent years of exile in Belgium. ⊠ *Rue de la Régence 3.* ☜ *Free.* ☉ *Tues.–Sun. 10–noon and 1–5.*

★ ⓬ **Musée d'Art Moderne** (Museum of Modern Art). Rather like the Guggenheim Museum in reverse, this modern museum burrows underground and circles downward eight floors. You can reach it by an underground passage from the Museum of Ancient Art, or you can enter it from the house on Place Royale where Alexandre Dumas (père) once lived and wrote. Although the collection is mainly Belgian and French art of the past 100 years, the museum highlights modern Belgian artists who have acquired international prominence, such as the expressionist James Ensor and the surrealists Paul Delvaux and René Magritte. You'll also discover several others who deserve wider recognition, adding the pleasure of discovery to this art experience. Note that lunch hours at the two museums are staggered so as not to inconvenience visitors. ⊠ *Place Royale 1.* ☜ *Free.* ☉ *Tues.–Sun. 10–1 and 2–5.*

Musée des Enfants. There are few kids who don't fall in love with this Children's Museum, even though its purpose is educational for 2- to 12-year-olds: learning to handle both objects and emotions. Kids get to plunge their arms into sticky goo, dress up in eccentric costumes, crawl through tunnels, and take photographs with an oversize camera. ⊠ *Rue du Bourgmestre 15,* ☎ *02/640–0107.* ☜ *BF180.* ☉ *Sept.– July, Wed. and weekends 2:30–5. Trams 93 and 94.*

★ **Musée Horta.** The house where Victor Horta (1861–1947), the creator of Art Nouveau, lived and worked until 1919, is the best place to see his joyful interiors and furniture. Horta's genius lay in his ability to create a sense of opulence and spaciousness where little space existed. Lamps hang from the ceilings like tendrils, and mirrored skylights evoke giant butterflies with multicolored wings of glass and steel. For examples of how Horta and his colleagues transformed the face of Brussels in little more than 10 years, ride down Avenue Louise to Vleurgat, and walk along Rue Vilain XIIII, to the area surrounding the **ponds of Ixelles.** ⊠ *Rue Américaine 25,* ☎ *02/537–1692.* 🖃 *BF100 (weekends BF200).* ☉ *Tues.–Sun. 2–5:30. To house: Tram 91 or 92 to Ma Campagne. To Ixelles: Tram 93 or 94.*

🖑 **Oceade.** Attractions here include water slides and a wave pool. ⊠ *Boulevard du Centenaire 20, next to Mini-Europe,* ☎ *02/478–4944.* 🖃 *BF430.* ☉ *Tues.–Thurs. 2–10, Fri. 2–midnight, Sat. 11 AM–midnight, Sun. 10–8.*

⑮ Palais de Justice. Many a nasty comment—"the ugliest building in Europe," for instance—has been made about Leopold II's giant Law Courts, on the site of the old Gallows Hill, but it sure strikes fear into the heart of the malefactor. The terrace in front of it offers great views of the Lower Town and, to the northwest, another huge and eccentric building, the Basilique, begun in 1905 but not completed until 1970. On its right, straight north, you can see the Atomium. ⊠ *Place Poelaert.* 🖃 *Entrance hall free.* ☉ *Office hours.*

Parc de Bruxelles. This was once a game park, but in the late 18th century it was tamed into rigid symmetry and laid out in the design of Masonic symbols. The huge **Palais Royal** occupies the entire south side of the park. It was built by Leopold II at the beginning of this century on a scale corresponding to his own megalomaniacal ambitions. The present monarch, King Albert, comes here for state occasions, although he lives at Laeken Palace on the outskirts of Brussels. ⊠ *Place des Palais, Rue Royale, adjacent to Place Royale.* 🖃 *Palais Royal free.* ☉ *July 22–early Sept., Tues.–Sun. 10–4.*

⑩ Place du Petit-Sablon. The other half of the Grand Sablon (☞ *above*), this part of the square is surrounded by a magnificent wrought-iron fence, topped by 48 small bronze statues representing the city's guilds. Inside the peaceful garden stands a double statue of the Flemish patriots, Counts Egmont and Hoorn, on their way to the Spaniards' scaffold in 1568. Also on the square is the **Musée Instrumental** (Musical Instruments Museum), with more than 4,000 instruments, one of the largest museums of its kind in the world. The saxophone family is well represented here, as befits the country of its inventor, Adolphe Sax. The collection is scheduled to be transferred to a house on the Place Royale that is now undergoing restoration. ⊠ *Place du Petit Sablon 17.* 🖃 *Free.* ☉ *Tues., Thurs., Sat. 2:30–4:30, Wed. 4–6, Sun. 10:30–12:30.*

⑭ Place Louise. There's a certain type of young Belgian matron, tall, blond, bejeweled, and freshly tanned whatever the season, whose natural urban habitat is around Place Louise. The most expensive shops are along Boulevard Waterloo. Prices are somewhat lower on the other side of the street, on Avenue de la Toison d'Or, which means the Golden Fleece, a name some find amusing. Additional shops and boutiques line both sides of Avenue Louise and the Galerie Louise, which burrows through the block to link Avenue de la Toison d'Or with Place Stéphanie. This is an area for browsing, window-shopping, movie-going, and café-sitting; in short, for enjoying the good life.

NEED A BREAK? | **Nemrod** (⊠ Boulevard de Waterloo 61, ☎ 02/511–1127) is a pleasant café-pub dressed up as a hunting lodge with a blazing fire, very popular for a shopping break or before a show.

★ ⑬ Place Royale. Although the Royal Square was built in the French style by Austrian overlords, it is distinctly Belgian. White and elegantly proportioned, it is the centerpiece of the Upper Town, which became the center of power in the 18th century. The equestrian statue in its center, representing Godefroid de Bouillon, Crusader and King of Jerusalem, is a romantic afterthought. The buildings are being restored one by one, leaving the facades intact. Place Royale was built on the ruins of the Palace of the Dukes of Brabant, which had burned down. The area is now being excavated, and eventually it will be possible to visit the underground digs and see the main hall, Aula Magna, where Charles V was crowned Holy Roman Emperor in 1519 and where, 37 years later, he abdicated to retire to a monastery. The church on the square, **St-Jacques-sur-Coudenberg,** was originally designed to look like a Greek temple. After the French Revolution reached Belgium, it did, in fact, briefly serve as a "Temple of Reason." The Art Nouveau building-ing on the northwest corner is the former Old England department store, soon to house the Musical Instruments Museum when it moves from cramped quarters in the Petit Sablon.

On or near Place Royale are the neoclassical courtyard of the **Palace of Charles of Lorraine;** the **Hotel Ravenstein,** built in the 15th century and the only surviving aristocratic house from that period; and the **Palais des Beaux-Arts,** an Art Deco–style concert hall, designed in the 1920s by Victor Horta after a visit to the United States.

Dining and Lodging

There are more than 1,600 restaurants in Brussels (whose population is ½ that of New York), and 25 are internationally acclaimed. Belgians take the pleasures of the table seriously and are happy to save up to give themselves, their families, and friends a treat. If you don't want two full restaurant meals a day, there are plenty of snack bars for a light midday meal, and most cafés serve sandwiches and light hot meals both noon and night. The city is also richly endowed with good and mostly inexpensive Asian restaurants.

Hotels in Brussels are usually a mixture of the cozy and the cosmopolitan. While some hostelries are postwar, modern, and—at first glance—somewhat impersonal, explore a little further and you'll find a charming and welcoming ambience beneath their businesslike exterior. As home to the European Commission, the city attracts many businesspeople, who tend to book mid-week. Look for savings on weekend rates.

For price categories, *see* The Pleasures of Dining and Lodging at the beginning of this chapter.

$$$$ ✕ **Comme Chez Soi.** Pierre Wynants, the perfectionist owner-chef, has
★ decorated his bistro-size restaurant in Art Nouveau style. The superb cuisine, excellent wines, and attentive service complement the warm decor. Wynants is ceaselessly inventive, and earlier creations are quickly relegated to the back page of the menu. One all-time favorite, fillet of sole with a white wine mousseline and shrimp, is, however, always on the menu. ✉ *Place Rouppe 23,* ☎ *02/512–2921,* FAX *02/511–8052. Reservations essential. Jacket and tie. AE, DC, MC, V. Closed Sun.–Mon., July, Dec. 25–Jan. 1.*

$$$$ ✕ **L'Ecailler du Palais Royal.** This seafood-only restaurant, just off the Grand Sablon, feels like a comfortable club, and many of the clients seem to have known each other and the staff for years. Risotto of prawns in champagne, baked lobster custard, and the best turbot you're likely to taste for a long time are among the delicacies offered. ✉ *Rue Bodenbroek 18,* ☎ *02/512–8751. Reservations essential. Jacket and tie. AE, DC, MC, V. Closed Sun., Easter wk, Aug.*

$$$$ ✕ **La Truffe Noire.** Luigi Ciciriello's "Black Truffle" attracts a sophis-
★ ticated clientele with its modern design, well-spaced tables, and a cuisine that draws on classic Italian and modern French cooking. Carpaccio
is prepared at the table and served with long strips of truffle and
Parmesan. Entrées include ravioli filled with minced truffles and wild
mushrooms, John Dory stuffed with truffles and leeks, and leg of
Pauillac lamb in pie crust. ✉ *Boulevard de la Cambre 12,* ☎ *02/640–
4422. Reservations essential. Jacket and tie. AE, DC, MC, V. No lunch
Sat. Closed Sun., Easter wk, 2nd ½ of Aug., Christmas wk.*

$$$$ ✕ **Maison du Cygne.** With decor to match its classic cuisine, this
restaurant is set in a 17th-century guild hall on the Grand'Place. It's
the place to go for power dining. The formal dining room upstairs features paneled walls hung with Old Masters, and a small room on the
mezzanine contains two priceless Bruegels. Service is flawless in the grand
manner of old. Typical French-Belgian dishes include *lotte aux blancs
de poireaux* (monkfish and leeks), a specialty. ✉ *Rue Charles Buyls
2,* ☎ *02/511–8244. Reservations essential. Jacket and tie. AE, DC,
MC, V. No lunch Sat. Closed Sun. and 3 wks in Aug.*

$$$$ ✕ **Villa Lorraine.** Generations of American business travelers have
been introduced to the three-hour Belgian lunch at the opulent Villa,
on the edge of the Bois de la Cambre. The green terrace room is light
and airy, and there's alfresco dining under the spreading chestnut tree.
You can feast on such standbys as red mullet in artichoke vinaigrette,
crayfish cooked in chicken stock with white wine and a dash of Ar-
magnac, and duckling with peaches and green pepper. ✉ *Avenue du
Vivier-d'Oie 75,* ☎ *02/374–3163. Jacket and tie. AE, DC, MC, V. Closed
Sun. and July.*

$$$ ✕ **Castello Banfi.** On the Grand Sablon in beige-and-brown post-
modern surroundings, you can enjoy classic dishes with added refine-
ments, such as toasted pine kernels with pesto. There's excellent
carpaccio with Parmesan and celery, red mullet with ratatouille, and
unbelievable mascarpone. The quality of the ingredients (sublime olive
oil, milk-fed veal imported from France) is very high. The wine list is
strong on fine Chianti aged in wood. ✉ *Rue Bodenbroek 12,* ☎ *02/
512–8794. Jacket and tie. AE, DC, MC, V. No dinner Sun. Closed Mon.
and 2nd ½ of Aug.*

$$$ ✕ **La Porte des Indes.** This is the city's foremost Indian restaurant—
the creation of Karl Steppe, a Belgian antiques dealer turned restau-
rateur. The gracious staff wears traditional Indian attire. The plant-filled
lobby, wood carvings, and soothing blue-and-white decor provide a
restful backdrop. The cuisine ranges from a mild pilaf to a spicy *vin-
daloo* (very hot curry). The "brass tray" offers an assortment of specialties. A vegetarian menu is also available. ✉ *Avenue Louise 455,*
☎ *02/647–8651. AE, DC, MC, V. Closed Sun.*

$$$ ✕ **Les Capucines.** This pleasant restaurant stands out amid the medi-
ocrity of most eateries in the Place Louise shopping area. The dining
room is inviting, decorated in shades of green, with huge flower ar-
rangements. Chef Pierre Burtonboy prepares dishes such as grilled fil-
let of sea bream on a bed of shredded leek dressed with nut oil; lamb
interleaved with goose liver, rolled and encased in pastry, with rosemary
and thinly sliced potatoes; bitter chocolate mousse with crème anglaise;
and iced peach soup with mint. ✉ *Rue Jourdan 22,* ☎ *02/538–6924.
AE, DC, MC, V. No dinner Mon. Closed Sun., 2 wks in Sept.*

$$$ ✕ **Ogenblik.** This small, split-level restaurant, in a side alley off the
★ Galeries St-Hubert, has all the trappings of an old-time bistro: green-
shaded lamps over marble-topped tables, sawdust on the floor, and laid-
back waiters. There's nothing casual about the cuisine, however: boned
chicken with sweetbreads and goose liver, mille-feuille (thin layers of
puff pastry separated by filling) of lobster and salmon, saddle of lamb

Central Brussels Dining and Lodging

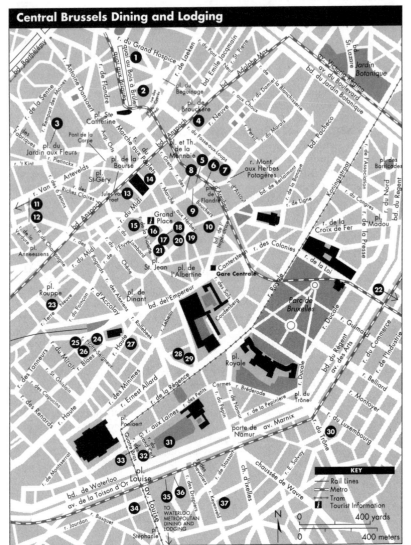

Dining

Adrienne, **36**

Au Vieux Saint Martin, **27**

Aux Armes de Bruxelles, **8**

Aux Marches de la Chapelle, **24**

Boccaccio, **20**

Brasserie Georges, **49**

Cappuccino, **38**

Castello Banfi, **28**

Chez Jean, **18**

Comme Chez Soi, **23**

Falstaff, **13**

Gallery, **33**

In't Spinnekopke, **3**

La Fine Fleur, **43**

La Porte des Indes, **47**

La Quincaillerie, **46**

La Roue d'Or, **21**

La Truffe Noire, **48**

L'Ecailler du Palais Royal, **29**

La Grande Porte, **25**

Le Faste Fou, **32**

Léon de Bruxelles, **9**

Les Capucines, **34**

Les Petits Oignons, **26**

Maison du Cygne, **16**

Ogenblik, **6**

Villa Lorraine, **50**

Vincent, **5**

Lodging

Alfa Louise, **45**

Amigo, **15**

Beau-Site, **42**

Cadettt, **44**

Château du Lac, **51**

Clubhouse, **41**

Conrad, **39**

Gerfaut, **11**

Hilton, **31**

Le Dixseptième, **19**

Manos Stephanie, **40**

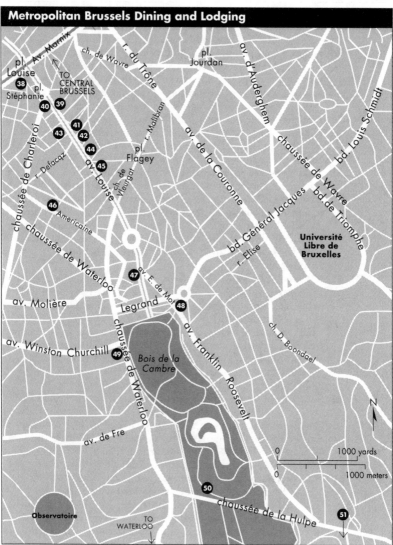

Metropolitan Brussels Dining and Lodging

Matignon, **14**
Metropole, **4**
Montgomery, **22**
Mozart, **17**
Novotel, **10**
Orion, **1**
Radisson SAS
Hotel, **7**
Royal Windsor
Hotel, **12**
Sofitel, **35**
Stanhope, **30**

Sun, **37**
Welcome Hotel, **2**

with spring vegetables. The selection of Beaujolais is particularly good. ⊠ *Galerie des Princes 1,* ☎ *02/511–6151. No reservations after 8. AE, DC, MC, V. Open until midnight. Closed Sun.*

\$\$ ✕ **Aux Armes de Bruxelles.** Hidden among the tourist traps in the Ilôt Sacré, this restaurant attracts a largely local clientele with its slightly tarnished middle-class elegance and its Belgian classics: turbot *waterzooi* (a creamy stew of potatoes, vegetable, and fish), a variety of steaks, mussels prepared every which way, and french fries, which the Belgians believe, with some justification, they prepare better than anyone else. The place is cheerful and light, and service is friendly if frequently overstretched. ⊠ *Rue des Bouchers 13,* ☎ *02/511–2118. AE, DC, MC, V. Closed Mon. and June.*

\$\$ ✕ **Aux Marches de la Chapelle** (formerly Les Brigittines). This very at-
★   tractive restaurant, opposite the Eglise de la Chapelle near the Grand Sablon, has listened to its clientele and converted from haute cuisine to simpler but high-quality brasserie fare, including traditional cassoulet and sauerkraut. One of the Belle Epoque rooms is dominated by a splendid old bar, the other by an enormous open fireplace. ⊠ *Place de la Chapelle 5,* ☎ *02/512–6891. AE, DC, MC, V. No lunch Sat. Closed Sun. and Aug.*

\$\$ ✕ **Brasserie Georges.** This hugely successful brasserie was the first in
★   Brussels and is still the best. You'll find a splendid display of shellfish at the entrance, an Art Deco interior with tile floor and potted palms, and fast, friendly service by waitresses in black and white. The fare includes traditional dishes, such as sauerkraut, poached cod, and potted duck, as well as more adventurous dishes such as salmon tartare and swordfish chop with a light chicory curry. Twenty-five different wines are sold by the glass. ⊠ *Avenue Winston Churchill 259,* ☎ *02/ 347–2100. AE, DC, MC, V. Open until midnight.*

\$\$ ✕ **In 't Spinnekopke.** This is where true Brussels cooking has survived and continues to flourish. Its low ceilings and benches around the walls have remained from its days as a coach inn in the 18th century. You can choose from among 100 artesian-well beers. Many of the dishes are made with beer. ⊠ *Place du Jardin aux Fleurs 1,* ☎ *02/511–8695. AE, DC, MC, V. No lunch Sat. Closed Sun.*

\$\$ ✕ **La Fine Fleur.** This neighborhood restaurant, a stone's throw from Avenue Louise, attracts a young, artistic clientele. Leafy plants proliferate, and French *chansons* from the stereo set the mood. The owner, an artist, designed the minimalist decor and serves a sort of minimalist cuisine, which includes such happy surprises as carpaccio with cèpes, and scallops with horseradish—but portions are not large. Arrive after nine to experience the place at its busiest. ⊠ *Rue de la Longe Haie 51,* ☎ *02/647–6803. AE, DC, MC, V. No lunch Sat. Closed Sun., 2 wks at Easter, 2 wks in Aug.*

\$\$ ✕ **La Quincaillerie.** The name means "The Hardware Store," and that's
★   precisely what this place used to be. It still looks the part, except now there are tables perched on the narrow balcony and an oyster bar downstairs. The youngish clientele is served by even younger waitresses, who run up and down the stairs with heavy trays. The menu consists mostly of brasserie grub, such as baked ham knuckle, but it's enlivened by dishes that include salmon fillet, honey-baked Peking duck, and excellent game. The upwardly mobile have a soft spot for this place. ⊠ *Rue du Page 45,* ☎ *02/538–2553. AE, DC, MC, V. Open until midnight.*

\$\$ ✕ **La Roue d'Or.** The murals here pay extravagant homage to Magritte, the great surrealist. Bowler-hatted gentlemen ascend serenely to the ceiling, a blue sky inhabited by tropical birds. The good cuisine includes traditional Belgian fare as well as such staples of the French brasserie repertoire as lamb's tongue vinaigrette with shallots, pig's feet salad, or veal kidneys with watercress cream. The *escargots à la bour-*

guignonne (snails in their shells with a garlic-butter sauce) is outstanding. Go elsewhere if you're seeking a quiet meal; the noise level here can be quite high. ⊠ *Rue des Chapeliers 26,* ☎ *02/514–2554. AE, DC, MC, V. Closed weekends and mid-July–mid-Aug.*

$$ ✕ **Les Petits Oignons.** This airy 17th-century restaurant, in the heart of the Marolles, has been furnished with plants and bright modern paintings. It places no demands on your palate, but the ambience makes you feel good, and you are well looked after. Pâté of goose liver with champagne *ratafia* (liqueur) and leg of lamb with potatoes au gratin are among the choices. ⊠ *Rue Notre-Seigneur 13,* ☎ *02/512–4738. AE, DC, MC, V. Closed Sun. and Aug.*

$$ ✕ **Vincent.** In a town where most of the more fashionable places now concentrate on seafood, Vincent remains unapologetically a red-meat stronghold. Sides of beef and big slabs of butter in the window announce what awaits you. You pass through the kitchen on your way to the dining room, which is decorated with hand-painted tiles. ⊠ *Rue des Dominicains 8,* ☎ *08/511–2303. AE, DC, MC, V. Closed Aug.*

$ ✕ **Adrienne.** It's the huge cold buffet that packs them in year after year at this upstairs restaurant, just around the corner from Avenue Toison d'Or. The look is rustic, with red-and-white-check tablecloths; you can eat on the terrace in summer. The location is great for uptown shopping and movies, and it's also fun for kids. ⊠ *Rue Capitaine Crespel 1A,* ☎ *02/511–9339 (2nd location near Atomium,* ☎ *02/478–3000). AE, DC, MC, V. Closed Sun.*

$ ✕ **Au Vieux Saint Martin.** Even when neighboring restaurants on
★ Grand Sablon are empty, this one is full. A rack of glossy magazines is a thoughtful touch for lone diners, and you're equally welcome whether you order a cup of coffee or a full meal. The short menu emphasizes Brussels specialties; portions are generous. A wine importer, the owner serves unusually good wine for the price, by the glass, or by the bottle. The red walls are hung with large, contemporary paintings, and picture windows overlook the pleasant square. A brass plaque marks the table where President Bill Clinton relaxed during a Brussels walkabout. The kitchen is open daily from noon until midnight. ⊠ *Grand Sablon 38,* ☎ *02/512–6476. Reservations not accepted. No credit cards.*

$ ✕ **Boccaccio.** The Moroccan husband and Swedish wife who own the restaurant serve generous portions of Italian-inspired food in this super friendly hole-in-the-wall, shaped like a diner with a tiny kitchen at one end. It's popular with airline crews—not a bad recommendation. ⊠ *Rue du Marché-aux-Fromages 14,* ☎ *02/512–2929. AE, DC, MC, V. Closed Sun.*

$ ✕ **Cappuccino.** This sleek, Italian-chic café, strategically located in the heart of the uptown shopping area, serves cocktails, coffee, ice cream, sandwiches, and a few Italian standards, including pizza and lasagna. ⊠ *Avenue Louise 35,* ☎ *02/538–5232. Reservations not accepted. AE, DC, MC, V.*

$ ✕ **Chez Jean.** Jean Cambien runs a reliable restaurant, unchanged since 1931, with oak benches against the walls, backed by mirrors on which the dishes of the day are written in whitewash. Waitresses in black and white serve poached cod, mussels cooked in white wine, chicken waterzooi, and other Belgian dishes. ⊠ *Rue des Chapeliers 6,* ☎ *02/ 511–9815. No credit cards. Closed Sun.–Mon.*

$ ✕ **Falstaff.** Some things never change, and Falstaff is one of them. This
★ huge tavern, with an interior that is pure Art Nouveau, fills up for lunch and keeps going until 5 AM, with an ever-changing crowd, from students to pensioners. Cheerful waitresses punch in your orders for onion soup, filet mignon, salads, and other straightforward dishes on electronic order pads. Falstaff II (⊠ Rue Henri Maus 25) has the same food but not the ambience. The jury is still out on the latest, more up-

scale addition to this empire, Falstaff-Gourmand (✉ Rue des Pierres 38, ☎ 02/512–1761). ✉ *Rue Henri Maus 19,* ☎ *02/511–8789. AE, DC, MC, V.*

$ ✕ Gallery. Here's a Vietnamese restaurant that looks like an art gallery, with contemporary black chairs and tables, artfully suspended spotlights, and an exhibit of black-and-white photographs. The kitchen holds no surprises, but the food is well prepared and the helpings generous. Many come here for the large and well-stocked bar. ✉ *Rue du Grand Cerf 7,* ☎ *02/511–8035. AE, DC, MC, V. No lunch Sun. Closed 1st ½ of Aug.*

$ ✕ La Grande Porte. A long-time favorite in the Marolles area that makes no concession to fashion or style, this old place has a player piano and offhand but jovial waiters. It serves copious portions of popular Brussels specialties, such as *ballekes à la marolienne* (spicy meatballs) and *carbonade à la flamande* (beef and onions stewed in beer). The later the evening, the livelier the atmosphere and the greater the demand for its famous onion soup. ✉ *Rue Notre-Seigneur 9,* ☎ *02/512–8998. DC. Closed July.*

$ ✕ Le Faste Fou. Well situated in the Place Louise area, this is a popular lunch place for office workers. There is counter service downstairs and table service upstairs in a bare and noisy dining room devoid of decor; friendly servers and good food make up for it. The menu offers substantial salads and complete meals. ✉ *Rue du Grand-Cerf 21,* ☎ *02/511–3832. Reservations not accepted. AE, DC, MC, V. Closed Sun.*

$ ✕ Léon de Bruxelles. For reasons known only to themselves, the pro-
★ prietors of the old Chez Léon, known to every Bruxellois for the past 100 years, have changed its name. Even though prices have been edging upward lately, it continues to do a land-office business and has over the years expanded into a row of eight old houses. Heaping plates of mussels and other Belgian specialties, such as eels in a green sauce, are served nonstop, accompanied by arguably the best french fries in town. ✉ *Rue des Bouchers 18,* ☎ *02/511–1415. Reservations not accepted. AE, DC, MC, V.*

$$$$ ✕▦ Conrad. Opened in 1993 on the elegant Avenue Louise, this hotel combines the classic facade of an 1865 mansion with a sleek, deluxe American interior. Rooms come in many different shapes but are all spacious and have three telephones, a desk, bathrobes, and in-room checkouts. The intimate, gourmet Maison de Maître restaurant wins good reviews, and Cafe Wiltcher's offers all-day dining. The large piano bar is pleasantly chummy. President Clinton stayed here on a recent trip to Brussels. ✉ *Avenue Louise 71,* ☎ *02/542–4242,* ℻ *02/542–4300. 254 rooms, 15 suites. 2 restaurants, 2 bars, convention center, conference and banquet facilities, parking (fee), shops. Breakfast not included. AE, DC, MC, V.*

$$$$ ✕▦ Hilton. One of the first high-rises in Brussels back in the 1960s, it outclasses most other Hiltons in Europe and is continuously being refurbished floor by floor. The corner rooms are the most desirable. There are four floors of executive rooms, with a separate check-in area. The location near the Porte Louise is great for upscale shopping. There is a fine panoramic view from the 27th-floor restaurant, the En Plein Ciel (buffet lunch only). The second-floor restaurant, the Maison du Boeuf, is one of the best in town, and the ground-floor Café d'Egmont stays open around the clock. ✉ *Boulevard de Waterloo 38,* ☎ *02/504–1111,* ℻ *02/504–2111. 420 rooms, 30 suites. 3 restaurants, 2 bars, sauna, shops, convention center, parking (fee). Breakfast not included. AE, DC, MC, V.*

$$$$ ✕▦ Montgomery. The owners of this 1993 hotel set out to create new standards of service for the business traveler, and, for the most part, they have succeeded. Fax machines, three telephones (with a private line for incoming calls), good working desks, safes, triple-glazed windows, and bathrobes are standard. Rooms are decorated in Chinese, English (for those who like frills and furbelows), or cool, clean colonial style. There's a library bar-restaurant with a wood-burning fireplace, and the small meeting rooms are well appointed. The location is convenient to the European Commission. ⊠ *Avenue de Tervueren 134,* ☎ *02/741–8511,* ☏ *02/741–8500. 61 rooms, 2 penthouses, 1 suite. Restaurant, bar, health club, library, meeting rooms, parking (fee). Breakfast not included. AE, DC, MC, V.*

$$$$ ✕⌸ **Radisson SAS Hotel.** Next to the Opera, near the northern end of ★ the Galeries St-Hubert, this hotel opened in 1990 and was an instant success. The floors are decorated in a variety of styles—Asian (wicker furniture and Asian art), Italian (art deco fixtures and furnishings), and Scandinavian (light-wood furniture and parquet flooring). The greenery-filled atrium incorporates a 10-foot-high section of the 12th-century city wall. The Sea Grill is a first-rate seafood restaurant, and Danish open-face sandwiches are served in the atrium's café. A copious buffet breakfast is included. There's no extra charge for children under 15. ⊠ *Rue du Fosse-aux-Loups 47,* ☎ *02/219–2828,* ☏ *02/219–6262. 281 rooms. 3 restaurants, 2 bars, sauna, health club, business services, convention center, parking (fee). AE, DC, MC, V.*

$$$$ ✕⌸ **Royal Windsor Hotel.** The Royal Windsor, which opened in 1974 and is near the Grand'Place, has been refurbished. All rooms have blond-wood paneling and marble bathrooms. They are, however, on the small side. The lobby is businesslike, with leafy plants, comfortable sofas and chairs placed around marble-topped tables, and music wafting in from the adjacent piano bar. The elegant dining room, Les Quatre Saisons, serves light, imaginative, and expensive French cuisine. ⊠ *Rue Duquesnoy 5,* ☎ *02/511–4215,* ☏ *02/511–6004. 280 rooms. Restaurant, piano bar, health club, dance club, convention center, parking (fee). AE, DC, MC, V.*

$$$$ ✕⌸ **Stanhope.** This small hotel is the most expensive in Brussels and operates on the principle that if you have to ask the price, you can't afford it. It was created out of three adjoining town houses. All the rooms and suites have high ceilings, marble bathrooms, and luxurious furniture, but no two are alike, and each has its own name. The Linley, for example, features furniture handmade by Viscount Linley, nephew of the Queen of England. You can have English-style afternoon tea in the ground-floor salon, and the downstairs bar serves caviar. ⊠ *Rue du Commerce 9,* ☎ *02/506–9111,* ☏ *02/512–1708. 25 rooms, 25 suites. Restaurant, bar, tea shop, sauna, health club, meeting rooms, parking (fee). AE, DC, MC, V.*

$$$ ✕⌸ **Amigo.** Just a block from the Grand'Place and decorated in Span-★ ish Renaissance with touches of Louis XV, the Amigo looks more turn-of-the-century than 1950s, when it was built. Public spaces and guest rooms were refurbished in 1993. Rooms vary in furnishings, size, and price; those on higher floors, with views over the surrounding rooftops, are more expensive. Bathrooms are on the small side. Amigo is popular with those who like understated luxury. The service is excellent. ⊠ *Rue d'Amigo 1–3,* ☎ *02/547–4747,* ☏ *02/513–5277. 183 rooms. Restaurant, bar, meeting rooms, parking (fee). AE, DC, MC, V.*

$$$ ✕⌸ **Château du Lac.** Half an hour from the city center and a good ★ choice for those who want a peaceful home base from which to visit the capital and the provinces, this mock-Florentine castle is a former Schweppes bottling plant. The large rooms are light beige and well furnished, and the decor in the public rooms is contemporary, mostly white with red details. The splendid restaurant, Le Trèfle à Quatre, where Michel Haquin is chef, is itself worth a visit here, not only for his superb cuisine, focusing on fish and game, but also for the views over the lake. ⊠ *Avenue du Lac 87, Genval,* ☎ *02/654–1122,* FAX *02/653–6200. 38 rooms. Restaurant, bar, pool, sauna, convention center. AE, DC, MC, V.*

$$$ ✕☷ **Metropole.** Stepping into the Metropole, you would think you were on the *Orient Express.* The hotel has been restored to the palace it was during the Belle Epoque. The lobby sets the tone, with its enormously high coffered ceiling, chandeliers, marble, and Oriental carpets. The theme is carried through in the bar with potted palms, deep leather sofas, and Corinthian columns; in the café, which opens onto the sidewalk of Place de Brouckère; and in the Alban Chambon restaurant (named for the architect). The rooms are understated modern in varying shades of pastel (some with trompe l'oeil murals), with furniture upholstered in the same material as the bedspreads. ⊠ *Place de Brouckère 31,* ☎ *02/217–2300,* FAX *02/218–0220. 410 rooms. Restaurant, bar, café, convention center, airport shuttle. AE, DC, MC, V.*

$$ ✕☷ **Cadettt.** The concept of the Cadettt (part of the Swiss Mövenpick Group) is to offer superior rooms with limited services, at moderate rates. Completed in 1991, this hotel has large rooms, each with blond-wood furniture, a Lay-Z-Boy chair, and good work space. The beige-and-green atrium bar and restaurant serves generous Swiss breakfasts and a limited selection of specialties for lunch and dinner. The basement wine bar has a separate entrance. ⊠ *Rue Paul Spaak 15,* ☎ *02/645–6111,* FAX *02/646–6311. 128 rooms. Restaurant, 2 bars, sauna, health club, meeting rooms, parking (fee). Breakfast not included. AE, DC, MC, V.*

$$ ✕☷ **Manos Stephanie.** The Louis XV furniture, marble lobby, and an-
★ tiques set a standard of elegance seldom encountered in a hotel in this price category. The rooms have rust-colored carpets, green bedspreads, and good-size sitting areas. The hotel, opened in 1992, occupies a grand old town house, so the rooms are not rigidly standardized; the split-level Room 103 is especially appealing. The atrium restaurant is enlivened by gaily striped chair coverings. ⊠ *Chaussée de Charleroi 28,* ☎ *02/539–0250,* FAX *02/537–5729. 55 rooms. Restaurant, bar, meeting rooms. AE, DC, MC, V.*

$$ ✕☷ **Novotel.** A stone's throw from the Grand'Place, this hotel was built in 1989 but with an old-look, gabled facade. Some French lodging chains mass-produce hotels that are functional but motel-like, and this one is no exception. The rooms have white walls and russet carpets; all come with a sofa that can sleep an extra person, some with an additional roll-away bed. There's no extra charge for children under 16. The Grill serves French hotel-chain cuisine; it's acceptable but far from exciting. ⊠ *Rue du Marché-aux-Herbes 120,* ☎ *02/514–3333,* FAX *02/511–7723. 136 rooms. Restaurant, bar, no-smoking floor, meeting rooms, parking (fee). AE, DC, MC, V.*

$ ✕☷ **Matignon.** Only the facade was preserved in the conversion of this Belle Epoque building to a hotel in 1993. The lobby is no more than a corridor, making room for the large café-brasserie that is part of the family-owned operation. Rooms are small but have generous beds, blow-dryers, and large-screen TVs, a welcome change from the dinky TVs you find in most other European budget hotels. Windows are double-glazed, and that's important in this busy spot across the street from the Bourse and two blocks from the Grand'Place. The five duplex suites are an especially good value. ⊠ *Rue de la Bourse 10,* ☎ *02/511–0888,* FAX *02/513–6927. 22 rooms. Restaurant, bar. Advance payment requested. AE, DC, MC, V.*

$ ✕☷ **Welcome Hotel.** Among the charms of the smallest hotel in Brus-
★ sels are the young owners, Michel and Sophie Smeesters. The six rooms, with king- or queen-size beds, are as comfortable as those in

far more expensive establishments. Plans to add four more rooms are well advanced. This little hotel is much in demand, so book early. There's a charming breakfast room, and around the corner on the fish market, Michel doubles as chef of the excellent seafood restaurant La Truite d'Argent, where hotel guests get a special rate. ⊠ *Rue du Peuplier 5,* ☎ *02/219–9546,* ℻ *02/217–1887. 6 rooms with bath. 2 restaurants, meeting rooms. AE, DC, MC, V.*

$$$ 🏨 **Sofitel.** Opened in 1989, the six-floor Sofitel has a great location opposite the Hilton. There's a chic shopping arcade on the ground floor, and you reach the lobby on an escalator. Public rooms and bedrooms are decorated in warm brown and beige tones. Bathroom telephones and bathrobes are standard. The restaurant, at the back of the lobby, has been downgraded to a buffet breakfast room, but there is good room service. ⊠ *Avenue de la Toison d'Or 40, 1050,* ☎ *02/514–2200,* ℻ *02/514–5744. 171 rooms. Breakfast room, bar, meeting rooms. Breakfast not included. AE, DC, MC, V.*

$$ 🏨 **Alfa Louise.** Opened in 1994 on the prestigious Avenue Louise, this hotel is distinguished by its large rooms with sitting areas and office-size desks, making it an excellent choice for budget-minded business travelers. Bathrobes and room safes are additional conveniences. There's a jazz piano bar off the lobby. ⊠ *Avenue Louise 212, 1050,* ☎ *02/644–2929,* ℻ *02/644–1878. 40 rooms. Bar, breakfast room, meeting rooms. AE, DC, MC, V.*

$$ 🏨 **Beau-Site.** Gleaming white and with flower boxes suspended from the windowsills, this former office building, opened as a hotel in 1993, makes a smart impression. The location (a block from the upper end of Avenue Louise) and the attentive staff are big pluses. The good-size rooms come in shapes other than the standard cube, and bathrooms have blow-dryers and bidets. The complimentary buffet breakfast includes bacon and eggs. ⊠ *Rue de la Longue Haie 76, 1000,* ☎ *02/640–8889,* ℻ *02/640–1611. 38 rooms with bath. Breakfast room. AE, DC, MC, V.*

$$ 🏨 **Clubhouse.** The large, blue-carpeted lobby, which opens on a small garden and has a fire in the open hearth on chilly days, is particularly inviting. The location, on a quiet side street off the elegant Avenue Louise, is another plus. The rooms have pastel walls, salmon-pink carpeting, flower-patterned bedspreads and curtains, and a sofa, easy chair, and desk. ⊠ *Rue Blanche 4, 1000,* ☎ *02/537–9210,* ℻ *02/537–0018. 81 rooms. Bar, meeting rooms, parking (fee). AE, DC, MC, V.*

$$ 🏨 **Le Dixseptième.** Opened in 1993, this hotel occupies the stylishly
★ restored 18th-century residence of the Spanish ambassador. Rooms surround a pleasant interior courtyard, and suites are up a splendid Louis XVI staircase. Named for Belgian artists, all units have whitewashed walls, plain floorboards, exposed beams, suede sofas, and colorful draperies. Suites have working fireplaces and fax machines; one has a separate office. ⊠ *Rue de la Madeleine 25, 1000,* ☎ *02/502–5744,* ℻ *02/502–6424. 12 rooms, 13 suites. Breakfast room–bar, kitchenettes. AE, DC, MC, V.*

$ 🏨 **Gerfaut.** In this cheerful hotel opened in 1991, the rooms—in light beige with colorful bedspreads—are of reasonable size. Rooms with three and four beds are available at modest supplements. Breakfast is served in the bright and friendly Winter Garden room. The location near the Gare du Midi (South Station), though not choice, provides an opportunity to see a part of Brussels most tourists ignore. ⊠ *Chaussée de Mons 115–117, 1070,* ☎ *02/522–1922,* ℻ *02/523–8991. 48 rooms. Bar. AE, DC, MC, V.*

$ 🏨 **Mozart.** Although it's up a flight of stairs and there's no elevator, this hotel, opened in 1993, is attractive and spacious. The rooms, all with refrigerators and showers, are decorated in shades of salmon and have oak beams. Breakfast is served in a cozy nook. The multilingual Ben, the Moroccan owner, and his Swedish wife also run the remarkably inexpensive Boccaccio restaurant (☞ *above*) across the street. ⊠ *Rue Marché aux Fromages 15A, 1000,* ☎ *02/502–6661,* 𝔽𝔸𝕏 *02/502–7758. 23 rooms. Breakfast room. AE, DC, MC, V.*

$ 🏨 **Orion.** This former residential hotel has converted to a regular hotel operation. The whitewashed surfaces are offset by bright red details. Rooms have pull-out twin beds, and junior suites sleep four. All have fully equipped kitchenettes. Rooms on the courtyard are the quietest. ⊠ *Quai au Bois-à-Brûler 51, 1000,* ☎ *02/221–1411,* 𝔽𝔸𝕏 *02/221–1599. 169 rooms. Breakfast room, meeting rooms, parking (fee). AE, DC, MC, V.*

$ 🏨 **Sun.** Rooms are on the small side and the bathrooms are cramped, but the beds have firm mattresses, there are in-room safes, and decor is a pleasant pastel green. The attractive breakfast room has a striking glass mural; snacks are served there during the day. The hotel is on a quiet but slightly dilapidated side street off the busy Chaussée d'Ixelles. ⊠ *Rue du Berger 38, 1050,* ☎ *02/511–2119,* 𝔽𝔸𝕏 *02/512–3271. 22 rooms with bath or shower. Breakfast room, parking (fee). AE, DC, MC, V.*

Nightlife and the Arts

Nightlife

By 11, most Bruxellois have packed up and gone home. But around midnight, bars and cafés fill up again, as the night people take over, and some stay open till dawn. In this city, people provide their own entertainment, and nightclubs, though they exist, are likely to disappoint.

BARS AND LOUNGES

There's a café on virtually every street corner, and they are all taprooms in disguise. The Belgians consume vast quantities of beer, some of it with a 10% alcohol content. **Moeder Lambic** (⊠ Rue de Savoie 68 in St-Gilles) claims to stock 600 Belgian beers and a few hundred more foreign ones. **Fleur en Papier Doré** (⊠ Rue des Alexiens 53) was the hangout for surrealists, dadaists, and other artists, and their spirit lingers on. **Ultième Hallucinatie** (⊠ Rue Royale 316) is Art Nouveau. People meet for a drink at all hours in the **Falstaff** (⊠ Rue Henri Maus 19), **Le Perroquet** (⊠ Rue Watteeu 31, off the Grand Sablon), or **'t Kelderke** (⊠ Grand'Place 15). If you like Gypsy music, try the late-night **Ateliers de la Grande Ile** (⊠ Rue de la Grande Ile 33).

Brussels's sizable black population, hailing mostly from Zaire and mostly French-speaking, has its own hangouts. One such is **Kwassa Quoisa** (⊠ Rue de Boetendael 113 in Uccle, ☎ 02/344–9836); another is the disco **L'Ecume des Nuits** (⊠ Galerie Louise 122A, entrance, Place Stéphanie, ☎ 02/512–9147). **Chaussée de Wavre** is the principal street for African shops, bars, and restaurants.

A popular non-ethnic nightspot is **Rick's Café Américain** (⊠ Avenue Louise 344, ☎ 02/648–1451). The **James Joyce** (⊠ Rue Archimède 34, ☎ 02/230–9894) and the **Kitty O'Shea** (⊠ Boulevard de Charlemagne 42, ☎ 02/230–7875) are as Irish as they come. Among the most popular **hotel bars** are those in the Hilton, the Amigo, and the Métropole (☞ Dining and Lodging, *above*). **Le Cerf** (⊠ Grand'Place 20) is the most popular bar in the heart of the city; hot toddies are a specialty.

CABARETS

Show Point (⊠ Place Stephanie 14, ☎ 02/511–5364) offers striptease. **Chez Flo** (⊠ Rue au Beurre 25, ☎ 02/512–9496) has transvestite shows. **Do Brasil** (⊠ Rue de la Caserne 88, ☏ 02/513–5028) features Latin American entertainment.

DISCOS

Action starts at midnight in most of the discos. **Griffin's** (⊠ Royal Windsor Hotel, Rue Duquesnoy 5, ☏ 02/505–5555) appeals to young adults and business travelers. **Le Mirano Continental** (⊠ Chaussée de Louvain 38, ☏ 02/218–5772) attracts a self-styled jet set. **Le Garage** (⊠ Rue Duquesnoy 16, ☏ 02/512–6622) draws a younger crowd; Sunday is gays only. The trendy favor **Jeux d'Hiver** (⊠ Chemin du Croquet 1A, ☏ 02/649–0864), a members-only club in the Bois de la Cambre (Thursday and Friday); you'll be admitted if you look the part.

GAY BARS

Tels Quels (⊠ Rue du Marché au Charbon 81, ☏ 02/512–4587); **Why Not** (⊠ Rue des Riches Claires 7, ☏ 02/512–7587); and, for lesbians, **Le Féminin** (⊠ Rue Bourgal 9, ☏ 02/511–1719).

JAZZ

There are two contemporary Belgian jazz greats: Toots Thielemans (on harmonica) and the guitarist Philip Catherine, and if you're lucky you might catch one of them in Brussels. Among the best jazz venues are **Travers** (⊠ Rue Traversière 11, ☏ 02/218–4086); **Kaai** (⊠ Quai aux Pierre de Taille 39, ℻ 02/502–1275); **Preservation Hall** (⊠ Place de Londres 4, ☏ 02/502–1597); **Sounds** (⊠ Rue de la Tulipe 28, ☏ 02/512–9250); **New York Café Jazz Club** (⊠ Chaussée de Charleroi 5, ☏ 02/534–8509); and **L'Archiduc** (⊠ Rue Antoine Dansaert 6, ☏ 02/512–0652).

The Arts

A glance at the "What's On" supplement of the weekly English-language newsmagazine *The Bulletin* reveals the breadth of the offerings in all categories of cultural life. Tickets for most events can be purchased by calling **Free Time Line** (☏ 02/538–3131) or **Ticketel** (☏ 02/675–5414).

FILM

First-run English-language and French movies predominate. The most convenient movie theater complexes are **Acropole** (⊠ Avenue de la Toison d'Or, ☏ 02/511–4238) and **UGC de Brouckère** (⊠ Place de Brouckère, ☏ 02/218–0607). The biggest—26 theaters—is the futuristic **Kinepolis** (⊠ Avenue du Centenaire 1, Heysel, ☏ 02/478–0450). The **Musée du Cinéma** (⊠ Rue Baron Horta 9, ☏ 02/507–8370) shows classic and silent movies (BF50 if 24 hours in advance; BF80 at the door).

MUSIC

The principal venue for classical music concerts is the **Palais des Beaux-Arts** (⊠ Rue Ravenstein 23, ☏ 02/507–8200). Many chamber music concerts and recitals are held in the more intimate **Conservatoire Royale** (⊠ Rue de la Régence 30, ☏ 02/511–0427). There are many concerts in various churches, especially the **Eglise des Minimes** (⊠ Rue des Minimes 62).

If you're going to be in Brussels in the spring, try to take in some of the concerts that are part of the **Queen Elisabeth Music Competition** (the penultimate round is at the Conservatoire Royale, the final week at the Palais des Beaux-Arts), for pianists, violinists, singers, and composers in successive years. The monthlong **Ars Musica** (☏ 02/512–1717) festival of contemporary music is in February and March of each year, held in various locations.

The principal venue for rock concerts is the **Forest National** (⊠ Avenue du Globe 36, ☏ 02/347–0355). For more rock and pop, as well as French *chanson*, check the **Cirque Royal** (⊠ Rue de l'Enseignement

81, ☎ 02/218–2015) and **Centre Culturel le Botanique** (⊠ Rue Royale 236, ☎ 02/218–3732).

The national opera house is the excellent **Théâtre Royal de la Monnaie** (⊠ Place de la Monnaie, ☎ 02/218–1211); this is where the 1830 revolution started. Inflamed by the aria starting "Amour sacré de la patrie" (Sacred love of your country) in Auber's *La Muette de Portici*, members of the audience rushed outside and started rioting. The brief and largely unbloody revolution against the Dutch established the Belgian nation state. Visiting opera and dance companies often perform at the **Cirque Royal** (⊠ Rue de l'Enseignement 81, ☎ 02/218–2015). Dance is among the liveliest arts in Belgium. Anne Teresa De Keersmaeker is the choreographer-in-residence at the opera house, but her group, *Rosas,* also performs at the Cirque and at **Lunatheater** (⊠ Square Sainctelette 20, ☎ 02/201–5959) as do the Royal Flanders Ballet and other groups.

Nearly all the city's 30-odd theaters stage French-language plays; only a few present plays in Dutch. Talented amateur groups also put on occasional English-language performances. Avant-garde performances are the most rewarding. Check what's on at **Théâtre Varia** (⊠ Rue du Sceptre 78, ☎ 02/640–8258), **Théâtre du Residence Palace** (⊠ Rue de la Loi 155, ☎ 02/231–0740), **Théâtre de Poche** (⊠ Bois de la Cambre, ☎ 02/649–1727), and **Rideau de Bruxelles** (⊠ Palais des Beaux-Arts, Rue Ravenstein 23, ☎ 507–83610.)

Outdoor Activities and Sports

Golf

The top clubs in the area are **Royal Golf Club de Belgique** (⊠ Château de Ravenstein, Tervuren, ☎ 02/767–5801), **Royal Waterloo Golf Club** (⊠ Vieux Chemin de Wavre 50, Ohain, ☎ 02/633–1850), and **Keerbergen Golf Club** (⊠ Vlieghavenlaan 50, Keerbergen, ☎ 015/234961). For more information, call the **Royal Belgian Golf Federation** (☎ 02/672–2389).

Health and Fitness

Several hotels have well-equipped fitness centers open to the public. The best are at the **Europa Brussels** (⊠ Rue de la Loi 107, ☎ 02/230–1333), **Holiday Inn** (⊠ Holidaystraat 7, Diegem, ☎ 02/720–5865), **John Harris Fitness** at the Radisson SAS Hotel (⊠ Rue du Fossé-aux-Loups 47, ☎ 02/219–8254), and **Sheraton** (⊠ Place Rogier 3, ☎ 02/224–3111). Fees average BF1,000 a session. Prices are considerably lower at independent health clubs, such as **European Athletic City** (⊠ Avenue Winston Churchill 25A, ☎ 02/345–3077) and **California Club** (⊠ Chaussée d'Ixelles 298–300, ☎ 02/640–9344).

Jogging

For in-town jogging, use the **Parc de Bruxelles** (⊠ Rue de la Loi to the Palace); for more extensive workouts, head for the **Bois de la Cambre** (⊠ Southern end of Avenue Louise), a natural park that is a favorite among joggers and families with children. The park merges on the south into the beech woods of the 11,000-acre **Forêt de Soignes,** extending as far south as Genval with its lake and restaurants.

Spectator Sports

Going to the races is second in popularity only to soccer, and there are three major racecourses: **Boitsfort** (⊠ Chaussée de la Hulpe 51, ☎ 02/660–2839), which has an all-weather flat track; **Groenendael** (⊠

Sint-Jansberglaan 4, Hoeilaart, ☎ 02/673–6792), for steeplechasing; and **Sterrebeek** (✉ Du Roy de Blicquylaan 43, Sterrebeek, ☎ 02/767–5475), for trotting and flat racing. For more information, contact the **Jockey Club de Belgique** (☎ 02/672–7248).

SOCCER

Soccer is the most popular spectator sport, and the leading club, **Anderlecht,** has many fiercely loyal fans. Their home pitch is Parc Astrid (✉ Avenue Theo Verbeeck 2, ☎ 02/522–1539). Major international games are played at the former Heysel Stadium, now rebuilt and renamed **Stade Roi Baudouin** (✉ Avenue du Marathon 135, ☎ 02/479–3654). For information and tickets, contact the **Maison du Football** (✉ Avenue Houba de Strooper 145, ☎ 02/477–1211), which is open weekdays from 9 to 4:15.

Swimming

Hotel swimming pools are few and far between. Among covered public pools, the best are **Calypso** (✉ Avenue Wiener 60, ☎ 02/673–7619), **Longchamp** (✉ Square de Fré 1, ☎ 02/374–9005), and **Poseidon** (✉ Avenue des Vaillants 4, ☎ 02/762–1633).

Tennis

Popular clubs include the **Racing Club** (✉ Avenue des Chênes 125, ☎ 02/374–4181), **Royal Leopold** (✉ Avenue Dupuich 42, ☎ 02/344–3666), and **Wimbledon** (✉ Chaussée de Waterloo 220, Rhode-St-Genèse, ☎ 02/358–3523). For more information contact the Fédération Royale Belge de Tennis (Royal Belgian Tennis Federation, ☎ 02/217–2365).

Shopping

The Belgians started producing high-quality luxury goods in the Middle Ages, and this is what they are skilled at. This is not a country where you pick up amazing bargains. Value added tax (TVA) further inflates prices, but visitors from outside the European Union can obtain refunds.

Shopping Districts

The stylish shopping area for clothing and accessories comprises the upper end of **Avenue Louise** and includes **Avenue de la Toison d'Or,** which branches off at a right angle; **Boulevard de Waterloo,** on the other side of the street; **Galerie Louise,** which links the two avenues; and **Galerie de la Toison d'Or,** another gallery two blocks away. The **City 2** mall on Place Rogier and the pedestrian mall, **Rue Neuve,** are fun and inexpensive shopping areas (but not recommended for women alone after dark). The **Place du Grand-Sablon** and adjoining streets and alleys is where you will find antiques dealers and smart art galleries. The **Galeries St-Hubert** is a rather stately shopping arcade lined with upscale shops selling men's and women's clothing, books, and interior design products. In the **Rue Antoine Dansaert** and **Place du Nouveau Marché aux Grains,** near the Bourse, a number of boutiques feature fashions by young designers, and interior design, and art shops.

Department Stores

The best Belgian department store is **Inno** (✉ Rue Neuve 111, ☎ 02/211–2111; ✉ Avenue Louise 12, ☎ 02/513–8494; ✉ Chaussée de Waterloo 699, ☎ 02/345–3890). Others, such as **C&A** and **Marks & Spencer,** are clustered at the Place de la Monnaie end of Rue Neuve.

Street Markets

Bruxellois with an eye for fresh farm produce and low prices do most of their food shopping at the animated open-air markets in almost every borough. Among the best are those in **Boitsfort** in front of the Maison Communal on Sunday mornings; on **Place du Châtelain,** Wednesday afternoons; and on **Place Sainte-Catherine,** all day, Monday through Saturday. In addition to fruits, vegetables, meat, and fish, most markets include traders with specialized products, such as wide selections of cheese and wild mushrooms. The most exotic market is the Sunday morning, **Marché du Midi,** where the large North African community gathers to buy and sell foods, spices, and plants, transforming the area next to the railway station into a vast bazaar.

In the Grand'Place there's a **Flower Market,** daily, except Monday, and a **Bird Market,** Sunday mornings. You need to get to the flea market, **Vieux Marché** (⊠ Place du Jeu de Balle) early. It's open daily 7–2. The **Antiques and Book Market** (⊠ Place du Grand-Sablon), Saturday 9–6 and Sunday 9–2, is frequented by established dealers.

Specialty Stores

BOOKS

Tropismes (⊠ Galerie des Princes 11, ☎ 02/512–8852) carries more than 40,000 titles and will help you find out-of-print books. **Libris** (⊠ Espace Louise, ☎ 02/511–6400) is very well stocked with current French-language titles. The **Galerie Bortier** (⊠ Rue de la Madeleine–Rue St. Jean) is a small, attractive arcade devoted entirely to rare and secondhand books. It was designed by the architect responsible for the Galeries St- Hubert. Shops specializing in comic strip albums include those at Chaussée de Wavre Nos. 167, 179, and 198, and the **Tintin Shop** (⊠ Rue de la Colline 13, off Grand'Place).

English-language bookstores include **House of Paperbacks** (⊠ Chaussée de Waterloo 813, Uccle, ☎ 02/343–1122); **Librairie de Rome** (⊠ Avenue Louise 50b, ☎ 02/511–7937); and **W. H. Smith** (⊠ Boulevard Adolphe Max 71–75, ☎ 02/219–2708), which carries hard covers, paperbacks, and periodicals. The *International Herald Tribune* and the *Wall Street Journal* are sold by almost all newsdealers.

CHOCOLATES

Godiva (⊠ Grand'Place 22 and other locations) is the best known. **Neuhaus** (⊠ Galerie de la Reine 25–27 and other locations) is the runner-up and is preferred by many. **Leonidas** (⊠ Chaussée d'Ixelles 5 and other locations) is the budget alternative, still high quality. The best handmade pralines, which are the crème de la crème of Belgian chocolates, are made and sold at **Nihoul** (⊠ Avenue Louise 298–302, ☎ 02/648–3796), **Mary** (⊠ Rue Royale 73, ☎ 02/217–4500), and **Wittamer** (⊠ Place du Grand Sablon 12, ☎ 02/512–3742).

CRYSTAL

The Val-St-Lambert mark is the only guarantee of handblown, hand-engraved lead crystal vases and other glass. You can buy it in many stores; the specialist is **Art et Sélection** (⊠ Rue du Marché-aux-Herbes 83, ☎ 02/511–8448)

LACE

Manufacture Belge de Dentelle (⊠ Galerie de la Reine 6–8, ☎ 02/511–4477) and **Maison F. Rubbrecht** (⊠ Grand'Place 23, ☎ 02/512–0218) sell local handmade lace. Lace sold in the souvenir shops is likely to come from the Far East. An introductory visit to the **Musée du Costume et de la Dentelle** (⊠ Rue de la Violette 6, ☎ 02/512–7709) is a good idea if you're planning to shop for lace.

LEATHER GOODS

Delvaux (⊠ Galerie de la Reine 31, ☎ 02/512–7198; ⊠ Boulevard de Waterloo 27, ☎ 02/513–0502) makes outstanding, classic handbags, wallets, belts, and attaché cases. Be prepared to part with a hefty sum, but the Delvaux products last and last.

Brussels A to Z

Arriving and Departing

BY CAR

Belgium is covered by an extensive network of four-lane highways. Brussels is 204 kilometers (122 miles) from Amsterdam on E19; 222 kilometers (138 miles) from Düsseldorf on E40; 219 kilometers (133 miles) from Luxembourg City on E411; and 308 kilometers (185 miles) from Paris.

Drivers piggy-backing on Le Shuttle through the Channel Tunnel have another 213 kilometers (128 miles) to go from Calais to Brussels; the route via Oostende is the fastest, even though on the Belgian side the highway stops a few kilometers short of the border. Those taking the ferry to Oostende are 115 kilometers (69 miles) from Brussels on the six-lane E40.

Brussels is surrounded by a beltway, marked RING. Exits to the city are marked CENTER. Among several large underground parking facilities, the one close to the Grand'Place is particularly convenient for users of downtown hotels.

BY BUS

Eurolines offers up to three daily express bus services from Amsterdam, Berlin, Frankfurt, Paris, and London. The Eurolines Coach Station is located at CCN Gare du Nord (✉ Rue du Progrès 80, ☎ 02/203–0707).

From London, the **City Sprint** bus connects with the Dover–Calais Hovercraft, and the bus then takes you on to Brussels. For reservations and times, call **Hoverspeed** (☎ 01304/240241).

BY PLANE

All flights arrive at and depart from **Zaventem** (☎ 02/732–3111), Brussels's National Airport. **Sabena, American, Delta** and **United** fly into Brussels from the United States. **Sabena, British Midland,** and **British Airways** fly to Brussels from London's Heathrow Airport; **Air UK,** from Stansted; and **British Airways,** from Gatwick. Several regional centers in the United Kingdom also have direct flights to Brussels, as do all capitals in Europe and a growing number of secondary cities. The no-frills airline **Virgin Express** offers scheduled flights to and from a growing number of cities on the Continent.

Express trains leave the airport for the Gare du Nord and Gare Centrale stations every 20 minutes (one train an hour continues to the Gare du Midi). The trip takes 20 minutes and costs BF125 one way in first class, BF85 second class. The trains operate 6 AM to midnight.

Taxis are plentiful. A taxi to the city center takes about half an hour and costs about BF1,000. You can save 25% on the fare by buying a voucher for the return trip if you use the Autolux taxi company. Beware freelance taxi drivers who hawk their services in the arrival hall.

Courtesy buses serve airport hotels and a few downtown hotels. Inquire when making reservations.

BY TRAIN

Eurostar trains from London (Waterloo) use the Channel Tunnel to cut travel time to Brussels (Gare du Midi) to 3¼ hours. Trains stop at Ashford (Kent) and Lille (France). At press time (fall 1996) there were seven daily services, and a first-class, one-way ticket cost BF5,210; second class, BF3,680. A number of promotional fares are available. Eurostar is operated by London & Continental Railways, a new consortium, which promises great improvements in distribution and marketing.

Conventional train services from London connect with the Ramsgate–Oostende ferry or Jetfoil, and from Oostende the train takes you to Brussels. The whole journey, using Jetfoil, takes some six hours; by ferry, about nine hours. For more information, contact **British Rail** (☎ 0171/834–2345).

Brussels is linked with Paris, Amsterdam, and Liège by new **Thalys** high-speed trains, which operate at full TGV speed on French tracks; in Belgium and Holland, until new tracks have been laid, they provide a slower but very comfortable ride. **Belgian National Railways** (SNCB; ☎ 02/203–3640) is the national rail line.

Getting Around
BY METRO, TRAM, AND BUS
The metro, trams, and buses operate as part of the same system. All three are clean and efficient, and a single ticket, which can be used on all three, costs BF50. The best buy is a 10-trip ticket, which costs BF320, or a one-day card costing BF125. You need to stamp your ticket in the appropriate machine on the bus or tram; in the metro, your card is stamped as you pass through the automatic barrier. You can purchase these tickets in any metro station or at newsstands. Single tickets can be purchased on the bus.

Detailed maps of the Brussels public transportation network are available in most metro stations and at the Brussels tourist office in the Grand' Place (☎ 02/513–8940). You get a map free with a Tourist Passport (also available at the tourist office), which, for BF220, allows you a one-day transport card and BF1,000 worth of museum admissions.

BY TAXI
Call **Taxis Verts** (☎ 02/349–4949) or **Taxis Oranges** (☎ 02/513–6200). You can also catch one at cab stands around town. Distances are not great, and a cab ride costs between BF250 and BF500. Tips are included in the fare.

Contacts and Resources
CAR RENTALS
Avis (☎ 02/726–9488). **Budget** (☎ 02/646–5130). **Europcar/Interrent** (☎ 02/640–9400). **EuroDollar** (☎ 02/735–6005). **Hertz** (☎ 02/513–2886).

DOCTORS AND DENTISTS
Doctor (☎ 02/479–1818). **Dentist** (☎ 02/426–1026).

EMBASSIES
U.S. Embassy (⊠ Boulevard du Régent 27, ☎ 02/513–3830); **Canadian** (⊠ Avenue de Tervuren 2, ☎ 02/741–0611); **British** (⊠ Rue d'Arlon 85, ☎ 02/287–6211).

EMERGENCIES
Police (☎ 101); **Accident and Ambulance** (☎ 100).

GUIDED TOURS
De Boeck Sightseeing (☎ 02/513–7744) operates city tours (BF750) with multilingual cassette commentary. Passengers are picked up at major hotels and at the tourist office in the Town Hall. More original are the tours run by **Chatterbus** (⊠ Rue des Thuyas 12; reservations through Brussels tourist office, ☎ 02/513–8940). Tours include visits on foot or by minibus to the main sights (BF600) and a walking tour that includes a visit to a bistro (BF250). Tours are operated early June through September.

ARAU (⊠ Boulevard Adolphe Max 55, ☎ 02/219–3345) organizes thematic city bus tours from March through November, including "Brussels 1900: Art Nouveau," "Alternative Brussels," and "Brussels 1930: Art Deco." The cost is BF500 for a half-day tour.

De Boeck Sightseeing Tours (⊠ Rue de la Colline 8, Grand'Place, ☎ 02/513–7744) visits Antwerp, the Ardennes, Brugge, Ghent, Ieper, and Waterloo.

Qualified guides are available for individual tours from the Tourist Information Brussels (TIB) in the Town Hall (☎ 02/513–8940). Three hours costs BF3,000, and up to 20 people can share the same guide.

LATE-NIGHT PHARMACIES
One pharmacy in each district stays open 24 hours; the roster is posted in all pharmacy windows. In an emergency call 02/479–1818.

LODGING
Tourist Information Brussels (TIB) publishes an annual hotel guide listing prices and facilities. You can obtain a copy by writing to TIB (⊠ Hôtel de Ville, 1000 Brussels). It contains a reservation form, to be sent to Belgian Tourist Reservations (⊠ Boulevard Anspach 111, 1000 Brussels, ☎ 02/513–7484, ⅅⅫ 02/513–9277). If you arrive in Brussels without reservations, check the TIB (⊠ Grand'Place, ☎ 02/513–8940); they don't give up until they've found you a place. The youth organization **Acotra** (⊠ Rue de la Madeleine 53, ☎ 02/512–8607) has a room-finding service for youth hostels. These services are free, but you will be asked for a deposit, which is then deducted from your hotel bill.

TRAVEL AGENCIES
American Express (⊠ Place Louise 2, ☎ 02/512–1740). **Carlson/Wagonlit Travel** (⊠ Boulevard Clovis, ☎ 287–8110).

VISITOR INFORMATION
Tourist Information Brussels (TIB; ☎ 02/513–8940), in the Hôtel de Ville on the Grand' Place, is open daily 9–6 during the main tourist season (off-season, Sunday 10–2; December through February, closed Sunday). The main tourist office for the rest of **Belgium** is near the Grand'-Place (⊠ Rue Marché-aux-Herbes 63, ☎ 02/504–0390) and is open weekdays 9–7, weekends 9–1 and 2–7 (in winter the office closes at 6 PM and is closed Sunday mornings).

EXCURSIONS FROM BRUSSELS

Waterloo

19 km (11 mi) south of Brussels—see Belgium map for placement.

Waterloo, like Stalingrad or Hiroshima, changed the course of history. In sheer bloodiness, it was to be exceeded only by the Battle of the Somme in World War I. It has become a word so charged with symbolism that visitors are sometimes surprised that there actually is such a place. But there is, and a popular town it is, especially among expats. At one time, so many American families lived in Waterloo that it became known as Scarsdale East. Now there are so many Scandinavians that some Waterloo shopkeepers have learned basic Swedish.

The Duke of Wellington spent the night of June 17, 1815, at an inn in Waterloo, where he established his headquarters. When he slept there again the following night, Napoléon had been defeated. The inn in the center of this pleasant, small town is now the **Wellington Museum**. It presents the events of the 100 days leading up to the Battle of Waterloo, maps and models of the battle itself, as well as military and Wellington memorabilia in well laid-out displays ⊠ *Chaussée de Brux-*

elles 147, ☎ *02/345–7806.* ⊠ *BF80.* ☉ *Apr.–mid-Nov., daily 9:30–6:30; mid-Nov.–Mar., daily 10:30–5.*

The actual **Waterloo Battlefield** is just south of the town (sign-posted "Butte de Lion"). This is where Wellington's troops received the onslaught of Napoléon's army. A crucial role in the battle was played by some of the ancient, fortified farms, of which there are many in this area. The farm of Hogoumont was fought over all day; 6,000 men, out of total casualties of 48,000, were killed here alone. Later in the day, fierce fighting raged around the farms of La Sainte Haye and Papelotte. In the afternoon, the French cavalry attacked, in the mistaken belief that the British line was giving way. Napoléon's final attempt was to send in the armored cavalry of the Imperial Guard, but at the same time the Prussian army under Blücher arrived to engage the French from the east, and it was all over. The battlefield is best surveyed from the top of the **Butte du Lion**, a pyramid 226 steps high and crowned by a 28-ton lion, which was erected by the Dutch 10 years later.

The visitor facilities at the battlefield were long below par, and some of the tackiness remains, including some restaurants and a seedy wax museum. The new **visitors center** is an improvement, offering an audiovisual presentation that explains the progress of the battle, followed by a mood-setting film of the fighting, as seen through the eyes of children. You can buy souvenirs here, too—from tin soldiers to T-shirts—as well as tokens for other attractions.The adjacent **Battle Panorama Museum** contains a vast, circular painting of the charge of the French cavalry, executed with amazing perspective and realism. First unveiled in 1912, it was recently restored. ⊠ *Route du Lion 252-254,* ☎ *02/385–1912.* ⊠ *BF300, including the Butte du Lion and Panorama.* ☉ *Apr.–Oct., daily 9:30–6:30; Nov.–Mar., daily 10:30–4.*

Judging by the prevalence of souvenirs and images of Napoléon, you could be forgiven for thinking that the battle was won by the French. In fact, there were Belgian soldiers fighting on both sides. Those particularly interested in Napoléon's last days as emperor will want to visit his headquarters at what is now the small **Musée du Caillou** in Genappe, south of the battlefield. It contains the room where he spent the night before the battle, his personal effects, and objects found in the field. ⊠ *Chaussée de Bruxelles 66,* ☎ *02/384–2424.* ⊠ *BF60.* ☉ *Apr.–Sept., Tues.–Sun. 10:30–6:30; Nov.–Mar., Tues.–Sun. 1:30–5.*

Dining and Lodging

$$ ✕ **L'Auberge d'Ohain.** This country inn northeast of Waterloo has an
★ elegant dining room decorated in shades of peach and champagne, and a kitchen capable of great things: carpaccio of scallops with basil and olive oil, fillet of sole with asparagus in a parsley broth, and lightly curried lobster fricassee. The four-course *menu découverte* (tasting menu) is an excellent value. ⊠ *Chaussée de Louvain 709,* ☎ *02/653–6497. AE, DC, MC, V. Closed Sun.–Mon. and 2nd ½ of July.*

$ ✕ **L'Amusoir.** Popular with resident Americans, this is an unpretentious steak house in an old wooden building in the center of town. It serves excellent filet mignon, prepared with a variety of sauces. ⊠ *Chaussée de Bruxelles 121,* ☎ *02/353–0336. AE.*

$$ ✕▥ **Le 1815.** This new, small hotel is actually on the battlefield. Each room is named for one of the participating generals and decorated with his portrait. The style is art deco, but with details evocative of the period of the battle. The restaurant is much better than those clustered at the foot of the Butte du Lion. ⊠ *Rte. du Lion 367,* ☎ *02/387–0060,* ⴼⴰⵅ *02/387–1292. 14 rooms with bath. Restaurant, bar, miniature golf. AE, DC, MC, V.*

Mechelen

28 km (17 mi) north of Brussels and about the same distance from Antwerp (avoid the exit for the almost identically named Machelen, a Brussels suburb)—see Belgium map for placement.

Mechelen (Malines in French) preserves its medieval past in many ways as perfectly as does the more famous Brugge (Bruges) but on a smaller scale. There are far fewer tourists, an important plus if you are uncomfortable with crowds. Mechelen is also an important ecclesiastical center, being the residence of the Roman Catholic Primate of Belgium. The city is the center of vegetable production, especially asparagus, whose stalks reach their height of perfection in May, and *witloof,* the Belgian delicacy known elsewhere as chicory or endive.

Mechelen's brief period of grandeur coincided with the reign (1507–30) of Margaret of Austria. She established her devout and cultured court in this city while she served as regent for her nephew, who later became Emperor Charles V. The philosophers Erasmus and Thomas More were among her visitors, as were the painters Albrecht Dürer and Van Orley (whose portrait of Margaret hangs in the Musée d'Art Ancien in Brussels), and Josquin des Prés, the master of polyphony.

★ **Sint-Romboutskathedraal,** completed in the 1520s, represents a magnificent achievement by three generations of the Keldermans family of architects, who were active in cathedral building throughout Flanders. The beautifully proportioned tower, 318 feet high, was intended to be the tallest in the world, but the builders ran out of money before they could reach their goal. Inside are two remarkable 40-ton carillons of 49 bells each; carillon-playing was virtually invented in Mechelen, and student carillonneurs still come here from all over the world. The best place to listen to the bells is in the Minderbroedersgang. The interior of the cathedral is spacious and lofty, particularly the white sandstone nave dating from the 13th century. Chief among the art treasures is Van Dyck's *Crucifixion* in the south transept. ⊠ *Grote Markt.* ⊙ *Mon.–Sat. 9:30–4 (until 7 in summer), Sun. 1–5; check tourist office for tower tours; carillon concerts Sat. at 11:30 AM, Sun. at 3, Mon. at 8:30 PM.*

Seldom have two parts of a single building had such vividly contrasting styles as does the **Stadhuis** (Town Hall). To the right is the Gothic, turreted, 14th-century *Lakenhalle* (Cloth Hall). To the left is the flamboyant palace commissioned by Charles V to accommodate the *Grote Raad* (Grand Council) of the Burgundian Netherlands. Work was abandoned in 1547 but resumed and completed in the 20th century in accordance with the Keldermans' original plans. ⊠ *Grote Markt.* ⊙ *Guided tours (from the tourist office) start at 2 PM weekends Easter–June and Sept., daily July–Aug.*

NEED A BREAK?

The smallest café in Mechelen is the **Borrel Babel** in the charming Sint Romboutshof, behind the cathedral. Different varieties of *genever* (Dutch gin) are the potent specialty.

The **Koninklyke Manufactuur/Manufacture Royale Gaspard De Wit** (Royal Tapestery Manufacture) is the best place to understand and distinguish between different styles of tapestry weaving, and one of the few places where this ancient and glorious art is still practiced. Official opening hours are severely restricted, but see what the Tourist Office can do for you at other times. ⊠ *Schoutetstraat 7,* ☎ *015/202905.* 🎫 *Guided tours of workshops and collection of antique and contemporary tapestries BF150.* ⊙ *Tours Sat. at 10:30 (except July).*

Haverwerf and Zoutwerf, oats and salt, respectively, were loaded on these old wharfs on the river Dijle. On the Haverwerf stand three remarkable houses. The green one, called Paradise, is Gothic, with a relief showing the banishment of Adam and Eve. In the middle stands the Little Devils, with a 15th-century timber facade decorated with carved satyrs. The red one, St. Joseph, is a Baroque house from 1669. On the Zoutwerf stands the old fishmongers' guild hall from the 16th century, embellished by a magnificent golden salmon.

At **Planckendael Animal Farm,** more than 1,000 animals lead a life of near-freedom in this vast park, which features an adventure trail for children, a large playground, and a children's farm. The park can be reached by boat from Mechelen (Colomabrug), with departures every 30 minutes from 9 to 8:30. ⊠ *Leuvensesteenweg 582, Muizen.* ☎ *015/414921.* *BF380.* *Daily 9–5 (until 6:30 in summer).*

Speelgoedmuseum Mechelen (Mechelen Toy Museum) has more than 8,000 tin soldiers standing ready to do battle on a model of Waterloo. This large museum also has a vast collection of toys and games, both ancient and modern, and there's a play area for young and old. ⊠ *Nekkerspoel 21,* ☎ *015/557075.* *BF120.* *Tues.–Sun. 10–5.*

Dining

$$$ ★ ✕ **D'Hoogh.** In a grand graystone mansion on the Grote Markt, its second-floor dining room looking over the square, this glamorous landmark presents top-quality *cuisine du marché* (whatever is freshest): smoked eel terrine with pistachios, poached goose liver in port jelly with caramelized apples, turbot and zucchini spaghetti in vinaigrette and olive oil, and, in April and May, the most wonderful asparagus imaginable. ⊠ *Grote Markt 19,* ☎ *015/217553. Reservations essential. AE, DC, MC, V. No lunch Sat., no dinner Sun. Closed Mon. and 1st 3 wks of Aug.*

$$ ★ ✕ **De Wingerd.** This superb fish restaurant is right on the Fish Market, where the standards are the highest and the products the freshest. Follow the recommendations of the pleasant and knowledgeable staff. In good weather, you can dine alfresco on the pleasant square. ⊠ *Vismarkt 1,* ☎ *015/206700. AE, DC, MC, V. Closed Mon.–Tues. and Aug.*

$ ✕ **'t Korenveld.** This tiny, old-fashioned bistro has been primly restored and decked with pretty floral wallpaper and tiled tabletops. Its cuisine is unpretentious, featuring simple fish and steaks at low prices. It adjoins the Alfa Hotel and has some tables in their bar. ⊠ *Korenmarkt 20,* ☎ *015/421469. AE, DC, MC, V. Closed Mon.*

Leuven

26 km (16 mi) east of Brussels—see the Belgium map for placement.

Leuven (Luvain), like Oxford, is a place where underneath the hubbub of daily life you sense an age-old devotion to learning and scholarship. Its ancient Roman Catholic university, founded in 1425, was one of Europe's great seats of learning in the Middle Ages. One of its rectors was elected Pope Adrian VI. Erasmus taught here in the 16th century, as did the cartographer Mercator and, in the following century, Cornelius Jansen, whose teachings inspired the anti-Jesuit Jansenist movement. The city was pillaged and burned by the Germans in 1914, when 1,800 buildings, including the university library, were destroyed; in 1944 it was bombed again. In the 1960s, severe intercultural tensions caused the old bilingual university to split into a French-language and Dutch-language university. The French speakers moved their university south of the linguistic border to the new town of Louvain-la-Neuve; the Dutch-speakers remained in Leuven. Present-day **Katholieke**

Universiteit Leuven has a student body of more than 25,000, including about 1,000 seminarians from many different countries.

★ Every Flemish town prides itself on its ornate, medieval **Stadhuis** (Town Hall). This one escaped the 1914 fire because it was occupied by German staff. It is the work of Leuven's own architectural master of Flamboyant Gothic, Mathieu de Layens, who finished it in 1469 after 21 years' work. In photographs it looks more like a finely chiseled reliquary than a building; it is necessary to stand back from it to fully appreciate the vertical lines in the mass of turrets, pinnacles, pendants, and niches, each with its own statue. The interior contains some fine 16th-century sculpted ceilings. ⊠ *Grote Markt.* ☉ *Guided tours (from the tourist office) weekdays at 11 and 3, weekends at 3.*

NEED A
BREAK? Under the Town Hall, and adjoining a small beer museum, is the **Raadskelder** café, strategically located to help revive tired city officials and tourists.

Sint Pieterskerk, Leuven's Collegiate Church of St. Peter, has had a troubled architectural history. A shifting foundation led to the shortening of the tower in the 17th century and to the replacement of the spire with a cupola in the 18th. The interior, however, is remarkable for the purity of the Gothic nave. The ambulatory and choir are closed for restoration, but some treasures usually found there include *The Last Supper,* by Leuven's 15th-century official painter, Dirk Bouts, and are on temporary display in the nave. ⊠ *Grote Markt.* ☜ *Free.* ☉ *Tues.–Sat. 10–noon and 2–5, Sun. 2–5; mid-Mar.–mid-Oct., also Mon. 10–noon and 2–5.*

Stedelijk Museum Vander Kelen-Mertens (Municipal Museum) gives you an idea of how Leuven's upper crust lived 100 years ago. The building, which dates from the 16th century, was originally a college. It became the burgomaster's residence in the 19th century. A series of rooms in different styles reflect his taste. The art collection includes works by Albrecht Bouts (died 1549), son of Dirk, and Quentin Metsys (1466–1530), a remarkable portraitist, as well as Brabantine sculptures from the 15th and 16th centuries. ⊠ *Savoyestraat 6.* ☎ *016/226906.* ☜ *BF50.* ☉ *Tues.–Sat. 10–5, Sun. 2–5.*

Every Flemish city worth its salt also has a *begijnhof* (beguinage), a city within a city, formerly inhabited by members of a Christian sisterhood dating from the 13th century. The original members were widows of fallen Crusaders. **Groot Begijnhof** is the largest in the country. It is half a mile down Naamsestraat, past several university colleges (the American College is at No. 100). This quiet retreat numbers 72 tiny, whitewashed houses, with religious statues in small niches, dating mostly from the 17th century, grouped around the early Gothic Church of St. John the Baptist. The houses have been carefully restored and all but one are lived in by university staff.

Dining

$$$ ✕ **Belle Epoque.** This grand urban town house by the station offers the most lavish dining in Leuven, served with considerable pomp in an Art Nouveau setting. Try the smoked salmon filled with eel mousse, and wild hare, in season. There's also a pleasant terrace. ⊠ *Bondgenotenlaan 94,* ☎ *016/223389. Reservations essential. AE, DC, MC, V. Closed Sun.–Mon. and 3 wks in July–Aug.*

$ ✕ **Domus.** Tucked into a back street off the Grote Markt, this café adjoins the tiny Domus brewery, famous for its honey beer. The ambience is young and casual, the decor authentically rustic: craggy old beams, a brick fireplace, a labyrinth of separate rooms, bric-a-brac, and paisley table throws. The menu offers well-prepared omelettes, chicken à la king, and a cream gratin of endive, ham, and cheese, as well as several salads and cold plates. ⊠ *Tiensestraat 8,* ☎ *016/201449. No credit cards.*

Excursions from Brussels A to Z

Waterloo
ARRIVING AND DEPARTING
Bus W from Brussels (Place Rouppe) runs at half-hour intervals. There is also frequent commuter train service.

GUIDED TOURS
De Boeck Sightseeing (☎ 02/513–7744), operates half-day tours from Brussels.

Expert guides, **Les Guides 1815** (⊠ Route du Lion 250, ☎ 02/385–0625), can be hired to take you around the battlefield for one-hour (BF1,400) and three-hour tours (BF2,200); group tours in English (BF100 per person) are weekends at 4, July through August.

VISITOR INFORMATION
Waterloo Tourist Office: ⊠ Chaussée de Bruxelles 149, ☎ 02/354–9910. ⊙ Apr.–Nov. 15, daily 9:30–6:30; Nov. 16–Mar., daily 10:30–5.

Mechelen
ARRIVING AND DEPARTING
The train trip from Brussels takes 15 minutes.

GUIDED TOURS AND VISITOR INFORMATION
Dienst voor Toerisme (City Tourist Office) organizes walks to explore historic Mechelen and also distributes tourist information. ⊠ *Stadhuis (Town Hall), Grote Markt 21,* ☎ *015/297655.* ⊡ *Tours BF60.* ⊙ *Tours Easter–Sept. weekends; July–Aug. daily; June–mid-Sept., Mon.*

Leuven
ARRIVING AND DEPARTING
By car, take the motorway toward Liège; the Leuven exit is marked. The train takes 20 minutes.

GUIDED TOURS AND VISITOR INFORMATION
There are no regularly organized guided tours of Leuven, but you can arrange with the tourist office for an English-speaking personal guide (BF1,200) for two hours. ⊠ *City Tourist Office, Leopold Vanderkelenstraat 30,* ☎ *016/211539.* ⊙ *Weekdays 9–5, Sat. (and Sun. Mar.–Oct.) 10–5.*

HAINAUT

Hainaut is a proud old region that was the nursery of French kings, the rich dowry of dynastic marriages, and for many years the buffer between expansionist France and quarrelsome Flanders. You'll see land scarred by the industrial revolution and ancient, fortified farms turned into centers of highly productive agriculture; cathedrals spared the ravages of war; and parks and châteaux that are reminders of the feudal world that was.

Most visitors explore Hainaut as an excursion from Brussels, or as a stopover en route to France. One can also cut across from Bouillon in southwest Luxembourg, through France along the scenic, winding road beside the Semois River, and begin the tour of Hainaut in Chimay, in reverse order to the itinerary suggested here.

In case you want to see the world.

At American Express, we're here to make your journey a smooth one. So we have over 1,700 travel service locations in over 120 countries ready to help. What else would you expect from the world's largest travel agency?

do more®

AMERICAN EXPRESS

Travel

In case you want to be welcomed there.

We're here to see that you're always welcomed at establishments everywhere. That's why millions of people carry the American Express® Card – for peace of mind, confidence, and security, around the world or just around the corner.

do more

In case you're running low.

We're here to help with more than 118,000 Express Cash locations around the world. In order to enroll, just call American Express before you start your vacation.

do more

AMERICAN EXPRESS

Express Cash

And just in case.

We're here with American Express® Travelers Cheques and Cheques *for Two*.® They're the safest way to carry money on your vacation and the surest way to get a refund, practically anywhere, anytime.

Another way we help you...

do more®

AMERICAN
EXPRESS

Travelers
Cheques

Attention! As you drive south from Brussels through Flemish Brabant, Tournai is signposted as Doornik. This changes to Tournai as you cross the linguistic border at Enghien/Edingen.

Numbers in the margin correspond to points of interest on the Hainaut map.

Gaasbeek

16 *15 km (9 mi) west of Brussels, 29 km (18 mi) northwest of Nivelle.*

In Gaasbeek you are in Bruegel country, almost as if you stepped inside one of his paintings of village life. The area is called Pajottenland, and you may be familiar with the landscape from Bruegel's works, many of which were painted here. From the terrace of the **Château of Gaasbeek** you have a panoramic view of this landscape. The rulers of Gaasbeek once lorded it over Brussels, and the townspeople took terrible revenge and razed the castle. Restored in the 19th century, it contains outstanding 15th- and 16th-century tapestries. Rubens's will is among the documents in the castle archives. The surrounding park is popular with picnickers. ⊠ *Kasteelstraat 40,* ☎ *02/532–4372.* ⊠ *BF120.* ⊗ *Apr.–June and Sept.–Oct., Tues.–Thurs. and weekends 10–5; July–Aug., Sat.–Thurs. 10–5.*

En Route Beersel is just off the motorway as you head south from Brussels. It is the site of a stark 13th-century fort, the **Kastel van Beersel,** surrounded by a moat, which was part of Brussels's defenses. The interiors are empty, except for one room, which is a well-equipped torture chamber. ⊠ *Lotsestraat,* ☎ *02/331–0024.* ⊠ *BF60.* ⊗ *Mar.–mid-Nov., Tues.–Sun. 10–noon and 2–6; mid-Nov.–Dec. and Feb., weekends 10:30–5.*

In Attre, near Ath, stands the splendid **Château d'Attre,** built in 1752 and preserved intact. It is still inhabited, and visits are limited to the salons and drawing rooms of the ground floor. Among its treasures are paintings by Franz Snyders and Murillo. The semi-wild park surrounding the château has great charm. ⊠ ⊠ *BF120.* ⊗ *Apr.–Oct., weekends 10–noon and 2–6; July–Aug., Thurs.–Tues. 10–noon and 2–6.*

Park Paradisio is an ornithologist's dream come true. On a former monastic domain, amidst old ruins, bushes, ancient trees, a river, and three lakes, more than 2,500 birds of 400 different species live in semi-liberty. Birds of prey live inside a 50-foot-high cage of 30,000 square feet, which visitors may enter. Special care is taken with birds of endangered species so that their offspring can be returned to the wild. There's also a children's farm, restaurants, and a playground. The park is near Attre. ⊠ *Domaine de Cambron, Cambron,* ☎ *068/454653.* ⊠ *BF385.* ⊗ *Apr.–Oct., daily 10–6.*

Tournai

17 *86 km (52 mi) southwest of Brussels, 48 km (29 mi) west of Mons, 28 km (17 mi) east of Lille (France).*

Tournai was an important center when the Roman legions were still marching around these parts. Clovis, the Merovingian king who became the first Christian ruler of France, was born here in 465. At various times, Tournai has been English, French, and Austrian. Through these vicissitudes the city remained a flourishing center of art. The German bombardment in May 1940 destroyed virtually all the priceless old buildings, with the exception of a few Romanesque houses from the 12th century—unique in Western Europe—and a handful of 14th- and 15th-century Gothic buildings.

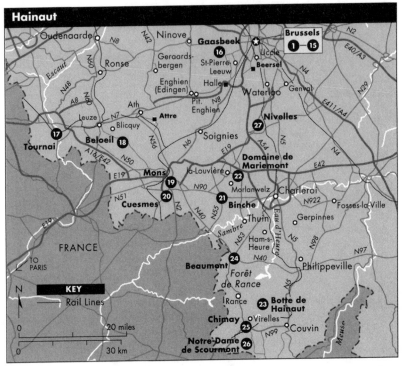

Hainaut

★ The **Cathédrale Notre-Dame,** with its five towers, all different, dominates the city today. Begun in 1110 and completed in 60 years, it is the most original work of religious architecture in Belgium and the beginning of a distinctive style that spread from Tournai down the river Escaut (Scheldt). You get the best general view of the cathedral from Place Paul-Emile Janson, and you need to walk around it to get the full effect of its vast proportions and the massive silhouettes of its five towers. Inside is an overpowering Renaissance screen in polychrome marble, contrasting with the Romanesque purity of the nave. The transept, almost a cathedral within the cathedral, contains what remains of 12th-century frescoes and well-restored 14th-century windows. In the chapels are paintings by Rubens (the magnificent *Purgatory*), Pourbus the Elder, and Martin de Vos. Foremost among the objects in the treasury are reliquaries in gilded copper and silver by two of the great 13th-century silversmiths and masters of Art Mosan, Nicholas de Verdun, and Hugo d'Oignies. ⊠ *Place Paul-Emile Janson.* ☉ *Cathedral Apr.–Oct., daily 8:30–1 and 2–6; Nov.–Mar., daily 9–noon and 2–6; Treasury Apr.–Oct., weekdays 10–11:45 and 2–5:30, weekends 8:30–noon and 2–6; Nov.–Mar., daily 9–noon and 2–4.*

NEED A **A l'Bancloque** (⊠ Rue des Chapeliers 46, ☎ 069/222149) is a classic
BREAK? Belgian drinking room with high, coffered ceilings and an old stone fireplace.

The 240-foot-high **Beffroi** (Belfry) on the Grand'Place is the oldest in this land of old belfries, dating from 1188. Hanging here are two bells from 1392 and a 15th-century carillon. It cannot be visited, as it is undergoing restoration.

The **Pont des Trous** is a rare example of a 13th-century fortified bridge built to control river access. The bridge was blown up in 1940; it was rebuilt after the war and raised 8 feet to allow river traffic to pass through—exactly what the old bridge was built to prevent. Sightseeing boats leave from the landing stage below the bridge.

The new **Musée de la Tapisserie** (Tapestry Museum) vividly illustrates the long and profitable tradition of tapestry-making in Tournai and displays an outstanding selection of tapestries from the Middle Ages to the present day. In the contemporary section there are demonstrations of tapestry weaving every weekday. ⊠ *Place Reine Astrid,* ☎ *069/ 234285.* ☞ *BF80.* ⊙ *Wed.–Mon. 10–noon and 2–5:30.*

The star-shaped **Musée des Beaux Arts** was designed by Victor Horta, the master Art Nouveau architect, so as to allow a maximum of natural light. Its exceptional collection of early Flemish art includes works by native son Roger de la Pasture, better known as Roger Van der Weyden, who is represented by a Nativity scene and the *Salve Regina* triptych; and Impressionist masterpieces such as Manet's *Couple d'Argenteuil,* and modern Belgian art. ⊠ *Enclos Saint-Martin,* ☎ *069/222045.* ☞ *BF80.* ⊙ *Wed.–Mon. 10–noon and 2–5:30.*

Ⓒ The **Centre de Loisirs de l'Orient** is a family-oriented leisure center with boats, games, barbecues, swimming pool, and a waterside pub. ⊠ *Chemin de Mons 8 (exit 32),* ☎ *069/222635.* ☞ *Free.* ⊙ *Apr.–mid-Sept., daily 10–10.*

Ⓒ The **Archeosite** is an open-air museum and experimental archaeological center, with prehistoric dwellings with mud walls and thatched roofs reconstructed in accordance with archaeological findings. Activities include basketwork, weaving, pottery, bronze casting, and iron ore processing. ⊠ *Rue de l'Abbaye 15, Aubechies,* ☎ *069/671116.* ☞ *BF100.* ⊙ *Nov.–Easter, weekdays 9–5; Easter–Oct., weekdays 9–5, weekends 2–6.*

★ ⑱ **Beloeil** is the magnificent, fairy-tale château of the Prince de Ligne, whose ancestors have lived here since the 14th century. The 17th-century château is partially a reconstruction from the original plans, following a fire in 1900. It contains fine furniture and tapestries, and the heirlooms include gifts from Marie Antoinette and Catherine the Great, friends of the Maréchal de Ligne; his grandson was offered, but refused, the Belgian crown. The elegant park, with a 5-kilometer (3-mile) vista, is patterned after Versailles. ⊠ *Rue du Château 11, Beloeil,* ☎ *069/689426.* ☞ *BF280 (tour of castle BF500 extra).* ⊙ *Apr.–Sept., daily 10–6.*

Dining and Lodging

$$$ ✕ **Le Pressoir.** Tucked away at the end of the Marché aux Poteries, between the cathedral and the Beffroi, this elegant but unpretentious restaurant combines historical atmosphere (exposed brick, illuminated oil paintings) with surprising urbanity: The bar draws BCBG (*bon chic–bon genre*) clientele, and the restaurant hosts visiting VIPs. Try the saffron-perfumed bouillabaisse of *rouget* (red mullet) or confit of farm pigeon with young turnips. ⊠ *Marché aux Poteries 2,* ☎ *069/223513. AE, DC, MC, V. No dinner Mon., Wed., Thurs. Closed Tues., Carnival wk, last 3 wks of Aug.*

$ ✕ **Bistro de la Cathédrale.** This modernized, brightly lighted storefront restaurant offers a few very reasonable fixed-price menus and large portions of good, simple, well-prepared food: fresh oysters, salads of *crevettes grise* (tiny shrimp), sole meunière, rabbit with prunes. The ambience is casual, the staff friendly. ⊠ *Vieux Marché aux Poteries 15,* ☎ *069/210379. AE, DC, MC, V.*

$ ✕ **Ô Pères au Quai.** On the riverside behind the columns of a 17th-century house, this value-for-money restaurant consists of one room, where meat is grilled in the large fireplace, and a pleasant garden. For starters, there's an hors-d'oeuvre buffet. Fixed-price menus include wine. ⊠ *Quai Notre-Dame 18,* ☎ *069/232922. AE, DC, MC, V. No lunch Sat., no dinner Mon.*

$$$ 🏨 **Le Panoramique.** As the name indicates, this hotel has sweeping views from its hilltop location a couple of miles from the center of town. Almost all of the modern rooms have bays opening onto a balcony. This is more like a ski resort than an ordinary hotel, long on comfort, short on charm. ⊠ *Place de la Trinité 2, Mont Saint-Aubert,* ☎ *069/233111,* FAX *069/233323. 23 rooms with bath. Restaurant, meeting rooms, indoor pool. AE, DC, MC, V.*

$$ 🏨 **Holiday Inn Garden Court.** This is a fully modernized chain-style business hotel at the foot of the cathedral in the center of town. Some rooms look onto the small square. ⊠ *Place St-Pierre,* ☎ *069/215077,* FAX *069/215078. 45 rooms. Restaurant, café, meeting rooms. AE, DC, MC, V.*

$ 🏨 **L'Europe.** Well placed on the Grand'Place, with rooms looking out toward the Beffroi and historic architecture, this is a comfortable hotel in an old step-gabled house. The rooms have been cheaply redecorated but with a lavish touch; most have toilets down the hall. The restaurant-tavern downstairs draws crowds of locals for stone-grilled meats. ⊠ *Grand'Place 36,* ☎ *069/224067. 8 rooms. Restaurant-tavern. AE, MC.*

Outdoor Activities and Sports

TENNIS

Try the **Waux-Hall** (⊠ Avenue Reine Astrid 22, Mons, ☎ 065/337923); or **Plaine de Jeux Bozière** (⊠ Avenue Bozière 1B, Tournai, ☎ 069/223586).

Mons

⑲   *48 km (29 mi) east of Tournai, 67 km (40 mi) south of Brussels, 72 km (43 mi) west of Namur.*

The hilly streets of Mons, lined with elegant, if grimy, 17th- and 18th-century brick houses, have considerable charm. At the highest point stands a remarkable **belfry,** known locally as *le château,* for it stands next to what once was the castle of the counts of Hainaut. Built in the 17th century, it's a Baroque tower, 285 feet high, crowned by an onion dome. Because it is undergoing restoration, the tower cannot be visited, but the work doesn't stop the bells of the carillon from ringing in the hours.

Mons has had its share of misfortunes. Like most of Wallonia's cities, it was repeatedly occupied and lost by the troops of Louis XIV, of the French Revolution, and of Napoléon. It was at Mons in August 1914 that the British Expeditionary Force first battled the Germans. Many of the self-styled Old Contemptibles spoke of a vision of the "Angels of Mons" helping them hold their position longer than seemed possible. Thirty years later, further destruction was wrought by a running battle between advancing American troops and the retreating Germans.

The **Hôtel de Ville** (Town Hall) in the Grand'Place is largely the work of Matthieu de Layens, the master of the Town Hall in Leuven, which to some extent it resembles. Next to the door stands a forged-iron statuette of a monkey. If you touch its head with your left hand, it will bring you good luck, as it has done for believers since the Middle Ages.

NEED A   **Le St-Germain-Saey** (⊠ Grand'Place 12) is an excellent pastry shop
BREAK?   where you can also have a sandwich or a more ambitious meal.

The **Collégiale Sainte-Waudru** (Collegiate Church of St. Waudru), named for the wife of a Merovingian dignitary who, legend has it, founded a monastery in the 7th century around which the city developed. The church was begun in 1450 by the women of St. Waudru's Noble Chapter of Secular Canonesses. The elaborately decorated Car d'Or (Golden Coach), which carries the reliquary of St. Waudru on a once-a-year procession through the streets on Trinity Sunday (eighth Sunday after Easter), stands in the nave next to doors that are opened only on special occasions. The precious objects in the treasury include what is purported to be Saint Waudru's ring. ⊠ *Place du Chapitre.* ⊡ *Treasury BF30.* ⊙ *May–Sept., Tues.–Sun. 2–5.*

★ **Grand-Hornu** is a remarkable example of early industrial architecture seeking to humanize working conditions, in an area dotted with conical slag heaps, reminders of a coal-mining past. The vast complex of workshops, offices, and housing, including a library, dance hall, and bathhouse, was built by Henri De Gorge in the early 19th century in neoclassical style, with arcades, pediments, and half-moon windows. It served its purpose for well over a century. Fortunately it was rescued from demolition and is now a multipurpose cultural center. ⊠ *Rue de Wasmes, Hornu,* ☎ *065/770712.* ⊡ *BF100.* ⊙ *Mar.–Sept., Tues.–Sun. 10–noon and 2–6; Oct.–Feb., Tues.–Sun. 10–noon and 2–4.*

⓴ **Cuesmes** was once home to **Vincent van Gogh.** He came to the Borinage, the area south of Mons, as a preacher in 1878 and stayed with a family of miners, the Decrucqs. It was here that he began drawing the landscape and scenes of the miners' lives. The house still stands. The original environment has been reconstructed; there is an exhibition of reproductions of his work and an audiovisual presentation. ⊠ *Rue du Pavillon 3, Cuesmes,* ☎ *065/335580.* ⊡ *BF50.* ⊙ *Tues.–Sun. 10–6.*

Dining and Lodging

$$ ★ ✕ **Alter Ego.** This handsome, stylish brasserie offers regionally inspired cuisine: head cheese with sweet garlic, saddle of rabbit with rosemary, and outstanding chocolate mousse. You get excellent value for your money here. ⊠ *Rue Nimy 6,* ☎ *065/351730. AE, DC, MC, V. No dinner Sun. Closed Mon., mid-July–mid-Aug.*

$ ✕ **Le Sans-Soucis.** This elegant tearoom (open until 7), with lamps on the tables, English china, fresh flowers, and piped-in classical music, serves the best light lunches in town: quiches, vegetable tarts, good salads, followed by marvelous cakes. ⊠ *Rue d'Havré 79,* ☎ *065/319333. Closed Sun.*

$$ ✕▦ **Casteau Resort Hotel.** The setting is peaceful for this modern hotel some 8 kilometers (5 miles) northeast of Mons, which makes a good base for exploring the region. Rooms are pretty standard, but with thoughtful amenities, such as a trouser press. The restaurant menu has some unusual items, including brioche with smoked eel and a poached egg. ⊠ *Chaussée de Bruxelles 38, Casteau,* ☎ *065/728741,* FAX *065/728744. 71 rooms. Restaurant, tennis courts, horseback riding, convention center. AE, DC, MC, V.*

$$ ★ ✕▦ **Château de la Cense au Bois.** This 19th-century château in a 40-acre park on the outskirts of Mons has luxurious and tasteful rooms. Each room is different from the others, but all have large beds, large bathrooms, and a view of the park. There is no obligation to eat in the restaurant, **L'Oscière Gris,** which serves ambitious French cuisine. ⊠ *Route d'Ath 135, Nimy,* ☎ *065/316000,* FAX *065/361155. 10 rooms. Restaurant ($$$; closed Mon.; no dinner Sun.), bicycles. AE, DC, MC, V. Closed 2nd ½ of Jan., 2nd ½ of July.*

Outdoor Activities and Sports

GOLF

There's a public 18-hole golf course west of Mons, **Golf Public** (⊠ Rue du Mont Garni 3, Baudour, ☎ 065/622719).

TENNIS

☞ Outdoor Activities and Sports *in* Tournai, *above*.

Binche

㉑ *16 km (10 mi) east of Mons, 62 km (37 mi) south of Brussels.*

Binche is the only remaining walled city in Belgium, and its center is still intact behind 25 towers and 2¼ kilometers (1½ miles) of ramparts. However, its biggest claim to fame is that it is the **Carnival Capital of Belgium.** The carnival begins the Sunday before Ash Wednesday, when hundreds of transvestite "Mam'zelles" dance in the streets to the music of fiddles, barrel organs, and drums, and then 1,500 Binche dancers form a procession. Shrove Tuesday, the day before Ash Wednesday, is the big day. The dancers, or Gilles, have celebrated the springtime rites since the 14th century. They dance with dignity and gravity, repeating ritual gestures such as ringing cow bells and distributing—throwing, actually—oranges. They assemble at dawn and go from house to house in fantastic costumes emblazoned with red and yellow heraldic lions. In the morning they wear wax-covered masks on which are painted green glasses, whiskers, and moustaches. In the afternoon, their enormous hats are crowned with huge plumes of ostrich feathers. To the rhythm of drums, the Gilles move through the streets in a slow, shuffling dance. The day ends with fireworks, but the Gilles continue dancing through the night. Traditionally, they drink nothing but champagne.

The **Musée International du Carnaval et du Masque** has been installed in the former Augustine college. It contains one of the world's finest collections of masks and costumes from all over the world, and there's an audiovisual presentation of the local carnival, in case you're in Binche at the wrong time for the real thing. ⊠ *Rue du St-Moustier 10,* ☎ *064/ 335741.* ☑ *BF150.* ☉ *Apr.–Oct., Mon.–Thurs. 9–noon and 2–6, Sat. 2–6; Nov.–Mar., Mon.–Thurs. 9–noon and 2–6, weekends 2–6. Closed during Carnival.*

★ The **Plan Incliné de Ronquières** is a grandiose engineering feat that did not bring about all the results that were hoped for. This mile-long "sloping plane" was designed to allow river traffic to enter hugh tanks, which were winched up 225 feet to a higher level, avoiding time-consuming locks. Now a new attraction has been added, in the tower overlooking the installation, which they hope will bring in the multitudes. To experience *Un Bateau, une Vie* (A Boat, a Life), visitors are issued infrared helmets that provide an interactive virtual-reality experience. You have the impression of following a boatman down into his barge, experiencing the traditional as well as the modern way of life on the canal, and sharing the confidences of its people. ⊠ *Halfway between Binche and Brussels,* ☎ *065/360464.* ☑ *Virtual-reality show BF250; boat trip BF100.* ☉ *Show: June–Sept., daily 10–7 (last ticket at 5); boats May–Sept., Tues. and Thurs.–Sun. noon, 2, 3:30, 5:30.*

㉒ The **Domaine de Mariemont** is a 110-acre English-style park, one of the most attractive parks in Belgium. It is embellished with sculptures by a number of artists, including Auguste Rodin and Constantin Meunier. Only ruins remain of the châteaux that once stood here, but there is a well-laid-out museum containing excellent collections of ancient and Chinese art, archaeological finds, and Tournai porcelain. ⊠ *Chaussée de Mariemont,* ☎ *064/212193.* ☑ *Free.* ☉ *Tues.–Sun. 10–6.*

Charleroi, a much larger town and former capital of the "Black Country," 20 kilometers (12 miles) east of Binche, has been hard hit by a recession that has made steel production almost obsolete. The city has some excellent museums. The **Musée de la Photographie** tells the story of photography from its infancy to the present day and mounts excellent temporary exhibitions. ⊠ *Avenue P. Pastur 11,* ☎ *071/435810,* ☜ *BF150.* ⊘ *Tues.–Sun. 10–6.*

☾ The **Musée des Sciences de Parentville** is a playful, family-oriented science museum, with laboratory and interactive displays, plus a playground with scientific games. ⊠ *Rue de Villers 227, Couillet,* ☎ *071/ 600300.* ☜ *BF130.* ⊘ *Weekdays 9:30–5:30, Sun. 10–6.*

Dining

$ ✕ **L'Industrie.** This is one of the few places serving the Binche specialty, *doubles* (buckwheat pancakes filled with cheese), but order by telephone the day before. This gracefully aging restaurant is so discreet that you might well miss it. It's on the corner of Grand'Place and Rue de la Hure. Head cheese, eel with herb sauce, and mussels are standard menu items. ⊠ *Grand'Place 4,* ☎ *064/331053. No dinner Mon., Tues. Closed Wed.*

Botte de Hainaut

㉓ The **Botte de Hainaut** extends some 50 kilometers (30 miles) south from Charleroi into France. This boot-shaped area is rich in wooded valleys, villages, châteaux and lakes.

☾ The **Eau-d'Heure Lakes** is a wild, wooded 4,500-acre park with trails, as well as aquaria, an ecological museum, and a panoramic tower. ⊠ *Boussu-lez-Walcourt,* ☎ *071/633534.* ☜ *BF180.* ⊘ *Easter–Sept., daily 9–6.*

㉔ The **Tour Salamandre** in **Beaumont** is all that remains of a major fortified castle built in the 11th century. The tower has been restored and houses a museum of local and regional history. ⊠ *Beaumont,* ☎ *071/ 588191.* ☜ *BF50.* ⊘ *May–Sept., daily 9–noon and 2–7; Oct., Sun. 10–noon and 2–5.*

㉕ All the way south is **Chimay,** a small town with vivid memories of the great nation to the south. It was the home of Froissart, the 14th-century historian whose chronicles furnished the background information for some of Shakespeare's plays. Later, Chimay became the home of Madame Tallien, a great beauty who was known to revolutionary France as Notre Dame de Thermidor. She narrowly escaped the guillotine, married her protector, Citizen Tallien, and persuaded him to instigate the overthrow of Robespierre. Eventually she was again married, to François-Joseph Caraman, prince de Chimay, and ended her days in peace and dignity as mistress of the **Château de Chimay.** The warrent for her arrest, signed by Robespierre, is preserved at the château, along with other Franch memorabilia, such as the baptismal robe worn by Napoléon's son, the king of Rome. ⊠ *Grand'Place,* ☎ *060/211846.* ☜ *BF200.* ⊘ *Guided tours Mar.–Nov., daily 10–noon and 2–6.*

㉖ **Notre-Dame de Scourmont** is a Trappist monastery whose monks produce some of the best cheese and most potent beer in Belgium. Although the monastery is not open to the public, except for retreats, you can purchase beer and cheese there. ⊠ *About 1 mi south of Chimay.*

Dining and Lodging

$$ ✕☷ **Hostellerie du Gahy.** Overlooking a large garden, this small inn has six rooms decorated in traditional style. The cuisine is ambitious: Try the lobster with vanilla flavoring in puff pastry or quails stuffed

with foie gras. Half board (a good buy) is obligatory in summer. ✉ *Rue Gahy 2, Momignies, Chimay,* ☎ *060/511093,* FAX *060/512879. 6 rooms with bath. Restaurant. AE, DC, MC, V. No dinner Sun. and Wed. Closed Mon.*

$ ✕🏠 **Le Virelles.** Just north of Chimay, in the open greenery around the
★ Etang de Virelles, this old country inn offers simple, regional cooking in a pretty, well-weathered beam-and-copper setting. You can have trout or *escavèche* (spicy, cold marinade of cooked fish), or a more ambitious, multicourse menu based on regional freshwater fish and game. Rooms, named after field flowers, are simple and cozy, some with four-poster beds. The adjacent nature reserve is great for long walks. ✉ *Rue du Lac 28, Virelles,* ☎ *060/212803,* FAX *060/212458. 7 rooms with bath or shower. Restaurant, café. AE, DC, MC, V. No dinner Tues. Closed Wed. (except July–Aug.).*

Outdoor Activities and Sports

ARCHERY

You can practice crossbow shooting in Beaumont at the **Arbaletriers Beaumontois** (✉ Parc de Paridaens, ☎ 071/588255) or archery at the **Club Saint-Sebastien** (✉ Rue de Mons 3, ☎ 060/588462).

HORSEBACK RIDING

Horseback riding is popular in many parts of the province, particularly in the less densely populated south. In Chimay you can arrange treks with the **Centre Equestre des Fagnes** (✉ Rue de la Fagne 20, ☎ 060/411169).

Nivelles

㉗ *34 km (21 mi) south of Brussels, 13 km (8 mi) west of Villers-la-Ville.*

★ **La Collégiale Sainte-Gertrude** (St. Gertrude's Collegiate Church), the pride of Nivelles, is, in fact, a reconstruction. This old town suffered terribly from bombardment in May 1940, when more than 500 buildings were destroyed, including the original church dating from the 7th century when the Merovingian kings ruled the land. Reparations from Germany paid for the rebuilding of the church, Belgium's finest Romanesque building, whose beauty derives from its severe simplicity. A peculiarity is the two choirs, one symbolizing the power of the Holy Roman Emperor and the other that of the Pope. The church is named for the daughter of Pepin the Old, St. Gertrude, who founded a convent in Nivelles in about 650. The crypt contains the burial vaults of St. Gertrude and her parents. ✉ *Grand'Place,* ☎ *067/215413.* 🎫 *BF90.* ☼ *Weekdays 9–6 (Oct.–Mar. until 5); guided tours weekdays at 1:30, 3, and 4:30, weekends at 2 and 3:30.*

NEED A
BREAK?
Locals swear by **Pâtisserie Courtain** (✉ Blvd. Fleur de Lys 14) for the local Nivelles specialty, *tarte al djote,* a succulent cheese and vegetable pie, served hot.

Villers-la-Ville

36 km (22 mi) south of Brussels, 15 km (9 mi) southwest of Ottignies/Louvain-la-Neuve, 13 km (8 mi) east of Nivelles.

★ The **Abbey Ruins,** at the crossroads north of the village, dates from 1147. St. Bernard himself is believed to have laid the foundation stone, and as usual the Cistercians had a knack for building their monasteries in spots of great natural beauty. The abbey became one of Europe's most important and wealthy. It was repeatedly expanded, but it all ended when the French Revolution reached Belgium and the abbey was burned, sacked, and relegated to a quarry for building material. Cistercian masonry is, however, not easily destroyed, and the walls and vaults of cloister, dormitories, refectory, and chapter hall form an impressive architectural unit. Open-air concerts and drama performances are staged here every summer. ☎ 071/879555. 🎫 BF80; guided visits (Sun. at 3) BF150. ☉ Apr.–Oct., Mon.–Tues. noon–4, Wed.–Sun. 10–6; Nov.–Mar., Wed.–Fri. 1–5, weekends 11–5.

Hainaut A to Z

Arriving and Departing

BY CAR

Roads leading south from Brussels pass through Flemish-speaking Brabant; thus roads are signposted to Bergen (Mons), Doornik (Tournai), and Rijsel (Lille). The E19 motorway from Brussels to Paris passes Mons on the way. The E42 from Liège joins the E19 before Mons and branches off from it between Mons and the border to continue to Tournai and Lille. South of Charleroi, roads are mostly two-lane highways.

BY TRAIN

There is one local train an hour from Brussels to Tournai (55 minutes) and one to Mons (45 minutes). Three of the express trains to Paris also stop at Mons. There are two trains an hour to Charleroi (40 minutes).

Getting Around

Tournai, Mons, and Charleroi are linked by rail, with one train an hour taking a half hour between each stop. Excursions to destinations other than these principal cities are best made by car.

Contacts and Resources

GUIDED TOURS

City tours are organized on request by the individual tourist offices in Tournai, Mons, Charleroi, and Binche. For tours of the southern part of the province, contact the tourist office in Beaumont (☞ Visitor Information, below).

VISITOR INFORMATION

Province of Hainaut (✉ Rue des Clercs 31, Mons, ☎ 065/360464). **Beaumont** (✉ Grand'Place 10, ☎ 071/588191). **Binche** (✉ Rue St-Paul 14, ☎ 064/333721). **Charleroi** (✉ Avenue Mascaux 100, Marcinelle, ☎ 071/448711). **Mons** (✉ Grand'Place 22, ☎ 065/335580). **Tournai** (✉ Vieux Marché-aux-Poteries 14, ☎ 069/222045).

FLANDERS: GHENT, BRUGGE, AND THE NORTH SEA COAST

Brugge and Ghent, the art cities of Flanders, represent the magnficient flowering of the late Middle Ages. Here, Flemish painters arrived in the 15th century and left behind some incomparable treasures—Jan van Eyck's *Adoration of the Mystic Lamb* altarpiece and Hans Memling's St. Ursula Shrine, to name but two. Long before, the region had attracted other visitors—the Vikings. It was to fend off these marauders that Baldwin of the Iron Arm, first Count of Flanders, built the original fortifications at both Brugge and Ghent. The cities came to prominence as centers of the cloth trade. Flemish weavers had been renowned since Roman times, but it was in the Middle Ages, when they began using the finest wool from England, Scotland, and Ireland, that their products became truly superior. Thus, the English acquired an interest in keeping Flanders from the French. This early form of industrialization also prepared the groundwork for communal strife, pitting common weavers against patrician merchants. The destinies of the two cities diverged in the 19th century. Brugge settled into a graceful decline from which it has only roused itself in the last few decades. Ghent, however, embraced the industrial revolution, becoming an important textile center once more.

The cities of Kortrijk and Ieper, to the south, recall the long history of battles fought in the region since the time of Julius Caesar. In the Hundred Years' War, Flemish pikemen unhorsed French cavalry in the Battle of the Golden Spurs; in the War of the Spanish Succession, Marlborough confronted Louis XIV on Flemish soil; and in World War I, the unspeakable No Man's Land stretched across Flanders Fields. Today, the North Sea coast continues to be irresistible to invaders, but of a more peaceful kind, drawn by fresh air, sand, and calm.

Pleasures and Pastimes

ART

The art of oil painting was invented in Flanders in the 15th century, and there are those who feel that it has not been bettered since the days of Jan Van Eyck, Hans Memling, and their friends and followers. Although much of their output was pilfered by Spanish and Austrian overlords, a treasure trove remains in Flanders's museums and churches. Nor should you overlook the work of modern masters, such as James Ensor and Paul Delvaux, who lived and worked here.

BICYCLING

The towpaths of the poplar-lined canals seem to have been built for bicycle riders. In this country, there is no obstacle other than the wind. You can rent mountain bikes and join organized tours, and there's a network of cabins especially for two-wheeled travelers.

DINING

Naturally, this is seafood country: Brugge ships in fresh fish daily from its port, Zeebrugge; and the coast towns serve North Sea delicacies directly from the source, at terrace restaurants whipped by sand and salt air. Even in landlocked Ghent, some 50 kilometers (30 miles) from the coast, locals snack on whelks and winkles (sea snails) as if they were popcorn. You'll inevitably find sole and turbot poached, *barbue* (brill) grilled or broiled, and a limited choice of classic sauces: grilled fish with rich béarnaise or mustard sauces and poached fish with only slightly lighter sauce mousseline.

When the Flemish aren't eating their fish straight or in a blanket of golden sauce, they consume it in the region's most famous dish, fish waterzooi. The citizens of Ghent have a chicken version of the dish.

Fish is the staple of everyday Flemish cuisine. The essentials are *mosselen* (mussels) and *paling* (eels), the latter as common a source of protein here as chicken or beef is elsewhere. Their flesh is firm, fatty, and sweet, served in long cross-sections that contain an easy-to-remove backbone. The most prevalent preparation by far is "in green," stewed in a heady mix of sorrel, tarragon, sage, mint, and parsley. The side dish? *Frites* (fries), of course.

For two vegetable delicacies of Flanders, it's worth arranging your visit to be here in springtime: asparagus, white and tender, served either in sauce mousseline or with the traditional Flemish garnish of chopped hard-boiled egg and melted butter; and the rarer, expensive hops sprouts, sweet, delicate shoots of the hops plant, abundant in March and April in beer-making country.

For dining price categories, *see* The Pleasures of Dining and Lodging at the beginning of this chapter.

The Middle Ages and the Renaissance come alive, particularly in Ghent and Brugge, and especially in the works of the great Flemish Primitives, whose paintings portray dress, lifestyle, and cityscapes of the 15th and 16th centuries. Many buildings are equally evocative, although later renovations have to be taken into account.

The Counts of Flanders were replaced by the Dukes of Burgundy, followed by the Hapsburg Emperors of Spain and Austria. Dynastic marriages changed the destiny of nations, and such events are brought to life in colorful pageants. There are many corners of Flanders Fields that are forever England. The beautifully maintained war cemeteries are visually a total contrast with the trenches yet bring them inexorably to mind.

LODGING

Unlike Antwerp and Brussels, Brugge is not a conference town but its opposite: This is where city residents like to get away for romantic weekends. Brugge is happy to accommodate them with honeymoon suites and other romantic trappings. Many hotels also work hard to supply appropriately Old Flemish decor in the public areas and, when possible, in the rooms. Recent changes in fire codes left Brugge struggling between the need to install fire escapes and the desire to preserve its historic landmarks. The results are discreet but comforting in this city that often glows with a thousand wood-burning hearths. Ghent, like Brugge, aims at weekend visitors but hasn't developed an industry of romantic hotels; lodgings, with few exceptions, are modern. In Ghent you can, however, stay in the oldest hotel in the world, in business since the 13th century. In these historic towns, even modern hotel chains blend in with the local architecture.

Check with the tourist offices of Brugge and Ghent for package arrangements that include room reservations and some restaurant meals, for a reasonable fixed price. Coast hotels aim for longer visits and often offer half-board plans; in summer, be sure to book well in advance.

For lodging price categories, *see* The Pleasures of Dining and Lodging at the beginning of this chapter.

WATER SPORTS

The Belgian coast, with its prevailing breeze and wide, sandy beaches, offers splendid opportunities for sailing, swimming, windsurfing, sand yachting, and other sports. Even horseback riding is a semi-aquatic sport here, with horses splashing along the water's edge at full stretch.

Exploring Flanders

The wealth of the Flemish cities was created by the weaving trade. The sumptuous clothing, so lovingly depicted in numerous paintings, was all locally produced. The merchants built their magnificent houses in Flemish style, and they engaged Flemish artists to paint their portraits. Flemish architects designed the churches and town halls. All of this combined to create a remarkable homogeneity, and in that sense, Brugge and Ghent are twin towns, and Kortrijk, Ieper, and the others are the closest of kin. It also helped shape the Flemish identity. Even today, a Fleming would, if left to his own devices, build himself a home that would not look out of place in medieval Brugge or Ghent.

If you ask the locals to define Flanders, you will almost always start a heated argument. Politically, it means the part of Belgium that lies north of the linguistic border, except Brussels. Many Flemish people contend that Brussels, too, is Flemish, which is historically correct but politically a bone of contention. However, nobody can dispute that only two provinces, to the west of Antwerp and Brussels, bear the name: East Flanders and West Flanders. It is a small area, but enormously rich in history and art.

Numbers in the text correspond to numbers in the margin and on the maps.

Great Itineraries

You can reach the remotest corner of Belgium in little more than an hour and a half. Many visitors cover the area of East and West Flanders through one-day excursions from Brussels, but it's a shame to spend two or three hours traveling each day and missing out on the pleasure of spending evenings soaking up the atmosphere of Ghent and Brugge.

IF YOU HAVE 2 DAYS

See **Ghent** ㉘ the first day, walking along the river to view the guild halls on the banks of the Graslei, visiting the ancient Castle of the Counts, Town Hall and Belfry, and, above all, St. Bavo's Cathedral, containing one of the world's greatest paintings, Van Eyck's *Adoration of the Mystic Lamb*. Proceed to **Brugge** ㊳, and spend a full day visiting Burg, its ancient center. Wander along its canals, and then visit the Groningen Museum to see the paintings by the Flemish Primitives and the Memling Museum for those of Brugge's greatest artist, followed by visits to the Minnewater "Lake of Love" and the serenely peaceful Begijnhof.

IF YOU HAVE 5 DAYS

Again, start with **Ghent** ㉘. In the evening, after dinner, walk again through the historic center, whose highlights are magically floodlit at night. On the second day, take a boat down the attractive river Leie, or rent a bike and ride along its banks, to visit the villages much frequented by artists a century ago. On the third day, visit **Kortrijk** (50), where Flemings defeated the French in 1302, and tour the World War I battlefields and war cemeteries around **Ieper** (51), proceeding to **Brugge** ㊳ in the evening for two days. This gives you time to see the parts of Brugge less frequented by tour groups and to take a side trip by canal boat through the polder to medieval **Damme** ㊾, where goods from Brugge were transshipped to larger vessels.

IF YOU HAVE 7 DAYS

Do all of the above, and then treat yourself to two days in **Oostende** (54), spending one day seeing its remarkable modern museum and the art of James Ensor, the other relaxing on the beach or taking the coastal tram to explore resorts such as **De Panne** (55) to the west or **Knokke** (59) to the east.

When to Tour Flanders

Almost any time of year is fine for visiting this region, although January and February may be too chilly for sightseeing on foot. Some restaurants along the coast close for the winter months, but many people enjoy walking along the beaches when the sea air is bracing and visiting Brugge in early spring or late fall, when there are few tourists. Museums in Brugge and Oostende are closed on Tuesday; in the rest of the country the closing day is generally Monday.

Ghent: Gateway to Flanders

㉘ *55 km (33 mi) northwest of Brussels, 60 km (36 mi) southwest of Antwerp.*

There are those who come to Ghent regularly for no other reason than to feast their eyes on Van Eyck's masterpiece in St. Bavo's Cathedral.

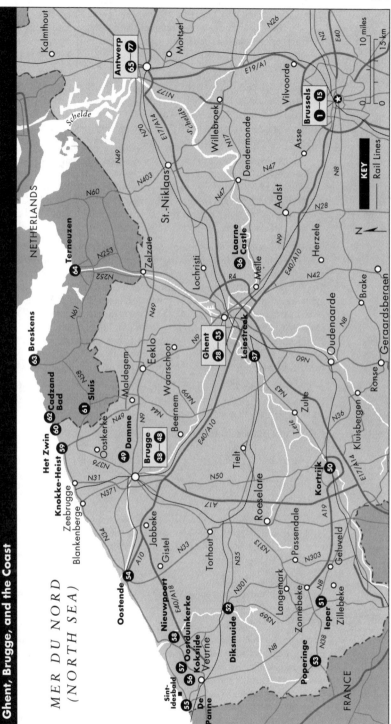

Ghent, Brugge, and the Coast

You can come back to *The Adoration of the Mystic Lamb* many times and still find new things to contemplate and admire. The painting is the number one treasure of historic Ghent. The seat of the regional government of Flanders, Ghent is a lively town with lots to offer in politics, business, and the arts.

The city developed around two 7th-century abbeys, Sint-Pieter (St. Peter) and Sint-Baafs (St. Bavo), and the 9th-century castle of Gravensteen, which dominates the river Leie. The canal joining Ghent and Damme, Brugge's port, was dug in the 13th century—100 years later, more than 5,000 men were working at the weaver's trade in Ghent.

In the early Middle Ages, the wealthy burghers were loyal to the counts of Flanders, who owed allegiance to the kings of France. But the weavers were dependent for their livelihood on wool shipments from England, France's enemy in the Hundred Years' War. In 1302 the weavers took up arms against the French, defeating them in a battle that, to this day, is vividly recalled by Flemish patriots.

In 1448, the people of Ghent refused to pay a salt tax imposed by Philip the Good, Duke of Burgundy. For five years their militia stood firm against Philip's troops, and when they were finally overwhelmed, 16,000 townspeople perished. Ghent continued to rebel, again and again, against perceived injustices. The emperor himself, Charles V, who was born in Ghent, was not immune to their wrath. He responded by razing the St. Bavo Abbey and suppressing the rights of Ghent's residents. Religious fervor was added to this volatile mixture when the Calvinist iconoclasts proclaimed the city a republic in 1577, only to be overthrown by Spanish forces seven years later.

In the 18th century, French armies marched on Ghent on four different occasions. This did little to dampen the conflict between French and Flemish speakers in the city.

Ghent was rescued from economic oblivion by a daring young man named Lieven Bauwens, who, in 1800, smuggled a spinning jenny out of Britain in a reversal of what had happened hundreds of years earlier, when Flemish weavers emigrated to England. Bauwens's exploit provided the foundation for a textile industry that employed 160,000 workers a century later.

To facilitate textile exports, a new canal was built to link Ghent's inland port with the North Sea. It remains vital to modern industrial development, such as a Volvo assembly plant. Today, huge car carriers filled with Hondas sail up the canal to Ghent.

The city's true Flemish name is Gent; the English variant, Ghent, exists only to prevent mispronunciation. French-speakers call the city Gand.

Exploring Ghent

★ ㉙ The best way to begin a tour of Ghent is to view the three medieval towers from **St. Michael's Bridge.** The closest is the tower of **Sint-Niklaaskerk** (St. Nicholas's Church), the parish church of Ghent's merchants. Its sober style is sometimes called Scheldt Gothic, for it traveled down the river Scheldt from Tournai, where it originated. Next comes the **Belfort** (Belfry), begun in 1314 but not completed until 1913, when the spire with its gilded details was added, based on the original 14th-century elevation. In the background stands the honey-colored sandstone tower of **Sint-Baafskathedraal** (St. Bavo's Cathedral), begun in the 13th century but finished in the 16th in the ornate Brabantine Gothic style.

201

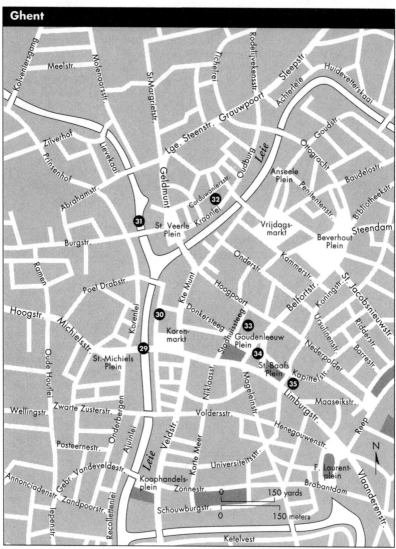

Ghent

Belfort, **34**

Graslei, **30**

Gravensteen, **31**

Museum voor
Volkskunde, **32**

Sint
Baafskathedraal, **35**

St. Michael's
Bridge, **29**

Stadhuis, **33**

★ **㉚** **Graslei** is a magnificent row of guild houses, best seen from across the river Leie. The **Vrije Schippers** (Free Bargemen), at No. 14, is a late Gothic building from 1531, when the guild dominated inland shipping. No. 11 is the **Korenmetershuis** (Grain Measurers' House), a late Baroque building from 1698. Next to it is the narrow Renaissance **Tolhuis** (Toll House), where taxes were levied on grain shipments. It stands side by side with the brooding, Romanesque **Koornstapelhuis** (Granary), which was built in the 12th century and served its original purpose for 600 years; this was where the grain claimed by the tax collectors was stored. The guild house of the **Metselaars** (Masons), finally, is a copy of a house from 1527. The original, which stands near the transept of St. Nicholas's Church, has also recently been restored. Every night in season (and Friday and Saturday nights, November through April), the Graslei and all other historic monuments are illuminated from sunset to midnight.

NEED A
BREAK?

If you're wandering around after 7, stop in at **Tap en Tepel** (✉ Gewad 7, ☎ 09/223–9000; closed Sun.–Tues. and Aug.), a wine and cheese house filled with flickering candles and lined with shelves of wine bottles.

㉛ **Gravensteen,** the castle of the counts of Flanders, resembles an enormous old battleship, improbably steaming down the Lieve Canal. From its windswept battlements, there's a splendid view over the rooftops of old Ghent. Rebuilt a number of times—most recently in the 19th century to reflect what the Victorians thought a medieval castle should look like—it has little in common with the original fortress conceived by Count Baldwin of the Iron Arm to discourage marauding Norsemen. Its purpose, too, changed from protection to oppression as the conflict deepened between feudal lords and unruly townspeople. One of the rooms contains an exhibition of instruments of torture, and there is an *oubliette* (secret dungeon), deep below the floor of another room. It was here, too, that the Continent's first spinning mule was installed after being spirited away from England; soon the castle's chambers were invaded by clattering loom, and Ghent became a textile center to rival Manchester. ✉ *Sint-Veerleplein,* ☎ 09/225–9306. ✉ BF100. ☉ *Daily 9–6 (Oct.–Mar. until 5).*

㉜ **Museum voor Volkskunde** (Folklore Museum), the **Kraanlei** waterfront, on which it stands, and **Patershol,** the quarter right behind it, form an attractive and evocative ensemble. The museum consists of a score of small, 16th-century almshouses, surrounding a garden, that have been reconstructed to convey an idea of life in Ghent 100 years ago: One room is a grocer's shop, another a tavern, a third a weaver's workshop, and there are several ordinary rooms. ✉ *Kraanlei 65,* ☎ 09/223–1336. ✉ BF180. ☉ *Apr.–Oct., daily 9–12:30 and 1:30–5:30; Nov.–Mar., Tues.–Sun. 10–noon and 1:30–5.*

Two Baroque houses along **Kraanlei** have elaborately decorated facades. The panels of No. 79 represent the five senses, crowned by a figure of a flute player, while those of No. 77 illustrate six acts of mercy. The house used to be an inn, and hospitality to travelers was considered the seventh act of mercy. The **Patershol** quarter used to house many of the textile workers from the Gravensteen, and it eventually turned into a badly neglected slum. But lately Patershol has become a desirable address for young and well-to-do families who have converted many of the small houses for their use, interspersed with smart cafés and restaurants.

NEED A
BREAK?

Café Evaluna (✉ Kraanlei 27, ☎ 09/233–3033), in a Renaissance building, serves excellent cakes as well as light and inexpensive lunches.

③③ The **Stadhuis** (Town Hall) is an early example of what raising taxes can do to a city. In 1516, Antwerp's Domien de Waghemakere and Mechelen's Rombout Keldermans, two prominent architects, were called in to build a town hall that would put all others to shame. But before the building could be completed, Emperor Charles V imposed new taxes that drained the city's resources. When work resumed in 1580, during the short-lived Protestant Republic, it was completed in a stricter and more economical style. Among its features are the tower on the corner of Hoogpoort and Botermarkt, the balcony expressly built for announcements and proclamations and, above all, the lacelike tracery that embellishes its facade. ⊠ *Botermarkt,* ☎ *09/223–9922.* ⛩ *BF60.* ☉ *Guided visits only, Apr.–Oct., Mon.–Thurs. at 3.*

③④ The **Belfort** (Belfry), 300 feet high, symbolizes the power of the guilds in the 14th century. The Belfry contained the documents listing the privileges of the city, jealously guarded behind double doors with triple locks, and bells that were rung in moments of danger, until Charles V ordered them removed. Now a 52-bell carillon, said by experts to be the best in the world, hangs on the fifth floor, and one of the damaged old bells rests at the foot of the tower. There's an elevator to whisk you to the top. ⊠ *Sint-Baafsplein,* ☎ *09/233–3954.* ⛩ *BF80; guided visits BF100.* ☉ *Apr.–early Nov., daily 10–12:30 and 2–5:30; guided visits at 10 min past the hr.*

The Belfry is adjoined by the **Lakenhalle** (Cloth Hall). Its vaulted basement was used as a prison for 150 years and is now a restaurant.

★ **③⑤** **Sint Baafskathedraal** (St. Bavo's Cathedral) contains one of the greatest treasures in Christendom, *The Adoration of the Mystic Lamb.* Now in the De Villa Chapel, to the left of the entrance, the masterpiece is a stupendous polyptych by Jan van Eyck, completed in 1432. It has a history as tumultuous as that of Ghent itself. When the iconoclasts smashed St. Bavo's stained-glass windows and other treasures, the painting was hidden in the tower. Napoléon had it carried off to Paris. Joseph II of Austria found the panels of Adam and Eve prurient because theirs were the first naturalistically depicted human bodies in Western art. They disappeared and remained lost for 100 years. The other side panels were sold and hung in a Berlin museum. In 1920 the masterpiece was again complete, but 14 years later a thief removed the panels on the lower left side. He returned the St. John the Baptist panel, but apparently died while waiting for a ransom for the panel of the Righteous Judges. Most people believe the panel is hidden somewhere in Ghent, possibly even in the cathedral. The whole altarpiece was sent to France for safekeeping during World War II, but the Germans located and stole it. American troops eventually discovered it in an abandoned salt mine in Austria.

The central panel is based on the Book of Revelations: "And I looked, and, lo, a Lamb stood on the mount Sion, and with him an hundred forty and four thousand, having his Father's name written in their foreheads." There are not quite that many people in the painting, but it does depict 248 figures and 42 different types of flowers, each botanically correct. But statistics do not even suggest its grandeur. It uses a miniaturist technique to express the universal; realism to portray spirituality; and the blood of the sacrificial lamb mixes with the fountain of life to redeem the world. To the medieval viewer, it was an artistic *Summa Theologica,* a summation of all things revealed about the relationship between God and the world. An old tradition identifies the horseman in the foreground of the panel, to the immediate left, as Hubert van Eyck, Jan's brother, while the fourth figure from the left is believed to be Jan himself. It is now thought by art historians that Hubert, once believed to be co-creator of the luminous oil panels, was merely the carver of the imposing wooden frame of the altarpiece. As for the paintings themselves, Jan used brushes so delicate that the finest consisted of a single boar's bristle. The work was completed on May 6, 1432.

Originally dedicated to St. John, the cathedral became the site for the veneration of St. Bavo, Ghent's own saint, after Charles V had the old Abbey of St. Bavo razed. The Order of the Golden Fleece, instituted in Brugge by Philip the Good in 1430, was convened here in 1559 by Philip II of Spain. It is still in existence, currently presided over by King Juan Carlos of Spain as grand master. The coats of arms of the 51 knights who first belonged to the Order still hang in the south transept. The cathedral's remarkably ornate pulpit is carved in white Italian marble and black Danish oak. In one of the radiating chapels hangs a Rubens masterpiece, *Saint Bavo's Entry into the Monastery.* ⊠ *Sint-Baafsplein.* 🎫 *Cathedral free; De Villa Chapel BF60.* ⊘ *Cathedral daily 8:30–6; chapel Apr.–Oct., Mon.–Sat. 9:30–noon and 2–6, Sun. 1–6; Nov.–Mar., Mon.–Sat. 10:30–noon and 2:30–4, Sun. 2–5. No visits to cathedral or chapel during services.*

Klein Begijnhof was founded in 1234 by Countess Joanna of Constantinople. Southeast of the city center, it is the best preserved of Ghent's three beguinages. It is protected by a wall and portal. The small houses, each identified by a statue of a saint and surrounding a spacious green, are still occupied by a small number of Beguines, leading the life stipulated by their founder 750 years ago. They are the last of their kind. You may walk through the Klein Begijnhof (quietly, please), but the houses cannot be visited. ⊠ *Lange Violettenstraat 71.*

🕑 The **School Museum Michel Thiery,** in St. Peter's Abbey, is an original institution, with different sections focusing on geography and various sciences, but the biggest attraction is a sound-and-light show featuring a large-scale model of Ghent as it was 400 years ago. ⊠ *Sint-Pietersplein 14,* ☎ *09/222–8050.* 🎫 *BF80.* ⊘ *Mon.–Thurs. and Sat. 9–12:15 and 1:30–5:15, Fri. 9–12:15.*

Museum voor Schone Kunsten (Museum of Fine Arts), a neoclassical museum in Citadel Park, is one of Belgium's finest, featuring paintings and sculptures from the Middle Ages to the early 20th century. Its collections include two outstanding paintings by Hieronymus Bosch, *Saint Jerome* and *The Bearing of the Cross;* in the latter, Christ is shown surrounded by grotesque faces of unmitigated cruelty. There is also a fine selection of works from the flowering of Belgian art around the turn of the century. ⊠ *Nicolaas de Liemaeckereplein 3,* ☎ *09/222–1703.* 🎫 *BF80.* ⊘ *Tues.–Sun. 9–5.*

The lively **Museum van Hedendaagse Kunst** (Museum of Contemporary Art), also in Citadel Park, includes, in addition to hyperrealism, pop art and works of great vitality by artists of the COBRA Group from Copenhagen, Brussels, and Amsterdam. ⊠ *Hofbouwlaan 28,* ☎ *09/221–1703.* 🎫 *BF80.* ⊘ *Tues.–Sun. 9:30–5.*

36 **Laarne Castle,** one of the best-preserved medieval strongholds in the country, lies 13 kilometers (8 miles) east of Ghent. Built in the 14th century to protect the city's eastern approaches, it was converted to peaceful use in the 17th; inside are fine examples of Brussels tapestry weaving and an outstanding collection of silver from the 15th to the 18th century. ⊠ *Rte. R4, Exit 5, Heusden–Laarne,* ☎ *09/230–9155.* 🎫 *BF120.* ⊘ *July–Aug., daily 10–noon and 2–6; Sept.–Dec. and Feb.–June, Tues.–Sun. 10–noon and 2–6.*

37 The **Leiestreek** (Lie Region), just south of Ghent, is a charmingly bucolic area that has attracted many painters. The fact that they are not widely known abroad makes it even more pleasant to discover their work in its original setting. The best way to enjoy the banks of the Leie is by rented motorboat or bike. **Sint-Martens-Latem,** with its 15th-century wooden windmill, was home to Gustave van de Woestyne, an artist who worked in the early years of this century. He was followed, after World War I, by Constant Permeke and the expressionists. In the neighboring village of **Deurle,** the house and studio of the Ghent painter Gust De Smet has been turned into the **Museum Dhondt-Dhaenens.** It contains a major collection of expressionist paintings, including works by Permeke, Van den Berghe, and Albert Servaes. ⊠ *Take Rte. N466 from Exit 13.* ☒ *BF50.* ⊙ *Mar.–Nov., Wed.–Fri. 2–6, weekends 10–noon and 2–4.*

In the village of **Deinze,** beside an attractive Gothic church next to the river, you'll find the **Museum van Deinze en Leiestreek,** with works by the Impressionist Emile Claus, as well as by the Latem group of painters. ⊠ *Lucien Matthyslaan 3,* ☎ *09/386–0011.* ☒ *BF40.* ⊙ *Weekdays 2–5:30, weekends 10–noon and 2–5.*

Dining and Lodging

$$$ ✕ **Waterzooi.** In the shadow of the Castle of the Counts, this tiny restaurant is named for Ghent's contribution to Belgian gastronomy, a creamy fish and vegetable stew. Specialties include turbot with three pepper sauces and lobster-filled ravioli with estragon. ⊠ *Sint-Veerleplein 2,* ☎ *09/225–0563. Reservations essential. Jacket and tie. AE, DC, MC, V. Closed Wed., Sun., and 1st 3 wks in Aug.*

$$ ✕ **Buikske Vol.** Probably the best among the nouveau-chic of Patershol's trendy eateries, this restaurant likes to surprise diners with unusual combinations, such as filet of Angus beef with onion confit, or crispy sweetbreads with rabbit. ⊠ *Kraanlei 17,* ☎ *09/225–1880. AE, MC, V. No lunch Sat., no dinner Wed. Closed Sun., Easter wk, and 1st ½ of Aug.*

$$ ✕ **Het Cooremetershuis.** One flight up from the Graslei, in an ancient
★ guild house, this venturesome little restaurant serves well-executed, contemporary dishes, such as langoustine-and-basil salad, filet of lamb with lentils, and John Dory with a parsley coulis. ⊠ *Graslei 12,* ☎ *09/223–4971. Reservations essential. AE, DC, MC, V. Closed Wed., Sun., and July 15–Aug. 15.*

$ ✕ **'t Hietekoekske.** Although the name of this lunch-only restaurant means pancakes in the Ghent dialect, the menu also offers a few elegant and simple daily specials. The ambience is casual and comfortable, suitable also for an afternoon snack in this shopping neighborhood. ⊠ *Bennesteeg 1,* ☎ *09/223–7566. No credit cards. No dinner. Closed Sun.*

$ ✕ **Taverne Keizershof.** Touristy taverns are much the same all over Belgium, but this one is popular with locals as well, always a good sign. The daily plates are large portions of good, solid foods, and all-day snacks include toasted sandwiches and spaghetti. ⊠ *Vrijdagmarkt 47,* ☎ *09/223–4446. MC, V. Closed Sun.*

$$$ ✕▦ **Novotel.** Though part of a cookie-cutter, look-alike hotel chain, this modern lodging merits mention not only because of its location, in the center of the tourist and shopping area, but also because it manages to compress a sprawl of business-class luxuries—lounges, garden, swimming pool—into a small urban space. Some windows open onto an inner courtyard, with its pool and greenery, and some take in the city monuments; decor is slick and standardized. ⊠ *Goudenleeuwplein 5,* ☎ *09/224–2230,* FAX *09/224–3295. 117 rooms. Restaurant, bar, pool. AE, DC, MC, V.*

$$$ ✕🏨 **Sofitel.** The Ghent outpost of this top-of-the-line, comfortable French hotel chain, decorated in warm brown-and-beige house colors, is located in the heart of the old city. ⊠ *Hoogpoort 63,* ☎ *09/233–3331,* 🅵🅰🆇 *09/233–1102. 127 rooms with bath. Restaurant, bar, health club, convention center, parking (fee). AE, DC, MC, V.*

$$ ✕🏨 **Sint Jorishof.** Napoléon stayed here. So did Emperor Charles V and Mary of Burgundy, for this is the oldest hotel in the world. Needless to say, the step-gabled old inn has been much tinkered with over the centuries, but a great deal of the Gothic spirit has been preserved, especially in the reception area and restaurant, which serves classic French fare. Rooms are less atmospheric, though new and attractive, with peach-tinted wood and Florentine textile prints. ⊠ *Botermarkt 2,* ☎ *09/224–2424,* 🅵🅰🆇 *09/224–2640. 28 rooms with bath (some in annex across street). Restaurant, conference rooms, parking (fee). AE, DC, MC, V.*

$$ 🏨 **Gravensteen.** This handsome, 19th-century mansion has been completely refurbished in Second Empire style. The historic atmosphere of the grand public spaces compensates, perhaps, for the small but personalized rooms. The canal-front location, a few steps from the Castle of the Counts, is a great plus. ⊠ *Jan Breydelstraat 35,* ☎ *09/225–1150,* 🅵🅰🆇 *09/225–1850. 17 rooms with bath. Bar, breakfast room, lounge, parking (fee). AE, DC, MC, V.*

$ 🏨 **Erasmus.** From the flag-stoned and wood-beamed library-lounge to
★ the stone mantels in the bedrooms, every inch of this noble 16th-century home has been scrubbed, polished, and decked with period ornaments. Even the tiny garden has been carefully manicured. The couple that runs the hotel does everything from answering the bell pull at night to serving breakfast in the parlor. ⊠ *Poel 25,* ☎ *09/224–2195,* 🅵🅰🆇 *09/233–4241. 11 rooms with bath. Breakfast room, lobby lounge. AE, DC, MC, V. Closed mid-Dec.–mid-Jan.*

Nightlife and the Arts

Nightlife

As in most Belgian towns, nightlife in Ghent is a laid-back affair. A few cabarets exist, but the Gentenaars much prefer their pubs and cafés. **Backstage** (⊠ Sint-Pietersnieuwstraat 128, ☎ 09/233–3535), a café-restaurant across from the Vooruit center, presents occasional classical and jazz concerts. **Cirque Central** (⊠ Hoogpoort 32, ☎ 09/225–1416) is both a café and a disco with an under-25 crowd. The **Brasserie Abajour** (⊠ Oudburg 20, ☎ 09/223–4208), relaxed, with a cool jazz and art deco ambience, overlooks the Leie.

The Arts

Cultural life in Ghent is lively and varied, and it's worthwhile checking *The Bulletin*'s "What's On" section under the heading "Other Towns." Many events take place in the **Kunstencentrum Vooruit** (Vooruit Arts Center; ⊠ Sint-Pietersnieuwstraat 123, ☎ 09/225–5643), which includes two concert halls, a ballroom, a theater, 10 smaller halls, and an art gallery.

De Vlaamse Opera (Flemish Opera House; ⊠ Schouwburgstraat 3, ☎ 09/225–2425), which has been restored, has a splendid ceiling and chandelier. Its eight annual productions (co-produced with the Royal Flanders Opera of Antwerp) are of high international standards.

Shopping

Veldstraat and the **Langemunt** are major shopping streets. There are also several exclusive shopping galleries, where boutiques are interspersed with cafés and restaurants, such as the **Bourdon Arcade** (Gouden

Leeuwplein) and **Braempoort** (between Brabantdam and Vlaanderen-straat). **Voldersstraat** is where the smartest fashion boutiques are located.

The largest market is on the attractive and historic **Vrijdagmarkt,** held Friday from 7 to 1 and Saturday from 1 to 6. This is where leaders have rallied the people of Ghent from the Middle Ages to the present day.

Many visitors take home a supply of "Gentse Mokken," syrup saturated biscuits available from any pastry shop.

Ghent A to Z

Arriving and Departing

BY CAR

From Brussels, Ghent is reached via the six-lane E40, which continues to Brugge and the coast. Traffic can be bumper-to-bumper on summer weekends. Ghent is 60 kilometers (36 miles) from Antwerp on the E17 and 292 kilometers (175 miles) from Paris on the E15/E17.

BY TRAIN

Non-stop trains depart on the hour, and 27 minutes past the hour, from Brussels South (Gare du Midi). Travel time to Ghent is 28 minutes. For train information call 02/203–3640 or 09/221–4444.

Getting Around

Since most of the sights are within a radius of half a mile from the Stadhuis (Town Hall), by far the best way to see them is **on foot.**

You can rent **bikes** at the train station at a reduced rate, or at **Ganesh & Co.** (⊠ Zwartessustersstraat 30, ☉ Mon.–Sat. 10–6).

Motorboats for trips around the Ghent waterways and/or down the river Leie can be rented from **Minerva** (☎ 09/221–8451) for BF850 per hour and BF2,500 for four hours, weekends slightly higher. Boats take four to five people and no license is required. Embarkation is at the landing stage at Coupure/Lindenlei. Larger boats with helmsman are also available for BF2,000 per hour.

There are **taxi** stands at the railway station and at major squares.

For **car rental,** try **Avis** (⊠ Kortrijkse Steenweg 676, ☎ 09/222–0053).

If you arrive by train, take **Tram 1, 11, or 12** (fare: BF50) for the city center.

Guided Tours

Sightseeing **boats** depart from the landing stages at Graslei and Korenlei for 35-minute trips on the Ghent waterways, Easter through October (BF150).

You can arrange for a **taxi** with an English-speaking driver/guide (☎ 09/223–2323).

Horse-drawn carriages wait in Sint-Baafsplein. A half-hour trip for up to four people is BF700 and gives you a general idea of the town center.

Guided Walks

Your Ghent experience can be much enhanced by a personal guide. Call **Gidsenbond van Gent** (Association of Ghent Guides, ☎ 09/233–0772). The charge is BF1,500 for the first two hours, BF600 per additional hour.

Outdoor Activities and Sports

Ghent has an extensive sports and recreation center only minutes from the city, the 250-acre **Blaarmeersen** (⊠ Zuiderlaan 5, ☎ 09/221–8266).

It is equipped with outdoor and indoor tennis courts, squash courts, a roller-skating track, jogging and cycling tracks, and facilities for windsurfing, sailing, canoeing, and camping.

Visitor Information

The **Dienst voor Tourisme** (Tourist Service; ⊠ Predikherenlei 2 ☎ 09/225–3641) has a satellite office in the Town Hall (⊠ Botermarkt, ☎ 09/266–5232).

Brugge: A Medieval Wonder

③⑧ *96 km (58 mi) northwest of Brussels, 45 km (27 mi) west of Ghent, 28 km (17 mi) east of Oostende.*

Brugge belongs to the world. Few other places have so well preserved their ancient heritage. Visitors flock here in numbers that occasionally seem overwhelming, but there are always quiet corners in this city offering refuge, where time appears to have stood still. The city may be better known by its French name, Bruges, but you'll score points with the locals by using the correct Flemish name.

Brugge is where Flemish painting began. In fact, painting with oil was invented by Van Eyck in the 1420s, and the technique was taken to Italy by his pupil Petrus Christus. The art of the so-called Flemish Primitives represented a revolution in realism, portraiture, and perspective; it brings their era alive in astonishing detail. Jan van Eyck was named court painter to Philip the Good, Duke of Burgundy, who married Isabella of Portugal in a ceremony of incredible luxury in Brugge's Prinsenhof in 1429.

Linked with the estuary of the Zwin on the North Sea by a navigable waterway, Brugge was one of the most active members of the Hanseatic League in the 13th century. It exported Flemish cloth and imported fish from Scandinavia, furs from Russia, wine from Gascony, and silk from Venice. Italian merchants from Lombardy, Tuscany, and Venice set themselves up in Brugge, and the town established Europe's first stock exchange.

In 1301, the French queen Jeanne of Navarre was annoyed by the finery flaunted by the women of Brugge. "I thought I alone was queen," she said, "and here I am surrounded by hundreds more." The men of Brugge, in return, were annoyed at being requested to pay for the French royal couple's lavish reception. One fine morning in May 1302, they fell upon and massacred the French garrison and then went on with the men of Ghent and Ieper to defeat the French chevaliers in the epic Battle of the Golden Spurs.

The last Burgundian feast in Brugge was the wedding of Duke Charles the Bold to Margaret of York, sister of England's Edward IV, in 1468. At the end of the century adversity struck. Flemish weavers had emigrated across the Channel and taught their trade to the English, who became formidable competitors. Even worse, the Zwin had begun to silt up, and the people of Brugge did not have the will or the funds to build the canal that might have saved their industry. Instead, trade and fortune switched to Antwerp.

Today the principal industry in Brugge is tourism. In the 19th century, British travelers on their way to view the battlefield of Waterloo rediscovered Brugge and spread its fame as a perfectly preserved medieval town. A novel by Georges Rodenbach, *Bruges-la-Morte* (Bruges, the Dead), brought more visitors but created an image that has been difficult to throw off. Brugge, the administrative center of West Flanders, incorporates within its city limits the new port of Zeebrugge, and fields fiercely competitive soccer teams.

Exploring Brugge

㊴ Most tours of Brugge begin at the **Markt,** which has been a market square since 958. In the middle stands the statue of the city's medieval heroes, Jan Breydel and Pieter De Coninck, who led the commoners of Flanders to their short-lived victory over the aristocrats of France. The west and north sides of the market square are lined with old guild houses. Most of them shelter restaurants of unremarkable quality that spill out onto the sidewalk. On the east side stand the provincial government house and the post office, an excellent pastiche of Burgundian Gothic. On the south side of the Markt stands the **Belfort** (Belfry), rising to a height of 270 feet. It commands the city and the surrounding countryside with more puissance than grace. The octagonal lantern that crowns the tower, added in the 15th century, contains the 47 bells of the remarkable Brugge carillon. ▨ *BF100.* ☉ *Apr.–Sept., daily 9:30– 5; Oct.–Mar., daily 9:30–12:30 and 1:30–5. Carillon concerts: June 15–Sept., Mon., Wed., Sat. 9–10 PM, Sun. 2:15–3; Oct.–June 14, Wed. and weekends 2:15–3.*

★ ㊵ Burg is an enchanted square, never more so than when discreetly floodlit after dark. The Burg derives its name from the fortress built by Baldwin of the Iron Arm, which is long since gone. So is, alas, the Carolingian Cathedral of St. Donaas, built around 900 and wantonly destroyed by French Republicans in 1799; the cathedral's site is now a small park. In the corner of the square stands the small **Heilig Bloed Basiliek** (Basilica of the Holy Blood). The Lower Chapel has kept its pure, austere 12th-century Romanesque character, with massive pillars supporting a low, vaulted roof. The vivid colors of the painted statuary, restored to its 13th-century vividness, come almost as a shock. The baptismal scene carved on the tympanum is original. A beautiful Gothic external stairway leads to the Upper Chapel, which was twice destroyed—by Protestant iconoclasts in the 16th century and by French Republicans in the 18th—but both times rebuilt. The last reconstruction is not to everyone's taste. The phial, thought to contain a few drops of the blood of Christ, was brought from Jerusalem to Brugge in 1149 by Derick of Alsace. It is exposed here every Friday, and on Ascension Day it is carried through the streets in the magnificent Procession of the Holy Blood, a major pageant that combines religious and historical elements. There is a small museum next to the basilica containing the 17th-century reliquary. ▨ *BF40.* ☉ *Apr.–Sept., daily 9:30–noon and 2–6; Oct.–Mar., daily 10–noon and 2–4 (closed Wed. PM).*

Also on Burg square is the **Stadhuis** (Town Hall), a jewel of Gothic architecture in white sandstone, with strong vertical lines. Built at the end of the 14th century, it marked the transition of power from the nobility to the city aldermen and served as the model for all the other town halls that adorn every self-respecting Flemish town. The statues that originally embellished the facade were smashed by the French Republicans and have been replaced by modern replicas. Inside, a staircase ascends to the Gothic Hall, which has a marvelous double-vaulted timber roof. Its 19th-century frescoes relate a romantic version of the history of Brugge. ▨ *BF60.* ☉ *Apr.–Sept., daily 9:30–5; Oct.–Mar., daily 9:30–12:30 and 2–5.*

The Town Hall is linked with the graceful **Oude Griffie,** the former Recorder's House, by a bridge arching over the narrow Blinde Ezelstraat. Two centuries younger than its neighbor, it is a mixture of Gothic and Flemish Renaissance elements. Squeezed into the corner

Brugge

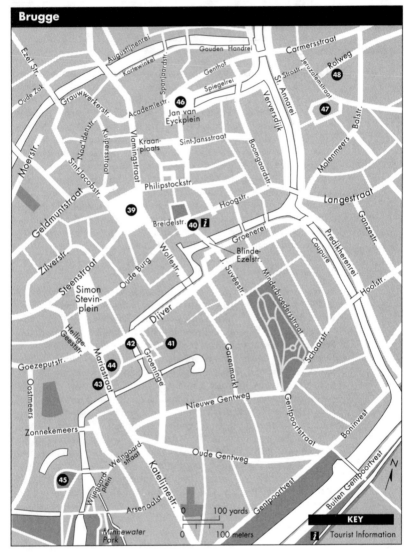

Begijnhof, **45**

Brangwyn
Museum, **42**

Burg, **40**

Groeninge
Museum, **41**

Jan Van Eyckplein, **46**

Markt, **39**

Memling
Museum, **43**

Museum voor Volks
kunde, **48**

Onze-Lieve-
Vrouwekerk, **44**

St. Anne Quarter, **47**

next to the Oude Griffie is the tiny **Museum van het Brugse Vrije** (Museum of the Brugge County Council), a remnant of the 15th-century Brugse Vrije county hall. Its principal treasure is the courtroom with its huge oak and black-marble chimney piece. A large bas-relief depicts a robust, nearly life-size Charles V, carved in dark oak and marble by Lancelot Blondeel while the emperor was still a young man. ✉ *BF20.* ☺ *Feb.–Dec., Tues.–Sun. 10–noon and 1:30–5.*

NEED A
BREAK?

Opus 4 is reached through the shopping gallery Ten Steeghere, which starts next to the basilica. Overlooking a pleasant stretch of canal, it's a good place for a quiet beer, snack, or cake.

★ The **Reien** (canals), with their old hump-back stone bridges, give Brugge its character. They open up the perspective and impose their calm so that we're able to contemplate the old city and see it as it really was. The view from the **Meebrug** is especially good. Farther along the **Groenereit** and the **Godshuizen De Pelikaan** canals are almshouses dating from the early 18th century. There are several such charitable buildings in the city, tiny houses built by the guilds for the poor, some still serving their original purpose. **Steenhouwersdijk** overlooks the brick rear gables that were part of the original county hall. Just beyond the Vismarkt (Fish Market), where fresh seafood from Zeebrugge is sold Tuesday through Saturday, is the little **Huidenvettersplein** (Tanners' Square), with its 17th-century guild house. Next to it, from the **Rozenhoedkaai** canal, the view of the heart of the city includes the pinnacles of the town hall and basilica and the belfry: the essence of Brugge.

★ ④ **Groenine Museum** is one of the world's important galleries. In the very first room hangs Jan van Eyck's wonderfully realistic *Madonna with Canon Van der Paele.* Van Eyck achieved texture and depth through multiple layers of oil and varnish, and his technique has withstood the ravages of more than five centuries. All the Flemish Primitives and their successors—Petrus Christus, Hugo Van der Goes, Hans Memling, Hieronymus Bosch, Roger Van der Weyden, Gerard David, Pieter Bruegel (both Elder and Younger), Pieter Pourbus—are represented at this feast. The survey of Belgian art continues through the romantics and realists to surrealists and contemporary artists. The Groeninge is set back from the street in a diminutive park behind a medieval gate. Although it is blessedly small, such are its riches that it warrants a half-day or more. ✉ *Dijver 12,* ☎ *050/339911.* ✆ *BF200; combination ticket (includes the Gruuthuse, Memling, and Brangwyn museums) BF400.* ☺ *Apr.–Sept., daily 9:30–5; Oct.–Mar., Wed.–Mon. 9:30–12:30 and 2–5.*

NEED A
BREAK?

The attractive **Taverne Groeninge** (✉ Dijver 13) is decorated with works by Frank Brangwyn.

④ The **Brangwyn Museum,** in an 18th-century house, contains an outstanding collection of lace, a craft long and lovingly practiced in Brugge. The house also contains hundreds of drawings and paintings by Frank Brangwyn (1867–1956). His father was an architect who, like a number of other British romantics, settled in Brugge, and the son stayed on to paint many an homage to his adopted city. ✉ *Dijver 16,* ☎ *050/339911.* ✆ *BF80.* ☺ *Apr.–Sept., daily 9:30–5; Oct.–Dec. and Feb.–Mar., Wed.–Mon. 9:30–12:30 and 2–5.*

The **Gruuthuse Museum** was the home of Lodewijk Van Gruuthuse, a prominent and powerful nobleman of the Netherlands in Burgundian times. He financed Edward IV's campaign to regain the throne of England in 1461. Room 6 is an attractive Gothic interior with a 15th-century mantelpiece and stained-glass windows. It is next door to the Brangwyn Museum (☞ *above*). ✉ *Dijver 17,* ☎ *050/339911.* 🔳 *BF130.* ⊘ *Apr.–Sept., daily 9:30–5; Oct.–Mar., Wed.–Mon. 9:30–12:30 and 2–5.*

★ ❹❸   The **Memling Museum** contains just six works, but they are of breathtaking quality and among the greatest—and certainly the most spiritual—of Flemish Primitives. Hans Memling (ca. 1440–94) was born in Germany but spent the greater part of his life in Brugge. In *The Altarpiece of St. John the Baptist and St. John the Evangelist,* two leading personages of the Burgundian court are believed to be portrayed: Mary of Burgundy (buried in the church across the street) as St. Catherine, and Margaret of York as St. Barbara. The "paintings within the painting" give details of the lives of the two saints. The miniature paintings that adorn the St. Ursula Shrine are marvels of fine detail and poignancy; Memling's work gives recognizable iconographic details about cities, such as Brugge, Cologne, Basel, and Rome. The Memling Museum is inside the medieval **Sint-Janshospitaal,** which was founded in the 12th century and remained in use until the early 20th. The middle ward, the oldest of three, was built in the 13th century in Romanesque style. There is a fascinating painting from the 18th century that shows patients arriving by sedan chair and being fed and ministered to by sisters and clerics. ✉ *Mariastraat 38,* ☎ *050/332562.* 🔳 *BF130.* ⊘ *Apr.–Sept., Wed.–Mon. 9:30–5; Oct.–Mar., Wed.–Mon. 9:30–noon and 2–5.*

❹❹   **Onze-Lieve-Vrouwekerk** (Church of Our Lady) has a tower 400 feet high, which makes it the highest brick construction in the world. While brick permits you to build high, it cannot be sculpted like stone; hence the tower's somewhat severe look. The church's most precious treasure is the small *Virgin and Child,* an early work by Michelangelo, who sold it to a merchant from Brugge when the original client failed to pay. Carved in white marble, it sits in a black marble niche in an altar at the end of the south aisle. The choir contains two mausoleums: that of Mary of Burgundy, who died in 1482 at the age of 25 after a fall from her horse; and that of her father, Charles the Bold, killed in 1477 while laying siege to Nancy in France. Mary was as well loved in Brugge as her husband, Maximilian of Austria, was disliked. Her finely chiseled effigy captures her beauty. ✉ *Gruuthusestraat.* ⊘ *Apr.–Sept., daily 10–11:30 and 2:30–5 (Sat. until 4); Oct.–Mar., 10–11:30 and 2:30–4:30 (Sat. until 4). Closed Sun.* AM *except to worshipers.*

★ ❹❺   The **Begijnhof** (Beguinage) has been an oasis of peace for 750 years. This serene cluster of small, whitewashed houses surrounding a pleasant green is at its best in spring, when daffodils bloom and sunlight, dappled by high poplars, falls over the lawns. The Begijnhof (Beguinage in French) was founded in 1245 by Margaret, Countess of Constantinople, to bring together the Beguines, many of them widows of Crusaders. The congregation flourished for 600 years. The Beguines have been replaced by Benedictine sisters, and you may join them, discreetly, for vespers in their small church of St. Elizabeth. Although most of the present-day houses are from the 16th and 17th centuries, they have maintained the architectural style of the houses that preceded them. One house has been set aside as a small museum. Visitors are asked to respect the silence. ✉ *Monasterium de Wijngaard, Oud Begijnhof,* ☎ *050/330011.* 🔳 *Free; BF50 for a house visit.* ⊘ *Apr.–Sept. daily 10–noon and 1:45–5:30; Oct.–Nov. and Mar., daily 10:30–noon and 1:45–5; Dec.–Feb., Wed.–Thurs. and weekends 2:45–4:45, Fri. 1:45–6.*

Minnewater is romantically but incorrectly termed "the Lake of Love." More prosaically, this man-made lake was created in the 13th century to expand the city harbor and it often accommodated more than 100 ships. The swans of Minnewater evoke an etymological legend or perhaps a historical truth: In 1488, six years after his wife's death, Maximilian of Austria was imprisoned by the people of Brugge, and his advisor, Pieter Lanchals, was decapitated. Because the name *Lanchals* is very close to the Dutch word for "long neck," when Maximilian was freed, he ordered Brugge to expiate its crime by keeping swans in the canals of the city in perpetuity. Maximilian went on to become emperor; his grandson was Charles V. ☒ *Next to the Begijnhof.*

NEED A BREAK? | **Straffe Hendrik,** on the delightful Walplein Square, is a brewery pub, part of the Henri Maes brewery, which you can tour. "Straffe" means strong, and this beer, at more than 9%, is all of that.

46 **Jan Van Eyckplein** is a colorful square with a statue of the painter, at the center of Hanseatic Brugge. Located where the present-day canal ends, it includes the old **Tolhuis** (Customs House), built in 1477, where vehicles on their way to market had to stop; and **Poortersloge,** a late Gothic building with a slender spire, owned by the guild of porters and used as a meeting place for the burghers. The rampant bear that occupies one niche represents the legendary bear speared by Baldwin of the Iron Arm; it became the symbol of the city.

Spanjaardstraat leads up to the quay where goods from Spain were unloaded. The house at No. 9 was where St. Ignatius of Loyola stayed when he came to Flanders on holidays from his studies in Paris. Directly ahead are the three arches of the **Augustijnenbrug.** Dating from 1391, it's the oldest bridge in Brugge. On the other side of the canal, **Augustijnenrei** is one of the loveliest quays.

Huize ter Buerze (House of Purses) stands on the intersection of Academiestraat and Vlamingstraat. Built in 1453 and recently carefully restored, this was where money was exchanged. The name lives on as the modern Beurs, or Bourse. The houses of the Venetian and Florentine merchants have disappeared, but the Genoese trading house, now known as the **Saaihalle** (Serge Hall), still stands, just across the narrow Grauwwerkerstraat from the House of Purses. The original crenelated curtain wall has been replaced by a bell-shaped gable.

NEED A BREAK? | **Vlissinghe** (☒ Blekersstraat 2A) is the oldest pub in Brugge; people have been enjoying the beer here since 1552, and it hasn't changed much. You can also relax among the rosebushes in the courtyard.

47 The **St. Anne Quarter** illustrates how yesteryear's poverty becomes today's picturesque sights. The small houses that now look so tidy were the homes of last century's truly needy. By way of contrast, the 17th-century **Sint-Annakerk** (St. Anne's Church) is filled with riches, sculpted wood, and copper and enormous paintings. ☒ *Sint-Annaplein.* 🖼 *Free.* ☉ *Apr.–Sept., Mon.–Sat. 10–noon and 2–4 (Sat. closed PM).*

The striking **Jeruzalemkerk** (Jerusalem Church), which dates to the late 15th century, was built by two pilgrims returning from the Holy Land, copying the Church of the Holy Sepulchre in Jerusalem, as it was then. It is still privately owned. The black marble mausoleum of the pilgrims Anselm Adornes and his wife occupies a central position. ☒ *Jeruzalemstraat 3.* 🖼 *Free.* ☉ *Weekdays 10–noon and 2–6, Sat. 10–noon and 2–5.*

48 The **Museum voor Volkskunde** (Folklore Museum) is housed in a row of whitewashed almshouses, originally built for retired shoemakers, and contains various reconstructed interiors: grocery shop, living room, tavern. ⊠ *Rolweg 40,* ☎ *050/330044.* 🎟 *BF80.* ☉ *Daily 9:30–noon and 2–5; Oct.–Mar., closed Tues.*

The **Kantcentrum** (Lace Center) is a foundation that aims to maintain the quality and authenticity of this ancient craft. The center includes a lace museum in the Jerusalem almshouses in Balstraat and a lace school where youngsters are taught the intricate art of the bobbins. ⊠ *Peperstraat 3 (next to the Folklore Museum),* ☎ *050/330072.* 🎟 *BF40.* ☉ *Weekdays 10–noon and 2–6, Sat. 10–noon and 2–5.*

49 Damme, 7 kilometers (4 miles) north of Brugge, allows you to experience the peaceful polder landscape. You can go there by miniature paddle steamer, the *Lamme Goedzak,* on a canal lined with tall and slender poplars, all slightly bent by the prevailing breeze. Damme owes its place in history to a tidal wave in 1134 that opened up an inlet of the sea, from the Zwin to the neighborhood of Brugge, whose people were quick to build a canal to link up with it. Damme became an important port that held exclusive rights to import such varied commodities as wine from Bordeaux and herring from Sweden. The "Maritime Law of Damme" became the standard for Hanseatic merchants.

It was in Damme's **Onze-Lieve-Vrouwekerk** (Church of Our Lady) that Charles the Bold and Margaret of York were married. On the facade of the **Stadhuis** (Town Hall) you can see their effigies, the noble duke presenting the wedding ring to his fiancée. Damme is believed to have been the home of the legendary Till Eulenspiegel, whose merry pranks, detailed in Charles de Coster's novel, were often directed at the Spanish occupying force.

🖙 The **Boudewijn Park and Dolphinarium** offers 30-odd family attractions, including dolphin and ice shows. All shows are wheelchair-accessible. ⊠ *A. De Baeckestraat 12, St-Michiels, 2 km (about 1 mi) south of Damme,* ☎ *050/383838.* 🎟 *BF510 for all attractions; BF180 Dolphinarium only.* ☉ *Park: Easter–May, daily noon–6; May–Sept., daily 10–6; Sept., Wed. and weekends noon–6. Dolphinarium: daily, shows at 11 and 4, more during peak season.*

Dining and Lodging

$$$$ ✕ **De Karmeliet.** In a lovely 18th-century house with a graceful En-
★ glish garden, this culinary landmark offers Bresse pigeon in truffle juice, ravioli of *foie d'oie* (goose liver), and crisp potato nests with langoustine. The wine cave lives up to the kitchen's standard, which is stratospheric; the ambience is genteel, the service flexible and pleasant. ⊠ *Langestraat 19,* ☎ *050/338259. Reservations essential. AE, DC, MC, V. No dinner Sun. Closed Mon.*

$$$$ ✕ **De Witte Poorte.** Under low brick vaults and stone arches, with rear
★ windows looking onto a lush little garden, this formal restaurant offers rich, contemporary French cooking, with an emphasis on seafood. Specialties include crayfish ragout, langoustine waterzooi, sole with Zeeland oysters, and a superb dessert cart. ⊠ *Jan Van Eyckplein 6,* ☎ *050/ 330883. AE, DC, MC, V. Closed Sun.–Mon.*

$$$$ ✕ **Den Gouden Harynk.** Few of his colleagues can claim the natural flair of chef Philippe Serruys. Holding forth in a small, unpretentious, antiques-filled dining room just south of the Dijver, he serves international cuisine with an artist's gift, not only for presentation but also for planning, pacing, and inspired combinations. The menu offers langoustines brushed with a light curry blend or *foie d'oie* (goose liver) on a bed of rhubarb with pink peppercorns. ⊠ *Groeninge 25,* ☎ *050/ 337637. AE, DC, MC, V. Closed Sun.–Mon.*

$$$ ✕ **'t Bourgoensche Cruyce.** In one of the most medieval-looking buildings in Brugge (though its weathered timbers and sharp-raked roofs were rebuilt at the turn of the century), this restaurant also has one of the most romantic canal-side settings: Dining-room windows shed warm light over the water, the reflections tinted by the salmon- and copper-colored decor. The cuisine is equally appealing, including delicate smoked halibut, tender scallops, wild mushrooms, and saddle of hare. ⊠ *Wollestraat 41,* ☎ *050/337926. AE, MC, V.*

$$$ ✕ **De Waterput.** This small, whitewashed farmhouse, in the middle of
★ the polder-land, has a superb restaurant presided over by a most original chef, Willy Bataillie. There's no menu, because he uses only those products that are freshest and the best on any given day. A meal might include home-smoked wild salmon, John Dory with chives, wild duck with small onions, or crêpes suzette. ⊠ *Rondsaartstraat 1, Oostkerke, 9 km (5 mi) north of Brugge,* ☎ *050/599256. Reservations essential. Jacket and tie. AE, DC, MC, V. Closed Tues.–Wed., Thurs. off-season, mid-Nov.–mid-Dec.*

$$ ✕ **Breydel–De Coninck.** Directly en route between the Markt and Burg, this no-frills restaurant is known to everyone in Brugge, but they don't speak about it for fear it will be invaded by tourists. The place is famous for the freshness of its mussels and other seafood. Austere pink plastic tablecloths and vinyl banquettes leave the focus on the basics, and while there are token offerings of eel and steak, nothing could be more basic than a huge crock heaped high with shiny, blue-black shells. ⊠ *Breidelstraat 24,* ☎ *050/339746. AE, MC, V. Closed Wed. and June.*

$$ ✕ **'t Paardje.** Off the beaten tourist track, this family-owned little restaurant concentrates all efforts on a few specialties: Mussels are prepared in six variations, eel in eight, and steak in eleven. Its terra-cotta and lace decor is cozy, clean, and unpretentious, and its cooking dependably good. ⊠ *Langestraat 20,* ☎ *050/334009. MC, V. Closed Mon.–Tues. nights.*

$–$$ ✕ **Sint Joris.** Among the dozen or so competitive brasseries crowded along the Markt, this low-key spot maintains a more civilized profile than its neighbors do. Flowers, linens, candles, a roaring fire, and a comfortable clutter of ceramics and copper warm the dining room, and you'll find a choice of either sheltered or open terrace. The cooking is a cut above average, as well, and regional dishes are exceptionally well prepared: fish-based waterzooi, eel in green sauce, and mussels. ⊠ *Markt 29,* ☎ *050/333062. AE, DC, MC, V.*

$–$$ ✕ **Steakhouse De Tassche.** Though you may feel far removed from the romance of old Brugge, you'll be compensated by the attention, commitment to detail, and overall sincerity of this restaurant, run by a husband-and-wife team. A wide range of simple dishes, from inexpensive steak and fries to grilled sole, are served in a setting of pink damask and copper. The cooking comes from the heart: Even the fries are hand-cut, and the chef cruises the dining room like a true gastronome. ⊠ *Oude Burg 11,* ☎ *050/331282. DC, MC, V.*

$ ✕ **Staminee De Garre.** Tucked in an alley off the well-worn Breidel-
★ straat, this tiny two-tiered coffeehouse is a brick-and-beam oasis, offering Mozart and magazines along with plunger coffee and 136 beers—four of them variations on the house brew. There are simple cold platters and grilled sandwiches, attractively served, and traditional nibbles of cheese with the heartier beers. ⊠ *Off Breidelstraat,* ☎ *050/ 341029. No credit cards.*

$ ✕ **Taverna Curiosa.** Don't be put off by the aggressive posters, menus, and broadcast music that spill onto the street: Downstairs, this cross-vaulted crypt makes a comfortable, atmospheric hideaway from tourist traffic. It's an ideal place for conversation, a light meal, and one of the myriad beers offered, many of them local. Snacks include omelettes, sandwiches, and *visschotel* (smoked fish plates), as well as pancakes and ice cream. ⊠ *Vlamingstraat 22,* ☎ *050/342334. AE, MC, V. Closed Mon.*

$ ✕ **Tom Pouce.** Despite its somewhat stuffy air—heavy velour drapes, splashy carpet, cracked crockery, noisy open service bar—this old urban tearoom dominates the Burg every afternoon. Tourists, shoppers, and loyal retirees dig into warm apple strudel, airy waffles, and the tour de force: hot *pannekoeken,* pancakes that are light, eggy, and vanilla-perfumed, with a pat of butter and a sprinkle of dark brown sugar. There are lunch plates as well. ⊠ *Burg 16–17,* ☎ *050/330336. AE, DC, MC, V. Closed Mon.*

$$$$ ✕🏨 **Holiday Inn Crowne Plaza.** There was inevitable skepticism when Holiday Inn got permission to build a hotel right on the Burg in the heart of the city, but the critics have been confounded: The new redbrick hotel, with a red-tile roof and modern steel gables, fits in remarkably well with its surroundings. Rooms are large, modern, and decorated in muted colors; the best ones have steps leading up to them, and darkwood ceiling beams, giving you the feeling of being in the eaves. On display in the basement are remnants of the old ramparts and artifacts found during construction. ⊠ *Burg 10,* ☎ *050/345834,* 🆁🆇 *050/345615. 96 rooms. Restaurant, bar, pool, sauna, health club, convention center, parking (fee). AE, DC, MC, V.*

$$$–$$$$ ✕🏨 **Die Swaene.** Lavishly decorated in every period excess, this hotel
★ tries harder. Its location—facing one of the prettier canals in the heart of the tourist center—makes it particularly appropriate for splurging honeymooners, who will be rewarded with swaged tulle, crystal, and any number of marble nymphs. Its most popular room is a relatively subdued converted Flemish kitchen with stone fireplace and carved fourposter. The romantic, candlelit French restaurant serves such specialties as goose liver with caramelized apples, and lobster-and-spinach lasagna. ⊠ *Steenhouwersdijk,* ☎ *50/342798,* 🆁🆇 *050/336674. 24 rooms with bath. Restaurant ($$$$), bar. AE, DC, MC, V.*

$$–$$$ ✕🏨 **De Castillion.** This hotel is named for a bishop whose residence it was in the 18th century. Some of the guest rooms have cherrywood period furniture; others are furnished in a modern style. The restaurant's offerings include filet mignon of venison in a Pomerol stock, duck's liver, and a fricassee of monkfish and wild salmon. The fixed-price menus are great value for the money. Pre-dinner drinks and post-prandial coffee are served in the handsome Art Deco salon, which is decorated in shades of blue and green. ⊠ *Heilige Geetstraat 1,* ☎ *050/343001,* 🆁🆇 *050/339475. 18 rooms with bath, 2 suites. Restaurant, sauna, meeting rooms. AE, DC, MC, V.*

$$$$ 🏨 **De Tuileriëen.** This stately 15th-century mansion was converted to
★ a sumptuous hotel in 1988 and furnished with genuinely patrician taste: discreet antique reproductions, weathered marble, and warm mixedprint fabrics in shades of celadon, slate, and cream. The firelighted bar is filled with cozy tartan wingbacks, and the breakfast room has a massive mantel and a coffered ceiling. Despite its aristocratic air, this is a welcoming stop. Caveat: Canal views entail traffic noise; courtyard rooms are quieter. ⊠ *Dyver 7,* ☎ *50/343691. 26 rooms. Bar, breakfast room, indoor pool, sauna, free parking. AE, DC, MC, V.*

$$$ 🏨 **Bryghia.** Restored in 1965 and renovated in 1989, this 15th-century landmark (once a German/Austrian trade center) has seamless modern decor, with beechwood cabinetry and soft pastel florals. The management works hard on details of comfort, offering in-room teakettles, flowers, valet parking, and mosquito repellent when the canal

waters run slow. ⊠ *Oosterlingenplein 4,* ☎ *50/338059. 18 rooms with bath. Breakfast room. AE, DC, MC, V.*

$$$ ⊞ **Oud Huis Amsterdam.** Packaged like a fine gift, this snug, central
★ retreat occupies two noble 17th-century houses, combining the grace of another era with the polish and luxury of a new first-class property. Antique details—tooled Cordoba leather wallpaper, rough-hewn rafters, and Delft tiles—have been preserved, and services, such as international newspapers and umbrellas, have been added. Owner Philip Traen has even mounted ancestral art in an Old Master vein. Rooms with canal views also overlook a busy street; back rooms with roofline views are calmer. ⊠ *Spiegelrei 3,* ☎ *50/341810. 18 rooms with bath. Bar. AE, DC, MC, V.*

$$–$$$ ⊞ **Wilgenhof.** Halfway between Brugge and Damme, and a stone's throw from the canal, this bucolic mansion-on-the-polder is a good base for excursions in either direction and to the coast, which is just 12 kilometers (7 miles) away. Rooms are pleasant but fairly basic. ⊠ *Polderstraat 151,* ☎ *050/362744,* 𝕗𝕒𝕩 *050/362821. 6 rooms with bath. Breakfast room. AE, DC, MC, V.*

$$ ⊞ **Egmond.** Gracefully situated in the lush Minnewater park, this
★ manorlike inn offers garden views from every room, as well as the occasional skylight, parquet floor, fireplace, or dormer-sloped ceiling. Breakfast is served in an oak-beamed hall with a Delft-tiled fireplace. With the park in front and the quiet Beguinage behind, you may feel pleasantly isolated from the bustle of the center, though it's only 10 minutes' walk. ⊠ *Minnewater 15,* ☎ *50/341445,* 𝕗𝕒𝕩 *050/342940. 9 rooms with bath. Breakfast room.*

$$ ⊞ **Europ.** Run by an enthusiastic young management team, this midprice hotel focuses less on historic atmosphere than on basic comforts: Good big beds with Swiss-flex construction are in every room, and the breakfast buffet is generous. The hotel was first built in a 1789 house, with a modern wing added in 1970—but the current decor is spare and contemporary in both parts. ⊠ *Augustijnenrei 18,* ☎ *50/337975. 31 rooms, 28 with bath. Bar. AE, DC, MC, V.*

$$ ⊞ **Pandhotel.** This hotel was built as a private mansion in the 1830s and renovated as a hotel in 1979. A member of the Romantik chain, it mixes a jewel-box neoclassical decor with modern touches—dark ceramic baths, a skylighted breakfast room. Junior suites are decorated with Ralph Lauren fabrics. The hotel offers competitively priced two- and three-night packages. ⊠ *Pandreitje 16,* ☎ *50/340666. 24 rooms with bath. Breakfast room, bar. AE, DC, MC, V.*

$$ ⊞ **Ter Brughe.** A renovation of this 15th-century step-gabled house, in 1989, created a slick, modern, efficient hotel in which the decor might seem generic (beige and bamboo) but for those heavy beams, tempera murals, and leaded-glass windows. There are exposed brick barrel vaults in the bar, and you can throw bread to the ducks from the breakfast room, which opens directly onto the canal. ⊠ *Oost-Gistelhof 2,* ☎ *50/340324. 24 rooms with bath. Bar. AE, DC, MC, V.*

$ ⊞ **De Pauw.** Homey and warmly furnished, from the fresh flowers and
★ doilies to the bronzed baby booties in the breakfast parlor, this is a welcoming little inn passed on from mother to daughter. Every room has a name instead of a number, needlepoint cushions, and old framed prints. (Two rooms with shower down the hall are super values.) Breakfast, which includes six kinds of bread, plus cold cuts and cheese, is served on pretty china. ⊠ *Sint-Gilliskerkhof 8,* ☎ *50/337118. 8 rooms, 6 with bath. Breakfast room. AE, DC, MC, V.*

$ ⊞ **Fevery.** The living quarters of the family seem to spill over into the lounge area of this friendly, comfortable hotel; the magazines and knickknacks make you feel like family guests. There's even a baby monitor so parents can relax with a drink downstairs after putting a child to bed. The room decor was upgraded (new carpet, fresh chenille) in 1993, and all rooms have bathrooms. ⊠ *Collaert Mansionstraat 3,* ☏ *50/331269. 11 rooms with bath. Bar. AE, DC, MC, V.*

$ ⊞ **Jacobs.** With all its plush and crystal in the public rooms, this spot may look posh, but the staff is young and friendly, and the breakfast tables are garnished with plastic waste buckets. There are inexpensive no-bath rooms, as well as full-facility doubles, with homey, plain decors. ⊠ *Baliestraat 1,* ☏ *50/339831. 26 rooms, 24 with bath. Bar. AE, MC, V.*

Nightlife and the Arts

Nightlife
Among the nicest hotel bars are **The Meeting** at the Oud Huis Amsterdam (⊠ Spiegelrei 3, ☏ 050/341810), **De Medici** (⊠ Potterierei 15, ☏ 050/339833), and **Academie** (⊠ Wijngaardstraat 7–9, ☏ 050/332266).

Discos, mostly catering to a clientele not much older than 20, are clustered around Eiermarkt, back of the Markt: **Coolcat** (⊠ Eiermarkt 11, ☏ 050/340527), **Ambiorix** (⊠ Eiermarkt 11 bis, ☏ 050/337400), **The Pick** (⊠ Eiermarkt 12, ☏ 050/337638); and, at 't Zand, **Ma Rica Rokk** (⊠ 't Zand 8, ☏ 050/338358) and **Graffiti** (⊠ 't Zand 9, ☏ 050/336909). **Villa Romana** (⊠ Kraanplein 1, ☏ 050/343453) attracts an older crowd.

The Arts
The monthly *Agenda Brugge* (at the tourist office) gives details of all events in the city. Also check listings in *The Bulletin*.

The **Festival of Flanders** is the umbrella organization for music festivals in all major Flemish cities. For program information, contact Festival van Vlaanderen (⊠ Place Flagey 18, Brussels 1050, ☏ 02/648–1484).

The **Stadsshouwburg** (City Theater) in Vlamingstraat (☏ 050/338167) presents both musical and drama performances.

Outdoor Activities and Sports

Multi-Sports
Check out the city's **Sports Service** (⊠ Walweinstraat 20, ☏ 050/448322). The green city wall is pleasant for jogging. For a more extensive workout, try the Tillegembos Provinvial Domain in St-Michiels.

Swimming
Try the Olympic-size pool at the new **Provinciaal Olympisch Zwembad** (⊠ Olympia Park, Doornstraat, St-Andries, ☏ 050/390200). There's also a sauna and solarium.

Tennis
Check out the **Bryghia Tennis Club** (⊠ Boogschutterslaan 37, St-Kruis, ☏ 050/353406). Indoor courts cost BF350 for one hour, outdoor courts BF400 per hour.

Shopping

Brugge has many trendy boutiques and shops, especially along **Steenstraat** and **Vlamingstraat,** both of which branch off from the Markt. **Ter Steeghere** mall, which links the Burg with Wollestraat, deftly integrates a modern development into the historic center. The largest and most pleasant mall is the **Zilverpand** off Zilverstraat, where 50-odd shops cluster in Flemish gable houses around a courtyard with sidewalk cafés.

Your passport around the world.

- Worldwide access
- Operators who speak your language
- Monthly itemized billing

MCI Calling Card

415 555 1234 2244
J.D. SMITH

Use your MCI Card® and these access numbers for an easy way to call when traveling worldwide.

Austria (CC)♦†	022-903-012
Belarus	
From Gomel and Mogilev regions	8-10-800-103
From all other localities	8-800-103
Belgium (CC)♦†	0800-10012
Bulgaria	00800-0001
Croatia (CC)★	99-385-0112
Czech Republic (CC)♦	00-42-000112
Denmark (CC)♦†	8001-0022
Finland (CC)♦†	9800-102-80
France (CC)♦†	0800-99-0019
Germany (CC)†	0130-0012
Greece (CC)♦†	00-800-1211
Hungary (CC)♦	00▼800-01411
Iceland (CC)♦†	800-9002
Ireland (CC)†	1-800-55-1001
Italy (CC)♦†	172-1022
Kazakhstan (CC)	1-800-131-4321
Liechtenstein (CC)♦	155-0222
Luxembourg†	0800-0112
Monaco (CC)♦	800-90-19

Netherlands (CC)♦†	06-022-91-22
Norway (CC)♦†	800-19912
Poland (CC)✤†	00-800-111-21-22
Portugal (CC)✤†	05-017-1234
Romania (CC)✤	01-800-1800
Russia (CC)✤♦	747-3322
For a Russian-speaking operator	747-3320
San Marino (CC)♦	172-1022
Slovak Republic (CC)	00-42-000112
Slovenia	080-8808
Spain (CC)†	900-99-0014
Sweden (CC)♦†	020-795-922
Switzerland (CC)♦†	155-0222
Turkey (CC)♦†	00-8001-1177
Ukraine (CC)✤	8▼10-013
United Kingdom (CC)†	
To call to the U.S. using BT ■	0800-89-0222
To call to the U.S. using Mercury ■	0500-89-0222
Vatican City (CC)†	172-1022

To sign up for the MCI Card, dial the access number of the country you are in and ask to speak with a customer service representative.

http://www.mci.com

It helps to be pushy in airports.

Introducing the revolutionary new TransPorter™ from American Tourister® It's the first suitcase you can push around without a fight. TransPorter's™ exclusive four-wheel design lets you push it in front of you with almost no effort–the wheels take the weight. Or pull it on two wheels if you choose. You can even stack on other bags and use it like a luggage cart.

Stable 4-wheel design.

TransPorter™ is designed like a dresser, with built-in shelves to organize your belongings. Or collapse the shelves and pack it like a traditional suitcase. Inside, there's a suiter feature to help keep suits and dresses from wrinkling. When push comes to shove, you can't beat a TransPorter™. For more information on how you can be this pushy, call 1-800-542-1300.

Shelves collapse on command.

American Tourister®

Making travel less primitive®

©1996 American Tourister®

Street Markets

The Burg is the setting for the **Wednesday Market** (weekly except July and August) with flowers, vegetables, and fruit. The biggest is the **Saturday Market** on 't Zand. The **Fish Market** is held, appropriately, on the Vismarkt, daily except Sunday and Monday. All three are morning events, from 8 to approximately 12:30. On Saturday and Sunday afternoons (March through October) there's a **Flea Market** along the Dijver.

Specialty Stores

Some of the best known of Brugge's many **art and antiques** dealers are **'t Leerhuis** (⊠ Groeninge 35, ☎ 050/330302), which specializes in contemporary art; **Guyart** (⊠ Fort Lapin 37, ☎ 050/332159), which is both an art gallery and a tavern; **Papyrus** (⊠ Walplein 41, ☎ 050/336687), specializing in silverware; and **Classics Kunstatelier** (⊠ Oude Burgstraat 32–24), which has the best selection of Flemish hangings.

Brugge has been a center for lace making since the 15th century, and such intricate variations on the art as the rose pattern and the fairy stitch, which requires more than 300 bobbins, were developed here. Most tourists buy lace as a souvenir costing a few hundred francs, and you can find it in a great many souvenir shops. Handmade lace in intricate patterns, however, takes a very long time to produce, and this is reflected in the price. For work of this type, you should be prepared to part with BF10,000 or more. The best shop for the serious lace lover is **'t Apostelientje** (⊠ Balstraat 11, ☎ 050/337860), which is also a museum (admission free). You'll find it in the St. Anne Quarter, just behind the church.

Brugge A to Z

Arriving and Departing

BY BOAT

Sally Line (in the U.K., ☎ 01843/595522) car ferry has up to six sailings a day from Ramsgate to Oostende (four hours). **North Sea Ferries** (in the U.K., ☎ 01482/77177) offers overnight sailings from Hull to Zeebrugge (14 hours). Foot passengers only are carried by **Jetfoil** from Ramsgate to Oostende (1 hour, 40 minutes, up to four daily crossings). All connect with trains that stop at Brugge.

BY CAR

Brugge is 5 kilometers (3 miles) north of the E40 motorway that links Brussels with Ghent and Oostende. It is 126 kilometers (76 miles) from the Le Shuttle terminus at Calais.

BY TRAIN

There are two trains an hour from Brussels (50 minutes) and three trains an hour from Ghent (22 minutes) and from Oostende (15 minutes). For train information in Brugge call 050/382382; in Oostende call 059/701517.

Getting Around

The center of Brugge is best seen on foot. The winding streets may confuse your sense of direction, but if you look up, there's always the Belfry to guide you back to the Markt. Sturdy footwear is recommended. Key sights are illuminated after sunset, giving the old city an enchanted air and making evening walks very special.

Access for cars and coaches into the old city is severely restricted. There are huge car parks at the railway station and near the exits from the ring road.

BY BICYCLE

A bike is excellent for getting around Brugge and environs. Bikes can be rented at the **railway station** (BF150 per day with a valid train ticket), at **Eric Popelier** (⊠ Hallestraat 14, around the corner from the Belfry, ☎ 050/343262; BF150 for four hours, BF250 for the day), at **Koffiebontje** (⊠ Hallestraat 4, ☎ 050/338027; same rates), or at **De Ketting** (⊠ Gentpoortstraat 23, ☎ 050/344196; same rates). Several hotels provide bikes free of charge for their guests.

BY BUS

The **De Lijn** bus company (☎ 078/113663; fare BF40, 10-trip tickets BF230) runs most buses every 20 minutes, including Sunday. New minibuses, designed to penetrate the narrow streets, are now in service.

BY CAR

Impossible in town; great as a means of visiting battlefields and the coast. For car rental, try **Europcar/InterRent** (⊠ Spoorwegstraat 106, ☎ 050/385312).

BY TAXI

There are large taxi stands at the railway station (☎ 050/384660) and at the Markt (☎ 050/334444).

Guided Tours

BY BICYCLE

Bruges with Bart (☎ 050/333709) offers tours of the city beginning at 10 every day on the Markt. They last just under two hours and cost BF350.

The **Back Road Bike Co.** (☎ 050/343045) organizes tours covering six villages near Brugge. Mountain bikes are supplied, and the guided four-hour rides take only back roads.

BY BOAT

Independent motor launches depart from five jetties along the Dijver and Katelijnestraat as soon as they are reasonably full (every 15 minutes or so). The trips take just over half an hour. 🎫 *BF150.* ☼ *Mar.–Nov., daily 10–6; Dec. and Feb., weekends 10–6.*

BY CARRIAGE

You may have to wait for more than an hour for a short ride with inadequate commentary and then be asked for "something for the horse." Kids love it, however. Carriages wait in the Burg (BF800; Wednesday mornings at the Belfry).

BY MINIBUS

The 50-minute **Sightseeing Line** tour gives a good, if impersonal, overview of Brugge's attractions. No visits are included, and the commentary is taped. ⊠ *The Markt,* ☎ *050/311315.* 🎫 *BF330.* ☼ *July–Aug., hourly 10–7; Jan.–Feb., 11–1.*

Quasimodo Tours (☎ 050/370470; BF840) operates a "Fields of Flanders" full-day bus tour on Monday and Saturday, April 1 through October 31.

PERSONAL GUIDES

You can book an English-speaking guide through the **tourist office** (☎ 050/448686). Guides charge a minimum of BF1,200 for two hours, BF500 per extra hour. In July and August, groups are consolidated at the tourist office every day at 3; cost per person is BF100 (children free).

Visitor Information

Toerisme Brugge (Brugge Tourist Office): ⊠ Burg 11, ☎ 050/448686.

"Flanders Fields": The Historic Battlefields

"Flanders Fields" evoke both the pastoral peace of fields ready for harvest, dotted with crimson poppies, and the terrible war that shattered it; Simon Schama has called it "the blood-polluted source of all our sorrows." The provinces of West and East Flanders form the original, big-sky "platte land," the flat land that haunted Jacques Brel's imagination. It seems to induce a touch of wistfulness, and considering the many battles waged around here, this is understandable. The historic sites are testimony to the unique spirit of the Belgian people who, centuries ago, thought nothing of taking on the might of France or Spain.

The highways south from Brugge and Ghent point in the direction of "Flanders Fields," where decisive battles have been waged since the time of Julius Caesar. Here, longbowmen fought cavalry in heraldic colors, and here, the horrors of World War I were played out.

Kortrijk

⑩ *51 km (31 mi) south of Brugge, 45 km (27 mi) southwest of Ghent, 90 km (54 mi) southwest of Brussels.*

Kortrijk (Courtrai in French) was the flax capital of Europe in the Middle Ages and the uncontested producer of damask during the Renaissance. Today it is a center of carpet and furniture-fabric production, with shops and restaurants that attract well-to-do customers from the entire region.

The Battle of the Golden Spurs (which the French call the Battle of Courtrai) was fought immediately outside the city walls, close to the present Groeningelaan. On that fateful July 11, 1302, the poorly armed weavers and other craftsmen from Brugge, Ghent, and Ieper took on the flower of French nobility. The battle had actually been going well for the French infantrymen, but they were brushed aside by the mounted knights, who were spoiling for a fight. A hidden canal, the Groeninge, was the Flemings' greatest ally; many of the knights plunged into it, to be speared by the Flemish pikemen. After the battle, 700 pairs of golden spurs were removed from the bodies and triumphantly hung in the Church of Our Lady in Kortrijk as a votive offering. This story has a sequel: Eighty years later the French returned, defeated the Flemings, burned the city, and retrieved their spurs. The **Groeningeabdij Museum** depicts the history of Kortrijk and the Battle of the Golden Spurs and has displays of locally produced damask and silver. ⊠ *Houtmarkt,* ☎ *056/257892.* 🎫 *Free.* ☉ *Tues.–Sun. 10–noon and 2–5.*

The **Broeltoren,** on either side of the river Leie, are what remain of the medieval fortifications. A 45-foot-high neo-Gothic monument was erected on the spot where the Battle of the Golden Spurs was fought in 1302, and it is commemorated on the weekend closest to July 11 with a parade or a tournament (for information, ☎ 056/239371). These are curiously low-key affairs, given the importance of the battle in the annals of Flemish nationalism.

The **Begijnhof** (Beguinage), with its cobbled streets and whitewashed houses, is an oasis of calm in this busy city. The adjoining **Onze-Lieve-Vrouwekerk,** the church where the Golden Spurs once hung, contains a beautiful alabaster figure of St. Catherine from 1380, standing in the Chapel of the Counts of Flanders.

| NEED A BREAK? | The elegant **Tea Room D'haene** (⊠ Sint Maartenskerkstraat 4–1) serves very good pancakes, waffles, and pastries throughout the day, and pleasant light lunches. |

The **Nationaal Vlasmuseum** (National Flax Museum), in an old farmhouse, tells the story of flax-growing and linen-making in a series of lifelike tableaux. The river Leie, which passes through Kortrijk on its way to Ghent, was known as the Golden River in the Middle Ages because of the fields of flax on its banks. ⊠ *Etienne Sabbelaan 4,* ☎ *056/210138.* ⊡ *BF90.* ☉ *Mar.–Nov., Tues.–Fri. 9:30–12:30 and 1:30–6, Mon. 1:30–6, weekends 2–6.*

Dining and Lodging

$ ✕ **Restaurant Beethoven.** This intimate restaurant specializes in a variety of grilled meats. The chicken with saffron sauce is also popular, and there's a daily special that's generously served and competitively priced. ⊠ *Onze-Lieve-Vrouwestraat 8,* ☎ *056/225542. No credit cards. No dinner Wed. Closed Mon.*

$$$$ ✕🏠 **Gastronomisch Dorp Eddy Vandekerckhove.** Just south of Kortrijk, Eddy's "gastronomic village" is a gourmet's heaven. On the menu are such delicacies as new potatoes with langoustines and caviar, lobster and sea scallops with braised chicory and onion marmalade, and thinly sliced venison with *trompettes de la mort* (a kind of black mushroom) and celeriac mousse. The large, luxurious rooms overlook fields on one side and an exotic botanical garden and pond on the other. ⊠ *Sint-Anna 9,* ☎ *056/224756,* 🆕 *056/227170. 7 rooms with bath. Restaurant. AE, DC, MC, V. No dinner Sun. Closed Mon., Carnival wk, 2 wks in Sept.*

$$$ ✕🏠 **Damier.** This is a grand little hotel, impeccably renovated and in a superb location, right on Grote Markt. From its lavish café, with florid plasterwork and chandeliers, to its Laura Ashley rooms, to its beeswaxed oak wainscoting and Persian carpets, it exudes grace and seamless style; there are no musty corners or creaky halls hiding behind the decor. The hotel dates from the French Revolution, but its comforts are thoroughly modern. ⊠ *Grote Markt 41, B-8500,* ☎ *056/221547,* 🆕 *056/228631. 49 rooms. Restaurant, bar, outdoor café, sauna. AE, DC, MC, V.*

Ieper

🛈 *32 km (19 mi) west of Kortrijk, 52 km (31 mi) south of Brugge, 125 km (75 mi) west of Brussels, 91 km (85 mi) northeast of Calais.*

This is Ypres of World War I fame and shame, "Wipers" to the Tommies in the trenches, Ieper to the people who live here. The city was literally wiped off the face of the earth during the war. Today's Ieper is a painstaking reconstruction, which was not completed until after World War II.

Ypres Salient Memorial Museum shows the slow death of the old town during the war and how it affected not only soldiers but also civilians, buildings, and even livestock. The bayonets and guns, uniforms and helmets, medals and shells are all here, as well as useful maps of the battlefields and cemeteries, and poignant photographs of soldiers. The museum is housed on the second floor of the magnificent Lakenhall (Cloth Hall), a copy of a building that had stood here since 1304. ⊠ *Grote Markt,* ☎ *057/200724.* ⊡ *BF50.* ☉ *Apr.–mid-Nov., Tues.–Sun. 9:30–noon and 1:30–5:30.*

St. George's, a small Anglican church, contains an abundance of war memorabilia; the adjoining **Pilgrims' Hall** was built for those who visit Ieper looking for a relative's grave. ⊠ *Elverdingsestraat 1,* ☎ *057/216212.*

★ **Menin Gate** is among the most moving of war memorials. After World War I, the British built the vast arch in memory of the 300,000 soldiers who perished nearby. Every night at 8, traffic is stopped at the gate as buglers sound the Last Post. The practice was interrupted during World War II, but it was resumed the night Polish troops liberated the town, September 6, 1944.

Kasteelhof 't Hooghe is one of the few places where bomb craters can still be seen. A new museum, **Hooge Crater 1914–18,** has been installed in the old chapel. Items on display include bombs, grenades, rifles, and uniforms. ⊠ *Meenseweg 467, Zillebeke,* ☎ *057/468446.* ▩ *BF80.* ⊙ *Feb.–mid Dec., Thurs.–Tues. 10–7.*

Follow the signs via Canadalaan and Sanctuary Wood to **Hill 62,** where, in addition to photographs, weapons, and assorted objects salvaged from the field of battle, the owner has preserved some of the original trenches and tunnels on his land. You'll need to wear boots to inspect them. ⊠ *Canadalaan, Zillebeke,* ☎ *057/466373.* ▩ *BF100.* ⊙ *Daily 10–6.*

Some 44 million shells were fired over this stretch of the Western Front in the two world wars, and a fair number failed to explode. Flemish farmers still turn up about 200 every month, and the bomb disposal experts have to be called in. The poison-gas canisters cause special concern. **Tyne Cot,** near Passendale, a British cemetery with 12,000 graves, is the best known of more than 170 military cemeteries in the area. It is awe-inspiring, more austere than many other British cemeteries that dot the countryside, some as small and lovingly tended as a country graveyard.

❺ In **Diksmuide,** you can visit the so-called **Dodengang,** a network of trenches west of the town. Here, Belgian troops faced their German adversaries for four years. ⊠ *IJzerdijk 65,* ☎ *051/501716.* ▩ *BF60.* ⊙ *Apr.–June and Sept.–Oct., 9–noon and 1–5, July–Aug. 9–6.*

Like Ieper, Diksmuide has been completely rebuilt in its original style. The **IJzertoren,** a tower 275 feet high, has been erected in honor of the defenders. To many Flemish people it represents their struggle for autonomy.

The monument in the German war cemetery of **Praetbos-Vlasdo** conveys a touching message. It is a sculpture of two grieving parents by the great German artist Käthe Kollwitz, whose son was among the many young men who fell here.

❺ In **Poperinge,** you'll find one of the rare positive interludes of the war they called "great": **Talbot House,** founded by an Anglican priest, "Tubby" Clayton. It provided an opportunity for soldiers to get together, just south of the front line, regardless of rank, for mutual support and comradeship. Photographs and art by soldier artists are displayed, and the attic chapel can be visited. Talbot House became known also on the opposite side of the front as a symbol of peace. Today it provides free accommodations for young volunteers who help maintain the war cemeteries. ⊠ *Gasthuisstraat 43, Poperinge,* ☎ *057/333228.* ▩ *BF30.* ⊙ *Daily 9–noon and 2–5.*

Dining and Lodging

$$$ ✕ **D'Hommelkeete.** A low-slung Flemish farmhouse, where the rustic and the modern coexist, this is, according to experts, the best place to experience the elusive and expensive delicacy called *jets de houblon* (hop shoots). It is only available for three weeks in spring, so call ahead. Braised sea scallops with morel sauce, warm goose liver with Calvados, and venison *noisettes* (nuggets) are also recommended. ⊠ *Hoge Noenweg 3, Poperinge,* ☎ *057/334365. AE, DC, MC, V. No dinner Sun. and Wed. Closed Mon. and 2nd ½ of July.*

$ ✕ **'t Ganzeke.** Well used to feeding bus loads of people, this popular eatery acquits itself well with giant kebabs and large steaks, satisfying but unmemorable meals. ⊠ *Vandepeereboomplein 5, Ieper,* ☏ *057/200009. No credit cards.*

$$$ ✕▦ **Hostellerie Mont Kemmel** (Kemmelberg). This luxurious hotel and restaurant sit atop Flanders' highest mountain, altitude 475 feet. There's a panoramic view over "Flanders Fields" from the well-appointed rooms, and chef Solange Bentin cooks up sophisticated specialties, such as nettle-braised frogs' legs, and squab with a spice crust and port sauce. ⊠ *Berg 4, 8956 Kemmel,* ☏ *054/444145,* 𝔽𝔸𝕏 *054/444089. 16 rooms with bath. Restaurant, bar, golf privileges, tennis court. AE, DC, MC, V. No dinner Sun. Closed Mon., mid-Jan.–Feb., 1st wk of July.*

$$ ✕▦ **Regina.** Directly on Ieper's Grote Markt in a sturdy neo-Gothic brick building, this is a fresh, comfortable hotel, its generous spaces full of light, its rooms up-to-date. Everything has been upgraded except the windows; traffic noise is the only drawback. ⊠ *Grote Markt 45,* ☏ *057/219006. 17 rooms with bath. Restaurant, bar. AE, DC, MC, V.*

Flanders Battlefields A to Z

Arriving and Departing

BY CAR

Kortrijk is reached by the E40 from Brussels, branching off on the E17 from Ghent (which continues to Lille and Paris), or the A17 from Brugge. The easiest way to reach Ieper is via the A19 from Kortrijk, which peters out north of the city; highway N38 continues to Poperinge, where you're close to the French highway linking Lille with Dunkirk and Calais.

BY TRAIN

There's a train every hour from Brussels to Kortrijk. The trip takes 1 hour and 10 minutes. There are also several trains a day from Lille, where the *Eurostar* from London stops (but you must change stations from Lille Europe to Lille Flandres); the trip takes 35 minutes. To get to Ieper by train you have to change in Kortrijk to an infrequent local service that will take you to Ieper in 30 minutes and to Poperinge in 40 minutes.

Getting Around

Driving is definitely the best solution, because the various World War I sights are located in different directions from Ieper. Those sturdy of leg can, as usual, rent bikes at the railway station.

Guided Tours

Quasimodo Tours (☏ 050/370470) operates a "Fields of Flanders" full-day bus tour starting and ending at Brugge on Monday and Saturday, from April through October. The price is BF1,300.

Visitor Information

City Tourist Information Services (Dienst voor Toerisme) are at **Kortrijk** (⊠ Schouwburgplein 14a, ☏ 056/239371); **Ieper** (⊠ Stadhuis, Grote Markt, ☏ 057/200724); **Diksmuide** (⊠ Grote Markt 28, ☏ 051/510088); and **Poperinge** (⊠ Stadhuis, Markt 1, ☏ 057/334081).

The North Sea Coast

From De Panne in the southwest to Knokke in the northeast is only 65 kilometers (39 miles), but it's a considerable distance in terms of taste, from middle class to snob appeal. There's a total of 20 resorts, so close together that it's difficult to know where one ends and the next begins. You can walk for miles along the dike, flanked by modern apartment houses where flats are rented by the week or month. For many

Belgians, an apartment by the sea is the equivalent of a summer house. All along the coast, parents help their kids fly kites, youngsters ride pedal cars, horseback riders thunder by along the water's edge, lovers walk arm in arm, dogs chase sticks, children dig in the sand, and sun worshipers laze in deck chairs protected from the North Sea breezes by canvas windbreaks.

Belgians flock to the shore over the weekend year-round. Quite a few profess to like it best in the off-season, when you can walk along the beach in the pale winter sun, filling your lungs with bracing sea air, and then warm up in a cozy tavern with a plate of steaming mussels.

Oostende

⑤④ *115 km (69 mi) northwest of Brussels, 28 km (17 mi) west of Brugge, 98 km (59 mi) northeast of Calais.*

Oostende leads a double life, as a transportation and fishing center on the one hand, and as a somewhat old-fashioned, slightly naughty resort on the other. It is the largest town and the oldest settlement on the coast, with a history going back to the 10th century. It was a pirates' hideout for centuries, and it was from here that Crusaders set sail for the Holy Land. In the early 17th century, Oostende, which backed the Protestant cause, withstood a Spanish siege for three years.

One of Continental Europe's first railways was built between Oostende and Mechelen in 1838, eventually resulting in regular mail packet services to Dover, England, beginning in 1846. Oostende also drew its share of royalty: Queen Victoria herself came here for the sea air, and Leopold II built himself a sumptuous villa on the beach.

The **Albert I Promenade** is the fashionable area where shops and tearooms compete for attention with the view of the wide beach and the sea. At one end stands the **Casino** (Kursaal), which, in addition to gambling facilities, has a vast concert hall and exhibition space. The gaming rooms contain murals by master surrealist Paul Delvaux. ⊠ *Oosthelling,* ☎ *059/705111 or 059/707618 (reservations for shows).* ۞ *Gaming rooms 3 PM–dawn.*

The **Visserskai** (Fishermen's Wharf) is filled with an almost uninterrupted row of fish restaurants across from stalls where women hawk seafood in all its forms. ⊠ *Albert 1 Promenade, opposite end from the Casino.*

NEED A BREAK?
> **Jan's Café** (⊠ Van Iseghemlaan 60), where a giant sea monster is suspended above the bar, serves snacks and beer from noon to 11.

James Ensorhuis (James Ensor House) is an introduction to the strange and hallucinatory world of the painter James Ensor (1860–1949), who has only lately been recognized as one of the great artists of the early 20th century. Using violent colors to express his frequently macabre or satirical themes, he depicted a fantastic carnival world peopled by masks and skeletons. The displays in this house, which was his home and studio, include many of the objects found in his work, especially the masks, and copies of his major paintings. ⊠ *Vlaanderenstraat 27,* ☎ *059/502575.* ▣ *BF50.* ۞ *June–Sept., Wed.–Mon. 10–noon and 2–5; Oct.–May, weekends 2–5.*

A number of paintings and drawings by James Ensor, as well as works by expressionists such as Permeke and Brusselmans, can be seen in the **Museum voor Schone Kunsten** (Fine Arts Museum). ⊠ *Wapenplein,* ☎ *059/805335.* ▣ *BF50.* ۞ *Wed.–Mon. 10–noon and 2–5.*

Oostende also has a good modern art museum, the **Museum voor Moderne Kunst** (MMK), where contemporary artists are well represented by the likes of Pierre Alechinsky, Roger Raveel, and Paul Van Hoeydonck, whose statuette, *The Fallen Astronaut,* was deposited on the moon by the *Apollo XV* crew. ⊠ *Romestraat 11,* ☎ *059/508118.* ▨ *BF100.* ◷ *Wed.–Mon. 10–6.*

ↂ **Mercator,** the three-masted training ship of the Belgian merchant marine, is now moored close to the city center. Decks, fittings, and the spartan quarters have been kept intact, and there's a museum of mementoes brought home from the ship's exotic voyages. ⊠ *Vindictivelaan,* ☎ *059/705654.* ▨ *BF100.* ◷ *Apr.–Sept., daily 10–1 and 2–6 (July–Aug. until 7); Oct.–Mar., weekends 11–1 and 2–5.*

Provinciaal Museum Constant Permeke, the home of Belgium's outstanding expressionist painter and sculptor (1886–1952), is filled with some 150 of his paintings and virtually all his sculptures. Many of his paintings are somber, in shades of green and brown, drawn from the lives of peasants and fishermen. ⊠ *Gistelsesteenweg 341, Jabbeke (between Oostende and Brugge),* ☎ *050/811288.* ▨ *BF100.* ◷ *Tues.–Sun. 10–12:30 and 1:30–6 (until 5 in winter).*

Dining and Lodging

$$$ ✕ **Villa Maritza.** Bearing the name of an Austro-Hungarian countess who caught Leopold II's fancy, the 100-year-old villa, furnished in Renaissance Flemish style, serves a seafood cuisine based on the finest ingredients: lobster with Chinese truffles and caviar, sea scallops, and duck's liver served sweet-and-sour with sherry, plus the ultimate luxury, a sea view. ⊠ *Albert I Promenade 76,* ☎ *059/508808. Reservations essential. Jacket and tie. AE, DC, MC, V. No dinner Sun. (except July–Aug.). Closed Mon. and 2nd ½ of June.*

$$ ✕ **Lusitania.** This is arguably the best among the several restaurants that crowd the Visserskaik, and a little more expensive than its rivals. They all serve variations on the same seafood theme: salad of tiny, sweet shrimps, fish soup, grilled langoustines, and sole prepared in a variety of ways, including one that features béchamel sauce, shrimps, and mussels. ⊠ *Visserskai 35,* ☎ *059/701765. AE, DC, MC, V.*

$ ✕ **Zoe Grill.** The specialty here is spareribs, served at tiny tables covered with salmon-colored tablecloths. This good-natured restaurant, which stays open until midnight, faces the entrance to the cathedral. ⊠ *St. Petrus en Paulusplein 3,* ☎ *059/700820. MC, V. Closed Wed.*

$$$$ ✕▥ **Oostendse Compagnie/Le Vigneron.** This palatial villa, once a royal
★ residence, is right on the beach, with ocean views from the dining room with its splendid terrace and from the large bedrooms. The restaurant has had its ups and downs in recent years, but it's now firmly on an upward trajectory. Among its specialties are tempura of langoustines with new onions and ginger, roast turbot with spices, and pullet *à la vapeur* (steamed) with truffles. ⊠ *Koningstraat 79,* ☎ *059/704816,* ℻ *059/805316. 13 rooms with bath. Restaurant, beach. AE, DC, MC, V. No dinner Sun. Closed Mon., 1st 2 wks of Mar., Oct.*

$$$ ✕▥ **Andromeda.** So close to the Casino that you can practically hear the rolling of the dice, this luxury hotel has rooms in restful colors that match the sea. Junior suites come with balconies overlooking the beach. ⊠ *Kursaal Westhelling 5, 8400,* ☎ *059/704816,* ℻ *059/85316. 92 rooms with bath. Restaurant, bar, indoor pool, sauna, health club. AE, DC, MC, V.*

$$ ▥ **Old Flanders.** In a handsome brick building opposite the cathedral, this hotel offers family atmosphere, comfortable if nondescript rooms,

and a generous breakfast buffet. ⊠ *Jozef II Straat 49,* ☎ *059/806603,* FAX *059/801695. 15 rooms with bath. Bar, breakfast room. AE, DC, MC, V.*

Nightlife and the Arts

NIGHTLIFE

The closure rate among seasonal nightspots is high; make sure the place you select is still in business. The best bet along the coast is generally the local casino, where gambling underwrites the nightclub entertainment.

The **Sporting Club** (⊠ Oosthelling, ☎ 059/705111), which is run by the Casino, is the classiest nightspot in Oostende. Young male visitors from across the Channel, who arrive bent on a bender, head straight for **Langestraat,** where there's a wide choice of snack bars, beer joints, pizza houses, topless bars, and disco-clubs, including **Brazzaville,** the **Twilight,** and **Road 99.** The loudest and most densely packed disco is the **Dôme.** Local residents prefer the **Theatercafé-Bistro Bier Co.** (⊠ Alfons Pieterslaan 86) in the "Petit Paris" quarter, which is open from 11 AM to 2 AM. It has a fashionably unfinished look, there's a concert podium, and the atmosphere is convivial.

THE ARTS

Check *The Bulletin* under "Other Towns" for cultural activities. There are frequent retrospectives at Oostende's museums. Concerts of all kinds, from classical to rock, pop, and jazz, draw crowds from far away to the Oostende Casino's 1,700-seat hall (☎ 059/707618).

Outdoor Activities and Sports

RACING

The **Wellington Hippodrome** in Oostende (☎ 059/806055) is a top track for flat racing and trotting. Flat racing is July and August, Monday, Thursday, weekends, and bank holidays; trotting races (☎ 059/803636) are May through September, Friday at 6:45 PM.

De Panne

55 *31 km (19 mi) southwest of Oostende, 55 km (33 mi) southwest of Brugge, 143 km (86 mi) west of Brussels, 63 km (38 mi) northeast of Calais.*

De Panne is a family-friendly resort with the widest beach on the coast and sand dunes protected from developers. On the beach you can see sand yachts looking like sailboats on wheels, zipping along at up to 120 kph (72 mph). Riding horses along the beach and on trails through the dunes is also very popular. The royal family resided here during World War I because De Panne was part of that narrow band of Belgium that the Germans never occupied. The dunes west of the resort are a nature reserve, **Westhoek,** where you can roam around on your own; guided walks are organized in season. ⊠ *Dynastielaan,* ☎ *058/421818.*

Meli Park is a large family park complete with playground, action-oriented attractions, a nature park with animals and exotic birds, and a dream park where fairy-tale scenes are enacted. ⊠ *De Pannelaan 68, Adinkerke,* ☎ *058/420202.* ☒ *BF595.* ☉ *Apr.–1st wk Sept., daily 10:30–6 (July and Aug. until 7); rest of Sept., Wed. and weekends 10:30–6.*

★ **56** **Koksijde,** Sint-Idesbald, and Oostduinkerke are three small resorts, separated by just a few kilometers, that offer more than beach life. Koksijde has the highest dune on the coast, the **Hoge Blekker,** 108 feet high. Nearby are the ruins of the Cistercian **Duinenabdij** (Abbey of the Dunes) with an archaeological museum. ⊠ *Koninklijke Prinslaan 8,* ☎ *058/511933.* ☒ *BF100.* ☉ *June 15–Sept. 15, daily 10–6; Sept. 16–Dec. and Feb.–June 14, daily 9–noon and 1:30–5.*

The strikingly modern **Onze-Lieve-Vrouw ter Duinenkerk** (Our Lady of Sorrows of the Dunes Church), north of the Abbey, suggests both the dunes and the sea.

Many art lovers head for **Sint-Idesbald** to discover the **Paul Delvaux Museum.** It is dedicated to the painter, famous for his surrealist mix of nudes, skeletons, and trains, who recently died at the age of nearly 100. A pleasant outdoor restaurant is attached to the museum. ⊠ *Kabouterweg 42,* ☎ *058/521229.* ⊡ *BF150.* ☉ *July–Aug., daily 10:30–6:30; Apr.–June and Sept., Tues.–Sun. 10:30–6:30; Oct.–Dec., Fri.–Sun. 10:30–5:30.*

⑤⑦ At **Oostduinkerke** there are still some horseback shrimp fishers. At low tide, the sturdy horses, half immersed, trawl heavy nets along the shoreline. If you miss seeing them in action, you can study their unusual approach to fishing in the **National Fisheries Museum,** which contains interesting models of fishing boats over the past millennium. ⊠ *Pastoor Schmitzstraat 4,* ☎ *058/512468.* ⊡ *BF80.* ☉ *Apr.–Sept., daily 10–noon and 2–6.*

NEED A
BREAK?
In De Peerdevisscher (⊠ Pastoor Scmitzstraat 4), a traditional *estaminet* (old-style public house) converted into café and snack bar, continues the marine theme of the fisheries museum.

⑤⑧ **Nieuwpoort** is the country's premier yachting center, with some 3,000 leisure craft moored in the estuary. Nieuwpoort is also the home of a sizable fishing fleet, and amateur fishermen can participate in daylong sea fishing trips onboard the *Sportvisser* (⊠ Langebrug, ☎ 058/235600) or *Bounty* (⊠ Handelshaven, ☎ 058/2347300). Each charges BF1,000 per person. There's also a lively fish market and good wharfside seafood shops and restaurants. A monument to King Albert marks the spot where, in October 1914, the monarch gave the command to open the sluices of the river IJzer, inundating the polder and permanently halting the German advance.

Dining and Lodging

$$ ✕ **De Braise.** Run by the parents of Le Fox's chef, who ran Le Fox (☞ *below*) when it was a simple tavern, this is the Buyens family's return to their roots: an old-fashioned regional restaurant, offering updated, upgraded local cooking in a homey setting. Though the menu reads like a thousand others in the region—turbot poached or grilled, sauce hollandaise/dijonnaise, sole meunière—the portions are generous, the preparation superb, and the service sophisticated. ⊠ *Bortierplein 1,* ☎ *058/415999. AE, DC, MC, V. Closed Mon., Tues. in off-season, 2nd ½ of Jan., Oct.*

$ ✕ **Trois Suisses.** The specialties here—in what is more of a grill room than a restaurant—include juicy grilled fish, scampi, and tender beef. The waitresses are French; this part of the coast is favored by French-speaking Belgians and their friends from across the border. ⊠ *Nieuwpoortlaan 28,* ☎ *058/421977. Closed Thurs. AE, DC, MC, V.*

$$$ ✕ **Le Fox.** Chef Stéphane Buyens took over his parents' tavern and
★ created a prestigious, welcoming gastronomic retreat. Creating dishes such as roast langoustine tails in sea urchin butter, and turbot in an aromatic mix of 10 oils, herbs, and beet juice, he has drawn a loyal following. Guests stay in graciously furnished rooms (some have windows angled toward the waterfront) and work as many meals into the weekend as they can. The dining room is cozy and the ambience down to earth. ⊠ *Walckiersstraat 2,* ☎ *058/412855. 14 rooms with bath.*

*Restaurant, bar. AE, DC, MC, V. No lunch Tues. Closed Mon., 2nd
½ of Jan., 1st 3 wks of Oct.*

$$ ✕⊞ **Sparrenhof.** This is a self-contained oasis, cut off from the beach-
front scene but only 500 feet from the water. Its pretty pool is clois-
tered in a garden; many rooms face the greenery. The original building,
which has seven guest rooms, dates from the 1950s. The new wing is
flashy and modern. The restaurant is open year-round and has a wood-
burning fireplace and poolside tables. ⊠ *Koninginnelaan 26, B-8660,*
☎ *058/411328. 25 rooms with bath. Restaurant, bar, pool. AE, DC,
MC, V.*

Knokke-Heist

❺❾ *33 km (20 mi) northeast of Oostende, 17 km (10 mi) north of Brugge,
108 km (65 mi) northwest of Brussels.*

Knokke, to young Belgians of ample means, is where you go to show
off the latest fashions or with your newest flame. But those who in-
habit the old-money villas of Het Zoute, just inland from the beach,
would not dream of letting the world know about their chauffeurs and
butlers. Along the Kustlaan, on the leeward side of the dike, you'll find
a branch of virtually every fashionable shop in Brussels, all of them
open Sunday. The Casino has an enormous chandelier of Venetian crys-
tal, and some of the world's top entertainers come here to perform.
Gaming, however, is for members only.

NEED A   The Ibertplein square, widely known as the *Place M'as-tu-vu* (Did-you-
BREAK?   see-me Square), is a gathering place for the chic-at-heart. The newest
and most fashionable tearoom-restaurant is **Le Carré** (Albertplein 16,
☎ 050/611222), perfect for people-watching.

★ **❻⓿** **Het Zwin** is a remarkable 375-acre nature reserve and bird sanctuary.
Saltwater washes into the soil at certain times, making for some un-
usual flora and fauna. The best times to visit are in spring for the bird
migrations and from mid-July for the flowers, especially the native *Zwin-
neblomme,* or sea lavender. Rubber boots are a must, and binoculars
recommended. From the top of the dike there's a splendid view of the
dunes and inlets. Storks nest in the aviary, which also holds a large va-
riety of aquatic birds and birds of prey. A former royal villa, the Châlet
du Zwin, is now an attractive restaurant. ⊠ *Ooievaarslaan 8,* ☎
050/607086. ▣ *BF140.* ☉ *Daily 9–7 (Oct.–Mar. until 5).*

Zeeuwsch-Vlaanderen, The Netherlands

The Het Zwin nature preserve continues on the Dutch side of the bor-
der. Zeeuwsch-Vlaanderen, part of the Dutch province of Zeeland,
stretches 60-odd kilometers (about 36 miles) to the mouth of the
Scheldt, north of Antwerp. When Belgium declared its independence
in 1830, this Protestant province stayed with the Dutch, mostly for re-
❻❶ ligious reasons. The best-known town is **Sluis,** reached from Knokke
on N376 (N58 in the Netherlands). This small town shared the wealth
of Brugge, for it was on the waterway that linked Brugge with the sea.
Many Belgians come here to shop and bank.

❻❷ The beach proper begins with **Cadzand Bad,** which has several good
❻❸ hotels. Travelers also head for **Breskens,** where you can take a car ferry
to Vlissingen on Walcheren. Zeeuwsch-Vlaanderen is well suited for a
holiday with children precisely because the resorts are uncrowded, with
❻❹ wide and quiet beaches. N252 south, from the port city of **Terneuzen,**
links up with R4 to Ghent. There's a second car-ferry service east of
Terneuzen, from Kloosterzande on N60 to Kruiningen on Walcheren.

Going south on N60 you link up with N49 in Belgium, 26 kilometers (16 miles) from Antwerp.

Dining and Lodging

$$$$ ✕ **Ter Dijken.** Discretion and charm are the bywords at this restaurant, known for its terrace adjoining a magnificent garden. Langoustines with chives *au gratin,* croquettes of hand-peeled shrimp, and baked potato with caviar are among the favorites here. ⊠ *Kalvekeetdijk 137,* ☎ *050/608023. Reservations essential. Jacket and tie. AE, DC, MC, V. Closed Mon.–Tues., Jan., 10 days in Sept.*

$$ ✕ **New Alpina.** Despite token efforts at elegance, with pink linens and multiple stemware, this is a seafood diner at heart, where a friendly husband-and-wife team have served North Sea classics since 1970. Fresh *raie* (skate), turbot, sole, and shrimp are served with simple sauces; the multicourse, fixed-priced "Gourmet Menu" is a seafood feast. It's just off the beach, by the tourist office. ⊠ *Lichttorenplein 12,* ☎ *050/608985. V. No dinner Mon. Closed Tues.*

$$$$ ✕⌂ **La Réserve.** This vast country club of a hotel, complete with a salt-water treatment center and a man-made lake, was built as a private mansion in 1964. It was expanded, under various managements, into the enormous complex it is today. Flowers and antiques-like details do little to warm the airport-style public spaces, but guest rooms are bright and lovely, in soothing sponge-painted pastels. You can buy in as far as you like, from a simple bed-and-breakfast arrangement to a full-out Thalassa-treatment package. It's across from the Casino, three minutes from the beach. The restaurant is good and getting better. ⊠ *Elizabetlaan 158–160, Albertstrand,* ☎ *050/610606,* ℻ *050/603706. 112 rooms. Restaurant, bar, saltwater pool, beauty salon, massage, mineral baths, sauna, 4 tennis courts, windsurfing. AE, DC, MC, V.*

$$$ ✕⌂ **Katelijne.** This charming whitewashed brick auberge, built in the 1930s in traditional Flemish style, seems out of place amid the boutiques and snaking traffic of the beachfront. It offers an atmospheric retreat, with fireplace, Oriental runners, fringed plush furniture, and darkened timbers. The rooms are equally cozy and dated, though the marble-travertine baths are deluxe. There's a garden and terrace, and a welcoming copper-decked restaurant featuring fish. ⊠ *Kustlaan 166, Knokke-Zout,* ☎ *050/601216,* ℻ *0050/615190. 14 rooms with bath. Restaurant, bar. AE, MC, V.*

Nightlife and the Arts

The **Casino** (⊠ Zeedijk 507, ☎ 050/606010) offers dinner-dancing with two orchestras, gala nights with international stars, theater, movies, ballet, exhibitions, and two discos, **Number 1** (entrance on Zeedijk) and **Dubbel's** (entrance on Canada Square). Another favorite is the **Gallery Club** (⊠ Canada Square 22, ☎ 050/608133).

Outdoor Activities and Sports

For information about sports facilities throughout the region, contact **BLOSO** (Flemish Sports Association; ⊠ Rue des Colonies 31, Brussels, ☎ 02/510–3411). More detailed local information can be obtained for **Knokke** (☎ 050/604317); for **Oostende** (☎ 059/500529); and **De Panne** (☎ 058/412971). For information on water sports, contact Vlaamse Vereniging voor Watersport (⊠ Beatrijslaan 25, 2050 Antwerp, ☎ 03/219–6967).

GOLF

There is one 18-hole golf course at **De Haan** (☎ 059/235723) and two at **Knokke-Heist** (⊠ Caddiespad 14, ☎ 050/601616). For practice courses at other locations, contact local tourist offices.

SAILING

The coast, with its prevailing breeze, offers splendid sailing opportunities. Good yacht harbors include Blankenberge, Nieuwpoort, Oostende (☎ 059/706294), and Zeebrugge (☎ 050/544197).

SAND YACHTING

The best places are De Panne and Oostduinkerke, where the beach is up to 820 feet wide, and the facilities are excellent.

SWIMMING

Currents can be tricky, and you should swim only at beaches supervised by lifeguards. A green flag means bathing is safe; yellow, bathing is risky but guards are on duty; red, bathing is prohibited. Do not ignore warnings. Many resorts also offer good public outdoor pools.

TENNIS

Tournaments are held during the season at Oostende and Het Zoute. There are hundreds of courts along the coast; check with your concierge or the local tourist office.

WINDSURFING

Windsurfing is extremely popular and special areas have been set aside for it along many beaches. In Oostende, the Flemish Sports Association has set up a water-sports center (✉ Vicognedijk 30, ☎ 059/321564) on the Spuikom waterway (also used for oyster beds).

The North Sea Coast A to Z

Arriving and Departing

BY BOAT

Sally Line (in the U.K., ☎ 01843/595522) car ferry has up to six sailings a day from Ramsgate to Oostende (four hours). **North Sea Ferries** (in the U.K., ☎ 01482/77177) offers overnight sailings from Hull to Zeebrugge (14 hours). Foot passengers only are carried by **Jetfoil** from Ramsgate to Oostende (1 hour and 40 minutes, up to four daily crossings).

BY CAR

The six-lane E40 from Brussels passes both Ghent and Brugge en route to Oostende. On summer weekends, a better alternative is the N9 from Ghent via Brugge; for Knokke, you branch off on N49. A back road to the resorts southwest of Oostende is N43 from Ghent to Deinze, and then N35 to the coast. From Calais, the E40 has been completed on the French side, but a few kilometers of two-lane road remain before linking up with the rest of the E40 to Oostende and Brussels.

BY TRAIN

Oostende is the terminus of the Cologne–Brussels–Oostende railway line, which connects with ferry service to Ramsgate and the boat train to London. The trip from Brussels takes 1 hour and 10 minutes; from Ghent, 40 minutes; and from Brugge, 15 minutes. There's a train every hour. For train information in Oostende calll 059/701517. There's local, hourly train service from Ghent to De Panne (1 hour, 10 minutes), and direct service every hour from Brussels to Knokke (1 hour, 15 minutes) via Ghent and Brugge.

Getting Around

BY CAR

The coastal road, N34, is very busy in summer. Allow ample time for driving between resorts.

There's tram service—a happily preserved relic of another era—all the way from Knokke to De Panne. The trams are modern, and it's a pleasant ride, but don't expect uninterrupted views of the sea; the tram tracks are on the leeward side of the dike. The service runs every 15 minutes from Easter through September. Tickets cost from BF50 depending on distance. A one-day ticket comes to BF290; a five-day ticket is BF840. For information call 078/113663.

Contacts and Resources

GUIDED TOURS

Quasimodo (☎ 050/370470) runs all-day minibus tours from Brugge featuring a drive along the coast. They are operated Wednesday and Friday in season, with English-language commentary. The price is BF1,300.

Seastar operates regular sailings between Oostende and Nieuwpoort in July and August with two departures in each direction. The trip along the coast takes 1½ hours. ⊠ *Havengeul 17, Nieuwpoort,* ☎ *058/232425.* ▨ *BF450.*

River excursions onboard the *Jean Bart III* (☎ 058/232329) on the IJzer, through the polder from Nieuwpoort to Diksmuide and back, are operated daily in July and August.

VISITOR INFORMATION

For the area as a whole, **Westtoerisme** (⊠ Kasteel Tillegem, Brugge, ☎ 050/380296); **Knokke-Heist** (⊠ Zeedijk 660 (☎ 050/630380); **Nieuwpoort** (⊠ Marktplein 7, ☎ 058/224444); **Oostende** (⊠ Monacoplein 2, ☎ 059/701199); and **De Panne** (⊠ Zeelaan 21, ☎ 058/421818).

ANTWERP

In its heyday, Antwerp played second fiddle only to Paris. Thanks to artists such as Rubens, Van Dyck, and Jordaens, it was one of Europe's leading art centers. Its printing presses produced missals for the farthest reaches of the Spanish empire. It became, and has remained, the diamond capital of the world. Its civic pride was such that the Antwerp *Sinjoren* (patricians) considered themselves a cut above just about everybody else. They still do.

The word Antwerpen, Flemish for Antwerp, is very close to the word *handwerpen,* which means "hand throwing," and that, according to legend, is exactly what the Roman soldier Silvius Brabo did to the giant Druon Antigon. The giant would collect a toll from boatmen on the river and cut off the hands of those who refused, until Silvius confronted him, cut off the giant's own hand, and flung it into the river Scheldt. That's why there are severed hands on Antwerp's coat of arms.

Great prosperity came to Antwerp during the reign of Emperor Charles V. Born in Ghent and raised in Mechelen, he made Antwerp the principal port of his vast domain. It became the most important commercial center in the 16th century, as well as a center of the new craft of printing. The Golden Age came to an end with the abdication of Charles V in 1555. He was succeeded by Philip II of Spain, whose ardent Roman Catholicism brought him into immediate conflict with the Protestants of the Netherlands. In 1566, when Calvinist iconoclasts destroyed paintings and sculptures in churches and monasteries, Philip II responded by sending in Spanish troops. In what became known as the Spanish Fury, they sacked the town and killed thousands of citizens.

The decline of Antwerp had already begun when its most illustrious painters, Rubens, Jordaens, and Van Dyck, reached the peak of their fame. The Treaty of Munster in 1648, which concluded the Thirty Years' War, also sealed Antwerp's fate, for the river Scheldt was closed to shipping—not to be opened again until 1863, when a treaty obliged the Dutch, who controlled the estuary, to reopen it.

The huge and splendid railway station, built at the turn of the century, remains a fitting monument to Antwerp's second age of prosperity, during which it hosted universal expositions in both 1885 and 1894. In World War I, Antwerp held off German invaders long enough for the Belgian army to regroup south of the IJzer. In World War II, the Germans trained many V-1 flying bombs and V-2 rockets on the city, where Allied troops were debarking for the final push.

Antwerp today is Europe's second-largest port and has much of the zest often associated with a port. The city has traditionally taken pride in being open to influences from abroad and in welcoming newcomers to the city. Yet in recent elections, a large number of votes have been cast for Vlaamse Blok, a party of extreme right-wing tendencies.

Antwerp is known as the City of the Madonnas. On almost every street corner in the old section, you'll see a high niche with a protective statuette of the Virgin. People tend to think that because Belgium is linguistically split it is also religiously divided. This emphatically is not so. In fact, the Roman Catholic faith appears to be stronger and more unquestioning in Flanders than in Wallonia, where the anti-clericalism of fellow French-speakers has struck a responsive chord.

Pleasures and Pastimes

ART

Rubens is ever-present in Antwerp, and a genial presence it is. His house, his church, the homes of his benefactors, friends, and disciples are all over the old city. His wife also seems ever-present, for she frequently posed as his model for his portraits of the Virgin Mary. Rubens and his fellow Antwerper Van Dyck both dabbled in diplomacy and were knighted by the English monarch. Jacob Jordaens, less widely known, stayed close to Antwerp all his life; long regarded as an also-ran, he has only recently been recognized for his artistic genius.

In addition to being home to the Old Masters, Antwerp is also on the cutting edge in art. The sharpest designers and most far-out artists are here, rather than in the capital, and the galleries and modern art museum celebrate contemporary concepts.

DIAMONDS

The diamond trade has its own quarter in Antwerp, where the skills of cutting and polishing the gems have been handed down for generations by a tightly knit community. Multimillion-dollar deals are agreed upon with a handshake, and the industry has created its own Diamond High Council to establish strict quality control and high standards. There are some 1,500 diamond trading companies in Antwerp, many of them controlled by Hassidim, a Jewish sect. Some 85% of the world's uncut diamonds pass through Antwerp. With the exception of a few retail shops under the arches of the railway station, most of the diamond-cutting activity is handled discreetly and away from the public eye, but you can feast your eyes on the final product at a diamond museum and public showroom.

DINING

Antwerp remains remarkably conservative in its culinary tastes, focusing with understandable devotion on fish—presented with few frills in even the finest restaurants, often poached or steamed, and reasonably priced. From the chilled whelks and periwinkles (marine snails) picked out of their shells with pins, to piles of tender little *crevettes grises* (small shrimp), to the steamy white flesh of the mammoth turbot, the scent of salt air and fresh brine is never far from your table. The ubiquitous mussels and eels, showcased in mid-priced restaurants throughout the city center, provide a heavier, heartier version of local fish cuisine. Bought live from wholesalers, the seafood is irreproachably fresh.

For dining price categories, *see* The Pleasures of Dining and Lodging at the beginning of this chapter.

SHOPPING

Dedicated followers of fashion regard Antwerp as a trend-setter second only to Milan. Credit for this development goes to the so-called Antwerp Six and in equal measure to the remarkable designer who trained them, Linda Loppa. Ready-to-wear by Ann Demeulemeester, Dirk Bikkenbergs, Dries Van Nooten, and others can be found in New York's most expensive fashion boutiques. These designers command high prices in Antwerp, too, but in the shopping area just south of Groenplaats, prices are less astronomical.

Exploring Antwerp

Since many people arrive in Antwerp by train and the magnificent railway station is in the commercial center of the city, many form an immediate impression of Antwerp from the area that surrounds the station. This is a big mistake. Hop on the subway to Groenplaats, and walk past the cathedral and into the Grote Markt. This is where Antwerp begins. Although you can "do" Antwerp in a day, you would do much better with two days, allowing time to sample some of the great restaurants and the lively nightlife and to properly explore the rich collections of the Royal Museum of Fine Arts and other museums. Antwerp is also a good base for excursions throughout the province of the same name and neighboring Limburg. Antwerp can be visited year-round, but avoid Monday, when the museums are closed, for they are an integral part of enjoying this city. An excursion to the province of Limburg is best made in spring or summer; it is at its very best at apple-blossom time.

Numbers in the text correspond to numbers in the margin and on the Antwerp map.

A Good Walk

From the **Grote Markt** ⑥⑤ walk down Suikerrui toward the river, stopping en route at the **Etnografisch Museum** ⑥⑥. At the end of the street, turn right to the waterfront fortress, the **Steen** ⑥⑦. Walk up the block-long Repenstraat to the step-gabled **Vleeshuis** ⑥⑧. Proceed along Oude Beurs and its continuation, Wolstraat, turning left on Minderbroedersrui and then right on Keizerstraat, to **Rockoxhuis** ⑥⑨, the Renaissance home of Rubens's benefactor. Retrace your steps to the junction of Wolstraat and the church of **St. Carolus Borromeus** ⑦⓪ on the attractive Hendrik Conscienceplein. Walk down Wijngaardstraat in the direction of the Grote Markt, going around the cathedral to its entrance on Handschoenmarkt. The Gothic **Onze-Lieve-Vrouwe Kathedraal** ⑦① contains some of Rubens's greatest paintings. A few steps to the left, from the front of the cathedral, and you're in Koornmarkt. At No. 16 begins the **Vlaeykensgang** ⑦②, an old cobblestone lane. It merges into Pelgrimstraat. Turn right, then right again on Reyndersstraat, past the Baroque house of the painter Jacob Jordaens; then right on Hoogstraat and right again on Heilige Geeststraat, and you're at the **Plantin-More-**

Antwerp

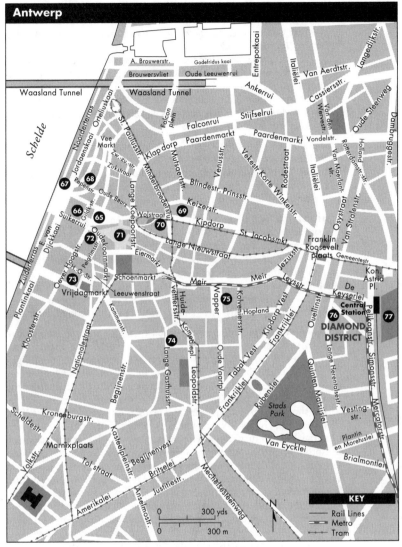

KEY

— Rail Lines

▬ Metro

┈┼┈ Tram

tus Museum ⑦, the printer's stately home and workshops. Cross the Vrijdagmarkt, and walk along Steenhouwersvest and Lombardenvest to Korte Gasthuisstraat, where you turn right and proceed to **Museum Mayer Van den Bergh** ⑦ with its outstanding Bruegels. By way of Huidevettersstraat and Meir, the main shopping area, you arrive at Wapper and **Rubenshuis** ⑦, the painter's home. Farther along Meir and its continuation, Leys and De Keyserlei, you arrive at the Diamond District, turning right on Appelmansstraat for **Diamondland** ⑦ and the Diamond Museum. De Keyserlei takes you on to Central Station and, on its other side, the **Antwerp Zoo** ⑦.

TIMING

Walking this route, with short stops at the museums, will take you four to five hours. Time permitting, you would be well advised to break at the Rubenshuis and see the Diamond District and the zoo the following day.

Sights to See

Centraalstation (Central Station). Next to the zoo, the neo-Baroque Centraalstation (Central Station) was built at the turn of the century during the reign of Leopold II of Belgium, a monarch not given to understatement. The magnificent exterior and splendid, vaulted ticket-office hall and staircases call out for hissing steam engines, peremptory conductors, scurrying porters, and languid ladies wrapped in boas. Alas, today most departures and arrivals are humble commuter trains.

Diamond District. Twenty-five million carats are cut and traded here every year, more than anywhere else in the world. The district occupies a few nondescript city blocks west of Central Station. Shop signs in Hebrew, and the distinctive clothing and ringlets worn by many Hasidic men, are the only clues that this area is any different from the rest of Antwerp. Below the elevated railway tracks, a long row of stalls and shops gleams with jewelry and gems, a bit like New York's West 47th Street. Diamond cutting began in Brugge but moved to Antwerp in the 16th century, along with most other wealth-creating activities. Antwerp's preoccupation with beauty and money helped the diamond trade flourish. Today the industry employs some 18,000 people, divided among 6,000 independent firms. In addition to cutters, grinders, and polishers, there are about 3,000 traders, of whom two-thirds are Jewish and one-fifth Indian, with a heavy sprinkling of Lebanese and Armenians. Nearly all come from long-established diamond families. Some of Antwerp's Jews managed to flee Belgium during World War II, but many more perished in the concentration camps.

⑦ **Diamondland.** A spectacular showroom, Diamondland was created to enable visitors to see some of the bustling activity. Because security is of the essence in this business, outsiders were not previously allowed to watch any of the activity inside. Diamondland has three floors of slide shows and films, showcases of rough and polished diamonds, and several diamond cutters at work. ⊠ *Appelmansstraat 33A,* ☎ *03/243–3612.* ☾ *Mon.–Sat. 9–6.*

⑥ **Etnografisch Museum** (Ethnographic Museum). This fascinating museum explores the art, myths, and rites of the native peoples of Africa, the Americas, Asia, and the South Seas. Among its 30,000 masks, tools, weapons, sculptures, and other objects are several unique pieces, some of them described in *La Musée Imaginaire,* André Malraux's famed compilation of the world's most important art and artifacts. ⊠ *Suikerrui 19,* ☎ *03/232–0882.* ▨ *BF75.* ☾ *Tues.–Sun. 10–5.*

⑥⑤ Grote Markt. The heart of the Old Town, the Grote Markt is dominated by a huge fountain splashing water over much of the square. It
is crowned by the figure of the legendary Silvius Brabo, who has been
about to fling the hand of the giant into the river Scheldt for the past
100 years. Another famous monster slayer, St. George, is perched on
top of a 16th-century guild house at Grote Markt 5, while the dragon
appears to be falling off the pediment. The triangular square is lined
on two sides by guild houses and on the third by the Renaissance **Stadhuis** (Town Hall). Antwerp's Town Hall was built in the 1560s during the city's Golden Age, when Paris and Antwerp were the only
European cities with more than 100,000 inhabitants. In its facade, the
fanciful fretwork of the late Gothic style has given way to the disci-
pline and order of the Renaissance; the public rooms are suitably impressive, though the heavy hand of 19th-century restoration work is
much in evidence. ✉ BF30. ☉ Mon.–Tues. and Thurs.–Fri. 8–6, Sat.
8–4; guided tours weekdays at 11, 2, and 3, Sat. at 2 and 3.

Koninklijk Museum voor Schone Kunsten (Royal Museum of Fine
Arts). A must for the student of Flemish art, the collection here is studded with masterworks from Bruegel to Ensor. The paintings here, re-
covered from the French after the fall of Napoléon, form the nucleus
of a collection of 2,500 works of art. For your first visit, you'll probably want to concentrate on Room H, devoted to Jacob Jordaens; Room
J, mostly monumental Rubens; and Room M, filled with Bruegels. The
collection of Flemish Primitives includes works by Van Eyck, Memling, Roger van der Weyden, Joachim Patinier, and Quinten Metsys.
On the ground floor there's a representative survey of Belgian art of
the past 150 years—Emile Claus, Rik Wouters, Permeke, Magritte, Delvaux, and especially James Ensor. ✉ Leopold de Waelplaats 1–9, ☎
03/238–7809. ✉ Free. ☉ Tues.–Sun. 10–5. Take Tram 8.

Ⓒ Mini-Antwerpen. The name says it all. Most, if not all, of Antwerp can
be found here, scaled down to kid size. The tour ends with a minisound-
and-sights show recounting the history of the city. ✉ Hangar 15,
Cockerillkaai, ☎ 03/237–0329. ✉ BF100. ☉ Daily 10–6.

★ ⑦④ Museum Mayer Van den Bergh. Bruegel's arguably greatest and most
enigmatic painting, Dulle Griet, is the showpiece here. Often referred
to in English as "Mad Meg," it portrays an irate woman wearing hel-
met and breastplate—a sword in one hand, and food and cooking utensils in the other—striding across a field strewn with the ravages and
insanity of war. There is no consensus on how to read this painting. Some
consider it one of the most powerful antiwar statements ever made. Others
claim that it denounces the Inquisition. Either way, nothing could be
further from the Bruegelian villages than this nightmare world. In 1894,
Mayer Van den Bergh bought Dulle Griet for BF488. Today it is priceless. There's one more Bruegel in the collection, his witty, miniature illustrations of Twelve Proverbs, based on popular Flemish sayings.

Mayer van den Bergh was a passionate art connoisseur who amassed
a private collection of almost 4,000 works in the 19th century. The collection includes treasures, such as a life-size polychrome statue from about
1300 of St. John resting his head on Christ's chest. It is, however, the
two Bruegel paintings that make this small museum a must. ✉ Lange
Gasthuisstraat 19, ☎ 03/232–4237. ✉ BF75. ☉ Tues.–Sun. 10–5.

NEED A   **De Foyer** (✉ Komedieplaats 18, ☎ 03/253–5517), highly popular with
BREAK?   the Antwerpers, occupies the rotunda of the 150-year-old, recently restored Bourla Theater and is a sight in its own right. A café, it serves
buffet lunch and light snacks and is open from noon to midnight.

Museum voor Hedendaagse Kunst (Museum of Contemporary Art). Known as MuHKA—ever since New York's Museum of Modern Art became known as M0MA—this museum has exhibitions that include contemporary painting, installations, video art, and experimental architecture. The museum is in a renovated grain silo a few blocks west of the Fine Arts Museum, near the waterfront. ✉ *Leuvenstraat 16–30*, ☎ *03/238–5960*. 🎫 *BF150*. ☉ *Tues.–Sun. 10–5. Take Bus 23*.

★ **⓲ Onze-Lieve-Vrouwekathedraal** (Our Lady's Cathedral). A miracle of soaring Gothic lightness, the Onze-Lieve-Vrouwekathedraal is landmarked by its 404-foot-high north spire—now restored to its original gleaming white and a beacon that can be seen from far away. Work started in 1352 and continued in fits and starts until 1584. Despite this, it is a totally homogeneous monument of stone and light, thanks to a succession of remarkable architects, including Peter Appelmans, Herman and Domien de Waghemakere, and Rombout Keldermans the Younger. The tower holds a 47-bell carillon (played Friday 11:30–12:30 and Monday in summer 8 PM–9 PM).

The cathedral's art treasures were twice vandalized, first by Calvinists in 1566, and again by the French revolutionary army at the end of the 18th century. The French even broke up the floor so that their horses would not slip on it. Some masterpieces were sold at auction and the rest carried off to Paris. Some, but by no means all, have subsequently been returned. Other works, either donated or purchased, make up an outstanding collection of 17th-century religious art, including four Rubens altarpieces, glowing with his marvelous red, allegedly fortified by pigeon's blood. The panels of *The Descent from the Cross* triptych—Mary's visit to Elizabeth (with the painter's wife as Mary) and the presentation of Jesus in the temple—are among the most delicate and tender biblical scenes ever painted. *The Assumption of the Virgin Mary*, painted for the high altar, shows the Virgin being carried upward by massed ranks of cherubs and cupids toward the angel waiting to crown her Queen of the Angels. *The Assumption* is skillfully displayed so that the rays of the sun illuminate it exactly at noon. ✉ *Handschoenmarkt*, ☎ *03/231–3033*. 🎫 *BF60*. ☉ *Weekdays 10–5, Sat. 10–3, Sun. 1–4*.

★ **⓳ Plantin-Moretus Museum.** This was the home and printing plant of an extraordinary publishing dynasty. For three centuries, beginning in 1576, the family printed innumerable bibles, breviaries, and missals; Christophe Plantin's greatest technical achievement was the *Biblia Regia* (in Room 16): eight large volumes containing the Bible in Latin, Greek, Hebrew, Syriac, and Aramaic, complete with notes, glossaries, and grammars.

The first three rooms were the family quarters, furnished in 16th-century luxury and containing several portraits by Rubens. Others remain as they were when occupied by accountants, editors, and proofreaders. The printing workshops are filled with Plantin's 16 printing presses. Two typefaces designed here, Plantin and Garamond, are still in use. The presses are in working order, and one can, in fact, purchase a copy of Plantin's sonnet, *Le bonheus de ce monde (An ode to contentment)*, in any of seven European languages, printed on an original press. ✉ *Vrijdagmarkt 22*, ☎ *03/233–0294*. 🎫 *BF75*. ☉ *Tues.–Sun. 10–5*.

NEED A BREAK?   **L'Entrepôt du Congo** (✉ Vlaamse kaai 42, ☎ 03/238-9232) is open 8 AM to 3 AM, serving whatever you need according to the time of day or night. It's a trendy place where the conversation gets more intellectual the later the evening.

Port of Antwerp. Although the Port of Antwerp is 88 kilometers (53 miles) from the sea, it is Europe's second largest port (after Rotterdam).

Giant locks facilitate navigation up the river Scheldt; the largest measures 550 yards by 75 yards. Every year, 100 million tons of goods are shipped here, serving a vast area stretching across half of Europe. Surprisingly, in the midst of all this hustle and bustle is a fishing village, Lillo, nestled among the enormous refineries, the tankers, and the buildings of the chemical industries. In Lillo, life continues as of old.

Provinciaal Diamantmuseum (Provincial Diamond Museum). This museum relates the history of the diamond trade in maps, models, and videos, and there's a complete 19th-century diamond workshop. Exceptional jewelry is displayed in the treasure room. ⊠ *Lange Herentalsestraat 31–33,* ☎ *03/231–8645.* ☑ *Free.* ☉ *Daily 10–5; demonstrations Sat. 2–5.*

NEED A
BREAK?

Beni Falafel (⊠ Lange Leemstraat 188, ☎ 03/218–8211) is a vegetarian snack bar in the heart of the Jewish quarter, where the ambience is at its greatest Thursday nights. In addition to falafel, the menu includes great soups, and there's take-out service. Beni closes for the Sabbath.

Provinciaal Museum voor Fotografie (Provincial Photography Museum). This collection celebrates the likes of Cartier-Bresson, William Klein, and Man Ray. There's also a display tracing the history of photography, from the "miragioscope" of the early 19th century to a James Bond camera disguised as a gun. Many consider this one of the world's leading photography museums. ⊠ *Waalse Kai 47,* ☎ *03/216–2211.* ☑ *Free.* ☉ *Tues.–Sun. 10–5.*

69 **Rockoxhuis.** This was the splendid Renaissance home of Rubens's friend and patron, Nicolaas Rockox, seven times mayor of Antwerp. A humanist and art collector, Rockox moved to this house in 1603. Two of the painter's works hang here. One is *Madonna and Child,* in fact a delicate portrait of his first wife, Isabella, and their son, Nicolaas; the other is a sketch for the *Crucifixion.* The collection also includes works by Van Dyck, Frans Snijders, Joachim Patinier, Jordaens, and David Teniers the Younger. The setting is important. Rather than being displayed on museum walls, the paintings are shown in the context of an upper-class Baroque home, furnished in the style of the period. A documentary video gives valuable information about Antwerp at that time. ⊠ *Keizerstraat 10,* ☎ *03/231–4710.* ☑ *Free.* ☉ *Tues.–Sun. 10–5.*

★ **75** **Rubenshuis.** A fabulous picture of the painter as patrician is presented here at Rubens's own house. Only the elaborate portico and temple, designed by Rubens in Italian Baroque style, were still standing three centuries after the house was built. Most of what we see is a reconstruction (completed in 1946), but from the master's own design. This was Rubens at the pinnacle of his fame. During this time he was appointed court painter to Archduke Albrecht and, with his wife, was sent on a diplomatic mission to Madrid, where he also painted some 40 portraits. He also conducted peace negotiations in London, on behalf of Philip IV of Spain. While in London he painted the ceiling of the Whitehall Banqueting Hall and was knighted by Charles I of Great Britain. The most evocative room in Rubens House is the huge studio. Drawings by Rubens and his pupils, as well as old prints, often re-create this room. In Rubens's day, visitors could view completed paintings and watch from the mezzanine, while Rubens and his students worked. Rubens completed about 2,500 paintings, nearly all characterized by the energy and exuberance that were his hallmark. A few Rubens paintings hang in the house, including a touching sketch in the studio of an Annunciation, and a self-portrait in the dining room. Unfortunately, his young widow promptly sold off some 300 pieces after

his death in 1640. ⊠ *Wapper 9,* ☎ *03/232–4747.* 🖾 *BF75.* ⊘
Tues.–Sun. 10–5.

⑦ St. Carolus Borromeus. A noted Jesuit church, St. Carolus Borromeus
also bears the imprint of Rubens. The front and tower are generally
attributed to him, and his hand can certainly be seen in the clustered
cherubim above the entrance. The church's facade suggests a richly decorated high altar, inviting the observer into the church. The interior
was once magnificent, but most of Rubens's frescoes were destroyed
by fire, and other works were carted off to Vienna when the Austrians banned the Jesuits. The square is one of the most attractive in
Antwerp, flanked by the harmonious Renaissance buildings of the Jesuit convent, now occupied by the City Library. ⊠ *Hendrik Conscienceplein 12,* ☎ *03/233–8433.* 🖾 *BF20.* ⊘ *Mon. and Wed.–Fri.
7:30–1, Sat. 7:30–noon and 3–6:15.*

NEED A
BREAK?

Het Elfde Gebod (⊠ Torfbrug 10) nestles under the cathedral. Its name
means the 11th Commandment. One of the most original of Antwerp's
many cafés, it is crammed with plaster saints and angels salvaged from
old churches. The beer is good, and you can have a pleasant meal of
bread and cheese.

⑥⑦ Steen. The Steen is 1,000 years old and looks it. A 9th-century fortress,
it was built to protect the western frontier of the Holy Roman Empire.
It was partially rebuilt 700 years later by Emperor Charles V. You can
distinguish the darker, medieval masonry extending midway up the walls,
from the lighter upper level of 16th-century work. The Steen was used
as a prison for centuries. Opposite the entrance is a cross where those
sentenced to death said their final prayers. It now houses the **National
Scheepvaartmuseum** (National Maritime Museum), where a large collection of models, figureheads, instruments, prints, and maps is on display. ⊠ *Steenplein,* ☎ *03/232–0850.* 🖾 *BF75.* ⊘ *Tues.–Sun. 10–5.*

The Steen is the only survivor of the original waterfront. Many houses
were torn down in the 19th century to make room for the wide,
straight quays that today are practically deserted, the port having
moved north of the city proper. The **Noorderterras,** a promenade starting at the Steen, is a popular place for a Sunday stroll along the Scheldt,
which here is 550 yards wide. "God gave us the river," say the Antwerpers, "and the river gave us all the rest."

★ **⑦ Vlaeykensgang.** A quiet cobblestone lane in the center of Antwerp, the
Vlaeykensgang seems untouched by time. The mood and style of the
16th century are perfectly preserved here. There is no better place to
linger on a Monday night when the carillon concert is peeling from the
cathedral. The alley ends in Pelgrimsstraat, where there is a great view
of the cathedral spire. **Jordaenshuis,** nearby, was the home of the painter
many saw as the successor of Rubens. It's a gem with many Baroque
touches—and with its very attractive courtyard rivals the Rubenshuis.
⊠ *Reyndersstraat 6,* ☎ *03/233–3033.* 🖾 *Free.* ⊘ *Tues.–Fri. 10–5.*

NEED A
BREAK?

De Groote Witte Arend (⊠ Leeuwenstraat 18), in another secret courtyard near the Jordaens house, is in a former convent. The background
music tends to be Vivaldi or Telemann and the menu lists 34 different
types of beer.

⑥⑧ Vleeshuis (Butchers' Hall). This remains one of the tallest buildings in
the Old City, even though it was completed in 1503. The designer was
Herman de Waghemakere, member of a family of architects who did
much to embellish their native city. The walls of Butchers' Hall were

built of alternating bands of brick and sandstone, creating an oddly pleasing layered effect. The ground floor was originally used as a meat market, while the upper floors were occupied by a banquet hall and council chambers. Today, most of the space is crammed with miscellaneous antiquities of local origin. ✉ *Vleeshouwersstraat 38–40,* ☎ *03/233–6404.* 🎫 *BF75.* ⏲ *Tues.–Sun. 10–5.*

The Vleehuis is the most prominent landmark of the Vleeshouwersstraat area, a residential neighborhood that has newly arisen in this historic district. Many ancient buildings remain, among them **De Spieghel** (The Mirror) off Oude Beurs at Spanjepandsteeg. Originally built for the archers' guild, it was bought in 1506 by Pieter Gillis, a leading humanist. At the beginning of his most famous work, Sir Thomas More describes how, on a visit to Antwerp, he is walking back from Mass in the cathedral with Gillis, when they encounter a traveler who tells them of his adventures on an island named Utopia. Erasmus, another friend of Gillis's, had the first edition of *Utopia* printed in Leuven.

(77) **Zoo.** The Antwerp Zoo houses its residents in style. Giraffes, ostriches, and African antelopes inhabit an Egyptian temple; a Moorish villa is home to the rhinoceroses; and a thriving okapi family grazes around an Indian temple. In part, this reflects the public's taste when the zoo was created 150 years ago. Today animals are allowed maximum space, and much research is devoted to endangered species. The zoo also has dolphin tanks, an aquarium, and a house for nocturnal animals. ✉ *Koningin Astridplein 26,* ☎ *03/231–1640.* 🎫 *BF425.* ⏲ *Daily 9–4:45 in winter, until 6:30 in summer.*

OFF THE BEATEN PATH

In **Berchem,** the 19th-century entrepreneur Baron Edouard Osy and his sister, Josephine Cogels, bought an old castle, demolished it, and built some refreshingly eccentric houses reflecting the eclectic tastes of that era. There are houses in Renaissance, Greek classical, and Venetian styles, but most of all, there are beautiful Art Nouveau buildings, especially at the southern end of Cogels Osylei and Waterloostraat. Berchem is southeast of the city center, the first stop on the line to Brussels. This is where international trains stop, rather than going into and backing out of Central Station.

Openluchtmuseum Middelheim (Middelheim Open Air Sculpture Museum) provides an excellent survey of three-dimensional art, from Rodin to the present. There are more than 300 sculptures in this very attractive setting, including ones by Henry Moore, Alexander Calder, and Zadkine. There is also a new pavilion that houses smaller or more fragile sculptures. Middelheim is just south of the city, above the tunnel for the expressway to Brussels. ✉ *Middelheimlaan 61,* ☎ *03/827–1534.* 🎫 *Free, except during special exhibitions.* ⏲ *Year-round Tues.–Sun. 10–sunset (5 PM in midwinter; 9 PM in summer).*

Dining

For dining price categories, *see* The Pleasures of Dining and Lodging at the beginning of this chapter.

$$$$ ★ ✕ **'t Fornuis.** In the heart of old Antwerp, this cozy restaurant, decorated in traditional Flemish style, serves some of the best food in the city, at the steepest prices. Barbary duck with peaches is one specialty, sweetbreads with wild mushrooms, another. ✉ *Reyndersstraat 24,* ☎ *03/233–9903. Reservations essential. Jacket and tie. AE, DC, MC, V. Closed weekends and 3 wks in Aug.*

$$$ ✕ **De Matelote.** In a house on a narrow street, this tiny bi-level restaurant has a mezzanine that is reached by a winding staircase. Chef Didier Garnich turns out such delicious creations as langoustines in a light curry sauce, sea scallops cooked with a stock of mushrooms and sorrel, and grilled asparagus with fresh morels and poached egg. The crème brûlée is outstanding. Local gourmets consider this the best seafood restaurant in town. ⊠ *Haarstraat 9,* ☎ *03/231–3207. Reservations essential. Jacket and tie. AE, DC, MC, V. Closed Sun., July.*

$$$ ✕ **Petrus.** Jean-Jacques De Busscher, the owner-chef, has named his small restaurant for Château Petrus, the prince of Pomerols (he sells the wine at about $400 a bottle). Serious wine lovers should visit the cellar, which stocks many great finds at much more affordable prices. The dining room has been completely redecorated. One specialty is a terrine of duck's liver interleaved with *filet d'Anvers* (lightly smoked beef). Sea scallops with deep-fried celery, sweetbreads on spicy bread, and gaspacho of fresh fruit are other current favorites. ⊠ *Kelderstraat 1,* ☎ *03/225–2734. Jacket and tie. AE, DC, MC, V. No lunch weekends. Closed Mon., 2 wks in July.*

$$ ✕ **Het Nieuwe Palinghuis.** This is an Antwerp landmark, with dark wood, pottery, and a comfortable relaxed air. Its seafood specialties—above all, its *paling* (eel)—are well prepared and reasonably priced. There's eel in green sauce, grilled turbot, grilled scallops, and sole in lobster sauce. ⊠ *Sint-Jansvliet 14,* ☎ *03/231–7445. AE, DC, MC, V. Closed Mon.–Tues. and June.*

$$ ✕ **Hungry Henrietta.** Father and son run this Antwerp institution, right next to the church of Sint-Jacob, where Rubens is buried. It's a stylish place, and quite large. In good weather you can dine in the garden. Filet of salmon with endives, quail salad, and leg of lamb are on the menu. ⊠ *Sint-Jacobsstraat 17,* ☎ *03/232–2928. AE, DC, MC, V. Closed weekends and Aug.*

$$ ✕ **In de Schaduw van de Kathedraal.** Cozier and more traditional than the wave of contemporary restaurants dominating the scene, it has a comfortable little dining room facing the cathedral square. In warm weather, you can dine on the terrace, in the shadow of the cathedral, the restaurant's namesake. Try the nutmeg-perfumed gratin of endive and *crevettes grises,* or steamed sole with scampi in fresh basil. ⊠ *Handschoenmarkt 17,* ☎ *03/232–4014. AE, DC, MC, V. Closed June–Sept., Tues.; Oct.–May, Mon.–Tues.*

$$ ✕ **Neuze Neuze.** Five tiny houses have been cobbled together to cre-
★ ate this handsome, split-level restaurant with plenty of nooks and crannies on different levels, whitewashed walls, dark brown beams, and a blazing fireplace. Warm smoked salmon with endive and a white beer sauce, scallops with rhubarb preserve, and goose liver meunière with caramelized pineapple are some of the dishes executed with the flair of pricier establishments. The genial patron, Domien Sels, is ever present. ⊠ *Wijngaardstraat 19,* ☎ *03/232–5783. AE, DC, MC, V. Closed Sun. and 3 wks in July.*

$$ ✕ **Sir Anthony Van Dijck.** Once one of Belgium's top gourmet restau-
★ rants, this dining spot is now a brasserie, serving fare such as salad liègeoise with smoked salmon and caramelized onions, duck à l'orange, and tuna steak. Diners sit under high, massive beams and stone pillars, surrounded by flowers and carved wood, at tables overlooking an interior courtyard. There are two seatings a night. ⊠ *Vlaykensgang, Oude Koornmarkt 16,* ☎ *03/231–6170. AE, DC, MC, V. Closed Sun., 1st 3 wks of Aug.*

$ ✕ **Kiekekot.** Antwerp students satisfy their craving for spit-roasted chicken and fries at this no-frills "chicken coop," which offers a juicy, golden half-chicken for little more than its retail price. ⊠ *Grote Markt*

35, ☎ *03/232–1502.* ⏱ *6 PM–4 AM (Fri.–Sat. till 6 AM). Reservations not accepted. No credit cards. Closed Tues.*

$ ✕ **Panaché.** This Antwerp institution, north of the Diamond District and close to Central Station, makes the best sandwiches in town. Good-value meals are served in the back room. ⊠ *Statiestraat 17,* ☎ *03/232–6905. Reservations not accepted. AE, DC, MC, V.*

$ ✕ **Rooden Hoed.** This atmospheric restaurant-tavern is pure Old Antwerp (the building itself dates from 1467), with high, dark wainscoting and plenty of pottery and knickknacks. Classic *cuisine bourgeoise* (country French) and Antwerp specialties are combined here—fish soup, sole, and mussels dominate. ⊠ *Oude Koornmarkt 25,* ☎ *03/233–2844. AE, MC, V. Closed Wed.–Thurs., mid-June–mid-July.*

$ ✕ **'t Brantyser.** This old café, with dark rafters, brick, and stucco, on two open levels, offers more than just drinks and the usual snacks: There are imaginative salads (endive with bacon and Roquefort), fish and meat dishes, and affordable specials. ⊠ *Hendrik Conscienceplein 7,* ☎ *03/233–1833. No credit cards. Closed Mon.*

$ ✕ **'t Hofke.** This restaurant is worth visiting for its location alone— it's in the Vlaeykensgang alley, where time seems to have stood still. The dining room has the look and feel of a private home, and the menu includes a large selection of inexpensive salads and omelettes, as well as more substantial fare. ⊠ *Oude Koornmarkt 16,* ☎ *03/233–8606. No credit cards. Closed Mon.*

$ ✕ **Ulcke van Zurich.** This trendy dinner spot occupies an old building where the young and young-at-heart enjoy chicken salad, spareribs, or chicken liver mousse with port, every night beginning at 6. It stays open late. ⊠ *Oude Beurs 50,* ☎ *03/234–0494. No credit cards.*

$ ✕ **Zuiderterras.** A stark, glass-and-black-metal construction, this riverside café and restaurant was designed by avant-garde architect bOb (his spelling) Van Reeth. Here you can have a light meal for about $15 and enjoy seeing the river traffic on one side and, on the other, a view of the cathedral and the Old Town. ⊠ *Ernest Van Dijckkaai,* ☎ *03/234–1275. Reservations not accepted. AE, DC, MC, V.*

Lodging

For lodging price categories, *see* The Pleasures of Dining and Lodging at the beginning of this chapter.

$$$$ ✕▥ **Antwerp Hilton.** Antwerp's newest luxury hotel, a five-story complex opened in 1993, incorporates the former fin de siècle Grand Bazaar department store and a gigantic ballroom seating 1,000. Rooms have mahogany doors, three telephones, safes, and executive desks. Afternoon tea is served in the marble-floored lobby, and lunch and dinner are offered in the redecorated and upgraded restaurant, Het Vijfde Seizoen. ⊠ *Groenplaats,* ☎ *03/204–1212,* ℻ *03/204–1213. 211 rooms. 2 restaurants, bar, no-smoking floors, sauna, health club, convention center, shops, parking (fee). AE, DC, MC, V.*

$$$ ✕▥ **Classic Hotel Villa Mozart.** This small, modern hotel in an old building is centrally located in a pedestrian area, next to the cathedral. The totally refurbished interior is modern, with the emphasis on business-class comforts: air-conditioning, electronic security. The rooms are slightly cramped—due, in part, to the generous beds—but many look out toward the cathedral. ⊠ *Handschoenmarkt 3–7,* ☎ *03/231–3031,* ℻ *03/231–5685. 25 rooms with bath. Restaurant, bar. AE, DC, MC, V.*

$$$$ ▥ **De Rosier.** Leaving would-be competitors in the deluxe market be- ★ hind by several laps, this is the only choice in town for luxury on an intimate scale. Cloistered behind double doors, this lovely hotel is nearly invisible from the narrow back street it faces, focusing inward, instead, on an aristocratic garden court. Its interior is sumptuously furnished. Downstairs, guests move freely from Louis XV to Empire to Victorian chinoiserie; rooms upstairs vary from skylighted, modernized garrets to the beamed-and-leaded-glass suite in pure Old Antwerp style, which has been favored by the likes of Madonna and Marlene Dietrich. The mansion dates from 1627. ⌧ *Rosier 21–23,* ☎ *03/225–0140,* ⅨⅩ *03/231–4111. 12 rooms with bath. Breakfast room, indoor pool. AE, DC, MC, V.*

$$$ ⊞ **Firean.** This Art Deco gem, built in 1929, was restored in 1986, not
★ only to its original architectural style but also to the welcoming grace of its era. It offers sweet relief to travelers benumbed by the uniformity of chain hotels. Its location—a residential neighborhood south of the center but on the route into town from the Brussels expressway—reinforces the tranquillity inside, expressed by fresh flowers, rich fabrics, and a tasteful mix of antiques and reproductions. The service is that of a family-owned and -operated establishment. Breakfast eggs come in floral-print cozies, and jazz piano is discreetly piped into public areas. The rooms themselves are quiet sanctuaries. A tram to the Old Town stops outside the door. ⌧ *Karel Oomsstraat 6,* ☎ *03/237–0260,* ⅨⅩ *03/238–1168. 11 rooms, 6 in annex next door, all with bath. Bar, breakfast room. AE, DC, MC, V. Closed ½ half of Aug., Dec. 24–1st weekend after Jan. 6.*

$$ ⊞ **Prinse.** Set well back from an Old Town street, this 400-year-old landmark with an interior courtyard opened as a hotel in 1990. It was once the home of 16th-century poet Anna Bijns. A member of the Relais du Silence (Quiet Inns) group, the hotel has a modern look, with black leather chairs, soft blue curtains, and tiled baths. Exposed beams give top-floor rooms more character. ⌧ *Keizerstraat 63,* ☎ *03/226–4050,* ⅨⅩ *03/225–1148. 30 rooms with bath. Breakfast room. AE, DC, MC, V.*

$ ⊞ **Pension Cammerpoorte.** Owned by the managers of the nearby Cammerpoorte Hotel, this small pension has been scrubbed and decorated with enthusiasm by its proud proprietor. Breakfast is served in a tidy brick-and-lace café downstairs. Rooms—on landings reached by a narrow staircase—are full of bright pastels and sad-clown art. ⌧ *Steenhouwersvest 55,* ☎ *03/231–2836,* ⅨⅩ *03/226–2968. 9 rooms with shower. Breakfast room. AE, DC, MC, V.*

$ ⊞ **Rubenshof.** Once a cardinal's residence, this hotel shows remnants of its former glory with a mixture of turn-of-the-century styles. Rooms were recently freshened, and the facade given a new coat of paint. The hotel is owned by a friendly Dutch couple, and the location is close to the Fine Arts Museum. ⌧ *Amerikalei 115-117,* ☎ *03/237–0789,* ⅨⅩ *03/248–2594. 24 rooms, 3 with bath. Breakfast room, free parking. AE, DC, MC, V.*

$ ⊞ **Scoutel.** This hotel, owned by the Boy Scouts but open to all ages and both sexes, is in a modern building five minutes' walk from Central Station. The double and triple rooms are simple but adequate; all have toilets and showers. Rates are lower for those under 25, and most of the guests *are* young people. Breakfast and sheets are included; towels can be rented. Guests are provided with front-door keys. ⌧ *Stoomstraat 3,* ☎ *03/226–4606,* ⅨⅩ *03/232–6392. 24 rooms with shower. Breakfast room, meeting room. No credit cards.*

Nightlife and the Arts

Nightlife

BARS

There are 2,500 taverns in Antwerp—one per 200 inhabitants. Many are in the Old Town. The most famous is probably the **Bierhuis Kul-**

minator (⊠ Vleminckveld 32–34, ☏ 03/232–4538), which stocks, cools, and pours 550 different kinds of beer, including EKU-28, the strongest beer on earth. **Pelgrom** (⊠ Pelgrimsstraat 15, ☏ 03/234–0809) is in a 16th-century tavern. **De Engel** (⊠ Grote Markt 3, ☏ 03/233–1252) is an ordinary café but the most popular in town. In **Blauwe Steen** (⊠ Ernest van Dijckkaai 34, ☏ 03/231–6710), you can listen to street musicians performing Antwerp music while you sip beer. **Beveren** (⊠ Vlasmarkt 2, ☏ 03/231–2225) is an old-fashioned café. **Il Mondo** (⊠ Grote Pieter Pot 6, no phone) is small and caters to the fashionable. **Het Spiegelbeeld** (⊠ Next to Il Mondo, ☏ 03/225–3010) is large and unpretentious.

DISCOS
Among the best-known is **Café Locale** (⊠ Waalsekaai 25, ☏ 03/238–5004) in the museum area south of the Old Town. At the **Café d'Anvers,** in the red-light district (⊠ Verversrui 15, ☏ 03/226–3870), the music is as mixed as the clientele. Other discos of note are **Prestige** (⊠ Anneessensstraat 18, ☏ 03/225–1717) and **New Casino** (⊠ Kloosterstraat 70, ☏ 03/237–8846). Check opening hours.

GAY BARS
These include **Oscar Wilde** (⊠ Van Schoonhovestraat 84, ☏ 03/226–1118) and **Marcus Antonius** (⊠ Van Schoonhovestraat 82, ☏ 03/231–4384) for gay men. For lesbians, there are **Shakespeare** (⊠ Oude Koornmarkt 24, ☏ 03/231–5058) and **Lady's Pub** (⊠ Waalsekaai 56, ☏ 03/238–5490).

JAZZ CLUBS
There isn't live music every night in these clubs, so check beforehand. Try **Swingcafé** (⊠ Suikerrui 13, ☏ 03/233–1478), **De Muze** (⊠ Melkmarkt 15, ☏ 03/226–0126), or **De Hopper** (⊠ Leopold De Waelstraat 2, ☏ 03/248–4933).

The Arts
Check *The Bulletin* for details on arts events in Antwerp.

Antwerp has acquired a reputation for innovative and exciting ballet, and its school is internationally renowned. The principal company is the **Koninklijk Ballet van Vlaanderen** (⊠ Royal Flanders Ballet, Britselei 80, ☏ 03/234–3438). The opera is **Koninklijke Vlaamse Opera** (⊠ Royal Flanders Opera, Frankrijklei 3, ☏ 03/233–6685).

The **Koninklijk Philharmonisch Orkest van Vlaanderen** (Royal Flanders Philharmonic) most frequently performs at **De Singel** (⊠ Desguinlei 25, ☏ 03/248–3800). Another venue for classical music is the **Koningin Elisabethzaal** (⊠ Koningin Astridplein 23, ☏ 03/233–8444). Visiting rock musicians perform at the Koningin Elisabethzaal and at the **Sportpaleis** (⊠ Schijnpoortweg 113, ☏ 03/326–1010).

The flagship of the more than two dozen theaters in Antwerp is the **Bourla Theater** (⊠ Komedieplaats, ☏ 03/231–0750), a marvelously restored 150-year-old theater, which is now the home of the **Koninklijke Nederlands Schouwburg** (Royal Dutch-Speaking Theater). Two other important theaters are **Vrije Val** (⊠ Namenstraat 7) and **Monty** (⊠ Montignystraat 3–5). The **Poppenschouwburg Van Campen** (⊠ Van Campen Puppet Theater, Lange Nieuwstraat 3, ☏ 03/237–3716) presents traditional puppet performances in Flemish dialect.

Outdoor Activities and Sports
Golf
The **Brasschaat Open Golf Club Center** (⊠ Miksebaan 248, Brasschaat, ☏ 03/653–1048) is 15 kilometers (9 miles) from the city center.

Skating

Two popular skating rinks are **Antarctica** (⊠ Moerelei 119, Wilrijk, ☎ 03/828–9928) and **Zondal** (⊠ Ruggeveldlaan 488B, Deurne, ☎ 03/325–0374).

Tennis

Courts at **Het Rooi** (⊠ Berchemstadionstraat 73, ☎ 03/239–6610) are available for BF200–BF300 per hour. Rates at **Beerschot** (⊠ Stadionstraat, ☎ 03/220–8687) are BF150 an hour. Try to book courts for as early in the day as you can.

Shopping

Antwerp takes pride in being young, with-it, and trendy, and this is reflected in the city's smart shops and boutiques.

Shopping Streets

The elegant **Meir,** together with its extension to the east, **De Keyserlei,** and at the opposite end, **Huidevettersstraat,** is where you will find the fashionable and long-established shops. Shopping galleries branch off from all three streets—**Century Center** and **Antwerp Tower** from De Keyserlei, **Patio** from Meir, and **Nieuwe Gaanderij** from Huidevettersstraat.

The boutiques along pedestrian malls often cater to more avant-garde tastes. The best-known area is **De Wilde Zee,** consisting of Groendalstraat, Wiegstraat, and Korte Gasthuisstraat. Another pedestrian area is **Hoogstraat,** between Grote Markt and Sint-Jansvliet, with its appendix, **Grote Pieter Potstraat.** Here you find good secondhand bookshops and all kinds of bric-a-brac.

Street Markets

Public auction sales of furniture and other secondhand goods are held on **Vrijdagmarkt** (Wednesday and Friday 9–noon). There's an antiques market on **Lijnwaadmarkt** (Easter–October, Saturday 9–5), just north of the cathedral. Antwerp's most popular and animated market is **Vogelmarkt** (the bird market, Sunday 9–1). On Oudevaartplaats (a block south from Rubenshuis on Wapper), the market also includes flowers and plants, fruit and vegetables, and lots of pets.

The **Rubensmarkt** (Rubens Market, August 15 annually) is held on the Grote Markt, with vendors in 17th-century costumes hawking everything under the sun.

Specialty Stores

CLOTHING

A group of fashion designers collectively known as the Antwerp Six has been making waves internationally with women's and, increasingly, men's ready-to-wear fashions. Two of them, Ann Demeulemeester and Dirk Bikkenbergs, are represented at **Louis** (⊠ Lombardenstraat 2, ☎ 03/232–9872). **Dries Van Nooten** has his own beautiful new boutique (⊠ Kammenstraat 18, ☎ 03/233–3419). Other leading fashion boutiques are **Modepaleis** (⊠ Nationalestraat 16, ☎ 03/233–9437) and **Closing Date** (⊠ Korte Gasthuisstraat 15, ☎ 03/232–8722).

DIAMONDS

Diamonds are tax-free and available at good prices to both individual customers as well as the many dealers who come to Antwerp for them. (Note: Tax-free does not mean duty-free when you return home.) If you are not an expert, you can rely on the advice given by the staff at **Diamondland** (⊠ Appelmansstraat 33A, ☎ 03/243–3612). The quality of the stones is guaranteed by a Diamond High Council certificate.

GIFTS

Calico House (✉ Zand 1, ☎ 03/233–6023) specializes in quilts and patchwork. **Extra Large** (✉ Oude Beurs 30, ☎ 03/232–9841) is a place for oversize, fun gifts.

Antwerp A to Z

Arriving and Departing

BY CAR

Antwerp is surrounded by a ring road from which expressways shoot off like spokes in a wheel. The city is 48 kilometers (29 miles) north of Brussels on the E19; 60 kilometers (36 miles) northwest of Ghent on the E17; 119 kilometers (71 miles) northwest of Liège on the A13.

BY PLANE

Deurne Airport (☎ 03/218–1211), 5½ kilometers (3 miles) from the city center, has several flights a day from London. **Brussels National Airport** (Zaventem) is linked with Antwerp by frequent bus service (hourly 7 AM–11 PM). The trip takes 50 minutes and costs BF250.

BY TRAIN

There are four to five trains an hour from Brussels, and the trip takes about 45 minutes. The train ride north to Rotterdam takes an hour. International Intercity trains between Paris and Amsterdam stop at Berchem Station south of the city center rather than entering the downtown Central Station (✉ Koningin Astridplein, ☎ 03/233–3915).

Getting Around

BY BUS

Municipal bus lines (☎ 03/218–1411) mostly begin outside Central Station in the Koningin Astridplein. Longer-distance buses start from the Franklin Rooseveltplaats.

BY TAXI

There are taxi stands in front of Central Station and at other principal points. It is often easier to call for one: Antwerp Taxi (☎ 03/238–3838), ATM (☎ 03/216–0160), or Metropole Taxi (☎ 03/231–3131).

BY TRAM AND SUBWAY

You can travel by tram all over central Antwerp. Some operate underground as the pre-Metro system. The most useful subway line for visitors links Central Station (Metro: Diamant) with the left bank via the Groenplaats (for the cathedral and Grote Markt). A BF40 ticket is good for one hour on all forms of public transport; BF105 buys unlimited travel for one day. Tickets are available at De Lijn offices (☎ 03/218–1411), the tourist office, and at the Diamant, Opera/Frankrijklei, and Groenplaats Metro stops.

Contacts and Resources

B&B RESERVATION AGENCIES

The City Tourist Office (✉ Grote Markt 15, ☎ 03/232–0103, FAX 03/231–1937) has made an inventory of bed-and-breakfast accommodations and short-listed the 25 best, with photographs, giving you a chance to pick the type of home where you'll feel most comfortable and an opportunity to learn something in advance about your hosts.

CAR RENTALS

Avis (✉ Plantin en Moretuslei 62, ☎ 03/218–9496). **Budget** (✉ Frankrijklei 70, ☎ 03/232–3500). **Hertz** (✉ Mechelsesteenweg 43, ☎ 03/233–2992).

Police (☎ 101). **Ambulance** (☎ 100). **Emergency Rooms:** Middelheim (⊠ Lindendreef 1, ☎ 03/280–3111); Stuivenberg (⊠ Lange Beeldekensstraat 267, ☎ 03/217–7111).

Touristram (☎ 03/480–9388) operates 50-minute tram tours with cassette commentary in the Old Town and old harbor area. Tickets (BF125) are sold on the tram. Departure is from Groenplaats every hour on the hour from 11 to 5, daily April–December; January–February, weekdays 1–5, weekends 11–5.

Qualified **personal guides** are available through the City Tourist Office, which requires two days' notice. The rates are BF1,200 for two hours and BF600 for each additional hour.

Flandria (☎ 03/231–3100) operates 50-minute boat trips on the river Scheldt, departing from the Steenplein pontoon (next to the Steen) daily every hour on the hour, 10–4, Easter–September (BF240), as well as boat tours of the port (2½ hours), which leave from Quay 13 near Londonstraat, May–August, daily 10:30 and 2:30; Easter–April and September, Sunday and bank holidays only (BF375).

The name of the pharmacy on night and weekend duty is displayed in all pharmacy windows.

American Express (⊠ Frankrijklei 21, ☎ 03/232–5920). **VTB** (⊠ Sint-Jacobsmarkt 45, ☎ 03/220–3232). **Huybrechts** (⊠ Carnotstraat 41, ☎ 03/231–9900).

The **Toerisme Stad Antwerpen** (Antwerp City Tourist Office; ⊠ Grote Markt 15, ☎ 03/232–0103, ℻ 03/231–1937), in the heart of the Old Town, is open Monday through Saturday 9–6 and Sunday 9–5. It will assist with hotel reservations. The **Toeristische Federatie Provincie Antwerpen** (Antwerp Provincial Tourist Office; ⊠ Karel Oomsstraat 11, ☎ 03/216–2810) will help plan trips throughout the province.

EXCURSION FROM ANTWERP

The northeast quarter of Belgium, composed of the provinces of Antwerp and Limburg, is not so frequently visited by travelers from abroad but is much loved by Belgians. It stretches from the sandy moors of Kempen (La Campine to French-speakers) in the north to the fertile plains of Haspengouw (La Hesbaye), with its prosperous-looking farms, orchards, and undulating fields. On the east, it borders the narrow Dutch corridor stretching south to Maastricht.

Until fairly recently, Limburg's economy was linked to its coalfields. Today it's the explosive growth of small businesses that has restored the province to a degree of prosperity. The economy also benefits from the Albert Canal, which leaves the Meuse just north of Liège to follow a course parallel to the river, and then veers off across the country to carry the heavy Liège traffic to Antwerp. Thanks to the canal, Genk is a center for the automotive and petrochemical industries. In spite of the presence of industry both light and heavy, this is a green and pleasant land.

Numbers in the margin correspond to points of interest on the Excursion from Antwerp map.

Kalmthout

18 km (11 mi) north of Antwerp on N11/N122 via Kapellen.

The **Kalmthoutse Heide** (heath) is a vast area of pines, sand dunes, and ponds, with flourishing bird life. The heath is crossed by marked paths. The **Arboretum** contains more than 6,000 trees in a 25-acre park, where you can wander freely across the lawns. It's a peaceful oasis with a varied range of colors every season, the presence of wild flowers providing a special accent. ⊠ *Heuvel 2,* ☎ *03/666–6741.* 🎫 *BF100.* ☉ *Mar. 15–Nov. 15, daily 10–5.*

Lier

★ **⑦** *17 km (10 mi) southeast of Antwerp on N10, 45 km (27 mi) northeast of Brussels on E19/N14 via Mechelen.*

The small town of Lier may seem a sleepy riverside town, but it has long attracted poets and painters and has even known its moment of glory. It was here in 1496 that Philip the Handsome of Burgundy married Joanna the Mad of Aragon and Castile, daughter of King Ferdinand and Queen Isabella of Spain. From that union sprang Emperor Charles V and his brother and successor as Holy Roman Emperor, the equally remarkable Ferdinand I of Austria.

The **Sint-Gummaruskerk (St. Gommaire's Church),** where they were wed, is yet another product of the De Waghemakere–Keldermans partnership, which worked so well in building the cathedral in Antwerp. It is well endowed with stained-glass windows from the 15th and 16th centuries, including those in the choir. They were the gift of Maximilian of Austria (father of Philip the Handsome), who visited in 1516 and is depicted in one of the windows, along with his wife, Mary of Burgundy.

The Kleine Nete flows straight through the heart of town; the Grote Nete and a canal encircle the center. Along the riverside, willows bend over the water, and across the river stands the **Zimmertoren,** a 14th-century tower renamed for Louis Zimmer, who designed its astronomical clock with 11 faces in 1930. His studio, where 57 dials show the movements of the moon, the tides, the zodiac, and other cosmic phenomena, is inside the tower. ⊠ *Zimmerplein 18,* ☎ *03/489–1111.* 🎫 *BF40.* ☉ *Daily 9–noon and 1–7 (in winter until 5).*

NEED A BREAK? **Van Ouytsels Koffiehoekje** (⊠ Rechtestraat 27, ☎ 03/480–2917) still roasts its own coffee. Don't pass up the delicious syrup-filled biscuits, *Lierse Vlaaikens,* which are the local specialty.

The **Begijnhof** (Béguinage) differs from most other Beguine communities in that its small houses line narrow streets rather than being grouped around a common. A Renaissance portico stands at the entrance, and on it a statue of St. Begge, who gave his name to this congregation and who probably derived his own from the fact that he was *un begue* (a stammerer). Beguines were members of ascetic or philanthropic communities of women, not under vows, founded in the Netherlands in the 13th century. ⊠ *Begijnhofstraat.*

Dining

$$ ✕ **'t Suyckeren Schip.** Just across from the church, this restaurant offers *cuisine bourgeoise* (French country): steaks with a variety of sauces, and five different preparations of sole. The setting has an informal, comfortable, brick-and-beams look. Sunday crowds come after church. ⊠ *Rechtestraat 49,* ☎ *03/489–0140. AE, DC, MC, V.*

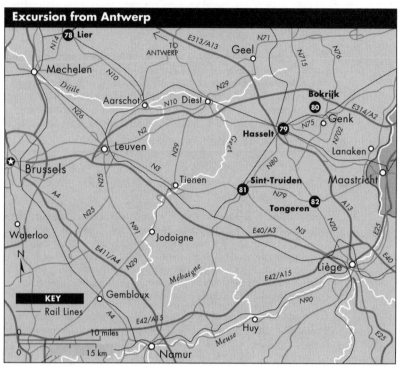

Excursion from Antwerp

$ ✕ **De Fortuin.** This is a tavern and restaurant, the former quite a bit cheaper. Shrimp croquettes are a specialty, and the service is friendly. In the summer you can eat on the terrace overlooking the river. ⊠ *Felix Timmermansplein 7,* ☎ *03/480–2951. No credit cards. Closed Mon.*

Hasselt

🟡 *77 km (46 mi) southeast of Antwerp, 82 km (49 mi) east of Brussels, 42 km (25 mi) northwest of Liège.*

Limburg has the youngest population in Belgium, and it is the province where the rate of development is fastest. This is particularly noticeable in Hasselt, a town with busy shopping streets, innovative museums, and lively music.

The **Nationaal Jenevermuseum** perpetuates Hasselt's slightly raffish distinction of having had gin distilling as its major industry. The museum dates from 1803 and is, in fact, one of the country's oldest surviving distilleries. *Jenever* means "gin" in Dutch, and a tour of the installations, which include changing exhibits, such as vintage gin advertisement posters, ends in the paneled tasting room. You can taste gin of various ages, flavors, and proofs from two dozen Belgian distilleries. ⊠ *Witte Nonnenstraat 19,* ☎ *011/241144.* 🎟 *BF90.* ☉ *Tues.–Sun. 10–5, weekends 2–6.*

Stadsmuseum Stellingwerf-Waerdenhof (Municipal Museum) is a strikingly modern space with white walls, red balconies, and large mirrors, installed in two beautifully converted mansions. Its collection consists of dramatically arranged Art Nouveau ceramics, church silverware (including the world's oldest monstrance, from 1286), and exhibits illustrating the history of the region. ⊠ *Maastrichterstraat 85,* ☎ *011/ 241070.* 🎟 *BF90.* ☉ *Tues.–Fri. 10–5, weekends 2–6.*

The third among Hasselt's unusual museums is the **Modemuseum** (Fashion Museum), installed in a 17th-century hospital building. The collection illustrates the development of fashion trends over the past two centuries. Today's fashion photographers, stylists, and designers of accessories are also represented. ✉ *Gasthuisstraat 11,* ☎ *011/239621.* ✍ *BF90.* ☉ *Tues.–Sun. 10–5, weekends 2–6.*

NEED A
BREAK?
't Stokerijke (✉ Hemelrijk 3) is where you can continue your education in Dutch gin—the owner is an expert. This is a convivial and attractive place, just behind the cathedral.

Japanse Tuin (Japanese Garden) is an exquisite gift from the Japanese city of Itami, Hasselt's twin city. The 6-acre park is one of great beauty and subtlety, with rocks, ponds, cherry trees, and 1,000 irises. There's also a Japanese teahouse. ✉ *Kapemolenpark,* ☎ *011/239544.* ✍ *BF100.* ☉ *Apr.–Oct., Tues.–Fri. 10–5, weekends 2–6.*

★ ⑳ **Bokrijk** is arguably the best and certainly the largest (1,360 acres) open-air museum and nature reserve in Europe. The museum, more than 90 acres in size, has more than 100 carefully restored buildings forming four small villages. There's also a small 16th-century urban area. The farm buildings have been transplanted from Limburg and other Flemish provinces. Each building has its own custodian, many of whom are gold mines of local folklore. The interiors are filled with old peasant furniture and utensils. There's a chapel, a windmill, a forge, and an inn, where you can enjoy traditional fare, such as spicy sausages, smoked ham, rich cheeses, and red Rodenbach beer. There's a full complement of artisans, at work in original costumes; a large playground with a children's village, chutes, pony rides, and other attractions; and a sports center with tennis courts, miniature golf, and even a soccer field.

The nature reserve shows the unspoiled Kempen country of heather and pine, sand and broom, with marshes and ponds frequented by waterfowl. Bokrijk is 6 kilometers (4 miles) northeast of Hasselt. ✉ *Domein Bokrijk, Genk,* ☎ *011/224575.* ✍ *Open-air museum BF250 (Apr.–June and Sept., Sun. and public holidays; July–Aug., daily), when 33 farmsteads are open and at least 10 craftsmen on duty; BF200 on "green days" (Apr.–June and Sept., Mon.–Sat.), when 22 farmsteads are open and at least 5 craftsmen on duty; BF100 on "blue days" (Oct., daily), when just a few cottages are open. Nature reserve free.* ☉ *Museum Apr.–Oct., daily 10–sunset; cottages close at 6 (5 in Oct.).*

Dining and Lodging

$ ✕ **De Egge.** This charming little one-horse restaurant offers the best efforts of a young couple who believe in their excellent taste: The decor is pretty and discreet, with whitewashed brick and café curtains, and the cooking is imaginative and beautifully executed. Try monkfish on a bed of leeks, or goat cheese brushed with honey and fresh thyme and served hot on a bed of julienne of apple, endive, and *mâche* (lamb's lettuce). ✉ *Walputstraat 23,* ☎ *011/224951. AE, DC, MC, V. Closed Thurs.*

$ ✕ **Majestic.** This big, leaded-glass tavern with high ceilings on the Grote Markt has a grand, historic feel. It draws locals for drinks, cards, snacks, and light meals: sandwiches, trout, steak, and an inexpensive menu of the day. ✉ *Grote Markt,* ☎ *011/223330. AE, DC, MC, V.*

$$$$ ✕🏠 **Scholteshof.** Owner-chef Roger Souvereyns created a mecca for
★ many a Belgian and foreign gourmet on his 18th-century farm 7 kilo-

meters (4 miles) west of Hasselt. He keeps adding new touches, his most recent being a beautiful fountain in the interior courtyard, where you can enjoy cocktails. There's also a sculpture-filled English garden and an extensive herb garden. A meal in the candlelit dining room is a romantic and relaxing experience; the imaginative menu includes such tempting creations as pumpkin soup with langoustines, carpaccio with a ball of caviar on green tomato jelly, sweetbreads roasted with rosemary, and grilled turbot with rhubarb mousse. For many, eating here is a once-in-a-lifetime experience; the checks are staggeringly high. Rooms are spacious and furnished with magnificent antiques. ⊠ *Kermtstraat 130, Stevoort,* ☎ *011/250202,* FAX *011/254328. 11 rooms, 7 suites. Reservations essential. Jacket and tie. AE, DC, MC, V. Closed Wed., 2 wks in Jan., 2 wks in July.*

$$ ✕▥ **Holiday Inn Hasselt.** Completed in 1990, this has become Hasselt's hotel of choice. Centrally located, it has been built to the same standards as apply to the chain worldwide. The design is post–Art Deco and the house color a light oyster gray. ⊠ *Kattegatstraat 1,* ☎ *011/242200,* FAX *011/223935. 107 rooms with bath. Restaurant, bar, pool. AE, DC, MC, V.*

Outdoor Activities and Sports

GOLF

There are excellent facilities at the **Vlaams-Japanese Golf & Business Club** (⊠ Vissenbroekstraat 15, ☎ 011/223793). Although the 18-hole course is for members only, the 9-hole training course is open to the public.

Sint-Truiden

⑧ *17 km (10 mi) southwest of Hasselt, 94 km (56 mi) southeast of Antwerp, 63 km (38 mi) east of Brussels, 35 km (21 mi) northwest of Liège.*

All around Sint-Truiden (Saint-Trond) thousands upon thousands of trees are in bloom in the spring, for this is the center of Haspengouw, the fruit-growing district. The town developed around the abbey founded by St. Trudo in the 7th century. The **Begijnhof** (Beguinage), dating from 1258, has a well-restored church, from the end of the 13th century. It is now the **Provinciaal Museum voor Religieuze Kunst** (Provincial Museum of Religious Art) and is known for its 38 frescoes, executed over four centuries. ⊠ *Begijnhof, off Speelhoflaan,* ☎ *011/691188.* ☜ *Free.* ☉ *Apr.–Oct., Tues.–Fri. 10–noon and 1:30–5, weekends 1:30–5.*

At the **Festraets Studio,** also in the Begijnhof, you can see the astronomical compensation clock, constructed by Camille Festraets out of 20,000 mechanical parts. It is more than 6 feet tall and weighs more than 4 tons. ⊠ *Begijnhof 24,* ☎ *011/686255.* ☜ *BF60.* ☉ *Visits Mar.–Oct., Tues.–Sun. at 3:45 and 4:45.*

Lace-making has been revived in Sint-Truiden over the past few decades with a great deal of originality. The results can be seen at the **Kantmuseum** (Lace Museum) in the school of the Ursuline Sisters. ⊠ *Naamse Straat 5,* ☎ *011/682356.* ☜ *BF30.* ☉ *Sun. and bank holidays 2–5.*

The **Sint-Gangulfskerk** (St. Gangulphe's Church) is worth the small detour to Diesterstraat. It is one of the few remaining Romanesque basilicas from the 11th century and has been carefully restored.

The **Sint-Leonarduskerk** (St. Leonard's Church) in Zoutleeuw, west of Sint-Truiden, dates from the 13th century and seems out of proportion for the town's current size. The church's great treasure is a tall paschal candlestick incorporating a Crucifixion scene, made by Renier van Thienen in 1453 and considered one of the finest brasswork pieces in Belgium. ☉ *Mon.–Sat. 9:30–noon and 1:30–6, Sun. 1:30–5 (winter Sun. 1:30–4).*

Dining and Lodging

$$$ ✕ **De Fakkels.** In an extravagantly decorated 19th-century town house, with tapestries, carved wood, leaded glass, and terrazzo floors, this ambitious restaurant offers well-executed French cooking: *pot-au-feu de St-Pierre aux raviolis de langoustines* (stew with lobster ravioli), sweetbreads on a bed of zucchini and mushrooms. ⊠ *Stationstraat 33,* ☎ *011/687634. AE, DC, MC, V. No dinner Sun. Closed Mon., last wk of Jan., 2nd ½ of Aug.*

$ ✕ **Century.** A classic old tavern/restaurant on the Grote Markt, with oak, green-velvet banquettes, and great windows framing the market scene, this simple spot is as comfortable for a drink as for a meal. Typical "snacks" include half a roasted chicken with fries and salad, omelettes, steaks, sole, and sandwiches. ⊠ *Grote Markt 5,* ☎ *011/688341. AE, DC, MC, V. No dinner Tues.*

$$ ✕▥ **Regency.** Expanded and renovated from its origins as an early 19th-century town house, this city hotel offers two styles: graceful old rooms with high, molded ceilings, and modern ones in the new wing. It's on a quiet street, close to the city center. ⊠ *Schepen Dejongstraat 43,* ☎ *011/684881. 30 rooms with bath. Restaurant, bar. AE, DC, MC, V.*

Tongeren

㊷ *20 km (12 mi) east of Sint-Truiden, 20 km (12 mi) southeast of Hasselt, 87 km (52 mi) east of Brussels, 19 km (11 mi) northwest of Liège.*

Tongeren (Tongres) started life as a Roman army encampment. It is one of Belgium's two oldest cities (the other being Tournai). This is where Ambiorix scored a famous but short-lived victory over Julius Caesar's legions in 54 BC. The Roman city was considerably larger than the present one; over the centuries, it was repeatedly sacked and burned. By the end of the 13th century, the city had retreated within its present limits and enjoyed the occasionally burdensome protection of the prince bishops of Liège. The Moerenpoort gate and sections of the ramparts remain from that period.

★ The **Onze-Lieve-Vrouwebasiliek** (Basilica of Our Lady) is one of the most beautiful Gothic monuments in the world. The original church was built on Roman foundations in the 4th century and was the first stone cathedral north of the Alps. After it was destroyed during a siege in 1213, construction of the Basilica began, taking three centuries to complete. The 12th-century Romanesque cloister of the original church is still intact. The Chapter House contains the Treasury, also known as the **Basilica Museum Tongeren.** This is the richest collection of religious art in the country, including a 6th-century ivory diptych of St. Paul, a Merovingian gold buckle from the same century, and a truly magnificent head of Christ sculpted in wood in the 11th century. The central nave, up to the pulpit, the choir, and the south transept, dates from 1240. The candlesticks and lectern, from 1372, are the work of Jehan de Dinant, one of the outstanding artists of metalworking who flourished in the cities of the Meuse valley. The basilica has excellent acoustics and is often used for symphony concerts. ⊠ *Grote Markt. Basilica Museum:* ☎ *012/390255.* ▱ *BF80.* ☉ *May–Sept., Tues.–Sun. 10–noon and 1:30–5; Oct.–Apr., by appointment.*

NEED A
BREAK? **De Pelgrim** (✉ Brouwerstraat 9, ☎ 012/238322) is an old-fashioned tavern, open late, that serves light and simple meals such as *omelette paysanne* (country omelette).

Gallo-Romeins Museum (Gallo-Roman Museum) is a fresh breath of air in the museum world, as different from dusty collections of ancient bric-a-brac as you can imagine. Opened in 1994, it displays objects in the same way they were found, allowing visitors to discover them in much the same way as they were discovered by archaeologists. The subterranean amphitheater uses visual and sound effects conceived by Stijn Coninx (director of the cult film *Daens*). The symbol of the exposition is a 12-faceted ball—several such objects have been found, and nobody knows what they represent or were used for. There's also an audiovisual space and a cafeteria. ✉ *Kielenstraat 15*, ☎ *012/233914.* 🎟 *BF200.* 🕙 *Mon. noon–6; Tues., Fri., and weekends 10–6; Wed.–Thurs. 10–9.*

Dining and Lodging

$$$$ ✕🛏 **Clos St. Denis.** This enormous 17th-century farmhouse with at-
★ tached barns has been completely restored as a fresh, elegant country inn, and one of Belgium's top restaurants. Chef Christian Denis serves extravagant fare: lobster tartare with chives; gratin of oysters in champagne and caviar; ravioli of *foie d'oie* (goose liver) in truffle cream. There's choucroute with suckling pig and mustard as well. Four dining rooms outdo each other for period luxury—burnished parquet, Persian runners, chinoiserie. ✉ *Grimmertingenstraat 24, Vliermaal-Kortessem*, ☎ *012/236096. Reservations essential. AE, DC, MC, V. Closed Mon.–Tues., 2nd ½ of July, 2 wks in Dec.–Jan.*

Excursion from Antwerp A to Z

Arriving and Departing

BY CAR

Lier is a short drive from Antwerp on the N10 or from Brussels on the E19/N14 via Mechelen. Hasselt is a straight drive, almost as the crow flies, from Antwerp on the A13/E313 motorway (which continues to Liège); from Brussels, take the E40/A2 via Leuven to Exit 26, then the E313 for the last few miles. Sint-Truiden is reached from Hasselt on the N80 and Tongeren on the N20 (they are linked by the N79); from Brussels take the E40 to Exit 25 for the N3 to Sint-Truiden, to Exit 29 for the N69 to Tongeren.

BY TRAIN

There are hourly trains from Antwerp to Lier (15 minutes), Hasselt (1 hour, 5 minutes), and Tongeren (1 hour, 40 minutes). There is also an hourly train from Brussels (Midi, Central, and Nord) taking 55 minutes to Sint-Truiden, 1 hour and 10 minutes to Hasselt.

Getting Around

If you're not driving, consider the humble bike. Hasselt, Sint-Truiden, and Tongeren are equidistant from one another, each leg of the triangle about 12 miles (☞ Outdoor Activities and Sports, *below*).

Contacts and Resources

EMERGENCIES

Police: ☎ 101. **Ambulance:** ☎ 100. The address of the on-duty **late-night pharmacy** is posted in all pharmacy windows.

GUIDED TOURS

At Lanaken, near the Dutch border east of Hasselt, you can rent a **horse and wagon** through the local tourist office (☎ 089/722467) and set off for a one-day excursion along a route mapped out for you, from May through October.

The Lanaken tourist office also takes bookings for a variety of **boat trips** on the Meuse and the South-Willems and Albert canals. *Stiphout Boat Trips,* ☎ *089/722467.* ⌨ *BF175–BF450.* ☉ *Apr.–mid-Sept.*

OUTDOOR ACTIVITIES AND SPORTS

For general information on sports facilities and opportunities, contact the **Sportdienst** (✉ Universiteitslaan 1, Hasselt, ☎ 011/237111).

Local tourist offices can supply maps and information on **bicycle trails.** Two of the most popular trails are the Trudofietsroute, 54 kilometers (32 miles) long, based on the travels of St. Trudo, and the Tongria route in Tongeren, 45 kilometers (27 miles) long.

VISITOR INFORMATION

The **Provincial Tourist Office for Limburg** is at Universiteitslaan 1, Hasselt (☎ 011/237450). **City Tourist Offices** are at Lombaardstraat 3, Hasselt (☎ 011/239540); Grote Markt 68, Sint-Truiden (☎ 011/686872); and Stadhuisplein 9, Tongeren (☎ 012/390255).

WALLONIA: FROM THE MEUSE TO THE ARDENNES

Rushing streams between steep rocks, high moorland and dense forests, feudal mountaintop castles, and hamlets with cottages of rough-hewn stone, rustic inns serving trout from the rivers and wild boar from the woods, Romanesque churches and prosperous fortified farms: This is Wallonia, an amazing variety of scenic and historic treasures, combined with the pleasures of good food and wine, served in atmospheric surroundings.

Wallonia, in southern Belgium, is everything that Flanders is not. While the northern part of the country is flat, Wallonia is hilly, even mountainous, attracting nature-lovers who enjoy walking, biking, and canoeing. If you like New England, you'll love Wallonia. Southerners all speak French; one in three also understands Walloon, a dialect descended from demotic Latin. The linguistic frontier corresponds roughly to the northern boundary of the Roman empire, and "Walas" was the name given to the Romanized Celts of the region. Today, the economy of rust-belt Wallonia has been overtaken by that of high-tech Flanders. The coal mines of Wallonia are a thing of the past, and the steel industry is fighting a tenacious battle to remain competitive. The Walloons are highly conscious of their culture and linguistic heritage and take pride in their separate identity within the framework of the nation.

Pleasures and Pastimes

CHÂTEAUX AND FORTS

Counts, dukes, and prince bishops lorded it over these parts for many centuries, and despite enthusiastic support for the French Revolution and, paradoxically, Napoléon, a feudal way of life continued well into the past century. A sizable number of châteaux of different sizes and shapes, reminders of how the ruling class lived, are scattered throughout the countryside. Many can be visited, including those still inhabited.

DINING

Eating in the Ardennes is one of the most straightforward pleasures Belgium has to offer. The territory is chockablock with atmospheric gray-stone inns. The cuisine is redolent of forest and farm, with ham, sausage, trout, and game in the forefront. The region's *charcuterie* (cured meats and sausages) is some of the best in central Europe. Ardennes sausage, neat and plump, is made with a blend of veal and pork and is smoked over smoldering oak; its flavor is a wholesome compromise between simple American summer sausage and the milder Italian salamis. The real charcuterie star is *jambon d'Ardennes,* ham that is salt-cured and delicately smoked so that its meat—surely the most succulent among its Parma and Westphalian competitors—slices up thin, moist, and tender, more like a superior roast beef than ham. Restaurants offer generous platters of it, garnished with crisp little gherkins and pickled onions or, if you're lucky, a savory onion marmalade. Trout offers diners a slightly lighter meal, though once poached in a pool of butter and heaped with toasted almonds, it may be as rich as red-meat alternatives. One pleasant low-fat alternative, though not always available, is *truite au bleu* (blue trout). Plunged freshly killed into a boiling vinegar stock, the trout turns steely blue and retains its delicate flavor.

For dining price categories, *see* The Pleasures of Dining and Lodging at the beginning of this chapter.

LODGING

Hotel rooms in this region tend to be low-priced, even if there's an outstanding restaurant downstairs. They usually fill up on weekends and during high season, June through August. If you prefer to eat somewhere other than in the hotel you've booked, clear it with the management: You're often expected (and sometimes obligated) to eat in their restaurant. Many hotels offer *demi-pension* (half-board) arrangements, as well as "gastronomic weekends," which include two or three lavish meals with two nights' lodging. Also available, and especially popular with families, are a wide variety of farmhouse accommodations and B&Bs.

For lodging price categories, *see* The Pleasures of Dining and Lodging at the beginning of this chapter.

THE OUTDOORS

To many visitors, this is the great attraction of Wallonia. Hiking on the high moors is an undemanding activity that attracts even the most sedentary. You need to be in somewhat better shape to shoot the rapids in a kayak, but you can pick your river in accordance with skill and the number of watery thrills and spills you are prepared for. Mountain bikes are readily available for hire, and in winter there's generally enough snow for a handful of ski lifts to stay open for a few hopeful weeks. Even if you remain in the comfort of your car, you can roll along rural routes and discover the real Wallonia. You crest a hill, and there's an unexpected vista of miles and miles of woods and lakes and fields; you turn a corner and find yourself in a village where every house has slate walls and a slate roof. You roll down the window and the fresh air is so incredible you have to stop.

Exploring Wallonia

Wallonia consists, west to east, of the provinces of Hainaut, Namur, and Liège and, to the southeast, Belgian Luxembourg. For too many people, this is an area you only pass through on the way to somewhere else: Hainaut on the way to Paris, Namur and Luxembourg on the way to Strasbourg or Burgundy, Liège on the way to Germany. To acquire the Wallonia habit, start by leaving the highway, stopping off in a city, or driving around the countryside—and arriving at your final destination a few hours or a couple of days late!

Numbers in the text correspond to numbers in the margin and on the Meuse and the Ardennes map.

Great Itineraries

IF YOU HAVE 2 DAYS
Start by visiting the magnificent caves at **Han-sur-Lesse** ⑧③, and then follow the river Lesse to its junction with the Meuse; visit **Dinant** ⑧④ and the area along the Meuse, ending up at ⚇ **Namur** ⑧⑤. The following day, explore Namur, then cross the plateau of Condroz and visit **Huy** ⑧⑥.

IF YOU HAVE 5 DAYS
Stay over in ⚇ **Liège** ⑧⑦; visit that city in the morning, and continue via Eupen to the moors and woodland of the **Hautes Fagnes**; visit **Malmédy** ⑧⑧ and **Stavelot** ⑧⑨, and stop at the original ⚇ **Spa** ⑨⓪. Proceed to tiny, delightful **Durbuy** ⑨①, then on to **La Roche-en-Ardenne** ⑨②, visit the war memorials in **Bastogne** ⑨③, stop at **St. Hubert** ⑨④, and finish the day in ⚇ **Bouillon** ⑨⑤. The following day, visit the ancient **Abbaye d' Orval** ⑨⑥ and the Roman town of **Arlon** ⑨⑦; or cut across the French Forêts de Château-Regnault along the winding Semois River to Belgian Hainaut.

When to Tour Wallonia

Wallonia is at its best April through June, and September through October. The Ardennes is very popular with Belgian and Dutch vacationers, especially during the school holiday season. Although this makes it very busy at that time, it is the best testimony that Wallonia has lots to offer for a family holiday.

The Meuse Valley

The Meuse River comes rushing out of France, foaming through narrow ravines. In Dinant it is joined by the Lesse and flows, serene and beautiful, toward Namur, watched over by ancient citadels. At Namur comes the confluence with the Sambre, tainted from its exposure to the industries of Charleroi. Here, the river becomes broad and powerful, and gradually the pleasure craft are replaced by an endless procession of tugboats and barges, before the Meuse reaches the sea in Holland under a different name, the Maas.

From the name of the river is derived the adjective "Mosan," used to describe an indigenous style of metalworking of extraordinary plasticity. It reached its finest flowering in the 12th and 13th centuries with masters such as Renier de Huy, Nicolas de Verdun, and Hugo d'Oignies. They worked with brass, copper, and silver to achieve artistic levels equal to those of the Flemish painters two centuries later.

Roman legions commanded by Julius Caesar marched up the Meuse valley 2,000 years ago and made it one of the principal routes to Cologne. Later, it served a similar purpose for Charlemagne, linking his Frankish and German lands. Little wonder that massive forts were built on the rocks dominating the invasion routes. Even so, the French came through here under Louis XIV and again under Napoléon. The Dutch, who ruled here for little more than a decade after Waterloo, expanded these fortifications. A century later, the Germans came through here, pushing west and south in World Wars I and II.

Han-sur-Lesse

★ ☾ ⑧③ *123 km (74 mi) southeast of Brussels, 64 km (38 mi) southeast of Namur, 77 km (46 mi) southwest of Liège.*

Han-sur-Lesse owes its fame to the magnificent **Grottes de Han** (Han Caves), which were rediscovered 150 years ago. The caves had provided refuge for threatened tribes since neolithic times. To tour them you board an ancient tram in the center of town that carries you to the mouth of the caves. There, multilingual guides take over and lead groups on foot

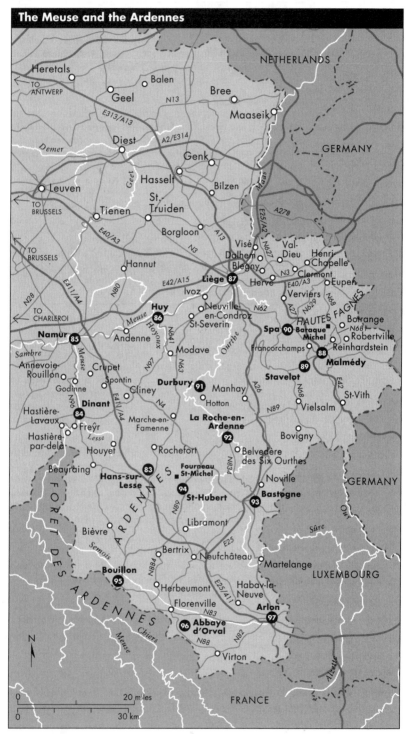

NETHERLANDS

GERMANY

TO
ANTWERP

Heretals

Balen

Geel

Bree

Maaseik

N13

Diest

A2/E314

Genk

E313/A13

Demer

Geet

Hasselt

Bilzen

Leuven

St.
Truiden

Tienen

TO
BRUSSELS

Borgloon

Visé

Val-
Dieu

Henri
Chapelle

A13

Dalhem

E40/A3

N3

Blegny

Clermont

Hannut

Vise

Eupen

N3

TO
BRUSSELS

N60

E42/A15

Liège **87**

Herve

Verviers

E40/A3

N28

E411/A4

Ivoz

N62

N629

N68

HAUTES FAGNES

TO
CHARLEROI

Huy **86**

Neuville-
en-Condroz

St-Severin

Spa **90**

Baraque
Michel

Botrange

N681

Robertville

Namur **85**

Andenne

Meuse

Hoyoux

N641

Modave

Ourthe

Francorchamps

88

Reinhardstein

Malmédy

Sambre

Meuse

Crupet

N97

N63

Stavelot

89

Annevoie-
Rouillon

Spontin

Durbury **91**

Manhay

A26

Godinne

N96

Cliney

N4

Hotton

N89

Vielsalm

St-Vith

Dinant **84**

Freÿr

Lesse

Marche-en-
Famenne

La Roche-en-
Ardenne

92

Bovigny

N68

E42

Hastière-
Lavaux

Hastière-
par-dela

Houyet

Rochefort

Belvedère
des Six Ourthes

Beauraing

Hans-sur-
Lesse **83**

Fourneau
St-Michel

N34

Noville

GERMANY

94

St-Hubert

Bastogne **93**

Bièvre

N89

Libramont

Oûr

Semois

Bertrix

N884

Neufchâteau

E25

Martelange

Sûre

LUXEMBOURG

Bouillon **95**

Herbeumont

E25/A4

Habay-la-
Neuve

N83

Florenville

Arlon **97**

N

Chiers

Abbaye
d'Orval **96**

N83

N82

Alzette

Meuse

N88

Virton

0   20 miles

0   30 km

FRANCE

through 3 kilometers (2 miles) of dimly lit chambers, with occasional glimpses of the underground river Lesse, past giant stalagmites, into the vast cavern called the Dome, 475 feet high, where a single torchbearer dramatically descends the steeply sloping cave wall. The final part of the journey is by boat on the underground river. The trip takes about 90 minutes. ⊠ *Rue J. Lamotte 2,* ☎ *084/377213.* 🖾 *BF275.* ⊘ *Apr.–Nov., daily 10–4:30, May–June until 5, July–Aug. until 6.*

☺ The **Réserve d'Animaux Sauvages** (Wildlife Reserve) is part of the domain of Han. A 625-acre park, it is filled with animals native to the region, such as wild boars, brown bears, bisons, wolves, and lynx. A panoramic coach takes you through the park, where you can observe the animals in their natural habitat. The trip takes one hour and 15 minutes. ⊠ *Rue J. Lamotte 2,* ☎ *084/377212.* 🖾 *BF210.* ⊘ *Mar.–Apr. and Sept.–Nov., daily 10–4:30; May–June, daily 10–5; July–Aug., daily 10–6.*

Château de Lavaux-Sainte-Anne is a superb, moat-encircled castle from the 12th century, rebuilt in the 16th century, and modified in the 18th. The towers and dungeon are medieval, the interior court Renaissance. The castle also houses a small hunting and nature museum with a fine ornithology section and an impressive restaurant (☞ Dining and Lodging, *below*). ⊠ *Rue du Château 10, Lavaux-Sainte-Anne.* 🖾 *BF175.* ⊘ *Mar.–Oct., daily 9–6; Nov.–Feb., daily 9–noon and 12:30–5.*

Dining and Lodging

$$$$ ✕🏠 **Château de Lavaux-Sainte-Anne.** The owner decided to plant an
★ herb garden in the courtyard, and then opened a restaurant in this moat-encircled castle. It rapidly became a great success, as the chef progressed from self-taught amateur to virtuoso. The stripped-down decor is off-set by a vast hunting painting, and *la patronne* handles the service as if to the manor born. Melt-in-your-mouth potatoes with goose liver and morels, carpaccio of sea scallops, and pikeperch with crackling skin are among the temptations. The smallish rooms ($$) are in an annex called Maison Lemonnier. ⊠ *Rue du Château 10, Lavaux-Sainte-Anne,* ☎ *084/388883,* 🖷 *084/388895. 8 rooms with bath. Restaurant, horseback riding. AE, DC, MC, V. Hotel and restaurant closed Mon.–Tues., mid-Dec.–mid-Jan., 1 wk May–June, 1 wk Aug.–Sept.*

$ ✕🏠 **Les Ardennes.** This is an acceptable roadhouse stopover for families visiting the caves, but most rooms are musty, with spongy beds and old bath fixtures; those overlooking the garden are more pleasant. Guests are required to eat in the hotel, which is no great punishment: There's honest regional cooking with some French fuss, friendly and competent service, and an unusually well-chosen wine list. ⊠ *Rue des Grottes 2, Han-sur-Lasse,* ☎ *084/377220,* 🖷 *084/378062. 26 rooms with bath. Restaurant ($$), bar, outdoor café. AE, DC, MC, V. Closed Wed. off-season and Jan.*

Dinant

❽❹ *40 km (24 mi) northwest of Han-sur-Lesse, 29 km (17 mi) south of Namur, 93 km (56 mi) southeast of Brussels, 80 km (48 mi) southwest of Liège.*

The drive toward Dinant is filled with stunning views of towering rock formations across the river from the road. **Freyr,** on the left bank, is considered the best rock-climbing center in Wallonia. The **Château de Freyr** is an impressive Renaissance building with beautiful interiors decorated with 17th-century woodwork and furniture. Louis XIV visited here during the siege of Dinant in 1675. Its park has been laid out in accordance with the design principles of Le Nôtre, the French land-

scape architect. ⊠ *Domaine de Freyr, Waulsort,* ☎ *082/222200.* 🖼
BF200. ⊗ *July–Aug., weekends, and bank holidays 2–6.*

Just before Dinant, the needle-shaped **Rocher Bayard** looms on the right
bank. Legend has it that Bayard, the steed of the legendary four Aymon
brothers, who were the implacable foes of Charlemagne, split the rock
with his hoof. The passage was widened by the troops of Louis XIV
as they advanced on the city.

Dinant has a most scenic but strategic location, which has led to its
involvement in an interminable series of wars. The 13th-century collegiate church of **Notre-Dame** huddles under the citadel. Its bulbous
blue bell tower is a 17th-century addition. Behind the church is the starting point for cable cars to the **Citadel,** which is not as old as you might
think—the ancient fortification was razed in 1818 by the Dutch, who
replaced it with a new fort just before they were ousted. The view is
splendid, and there is an arms museum, whose cannons and cannon
balls add to the military atmosphere. ⊠ *Le Prieuré 25,* ☎ *082/222119.*
🖼 *BF180, including cable car.* ⊗ *Apr.–Oct., daily 10–6; Nov.–Mar.,
daily 10–4.*

The French word *dinanderie,* meaning the art of brass- and copper-
working, is derived from Dinant, where it was developed in the 12th
century and spread downstream to Namur and Huy. The copperware
sold today in Dinant's souvenir shops is not, alas, of the same quality.
The **Dinanderie Museum** has a unique collection of weathercocks and
all manner of household utensils. ⊠ *Route de Givet 27,* ☎ *082/223864.*
🖼 *BF150.* ⊗ *Easter–Sept., Tues.–Sun. 1:30–6.*

But for Dinant, who knows what jazz would be like? This is the birthplace of **Adolphe Sax,** inventor of the saxophone and other musical
instruments. He died penniless, but today his image graces the BF200
note.

NEED A
BREAK?
Visit the **Patisserie Solbrun** to savor Dinant's two specialties: *flamiches*
(cheese, egg, and butter tarts), to be eaten piping hot; and the hard,
spicy *couques,* made of pastry and honey in many fanciful shapes. Although the town's streets are lined with cafés, this one has the advantage of a great river view.

🕃 **Mont-Fat,** 400 feet above Dinant, offers the combination of a guided
tour of prehistoric caves and a chairlift ride to an amusement area. ⊠
Rue en Rhée 15, ☎ *082/222783.* 🖼 *BF150.* ⊗ *May 1–14 and
Sept.–Oct. 20, Wed. 1–6 and weekends 11–6; May 16–Aug., Wed.
1–6, Thurs.–Tues. 11–6.*

La Merveilleuse, a cave whose many stalactites are remarkably white,
is located on the left bank, about 490 yards from the bridge, on the
road toward Philippeville. A visit takes about 50 minutes. ⊠ *Route
de Philippeville 142,* ☎ *082/222210.* 🖼 *BF180.* ⊗ *Mar.–May and
Sept.–Nov., daily 11–5; June–Aug., daily 10–6.*

Shooting the rapids of the **river Lesse** in a kayak has great appeal to
the adventure-minded. This is one of the liveliest tributaries of the Meuse,
which it joins just south of Dinant. The starting point is **Houyet.** The
21-kilometer (13-mile) ride takes you through two rapids and past the
eagle's-nest Walzin Castle, to Anseremme on the Meuse. Train service
to the starting point is available.

The moated **Château de Spontin,** east of the Meuse, is an excellent example of what this province has to offer. Of medieval origin, it has been

given a Renaissance brick superstructure. The drawbridge can still be operated, and there are secret staircases and lookouts. ⊠ *Chaussée de Dinant 8,* ☎ *083/699055.* ⊡ *Free.* ⊘ *Daily in season 10–5.*

In nearby **Crupet** stands a massive, river-encircled square dungeon from the 12th century. Also in the area is Purnode with its family-owned brewery, the **Brasserie du Bocq,** which has produced excellent beers since 1858. ⊠ *Rue de la Brasserie 4, Purnode,* ☎ *082/613737.* ⊡ *BF50.* ⊘ *Easter–Oct., Sun. at 2, 3, 4, and 5.*

Ⓒ At **Falaën,** west of the Meuse, you can rent pedal-powered, so-called gang cars for self-propelled trips on disused railway tracks along the scenic Molignée Valley. ⊠ *Les Draisines de la Molignée, Rue de Foy 21, Falaën,* ☎ *082/699079.* ⊡ *BF600 (1 hr)–BF800 (2 hrs).* ⊘ *Daily 10–6.*

Dining and Lodging

$$$ ✕ **Le Jardin de Fiorine.** Opened in May 1991 and a great success, this young, ambitious restaurant holds forth in a restored graystone mansion with a pretty garden behind. Specialties include a fine lobster and sweetbread salad, satiny lobster flan with Chablis, veal in tarragon and pears, and roast pigeon with corn cakes. ⊠ *Rue Georges Cousot 3,* ☎ *082/227474. AE, DC, MC, V. No dinner Sun. Closed Wed., 1st 3 wks of Lent, last wk in Aug.*

$$$ ✕ **Le Vivier d'Oies.** This country inn is in a lovely stone farmhouse with a modern stone-and-glass wing. The ambience is urbane, and the cuisine above reproach: goose liver sautéed with caramelized pears, crayfish with hearts of artichoke, trout with caviar. ⊠ *Rue Etat 7, Dorinne, northeast of Dinant, about 3 km (2 mi) east of Yvoir,* ☎ *083/699571. AE, DC, MC, V. No dinner Tues. Closed Wed., 2 wks June–July, 2 wks Sept.–Oct.*

$$ ✕ **Thermidor.** The decor may be on the stodgy side, but the cooking here is all it should be: traditional French cuisine, sauces made fresh on the spot, a few experiments in new combinations. Try the grilled salmon steak with fresh-whisked mustard sauce or chicken breast with a drizzle of vanilla butter. ⊠ *Rue Station 3,* ☎ *082/223135. AE, MC, V. No dinner Mon. Closed Tues.*

$ ✕🏠 **Auberge de Bouvignes.** This 1830 roadhouse combines beautifully restored architecture—beams, stonework, whitewashed brick—with an elegant decor and superb cooking. Its wine caves are blasted into the solid stone bluff behind, and its rustic bedrooms overlook the Meuse. Lobster dishes of all kinds are a specialty, including lobster ragout with asparagus, morels, and fresh pasta; or there may be Bresse pigeon with braised endive and truffles. ⊠ *Rue Fétis 112, Bouvignes-sur-Meuse, just north of Dinant,* ☎ *082/611600,* 🅵🅰🆇 *082/613093. 6 rooms with bath. Restaurant ($$$$). AE, DC, MC, V.*

$ ✕🏠 **Le Mosan.** In Anseremme, just upstream from Dinant, this welcoming old roadside hotel sits right on the riverbank. It's very well kept, with fresh, light decor in pretty pastels—worth the mild inconvenience of bathrooms across the hall. Downstairs, the traditional restaurant offers trout and steak, prepared in a dozen different ways, that you can enjoy either on the glassed-in porch or in the charming dining room—very good value for the money. ⊠ *Rue Dufrenne 2, Anseremme-Dinant,* ☎ *082/222450,* 🅵🅰🆇 *082/224679. 8 rooms without bath. Restaurant. AE, DC, MC, V.*

En Route From Dinant to Namur, the **Château et Jardins d'Annevoie** (Chateau and Gardens of Annevoie) present a happy blend of 18th-century French landscaping and romantic Italian garden design, remarkable for its use of natural waterfalls, fountains, and ponds to animate the gardens with their flower beds, lawns, statues, and grottoes. The water displays function without mechanical aids and have remained in working order for more than two centuries. The château blends perfectly with the gardens; the furniture, paneling, and family portraits all contribute to an ambience of elegant refinement. ⊠ *Route des Jardins 47,* ☎ *082/611555.* ⌑ *BF200.* ⊘ *Apr.–Oct., daily 9:30–6:30.*

Namur

★ ⑧⑤ *29 km (17 mi) north of Dinant, 64 km (38 mi) southeast of Brussels, 61 km (37 mi) southwest of Liège.*

Namur, at the confluence of the Meuse and the Sambre, takes pride in its beautifully preserved center, whose appealing streets are lined with pink-brick, 17th-century houses and, here and there, a rich Baroque church, all under the shadow of the Citadel, perched on the promontory overlooking the city. It is the seat of the body governing the affairs of the semiautonomous Walloon Region, chosen as a compromise acceptable to Charleroi and Liège, both of which are twice as large. Much of the center of Namur is a pedestrian zone, with cafés, art galleries, and boutiques. This is a university town, and the student population helps to liven up what passes for nightlife around the Rue St-Loup. Directly in the center is the quiet Place du Marché-aux-Légumes, with the Eglise de Saint-Jean Baptiste.

NEED A
BREAK?

The **Le XVIILe** (⊠ Place du Marché-aux-Légumes) is a new café in an old building, so named for its stucco, 18th-century ceiling. The specialty is pancakes with generous fillings.

The **Trésor Hugo d'Oignies** is a collection of the finest of the crosses, reliquaries, and other religious artifacts made by Brother Hugo d'Oignies for the monastery in nearby Oignies at the beginning of the 13th century. The finesse with which he worked the silver and enamel inlays, often depicting miniature hunting scenes, was remarkable, and Hugo d'Oignies has been recognized as one of the masters of Art Mosan. See the collection at the Institut des Soeurs de Notre-Dame. ⊠ *Rue Billiart 17,* ☎ *081/230342.* ⌑ *BF50.* ⊘ *Tues.–Sat. 10–noon and 2–5, Sun. 2–5.*

The **Musée Archéologique** (Archaeological Museum) contains Roman and Merovingian antiquities from the Namur area. It includes a collection of jewelry from the 1st to the 7th centuries with some magnificent specimens. It is installed in the handsome, 16th-century Butchers' Hall on the waterfront. ⊠ *Rue du Pont,* ☎ *081/231631.* ⌑ *BF80.* ⊘ *Tues.–Fri. 10–5, weekends 10:30–5.*

The **Musée Felicien Rops** honors an artist who was considered totally scandalous in his lifetime. Rops, a friend and illustrator of Baudelaire and other allegedly decadent French writers, was a master printmaker. A surrealist before his time, he created works that were, by turns, satirical and erotic. ⊠ *Rue Fumal 12,* ☎ *081/220110.* ⌑ *BF100.* ⊘ *Tues.–Sun. 10–5; Easter–Oct. until 6.*

The **Citadelle** (Citadel) commands fabulous views in all directions, where one can easily imagine the feelings of guards looking out for approaching armies. Namur was, in fact, besieged again and again for centuries on end. The 15th-century bastions were further fortified by the Spanish and, much later, the Dutch, who constructed their Fort d'Orange on the same site. Today you can reach the Citadel by car up the hairpin curves of a mile-long road called the Marvelous Route, or you can enjoy a scenic ride by cable car. ⊠ *Route Merveilleuse 8,* ☎ *081/226829.* ⌑ *BF195;*

cable car BF190 round-trip. ☼ *Easter–May, weekends 11–5; June–Sept., daily 11–5.*

There are several museums at the Citadel, including the **Musée Provincial de la Forêt** (Provincial Forestry Museum). Housed in an old hunting lodge, it gives an overview of the region's flora and fauna. ⊠ *Route Merveilleuse 9,* ☎ *081/743894.* ☑ *BF50.* ☼ *Apr.–Oct., daily 9–noon and 2–5.*

☾ The **Reine Fabiola** center, on the Citadel grounds, includes a large playground with miniature golf, go-carts, and electric cars. ⊠ *Route Merveilleuse,* ☎ *081/738413.* ☑ *BF100.* ☼ *May 1–14 and Sept.–Oct. 20, Wed. 1–6, weekends 11–6; May 15–Aug., Thurs.–Tues. 11–6, Wed. 1–6.*

Dining and Lodging

$$$ ✕ **Biétrumé Picar.** Noted chef Charles Jeandrain has now relocated to
★ Les Plante, a Namur suburb, and the new, verdant surroundings seem to give him new inspiration. The handsome dining room is tiled with flagstones from Jura, and the terrace, with its handsome view, is ideal in summer. The menu includes a creamy bouillon with green asparagus and turbot, sautéed langoustines with tomato and leek base, and rhubarb fricassee with caramelized peaches. ⊠ *Tienne Macquet 16,* ☎ *081/230739. Jacket and tie. AE, DC, MC, V. No dinner Sun. (except July–Aug.). Closed Mon.*

$$ ✕ **Le Temps des Cerises.** On a narrow street in old Namur, chockablock
★ with little restaurants, this retro café serves rich, hearty fare—fish soup with *rouille* (garlic and red-pepper sauce), homemade sausages, kidneys in garlic-juniper sauce—in artful and generous portions. The setting is charmingly Old Belgium, with lace café curtains, vintage postcards, knickknacks, and furniture and paneling painted a glossy cherry red. ⊠ *Rue des Brasseurs 22,* ☎ *081/225326. MC, V. No lunch Sat. Closed Sun.*

$ ✕ **Brasserie Henry.** In an attractive, high-ceiling building in old Namur, this is a place for traditional brasserie dishes, such as sauerkraut, steamed cod, and cassoulet. The restaurant is open until midnight. A children's menu is available. ⊠ *Place Saint-Aubain 3,* ☎ *081/220204. AE, DC, MC, V.*

$–$$$$ ✕▥ **Les Tanneurs.** This exquisite hotel is the creation of Christian Bou-
★ vier, who defied promoters prepared to demolish a row of ancient buildings in the heart of Namur. The interiors have been renovated with remarkable taste, using material such as oak and marble, and decorated with beautiful fabrics and delightful pictures. Each room is different, ranging from simple, inexpensive ones to a duplex deluxe. There are two restaurants: **L'Espièglerie** ($$$, no lunch Sat., closed Sun. and mid-July–mid-Aug.), serving delicacies such as quail stuffed with sweetbreads, and roast duck with figs; and **Grill des Tanneurs** ($), one flight up, which serves brasserie-type food. ⊠ *Rue des Tanneries 13,* ☎ *081/231999,* ℻ *081/229703. 16 rooms with bath. 2 restaurants, bar. AE, DC, MC, V.*

$$ ✕▥ **Beauregard.** Built into a wing of the Namur Casino, this is a polished, fashionable business hotel, with vivid color schemes (lime, salmon, teal) and sleek room decor. Rooms with wide views of the river cost slightly more. A breakfast buffet is served in a vast, windowed hall with river views. ⊠ *Avenue Baron de Moreau 1,* ☎ *081/230028,* ℻ *081/241209. 51 rooms. Restaurant, bar, breakfast room, casino. AE, DC, MC, V.*

$$ ✕▥ **Château de Namur.** This is primarily a hotel school, located in a grand old mansion built in 1930, that sits at the top of the Citadel's

bluff, high above the city. Much of the mansion's former grandeur is subjugated to its current role as a teaching vehicle. Public spaces are sparse and underfurnished, but rooms are comfortable and fresh, and the views are spectacular. Ask for a corner room, with double views. In the dining room, students practice the art of serving rough-edged but ambitious French cooking. ⊠ *Avenue de l'Ermitage 1,* ☎ *081/742630,* ℻ *081/742392. 29 rooms with bath. Restaurant, bar, tennis court, convention center. AE, DC, MC, V.*

$$ ✕🏠 **Novotel.** This French chain hotel is on the river, before you reach Namur coming from Dinant, in the heart of the strawberry-growing region. Worldwide standardization makes rooms, public areas, and restaurant rather impersonal. Riverside walks start at the door, and the staff will make all sorts of excursion arrangements. ⊠ *Chaussée de Dinant 1149, Wepion-Namur,* ☎ *081/460811,* ℻ *081/461990. 110 rooms. Restaurant, bar, indoor and outdoor pools, sauna, health club, meeting rooms. AE, DC, MC, V.*

$ ✕🏠 **Ferme du Quartier.** Just outside Namur, near the Bouge exit from the highway, this delightfully restored old stone farmhouse stands in a silent country oasis. Interiors are modern, in natural materials, with some brick-vaulted ceilings and beams. The locals dine in its simple, traditional restaurant on steaks, rabbit in mustard sauce, grilled salmon, or *pintadeau* (guinea fowl) in beer. Rooms in the converted barn are smaller but even quieter than those in the main house. ⊠ *Place Sainte-Marguerite 4, Bouge-Namur,* ☎ *081/211105,* ℻ *081/215918. 14 rooms with bath or shower. Restaurant, bar. AE, DC, MC, V. No dinner Sun. Closed July, last wk of Dec.*

En Route For a beautiful detour on the way to Huy, leave the N90 at Andenne and drive south via Ohey to Havelange. You are now in the heart of the fertile plateau of the **Condroz.** Continue on the N97 to Pont-de-Bonne and **Modave.** There, overlooking the Hoyoux, clearest and coldest of the rivers of the Ardennes, stands the 17th-century **Château des Comtes de Marchin.** Its elegant rooms feature stuccoed polychrone ceilings. The hydraulic machinery that brought water from the river to the cliff top was copied in France to bring water from the Seine to the Palace of Versailles. ☎ *085/411369.* 💷 *BF150.* ☉ *Apr.–mid-Nov., daily 9–6.*

Huy

86 *32 km (19 mi) east of Namur, 83 km (50 mi) southeast of Brussels 33 km (20 mi) southwest of Liège.*

Huy (pronounced "we"), where the Hoyoux joins the Meuse, is an ancient place; its city privileges of 1066 are the oldest that have been preserved in Europe. The Gothic **Eglise Collégiale de Notre-Dame** (Collegiate Church of Our Lady) has a rose window, the so-called Rondia, 30 feet in diameter. Its treasury contains several magnificent reliquaries, two of them attributed to Godefroy de Huy, who followed in the footsteps of Renier, also a native of Huy, a master of the Mosan style. 💷 *BF50.* ☉ *Mon.–Thurs. and Sat. 9–noon and 2–5, Sun. 2–5 except during services.*

The Grand'Place of Huy is dominated by a remarkable copper fountain, the **Bassinia,** a bronze cistern dating from 1406, decorated with saints. In the 18th century, the Austrians topped it with their double eagle. From the square you can wander through winding alleys to the old Franciscan monastery, which is now the **Musée Communal,** a mine of local folklore and history, with an exceptional Art Mosan oak carving of Christ. ⊠ *Rue Vankeerberghen 20,* ☎ *085/232435.* 💷 *BF60.* ☉ *Apr.–Oct., Mon.–Sat. 2–6, Sun. 10–noon and 2–6.*

For a great view of town and country, take a mile-long ride on the cable car, which will lift you from the left bank of the Meuse, across the river and to the cliff-top fort, **Citadelle,** part of the defenses built by the Dutch in the early 19th century. During World War II the Germans used it as a prison for resisters and hostages. It now contains a **Resistance and Concentration Camp Museum** composed of photographs, documents, and scale models. ⊠ *Chaussée Napoléon,* ☎ *085/215334.* ⊡ *BF120.* ☉ *Apr.–June and Sept., weekdays 10–5, weekends 10–6; July–Aug., daily 10–8; cable car July–Aug., daily.*

Mont Mosan Recreation Park is a large playground on the heights above Huy, complete with games, an inflatable village, a sea lion show, clowns, and miniature golf, to name a few. It's at the end of the cable-car line that also stops at the Citadel. ⊠ *Plaine de la Sarte,* ☎ *085/232996.* ⊡ *BF100.* ☉ *Mar. 20–Oct., daily 10–8.*

Dining and Lodging

$$ ✕⊡ **L'Aigle Noir.** The restaurant is the major drawing card here: seaweed-steamed sea scallops, fillet of sea bass in salt and mountain citrus fruit. The very comfortable rooms overlook the river, breakfast included. ⊠ *Quai Dautrebande 8,* ☎ *085/212341,* ℻ *085/236486. 10 rooms. Restaurant ($$$). AE, DC, MC, V. No dinner Wed. Closed early July–early Aug.*

$ ✕⊡ **Le Fort.** Tucked under the Citadel, across from the arching bridge over the Meuse, this is the simplest of roadhouses, but its rooms have been carefully decorated and maintained, and its owners pamper you in the unpretentious tavern downstairs. There's a brief, standard menu with trout, sole, or chicken, each with frites and salad, at reasonable prices. ⊠ *Chaussée Napoléon 6,* ☎ *085/212403,* ℻ *085/231842. 34 rooms, 25 with bath. Restaurant, bar. AE, DC, MC, V.*

The Meuse Valley A to Z

Arriving and Departing

BY CAR

Han-sur-Lesse is close to the E411 highway, which links Brussels with Luxembourg and runs south and east. Namur is close to the intersection of the E411 with the E42, which links Liège with Charleroi, Mons, and Paris, as well as with Tournai, Lille, and Calais.

BY TRAIN

There are two trains an hour from Brussels to Namur. The trip takes one hour from Brussels's Gare du Midi, 50 minutes from Brussels's Gare du Nord. It links up with a local service to Dinant (25 minutes). For train information in Namur, call 081/223675.

Getting Around

BY CAR

The most convenient way, by far, of getting around this region is by car. Public transportation services are scant. The E411 highway cuts through the region. Elsewhere, you travel chiefly on pleasant, two-lane roads, enjoying the scenery.

CAR RENTAL

Avis (⊠ Avenue des Combattants 31, Namur, ☎ 081/735906); **Europcar/InterRent, Square** (⊠ Léopold 20, Namur, ☎ 081/229157).

Contacts and Resources

GUIDED TOURS

Boat tours, ranging from short excursions to all-day trips, are available in both Dinant and Namur. Companies, for both, are in Dinant: **Compagnie des Bateaux** (⊠ Rue Daoust 64, ☎ 082/222315); **Bateau Ba-**

yard (⊠ Quai de Meuse 1, ☏ 082/223042); and **Bateau Ansiaux** (⊠ Rue du Vélodrome 15, ☏ 082/222325). With some advance planning, you could probably arrange to sail the entire length of the Meuse from France to Holland by sightseeing boats. In Huy, river trips are organized on the **Bateau Val Mosan** (⊠ Quai de Namur 1, ☏ 025/212915).

Guided walks are available April through September in **Mozet** the third Sunday of each month (☏ 085/842155), and in **Chardeneux** the first Sunday of each month (☏ 086/344407). In **Namur,** walking tours through the old city are organized every Monday, June through August at 2:30, starting from the Tourist Center (⊠ Square de l'Europe Unie, ☏ 081/246437), at the confluence of the Meuse and the Sambre. The price, per person, is BF100.

OUTDOOR ACTIVITIES AND SPORTS

Biking is a popular sport in this region. You can rent mountain bikes at **Kayaks Lesse & Lhomme** (⊠ Le Plan d'Eau, Han-sur-Lesse, ☏ 082/224397), **Kayaks Ansiaux** (⊠ Rue du Vélodrome 15, Anseremme-Dinant, ☏ 082/222325), and **Bill's Bike Evasion** (⊠ Chaussée de Namur 14, Profondeville, ☏ 081/414155). Check the local tourist office for more.

The sheer cliffs along the Meuse are excellent for **rock climbing.** Many hopeful mountaineers learn the skills here for more dramatic exploits. Contact **Club Alpin Belge** (⊠ Boulevard de la Meuse 9, Namur-Jambes, ☏ 081/303119).

Fishing is permitted on several stretches of the Meuse, and on some livelier tributaries, where it is mostly of the sitting-on-the-bank kind. Licenses can be purchased at local post offices (⊠ Rue St-Martin, Dinant; ⊠ Avenue Bovesse, Namur-Jambes).

The region is great for **horseback riding,** and several stables organize treks with overnight accommodations. Horses can be rented for about BF500 per hour. Contact the Provincial Tourist Office for a list of more than 20 stables.

The Lesse is one of the liveliest tributaries to the Meuse, great for **kayaking.** You can choose between the upper Lesse, where Lessive is the starting point, or the 21-kilometer (13-mile) ride from Hoyet, through two rapids and past the high cliffs holding Walzin Castle, to Anseremme on the Meuse, just south of Dinant. Most of the kayak-rental companies also have mountain bikes (☞ Biking, *above*); others include **Lesse Kayaks** (⊠ Place de l'Eglise 2, Anseremme, ☏ 082/224397) and **Kayaks Libert** (⊠ Quai de Meuse 1, Dinant, ☏ 082/226186). The season runs from April through October. Rentals start at BF650.

For **motor sports,** four-wheel-drive vehicles can be rented at Houyet from **Moens** (⊠ Rue du Pirli 4, Gendron-Celles, ☏ 082/667359). Following a test drive on a private circuit, drivers go along an adventure trail, fording rivers and climbing hills. Rentals start at BF4,000.

Sailing is extremely popular, with yacht harbors at Namur, Profondeville, Dinant, and Waulsort. Contact **Royal Nautique Club de Sambre et Meuse** (⊠ Chemin des Pruniers 11, Wepion, ☏ 081/461130).

VISITOR INFORMATION

For the entire region of **Wallonia:** Office de Promotion du Tourisme (⊠ Rue du Marché-aux-Herbes 61, Brussels, ☏ 02/504–0200); and **Province of Namur** (⊠ Parc Industriel, Rue Pieds d'Alouette 18, Naninne-Namur, ☏ 081/408010). City tourist offices: **Dinant** (⊠ Rue Grande 37, ☏ 082/222870); **Namur** (⊠ Square de l'Europe Unie, ☏ 081/246449); and **Huy** (⊠ Quai de Namur 1, ☏ 085/212915).

Liège and Environs

The people of Liège are the most Francophile among the Francophones. In fact, many Belgians feel that visiting Liège, gateway to the Ardennes, is almost like going abroad. The Liégeois, for their part, see little reason for going to Brussels; if they hanker for bright lights, they head for Paris. It was no accident that Georges Simenon could so easily transplant the cafés and streets of the Liège of his boyhood to Maigret's Paris.

The history of Liège differs fundamentally from that of the rest of the country. For 8 of its 10 centuries it was an independent principality of the Holy Roman Empire, from the time Bishop Notger transformed his bishopric into a temporal domain at the end of the 10th century. His successors had to devote as much time to the defense of the realm—much larger than the present province—as to pastoral concerns. The power of the autocratic prince bishops was also hotly contested by the increasingly independent-minded cities. The end was brought about by the French Revolution, which many Liégeois joined with enthusiasm. The ancient Cathedral of St. Lambert was razed, and the principality became a French *département*.

In the 19th century, after Belgian independence in 1830, the country saw an upsurge in industrial activity. The first European locomotive was built in Liège, and the Bessemer steel production method was developed here; it is to the burning furnaces that Liège owes its nickname *la cité ardente* (the Fiery City). Drawing on a centuries-old tradition of weapons manufacturing, the Fabrique Nationale started to build precision firearms, and Val-St-Lambert began to produce glassware that has gained wide renown. In August 1914 the forts of Liège kept the German invasion force at bay long enough for the Belgian and French troops to regroup; in 1944–1945, more than a thousand V1 and V2 missiles exploded in the city.

Liège

🔂 *33 km (20 mi) northwest of Huy, 97 km (58 mi) east of Brussels, 122 km (73 mi) southwest of Cologne.*

The bustling city of Liège—Luik to the Flemish and Dutch, Lüttich to the Germans—is quietly romantic. Surrounded by hills, it sits deep in the Meuse Valley at the confluence of the Meuse and Ourthe rivers. Here the Meuse is slate-gray, and pleasure craft play second fiddle to coal barges and tankers. Liège is a city riddled with secret courtyards, narrow medieval lanes, and steep, stepped streets. Above all, it is a city of joie de vivre, where you easily get into conversation with strangers. The institution that best expresses the Liège spirit is the *café chantant* (singing café), where everyone is welcome to burst into song and frequently does. At the same time, it must be admitted that the long years of crisis in the steel industry have taken their toll; the impact on the city's finances has been disastrous, and a dilapidated, worn-out look has settled over some areas.

Place de la Cathédrale is a pleasant square with flower beds in the center, lined with sidewalk cafés on two sides, and flanked by the north wall of the Gothic **Cathédrale St-Paul** (St. Paul's Cathedral). Inside, you'll see some handsome statues, including one of St. Paul, by Jean Delcour. Other graceful works by this 18th-century sculptor dot the old city. The cathedral's most highly prized possessions are in the Treasury, especially the *Reliquaire de Charles le Téméraire* (Reliquary of Charles the Bold), with gold and enamel figures of St. George, and the bold duke himself on his knees; curiously, their faces are identical. This reliquary was presented to Liège by Charles the Bold in 1471 in penance for having had the city razed three years earlier. ✉ *BF50.* ☉ *Daily (except during services) 10–noon and 2–5. Ring bell next to cloister door.*

NEED A
BREAK? **Le Panier Fleuri** (✉ Pont d'Avroy 20) is right out of the Belle Epoque. This combination tavern and brasserie serves Belgian beer, 200 brands of spirits, and 80 different permutations of ham and cheese on toast.

Vinâve-d'Ile, a charming and animated triangular square with a fountain graced by Delcour, adjoins Place de la Cathédrale. The **Eglise Saint-Denis** (Church of St. Denis) is one of the oldest in Liège, founded by Bishop Notger. It has a handsome reredos portraying the Suffering of Christ. ✉ *Place St-Denis, via Rue de la Cathédrale,* ☏ *04/223–5756.* ☉ *Mon.–Sat. 9–6, Sun. 9–11:30.*

Place Saint-Lambert is a true eyesore. What should be the city's most prestigious square has, in fact, been a hole in the ground for more than 20 years. It's as though the destruction of Cathédrale St-Lambert during the French Revolution cast a spell on the site. The word is that a solution has been agreed upon and work is about to start, but the Liégeois aren't holding their breath. On the other side of the square stands the enormous **Palais des Princes-Evêques** (Palace of the Prince Bishops), rebuilt at different stages since Notger's days. The present facade dates from 1734. It's worth picking your way across the square to have a peek inside the colonnaded 16th-century courtyard, which has remained unchanged. Each column is decorated with stone carvings of staggering variety. The palace is now used for government offices and law courts, which explains the presence of police and metal detectors.

Place du Marché is as old as the city itself. For centuries, this was where the city's commercial and political life was concentrated. A number of the old buildings surrounding it were among the 23,000 houses destroyed by German bombs. In the center stands the **Perron,** a large fountain sculpted by Jean Delcour, a symbol of municipal liberty.

NEED A
BREAK? The **Café à Pilori** (✉ Place du Marché 5) is another essentially Liégeois tavern, with a large fireplace and beamed ceiling. It serves light lunches and its own homemade brew.

La Batte is the animated riverfront of the old city. On Sunday from 9 to 2, it becomes a mile-long street market where you can buy anything, from bric-a-brac and foodstuffs, to songbirds and pets, to clothing, books, records, and toys. Visitors from neighboring Holland and Germany descend regularly on Liège to join the locals at the Sunday market, but it's not so much the merchandise that makes it attractive as the good-natured ambience.

The **Ilôt St-Georges** is an interesting example of urban archaeology. Twelve dilapidated buildings were taken apart, brick by brick, and put together again to form an attractive architectural whole. Here, too, is the new **Musée de l'Art Wallon,** containing works by Walloon artists from the 17th century to the present day, including Magritte and Delvaux. ✉ *En Féronstrée 86,* ☏ *04/221–9231.* ✉ *BF50.* ☉ *Thurs.–Sat. 1–6, Sun. 11–4:30.*

The **Musée d'Armes** (Arms Museum) is a handsome 18th-century mansion in the neoclassical style, opulently furnished. Napoléon slept here, at different times, with Josephine and Marie-Louise, and there's a portrait of him as First Consul, by Ingres. Since the Middle Ages, Liège has been famous for its arms manufacturing, and the collection reflects this with many rare and beautifully executed pieces. ⊠ *Quai de Maastricht 8,* ☎ *04/221–9416.* 🖾 *BF50.* ☉ *Mon., Thurs., and weekends 10–1; Wed. and Fri. 2–5.*

Musée Curtius, a patrician mansion built for the arms manufacturer Jean Curtin in the 16th century, contains 100,000 art and ornamental objects. One is a masterpiece, Bishop Notger's *Evangelistery,* an exquisite 10th-century manuscript of the gospels. On the ornamental cover is an ivory relief, carved in the year 1000, showing the bishop praying to Christ the King. The house is made of limestone and brick. ⊠ *Quai de Maastricht 13,* ☎ *04/221–9404.* 🖾 *BF50.* ☉ *Mon., Thurs., and Sat. 2–5; Wed. and Fri. 10–1.*

NEED A
BREAK?

A la Bonne Franquette (⊠ En Féronstrée 152) is a no-frills neighborhood eatery where you can enjoy a meal or snack.

★ The **Eglise St-Barthélemy** (St. Bartholomew's Church) contains Liège's greatest treasure, the Baptismal Font of Renier de Huy, which dates from between 1107 and 1118. This brass masterpiece of Art Mosan, weighing half a ton, is decorated with figures of the five biblical baptismal scenes in high relief. The scenes are of an extraordinary suppleness, and the font rests on 10 oxen, which are also varied and interesting. It is well displayed and well lit. During the French Revolution the font was hidden by the faithful, but the cover has disappeared. The church itself, consecrated in 1015, is one of the rare Romanesque churches that escaped being transformed into the Gothic style, retaining its original aspect of sober austerity. The nave has, however, been touched up in baroque fashion. ⊠ *Place St-Barthélemy,* ☎ *04/223–4998.* 🖾 *BF80.* ☉ *Daily 10–noon and 2–5 except during services.*

Impasses were the narrow mews where servants had their tiny houses in the days of the prince bishops. Prominent citizens lived along En Hors-Château. As late as the 1970s it was believed that the best approach to urban redevelopment was to tear down these houses. Luckily, common sense prevailed, and many small houses have been restored to mint condition. The **Impasse de la Vignette, de l'Ange** and its neighbor **Impasse de la Couronne** are fine examples. Here, as in many other places around Liège, you find a number of *potales* (wall chapels), devoted mostly to the Virgin or St. Roch, who was venerated as the protector against disease epidemics.

The **Montagne de Bueren** is a stairway with 373 steps ascending from Hors-Château toward the Citadel. The stairway is not much more than 100 years old, but it evokes the memory of Vincent van Bueren, a leader of the resistance against Charles the Bold. In 1468 he climbed the hill with 600 men, intending to fall upon the duke and kill him. Betrayed by their Liégeois accents, they lost their lives instead, and the city was pillaged and burned. Charles was loved in Burgundy, but he never had a good press in Liège. At the foot of the stairs, you can turn left through the cobbled **Impasse des Ursulines,** which leads to the small and peaceful Beguinage. Next to it stand old buildings rescued from demolition elsewhere in Liège, including a 17th-century post house. Continuing uphill, you come to a gate in the wall on the left. Push through it, and you're in a large and verdant hillside park.

The **Musée d'Art Religieux et d'Art Mosan** (Museum of Religious and Mosan Art) contains many fine pieces, including an 11th-century *Sedes Sapientiae* (Seat of Wisdom), a stiff and stern-faced, seated Virgin, reflecting a more austere age. ⊠ *Rue Mère Dieu 11,* ☎ *04/221–8944.* 🖾 *BF50.* ☉ *Tues.–Sat. 1–6, Sun. 11–4.*

The **Musée de la Vie Wallonne** (Museum of Walloon Life), in an old
Franciscan convent, has carefully reconstructed interiors that give a vivid
and varied idea of life in old Wallonie, from coal mines to farm kitchens
to the workshops of many different crafts. It even includes a court of
law, complete with a guillotine. One gallery is populated by the irreverent marionette *Tchantchès* and his band, who have always represented
the Liège spirit. ⊠ *Cour des Mineurs,* ☎ *04/223–6094.* 🎫 *BF80.* ◷
Tues.–Sat. 10–5, Sun. 10–4.

Outremeuse (On the Other Side of the Meuse) is a sort of alternative
Liège, the self-styled *Republique libre d'Outremeuse* (Free Republic).
Its inhabitants continue to speak Wallon, an ancient tongue of Latin
origin, and maintain old traditions. It was the home of two personages,
Georges Simenon and Tchantchès. Simenon left Liège as early as he could,
and only one of his more than 400 books, *Le pendu de Saint-Pholien,*
is set in the city; nevertheless the tourist office arranges occasional
Simenon walks for his fans. Tchantchès is strictly a local character, a
marionette that impersonates the "true Liégeois"—caustic, irreverent,
and funny. His home is the **Musée Tchantchès.** ⊠ *Rue Surlet 56,* ☎ *04/
342–7575.* 🎫 *BF40.* ◷ *Tues., Thurs. 2–4.*

The **Maison de la Métallurgie** (House of Metallurgy) is consecrated to
the industrial glory that was Liège's. It is a 19th-century steel mill, south
of Outremeuse, converted into a museum of industrial archaeology, including a 17th-century Walloon forge. ⊠ *Boulevard Raymond Poincaré
17,* ☎ *04/342–6563.* 🎫 *BF100.* ◷ *Weekdays 9–5, Sat. 9–noon.*

The **Musée d'Art Moderne et Contemporain** (Museum of Modern and
Contemporary Art) provides a useful survey of French and Belgian art
since the 1850s. Almost all the big names are represented in the collection of 700-odd paintings. The museum is located in an attractive
park south of Outremeuse, much favored by the Liégeois for a stroll
far away from the traffic. ⊠ *Parc de la Boverie 3,* ☎ *04/343–0403.*
🎫 *BF80.* ◷ *Tues.–Sat. 1–6, Sun. 11–4:30.*

The **Eglise St-Jacques** (St. James's Church) is a few blocks south of Liège's
center. The grimy exterior belies a wonderful interior in which marble,
stained glass, and polished wood combine to create an outstanding visual harmony. The glory of the church are the Gothic vaults, decorated
in intricate patterns of vivid blue and gold and containing myriad
sculpted figures. ⊠ *Place St-Jacques,* ☎ *04/222–1441.* ◷ *Weekdays
8–noon, Sat. 4–6.*

The **Cristalleries du Val St-Lambert** is one of Europe's great glassworks. It's located at Seraing, on the Meuse south of Liège. You can
see glassblowers and engravers at work, walk through well-restored
factory buildings from the 19th century, see an exhibition of museum
and contemporary glassware, and visit the shop. ⊠ *Rue du Val 245,
Seraing,* ☎ *04/337–0960.* 🎫 *BF125.* ◷ *Daily 9–5.*

The **Préhistosite de Ramioul** is a reconstruction of the world of prehistoric man. Different hypothetical dwellings give an idea of his technical aptitude, and visitors can try their hand at making pots and polishing
stones. The museum is next to the cave of Ramioul, where a new lighting system has brought out the beauty of the rock formations. Guided
visits explain the use of the cave by humans and its animal life. ⊠ *Rue
de la Grotte 128, Ivoz-Ramet, near Seraing,* ☎ *04/275–4975.* 🎫
BF290. ◷ *Easter–Oct., weekdays 9–5, weekends 11–6.*

Fort de Loncin has remained as it was at 5:15 PM on August 16, 1914,
when a German shell scored a direct hit, killing most of the garrison. ⊠ *Rue des Héros 15 bis, northeast of the city.* 🎫 *BF100.* ◷

Wed.–Sun. 10–6; winter, Wed.–Sun. 10–4; guided tours Apr.–Sept., Sat. at 2:30.

Fort de Battice brings memories of World War II. It held out against the Germans for 12 days in May 1940, while the German tanks rolled on into France. ✉ *Route d'Aubel, Battice, east of the city,* ☎ *087/311350.* ☐ *BF100.* ☉ *Last Sat. of Mar.–Nov., at 1:30.*

Cimetière Américain des Ardennes (American Cemetery) is one of two American war cemeteries and the final resting place for 5,327 soldiers of the U.S. First Army who fell in the Ardennes, at the Siegfried Line, and around Aachen. The memorial, decorated with an immense American eagle, contains a nondenominational chapel. ✉ *Route du Condroz 164, Neuville-en-Condroz, southwest of the city,* ☎ *04/371–4287.* ☐ *Free.* ☉ *Mid-Apr.–Sept., weekdays 9–6; Oct.–mid-Apr., weekdays 9–5.*

The **Cimetière de Henri-Chapelle** is the burial site of 7,989 GIs who fell here in the Battle of the Bulge during the last winter of World War II. The crosses and steles (commemorative stones) are arranged in arcs converging on the central monument, which also contains a small museum. From here, there is a great view over the plateau of Herve. ✉ *Route du Mémorial Américain, Hombourg,* ☎ *087/687173.* ☉ *Apr.–Sept., daily 8–6, Oct.–Mar., daily 8–5.*

The **Blegny Coal Mine** produced 1,000 tons of coal a day in its heyday. The wealth of Liège was based on coal, which was mined from the Middle Ages until 1980. An audiovisual presentation illustrates this history, and former miners lead tours of the surface and underground facilities. A complete visit takes 3½ hours. ✉ *Complexe Touristique de Blegny, Rue Lambert Marlet 23,* ☎ *04/387–4333.* ☐ *BF2902.* ☉ *Early Apr.–mid-Sept., daily 10–4:30; Mar. and mid-Sept.–Nov., weekends 10–4:30.*

☺ The **Wegimont Domaine,** an area of 50 acres surrounding a château, offers sporting facilities, fishing, rowing, swimming in a heated outdoor pool, miniature golf, and signposted walks. ✉ *Soumagne, east of the city,* ☎ *04/377–1020.* ☐ *BF100.* ☉ *May–Aug., daily 9–8.*

Dining and Lodging

$$$ ✕ **Au Vieux Liège.** There's good news at Old Liège. The cuisine is as
★ interesting as the remarkable building housing the restaurant: The Maison Havart, one of Belgium's extraordinary buildings, a sprawling, ramshackle cross-timbered beauty dating from the 16th century. Grilled monkfish Indian style, baby duck prepared with Armagnac, and lightly smoked sweetbreads with a spicy rosemary sauce are among the delicacies. Interiors, all creaking parquet and glossy wood beams, have been furnished in Old Master luxury—Delft tiles, brass, pewter, Oriental runners. ✉ *Quai de la Goffe 41,* ☎ *04/223–7748. Jacket and tie. AE, DC, MC, V. No dinner Wed. Closed Sun., Easter wk, mid-July–mid-Aug.*

$$$ ✕ **Chez Max.** There's never a dull moment at this wonderful, elegant brasserie run by the charismatic Alain Struvay. The brasserie cuisine is enlivened by specialties, such as lobster and langoustines au gratin, turbot in champagne sauce, very tender, lightly smoked salmon—and more than 100 brands of whiskey. There is a spectacular *banc d'écailler* (oyster and seafood display). ✉ *Place de la République Française 12,* ☎ *04/223–7748. AE, DC, MC, V. No lunch Sat. Closed Sun.*

$–$$ ✕ **Robert Lesenne.** Here's another celebrity chef, loved by most but not by all. The fixed-price menu offering a choice of 32 appetizers, entrées, and desserts is remarkable value for the money. Many are standards given a new twist; the hake comes with roast asparagus, the sweetbreads in a strudel. The handsome restaurant is soberly decorated in soft shades, offset by striking pictures. ✉ *Rue de la Boucherie 9,* ☎

04/222–0793. *Reservations essential. AE, DC, MC, V. No lunch Sat. Closed Sun. and 2nd ½ of July.*

$ ✕ **Café Lequet.** This wood-paneled, riverside restaurant was favored by the Simenon family, and it still serves honest, home-style cooking: chicken with endives, veal fricassee, mussels and fries. This is a favored hangout of yuppies—or to use the Belgain appelation, NPBU (*nouvelle petite bourgeoisie urbaine*). ⊠ *Quai sur Meuse 17,* ☎ *04/222–2134. No credit cards. No dinner Sun.*

$$$ ✕🖭 **Bedford.** Opened in 1994, this hotel on the banks of the Meuse is just a few blocks from major museums and the old city. The bright, air-conditioned rooms have leather armchairs and marble bathrooms with blow-dryers. The brasserie-style restaurant is in the oldest part of the hotel, which dates from the 17th century. ⊠ *Quai St-Léonard 36,* ☎ *04/228–8111,* 𝔽𝔸𝕏 *04/227–4575. 149 rooms. Restaurant, bar, meeting rooms. AE, DC, MC, V.*

$ ✕🖭 **Comfort Inn l'Univers.** A cut above most train-station hotels, this landmark has been kept up to date with double windows, sharp room decor (beige and burgundy), and a modernized brasserie-bar downstairs. ⊠ *Rue des Guillemins 116,* ☎ *04/252–2804,* 𝔽𝔸𝕏 *04/252–1653. 49 rooms. Restaurant, bar. AE, DC, MC, V.*

$$$ 🖭 **Holiday Inn.** Next to the Palais des Congrès, this is the hotel of choice for European Congress delegates and businesspeople. The lobby and guest rooms have recently been refurbished, and the riverfront location is very pleasant. ⊠ *Esplanade de l'Europe 2,* ☎ *04/342–6020,* 𝔽𝔸𝕏 *04/343–4810. 219 rooms. Bar, no-smoking rooms, indoor pool, health club, sauna, convention center, parking (fee). AE, DC, MC, V.*

$ 🖭 **Simenon.** Named for Liège's most famous native son and located ★   in his old neighborhood east of the river, this splendid Belle Epoque house has been converted into a theme hotel: Each room is named for one of the author's novels. Excellent homemade ice cream is served in the tearoom. ⊠ *Boulevard de l'Est 16,* ☎ *04/342–8690,* 𝔽𝔸𝕏 *04/344–2669. 11 rooms with bath. Lobby lounge, tearoom. AE, DC, MC, V.*

Nightlife and the Arts

Check times at **Infor-Spectacles** (⊠ En Féronstrée 92, ☎ 04/222–1111). You can also buy tickets there. For all sorts of events in Liège, look under "Other Towns" in *The Bulletin.*

CAFÉS AND DISCOS

The Liégeois have an amazing ability to stay up until all hours, and nightlife is booming on both sides of the Meuse. The Carré quarter, on the left bank, is favored by students and those who go to a show first and out afterward. Two *cafés chantant,* which are very typical of this city, should be tried: **Les Olivettes** (⊠ Rue Pied-du-Pont des Arches 6, ☎ 04/222–0708) and **Les Caves de Porto** (⊠ En Féronstrée 144, ☎ 04/223–2325). The latter is closed Tuesday and Thursday. Other cafés, with lots of traditional ambience, include **Le Seigneur d'Amay** (⊠ Rue d'Amay 12, ☎ 04/222–0044) and **La Taverne St-Paul** (⊠ Rue St-Paul 8, ☎ 04/223–7217) near the cathedral. Rue Tête-de-Boeuf contains some fashionable clubs and discos such as **Estoril** (☎ 04/221–0937). Or you may choose to finish the evening more quietly in an ambience of Liège folklore at the **Café Tchantchès** (⊠ Rue Grande-Beche, ☎ 04/343–3931), a true Liège institution.

JAZZ

The Roture quarter in Outremeuse is where people go for a full night's entertainment. There's hardly a house without a café, club, or jazz hangout. Here's where the best jazz clubs are, including **Le Lion s'envoile**

(✉ En Route 11, ☎ 04/342–9317), which has jazz Wednesday night, and **Le Cirque Divers** (✉ En Route 13, ☎ 04/341–0244). Both branch out from time to time into literary and other kinds of happenings.

MUSIC AND OPERA

Liège has its own opera company, the **Opéra Royal de Wallonie** (✉ Théâtre Royal, Rue des Dominicains, ☎ 04/223–5910). The city's symphony orchestra, **l'Orchestre Philharmonique de Liège,** has recorded prizewinning discs and tours internationally. The **Wallonie Chamber Orchestra** and other ensembles participate in the annual Festival de la Wallonie, with concerts also in Spa and Stavelot. The **Stavelot Music Festival** (☎ 080/862450) is held every August, with concerts in the old abbey.

PUPPET THEATER

On Wednesday at 2:30 and Sunday mornings at 10:30, you can see puppet theater featuring the irrepressible Tchantchès at the **Théâtre Royal Ex-Impérial de Roture** (✉ Rue Surlet 56, ☎ 04/342–7575) and the theater of the **Musée de la Vie Wallonne** (✉ Cour des Mineurs, ☎ 04/223–6094). The **Théâtre Al Botroule** (✉ Rue Hocheporte 3, ☎ 04/223–0576) has puppet shows for adults Saturday at 8, and for children Wednesday at 3.

THEATER

The most interesting theater performances in French or Walloon are generally at the **Théâtre de la Place** (✉ Place de l'Yser, ☎ 04/342–8118). It's worth checking out what's on at **Les Chiroux** (✉ Place des Carmes, ☎ 04/223–1960). The **Festival du Théâtre de Spa** (☎ 087/771700) is a showcase for the young and talented. Programs and information about the three-week August season are available from early June.

En Route Traveling from Liège to Malmédy, it is the trip itself, and especially the Hautes Fagnes, that is the big attraction. You leave the E40 motorway to Aachen at the exit for **Eupen,** where all the signs are in German, although you haven't crossed the border; this small town is the capital of Belgium's third (and by far the smallest) language group. From Eupen, you drive through dense woods that open up into the **Hautes Fagnes** (High Fens), a national park of almost 10,500 acres. Here the vistas open over vast tracts of moor, with bushes and copses harboring rich and varied vegetation and bird life. The marshland is waterlogged, and wooden walkways have been laid out across the area. You're well advised not to stray from them and to be exceedingly careful with matches during dry spells. Paths are clearly marked. **Baraque Michel** is the starting point for paths across the moors. At the à **Botrange** nature center, you can get a professional introduction to the flora and fauna of the High Fens. Parts of the area can only be visited with a guide, especially the peat bogs and the feeding areas of the *capercaillies* (large and very rare woodland grouse). You can book an individual guide in advance, and you can also rent boots and bikes. ✉ *Robertville,* ☎ *080/445781.* ▣ *BF150.* ☉ *Mon. 1–6, Tues.–Sun. 10–6; closed 2 wks in Nov.*

Schloss Reinhardstein, the loftiest and possibly the best-preserved medieval fortress in the country, is reached by a mile-long hike through the High Fens. It sits on a spur of rock overlooking the river Warche and has been in the hands of such illustrious families as the Metternichs, ancestors of Prince Metternich, who masterminded the Congress of Vienna in 1815. The castle has been well restored; the Hall of Knights and the Chapel are gems. ✉ *Robertville,* ☎ *080/446868.* ▣ *BF150.* ☉ *Tours mid-June–mid-Sept., Sun. at 2:15, 3:15, 4:15, and 5:15; July–Aug., also Tues., Thurs., and Sat. at 3:30.*

Malmédy

88 *57 km (34 mi) southeast of Liège, 156 km (94 mi) southeast of Brussels, 16 km (10 mi) southeast of Spa.*

Malmédy and its neighbor, Stavelot, formed a separate, peaceful principality, ruled by abbots, for 11 centuries before the French Revolution. The Congress of Vienna, redrawing the borders of Europe, handed it to Germany, and it was not reunited with Belgium until 1925. In a scene straight out of *Catch 22,* the center of Malmédy was destroyed by American bombers in 1944 after the town had been liberated. Still, there's enough left of the old town, where street signs are often in French and Wallon, for an interesting walk. Its carnival, beginning on the Saturday before Lent, is among the merriest in Belgium. To learn more about it, visit the **Musée du Carnaval.** ✉ *Place de Rome 11, 3rd floor (no elevator),* ☎ *080/337058.* 💳 *BF100.* ⏲ *July–Aug., Wed.–Mon. 3–6; Sept.–June, weekends 2:30–5:30.*

NEED A
BREAK? **Le Floreal** (✉ Place Albert-I 8) serves breakfast, lunch, dinner, and snacks, such as the local ham specialty, *jambon d'Ardennes.*

Dining and Lodging

$$$$ ✕🏨 **Hostellerie Trôs Marets.** Up the hill on the road toward Eupen, this inn offers a splendid view over the wooded valley. In fall, the fog hangs low over the nearby High Fens; in winter, cross-country skiing beckons. The main building contains the restaurant and five rustic, cozy rooms. A modern annex has suites (furnished in contemporary English style, with fireplaces) and a large indoor pool. The restaurant serves up such specialties as duck's liver with caramelized apples, asparagus in truffle vinaigrette, grilled duckling with honey, and Herve cheese soufflé with Liège liqueur. Half-board is a good value. ✉ *Route des Trôs Marets 2, Bévercé, 3 km (2 mi) north on N68,* ☎ *080/337917,* 📠 *080/339710. 5 rooms with bath, 4 suites. Restaurant, pool. AE, DC, MC, V. Closed mid-Nov.–Dec. 25.*

$ ✕🏨 **Ferme Libert.** This landmark is beautifully located on the edge of
★ the forest, a few miles north on the Eupen road. The architecture is traditional rustic, and the large dining room overlooks the valley. The menu is long on meat of all kinds, including ostrich, bison, and springbok. The ambience is similar to that of an Alpine resort, with skiing in winter (at least a few weeks), bracing walks the rest of the year. Half-pension is required on weekends. ✉ *Chaussée de Bévercé–Village 26, 4960 Bévercé,* ☎ *080/330247,* 📠 *080/339885. 18 rooms with bath, 22 with shower. Restaurant. AE, MC, V.*

Stavelot

89 *15 km (9 mi) southwest of Malmédy, 59 km (37 mi) southeast of Liège, 158 km (95 mi) southeast of Brussels.*

Although Stavelot is practically a twin town of Malmédy, its traditions differ. Here Carnival is celebrated on the fourth Sunday in Lent and is animated by about 2,000 *Blancs-Moussis* (White Monks), dressed in white with long capes and bright red long noses, who swoop and rush through the streets. The Blancs-Moussis commemorate the monks of Stavelot, who in 1499 were forbidden to participate in Carnival but got around it by celebrating Laetare Sunday (three weeks before Easter). Stavelot, too, was badly damaged in the Battle of the Bulge, but some picturesque old streets survived, particularly Rue Haute, off Place St-Remacle. The square is named for St. Remacle, who founded a local abbey in 647. His reliquary, now in the **Eglise Saint-Sébastien,** is one of the wonders of Art Mosan. Dating from the 13th century, it is 6½ feet long and decorated with statuettes, of the apostles on the sides and of Christ and the Virgin on the ends. ⊠ *Rue de l'Eglise 7,* ☎ *080/864437.* ⌑ *BF40.* ☉ *July–Aug., daily 9–noon and 2–5; rest of yr by appointment.*

Only a Romanesque tower remains of the original buildings that formed the **Ancienne Abbaye** (Old Abbey). The present buildings date from the 18th century, and the refectory has become a concert hall. The old stable has been converted into the **Musée d'Art Religieux Régional** (Regional Museum of Religious Art), and the vaulted cellars of the abbey have been put to somewhat anachronistic use in housing the **Musée du Circuit de Spa-Francorchamps** (Museum of the Spa-Francorchamp Racecourse), which displays Formula I racing cars, sports cars, and motorcycles illustrating the history of motor racing since 1907. ☎ *080/862706.* ⌑ *BF125; valid also for Museum of Religious Art.* ☉ *Daily 10–12:30 and 2:30–5:30 (Nov.–Mar. until 4:30).*

En Route The road from Stavelot runs through attractive landscape. The shortest—via Francorchamps—uses, in part, the Grand Prix racing circuit; prepare for detours in August. An alternative, even more rewarding route, is via **Coo;** kayak trips down the Amblève River start at the bottom of the waterfalls. Chairlifts take you up to **Telecoo,** a plateau where there's a splendid view of the Amblève River valley, an extensive amusement park, and a 200-acre Ardennes wildlife park (☎ 080/684265).

Dining and Lodging

$$ ✕⛌ **Le Val d'Amblève.** Their hotel having become a member of the
★ Romantik Hotels chain, the owners have spruced it up with new furniture. Rooms face a lawn with century-old trees. The restaurant's menu includes brill with asparagus and quail salad with croutons and bacon. ⊠ *Route de Malmedy 7,* ☎ *080/862353,* ﬀ *080/864121. 13 rooms with bath. Restaurant ($$$). AE, DC, MC, V. No dinner Thurs. Closed Mon., 3 wks in Jan.*

$ ✕⛌ **Hôtel d'Orange.** A former post house, this friendly hotel has been in the same family since 1789. Rooms are charming, and there's a range of fixed-price menus, including one for kids. Quail, ever popular in these parts, chicken à l'estragon, and lamb are staples on the menu. ⊠ *Devant les Capucins 8,* ☎ *080/862005,* ﬀ *080/864292. 22 rooms, 18 with bath or shower. Restaurant. AE, DC, MC, V. Closed Tues.–Wed. (except July–Aug.); 1 wk each in Jan., July, and Sept; weekdays Jan.–Feb.*

Spa

⑳ *18 km (11 mi) north of Stavelot, 38 km (23 mi) southeast of Liège, 139 km (83 mi) southeast of Brussels.*

Spa is, indeed, the spa from which all others have derived their name. The Romans came here to take the waters, and they were followed over the centuries by crowned heads, such as Marguerite de Valois, Christina of Sweden, and Peter the Great. Less welcome was Kaiser Wilhelm II, who established his general headquarters in Spa in 1918. By then Spa was already past its prime. During the 18th and 19th centuries, Spa had been the watering place of international high society, and many gracious houses remain from that period. The pleasures of "taking the cure" in beautiful surroundings were heightened in those days by high-stakes gambling, playing *pharaon* or *biribi* for rubles, ducats, piastres, or francs. Gambling in today's casino is more sedate. The **Casino** dates from 1763, making it the oldest in the world, but the present building is from the beginning of the century. Gaming rooms and the lobby are in Louis XVI style, a far cry from Las Vegas.

With its slightly geriatric air, Spa as a whole gives an impression of pleasantly faded elegance. The two best-known water sources in the center of town—locally known as *pouhons*—are the **Pouhon Pierre-le-Grant** and **Pouhon Prince-de-Condé,** which can be visited by tourists as well as *curistes* (people taking the cure). The price for a glass straight from the source is a modest BF7. ⊠ *Town center,* ☎ *087/772510.* ⊙ *Baths: Easter–Oct., daily 10–noon and 2–5:30; Nov.–Easter, weekdays 2–5, weekends 10–noon and 2–5.*

The **Grottes de Remouchamps,** once inhabited by primitive hunters, are beautifully lit underground caves where you can take the "longest subterranean boat ride in the world." ⊠ *Route de Louveigné,* ☎ *04/360–9070.* 🖃 *BF290.* ⊙ *Feb.–Nov., daily 9–6.*

The **Grotte de Comblain-au-Pont** was reopened in 1994 with modern lighting, allowing visitors to discover the caves on their own. There's an abandoned underground quarry and a 10-kilometer (6-mile) signposted walk laid out so that you can fully appreciate the geological and botanical riches of the region. ⊠ *Rue du Grand Pré 25, Comblain-au-Pont,* ☎ *04/369–4133.* 🖃 *BF330.* ⊙ *Apr.–mid-Nov., daily 10–5.*

Dining and Lodging

$$ ✕ **L'Art de Vivre.** Jean-François Douffet is the revelation of the dining
★ scene in Spa, with a fresh new approach that contrasts pleasantly with the old-fashioned gentility of his competitors. Sautéed goose liver accompanied by a potato pancake, and pikeperch with deep-fried basil leaves and ice cream with figs are among his creations. ⊠ *Avenue Reine Astrid 53,* ☎ *087/770444. AE, DC, MC, V. Closed Tues., Wed. (except July–Sept.).*

$$ ✕ **La Brasserie du Grand Maur.** This graceful 200-year-old city mansion
★ houses a lovely restaurant with a loyal clientele. Tartare of salmon, lamb infused with tomato and thyme, and duck's breast with raspberries and red currants are special favorites. The setting, all polished wood, linens, and antiques, enhances the meal. ⊠ *Rue Xhrouet 41,* ☎ *087/773616. AE, DC, MC, V. Closed Mon.–Tues., 3 wks Dec.–Jan., 2 wks in June.*

$–$$ ✕ **Old Inn.** A simple, slightly touristy little lunch stop on the main street across from the baths, this beamed and wainscoted restaurant serves inexpensive regional dishes (ham, game), as well as mussels and crepes. It's one step up from a tavern, with pink linens covered by paper mats with ads for local businesses. ⊠ *Rue Royale 17,* ☎ *087/773943. AE, DC, MC, V. Closed off-season, Wed.*

$$$ ✕🖼 **Cardinal.** Offering a real taste of old Spa, this grand urban resort
★ hotel opened in 1924—and was completely renovated in 1948. Its period decor and interior architecture are completely intact and as fresh as new. Have tea in the muraled salon, hot chocolate in the beautiful all-oak café, or dinner in the swanky chandeliered dining hall. Most rooms are 1948 modern (smooth gold oak paneling). ⊠ *Place Royale 21–27,* ☎ *087/771064,* 🖷 *087/771964. 29 rooms with bath. Restaurant, bar, tearoom. AE, DC, MC, V.*

Outdoor Activities and Sports

Boating

There's a yacht harbor along Boulevard Frère Orban in **Liège,** and water sports are popular upstream from the **Pont Albert I.** Another water-sports center is the Ile Robinson at **Visé.**

Canoeing and Kayaking

Virtually all the rivers of the Ardennes are great for canoeing, and the meandering Amblève is one of the best. Single or double kayaks can be rented at **Cookayak** (✉ Stavelot, ☎ 080/684265) for a 9-kilometer (5-mile) ride from Coo to Cheneux (about 1½ hrs) or a 23-kilometer (14-mile) ride to Lorcé (about 3½ hrs). Bus service back to the starting point is provided.

Golf

There are two 18-hole courses in the Liège area: the **Royal Golf Club du Sart Tilman** (✉ Route du Condroz 541, Angleur, ☎ 04/336–2021) and the **International Gomzé Golf Club** (✉ Sur Counachamps 8, Gomzé-Andoumont, ☎ 04/360–9207). At Spa, there's a lovely 18-hole golf course at **Balmoral** (✉ Avenue de l'Hippodrome 1, ☎ 087/771613).

Horseback Riding

The **Worriken Sports Center** (✉ Rue Worriken 9, Bütgenbach, ☎ 080/446961) offers horseback riding in the Hautes Fagnes region.

Motor Racing

Motor-sport fans know **Francorchamps** (near Spa) as one of the world's top racing circuits. The Formula I Grand Prix de Belgique race is run in August, and there are several other motorcycle and automobile races throughout the year. Contact Intercommunale du Circuit de Spa-Francorchamps (✉ Route du Circuit 55, Francorchamps, ☎ 087/275138) for information.

Skiing

Downhill and cross-country ski areas are dotted around the region. Equipment is generally available locally. Snow conditions vary wildly, however; check before setting out by calling **Belsud** (☎ 02/504–0280) in Brussels.

Swimming and Skating

The **Palais des Sports de Coronmeuse** in Liège (✉ Quai de Wallonie 7, ☎ 04/227–1324) provides facilities for swimming in a heated outdoor pool in summer and skating in winter.

Shopping

In Liège, the **Carré** is almost exclusively a pedestrian area, with boutiques, cafés, and restaurants. The most important shopping arcades are the **Passage Lemonnier** (✉ Between Vinâve d'Ile and Rue de l'Univérsité), **Galerie du Pont d'Avroy** (✉ Off the street of the same name), and **Galerie Nagelmackers** (✉ Between Place de la Cathédrale and Rue Tournant St-Paul).

Glassware from Val St-Lambert can be found in a number of shops and most advantageously at the factory shop (✉ Rue du Val 245, Seraing, ☎ 04/337–0960). **Firearms,** an age-old Liège specialty, are still handmade to order by some gun shops, notably Lebeau-Courally (✉ Rue St-Gilles 386, ☎ 04/252–4843). Keep in mind that only a licensed arms importer may carry arms into the United States.

Liège and Environs A to Z

Arriving and Departing

BY CAR

Liège is almost halfway to Cologne from Brussels on the E40. The city is also linked with Paris by the E42, which merges with E19 from Brussels near Mons, and Antwerp by the E313, and with Maastricht and the Dutch highway system by E25, which continues south to join the E411 to Luxembourg.

BY TRAIN

There are 20 trains a day from Brussels. The trip takes an hour by express train from Brussels Nord, 1 hour and 10 minutes from Brussels Midi. Local trains are 10 minutes slower. New Thalys high-speed trains cut 15 minutes off travel time from Brussels Midi. All express trains from Oostende to Cologne stop at Liège, so do international trains from Copenhagen and Hamburg to Paris. Liège's station is the **Gare des Guillemins** (☎ 04/252–9850).

Getting Around

BY BUS AND TRAIN

Local train services exist from Liège via Verviers to Eupen, and to Trois-Ponts (near Stavelot). From these points there is bus service to other localities.

In Liège, a single trip on a bus in the inner city costs BF36, and eight-trip cards sell for BF200.

BY CAR

This is by far the easiest, and if time is a problem, you can choose the highways that crisscross the province. To appreciate the region's scenic beauty, take the narrow roads that mostly follow the river valleys.

CAR RENTAL

Avis (⊠ Boulevard d'Avroy 238, Liège, ☎ 04/252–5500). **Hertz** (⊠ Boulevard d'Avroy 60, ☎ 04/222–4273).

BY TAXI

Taxis are plentiful in Liège and can be picked up at cab stands in the principal squares, or summoned by phone (☎ 04/367–6600).

Contacts and Resources

GUIDED TOURS

From Liège, one-day sightseeing **boat excursions** to Maastricht in the Netherlands are arranged Fridays in July and August. A visit to the Blegny Coal Mine and museum is included. Departures are from Passerelle on the right bank of the Meuse. For reservations call 04/387–4333.

You can hire an **English-speaking guide** from the Liège City Tourist Office (☞ Visitor Information, *below*). Rates are BF1,200 for two hours and BF600 per additional hour. If your French is up to it, you're welcome to join a guided walking tour with French commentary, starting from the city tourist office, July and August, Wednesday through Sunday, at 2, for BF140.

VISITOR INFORMATION

Province of Liège Tourist Office (⊠ Boulevard de la Sauvenière 77, ☎ 04/222–4210). **Liège City Tourist Office** (⊠ En Féronstrée 92, ☎ 04/221–9221). **Eupen** (⊠ Marktplatz 7, ☎ 087/553450). **Malmédy** (⊠ Place du Châtelet 10, ☎ 080/330250). **Spa** (⊠ Rue Royale 41, ☎ 087/772519). **Stavelot** (⊠ Ancienne Abbaye, ☎ 080/862706).

Belgian Luxembourg

The Belgian province of Luxembourg is almost twice as large as the independent Grand Duchy of Luxembourg. Luxembourg made common cause with Belgium against the Dutch in 1830, but while Belgium gained its freedom, the Grand Duchy was divided by decree of the major European powers, with the western part going to Belgium and the rest, as a sort of consolation prize, was handed to the unpopular William I of the Netherlands. It remained under Dutch domination for another 50-odd years. Luxembourg is the largest and, with just 200,000 inhabitants, by far the most sparsely populated province of Belgium. Here you can fill your lungs with fresh mountain air. It's a land of forests and dairy farms, slate-gray houses and fortresses perched on high rocks, swift streams and flowering meadows.

Durbury

★ ⑨ *40 km (24 mi) southwest of Spa, 51 km (31 mi) south of Liège, 119 km (71 mi) southeast of Brussels.*

Durbury had just 400 inhabitants until 20 years ago, when it unwillingly merged with surrounding parishes and became 20 times bigger. Before that, nothing much had changed since 1331, when Durbury received its city charter from John the Blind of Luxembourg. Wander around the narrow streets and soak up the atmosphere of a remarkably homogenous and well-preserved architecture, including the 16th-century, half-timbered grange where peasants would bring the part of the harvest due the lord of the manor.

In **Wéris,** one of the country's most beautiful villages, half-timbered houses and a great fortified farm surround an 11th-century Romanesque church. A number of megaliths bear witness to an older culture.

Dining and Lodging

$ ✕ **Le Moulin.** The mill dates from the 13th century, the cuisine from the 20th, and the seasoning comes from Provence: thyme, garlic, and saffron. Loin of lamb, duckling breast with honey and sherry, and seafood couscous are among the offerings. ⊠ *Place aux Foires 17,* ☎ *086/ 210084. AE, MC, V.*

$$ ✕🏨 **Le Sanglier des Ardennes.** Dominating the center of town, this inn-cum-luxury restaurant has a stone fireplace, beams, and public spaces punctuated by glass cases with perfume, leather, and French scarves for sale. Rooms are classic pastel-modern, and the bathrooms are large. The restaurant offers grand French cooking with some regional touches. Back windows overlook the Ourthe River. ⊠ *Rue Comte d'Ursel 99, 5480 Durbury,* ☎ *086/213262. 41 rooms. Restaurant ($$$$), bar, outdoor café. AE, DC, MC, V. Closed Thurs., Jan.*

La Roche-en-Ardenne

★ ⑨ *29 km (17 mi) south of Durbuy, 77 km (46 mi) south of Liège, 127 km (76 mi) southeast of Brussels.*

La Roche-en-Ardenne is marvelously situated and full of tourists. They're here for a good reason: The surroundings are the very essence of the Ardennes. The main attraction is a trip out of town to admire the view, and the principal part is played by the river Ourthe, a meandering stream that splashes through a landscape of great beauty. Follow N834 south and turn left on N843 to **Nisramont,** which has an excellent view. Cross the river and go left on N860 to Nadrin, and left again on N869 to the **Belvedère des Six Ourthes,** thus named because it has six different views of the meandering river. A 120-step climb to the top of the observation tower will reward you with a magnificent view of wooded hills and valleys. You can return on the pretty N860, following the banks of the Ourthe toward La Roche.

The **château,** whose ruins dominate the small town, dates from the 9th century. Subsequently it was added to by a long series of occupants, until the Austrians decided to partially dismantle it 200 years ago. The entrance is from Place du Marché. ☎ *061/212711.* 🎫 *BF70.* ☉ *Apr.–June and Sept., daily 10–noon and 2–5; July–Aug., daily 10–7; Oct.–Mar., weekends 10–noon and 2–4.*

La Roche-en-Ardenne suffered badly during the Battle of the Bulge, when some 70,000 shells hit the town. The **Musée de la Bataille des Ardennes** (Museum of the Battle of the Ardennes) displays uniforms, vehicles, weapons, and personal belongings found on the battleground. ⊠ *Rue Châmont 5,* ☎ *084/411725.* 🖃 *BF160.* ⊙ *Daily 10–6.*

Dining and Lodging

$$ ✕ **La Huchette.** Though a bit out of place in this hardy forest resort, this elegant and welcoming restaurant serves good, classic French cooking—delicate quenelles (dumplings) of pike in lobster broth, salmon tournedos in tarragon, pigeon with red cabbage—in a decidedly nonrustic setting of pink, brass, and terra-cotta. ⊠ *Rue de l'Eglise 6,* ☎ *084/411333. AE, MC, V. No dinner Tues. Closed Wed.*

$$ ✕🖾 **Hostellerie Linchet.** At the best address in an otherwise touristy town, this new hotel has large rooms that overlook the Ourthe valley. The restaurant offers splendid views and a traditional cuisine that includes such dishes as stuffed crayfish, poached trout in Alsatian white wine, and fillet of venison with truffle sauce; there's alfresco dining in season. ⊠ *Route de Houffalize 11,* ☎ *084/411223,* 🖷 *084/412410. 13 rooms. Restaurant ($$$). AE, MC, V. Closed Tues.–Wed., Mar., 3 wks June–July.*

$ ✕🖾 **Du Midi.** This tiny old cliffside hotel is worth a visit for the food, which is the Real Thing: straightforward regional specialties, simply and stylishly served. Game in season is superbly cooked (tenderloin of young boar in old port) and served with *gratin Dauphinois* (scalloped potatoes) and poached pear; there's also air-dried Ardennes ham with candied onions. The setting is local—oak, green plush, brass lamps, spinning-wheel chandeliers—though not old. The hotel is newly renovated, and all the rooms now have bath or shower. ⊠ *Rue Beausaint 6,* ☎ *084/411138,* 🖷 *084/412238. 8 rooms with bath or shower. Restaurant. AE, DC, MC, V. Closed 2nd ½ of June, 2nd ½ of Jan.*

$ ✕🖾 **Les Genets.** Even the rooms are pretty in this romantic old sprawl of a mountain inn, with its stenciled wallpaper and homey mixes of plaid, paisley, and chintz. Picture windows take in valley views on two sides. The restaurant offers gastronomic menus (grilled and smoked trout salad with hazelnut vinaigrette, pigeon in juniper). The hotel prefers guests to take half-board. ⊠ *Corniche de Deister 2,* ☎ *084/411877,* 🖷 *084/411893. 8 rooms, 7 with bath. Restaurant, bar. AE, DC, MC, V. Closed 3 wks June–July, 1st ½ of Jan.*

Bastogne

㉓ *34 km (20 mi) south of La Roche-en-Ardenne, 88 km (53 mi) south of Liège, 148 km (89 mi) southeast of Brussels.*

Bastogne is where General MacAuliffe delivered World War II's most famous response to a surrender request: "Nuts!" Although a number of Ardennes towns were destroyed during the Battle of the Bulge, Bastogne was the epicenter. The town was surrounded by Germans but held by the American 101st Airborne Division. The weather was miserable, making it impossible for supplies to be flown in to the Americans. On December 22, 1944, the Germans asked the U.S. forces to surrender. They didn't. On December 26 the skies cleared and supplies were flown in, but it took another month before the last German stronghold was destroyed. To this day, a Sherman tank occupies a place of honor in the center of town.

The **Colline du Mardasson** (Mardasson Hill Memorial) honors the Americans lost in the battle. The names of all U.S. Army units are inscribed on the wall, with a simple phrase: "The Belgian People Remembers Its American Liberators." Mosaics by Fernand Léger decorate the crypt with its three chapels, Protestant, Catholic, and Jewish. The **Bastogne Historical Center,** next to the memorial monument, is built in the shape of a five-pointed star. The ebb and flow of the battle are shown in multivision in the amphitheater, and there are also showings of a remarkable new film, including footage shot during the battle. The collections include authentic uniforms, arms, and wartime memorabilia. ⊠ *3 km (2 mi) east of Bastogne,* ☎ *061/211413.* ⊡ *BF245.* ☉ *Apr. and Sept.–Mar., daily 10–4; May–June, daily 9–5; July–Aug., daily 9–6.*

Dining and Lodging

$ ✕ **Wagon-Restaurant Léo.** Originally a tiny chrome railroad diner, this local institution has spilled over across the street into the new, chicly refurbished Bistro Léo. The restaurant serves huge platters of plain Belgian standards—mussels, trout in riesling, *filet Américain* (steak tartare), frites; in the bistro, cold ham plates, quiche, and homemade lasagna are the fare. ⊠ *Rue du Vivier 8,* ☎ *061/216510. MC, V.*

$ ✕⊡ **La Ferme au Pont.** On a country road between Bastogne and La
★ Roche, this idyllic little farmhouse inn is surrounded by forests, with the Ourthe rushing just behind it. Dating from 1747, with whitewashed brick, flower boxes on every sill, and a dining room with views of landscaped grounds, the inn offers good, simple cooking—grilled ham and smoked trout—and comfortable rooms decked with ivy-print fabrics. ⊠ *On N834, 16 km (10 mi) from Bastogne, near Ortho,* ☎ *084/433161. 7 rooms, 4 with bath. AE, DC, MC, V.*

$$ ⊡ **Melba.** A couple of minutes from Place MacAuliffe, this is a modern if somewhat anonymous hotel, with access for persons with disabilities. A large buffet breakfast is included, supplied from the patisserie of the same name. ⊠ *Avenue Mathieu 49-51,* ☎ *061/217778,* ⅨⅩ *061/215568. 24 rooms with bath. Breakfast room, meeting rooms. AE, MC, V.*

$ ⊡ **Du Sud.** Airy and solid in its new, postwar form, this straightforward little hotel kept its local atmosphere—oak details, game trophies, tile floors—and offers simple comforts. Back rooms are quietest. ⊠ *Rue de Marche 39,* ☎ *061/211114. 13 rooms with shower. Café. MC, V.*

Saint-Hubert

㉔ *28 km (17 mi) west of Bastogne, 25 km (15 mi) south of La Roche-en-Ardenne, 137 km (82 mi) southeast of Brussels.*

Saint-Hubert bears the name of the patron saint of hunters. According to legend, Hubert, hunting in these woods on Good Friday in 683, saw his quarry, a stag, turn its head toward him, and its antlers held a crucifix. Hubert lowered his bow and went on to become a bishop and a saint. On the first Sunday in September, the old **Basilica** has a special Mass that includes music played with hunting horns, followed by a historical procession; and on November 3, St. Hubert's Feast Day, there's a blessing of the animals in the Basilica. The Basilica is stunningly beautiful, with a late Gothic interior of noble proportions and luminosity. ⊠ *Place de l'Abbaye,* ☎ *061/612388.* ⊡ *BF25.* ☉ *Daily 9:30–5.*

Fourneau Saint-Michel has two interesting museums. One is an **Industrial Museum** that includes a preserved, 18th-century ironworks complex and shows ironworking techniques up to the 19th century. The other is an open-air **Museum of Rural Life,** with 25 structures, including thatched cottages, tobacco sheds, a chapel, and a school. ⊠ *Route de Nassagne, 7 km (4 mi) north of Saint-Hubert,* ☎ *084/210890.* ⊡ *BF100* *per museum.* ⏲ *Mar.–Dec. (Rural Life until mid-Nov.), daily 9–5 (in July–Aug. until 6).*

The **Euro Space Center** shows off the latest technology in a futuristic setting, with models (some full-scale) of the *Discovery* space shuttle, Mir space station, and the *Ariane* satellite launcher. There's an educational program as well for young and old. ✉ *Rue Devant-les-Hêtres 1, Transinne,* ☎ *061/656465.* 🎫 *BF395.* ⏲ *Mid-Feb.–Nov., daily 10–5.*

Dining and Lodging

$ ✕🏨 **Borquin.** In the shadow of the handsome Basilica, this small, friendly hotel comprises a few, reasonably comfortable rooms. The unabashedly kitschy restaurant serves honest and copious home-style cooking. ✉ *Place de l'Abbaye 6,* ☎ *061/611456,* FAX *061/612018. 9 rooms, 7 with bath. Restaurant. AE, DC, MC, V. Closed Wed. and 2nd ½ of Aug.*

Bouillon

(95) *56 km (34 mi) southwest of Saint-Hubert, 81 km (49 mi) southwest of La Roche-en-Ardenne, 161 km (97 mi) southeast of Brussels.*

In Bouillon, the Semois River curls around a promontory crowned by one of Europe's most impressive castles. This tiny town was capital of a duchy almost equally small, which managed to remain independent for 800 years. Its most famous native son, Godefroy de Bouillon, sold it to the Bishop of Liège in 1096 to improve his cash flow, before departing on the first crusade and becoming Defender of the Holy Sepulchre. Bouillon owed its independence to the **Château Fort,** an impressive example of medieval military architecture. Successive modifications have done little to alter the personality of this feudal stronghold, with its towers, drawbridge, guardroom, torture chamber, dungeons, and enormous walls. There's an outstanding view from the top of the Tour d'Autriche. Visits by torchlight are organized nightly (except Monday and Thursday) in July and August. In season, the town is packed with tourists. ☎ *061/466257.* 🎫 *BF140.* ⏲ *Mar.–June and Sept.–Nov., daily 10–5; July–Aug., daily 9:30–7; Dec. and Feb., weekdays 1–5, weekends 10–5.*

The **Musée Ducal** is installed in an 18th-century mansion in front of the château. Its collections illustrate the history of the Crusades; another section is devoted to the printing press that published Voltaire, Diderot, and other writers when they could not publish in France. ✉ *Rue du Petit 1,* ☎ *061/466956.* 🎫 *BF120.* ⏲ *Apr.–June and Sept.–Oct., daily 10–6; July–Aug., daily 9:30–7; Nov.–Dec., weekends 10–5.*

★ (96) **Abbaye d'Orval** was once one of Europe's richest and most famous monasteries. Founded by Italian Benedictines in 1070, it flourished for 700 years before being twice destroyed by French troops. The grandeur and nobility of the medieval and 18th-century ruins are remarkable. The tomb of Wenceslas, first Duke of Luxembourg, is in the choir of the abbey church, and outside it is the spring where Mathilde, Duchess of Lorraine, once dropped her wedding band, only to have it miraculously returned by a trout. The monastery was finally reconsecrated as a Trappist abbey in 1948. The monks are known not only for their spirituality but also for the excellence of their bread, cheese, and potent Trappist beer. ✉ *Villers-devant-Orval,* ☎ *061/311060.* 🎫 *BF80.* ⏲ *Daily (except Mon.* AM *in winter) 10–noon and 1:30–5:30.*

Dining and Lodging

$$$$ ✕🏨 **Auberge du Moulin Hideux.** Nestled in a valley amid leafy woods, this inn with a mill is synonymous with gracious living. The fountain is illuminated at night, swans glide in the small pond, and breakfast is

served on the flower-bedecked terrace. The cuisine is traditional but updated with a lighter touch; woodcock mousse, black and white *boudins* (blood sausage) with truffles, and fabulous game in season are among the menu highlights. The rooms, all with balconies, have been decorated with great taste by the owner herself. Interestingly, the name means the "Hideous Mill," a play on words from the fact that there used to be two mills, *il y a deux.* ⊠ *Route de Dohan 1, Noirefontaine, 4 km (just over 2 mi) north of Bouillon,* ☎ *061/467015,* FAX *061/467281. 10 rooms with bath, 3 suites. Restaurant, bar, bicycles. AE, DC, MC, V. Closed Dec.–mid-Mar.*

$$ ✕🏠 **Au Gastronome.** This auberge, once a roadside café, is one of Bel-
★ gium's top half-dozen restaurants. The chef explores the usual stellar routes of haute cuisine, without losing any of its freshness. A local delicacy is suckling pig, roasted in its crisp skin, its juices blending with those of its stuffing of green pepper and lime. The setting is a little stuffy, but rooms upstairs are pleasantly old-fashioned, in shades of pink and cream, with floral prints. All overlook the garden. ⊠ *Rue Bouillon 2, Paliseul, 15 km (9 mi) north of Bouillon,* ☎ *061/533064,* FAX *061/533891. 9 rooms with bath. Restaurant ($$$$). AE, DC, MC, V. No dinner Sun. Closed Mon., Jan., Carnival wk, 2 wks June–July.*

$$ ✕🏠 **De la Poste.** This is the most historic and atmospheric hotel in town, but not consistently the most comfortable. Since Napoléon III, Emile Zola, and Victor Hugo stayed at this 1730 stagecoach stop, its original rooms have been left virtually unchanged, balancing burnished oak and antiques with aged fixtures and small baths. The all-new annex, built in 1990, offers modern comfort. Downstairs, the grandeur remains intact, with a charming mix of Victorian antiques and rustic brocante. The restaurant stretches along the riverfront; the menu features French classics. ⊠ *Place St-Arnould 1, Bouillon,* ☎ *061/466506,* FAX *061/467202. 77 rooms, 68 with bath or shower. Restaurant, bar, outdoor café. AE, DC, MC, V.*

$ ✕🏠 **Auberge d'Alsace.** In the center of Bouillon, with the river Semois across the street and the château towering behind, is this ambitious little hotel-restaurant. Having had the interior rebuilt from the ground up, the proprietress has lavished the rooms with flashy fabrics, brass, lacquer, lace, and the occasional baldachin. Striking a similar tenuous balance between store-bought chic and Old Ardennes, the restaurant downstairs offers good cooking: monkfish with kiwi, curried shrimp, but also home-smoked trout and homemade *civet de marcassin* (stew of preserved young boar). ⊠ *Faubourg de France 3,* ☎ *061/466588,* FAX *061/468321. 18 rooms with bath or shower. Restaurant, café, outdoor café. AE, MC, V.*

Arlon

97 *55 km (33 mi) east of Bouillon, 187 km (112 mi) southeast of Brussels, 29 km (17 mi) west of Luxembourg.*

Arlon, like Tongeren to the north and Tournai to the west, has a Roman past, which is vividly present in the **Musée Luxembourgeois.** The museum contains a number of Roman tombstones from the first 300 years AD, sculpted with reliefs of mythical figures as well as scenes from daily life. The best-known and most vivid is *The Voyagers.* There is also a section of Merovingian objects and jewelry. ⊠ *Rue des Martyrs 13,* ☎ *063/219988.* 🎫 *BF100.* ☉ *Mid-June–mid-Sept., Mon.–Sat. 9–noon and 2–5, Sun. 10–noon and 2–7.*

Dining and Lodging

$ ✕ **Le Clos Saint-Donat.** This upstairs, downtown restaurant, decorated in pastel colors offset by showy copper, is a relaxing place to stop. The menu scales no heights: spring chicken with raisin sauce, blanquette of veal. Value-for-money fixed-price menus are available. ⊠ *Place Didier 31,* ☎ *063/233400. AE, MC, V. No lunch Sat., no dinner Sun. Closed 1st ½ of Sept.*

$$$ ✕▥ **Château du Pont-d'Oye.** Close to the French border in Habay-la-Neuve, about 8 kilometers (5 miles) north of Arlon, stands this graceful château on the edge of the forest, surrounded by ponds and ancient linden trees. The architectural splendor extends to the rooms and to the newly renovated restaurant, where a distinguished clientele enjoys lasagna of oyster mushrooms and tiny shrimps with sweet garlic, or crispy quail fillets with juice of truffle. Book very early. ⊠ *Rue du Pont d'Oye 1, Habay-la-Neuve,* ☎ *063/422148,* ▦ *063/423588. 18 rooms with bath. Restaurant, indoor pool, tennis courts. AE, MC, V. No dinner Sun. Closed Mon., 2nd ½ of Feb., last wk in Aug.*

Outdoor Activities and Sports

Biking
Biking in these parts requires strong legs. Mountain bikes can be rented from **Ardenne Adventures** and **Ferme de Palogne** (☞ Canoeing, *below*), and **Moulin de la Falize** (⊠ Vieille Route de France 33, Bouillon, ☎ 061/466200), a multisport facility with a swimming pool, bowling alleys, a sauna, and fitness room.

Canoeing, Kayaking, and Rafting
The rapid rivers of the Ardennes are ideal for all three sports. Equipment can be rented by day or by distance, generally with return transportation to the point of departure. For the river Ourthe, try **Ardenne Adventures** (⊠ La Roche-en-Ardenne, ☎ 084/411347; kayaks Apr.–Oct., rafting Nov.–Mar.) or **Ferme de Palogne** (⊠ Vieuxville, ☎ 086/212412). For the Semois River, go to **Saty Rapids** (⊠ Bouillon, ☎ 061/466200) or **Récréalle** (⊠ Alle-sur-Semois, ☎ 061/500381), which also functions as a general sports center, with facilities for table tennis, bowling, fishing, and volleyball.

Horseback Riding
Centre Equestre de Mont-le-Soie (⊠ Grand-Halleux, ☎ 080/216443) offers both instruction and guided trail rides.

Belgian Luxembourg A to Z

Arriving and Departing
BY CAR

The main arteries to and through the region are the E411 highway from Brussels, which can get very busy during school holidays, and the E25 from Liège, generally less traveled, which joins the E411 not far from the border with the Grand Duchy. When the E411 is busy, the N4 highway from Namur to Bastogne is often a good alternative. The N63 highway from Liège links up with the N4 at Marche-en-Famenne, and the N89 connects La Roche-en-Ardenne with Bouillon via Saint-Hubert. From this network of highways you are never more than a few miles from your destination.

BY TRAIN

Local trains from Brussels to Luxembourg stop at Jemelle (near Rochefort) and Libramont (halfway between Saint-Hubert and Bouillon). There's a train every hour, and the trip to Jemelle takes 1 hour and 5 minutes; to Libramont, 2 hours. The trains connect with local bus services.

Getting Around
BY CAR

This is the only way to see this area unless you have unlimited time. You need to slow down considerably as you get off the highway and start enjoying yourself. Looking at a road map, you'll see that lots of small local roads have a green line running alongside them, indicating areas of great natural beauty.

Contacts and Resources
GUIDED TOURS

This is not a specialty of this area. Check with the local tourist office for guided visits to local attractions.

VISITOR INFORMATION

The provincial tourist office for **Belgian Luxembourg** is at Quai de l'Ourthe 9, La Roche-en-Ardenne (☎ 084/411011). City tourist offices: **Arlon** (Rue des Faubourgs 2, ☎ 063/216360); **Bastogne** (Place MacAuliffe 24, ☎ 061/212711); **Bouillon** (Bureau du Château-Fort, ☎ 061/466257; during high season, Porte de France, ☎ 061/466289); **Durby** (Rue Comte d'Ursel, ☎ 086/212428); **La Roche-en-Ardenne** (Syndicat d'Initiative, Place du Marché 15, ☎ 084/411342); **Saint-Hubert** (Rue St.-Gilles, ☎ 061/613010).

BELGIUM A TO Z

This section details essential country-wide information: For further advice, also consult the A to Z section for each of the Belgium regions found throughout this chapter.

Arriving and Departing

From North America by Plane
AIRPORTS AND AIRLINES

All intercontinental, and the vast majority of other international flights, arrive at **Brussels National Airport** at Zaventem. The airport is linked with Antwerp by coach service and with all other Belgian cities by rail.

Sabena (☎ 02/723–2323), the Belgian national carrier, flies to Brussels from New York, Boston, and Chicago; **American Airlines** (☎ 02/508–7700), from New York and Chicago; **United** (☎ 02/646–5588), from Washington; **Delta** (☎ 730–8200), from New York and Atlanta.

Sample flying times are as follows: 6 hours, 50 minutes from New York to Brussels; and seven hours from Boston to Brussels. Return flights are about an hour longer.

From the United Kingdom
BY PLANE

Sabena (☎ 02/723–2323) and **British Midland** (☎ 02/772–9400) fly to Brussels from London (Heathrow); **British Airways** (☎ 02/725–3000) from London (Heathrow and Gatwick); and **Air UK** (☎ 02/507–7052), from London (Stansted). Other U.K. cities with direct or nonstop flights to Brussels include Birmingham, Manchester, Newcastle, Leeds, Bristol, Edinburgh, and Glasgow. Flying time from London to Brussels is 1 hour; Brussels to London is 1 hour, 10 minutes.

BY CAR

For information about using the Channel Tunnel, *see* Driving *in* the Gold Guide.

The ferry routes to Belgium are from Ramsgate to Oostende and from Hull to Zeebrugge. Unless you're traveling in the dead of winter, and sometimes even then, it's essential to book well in advance (☞ By Ferry, *below*). Rates vary according to the length of your vehicle, the time of your crossing, and whether you travel in peak, shoulder, or low season.

Both the **Automobile Association** (⌧ Fanum House, Basingstoke, Hants. RG21 2EA, ☎ 01345/500600) and the **Royal Automobile Club** (⌧ RAC House, Box 100, South Croydon CR2 6XW, ☎ 0181/686–2525) operate on-the-spot breakdown and repair services across Belgium. Both companies will also transport cars and passengers back to Britain in case of serious breakdowns. AA has 5-day, 12-day, and 31-day coverage; RAC offers 10-day and 31-day coverage.

BY FERRY
The principal route across the English Channel to Belgium is Ramsgate to Oostende, operated by **Sally Line** and, starting in March 1997, by a new company, **Holyman Sally** (⌧ Argyle Centre, York St., Ramsgate, Kent CT11 9DS, ☎ 01843/595522). The crossing by ferry has taken four hours; the new fast-craft catamarans will require 1 hour and 50 minutes.

BY TRAIN
For details on the Eurostar and Thalys high-speed trains, *see* Rail Travel *in* the Gold Guide.

Boat trains timed to meet ferries or catamarans at Ramsgate leave London and connect with onward trains at Oostende. Contact **Intercity Europe,** the international wing of BritRail, at London/Victoria station (☎ 0171/834–2345 for information or 0171/828–8092 for bookings).

BY BUS
City Sprint, operated by **Hoverspeed** (☎ 01304/240241), offers bus service to Dover, Hovercraft service to Calais, and another bus connection to Brussels or Antwerp. Both trips take about seven hours. **Eurolines** (☎ 0171/730–8235) has daily and overnight services, using the ferry to Oostende. The trip takes about 10½ hours.

CAR RENTALS
Major firms in Brussels include **Alamo** (☎ 02/753–2060); **Avis** (☎ 02/726–9488); **Budget** (☎ 02/720–1717); **Eurodollar** (☎ 02/735–6005); **Europcar/InterRent** (☎ 02/640–9400); **Hertz** (☎ 02/513–2886).

Guided Tours

General-Interest Tours
Listed below is a sample of the tours and packages that concentrate on Belgium. For tours that cover the Benelux region, *see* Tour Operators *in* Important Contacts A to Z.

FROM THE U.K.
Shearing Holidays (⌧ Miry La., Wigan, Lancashire WN3 4AG, ☎ 01942/824824) features a five-day city break centered in Brugge with excursions to Brussels and other places of interest. **Time Off Ltd.** (⌧ Chester Close, Chester St., London SW1X 7BQ, ☎ 0171/235–8070) has packages from two to seven nights to Brussels and Brugge.

Special-Interest Tours
FROM THE U.K.
The Belgium Travel Service (⌧ Bridge House, 55-59 High Rd., Broxbourne, Herts. EN10 7DP, ☎ 01992/456166) specializes in inclusive holidays on the Belgian coast and in the Ardennes, and it also organizes tailor-made individual tours to any part of Belgium. **Holts' Tours** (⌧ 15 Market St., Sandwich, Kent CT13 9DA, ☎ 01304/612248) organizes tours of World War I battlefields in France and Belgium, with

an emphasis on the Ypres battlefield. Waterloo and Battle of the Bulge tours are also available.

Package Deals for Independent Travelers

American Airlines Fly Away Vacations (☎ 800/832–8383) offers independent packages for as long as you like for visits to Brussels, Brugge, and Antwerp. **Extra Value Travel** (✉ 683 S. Collier Blvd., Marco Island, FL 33937, ☎ 813/398–4848 or 800/255–2847) offers self-drive tours of Belgium, including hotel choices and car rental. **Northwest WorldVacations** (☎ 800/692–8687) provides visitors to Brussels with preferred hotel and car-rental rates and tour options for a minimum of two nights. **Travel Bound** (✉ 599 Broadway, Penthouse, New York, NY 10012, ☎ 212/334–1350 or 800/456–8656) offers a weeklong "Brussels Grand" package for independent travelers. **United Vacations** (✉ 106 Calvert St., Harrison, NY 10528, ☎ 800/678–0949) will customize your itinerary in Belgium.

Languages

Belgium is bisected by a linguistic border, with Flemish spoken to the north and French to the south of it. Written Flemish is indistinguishable from Dutch, but spoken Flemish may include dialect variations. Some French speakers have Walloon, a separate German-influenced tongue, as a second language. German, spoken by 200,000 people at the eastern end of the country, is Belgium's third official language. Brussels is officially bilingual (Flemish/French).

Language is a sensitive subject in Belgium, loaded with political implications. A foreigner is well advised to use English rather than French in Flanders, even though both are widely understood. You will have no problem finding English-speakers in Brussels. In Wallonia you may have to muster whatever French you possess, but in tourist centers you will always be able to find people who speak some English.

Mail

Postal Rates

An airmail letter or postcard to the United States costs BF34 for up to 20 grams, BF60 for up to 50 grams. Letters (up to 20 grams) and postcards to the United Kingdom cost BF16; up to 50 grams, BF38. Airmail letters must have an "A PRIOR" sticker.

Receiving Mail

If you do not know where you will be staying, you can have mail sent care of **American Express** (✉ Place Louise 1, 1000 Brussels). The service is free for cardholders, otherwise BF50 per letter.

Money and Expenses

Currency

The monetary unit in Belgium is the Belgian franc. There are bills of 100, 200, 500, 1,000, 2,000, and 10,000 francs, and coins of 1, 5, 20, and 50 francs. At press time (fall 1996), one dollar was worth about BF32; one pound sterling, BF48; and one Canadian dollar, BF23.

What It Will Cost

Inflation is low to moderate, currently at less than 3%. Brussels, with its vast influx of business travelers and officials on EU business, has some very expensive hotels and restaurants, but some enterprising hoteliers and restaurateurs offer similar quality at much lower prices. Value Added Tax (TVA) is always included in the price quoted for accommodations and meals. It ranges from 6% on basic items to 21% (☞ Shopping, *below*).

SAMPLE COSTS
A cup of coffee in a café will cost you BF45–BF60; a glass of beer, BF35–85; a glass of wine, about BF100. Train travel averages BF7 per mile, the average bus/metro/tram ride costs BF50, theater tickets are about BF500, and movie tickets cost about BF250.

Outdoor Activities and Sports

Two organizations provide information on all sports facilities in the country: **BLOSO** (✉ Rue des Colonies 31, ☎ 02/510–3411), for Flemish speakers, and **ADEPS** (✉ Boulevard Léopold II 44, ☎ 02/413–2800), for French speakers.

Cycling
The flat land of Flanders is ideal for this sport, but it can get windy at times. The steep hills of the Ardennes separate the men from the boys. You can rent bikes cheaply at many railway stations, but they aren't your state-of-the-art models. Specialized rental shops exist in most tourist centers.

Golf
Until recently, golf was strictly a rich man's sport in Belgium, but it is becoming more popular, and there are now courses near all major cities. For locations, contact the **Fédération Royale Belge de Golf** (Royal Belgian Golf Federation; ✉ Chaussée de La Hulpe 110, 1000 Brussels, ☎ 02/672–2389).

Mountaineering
The Ardennes may not be the Alps, but the many cliffs, especially along the Meuse River valley, provide excellent opportunities for rock-face climbing. For information, call the **Club Alpin Belge** (✉ Boulevard de la Meuse 9, Namur-Jambes, ☎ 081/303119).

Tennis
There are tennis courts aplenty, but book early because this is a very popular sport. Your hotel concierge will generally help. For more information, contact the **Fédération Royale Belge de Tennis** (Royal Belgian Tennis Federation; ✉ Galerie Porte Louise 203, 1050 Brussels, ☎ 02/513–2920).

Water Sports
All along the coast, as well as on lakes and man-made bodies of water, you'll see large numbers of people windsurfing. For information on this and other water sports, contact the **Vlaamse Watersportvereinigen** (Flemish Water Sport Association; ✉ Beatrijslaan 25, Antwerp, ☎ 03/219–6967). Belgium's entire North Sea coast is one long beach, with many resorts packed tightly together (☞ The North Sea Coast, *above*).

Shopping

Good-quality lace is available in several shops in Brussels (but not in souvenir shops); even so, you may wish to wait until you've seen what is available in Brugge before making your choice. Similarly, if you're interested in fashion, wait until you've checked out the avant-garde boutiques in Antwerp. If your visit includes Liège, go first to the Val St.-Lambert factory shop before buying crystal elsewhere. Chocolate is best bought as close to departure as possible. In fact, some of the best brands (Godiva, Neuhaus, Daskalides) are available in the tax-free shop at the airport. The Godiva shop in Place Stéphanie will mail boxes anywhere in the world.

Many shops advertise that goods are available tax-free. There's a simpler option than those mentioned in the Gold Guide, but it requires trust. At the time of purchase by credit card, you pay the price without TVA and you also sign, with your card, a guarantee in the amount of the sales tax. You are given two invoices: One is your record and the other must be stamped by customs when you leave Belgium (or the last EU country on your itinerary). You must return the stamped invoice to the store within three months, or you forfeit the guarantee.

Student and Youth Travel

The youth information service in Brussels is **Infor-Jeunes** (☎ 070/233444), and there's also an English-language **Help Line** (☎ 02/648–4014), which provides both practical information and crisis intervention. **Acotra** (✉ Rue de la Madeleine 51, ☎ 02/512–7078) will help in finding inexpensive accommodations.

Youth hostels are inexpensive and numerous. For information on facilities in Wallonia, write to **Les Auberges de la Jeunesse** (Belgian Youth Hostels; ✉ Rue Van Oost 52, 1030 Brussels, ☎ 02/215–3100); for Flanders, **Vlaamse Jeugdherbergcentrale** (Flemish Youth Hostel Center; ✉ Van Stralenstraat 40, 2060 Antwerp, ☎ 03/232–7218).

Telephones

Local Calls

Pay phones work with Telecards, available in a number of denominations, starting at BF200. These cards can be purchased at any post office and at many newsstands. Most phone booths that accept Telecards have a list indicating where cards can be bought. Some public phones are still coin-operated, taking 5- and 20-franc coins. A local call costs between BF10 and BF20.

International Calls

The least expensive way is to buy a high-denomination Telecard and make a direct call from a phone booth. A five-minute call to the United States at peak time will cost about BF750 by this method. Most hotel rooms are equipped with direct-call telephones, but nearly all add a service charge that can be substantial. It's better to ask beforehand what service charges are applied.

To call collect or by credit card, to the United States, dial 0800/10010 for **AT&T**; 0800/10012 for **MCI**; or 0800/1014 for **US Sprint**; to the United Kingdom, dial 0800/10044 for **BT Direct.** Similar services now exist for most countries; consult the phone book under "Communications internationales manuelles."

Tipping

A service charge is included in restaurant and hotel bills, and tips are also included in the amount shown on the meter in taxis. Additional tipping is unnecessary unless you wish to say thank you for very good service. Hotel porters generally get a gratuity of BF100 for carrying bags to your room. Tip doormen BF50 for getting you a cab. Porters in railway stations ask a fixed per-suitcase price of BF60. In movie theaters, ushers expect a BF20 tip when you present the ticket. Washroom attendants get a BF10 tip. Hairdressers usually receive 10% to 20%.

Transportation: Getting Around

By Plane

There is no domestic air service.

By Train

The **Société Nationale des Chemins de Fer Belge** (⊠ SNCB/Belgian National Railways, Rue de France 85, 1070 Brussels, ☎ 02/203–3640) provides frequent train service—first and second class—from Brussels to all major cities in the country. Very few are more than an hour away. This means that you can, if you wish, see most of the country on day trips while remaining based in Brussels and traveling on reduced-price, same-day return tickets. Tickets are sold only at railway stations.

RAIL PASSES

Tourrail Tickets allow unlimited travel on the Belgian network for any five days during a one-month period. The price is BF2,995 first class and BF1,995 second class. A **Go-Pass,** available at BF1,360 for those between 12 and 26, is good for 10 one-way trips in a six-month period; it is not individual and can be used by a group traveling together. Rail passes can be bought in any Belgian railway station.

By Bus

Intercity bus travel is not well developed in Belgium. You can, however, reach a number of localities surrounding each city by the local bus company.

By Car

Belgium has a magnificent network of well-marked motorways and, in contrast with the railroads, they are not all spokes from the Brussels hub. You can, for instance, drive along fast, four-lane highways from Antwerp to Ghent, or Liège to Tournai or Brugge to Kortrijk, without passing through the capital. There are no tolls, and most highways are illuminated at night.

You must carry a warning triangle, to be placed well behind the car in case of a breakdown. There are emergency telephones at intervals along the motorways. The speed limit is 130 kph (80 mph) on motorways, 90 kph (56 mph) on secondary roads, and 50 kph (31 mph) in built-up areas. Driving with the flow may mean higher speeds than most U.S. drivers are accustomed to. At intersections, always check traffic from the right even if you're on a thoroughfare; Belgian drivers can be reckless in insisting on "priority on the right." Gas costs about the same as in other European countries, which means quite a bit more than in the United States (almost a dollar a liter).

Visitor Information

Contact the **Belgian Tourist Office**: in the United States and Canada (⊠ 780 3rd Ave., Suite 1501, New York, NY 10017, ☎ 212/758–8130, FAX 212/355–7675); in the United Kingdom (⊠ 29 Princes St., London W1R 7RG, ☎ 0171/629–0230).

4 Luxembourg

Tiny Luxembourg, nestled between Germany, France, and Belgium, has been a pawn of world powers for much of its 1,000 years. Today it looms large as a world financial powerhouse and one of Europe's most scenic countries. Come here for rambles through medieval villages and hilltop castles, strolls along riverbanks and through deep forests, and hearty meals in country inns. From sophisticated Luxembourg City, with its ancient fortifications and modern skyscrapers, to the Ardennes plateau, site of the World War II Battle of the Bulge, to the wineries along the Moselle, Luxembourg is 999 square miles of beauty, history, and good times.

By Nancy
Coons

Updated by
Eric Sjogren

THE CAPITAL OF TINY LUXEMBOURG greets visitors with an awe-inspiring view: Up and down the length of the Alzette River stretches a panorama of medieval stonework—jutting fortification walls, slit-windowed towers, ancient church spires, massive gates—as detailed and complete as a 17th-century engraving come to life. Then you abruptly enter the 20th century. The Boulevard Royal, little more than five blocks long, glitters with glass-and-concrete office buildings, each containing a world-class bank and untold, anonymous, well-sheltered fortunes.

Luxembourg, once sovereign to lands that stretched from the Meuse to the Rhine, was reduced over the centuries to being a pawn in the power struggles between its many conquerors. Until recently little more than a cluster of meager farms and failing mines, Luxembourg today enjoys newfound political clout and the highest per capita income in the world.

The Grand Duchy of Luxembourg, one of the smallest countries in the United Nations, measures only 2,597 square kilometers (999 square miles), less than the size of Rhode Island. It is dwarfed by its neighbors—Germany, Belgium, and France—yet from its history of invasion, occupation, and siege, you would think those square miles were filled with solid gold. In fact, it was Luxembourg's fortresses carved out of bedrock, its very defenses against centuries of attack, that rendered it all the more desirable.

It all started in 963, when Charlemagne's descendant Sigefroid, a beneficiary of the disintegration of Central Europe that followed Charlemagne's death, chose a small gooseneck, carved by the Alzette, to develop as a fortress and the capital of his considerable domain. Thanks to his aggressions and the ambitions of his heirs, Luxembourg grew continuously until, by the 14th century, its count, Henry IV, was powerful and important enough to serve as Henry VII, king of the German nations and Holy Roman Emperor. During that epoch, Luxembourg contributed no fewer than five kings and emperors, including Henry VII's son, the flamboyant John the Blind (Jean l'Aveugle), who, despite leading his armies to slaughter in the Battle of Crécy (1346), remains a national hero.

After John the Blind's death, Luxembourg commanded the greatest territory it would ever rule—from the Meuse to Metz and the Moselle—and its rulers, Charles IV, Wenceslas I and II, and Sigismund, carried the name of the House of Luxembourg to European renown. If Luxembourg had a golden age, this was it, but it was short-lived. Plague, the decay of feudalism, marital and financial intrigues among leaders who rarely, if ever, set foot in Luxembourg—all these factors finally left the duchy vulnerable, and Philip the Good, Duke of Burgundy, took it by storm in 1443.

From that point on, Luxembourg lost its significance as a geographical mass and took on importance as a fortress. It was controlled from 1443 to 1506 by Burgundy, from 1506 to 1714 by Spain (with a brief period, 1684–97, under Louis XIV of France), and from 1714 to 1795 by Austria; Napoléon took it from the Hapsburgs in 1795. Each, in taking the fortress, had to penetrate miles of outworks whose battlements filled the countryside. After having penetrated the outer defenses, the aggressors then faced a citadel perched on sheer stone cliffs, with weapons pointing at them from every direction and where the soldiers outnumbered the citizens. To take it by frontal attack was out of the question; the solution, usually, was siege and starvation.

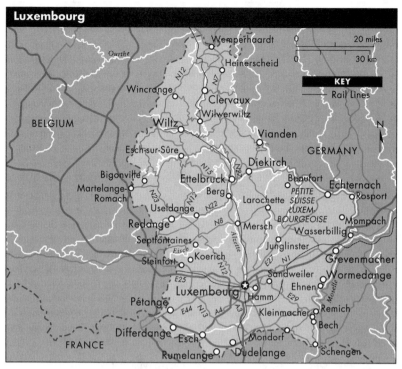

Having been torn and ravaged for 400 years by its conquerors' games of tug-of-war, Luxembourg continued to provoke squabbles well into the 19th century. The Congress of Vienna gave a territorially reduced Luxembourg independence of a sort. The Grand Duke of Luxembourg was also King of Holland when Belgium rebelled against Dutch rule in 1830. Only the presence of a Prussian garrison kept Luxembourg in the Dutch camp. Nine years later, Luxembourg was again partitioned, with the western half becoming a Belgian province. William II became the first and last Dutch Grand Duke to achieve popular acclaim; he created a parliament and laid the foundations for modern Luxembourg. In 1867 Luxembourg was declared an independent and neutral state by the Treaty of London, and its battlements were dismantled, stone by stone. What remains of its walls, while impressive, is only a reminder of what was once one of the great strongholds of Europe—the "Gibraltar of the North."

The Grand Duchy's neutrality was violated by the Germans in 1914. When World War I ended, the people of Luxembourg gave their confidence, by popular vote, to Grand Duchess Charlotte, who remained a much-loved head of state for 45 years until abdicating in favor of her son, Jean, in 1964. Grand Duke Jean is married to Grand Duchess Joséphine-Charlotte, the daughter of Belgium's King Leopold and his Swedish-born Queen Astrid. Their large family has remained untouched by the types of scandals that have marred the reputations of other royal houses.

In the late 19th century, breakthroughs in both farming and mining technology turned the country around. A new, efficient technique for purifying iron ore created an indispensable by-product, fertilizer, which started a boom that put Luxembourg on 20th-century maps. A steel industry was created and, with it, more jobs than there were local workers. Thousands of workers came from Italy, and later Portugal, to take up residence in Luxembourg. Even today, about 20% of the workforce lives outside Luxembourg and crosses the border daily going to and from work.

Most recently, Luxembourg has become one of the world's top financial centers, with 225 banks from throughout the world established in the Grand Duchy. The broadcasting and communications satellite industries are also important to the national economy.

Hitler was convinced that Luxembourg was part of the greater Germanic culture. Suppressing Luxembourgish and changing French names into German, he launched a campaign to persuade Luxembourgers to *Heim ins Reich*—come home to the fatherland as ethnic Germans. Yet a visit to any war museum will show that the Luxembourgers weren't having any of it, and that the majority has yet to forget that the German invasions left Luxembourg hideously scarred and that thousands of its men were conscripted during the German occupation and sent as so much cannon fodder to the Russian front.

The experiences of two world wars convinced Luxembourg that neutrality does not work. Native son Robert Schuman was one of the founding fathers of the Common Market that eventually became the European Union, with Luxembourg a charter member. The European Court of Justice and other European institutions are located in Luxembourg. The Grand Duchy is fiercely opposed to any suggestions that it would save a lot of money if all such bodies were in Brussels. It certainly won't happen during the lifetime of the present European Commission, whose president is the former, long-serving prime minister of Luxembourg, Jacques Santer.

Soldiers from Luxembourg serve with young men from France, Germany, and Belgium in the European Army. Small it may be, but the army is a powerful symbol of the unity that has replaced old enmities. The men from Luxembourg can communicate with their European brothers more easily than the others, because they are fluent in both French and German. French is the official language of the Grand Duchy, and the teaching of German is mandatory in the schools. They also have their own language, *Lëtzebuergsch,* descended from the language of the Rhineland Franks, which has the added advantage of being understood by virtually no one else, be they occupants, business partners, or tourists. This is the language in which the national motto is expressed: *Mir wölle bleiwe wat mir sin,* "We want to stay what we are." Today that means being a powerful, viable grand duchy in the heart of modern Europe.

The Pleasures of Dining and Lodging

Dining

"French quality, German quantity"—that's an apt and common description of Luxembourg cuisine. A quick study of local posted menus might lead visitors to think the locals eat nothing but *cuisine bourgeoise*—veal with cream and mushrooms, beef entrecôte with peppercorn sauce, veal *cordon bleu* (stuffed with ham and cheese)—all served in generous portions, with heaps of *frites* (french fries) on the side. Yet this tiny country has its own earthy cuisine, fresh off the farm: *judd mat gardebounen* (smoked pork shoulder with broad beans), *jambon d'Ardennes* (smoked ham served cold with pickled onions), *choucroute* (sauerkraut), batter-fried whiting, and spicy *gromperekichelcher* (fried potato patties). More upscale additions to the national specialties are *écrevisses* (crayfish), cooked with local wine, and all manner of trout.

Luxembourg has more star-studded French *gastronomic* restaurants per capita than any other European country. Many restaurants—including some of the top ones—offer a moderately priced luncheon menu. Ethnic restaurants present less expensive alternatives, and, given the sizable population of those of Italian descent, pasta and pizza have almost acquired the status of a national cuisine. Fast-food eateries are also present in force, especially in the capital.

Lunch takes place mostly between noon and 2. Dinner, except in the fanciest restaurants, tends to be earlier than the European norm, generally between 7 and 9.

CATEGORY	COST*
$$$$	over Flux 3,000
$$$	Flux 1,500–3,000
$$	Flux 750–1,500
$	under Flux 750

per person for a three-course meal including service and tax, but not beverages

Lodging

Hotels in Luxembourg are tidy and straightforward, rarely reaching the peaks of luxury, but equally rarely representing tremendous bargains. Most hotels in Luxembourg City are relatively modern and vary from the international style, mainly near the airport, to family-run establishments in town. Many of these, often filled with business travelers on weekdays, offer reduced rates on weekends. Outside the capital, hotels are often in picturesque buildings.

The Office National du Tourisme (⊠ ONT, B.P. 1001, L-1010 Luxembourg, ☎ 400808, FAX 404748) will make hotel reservations free of charge. Such bookings must be confirmed by the traveler. The ONT offices at the airport and railway station will make reservations for travelers arriving without one.

Inexpensive youth hostels are plentiful; many are set in ancient fortresses and castles. Most are linked by marked trails of 10 to 20 miles. For information, contact Centrale des Auberges Luxembourgeoises (⊠ Place d'Armes 18, B.P. 374, L-2013 Luxembourg, ☎ 225588). The Grand Duchy is probably the best-organized country in Europe for camping. It offers some 120 sites, all with full amenities. Listings are published annually by the national tourist office (⊠ ONT, B.P. 1001, L-1010 Luxembourg).

CATEGORY	COST*
$$$$	over Flux 8,000
$$$	Flux 5,000–8,000
$$	Flux 2,500–5,000
$	under Flux 2,500

for two persons sharing a double room, including service and tax

Exploring Luxembourg

There are those who arrive in Luxembourg by train in the morning, tour the city, and depart before dark. Yes, it can be done, but it's a shame to be left with just a fleeting memory, when a somewhat longer visit can leave a lasting impression. The Old Town of Luxembourg is of necessity small; there's not much space within the walls of a fortress built on a rock. This makes it eminently walkable, and there's an elevator to transfer you down to the level of the surrounding part of town. Short distances make it possible, too, to visit the rest of the country within the space of a few pleasant days.

One attractive region of Luxembourg goes by the nickname "Little Switzerland." In a way, that appellation could apply to the Grand Duchy as a whole. Whether you are walking, driving, or riding a bike, the pleasure of being surrounded by an attractive and well-tended countryside is ever present, from the vineyards along the Moselle to the steep hills and deep woods to the north.

Great Itineraries

Numbers in the text correspond to numbers in the margin and on the Luxembourg City and Luxembourg Ardennes maps.

IF YOU HAVE 2 DAYS

On the first day, take in the classic sights of ⚏ **Luxembourg City,** starting with a view from the **Viaduct** ① and the poignant **Monument of National Unity** ②. Stop at the French-built **Citadel of the Holy Spirit** ③, and visit the underground defense passages known as **Pétrusse Casemates**. You're now near **Notre-Dame Cathedral** ⑤ with its royal crypt. In the afternoon, start with the new, interactive **City Historical Museum** ⑥, which traces Luxembourg's 1,000-year history. At the **Maquette** ⑦ you can see what the fortress looked like in its glory days; then visit the **Grand Ducal Palace** ⑧. Next to it are the art treasures of the **National Museum** ⑨ and the ancient **Three Towers** ⑩. The **Bock** ⑪ is the site of the original 963 castle. Descending by elevator to the *Grund* (ground), stop at the **Museum of Natural History** ⑫ and the Baroque Church of St. John. Walk through the canyon park of the Petrusse valley and up to the old city, emerging onto the banking street, **Boulevard Royal** ⑬, and the main pedestrian shopping street, **Grand'rue** ⑭.

On the second day, allow ample time for the new **Wenzel Walk** through space and time. It leads from the Bock down into the valley, past ancient gates and ruins, over 18th-century military installations and along the Alzette valley, with audiovisual presentations along the way. Use the afternoon to re-enter the 20th century at **Kirchberg** ⑮, a plateau to the east of the old city and home to the European Union institutions, including the European Court of Justice. Here, too, are modern bank palaces of architectural and artistic interest.

IF YOU HAVE 3 DAYS

Follow the itinerary above, and on the third day, drive north to the Luxembourg Ardennes via **Diekirch** ⑯, whose Museum of Military History brings alive the Battle of the Bulge, then on to **Vianden** ⑰, home of one of the most spectacularly dramatic castles you're ever likely to see. Continue north to **Clervaux** ⑱, where there's another sprawling castle, now the permanent home of *The Family of Man* photo exhibition.

IF YOU HAVE 5 DAYS

Follow the itinerary above and stay overnight in ⚏ **Clervaux** ⑱. Turning south, stop in tiny **Esch-sur- Sûre** ⑲, circled by the river and dense forests, and continue on to **Bourscheid** ⑳ with its romantic castle ruins overlooking three valleys. Past Diekirch, head for **Larochette** ㉑ and its striking, step-gabled castle. At Reuland, you enter the Müllerthal and are now in the very pretty countryside known as **Petite Suisse** ㉒. Stop over at ⚏ **Echternach** ㉓. On the fifth day, visit this town on the river Sûre, which is the home of the unique and ancient dancing procession at Whitsun (Pentecost). Travel south along the Sûre River, which here forms the border with Germany until it meets the Moselle. The vineyards have been cultivated since Roman times and cover every slope. Pretty little **Ehnen** ㉔, a well-preserved village, is a good place for a stop to see the wine museum. Heading back toward Luxembourg City from Remich, stop at **Hamm** ㉕ to visit the American Military Cemetery, where

General George Patton is buried with 5,000 comrades-at-arms who fell during the liberation of Luxembourg.

When to Tour Luxembourg

April through October is a good time to visit the Grand Duchy, with spring and early fall being the best. Outside the capital, many museums and other attractions open at Easter and stay open through October. Landlocked Luxembourg is far enough from the sea so that winters are a bit colder and summers a bit warmer than in neighboring Belgium. Gourmets keen on sampling the best restaurants should note that a number of them are closed most of August.

LUXEMBOURG CITY

If you visit one place only in the Grand Duchy of Luxembourg, it will probably be Luxembourg-Ville (Luxembourg City), a city of 79,000 people in a nation of 400,000. Here, at leisure, you can explore all the must-sees—the fortifications, the old cobbled streets, the parks, the cathedral, the museums—and, after shopping, relax in a shaded terrace café, listening to street musicians or a brass band. The city is small enough to be done in a day if you are pressed for time. But if you have a bit more time, you may find quiet little Luxembourg a romantic base for day trips and a lovely place at night, with its illuminated monuments and walls and its inviting public squares.

Archaeology

The adventure of discovering a world of the past can be enjoyed to the fullest in old Luxembourg City, which has been declared a World Heritage Site by UNESCO. A walk has been laid out that lets you explore the 1,000-year history of the "Gibraltar of the North," and a new and exciting vertical museum allows you to contemplate the evolution of human habitation on this rock.

Castles

Luxembourg City was not the only place that knew how to defend itself. There are more than 50 feudal castles in this small country, of all sizes, ages, styles, and states of repair. You come around a bend in a road, or crest a hill, and in front of you there looms a feudal stronghold, dominating the surrounding landscape with its squat towers, slender turrets, and massive walls. They make you think again of what it took to create islands of peace in those turbulent times.

Dining

In the capital, as in the rest of the Grand Duchy, workers drop everything at noon and rush home to a leisurely hot meal, jamming the streets, then rush back at 2, jamming the streets once more. Most restaurants offer a relatively speedy *plat du jour* (daily, one-course special) for those who don't commute twice a day. Evening meals at home tend to be a cold supper of ham, sausage, dark bread, and cheese; the occasional meal out is usually a celebration, enjoyed at length. The Sunday noon meal is the most important of the week. Most Luxembourg restaurants are closed on Sunday, but country restaurants, never very far away, are booked with three-generation families, who spend the afternoon eating and drinking before an afternoon stroll, after which the men retire to the local pub.

Exploring Luxembourg City

391 km (243 mi) southeast of Amsterdam, 219 km (136 mi) southeast of Brussels, 29 km (18 mi) east of Arlon.

The capital goes by the same name as the country—the suffix "City" is added only as a convenience for foreigners, who may ask themselves if they have arrived at the right place when they see the sign *Lëtzebuerg*. Don't worry, it's just Luxembourg being Luxembourgish. When Luxembourgers themselves refer to visiting the capital, they merely say they are going *en ville* (to the city). Ranging from southern European blue-collar workers to international bankers and European civil servants, half of Luxembourg's modest population are foreigners. This has given the city a cosmopolitan sheen and enriched it with a variety of ethnic restaurants, but the Luxembourgers themselves remain essentially homebodies, who go home for lunch if they can and see no point in hanging about in town after dark. Those who do not fit into this pattern often dream of studies or careers in a foreign metropolis. This is why Luxembourg's year in the limelight as Europe's "City of Culture" in 1995 was so important to young people. It showed them that their culture has value to artists and performers from other parts of the world and that Luxembourg is much, much more than a tax haven or a meeting point for European Union politicians.

Numbers in the margin correspond to points of interest on the Luxembourg City map.

❶ From the **Viaduc,** which spans the Pétrusse valley, you'll have a first glimpse of the rocky ledges—partly natural, partly man-made—on which the city was founded. The Pétrusse, more of a brook than a river, is now contained by concrete, but the valley has become a singularly beautiful park. **❷** The **Monument de la Solidarité Nationale** (Monument of National Unity), at the end of the bridge, commemorates Luxembourg's World War II victims, its stark granite and steel suggesting the prisons and concentration camps where they suffered. The walls of the small chapel, containing a symbolic tombstone, are made entirely of stained glass. It was as a direct result of its war experiences that Luxembourg abandoned traditional neutrality for international cooperation.

❸ The 17th-century **Citadelle du St-Esprit** (Citadel of the Holy Spirit), with its typically wedge-shaped fortifications, was built by Vauban, the brilliant French military engineer, on the site of a former monastery. From the "prow" you'll enjoy wraparound views: the three spires of the cathedral, the curve of the Alzette, and the incongruous white tower of the European Parliament secretariat.

❹ **Place de la Constitution** is marked by the gilt *Gëlle Fra* (Golden Woman), on top of a tall column. This World War I memorial was destroyed by the Nazis in 1940 and rebuilt, with original pieces incorporated, in 1984. Here you'll find the entrance to the ancient **Casemates** (military tunnels) carved into the rocky Pétrusse fortifications. At the height of her power and influence, Luxembourg was protected by three rings of defenses comprising 53 forts and strongholds. During the many phases of the fortress's construction, the rock itself was hollowed out to form a honeycomb of passages running for nearly 24 kilometers (15 miles) below the town. Ten gates controlled admittance through the walls, and the town was, in effect, 440 acres of solid fort. The Casemates served not only defensive purposes but were also used for storage and as a place of refuge when the city was under attack. Two sections of the passages are open to the public. These sections contain former barracks, cavernous slaughterhouses, bakeries, and a deep well. ⊠ *Place de la Constitution.* 🚆 *Flux 70.* ☉ *Easter, Whitsun (Pentecost, 7th Sun. after Easter), and July–Sept., daily 10–5.*

❺ The **Cathédrale Notre-Dame,** in late Gothic style, has a fine portal sculpted by Daniel Muller of Freiburg and an attractive Baroque organ

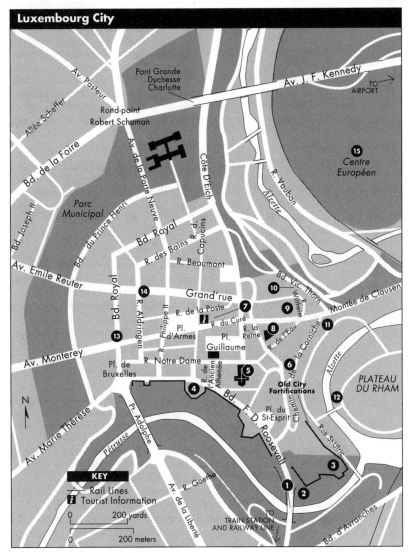

Luxembourg City

KEY

△ Rail Lines
🛈 Tourist Information

gallery. During the fortnight of national pilgrimage starting on the third Sunday after Easter, large numbers of Luxembourgers flock to their cathedral. The closing ceremony, attended by the royal family, is an event no politician can afford to miss, regardless of party and persuasion. The crypt, down a broad staircase, contains the tomb of John the Blind, the gallant 14th-century King of Bohemia and Count of Luxembourg, who fell at the Battle of Crécy in France during the Hundred Years' War. There, too, are the tombs of the grand-ducal dynasty. ⊠ *Rue Notre-Dame.* ◷ *Easter–Oct., weekdays 10–5, Sat. 8–6, Sun. 10–6; Nov.–Easter, weekdays 10–11:30 and 2–5, Sat. 8–11 and 2–5, Sun. 10–5.*

★ ❻ The **Musée d'Histoire de la Ville de Luxembourg** (Luxembourg City Historical Museum), a multimedia, interactive museum that opened in 1996, traces the development of the city over 1,000 years. Partially underground, its lowest five levels show the town's preserved ancient stonework. From a glass-wall elevator, you can enjoy a wonderful view of the ravine from the upper floors. ⊠ *Rue du Saint-Esprit,* ☎ 479627. ▦ *Flux 250.* ◷ *Tues.–Sun. 10–6, Thurs. 10–8.*

The old town's **three main squares** are diagonally aligned. One is the sloping, elegant **Place Clairefontaine,** with its graceful statue of Grand Duchess Charlotte and imposing 18th-century ministerial offices. The second square, **Place Guillaume,** is known locally as the Knuedler, a name derived from the girdle worn by Franciscan monks who once had a monastery on the site. On market days (Wednesday and Saturday mornings) the square is a mass of retail fruit and vegetable stands, vivid flower vendors, cheese and fish specialists, and a few remaining farmers who bring in their personal crop of potatoes, apples, cabbage, and radishes—as well as homemade jam, sauerkraut, and goat cheese. That's Grand Duke William II on the bronze horse; he reigned from 1840 to 1849, while Luxembourg was flush with new independence. The Hotel de Ville (Town Hall), its stairs flanked by two bronze lions, was inaugurated in 1844. The third square, **Place d'Armes,** was once the innermost heart of the fortified city. Today, lined with symmetrical plane trees and strung with colored lights, it is the most welcoming corner of town. In fine weather its cafés and benches are full of both locals and tourists. The bandstand has concerts every summer evening by visiting bands. Every second and fourth Saturday, a *brocante* (antiques/flea) market fills the square. The tourist office is on the southwest corner, in the **Cercle Municipal,** with its bas-relief of the Countess Ermesinde granting Luxembourg its charter of freedom in 1244.

❼ The **Forteresse de Luxembourg: Maquette,** behind the tourist office, has a relief model of the fortress at various stages of its construction. ⊠ *Rue du Curé,* ☎ 222809. ▦ *Flux 60.* ◷ *Easter–mid-Oct., Mon.–Sat. 10–12:30 and 2–6.*

❽ The **Grand Ducal Palace** is the city's finest building. It dates from the 16th century, and there is a distinct Spanish-Moorish influence in its elaborate facade. The Grand Ducal family used to live here; now it is used for business and entertaining. Official receptions are held in the festive hall on the second floor, and foreign envoys are received in the Hall of Kings. Its extensive art collection was dispersed during World War II but was returned afterward. Behind the palace is the oldest part of town, the **Marché-aux-Poissons,** site of the old fish market and originally the crossing point of two Roman roads. ⊠ *Rue du Marché-aux-Herbes.* ▦ *Flux 200; tickets sold only at the City Tourist Office (early booking recommended).* ◷ *Mid-July–early-Sept., Mon.–Tues. and Thurs.–Sat.; guided tours only (in English at 4).*

⑨ The **Musée National** (National Museum), set in an attractive row of 16th-century houses, has some outstanding paintings by the expressionist Joseph Kutter, probably Luxembourg's greatest artist. The art gallery includes a fine Cranach and two Turner watercolors of the Luxembourg fortress. The museum also hosts the spectacular Bentinck-Thyssen collection of 15th- to 19th-century art, including works by Bruegel, Rembrandt, Canaletto, and other masters. ⊠ *Marché-aux-Poissons,* ☎ *479330.* 🖭 *Free.* ⊙ *Tues.–Fri. 10–4:45, Sat. 2–5:45, Sun. 10–11:45 and 2–5:45.*

NEED A BREAK?

The **Welle Man** (⊠ Rue Wiltheim 12, ☎ 471783), on the street that runs alongside the National Museum, is the quintessential Luxembourgish museum bar. Sit on the tiny terrace and enjoy the magnificent view. Sip a glass of Elbling or Rivaner, local white wines, or try a *kir,* made from black-currant liqueur and white wine.

⑩ The **Trois Tours** (Three Towers) and the **Gate Saint-Michel** are among the city's most romantic sights. The oldest of the towers was built around 1050. During the French Revolution, the guillotine was set up in these towers. The gate stands at the bottom of Rue Wiltheim, and from here you can clearly see the source of Luxembourg's strength as a fortress.

★ **⑪** The **Bock** is Luxembourg's raison d'être. Jutting dramatically out over the valley, this cliff served as the principal approach to the town, as far back as Celtic and Roman times, until bridges were later constructed. The name comes from the Celtic *büück,* meaning the promontory supporting a castle. Over its farthest point looms the ruined tower of the castle of Sigefroid himself. He founded the fortress Lucilinburhuc in 963; it was expanded, over the centuries, from this dominant point.

Taking in vertiginous views of the valley, just as Sigefroid did, you'll see the Plateau du Rham across the way, on the right, and, before it, the massive towers of Duke Wenceslas's fortifications, which in 1390 extended the protected area. The blocklike *casernes* (barracks) were built in the 17th century by the French and function today as a hospice for the elderly. Below them, at the bottom of the valley, is the 17th-century Neumünster Abbey, which, from 1869 to 1984, served as the prison. Here, too, you can gain access to the underground casemates. At the entrance, the **Archaeological Crypt** provides an excellent introduction, with an audiovisual presentation depicting Luxembourg history from the 10th to the 15th centuries. 🖭 *Crypt and casemates Flux 70, casemates alone Flux 50.* ⊙ *Mar.–Oct., daily 10–5.*

NEED A BREAK?

On the Corniche, stop at the shady outdoor tables of the **Breedewée** (⊠ Rue Large 9, ☎ 222696) for a drink or a light, French-accented plat du jour.

★ The **Grund,** once considered dank and squalid, is suddenly in vogue. It is reached by taking an elevator down from Place du Saint-Esprit. You'll find chic restaurants, exclusive clubs, and skylighted, renovated town houses among the tumbledown laborers' homes. The new **Musée** **⑫** **d'Histoire Naturelle** (Museum of Natural History) is housed in a reconverted women's prison. The archaeological collections now housed in the Musée National (☞ *above*) will be transferred here. *Scheduled to open Jan. 1997 (but don't hold your breath).* ⊠ *Rue Munster 23,* ☎ *462–2321.* 🖭 *Admission not yet determined.* ⊙ *Tues.–Thurs. 2–6, Fri.–Sat. 10–6.*

The Baroque **Eglise de Saint-Jean** (Church of St. John), once the church of the Benedictines of Neumünster Abbey, who were expelled when the French Revolution hit Luxembourg, contains many treasures. One of its most important is a Black Madonna, whose protection against pestilence was prayed for over many centuries. The church passage along the river provides fabulous views of the side of the cliff and the towering fortifications on the other side of the Alzette. It leads to a former abbey courtyard, the **Tutesall,** where convicts formerly worked sewing bags. Today it is a stylish exhibition venue. Another building, the former men's prison, is being converted into a cultural center.

NEED A BREAK?   **Scott's Pub** (⊠ Bisserwé 4, ☎ 475352), at the bottom of the valley, is a gathering place for the English-speaking, where outdoor tables line the picturesque Alzette. It's the place to have a pint of bitter or sample the Anglo-American cuisine.

The **Vallée de la Pétrusse** is a broad park in a canyon, full of willows, cherry trees, and bluffs. Near the high Viaduc, you'll see the **Chapelle de Saint-Quirin** built into the rocks. The cave is said to have been carved by the Celts; it is known to have housed a chapel since at least the 4th century.

⓭ **Boulevard Royal**—Luxembourg's mini–Wall Street—was once the main moat of the fortress. You can reach it by walking up narrow switchbacks from the valley or by taking the elevator to Place du Saint-Esprit and cutting across on Boulevard Roosevelt. Lined with as many of the 225 foreign financial institutions as could squeeze onto the five-block street, Boulevard Royal is the symbol of a financial center where the securities trading operation has a higher turnover than that of the New York Stock Exchange. The pinstripe suits can get some relief from their labors through gazing at Niki de St. Phalle's large and brightly colored statue, *La Tempérance,* which adorns their street.

⓮ The **Grand'Rue** is Luxembourg's pedestrian-only shopping street. You'll find the same brands vying for your attention in little Luxembourg as in New York, but then, investment bankers have pockets here as deep as anywhere else. Pastry shops and sidewalk cafés add the middle-class touch so deeply typical of Luxembourg. There are pooper-scooper automats for the poodles, and the occasional street musician will, as likely as not, be playing a Bach partita.

⓯ The **Plateau Kirchberg** is, some claim, a moonscape of modern architecture. A number of banks, needing more space than available on Boulevard Royal, have put up huge edifices on Kirchberg, reached by the single-span Grande Duchesse Charlotte Bridge across the Pfaffenthal. Gottfried Boehm's glass-and-aluminum Deutsche Bank encloses a giant atrium, frequently used for art exhibitions, and Richard Meier's sober Hypobank is the perfect foil for an explosively dynamic sculpture by Frank Stella. The banks are cheek by jowl with the modernistic buildings of the European institutions, often accompanied by contemporary sculpture—the European Court of Justice, with sculptures by Henry Moore and Lucien Wercollier; the Jean Monnet Building, with a replica of Carl-Fredrik Reuterswärd's *Non-Violence*; the European Center, where the Council of Ministers meets; and others, whose presence in Luxembourg are visible reminders of the disproportionately important role played by this tiny country in the politics of the European Union.

The signposted **Valley of the Seven Châteaux** can be visited on a circle tour west of **Mersch,** 17 kilometers (10 miles) north of the capital, cutting west to **Reckange,** south to **Hollenfels, Marienthal,** and **Ansembourg** (which has an old castle in the heights and a new one in the valley below), then working west to **Septfontaines** and south to **Koerich.** The castles, in various stages of repair and representing a broad historical spectrum, have not been restored for visitors, but they loom above forests and over valleys much as they did in Luxembourg's grander days. Follow the road signs marked "Vallée des Sept Châteaux": This rather obscure and never-direct itinerary takes you through farmlands, woods, and—just outside Koerich, at **Goeblange**—to the foundations of two 4th-century **Roman villas**, their underground heating and plumbing systems exposed; the rough cobbles leading into the woods are original, too.

Dining

Luxembourg City has a wide variety of restaurants, offering everything from top French cuisine to simple local specialties; you'll also find an assortment of international choices and a plethora of pizzerias. It's easy to find a fixed-price menu or plat du jour by wandering from restaurant to restaurant, but beware: The best places are often booked up at weekday lunchtime; if you know where you want to eat, phone ahead. Dress is casual unless indicated otherwise.

Some of the best and most enjoyable restaurants are in the countryside, but in this small country this generally doesn't mean much more than a half hour's drive.

$$$$ ✕ **Clairefontaine.** Airy, bright, and ultrachic, this famed dining spot on
★ the city's most attractive square attracts government ministers and visiting dignitaries as well as genuine gourmets. Chef-owner Tony Tintinger's inspirations include a showcase of foie gras specialties, innovative fish dishes (soufflé of langoustines flavored with aniseed), and game novelties (tournedos of doe with wild mushrooms). ✉ *Place de Clairefontaine 9,* ☎ *462211. Reservations essential. Jacket and tie. AE, DC, MC, V. No lunch Sat. Closed Sun., 1 wk in May, 2 wks in Aug., 1st wk in Nov.*

$$$$ ✕ **L'Agath.** Franky Steichen is the rising star in Luxembourg gastron-
★ omy. His restaurant, on the edge of a park, is in Howald, well south of the city center. This does not stop the faithful from trekking to his place to enjoy sautéed langoustines with crispy potato pancakes, smoked salmon crêpes au gratin, and coriander-flavored fillet of lamb. The dessert trolley offers a dozen different sorbets. ✉ *Route de Thionville 274,* ☎ *488687. Reservations essential. Jacket and tie. AE, DC, MC, V. Closed Sun., Mon., mid-July–early Aug.*

$$$$ ✕ **Saint-Michel.** In a 16th-century building behind the Ducal Palace, warmly lighted and intimate, this gastronomic-astronomic restaurant is rich in historical atmosphere. It is owned by an inventive German chef, Joerg Glauben, who has introduced expense-account diners to his lobster salad with green asparagus tips, pigeon stuffed with foie gras and accompanied by rhubarb compote, and sumptuous desserts. The staff is young, skilled, and down to earth, and the ambience is genuinely welcoming. ✉ *Rue de l'Eau 32,* ☎ *223215. Reservations essential. Jacket and tie. AE, DC, MC, V. Closed weekends and 3 wks in Aug.*

$$$ ✕ **Am Pays.** Seriously good fish, such as grilled sea bass infused with basil, and saffron-flavored monkfish, is served in this bandbox bistro, which has booths downstairs and a more formal dining room up a winding staircase. Am Pays is virtually the only restaurant that stays open in August. ✉ *Rue du Curé 20,* ☎ *222618. AE, DC, MC, V. No lunch Sat. Closed Sun., 3 wks in Feb.*

$$$ ✕ **Bouzonviller.** The modern, airy dining room is a pleasure in itself with a magnificent view over the Alzette valley. Over the years, Christian Bouzonviller has built up a following among serious gourmets with dishes such as sea scallops in a wild mushroom bouillon, loin of veal with olive rissole, and original desserts, including a coffee-and-whisky tart. ✉ *Rue Albert-Unden 138,* ☎ *472259. Reservations essential. Jacket and tie. MC, V. Closed weekends and 3 wks in Aug.*

304

Dining
Am Pays, **11**
Ancre d'Or, **15**
Bacchus, **16**
Bouzonviller, **3**
Clairefontaine, **18**
Ems, **24**
Kamakura, **17**
L'Agath, **26**
La Lorraine, **8**
Mousel's Cantine, **13**
Oberweis, **12**
St-Michel, **14**
Taverne Bit, **2**
Times, **10**

Lodging
Auberge le
Châtelet, **22**
Carlton, **23**
Cottage, **25**
Cravat, **19**
InterContinental, **5**
Italia, **21**
La Cascade, **20**
Le Royal, **7**
Parc Belair, **9**
Romantik
Hotel/Grünewald, **4**
Sieweburen, **1**
Sofitel/Europlaza, **6**

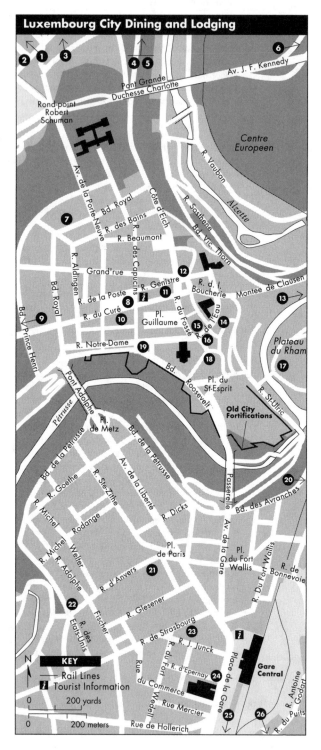

Luxembourg City Dining and Lodging

$$$ ✕ **La Lorraine.** Strategically located on the Place d'Armes, this restaurant in landlocked Luxembourg specializes in outstanding seafood. A shop around the corner shows off the coast-fresh quality of its fish and shellfish. Baked skate in hazelnut butter with capers and puff pastry with sole and morels are good bets. ⊠ *Place d'Armes 7,* ☎ *474620. AE, DC, MC, V. No lunch Sat. Closed Sun. and 2nd ½ of Aug.*

$$ ✕ **Ancre d'Or.** This tidy, friendly brasserie, just off Place Guillaume, serves a wide variety of traditional Luxembourgish specialties. Try the *judd mat gardebounen* (smoked pork with broad beans) or *treipen* (blood pudding), as well as lighter fare. The apple tart (Luxembourgish style, with custard base) is homemade. Portions are generous, service is friendly, and the clientele is local. ⊠ *Rue du Fossé 23,* ☎ *472973. MC, V. Closed Sun.*

$$ ✕ **Bacchus.** This Italian pizzeria attracts an upscale, downtown set, as much for its location in the historic center and its slick peach-and-brass decor as for its food, which is straightforward and reasonably priced. Wood-oven pizza and classic pastas are dependable choices. Reserve for a seat in the tranquil courtyard. ⊠ *Rue Marché-aux-Herbes 32,* ☎ *471397. AE, DC, MC, V.*

$$ ✕ **Kamakura.** If heavy Western cuisine palls, take the elevator down from Saint-Esprit to the Grund and try this elegant Japanese restaurant. A number of fixed-price menus offer a variety of delicate, nouvelle-accented dishes, artfully presented and graciously served. A la carte specialties, considerably more expensive, include impeccably fresh sashimi and light tempura vegetables. ⊠ *Rue Munster 2–4,* ☎ *470604. AE, DC, MC, V. Closed Sun.*

$$ ✕ **Mousel's Cantine.** Directly adjoining the great Mousel brewery, this fresh, comfortable café serves up heaping platters of local specialties—braised and grilled ham, sausage, broad beans, and fried potatoes—to be washed down with crockery steins of creamy *Gezwickelte Béier* (unfiltered beer). The front café is brighter, but the tiny fluorescent-lighted dining room has windows into the brewery. ⊠ *Montée de Clausen 46,* ☎ *470198. MC, V. Closed Sun.*

$$ ✕ **Times.** On a pedestrian street of art galleries and boutiques, you'll
★ also find this restaurant, offering excellent food at reasonable prices. Its narrow dining room is lined with Canadian cherrywood and is often filled with artists and journalists. The cuisine features ambitious creations, such as filet mignon of suckling pig cooked with tea, and many variations on the carpaccio theme (beef, tuna, and salmon). ⊠ *Rue Louvigny 8,* ☎ *222722. AE, DC, MC, V. Closed Sun.*

$ ✕ **Ems.** Across the street from the train station, this lively establishment with vinyl booths draws a loyal, local crowd. Many come for its vast portions of mussels in a rich wine-and-garlic broth, accompanied by french fries and a bottle of sharp, cold, and inexpensive Auxerrois or Rivaner. ⊠ *Place de la Gare 30,* ☎ *487799. Reservations not accepted. AE, DC, MC, V. No lunch Sat.*

$ ✕ **Oberweis.** Luxembourg's most famous patisserie also serves light
★ lunches. You select your meal at the counter (quiche lorraine, spinach pie, and the like), and it is served at your table. Beer and wine are available. ⊠ *Grand'Rue 19-20,* ☎ *470703. Reservations not accepted. AE, DC, MC, V. Closed Sun.*

$ ✕ **Taverne Bit.** With wooden tabletops and dark-wood banquettes, this is a cozy and very local pub, where you can drink a *clensch* (stein) of draft Bitburger beer (from just across the German border) and have a plate of sausage with good potato salad, a plate of cold ham, or *kachkeis,* the pungent local cheese spread, served with baked potatoes. It's just off the Parking Glacis. ⊠ *Allée Scheffer 43,* ☎ *460751. No credit cards. No lunch weekends.*

Lodging

Hotels in the city center are generally preferable to those clustered around the train station. There are also large, modern hotels near the airport and on the Plateau Kirchberg.

$$$$ ✕⌂ **InterContinental.** Rising above the outskirts of Luxembourg like a 20th-century château-fort, this modern, 19-story deluxe hotel opened in 1985 and competes directly with Le Royal (☞ *below*) downtown. Its rooms are gracious, with comfortable, wide beds. The restaurant, Les Continents, attracts locals for its upscale French cooking. ⊠ *Rue Jean Engling, L-1013 Dommeldange,* ☎ *43781,* ℻ *436095. 344 rooms. Restaurant, bar, café, indoor pool, sauna, health club, convention center, parking (fee). AE, DC, MC, V.*

$$$$ ✕⌂ **Le Royal.** This is the prestige place to stay, with its glass-and-mar-
★   ble lobby, surmounted by an enormous modern chandelier, and smaller lobbies on each floor. The rooms, surprisingly, are no more than standard modern. However, this is the kind of hotel where cellular phones are not allowed in the restaurants and where the gift shop sells "Les must de Cartier." The piano bar is popular, as is the brasserie–breakfast room Le Jardin, especially when the fountain terrace is open. The main restaurant, Le Relais Royal, is *the* place for power dining. ⊠ *Boulevard Royal 12,* ☎ *416161,* ℻ *225948. 180 rooms with bath. 2 restaurants, piano bar, indoor pool, barbershop, beauty salon, sauna, tennis court, exercise room, bicycles, parking (fee). AE, DC, MC, V.*

$$$$ ✕⌂ **Sofitel and Europlaza.** The Sofitel is the new, more expensive wing of the old Sofitel, renamed Europlaza ($$$). Built in 1993, the new Sofitel is more spacious than the Europlaza, although both share amenities. The Europlaza, which has a friendly, American feel to it, is a popular choice for those doing serious business with the Kirchberg institutions. ⊠ *Centre Européen,* ☎ *437761,* ℻ *438658. Sofitel: 104 rooms; Europlaza: 260 rooms. Restaurant, bar, coffee shop, indoor pool, sauna, conference center. AE, DC, MC, V.*

$$$ ✕⌂ **Cravat.** This charming Luxembourg relic—moderately grand, modestly glamorous—straddles the valley and the Old Town in the best location in the city. Though corridors have a dated, institutional air, the rooms are fresh and welcoming in a variety of tastefully retro styles. The art deco coffee shop has been freshened up but still draws fur-hatted ladies to tea. The prime minister and his cabinet can be found in the hotel tavern most Friday afternoons. ⊠ *Boulevard F.D. Roosevelt 29,* ☎ *221975,* ℻ *226711. 60 rooms with bath. Restaurant, bar, breakfast room, taproom. AE, DC, MC, V.*

$$$ ✕⌂ **Parc Belair.** This privately owned and family-run hotel, a few
★   blocks from the city center, was built just a few years ago. It stands on the edge of the Parc de Merl, next to an attractive playground. Rooms are a warm beige; those facing the park are the quietest. The complex includes a separate restaurant with outdoor café. A copious buffet breakfast is included. ⊠ *Avenue du X Septembre.109,* ☎ *442323,* ℻ *444484. 45 rooms with bath. Restaurant, breakfast room, playground, meeting rooms, parking (fee). AE, DC, MC, V.*

$$ ✕⌂ **Auberge le Châtelet.** At the edge of a quiet residential area but within easy reach of the station and the Old Town, this pleasant hotel (formerly the Auberge du Coin) has stone and terra-cotta floors, double windows, Oriental rugs, and tropical plants. Rooms are freshly furnished in knotty pine with new tile baths. There's a French restaurant and a comfortable oak-and-stone bar. The nine rooms in the adjoining annex cost slightly less. ⊠ *Boulevard de la Pétrusse 2,* ☎ *402101,* ℻ *403666. 32 rooms with bath. Restaurant, bar. AE, DC, MC, V.*

$$ ✕▥ **Italia.** This is a find: a former private apartment house converted into a hotel. Some rooms have the old plaster details and cabinetry left behind by the apartment dwellers. Rooms are solid and freshly furnished, all with private tile bathrooms. The restaurant downstairs is one of the city's better Italian eateries. ⊠ *Rue d'Anvers 15-17,* ☎ *486626,* ☞ *480807. 20 rooms with bath. Restaurant, bar. AE, DC, MC, V.*

$$ ✕▥ **La Cascade.** This turn-of-the-century villa has been converted
★ into a hotel of considerable charm and elegance. There's a good Franco-Italian restaurant and a lovely terrace overlooking the Alzette River. A bus stops outside to take you to the center, just over a mile away. ⊠ *Rue de Pulvermuhl 2,* ☎ *428736,* ☞ *428788–88. 9 rooms with bath. Restaurant, bar, meeting rooms, free parking. AE, DC, MC, V.*

$$ ✕▥ **Romantik Hotel/Grunewald.** A member of the Romantik group, the Grunewald is just outside the city and at the high end of its price category. The old-fashioned lounge is crammed with wing chairs, knickknacks, and old prints; rooms have Oriental rugs, rich fabrics, and Louis XV–style furniture. Rooms overlooking the garden are worth booking ahead; street-side windows are triple-glazed. There's an attractive garden and a terrace for alfresco breakfasts. The pricey restaurant (closed Sun.) serves rich, classic French cuisine. ⊠ *Route d'Echternach 10–14, L-1453 Dommeldange,* ☎ *431882,* ☞ *420646. 26 rooms with bath. Restaurant, meeting rooms. AE, DC, MC, V.*

$$ ✕▥ **Sieweburen.** At the northwestern end of the city is this attractively rustic hotel, opened in 1991; the clean, large rooms have natural-wood beds. There are woods in the back and a playground in front. The brasserie-style tavern, older than the rest of the property, is hugely popular, especially when the terrace is open. ⊠ *Rue des Septfontaines 36,* ☎ *442356,* ☞ *442353. 13 rooms with bath. Restaurant, taproom, playground, free parking. AE, DC, MC, V.*

$ ✕▥ **Cottage.** Modern budget hotels are few and far between. The one closest to the city (a 15-minute train ride away) is the motel-style but pleasant Cottage. ⊠ *Rue Auguste Liesch, L-3474 Dudelange,* ☎ *520591,* ☞ *520576. 45 rooms with bath. Restaurant, bar, free parking.*

$ ▥ **Carlton.** This vast hotel near the station, built in 1918, has a quiet inner court and is buffered from the Rue de Strasbourg scene by a row of stores. Budget travelers will find roomy, quiet quarters. The beveled glass, oak parquet, and terrazzo floors are original—but so are the toilets, all down the hall. Each room has antique beds, floral-print comforters, and a sink; wooden floors, despite creaks, are white-glove clean. ⊠ *Rue de Strasbourg 9,* ☎ *484802,* ☞ *486480. 50 rooms without toilet, 8 with shower. Bar, breakfast room. No credit cards.*

Nightlife and the Arts

Luxembourg City hosts a disproportionate number of arts events for its size. Watch for posters on kiosks, and check the tourist office on the Place d'Armes, where tickets to many events are sold. Tickets to events at the Municipal Theater (⊠ Rond-point Robert Schuman, ☎ 470895) are sold at its box office. The *Luxembourg News,* an English-language weekly translating local news from the city dailies, offers up-to-date events listings; it is sold at bookstores and magazine stands. *Weekend* and *Rendez-vous Lëtzebuerg,* both available at the tourist office, also offer listings.

Bars and Cafés

Lentzen Eck (⊠ Rue de la Boucherie 2, ☎ 222477) offers a traditional old-Luxembourg setting, plus a good list of the local liqueur, eaux-de-vie. **Chiggeri** (⊠ Rue du Nord 13-15, ☎ 228236), which draws a sophisticated international crowd (the owner is a literary editor), has a wide choice of beers and wines, plus midnight snacks. **Am Häffchen** (⊠ Bisserwée 9, ☎ 227166) serves drinks and meals in an intimate, retro setting, complete with bookshelves; **Bonaparte,** same management, same courtyard, has the ancient rockface as its back wall and serves up pasta and pizza as well as drinks. **Interview** (⊠ Rue Aldringen 21, ☎ 473665) draws a very young, stylish crowd (mostly students from the European School) to a setting of Warhol-esque urban decay. **Café des Artistes** (⊠ Montée du Grund, ☎ 461327) is an old, welcoming café with great ambience and a mostly middle-age clientele, where sing-along evenings make the chandeliers ring. The **George and Dragon** (⊠ Rue Albert Unden 217 [Rollingergrund], ☎ 474186) has an open fire, fish-and-chips, and Guinness stout on tap. **Yucatan** (⊠ Rue Notre-Dame 13, ☎ 226871) draws a stand-up local crowd for margaritas and, as an afterthought, a reasonable approximation of Mexican food.

Classical Music

Luxembourg is home to the **Orchestre Philharmonique du Luxembourg,** which performs a series of weekly concerts, usually on Thursday nights in the Municipal Theater and Friday nights at the new Conservatoire de Musique (⊠ Rue Charles Martel 33, ☎ 47962950). Watch for posters announcing "Concerts du Midi": They may feature Philharmonic Orchestra members as soloists or other professional chamber groups, and they are free. They take place at the Villa Louvigny, in the central municipal park. Though Luxembourg has no opera company of its own, several German companies perform here on tour every season.

Discos

Le Biblos (⊠ Avenue Monterey 10, ☎ 223229) stays open until 3 AM. **Casablanca** (⊠ Boulevard d'Avranches 36, ☎ 496940) is the current weekend hot spot. At **Jamaïque** (⊠ Rue Aldringen 23, ☎ 470822), there's a mix of soul and country music. **Didjeridoo** (⊠ Rue de Bouillon 41, ☎ 440049) in Hollerich, on the highway to Esch-sur-Alzette, is Luxembourg's largest disco.

Film

The best films in any language usually come to **Cine Utopia** (⊠ Avenue de la Faiencerie 16, ☎ 472109), where reservations are accepted by phone. A new cinema complex, **Utopolis,** is scheduled to open on Plateau Kirchberg in 1997.

Gay Bars

These include **Café Big Moon** (⊠ Rue Vauban 14, ☎ 431746), **Chez Gusty** (⊠ Côte d'Eich 101, ☎ 431223), and **Café du Nord** (⊠ Avenue Emile Reuter 30, ☎ 453284). There's a disco for lesbians the first Friday each month at **Café A** (⊠ Rue de Belvaux 29, ☎ 585499).

Jazz Clubs

Melusina (⊠ Rue de la Tour Jacob 145, ☎ 435922) is basically a disco (pop and techno on weekends) but also draws top local musicians and touring guests for occasional jazz concerts.

Theater

Good traveling plays in French and German pass through the municipal theater, the Théâtre Municipal de la Ville de Luxembourg, Rond-Point Robert Schuman, ☎ 470895. There also are English-language amateur productions from time to time.

Visual Arts

In addition to a number of art galleries, Luxembourg now has a permanent space for modern and contemporary art exhibitions. It was in the old **Casino Luxembourg** (⊠ Rue Notre-Dame 41, ☎ 225045) where Liszt played his last public concert. The casino was converted in 1995 into an exemplary exhibition venue.

Outdoor Activities and Sports

Biking

In Luxembourg City, you can rent bicycles for forays throughout the Grand Duchy from **Vélo en Ville** (✉ Rue Bisserné 8, ☎ 47962383), in the Grund.

Golf

The **Golf Club Grand-Ducal** (☎ 34090) at Senningerberg, about 7 kilometers (4 miles) east of the city, has narrow fairways surrounded by dense woods; it is open only to members of other private clubs. The **Kikuoka Country Club Chant Val** (☎ 356135) is at Canach, about 10 kilometers (6 miles) east of Luxembourg City.

Shopping

Since Luxembourg has only partially and recently abandoned its rural roots, its citizens are for the most part unsentimental about the traditional blue-and-gray crockery and burnished pewter that once furnished every home; nowadays, they prefer their local Villeroy & Boch vitroporcelain in jazzy, modern designs. All three types can be found in most home-furnishings and gift shops. For souvenirs, there are lovely photography books on Luxembourg's historic sites, as well as reproduced engravings of the city in all its fortified glory. *Taaken,* miniature cast-iron firebacks with bas-relief scenes of Luxembourg, are made by the Fonderie de Mersch and are available in gift and souvenir shops.

Because Luxembourg City is home to a large population of bankers and well-paid Eurocrats, as well as its own newly wealthy, it has an unusually high number of luxury and designer shops for such a tiny city. Clerks, however, are not always overwhelmingly friendly.

Shopping Districts

The best of high-end shopping is on the **Grand'Rue** and streets radiating out from it; shops along **Avenue de la Gare** and **Avenue de la Liberté,** both forking north from the train station, offer more affordable goods.

Department Stores

Rosenstiel (✉ Rue Philippe II 4–6) is a glamorous and smaller version of New York's Trump Tower, with atrium escalators, fountains, marble, brass, and a mix of independent boutiques. **Monopol** (✉ Grand'Rue 33, Avenue de la Gare 42, and Avenue de la Liberté 53) has more middle-brow goods.

Street Markets

The main **farmers' market** is held in Place Guillaume every Wednesday and Saturday morning. An **antiques fair** takes over the Place d'Armes every second and fourth Saturday. The annual **Braderie,** a massive, citywide sidewalk sale, slashes prices on the last weekend in August or the first weekend in September.

Specialty Shops

CHINA

Villeroy & Boch porcelain has been manufactured in Luxembourg since 1767. The factory outlet, on the edge of town, offers good reductions on virtually flawless goods, and rock-bottom bargains on pieces with slightly visible flaws. The factory (✉ Rue de Rollingergrund 330, ☎ 46–821278) is on the northwest edge of town. Bus 2 takes you there. The factory shop will not ship your purchases, but the glossy main shop will (✉ Rue du Fossé 2, between the Grand'Rue and Place Guillaume, ☎ 463343). The main shop has a wide selection of quality, full-price goods.

CHOCOLATES
Oberweis (✉ Grand'Rue 19, ☎ 470703) and **Namur** (✉ Rue des Capucines 27, ☎ 223408) are the city's finest patisseries, both with a mean sideline in *knippercher,* Luxembourg chocolates.

PRINTS
Correspondances (✉ Rue de la Boucherie 16, ☎ 252060) carries lovely antique engravings and maps of Luxembourg, along with a serious assortment of antique books. **Galerie Kutter** (✉ Rue des Bains 17, ☎ 223571) offers good framed prints and stationery taken from the works of Luxembourg watercolorist Sosthène Weiss, who painted Cézanne-like scenes of Luxembourg's Old Town. **Librairie Bruck** (✉ Grand'Rue 22, ☎ 499888717) sells maps and engravings in its showroom downstairs.

Luxembourg City A to Z

Arriving and Departing

BY CAR
The proper motorway exits for Luxembourg City are poorly indicated for newcomers; if you're arriving from France, watch for "Belgique/Brussels–Liège/Luxembourg aeroport" with "centre-ville" in fine italics; from Belgium, exit for Strassen and turn left on the route d'Arlon. From Germany, the motorway empties directly into the center.

BY PLANE
Findel Airport, 6 kilometers (4 miles) from the city center, serves the entire country. Luxair buses leave the airport hourly from 6 AM to 10 PM, heading nonstop for the train station. Tickets cost Flux 120. Luxembourg City Bus 9 leaves the airport at regular intervals for the main bus depot at the train station. Tickets are Flux 40. A taxi ride airport to city center costs about Flux 600.

BY TRAIN
Luxembourg has frequent train service from Brussels (under three hours) and Paris (Gare de l'Est, four hours). From Amsterdam, you travel via Brussels (six hours). Most connections from Germany channel through Koblenz. The train services of the Luxembourg National Railways (mainly one north–south and one east–west route) are supplemented by a bus network reaching virtually every locality.

Getting Around

BY BUS
Luxembourg City has a highly efficient bus service covering town and outlying areas. Get details about services at the information counter in the station arrivals hall. A 10-ride ticket costs Flux 300, available from the bus station in the Aldringen Center. Buses for other towns throughout the country leave from the train station. For information on bus routes or departures, call the information desk at the train station (☎ 492424).

BY CAR
A car is a liability in this small, walkable city. It's best to deposit your vehicle in a central parking area, either Parking Glacis, near the Grande-Duchesse Charlotte bridge, or Parking Knuedler, under Place Guillaume.

You can call for a cab (☎ 482233 or 405252) or pick one up at stands by the central post office and the train station.

Contacts and Resources

CAR RENTALS
Avis (✉ Place de la Gare 2, ☎ 489595). **Budget** (✉ Findel Airport, ☎ 437575). **Hertz** (✉ Rue de Cessange 20, ☎ 485485). **InterRent/Europcar** (✉ Route de Thionville 88, ☎ 487684; ✉ Findel Airport, ☎ 434588). **Rent-a-Car** (✉ Route de Longwy 191, ☎ 441938).

GUIDED TOURS
Sales-Lentz (✉ Rue du Curé 26, ☎ 461818) offers tours every morning from April through October. The tours, which cost Flux 290, leave from Platform 5 of the bus station (next to the railway station) or from the war memorial in Place de la Constitution. They visit the historic sights of the center, the area housing various branches of the European Union, and some of the villas on the city outskirts. Another tour takes in the monuments of Luxembourg City and the castle of Bourglinster. It costs Flux 320 and runs April, May, and October, weekends 2:30– 5:45; June through September, Tuesday, Thursday, Saturday, and Sunday, 2:30–5:45. Other more complete tours of the Grand Duchy are available to groups of 10 or more.

From April through October, guided **minitrain tours** (Flux 230) of the Old Town and the Pétrusse valley start from Place de la Constitution (☎ 461617).

You can rent a **self-guided city tour** with headphones and cassette at the bus booth on Place de la Constitution; the cost is Flux 180, with a refundable deposit of Flux 1,000.

The new **Wenzel Walk** allows visitors to experience 1,000 years of history in 100 minutes, though you are well advised to take your time. It is named for Wenceslas II, Duke of Luxembourg and Holy Roman Emperor (no relation to the "good king" of the Christmas carol), who played an important part in fortifying the city. The walk starts at the Bock and leads down into the valley, over medieval bridges, through ancient gates and past ancient ruins and exact reconstructions (always labeled as such). Two audiovisual presentations are included along the way. The walk also takes in French military architecture of the 17th century and a stroll along the Alzette River, which played an important role in the city's defense system. Good walking shoes and a reasonably sound constitution are required. The walk is signposted, with full explanations at each sight. A descriptive leaflet is available from the City Tourist Office in Place d'Armes, which also can provide a guide (Flux 1,600 regardless of the size of the group).

VISITOR INFORMATION
The **Luxembourg National Tourist Office (ONT)** maintains an information desk in the hall of the Railway Station and at Findel Airport, offering hotel reservations and tourist information. *Railway Station:* ☎ *481199;* ⊙ *Sept.–mid-July, daily 9–noon and 2–6:30; mid-July–Aug., daily 9–7. Findel Airport:* ☎ *40080821;* ⊙ *Daily 10–2 and 4–6:30.*

The **Luxembourg City Tourist Office** has pamphlets and brochures and general information about the city. ✉ *Place d'Armes,* ☎ *222809.* ⊙ *Mid-Sept.–mid-June, Mon.–Sat. 9–1 and 2–6; mid-June–mid-Sept., weekdays 9–7, Sat. 9–1, Sun. 10–noon and 2–6.*

THE LUXEMBOURG ARDENNES AND THE MOSELLE

Vast, rolling green hills and dense fir forests alternate in Luxembourg's northern highlands, the southeast corner of the rocky, wooded Ardennes plateau. Higher and harsher than the Duchy's southern *Bon Pays* (Good Country), with bitter winters and barren soil, it is relatively isolated and inaccessible; indeed, even in the 1940s, no one expected the Germans to attempt an attack across such rough and uneven terrain. They did, of course, twice. The second led to one of the most vicious conflicts in World War II, the Battle of the Ardennes, or the Battle of the Bulge. Throughout its history, the region has been the hunting grounds of kings and emperors, Celts, Romans, and Gauls; shaggy deer and great, bristling wild boar still occasionally charge across a forest road. Castles punctuate its hills and valleys, and rocky rivers and streams pour off its slopes, making this an attractive vacation area for northern Europeans to experience wilderness and medieval history.

The Mullerthal—or, as some insist on calling it, *Petite Suisse* (Little Switzerland)—northeast of the capital, presents a more smiling face. It's a hilly area of leafy woods, rushing brooks, and old farms, ideal for hiking along its multitude of marked trails or for a picnic. South of it begins the Moselle valley, where you can see Germany on the other side of the river. This land has been cultivated since time immemorial. Roman antiquities still surface from time to time. The south-facing hills are covered with vineyards producing the fruity white wines for which Luxembourg is famous. Many of the valley's small towns and villages remain attractively old-fashioned.

Wines and Spirits

Luxembourg takes pride in its Moselle wines. The vineyards stretch along the hills lining the Moselle River, taking maximum advantage of the region's muted sunlight. The best include a crisp Riesling or Auxerrois, a dry Pinot Gris or a rounder Pinot Blanc, and the rare, rosélike Pinot Noir. More commonplace varieties, often served in pitchers or by the glass, are Rivaner and Elbling. Luxembourg's Moselle wines lend themselves well to the French aperitif called *kir,* a glass of white wine tinted pale pink with a touch of *cassis* (black currant liqueur), a version of which is made in the castle village of Beaufort. Be sure to try the local liqueur, eaux-de-vie, made from the fruity essence of *quetsch* (a little blue plum), *mirabelle* (halfway between a plum and a yellow cherry), *kirsch* (cherry), or—for the hard core—grain, the last best mixed in a mug of strong coffee.

Numbers in the margin correspond to points of interest on the Luxembourg Ardennes map.

Diekirch

🔟 *33 km (20½ mi) north of Luxembourg City.*

Diekirch preserves memories of Roman culture, early Christianity, and the brutalities of World War II. This small, easygoing city, with a pleasant pedestrian shopping area, has several points of interest. **Eglise St-Laurent** (St. Lawrence's Church), a small, ancient Romanesque church, has portions dating from the 5th century. It was first built over the foundations of a Roman temple, the older parts functioning as a cemetery. In 1961, that lower section was uncovered and with it about 30 Merovingian sarcophagi, many of them containing intact skeletons. Since 1978, the cemetery has been restored and open to the public. Some of the ancient foundations of the church can be seen through a grate in the nave; you may enter the crypt by an exterior door on the right of the building. At the **Musée Municipal** (Municipal Museum), in the basement of the primary school, there are two more sarcophagi and remains found under the church, along with well-preserved Roman mosaics from the 4th century, found two blocks away. Diekirch is riddled with remains of Roman culture, though most of its treasures were carried away by invading Franks. ⊠ *Place Guillaume.* 🎫 *Flux 20.* ⊙ *Easter.–Oct., Fri.–Tues. 10–noon and 2–6.*

In the **Musée National d'Histoire Militaire** (National Museum of Military History), 10 life-size, authentically equipped dioramas depict personal aspects of the hardships of the Battle of the Bulge. Unlike the museum at Bastogne, this thoughtful, neutral effort sidesteps discussions of strategies and fronts; it brings out individual details instead, from yellowed letters and K rations to propaganda flyers—both German and American—scattered to demoralize already homesick soldiers at Christmastime. All paraphernalia are authentic period pieces. The staff often welcomes veterans personally. Other exhibits illustrate Luxembourg military history since the end of the Napoleonic Wars. ⊠ *Bamertal 10,* ☎ *808908.* 🎫 *Flux 150.* ⊙ *Easter–Oct., daily 10–noon and 2–6; Nov.–Easter, daily 12–noon and 2–6.*

The **Diewelselter,** an impressive dolmen (stone altar) attributed to the Celts, stands south of Diekirch, overlooking the town. No one is sure who piled the great stones that form this ancient arch—or how they did it.

Dining and Lodging

$$$$ ✕🏨 **Hiertz.** This small hotel-restaurant looks stark and uninviting from the outside, but inside, the tired old dining room has, after 30 years, finally been transformed into a jewel of a place. Sit in the hotel's pretty terraced garden for summer aperitifs and after-dinner coffee; for dinner, try carpaccio of langoustines with caviar, or turbot flavored with vanilla and raspberry vinegar. The hotel plays second fiddle to the food and is in a lower price category ($$), but rooms are comfortable; ask for one of the three back rooms facing the garden. ⊠ *Rue Clairefontaine 1, L-9201,* ☎ *803562,* 🇫🇦🇽 *808869. 9 rooms with bath. Restaurant. AE, DC, MC, V. No dinner Mon. Closed Tues., 2nd ½ of Aug.*

Outdoor Activities and Sports

BICYCLING
Bikes can be rented at **Camping de la Sûre** (☎ 809425) and in summer at local train stations.

Vianden

★ ⑰ *11 km (7 mi) northeast of Diekirch, 44 km (27½ mi) north of Luxembourg City.*

In Vianden you come face to face with one of Europe's most dramatic sights: Driving around the last bend, you suddenly see a full-length view of its spectacular **castle** rearing up on a hill over the village, replete with conical spires, crenelation, step gables, and massive bulwarks. Its dramatic position enhances the tiny village's medieval air, with its steep, narrow main street and shuttered houses crouched at the feet of the feudal lord. The castle was built on Roman foundations in the 9th century, but its most spectacular portions date from the 11th, 12th, and 15th centuries. A **chairlift** carries visitors up to 1,500 feet for a remarkable view of the Our valley. *Castle:* ☎ *849291.* 🎫 *Flux 120.* ⊙ *Mar. and Oct., daily 10–5; Apr.–Sept., daily 10–6; Nov.–Feb., daily 10–4. Chairlift:* 🎫 *Flux 160.* ⊙ *Easter–mid-Oct., daily 10–6.*

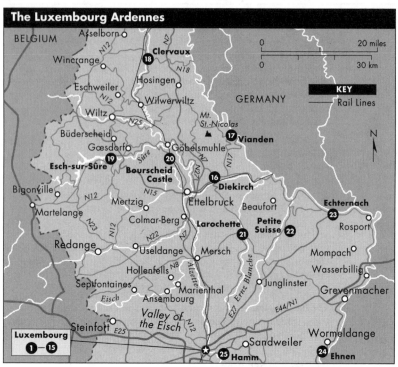

The Luxembourg Ardennes

BELGIUM
Asselborn
Wincrange
Clervaux **18**
Hosingen
N18
Eschweiler
Wilwerwiltz
GERMANY
Wiltz
Büderscheid
Goesdorf
Mt. St.-Nicolas ▲
17 Vianden
Esch-sur-Sûre **19**
Göbelsmuhle
Bourscheid Castle **20**
16 Diekirch
Bigonville
Ettelbruck
Beaufort
KEY
— Rail Lines
N
Martelange
Mertzig
Colmar-Berg
Larochette
Petite Suisse **22**
Echternach **23**
Rosport
Redange
Useldange
Mersch
Mompach
Wasserbillig
Hollenfells
Septfontaines
Marienthal
Junglinster
Grevenmacher
Ansembourg
Valley of the Eisch
Steinfort
Sandweiler
Wormeldange
Luxembourg **1 – 15**
25 Hamm
24 Ehnen

0   20 miles
0   30 km

The 13th-century **Gothic church**, in the valley below, once functioned as a Trinitarian monastery; its ancient cloisters have been restored to sparkling modernity. Down the hill, by the banks of the river Our, the **Musée Victor Hugo**, a museum, displays letters and memorabilia from the famous French author's sojourn here in 1871. ☎ 84257. ⌨ *Flux 45.* ☉ *Apr.–Oct., Wed.–Mon. 9:30–noon and 2–6.*

The **Musée de la Poupée et du Jouet** is a museum with a collection of 500 dolls and toys, including antiques dating to the 16th century. ⊠ *Grand'Rue 96,* ☎ *84591.* ⌨ *Flux 100.* ☉ *Easter–Oct., Tues.–Sun. 10–noon and 2–6.*

Dining and Lodging

$$$$ ✕⊞ **Oranienburg.** In the same family since 1880, this once-traditional
★ lodging has gone deluxe, decorating its rooms and restaurant in lush, new fabrics and modern, built-in fixtures. Only the café and stairwell retain the old-Vianden atmosphere, with game trophies and burnished oak. The restaurant, **Le Châtelain**, now contemporary and posh as well, attracts nonguests for its ambitious French cooking and its views toward the village and castle. The hotel café is much more modestly priced. ⊠ *Grand'Rue 126, L-9401,* ☎ *844224,* 🏧 *84333. 25 rooms with bath. Restaurant, café. AE, DC, MC, V. Restaurant closed Mon. off-season, Tues., 2 wks in Nov.; hotel and restaurant closed Jan.–mid-Mar.*

$ ✕⊞ **Aal Veinen.** Dark, cozy, and casual, this 1683 inn serves simple food—*bouchée à la reine* (chicken à la king) with frites, omelettes, cold sausage plates—and a wide selection of grilled meats, cooked in full view of the dining area over a sizzling wood fire. (If you've given up on pork chops, this is the place to get reacquainted.) Rooms upstairs are tidy and sparsely furnished, with some beams, stucco, and oak armoires. ⊠ *Grand'Rue 114, L-9401,* ☎ *84368,* 🏧 *84084. 8 rooms with bath. Restaurant, bar. MC, V.*

$ ✕🖾 **Heintz.** Expanded from its origins as a Trinitarian monastery, this atmospheric hotel has been in the family for four generations. During the war, owner Grandma Hansen worked with the Resistance, hiding hams, cash, and Luxembourgers with equal aplomb. The public spaces are rich with history, from the cross-vaulted oak café to the hallways filled with local antiques; rooms are simple and up-to-date. The oldest rooms, on the first floor, have antique oak furniture and original doors, but baths are down the hall; the best rooms are upstairs, with balconies over the garden and fountain. The restaurant ($$) offers French classics—grilled beef with béarnaise sauce, salmon in chives, and authentic German apple strudel with vanilla sauce. ⊠ *Grand'Rue 55, L-9410,* ☎ *84155,* ℻ *84559. 28 rooms, 26 with bath. Restaurant, café. AE, DC, MC, V. Restaurant closed Wed. (except mid-July–mid-Aug.), hotel and restaurant closed Nov.–Mar.*

Clervaux

★ **⑱** *31 km (19 mi) northwest of Vianden, 62 km (38½ mi) north of Luxembourg City.*

Clervaux, a forest village surrounded by deep-cleft hills, draws vacationers to hike, hunt, listen to Gregorian plainchant, and view *The Family of Man* photo exhibit in the sprawling castle. It was from this castle that Philip de Lannoi set forth in 1621 to make his fortune in America; one of his descendants was Franklin Delano Roosevelt. The old castle, virtually reduced to rubble in the Battle of the Bulge, has been completely restored. Two floors in the right wing of the castle house the noted exhibition of photo portraits of *The Family of Man*—considered by some to be the greatest photographic exhibition of all time—assembled by the great photographer Edward J. Steichen, a Luxembourg native. ☎ *5224241.* 🎫 *Flux 150.* ☉ *Mar.–Dec., Tues.–Sun. 10–6.*

Clervaux is also home to the striking **Benedictine Abbey of Saints Maurice and Maur,** built in 1910 in the style of the Abbey of Cluny, and perched high above town. Mass at 10:30 AM and vespers at 6:30 PM are celebrated with Gregorian plainchant. There's also an exhibition on the monastic life.

En Route   To enjoy the scenic route from Clervaux, head back toward Diekirch, but cut north (right) on a smaller road toward Mont St-Nicholas. It rewards you first with yet another spectacular view of Vianden and then with widespread views of the Our River valley from the summit.

⑲ Pretty little **Esch-sur-Sûre** is reached from Clervaux via Wilwerwiltz and Wiltz. Completely circled by densely forested hills, this miniature gooseneck on the river Sûre was once a stronghold, and its ruined **fortress-castle** still towers over the town (unrestored, but open to the public). Legend has it that an Esch Crusader brought home a Turk's head and hung it outside the castle gate and that it reappears to this day to warn of disaster; some claim to have seen it before the German invasion in 1940. The old textile factory (⊠ Route de Lutzhausen, ☎ 8993311) has been converted into a museum as part of a project, still in the planning stages, that will make the area surrounding Esch a national park.

Kids who finally tire of pouring imaginary boiling oil and shooting flaming arrows from Ardennes castles, and who balk at another uphill forest hike, will enjoy a trip to swim or windsurf on the waterfront of the
 Lac de la Haute Sûre, accessible on the south shore at Insenborn and on the north shore below Liefrange.

Following the green Sûre valley toward Goebelsmühle—along a quiet, winding road that is one of the most picturesque in the Grand Duchy— look for signs for Bourscheid Moulin-Plage, where you'll see the romantic ruins of **Bourscheid Castle.** It looms 500 feet above the Sûre River, with commanding views of three valleys. Restorations have made this rambling hodgepodge of towers and walls more accessible; the views are magnificent and there's a snack bar. ⊠ *Near N25,* ☎ *90570.* ⊡ *Flux 80.* ☉ *Apr.–June and Sept., daily 10–6; July–Aug., daily 10–7; Oct., daily 11–4.*

★ ❷⓿

★ ❷❶ From Bourscheid, follow signs to Lipperscheid, and from there via Diekirch to **Larochette,** which boasts a striking step-gabled castle that looks out over the town. The castle is privately owned and occupied, but adjoining ruins from an earlier incarnation (with evocative views over the small houses below) may be visited. ⊠ *Near N25.* ⊡ *Flux 50.* ☉ *Easter–Oct., daily 10–6.*

❷❷ At Reuland is the entrance to the Müllerthal, also known as Ernz Noire Valley, and **Petite Suisse,** an area of dense fir and beech forests, with high limestone bluffs and twisting brooks. There are *auberges* (inns) sprinkled along the roadside, with terrace tables and welcoming cafés.

At the top of the Ernz Noire valley, a short detour leads to **Beaufort,** where yet another splendid ruin, only partially restored to its 15th-century form, rises over green grounds full of sheep and forests full of walking trails. This one is well worth visiting: You can step into guard towers with archers' slits, look down wells, visit the kitchen fireplace, cross a drawbridge, and ogle torture equipment in a dungeon, including a rack. At the ticket counter, you can buy (or drink) samples of the local kirsch and cassis. ☎ *86002.* ⊡ *Flux 60.* ☉ *Apr.–Oct., daily 9–6.*

On the return from Beaufort, you can peer down the crevices at Werschrumsluff and Zickzackschluff, climb vantage points for vast panoramas of the landscape and the winding river Sûre at Perekop and Bildscheslay, and squeeze between the cliffs at the Gorge du Loup (Wolf's Throat) before arriving at Echternach.

Dining and Lodging

$$ ✕⊡ **Beau-Site.** This comfortable landmark in Esch-sur-Sûre is worth a visit enroute from Clervaux. At the edge of the village and overlooking the river, the hotel-restaurant has been updated with new woodwork and fresh tile. The rooms are modern, some with flower boxes and river views. The restaurant offers grilled meats and cream-sauce standards at prices slightly higher than average—but the portions are staggering, and the kitchen cuts no corners. ⊠ *Rue de Kaundorf 2, L-9650 Esch-sur-Sûre,* ☎ *89134,* ⅎⱯⵅ *899024. 18 rooms with bath. Restaurant, outdoor café. No credit cards. Closed 1st ½ of Jan.*

$–$$ ✕⊡ **Koener/International.** These two hotels, owned by brothers and adjoining a shared indoor pool, offer sleek modern details; rooms on the International side are somewhat more attractive (and more expensive: $$), with dark-green and brass decor. Neither half, aside from some rooms with forest views, has much Ardennes atmosphere, but both offer full comfort. *Koener:* ⊠ *Grand'Rue 14, L-9701,* ☎ *91002,* ⅎⱯⵅ *920826. International:* ⊠ *Grand'Rue 10, L-701,* ☎ *929391,* ⅎⱯⵅ *920492. 43/41 rooms. Restaurant, café, piano bar, indoor pool, sauna. AE, DC, MC, V. Koener closed mid-Jan.–mid-Mar.*

$ ✕⊡ **Le Commerce.** Directly below the castle and slightly apart from the hotel-packed center, this spacious hotel has been in the family for two generations and shows their pride: It combines slick, spare modernity—tile, stucco, polished oak—with homey old details (fringed lamps, heavy upholstery), and there's an open fireplace in the restaurant.

Some rooms have balconies over the river and hills. ✉ *Rue de Marnach 2, L-9709,* ☎ *91032,* FAX *929108. 54 rooms. Restaurant, bar, café. MC, V. Restaurant and hotel closed mid-Nov.–mid-Mar.*

The Arts

MUSIC AND THEATER

Wiltz, halfway between Clervaux and Esch-sur-Sûre, sponsors a popular theater and music festival in July, with performances and concerts in the outdoor amphitheater. Call or write ahead for ticket and schedule information (✉ Syndicat d'Initiative, L-9516 Wiltz, ☎ 957441).

Outdoor Activities and Sports

GOLF

There's an 18-hole course at **Eselborn** (☎ 929395), 3 kilometers (2 miles) northeast of Clervaux, with the inexpensive, 10-room **Hôtel du Golf** (☎ 929395) right by the course.

Echternach

㉓ *58 km (36 mi) southeast of Clervaux, 35 km (22 mi) northeast of Luxembourg City.*

Echternach dates from the 7th century and is the home of the only religious dancing procession remaining in the Western world. You wouldn't guess this at first glance, for modern Echternach is a flourishing tourist center all but adopted by the Germans across the Sûre, who fill its hotels, restaurants, and monuments every weekend. This ancient town was founded in 698 by Saint Willibrord, who came from Northumberland in England to establish a Benedictine abbey, which thrived until 1795. His remains are enshrined in the crypt of the **Basilica.** The early medieval basilica was destroyed in December 1944 and rebuilt in a modern style. The relics of the saint are contained in a neoclassical marble sarcophagus. Behind the elaborate carvings, you glimpse the simple tooled-stone sarcophagus cut in the 7th century. A few token traces of the original 7th-century chapel, founded by the saint himself, have been left exposed under heavy, modern repairs. On a hill just behind the basilica, a church, **Pierre et Paul,** stands on the remains of a Roman castellum and shows, in its spare architecture, signs of Merovingian, Romanesque, and Gothic influence. Every spring, the two churches host one of Luxembourg's most important arts events: the Echternach Festival of Classical Music.

On Whit Tuesday (eighth Tuesday after Easter), Echternach is transported to the Middle Ages: More than 10,000 pilgrims (most of them young people) from throughout the region come to town to join in—and tourists come to watch—the famous **Springprozession,** a dancing procession down the streets of the town, the marchers bouncing from one foot to the other, to the tune of a polka-like march. Their chanted prayer: "Holy Willibrord, founder of churches, light of the blind, destroyer of idols, pray for us." This unique pilgrimage has been repeated every year since the 15th century.

NEED A BREAK?

Just below Saints Peter and Paul's Church, have coffee and a generous piece of cake at the **Café-Tea Room Zimmer** and pick up something for later in the adjoining bakeshop-confectionery, perhaps the Echternach specialty, *Macarrons Moux.*

In the Middle Ages, Echternach was known throughout the Western world for another specialty, the exquisite *illuminations* (miniature illustrations) that accompanied the hand-copied texts produced by the Abbey's *scriptorium,* paintings that illustrated holy, hand-copied texts.

The original Abbey is long gone, but the magnificent quadrant of Abbey buildings from the 18th century remains and is of noble line and classical scale. Examples of the artwork produced in the Abbey can be viewed in the **Musée de l'Abbaye** (Abbey Museum) in the Abbey basement. The books displayed here are painstakingly executed reproductions of the originals, down to their gem-studded covers. The originals are now in various museums abroad. Even so, the exhibition provides an interesting introduction to the art of illumination in the Middle Ages. ⊠ *Flux 50.* ☉ *Apr.–Oct., daily 10–noon and 2–6; Nov.–Mar., weekends 2–5.*

Echternach's cobbled **Place du Marché,** in the old town center, offers a charming mix of Gothic arcades and restored medieval houses, festooned with wrought-iron signs and sculpted drain spouts; the arched and turreted 13th-century **Hôtel de Ville** (Town Hall) is its centerpiece.

En Route Leaving Echternach, follow signs for Wasserbillig/Trier and head south along the Sûre and the German border. You'll pass several small schnapps or eaux-de-vie distilleries, and their orchards. At Wasserbillig cut through town toward Grevenmacher; at the other end, you will come to the **Moselle River,** whose waters nourish Luxembourg's vineyards, cultivated since Roman times. The vines cover every exposed slope in sight, and the farther south you drive, the more romantic the scenery becomes. Graceful little **Wormeldange** is a key wine center; cut inland and follow signs up into Wormeldange-Haute (Upper Wormeldange) for sweeping views over the Moselle.

☙ The **Jardin des Papillons** (Butterfly Garden) in Grevenmacher seethes with fluttering wildlife, from butterflies to birds to tropical insects, all enclosed in an attractive greenhouse. ⊠ *Route du Vin,* ☎ *758539.* ⊠ *Flux 180.* ☉ *Apr.–mid-Oct., daily 9:30–5.*

NEED A BREAK? Stop at Wormeldange's enormous pink-stuccoed **Caves Cooperatives** to sample the local product. In a tidy adjoining pub, you can taste five wines served on a wrought-iron, vine-shaped rack. There's local grape juice, too, for the designated driver.

Dining and Lodging

$$$$ ✕ **La Bergerie.** One of the best restaurants in the country, La Bergerie
★ is in Geyershof, off the road to Luxembourg City. The 19th-century farmhouse nestles in an idyllic setting of forest and fields, with windows and a garden-terrace making the most of the expanse of greenery. The graceful, simple dining room features the cooking of owner-chef Claude Phal, whose specialties include classics (simple foie gras; steamed turbot in champagne sauce) and sophisticated experiments (smoked sole; young pigeon in pastry, its own juice caramelized). The strawberry gratin in orange butter uses fruit from the garden; all baked goods are made in the full-scale pastry kitchen. It's a family effort, with wife, son, and daughter-in-law running the restaurant and their offshoot hotel (☞ La Bergerie, *below*) in Echternach, 7 kilometers (4 miles) away, with free shuttle service. ⊠ *Geyershaff,* ☎ *79464. Reservations essential. AE, DC, MC, V. No dinner Sun. Closed Mon. and mid-Jan.–Feb.*

$ ✕▦ **Commerce.** Tucked back from Place du Marché, amid quiet side streets, and with an idyllic garden behind it, this simple hotel has been kept in top running order. Although rooms have fixtures of varying vintage, all have fresh decor. The restaurant and café are atmospheric, with oak wainscoting, beams, and pink linens; standard dishes (trout, bouchée à la reine) are moderately priced and well prepared. ⊠ *Place* *du Marché 16, L-6460,* ☎ *72301,* FAX *728790. 45 rooms. Restaurant, café. AE, MC, V. Closed mid-Nov.–mid-Feb.*

$$ ⌂ **La Bergerie.** Managed by the owners of the La Bergerie restaurant
★ (☞ *above*) outside town, this 1988 addition to the downtown hotel
scene is one of a kind: a small mansion, enclosed in a shady garden,
completely converted to creamy, modern luxury, with glistening tile baths,
opulent fabrics and cabinetry, and all the comforts—except a restau-
rant, which requires a pleasant shuttle ride into the countryside. Break-
fast is served beside a large bay window overlooking the garden and
fountain, or on the terrace; croissants come from the restaurant's pas-
try kitchen. ✉ *Rue de Luxembourg 47, L-6450,* ☎ *7285041,* FAX
*728508. 15 rooms with bath. Breakfast room, sauna. AE, DC, MC,
V. Closed Jan.–mid-Feb.*

The Arts
CLASSICAL MUSIC
The **Echternach Festival** of classical music is one of the most impor-
tant arts events in Luxembourg, bringing in world-class artists and en-
sembles and showcasing them in the basilica and the smaller Saints Peter
and Paul's Church. It takes place on weekends for a month during May
and June; tickets sell out quickly; write ahead to Lux-Festival (✉ B.P.
30, L-6401 Echternach).

Outdoor Activities and Sports
BICYCLING
Rent bikes from **Cycles Schmitt** (✉ Rue Ermesinde 27, ☎ 72148).

Ehnen

㉔ *52 km (32 mi) south of Echternach, 21 km (13 mi) east of Luxem-
bourg City.*

Tiny Ehnen, just down the road from Wormeldange, seems frozen in
time, with its narrow old streets, carved-wood doors, and unusual cir-
cular church. It's a popular excursion goal for city dwellers who want
to contemplate the river and sample the grape. Ehnen is home to a **Musée
du Vin** (Wine Museum), set in a typical group of Luxembourgish farm
buildings, with pink stucco and cobbled courts. Its rooms are full of
tools, equipment, and photographs of the wine-making industry, and
there's a demonstration vineyard planted with samples of each of the
local varietals. There are labels in English. ☎ *76026.* ⌐ *Flux 80.* ☉
Apr.–Oct., Tues.–Sun. 9:30–11:30 and 2–5.

A Possen is a 17th-century stone wine maker's house, restored and fur-
nished, in the small wine village, **Bech-Kleinmacher.** Its extraordi-
narily atmospheric displays include a "black kitchen," with a
ham-smoking chimney, and a cozy bedroom with a four-poster bed and
homespun linens; there are museum displays on the wine industry, and
a toy collection as well. There's also a **Waistuff** (wine *stube*), where
you can taste the local wine and sample dark bread smeared with pun-
gent *kachkeis,* Luxembourg's favorite cheese spread. ✉ *Rue Sandt 16,*
☎ *697353.* ⌐ *Flux 120.* ☉ *May–Oct., Tues.–Sun. 2–7; Nov.–Apr.,
Fri.–Sun. 2–7.*

㉕ At **Hamm,** on the outskirts of Luxembourg City, you'll find the **Amer-
ican Military Cemetery,** where General George Patton chose to be buried
with his men. More than 5,000 soldiers of the Third Army were buried
here, having died on Luxembourg soil; there are also 117 graves of un-
known soldiers. Each grave is marked with either a Star of David or
a simple cross, but they are not separated by race, rank, religion, or

origin—except for the 22 pairs of brothers, who lie side by side. Only Patton's cross, identical to the others, stands by itself.

From the parking lot, a small road, about a kilometer long, leads to Sandweiler, and across an intersection to the **German Military Cemetery,** which shelters more than twice as many war dead. Blunt stone crosses identify multiple burial sites, some marked with names and serial numbers, others marked simply *Ein Deutscher Soldat* (a German soldier).

Dining and Lodging

$$$$ ✕ **Lea Linster.** As the first woman to win France's top culinary award,
★   the Paul Bocuse d'Or, Lea Linster has earned international attention and keeps her modest farmhouse—once her mother's rustic café—full of prominent guests. Have a glass of champagne in the shady garden out back (cows may wander nearby), and then relax in the elegant dining room and enjoy her prizewinning dishes: lobster with truffled fettuccine au gratin, lamb in crisp potato crust, and hot chocolate soufflé. The wine list is weighted toward the high end, as are prices. ✉ *Rte. de Luxembourg 17, Frisange, 12 km (7 mi) south of Luxembourg City,* ☎ *668411. Reservations essential. AE, DC, MC, V. Closed Mon.–Tues.*

$$$ ✕ **A la Table des Guilloux.** Pierrick Guilloux was responsible for the Saint-
★   Michel restaurant in Luxembourg City, in its heyday one of Europe's finest, before "retiring" to the countryside to run this great little restaurant in a converted farmhouse. Here he cooks what he pleases, mostly dishes based on the traditions of his native Brittany. Trust his recommendations; few regret it. ✉ *Rue de la Résistance 17-19, Schouweiler, 13 km (8 mi) southwest of Luxembourg City,* ☎ *370008. No credit cards.*

$–$$ ✕ **Lëtzebuerger Kaschthaus.** Secure in her success in haute cuisine, Lea Linster hasn't forgotten her roots; in 1992 she opened her second dining spot, a simple farmhouse restaurant to cook nothing but Luxembourg specialties, superbly prepared and served without frills in a comfortable, old-fashioned setting. Print linens, stenciled wallpaper, and original ceramic flooring make everyone, from the young and hip to the senior citizens, feel at home. Try the green-bean soup, rich bouchée à la reine with sweetbreads, savory lentils with sausage, and mouthwatering fruit tarts. ✉ *Route de Bettembourg 4, Hellange, immediately off E25 between Bettembourg and Frisange,* ☎ *516573. AE, DC, MC, V. No lunch Wed. Closed Tues., 3 wks in Aug.–Sept., and Christmas wk.*

$ ✕▥ **Simmer.** This Moselle institution, built in 1863 and maintained
★   in a welcoming Victorian-rustic style, is the preferred riverfront retreat of the royal family and political luminaries, though its ambience remains comfortable and homey. Incorporating portions of a 1610 house and the founder's butcher shop, it was taken over by the current family in 1955 and built into an elegant hotel-restaurant. The details they added include a 17th-century fireplace in the dining room and carved oak grotesques paneling the salon. Rooms are spacious and solid, with dated glamour (brocade, gilt, crystal) and some antiques; in front, there are balconies, and in back small suites. Specialties in the restaurant ($$$) include braised *brochet* (pike) in cream and *sandre* (pike perch) in local Auxerrois; in summer, you can dine on the full-length, open-front porch. It's next door to the wine museum. ✉ *Route du Vin 117, L-5416 Ehnen,* ☎ *76030,* ℻ *76306. 17 rooms, 12 with bath. Restaurant, bar. AE, MC, V. Closed Feb., 2nd ½ of Nov.*

Nightlife and the Arts

For all its touristic charms, if you're interested in late nights and bright lights, this is not the region to linger in—head back for Luxembourg City. The one exception: The small treatment spa Mondorf-les-Bains, on the French border southeast of Luxembourg City, offers **Casino 2000**

(⊠ Rue Th. Flamang, ☎ 6610101), with full gaming facilities. Jacket and tie are required to play roulette and blackjack, but not for the slot machines.

Shopping

In Esch-sur-Sûre, you can buy very nice candles at the old *Käerzefabrik* (Candle Factory). But the most popular souvenirs of this region are meant to be consumed: Moselle wines, both sparkling and regular, can be tasted and purchased in gift packs from most of the wineries. Artisanale distilleries also sell their eaux-de-vie along the Moselle highway. At Beaufort, you can pick up a bottle of their house-label kirsch or cassis.

The Ardennes and the Moselle A to Z

Arriving and Departing

BY CAR

Driving is by far the most efficient and satisfying way to explore this region, and roads are well kept, though slow and winding. From Luxembourg City, follow signs for Ettelbruck (via route E 420/RN 7). An alternative—and very attractive—route is E27 toward Echternach, turning left almost immediately on the road to Larochette, and thence to Diekirch. The Moselle area is even closer to Luxembourg City, with no point more distant than a 40-minute drive.

BY BUS

Luxembourg buses connect throughout the Grand Duchy, both from Luxembourg City and from exterior towns. If you're staying outside the city, invest in the thick timetable, which has complete listings of connections.

BY TRAIN

Small rail lines out of Luxembourg City can carry you to Ettelbruck, Bourscheid, Clervaux, and Wiltz in the Ardennes, and to Wasserbillig on the Moselle, but other sites in these areas remain out of reach by train.

Contacts and Resources

GUIDED TOURS

Sales-Lentz (⊠ Rue du Curé 26, L-1368 Luxembourg City, ☎ 461818) offers coach tours to groups of 10 or more into the Ardennes or the Moselle area.

To view the Moselle by cruise boat, contact **Navigation Touristique** and its M.S. *Princess Marie-Astrid* (⊠ Route du Vin 10, L-6701 Grevenmacher, ☎ 758275); this graceful little ship stops at Wasserbillig, Grevenmacher, Wormeldange, Stadtbredimus, Remich, Bech-Kleinmacher, and Schengen. Meals are served en route. It runs, on average, twice a day between 11 AM and 6 PM from Easter through September; a comfortable itinerary for sightseers would be to leave Remich at 2:30, arrive at Schengen at 3:10, then double back to Remich by 4.

Most of the wine houses along the Moselle offer guided tours and tastings. Contact **Bernard-Massard** (⊠ Rue du Pont 8, L-6773 Grevenmacher, ☎ 75545), **St-Martin** (⊠ L-5570 Remich, ☎ 699091), and **St-Rémy** (⊠ L-5501 Remich, ☎ 69084).

VISITOR INFORMATION

Syndicat d'Initiative (tourist offices) are located at **Clervaux** (⊠ Château, ☎ 920072), **Diekirch** (⊠ Esplanade 1, ☎ 803023), **Echternach** (⊠ Porte Saint-Willibrord [Basilica], ☎ 72230), **Esch-sur-Sûre** (⊠ Parking, ☎ 89367), **Remich** (⊠ Gare Routière, ☎ 698488), and **Vianden** (⊠ Maison Victor Hugo, ☎ 84257).

LUXEMBOURG A TO Z

Arriving and Departing

From North America by Plane

AIRPORTS AND AIRLINES

Icelandair is the only airline to offer direct flights from the United States (New York; Boston; Washington, D.C.; Fort Lauderdale; and Halifax, Nova Scotia), with a stopover in Reykjavik. However, most of the main international airlines—**British Airways, Northwest, KLM, Sabena**—offer connections (usually with **Luxair**) allowing you to fly to London, Amsterdam, or Brussels, then connect into Luxembourg as a final destination with little or no additional cost. All flights land at **Findel Airport,** 6 kilometers (4 miles) from the city center. Their numbers, locally and in the United States: British Airways, ☎ 348347 or 800/247–9297; KLM, ☎ 424842; Icelandair, ☎ 40272727 or 800/223–5500; Luxair, ☎ 47982690; Sabena, ☎ 221212.

FLYING TIME

New York–Brussels, eight hours, plus Brussels–Luxembourg, 45 minutes; New York–Reykjavik, six hours, and Fort Lauderdale–Reykjavik, 7½ hours, plus Reykjavik–Luxembourg, three hours.

From the United Kingdom

BY PLANE

Luxair, the Luxembourg airline that connects to all major airports in Europe, has regular flights to London Heathrow, London Stansted, and Manchester (in Luxembourg, reservations, ☎ 436161; information, ☎ 47982311; in the U.K., ☎ 0191/745–4254). **British Airways** (in Luxembourg, ☎ 348347; in the U.K., ☎ 0181/897–4000) also has regular flights to and from Luxembourg.

Flying time from London to Luxembourg is 1 hour and 15 minutes.

BY CAR AND FERRY

The entire Benelux region is easily accessible in a day from London and the southeast. Nearly all ferries from Britain to the Continent take cars, as does the long-awaited Channel Tunnel. Several companies operate sailings direct to the Belgian ports of Oostende and Zeebrugge. Sailings are most frequent from the south coast ports; during the summer months there are up to six sailings a day from Ramsgate to Oostende, by **Sally Line** (☎ 01843/595522). The quickest (but most expensive) ferry crossing is from Dover to Calais via the Hovercraft link, operated by **Hoverspeed** (☎ 01304/240241). After a mere 35-minute crossing, you continue south from Calais to Lille and cut across Belgium, via Mons, Charleroi, and Namur, to reach Luxembourg. If weather and short queues permit, you'll make it from the south coast to Luxembourg in five hours. You also can take a standard ferry from Dover to Calais, with P&O alternating departures with **Stena** (☎ 01233/647047).

Fares vary considerably according to season, journey time, number of passengers, and length of vehicle. However, the approximate cost of crossing the Channel by ferry on one of the short sea routes in high summer, with an average vehicle of 4¼ meters (14 feet) and two adult passengers, works out to about £110 one way. By traveling off-peak, early in the morning or late evening, or in June and September, you can reduce costs.

BY TRAIN

☞ The Channel Tunnel *in* the Gold Guide.

Car Rentals

Luxembourg has among the lowest car-rental rates in Europe, as well as easy pickup at the airport and at the train station in Luxembourg City.

Customs and Duties

On Arrival

Americans and other non-EU members are allowed to bring in no more than 200 cigarettes, 50 cigars, 1 liter of spirits or sparkling wine, 2 liters of wine, 50 grams of perfume, and .25 liters of toilet water. **EU members** may bring in 300 cigarettes (200 if bought in a duty-free shop), 75 cigars, 1.5 liters of spirits or sparkling wine, 5 liters of wine, 75 grams of perfume, and .375 liters of toilet water.

On Departure

U.S. citizens may take home $400 worth of foreign merchandise as gifts or for personal use without having to pay duty, provided they have been out of the country for more than 48 hours and provided they have not claimed a similar exemption within the previous 30 days. Every member of a family is entitled to the same exemption, regardless of age, and the exemptions can be pooled. For the next $1,000 worth of goods, inspectors will assess a flat 10% duty, based on the price actually paid, so it is a good idea to keep your receipts. Included in the $400 allowance for travelers over the age of 21 are 1 liter of alcohol, 100 cigars, and 200 cigarettes. Any amount in excess of those limits will be taxed at the port of entry, and it may be additionally taxed in the traveler's home state. You may not take home meats, fruits, plants, soil, or other agricultural items.

Canadian citizens may take home 50 cigars, 200 cigarettes, and 40 ounces of liquor. Be sure to carry receipts for your purchases abroad, as any totaling more than $300 will be taxed.

British citizens may take home the same quantity of goods they were allowed to carry into Luxembourg (listed above). Because of strict rabies control, no pets or animals may be brought into the United Kingdom.

Guided Tours

General-Interest Tours

Listed below is a sample of the tours and packages that concentrate on Luxembourg. *See* Tour Operators *in* Important Contacts A to Z for tours that cover the Benelux region. Most tour operators request that bookings be made through a travel agent—there is no extra charge for doing so. For additional resources, contact your travel agent or the tourist office of Luxembourg.

FROM THE U.S.

Olson Travelworld (⌧ 1145 Clark St., Stevens Point, Wisconsin 54481, ☏ 715/345–0505 or 800/421–2255) tailors excursions in Luxembourg for groups.

FROM THE U.K.

Time Off Ltd. (⌧ Chester Close, Chester St., London SW1X 7BQ, ☏ 0171/235–8070) has packages from two to seven nights to Luxembourg.

Package Deals for Independent Travelers

Extra Value Travel (⌧ 683 S. Collier Blvd., Marco Island, FL 33937, ☏ 813/398–4848 or 800/336–4668) offers self-drive tours of Luxembourg that include hotel choices and car rental. **Travel Bound** (⌧

599 Broadway, Penthouse, New York, NY 10012, ☎ 212/334–1350 or 800/456–8656) offers tailored air-hotel packages to Luxembourg.

Language

Luxembourg is a linguistic melting pot. Although its citizens speak Lëtzeburgesch (Luxembourgish), a language descended from an ancient dialect of the Moselle Franks, they are educated in German and French, completing higher studies in French. The current generation also learns English and is, for the most part, easily conversant. The language used for government documents is French, but many are translated into German as well; a simple church service will often include German, French, Luxembourgish, and a trace of Latin. Within the tourist industry, most Luxembourgers you'll meet will speak some English with you, but they'll talk *about* you in Luxembourgish.

Mail

Postal Rates

Airmail postcards and letters weighing less than 20 grams cost Flux 25 to the United States. Letters and postcards to the United Kingdom cost Flux 16.

Receiving Mail

Mail can be sent care of American Express (⊠ Avenue de la Porte-Neuve 34, L-2227 Luxembourg). This service is free for holders of American Express cards or traveler's checks.

Money and Expenses

Currency

The Luxembourg franc (abbreviated Flux) is equal to the Belgian franc and used interchangeably with it within Luxembourg. Notes come in denominations of 100, 1,000, and 5,000 francs. Coins are issued in denominations of 1, 5, 20, and 50 francs; you will rarely be required to use the 50-centime piece. Be careful not to mix up French 10-franc pieces with Belgian and Luxembourgian 20-franc coins; the French coin is three times as valuable. At press time, rates of exchange averaged Flux 32 to the U.S. dollar, Flux 48 to the pound sterling, and Flux 23 to the Canadian dollar. Rates fluctuate daily, so be sure to check at the time you leave.

What It Will Cost

As Luxembourg continues to prosper, the cost of living increases annually, but hotel and restaurant prices tend to be up no more than 5% over last year's. Because of Luxembourg's low VAT (Value Added Tax), gasoline, cigarettes, and liquor continue to be notably cheaper here than in neighboring countries; you'll find combination gas station/liquor stores clustered at every border crossing. High-octane, unleaded gas costs about Flux 24 a liter; in Belgium, you'll pay 8 or 9 francs more.

SAMPLE COSTS

Cup of coffee, Flux 50; glass of beer, Flux 40; movie ticket, Flux 200; taxi ride, 4¾ kilometers (3 miles), Flux 500 (10% higher nights, 25% higher Sunday).

Taxes

VAT is 15%, except for hotels and restaurants, where it is 3%. The airport tax (payable with your ticket) is Flux 120. Purchases of goods for export (to non-EU countries only) may qualify for a refund; ask the shop to fill out a refund form. You must have the form stamped by customs officers on leaving the European Union. A minimum purchase of Flux 3,000 is required before you're eligible for a refund.

Opening and Closing Times

Most shops open at 9 and close at noon, reopening at 1:30 or 2 and closing for the night at 6. Many banks now stay open through the lunch hour, opening at 8:30 and closing at 4:30. Nearly all shops are closed Monday mornings.

Outdoor Activities and Sports

Biking

Biking is a very popular sport in the Grand Duchy. Good routes include Ettelbruck–Vianden and Luxembourg City–Echternach. The **Luxembourg National Tourist Office**—as well as those of Luxembourg City, Diekirch, and Mersch—all publish booklets and maps suggesting cycling tours within Luxembourg. Also contact the **Fédération du Sport Cycliste Luxembourgeois** (⊠ B.P. 1074, L-1010 Luxembourg, ☎ 292317).

Boating and Water Sports

The Wiltz and the Clerve rivers offer challenging waters for small craft or canoes, but the Our, with its wooded gorges, is the wildest; the Sûre is most rewarding, for its length and for the thrills it offers. For further information, write to the **Fédération Luxembourgeoise de Canoë et de Kayak** (⊠ Rue de Pulvermuhle 6, Luxembourg). People windsurf and sail on Lac de la Haute Sûre.

Camping

Visitors from all over Europe, especially the Netherlands, descend on Luxembourg's campgrounds every summer, making them sociable, crowded places, often near forests and riverfronts. Write for the pamphlet "Camping/Grand-Duché de Luxembourg," available through the national tourist office. The **Fédération Luxembourgeoise de Camping et de Caravaning** (⊠ Route d'Esch 31, L-4450, Esch-sur-Alzette, ☎ 591274) also publishes camping information.

Fishing

If you're in search of trout, grayling, perch, or dace—as well as relaxation—apply for a government fishing permit from the **Administration des Eaux et Forêts** (⊠ B.P. 411, L-2014 Luxembourg, ☎ 405310), and a local permit from the owner of the waterfront, which in many cases is your hotel.

Hiking and Walking

Luxembourg is full of well-developed forest trails, often on state lands with parking provided. The book *171 Circuits Auto-pedestres,* which includes 171 maps of walking itineraries, is available in bookshops for Flux 895. Trails will be full of strollers late Sunday afternoon, the traditional time for such outings.

Telephones

Local Calls

Public phones are relatively rare, except at post offices and in cafés. A local call costs Flux 5 or 10. No area codes are necessary within the Grand Duchy.

International Calls

To dial direct internationally, start with the country code (001 for the United States, 0044 for the United Kingdom), and then dial the local number. A **Telekaart,** available with 50 or 150 time units, works in specially equipped booths, usually in post offices, where they are sold. To make an international call without direct access, you must first dial 0010.

The cheapest way to make an international call is to dial direct from a public phone; in a post office, you may be required to make a deposit before the call. To reach an **AT&T** long-distance operator, dial 0800–0111; for **MCI,** 0800–0112; for **Sprint,** 0800–0115.

COUNTRY CODE
The country code for Luxembourg is 352.

Operators and Information
For international information, dial 016; for local information, 017.

Tipping

In Luxembourg, service charges of 15% are included in restaurant bills; for a modest meal, most people leave the small change. At a grander restaurant, you will be expected to leave a larger tip—up to 10% extra when a large staff is involved. For porters, a tip of Flux 50 per bag is adequate. Cab drivers expect a tip of about 10%.

Transportation: Getting Around

By Train
Train travel within the Grand Duchy is limited; a north–south line connects Luxembourg City with Clervaux in the north and Bettembourg in the south, and another line carries you to Grevenmacher and Wasserbillig, along the Moselle. For additional information, write or call the **Chemins de Fer Luxembourgeois** (✉ CFL, Place de la Gare 9, B.P. 1803, L-1018 Luxembourg, ☎ 492424).

By Bus
The Luxembourg bus system carries passengers to points throughout the Grand Duchy; most buses leave from the train station. You can buy an *horaire* (bus schedule) to plan complex itineraries, or you can ask at the tourist office for suggestions on how to get to Vianden or Echternach from Luxembourg City, for example. The **Oeko-Billjee,** a special day ticket (Flux 160), allows you to travel anywhere in the country by bus (including city buses) or rail, from the time you first use it until 8 AM the next day. They're available at the **Centre Aldringen,** the underground bus station in front of the central post office (✉ Avenue Monterey 8A at the corner of Rue Aldringen) or at any train station.

By Car
The best way to see Luxembourg, outside of Luxembourg City, is by car. Castles and attractive villages are scattered around and connected by pleasant, well-maintained country roads. *Priorité à droite* (yield to the right) applies here and should be strictly observed; drivers may shoot out from side streets without glancing to their left. Speed limits are 50 kph (31 mph) in built-up areas, 90 kph (55 mph) on national highways, and 120 kph (75 mph) on expressways.

Visitor Information

The **Luxembourg National Tourist Office** for the United States and Canada: ✉ 17 Beekman Pl., New York, NY 10022, ☎ 212/935–8888, FAX 212/935–5896. In the United Kingdom: ✉ 122 Regent St., London W1R 5FE, ☎ 0171/434–2800).

DUTCH VOCABULARY

English	Dutch	Pronunciation

Basics

English	Dutch	Pronunciation
Yes/no	Ja, nee	yah, nay
Please	Alstublieft	**ahls**-too-bleeft
Thank you	Dank u	**dahnk** oo
You're welcome	Niets te danken	neets teh **dahn**-ken
Excuse me, sorry	Pardon	pahr-**don**
Good morning	Goede morgen	**hoh**-deh **mor**-ghen
Good evening	Goede avond	**hoh**-deh **ahv**-unt
Goodbye	Dag!	dah

Numbers

English	Dutch	Pronunciation
one	een	ehn
two	twee	tveh
three	drie	dree
four	vier	veer
five	vijf	vehf
six	zes	zehss
seven	zeven	**zeh**-vehn
eight	acht	ahkht
nine	negen	**neh**-ghen
ten	tien	teen

Days of the Week

English	Dutch	Pronunciation
Sunday	zondag	**zohn**-dagh
Monday	maandag	**mahn**-dagh
Tuesday	dinsdag	**dinns**-dagh
Wednesday	woensdag	**voons**-dagh
Thursday	donderdag	**don**-der-dagh
Friday	vrijdag	**vreh**-dagh
Saturday	zaterdag	**zah**-ter-dagh

Useful Phrases

English	Dutch	Pronunciation
Do you speak English?	Spreekt U Engels?	sprehkt oo **ehn**-gls
I don't speak Dutch	Ik spreek geen Nederlands	ihk sprehk **ghen** **Ned**-er-lahnds
I don't understand	Ik begrijp het niet	ihk be-**ghrehp** het neet
I don't know	Ik weet niet	ihk **veht** ut neet
I'm American/ English	Ik ben Amerikaans/ Engels	ihk ben Am-er-ee-**kahns**/Ehn-gls

Where is . . .	Waar is . . .	vahr iss
the train station?	het station?	heht stah-**syohn**
the post office?	het postkantoor?	het **pohst**-kahn-tohr
the hospital?	het ziekenhuis?	het **zeek**-uhn-haus
Where are the restrooms?	waar is de WC?	**vahr** iss de **veh**-seh
Left/right	links/rechts	leenks/rehts
How much is this?	Hoeveel kost dit?	hoo-**vehl** kohst deet
It's expensive/ cheap	Het is te duur/ goedkoop	het ees teh **dour**/ **hood**-kohp
I am ill/sick	Ik ben ziek	ihk behn zeek
I want to call a doctor	Ik wil een docter bellen	ihk veel ehn **dohk**-ter **behl**-len
Help!	Help!	help
Stop!	Stoppen!	**stop**-pen

Dining Out

Bill/check	de rekening	de **rehk**-en-eeng
Bread	brood	brohd
Butter	boter	**boh**-ter
Fork	vork	fork
I'd like to order	Ik wil graag bestellen	Ihk veel khrah behs-**tell**-en
Knife	een mes	ehn mehs
Menu	menu/kaart	men-**oo**/kahrt
Napkin	en servet	ehn ser-**veht**
Pepper	peper	**peh**-per
Please give me . . .	mag ik [een] . . .	mahkh ihk [ehn] . . .
Salt	zout	zoot
Spoon	een lepel	ehn **leh**-pehl
Sugar	suiker	**sigh**-kur

FRENCH VOCABULARY

	English	French	Pronunciation

Basics

	Yes/no	Oui/non	wee/no
	Please	S'il vous plaît	seel voo play
	Thank you	Merci	mare-**see**
	You're welcome	De rien	deh ree-**en**
	Excuse me, sorry	Pardon	pahr-**doan**
	Good morning/ afternoon	Bonjour	bone-**joor**
	Good evening	Bonsoir	bone-**swar**
	Goodbye	Au revoir	o ruh-**vwar**

Numbers

	one	un	un
	two	deux	dew
	three	trois	twa
	four	quatre	**cat**-ruh
	five	cinq	sank
	six	six	seess
	seven	sept	set
	eight	huit	wheat
	nine	neuf	nuf
	ten	dix	deess

Days of the Week

	Sunday	dimanche	dee-**mahnsh**
	Monday	lundi	lewn-**dee**
	Tuesday	mardi	mar-**dee**
	Wednesday	mercredi	mare-kruh-**dee**
	Thursday	jeudi	juh-**dee**
	Friday	vendredi	van-dra-**dee**
	Saturday	samedi	sam-**dee**

Useful Phrases

	Do you speak English?	Parlez-vous anglais?	**par**-lay vooz ahng-**glay**
	I don't speak French	Je ne parle pas français	jeh nuh parl pah fraun-**say**
	I don't understand	Je ne comprends pas	jeh nuh kohm-prahn **pah**
	I don't know	Je ne sais pas	jeh nuh say **pah**
	I'm American/ British	Je suis américain/ anglais	jeh sweez a-may-ree-**can**/ahng-**glay**

Where is . . .	Où est . . .	oo ay
the train station?	la gare?	la gar
the post office?	la poste?	la post
the hospital?	l'hôpital?	low-pee-**tahl**
Where are the restrooms?	Où sont les toilettes?	oo son lay twah-**let**
Left/right	A gauche/à droite	a goash/a drwat
How much is it?	C'est combien?	say comb-bee-**en**
It's expensive/ cheap	C'est cher/pas cher	say sher/pa sher
I am ill/sick	Je suis malade	jeh swee ma-**lahd**
Call a doctor	Appelez un docteur	a-pe-lay un dohk-**tore**
Help!	Au secours!	o say-**koor**
Stop!	Arrêtez!	a-ruh-**tay**

Dining Out

Bill/check	l'addition	la-dee-see-**own**
Bread	du pain	due pan
Butter	du beurre	due bur
Fork	une fourchette	ewn four-**shet**
I'd like . . .	Je voudrais . . .	jeh voo-**dray**
Knife	un couteau	un koo-**toe**
Menu	la carte	la cart
Napkin	une serviette	ewn sair-vee-**et**
Pepper	du poivre	due **pwah**-vruh
Salt	du sel	dew sell
Spoon	une cuillère	ewn kwee-**air**
Sugar	du sucre	due **sook**-ruh

INDEX

NOTES

NOTES

NOTES

Fodor's Travel Publications

Available at bookstores everywhere, or call 1–800–533–6478, 24 hours a day.

Gold Guides
U.S.

Alaska

Arizona

Boston

California

Cape Cod, Martha's
Vineyard, Nantucket

The Carolinas & the
Georgia Coast

Chicago

Colorado

Florida

Hawai'i

Las Vegas,
Reno, Tahoe

Los Angeles

Maine, Vermont,
New Hampshire

Maui & Lana'i

Miami & the Keys

New England

New Orleans

New York City

Pacific North Coast

Philadelphia &
the Pennsylvania
Dutch Country

The Rockies

San Diego

San Francisco

Santa Fe, Taos,
Albuquerque

Seattle & Vancouver

The South

U.S. & British
Virgin Islands

USA

Virginia & Maryland

Washington, D.C.

Foreign

Australia

Austria

The Bahamas

Belize & Guatemala

Bermuda

Canada

Cancún, Cozumel,
Yucatán Peninsula

Caribbean

China

Costa Rica

Cuba

The Czech Republic
& Slovakia

Eastern &
Central Europe

Europe

Florence, Tuscany
& Umbria

France

Germany

Great Britain

Greece

Hong Kong

India

Ireland

Israel

Italy

Japan

London

Madrid & Barcelona

Mexico

Montréal &
Québec City

Moscow, St.
Petersburg, Kiev

The Netherlands,
Belgium &
Luxembourg

New Zealand

Norway

Nova Scotia, New
Brunswick, Prince
Edward Island

Paris

Portugal

Provence &
the Riviera

Scandinavia

Scotland

Singapore

South Africa

South America

Southeast Asia

Spain

Sweden

Switzerland

Thailand

Tokyo

Toronto

Turkey

Vienna & the Danube

Fodor's Special-Interest Guides

Alaska Ports of Call

Caribbean Ports
of Call

The Complete Guide
to America's
National Parks

Disney Like a Pro

Family Adventures

Fodor's Gay Guide
to the USA

Halliday's New
England Food
Explorer

Halliday's New
Orleans Food
Explorer

Healthy Escapes

Kodak Guide to
Shooting Great Travel
Pictures

Nights to Imagine

Rock & Roll
Traveler USA

Sunday in New York

Sunday in
San Francisco

Walt Disney World for
Adults

Walt Disney World,
Universal Studios
and Orlando

Wendy Perrin's Secrets
Every Smart Traveler
Should Know

Where Should We
Take the Kids?
California

Where Should We
Take the Kids?
Northeast

Worldwide Cruises
and Ports of Call

Special Series

Affordables
Caribbean
Europe
Florida
France
Germany
Great Britain
Italy
London
Paris

Bed & Breakfasts and Country Inns
America
California
The Mid-Atlantic
New England
The Pacific Northwest
The South
The Southwest
The Upper Great Lakes

Berkeley Guides
California
Central America
Eastern Europe
Europe
France
Germany & Austria
Great Britain & Ireland
Italy
London
Mexico
New York City
Pacific Northwest & Alaska
Paris
San Francisco

Compass American Guides
Alaska
Arizona
Canada
Chicago
Colorado
Hawaii
Hollywood
Idaho
Las Vegas

Maine
Manhattan
Montana
New Mexico
New Orleans
Oregon
San Francisco
Santa Fe
South Carolina
South Dakota
Southwest
Texas
Utah
Virginia
Washington
Wine Country
Wisconsin
Wyoming

Citypacks
Atlanta
Hong Kong
London
New York City
Paris
Rome
San Francisco
Washington, D.C.

Fodor's Español
California
Caribe Occidental
Caribe Oriental
Gran Bretaña
Londres
Mexico
Nueva York
Paris

Exploring Guides
Australia
Boston & New England
Britain
California
Caribbean
China
Egypt
Florence & Tuscany
Florida
France

Germany
Ireland
Israel
Italy
Japan
London
Mexico
Moscow & St. Petersburg
New York City
Paris
Prague
Provence
Rome
San Francisco
Scotland
Singapore & Malaysia
Spain
Thailand
Turkey
Venice

Fodor's Flashmaps
Boston
New York
San Francisco
Washington, D.C.

Pocket Guides
Acapulco
Atlanta
Barbados
Budapest
Jamaica
London
Munich
New York City
Paris
Prague
Puerto Rico
Rome
San Francisco
Washington, D.C.

Mobil Travel Guides
America's Best Hotels & Restaurants
California & the West
Frequent Traveler's Guide to Major Cities
Great Lakes

Mid-Atlantic
Northeast
Northwest & Great Plains
Southeast
Southwest & South Central

Rivages Guides
Bed and Breakfasts of Character and Charm in France
Hotels and Country Inns of Character and Charm in France
Hotels and Country Inns of Character and Charm in Italy
Hotels and Country Inns of Character and Charm in Paris
Hotels and Country Inns of Character and Charm in Portugal
Hotels and Country Inns of Character and Charm in Spain

Short Escapes
Britain
France
Near New York City
New England

Fodor's Sports
Golf Digest's Best Places to Play
Skiing USA
USA Today The Complete Four Sport Stadium Guide

Fodor's Vacation Planners
Great American Learning Vacations
Great American Sports & Adventure Vacations
Great American Vacations
Great American Vacations for Travelers with Disabilities
National Parks and Seashores of the East
National Parks of the West

WHEREVER YOU TRAVEL, *H*ELP IS NEVER FAR AWAY.

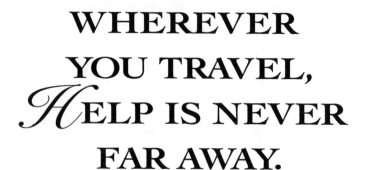

From planning your trip to providing travel assistance along the way, American Express® Travel Service Offices are always there to help.

Netherlands

American Express Travel Service
Van Baerlestraat 39
Amsterdam
20/673 8550

American Express Travel Service
92 Meent
Rotterdam
10/280 3040

American Express Travel Service
Venestraat 20
The Hague
70/370 1210

Belgium

American Express Travel Service
Frankrijklei 21
Antwerp
3/232 5920

American Express Travel Service
2 Place Louise
Brussels
2/676 2727

Luxembourg

American Express Travel Service
34 Avenue de la Porte Neuve
Luxembourg
228 555

Travel

http://www.americanexpress.com/travel